CAMBRIDGE UNIVERSITY PRESS

Cambridge, New York, Melbourne, Madrid, Cape Town, Singapore, São Paulo

Cambridge University Press
The Edinburgh Building, Cambridge CB2 2RU, UK

Published in the United States of America by Cambridge University Press, New York

www.cambridge.org
Information on this title: www.cambridge.org/9780521859950

© World Trade Organization 2003, 2005

This book is in copyright. Subject to statutory exception
and to the provisions of relevant collective licensing agreements,
no reproduction of any part may take place without
the written permission of Cambridge University Press.

First published 2005

Printed in the United Kingdom at the University Press, Cambridge

A catalogue record for this book is available from the British Library

ISBN-13 987-0-521-85995-0 hardback
ISBN-10 0-521-85995-6 hardback

Cambridge University Press has no responsibility for
the persistence or accuracy of URLs for external or
third-party internet websites referred to in this book,
and does not guarantee that any content on such
websites is, or will remain, accurate or appropriate.

WORLD TRADE ORGANIZATION

Dispute Settlement Reports

2003
Volume V

Pages 1725-2305

CAMBRIDGE
UNIVERSITY PRESS

THE WTO DISPUTE SETTLEMENT REPORTS

The *Dispute Settlement Reports* of the World Trade Organization (the "WTO") include panel and Appellate Body reports, as well as arbitration awards, in disputes concerning the rights and obligations of WTO Members under the provisions of the *Marrakesh Agreement Establishing the World Trade Organization*. The *Dispute Settlement Reports* are available in English, French and Spanish. Starting with 1999, the first volume of each year contains a cumulative index of published disputes.

This volume may be cited as DSR 2003:V

TABLE OF CONTENTS

Page

Argentina - Definitive Anti-Dumping Duties on Poultry from Brazil (WT/DS241)

Report of the Panel 1727

Cumulative Index of Published Disputes 2297

ARGENTINA - DEFINITIVE ANTI-DUMPING DUTIES ON POULTRY FROM BRAZIL

Report of the Panel
WT/DS241/R

*Adopted by the Dispute Settlement Body
on 19 May 2003*

TABLE OF CONTENTS

		Page
I.	INTRODUCTION	1734
II.	FACTUAL ASPECTS	1735
III.	PARTIES' REQUESTS FOR FINDINGS AND RECOMMENDATIONS	1737
	A. Brazil	1737
	B. Argentina	1742
IV.	ARGUMENTS OF THE PARTIES	1742
V.	ARGUMENTS OF THE THIRD PARTIES	1742
VI.	INTERIM REVIEW	1743
	A. Previous Mercosur Proceedings	1743
	B. Claim 10	1744
	C. Claim 11	1744
	D. Claim 13	1744
	E. Claim 17	1745
	F. Claim 21	1746
	G. Claim 22	1746
	H. Claim 27	1746
	I. Claims 28 - 30	1747
VII.	FINDINGS	1747
	A. Preliminary Issues	1747
	1. Disclosure of Written Statements - Article 18.2 of the DSU	1747
	(a) Arguments of the Parties / Third Parties	1747
	(b) Evaluation by the Panel	1749
	2. Previous Mercosur Proceedings	1751
	(a) Arguments of the Parties / Third Parties	1751

Report of the Panel

			Page
		(b) Evaluation by the Panel	1755
B.	General Issues		1759
	1.	Standard of Review	1759
	2.	Burden of Proof	1761
C.	Claims Concerning the Initiation of the Investigation / Alleged Procedural Violations During the Course of the Investigation		1762
	1.	Sufficiency of Evidence to Justify Initiation of the Investigation - Claims 2, 4, 6 and 8	1762
		(a) Arguments of the Parties	1762
		(i) Claim 2	1762
		(ii) Claim 4	1763
		(iii) Claim 6	1763
		(iv) Claim 8	1764
		(b) Evaluation by the Panel	1764
		(i) Claim 2	1766
		(ii) Claim 4	1769
		(iii) Claim 6	1771
		(iv) Claim 8	1772
		(c) Conclusion	1772
	2.	Sufficiency of the Application - Claims 1 and 5	1772
		(a) Arguments of the Parties	1772
		(i) Claim 1	1772
		(ii) Claim 5	1773
		(b) Evaluation by the Panel	1774
	3.	Failure to Reject the Application - Claims 3, 7 and 31	1775
		(a) Arguments of the Parties	1775
		(i) Claims 3 and 7	1775
		(ii) Claim 31	1776
		(b) Evaluation by the Panel	1776
		(i) Claim 31	1776
		(ii) Claims 3 and 7	1778
		(c) Conclusion	1778
	4.	Simultaneous Examination of the Evidence and Failure to Reject the Application - Claim 9	1778
		(a) Arguments of the Parties / Third Parties	1778

				Page
	(b)		Evaluation by the Panel	1779
	(c)		Conclusion	1782
5.			Failure to Notify Known Exporters - Claim 10	1782
	(a)		Arguments of the Parties	1782
	(b)		Evaluation by the Panel	1783
	(c)		Conclusion	1785
6.			Failure to Give 30 Days to Reply to the Questionnaire / Failure to Provide the Injury Questionnaire - Claim 11	1785
	(a)		Arguments of the Parties	1785
	(b)		Evaluation by the Panel	1786
	(c)		Conclusion	1788
7.			Failure to Make Evidence Available Promptly to Certain Brazilian Exporters - Claim 12	1788
	(a)		Arguments of the Parties	1788
	(b)		Evaluation by the Panel	1789
	(c)		Conclusion	1790
8.			Interested Party's Right to Defend Its Interests - Claim 13	1790
	(a)		Arguments of the Parties	1790
	(b)		Evaluation by the Panel	1791
	(c)		Conclusion	1792
9.			Failure to Provide the Full Text of the Written Application in a Timely Manner - Claim 14	1792
	(a)		Arguments of the Parties	1792
	(b)		Evaluation by the Panel	1793
	(c)		Conclusion	1795
10.			Use of Facts Available - Claims 15, 17 and 19	1795
	(a)		Arguments of the Parties	1795
		(i)	Claim 15	1795
		(ii)	Claim 17	1796
		(iii)	Claim 19	1797
	(b)		Evaluation by the Panel	1797
		(i)	Claim 15	1797
		(ii)	Claim 17	1798
		(iii)	Claim 19	1799
	(c)		Conclusion	1803

				Page
	11.	Failure to Provide a Public Notice of Conclusion of an Investigation - Claims 16, 18 and 20		1803
		(a)	Arguments of the Parties	1804
			(i) Claim 16	1804
			(ii) Claim 18	1804
			(iii) Claim 20	1804
		(b)	Evaluation by the Panel	1804
		(c)	Conclusion	1805
	12.	Calculation of an Individual Margin of Dumping - Claim 22		1805
		(a)	Arguments of the Parties	1805
		(b)	Evaluation by the Panel	1806
		(c)	Conclusion	1807
	13.	Essential Facts - Claim 21		1807
		(a)	Arguments of the Parties / Third Parties	1807
		(b)	Evaluation by the Panel	1808
		(c)	Conclusion	1810
D.	Conduct of the Investigation and Final Affirmative Determination			1810
	1.	Failure to Make an Adjustment for Freight Costs - Claim 23		1810
		(a)	Arguments of the Parties	1810
		(b)	Evaluation by the Panel	1811
		(c)	Conclusion	1813
	2.	Failure to Make Various Adjustments for Differences Reported by JOX - Claim 24		1813
		(a)	Arguments of the Parties	1813
		(b)	Evaluation by the Panel	1814
		(c)	Conclusion	1815
	3.	Differences in Physical Characteristics Justifying an Adjustment - Claim 25		1815
		(a)	Arguments of the Parties	1815
		(b)	Evaluation by the Panel	1816
		(c)	Conclusion	1817
	4.	Period of Collection of Dumping Data - Claim 26		1817

				Page
	(a)		Arguments of the Parties / Third Parties	1817
	(b)		Evaluation by the Panel	1818
	(c)		Conclusion	1818
5.			Sampling of Domestic Sales Transactions - Claim 27	1818
	(a)		Arguments of the Parties	1818
	(b)		Evaluation by the Panel	1818
	(c)		Conclusion	1820
6.			Injury Determination - Claim 32	1820
	(a)		Arguments of the Parties	1820
	(b)		Evaluation by the Panel	1822
	(c)		Conclusion	1824
7.			Failure to Explain Why the CNCE Examined 1999 Data for Certain Injury Factors but not Others - Claim 33	1824
	(a)		Arguments of the Parties	1824
	(b)		Evaluation by the Panel	1824
	(c)		Conclusion	1825
8.			Failure to Exclude the Effect of Non-Dumped Imports in the Injury Determination - Claims 34 - 37	1825
	(a)		Arguments of the Parties / Third Parties	1825
	(b)		Evaluation by the Panel	1826
	(c)		Conclusion	1828
9.			Failure to Examine Each of the Injury Factors and Indices Having a Bearing on the State of the Domestic Industry - Claims 38 - 40	1828
	(a)		Arguments of the Parties / Third Parties	1828
	(b)		Evaluation by the Panel	1828
		(i)	Productivity	1829
		(ii)	Factors Affecting Domestic Prices	1829
		(iii)	Magnitude of the Margin of Dumping	1831

					Page
			(iv)	Actual and Potential Negative Effects on Cash Flow, Growth, Ability to Raise Capital, or Investments	1832
			(c)	Conclusion	1834
		10.	Domestic Industry - Claim 41		1834
			(a)	Arguments of the Parties / Third Parties	1834
			(b)	Evaluation by the Panel	1836
			(c)	Conclusion	1837
		11.	Imposition of Variable Duties - Claims 28 - 30		1838
			(a)	Arguments of the Parties / Third Parties	1838
			(b)	Evaluation by the Panel	1839
			(c)	Conclusion	1845
	E.	Violation of Article VI of GATT 1994 and Article 1 of the AD Agreement			1845
			(a)	Arguments of the Parties	1845
			(b)	Evaluation by the Panel	1846
			(c)	Conclusion	1846
VIII.	CONCLUSIONS AND RECOMMENDATION				1846
	A.	Conclusions			1846
	B.	Nullification or Impairment			1848
	C.	Recommendation			1848

LIST OF ANNEXES

ANNEX A

Brazil

Contents		Page
Annex A-1	First Written Submission of Brazil	A-1851
Annex A-2	First Oral Statement of Brazil	A-1964
Annex A-3	Second Written Submission of Brazil	A-1978
Annex A-4	Replies of Brazil to Questions of the Panel - First Meeting	A-2008
Annex A-5	Second Oral Statement of Brazil	A-2040
Annex A-6	Replies of Brazil to Questions of the Panel - Second Meeting	A-2054
Annex A-7	Comments of Brazil on the Responses of Argentina to the Panel's and to Brazil's Questions - Second Meeting	A-2067

ANNEX B

Argentina

Contents		Page
Annex B-1	First Written Submission of Argentina	B-2092
Annex B-2	First Oral Statement of Argentina	B-2160
Annex B-3	Second Written Submission of Argentina	B-2173
Annex B-4	Replies of Argentina to Questions of the Panel - First Meeting	B-2188
Annex B-5	Second Oral Statement of Argentina	B-2215
Annex B-6	Replies of Argentina to Questions of the Panel - Second Meeting	B-2233
Annex B-7	Replies of Argentina to Questions of Brazil - Second Meeting	B-2247
Annex B-8	Comments of Argentina on the Responses of Brazil to the Panel's Questions - Second Meeting	B-2248
Annex B-9	Comments of Argentina on the Second Oral Statement of Brazil	B-2252

Report of the Panel

ANNEX C

Third Parties

Contents		Page
Annex C-1	Third Party Submission of Canada	C-2254
Annex C-2	Third Party Submission of the European Communities	C-2258
Annex C-3	Third Party Submission of Guatemala	C-2271
Annex C-4	Third Party Submission of Paraguay	C-2276
Annex C-5	Third Party Submission of the United States	C-2278
Annex C-6	Third Party Oral Statement of Paraguay	C-2284
Annex C-7	Third Party Oral Statement of Chile	C-2286
Annex C-8	Third Party Oral Statement of the United States	C-2287
Annex C-9	Third Party Oral Statement of Canada	C-2289
Annex C-10	Third Party Oral Statement of the European Communities	C-2290
Annex C-11	Replies of the European Communities to Questions of the Panel	C-2293
Annex C-12	Replies of the United States to Questions of the Panel	C-2295

I. INTRODUCTION

1.1   On 7 November 2001, Brazil requested consultations with Argentina pursuant to Article 4 of the *Understanding on Rules and Procedures Governing the Settlement of Disputes* (the "*DSU*"), Article XXII of the *General Agreement on Tariffs and Trade 1994* (the "*GATT 1994*"), Article 17 of the *Agreement on Implementation of Article VI of the General Agreement on Tariffs and Trade 1994* (the "*AD Agreement*"), including Article 17.4 thereof, and Article 19 of the *Agreement on Implementation of Article VII of GATT 1994* (the "*Agreement on Customs Valuation*") concerning the Argentine anti-dumping measures imposed in respect of imports of poultry from Brazil.[1] Argentina and Brazil held consultations on 10 December 2001, but failed to settle the dispute.

1.2   On 19 November 2001, the European Communities requested, pursuant to Article 4.11 of the *DSU*, to be joined in the consultations.[2]

1.3   On 25 February 2002, Brazil requested the establishment of a panel pursuant to Article XXII of the *GATT 1994*, Article 17 of the *AD Agreement* and Article 6 of the *DSU*.[3]

1.4   At its meeting on 17 April 2002, the Dispute Settlement Body (the "DSB") established this Panel in accordance with Article 6 of the *DSU* to examine the matter referred to the DSB by Brazil in document WT/DS241/3. At that meeting, the parties

---

[1] WT/DS241/1.
[2] WT/DS241/2.
[3] WT/DS241/3.

to the dispute also agreed that the Panel should have standard terms of reference. The terms of reference are, therefore, the following:

> "To examine, in the light of the relevant provisions of the covered agreements cited by Brazil in document WT/DS241/3, the matter referred by Brazil to the DSB in that document, and to make such findings as will assist the DSB in making the recommendations or in giving the rulings provided for in those agreements."

1.5 On 17 June 2002, Brazil requested the Director-General to determine the composition of the Panel, pursuant to paragraph 7 of Article 8 of the *DSU*. This paragraph provides:

> "If there is no agreement on the panelists within 20 days after the date of the establishment of a panel, at the request of either party, the Director-General, in consultation with the Chairman of the DSB and the Chairman of the relevant Council or Committee, shall determine the composition of the panel by appointing the panelists whom the Director-General considers most appropriate in accordance with any relevant special or additional rules or procedures of the covered agreement or covered agreements which are at issue in the dispute, after consulting with the parties to the dispute. The Chairman of the DSB shall inform the Members of the composition of the panel thus formed no later than 10 days after the date the Chairman receives such a request".

1.6 On 27 June 2002, the Director-General accordingly composed the Panel as follows:[4]

Chairman: Mr. Harsha V. Singh
Members: Ms. Enie Neri de Ross
Mr. Michael Mulgrew

1.7 Canada, Chile, the European Communities, Guatemala, Paraguay and the United States reserved their rights to participate in the Panel proceedings as third parties.

1.8 The Panel met with the parties on 25-26 September 2002 and 26 November 2002. It met with the third parties on 26 September 2002.

1.9 The Panel submitted its interim report to the parties on 25 February 2003. The Panel submitted its final report to the parties on 8 April 2003.

II. FACTUAL ASPECTS

2.1 This dispute concerns the imposition by Argentina of anti-dumping measures on imports of poultry from Brazil.

2.2 On 2 September 1997, the Centro de Empresas Procesadoras Avícolas (the "CEPA") filed an application for the initiation of an anti-dumping investigation with the Under-Secretariat for Foreign Trade (the "SSCE"), which subsequently became the Under-Secretariat for Industry, Trade and Mining (the "SSICM"). CEPA alleged that imports of poultry from Brazil into Argentina were taking place at dumped prices and that these imports represented a threat of material injury to the domestic

---

[4] WT/DS241/4.

industry.⁵ On 23 September 1997, the National Foreign Trade Commission (the "CNCE") issued an opinion regarding the representativeness of the domestic industry and, on 21 November 1997, the SSCE accepted the application presented by CEPA.

2.3   On 7 January 1998, the Department of Unfair Trading Practices and Safeguards (the "APCDS"), which subsequently became the Directorate of Unfair Competition (the "DCD"), concluded in its Report on the Feasibility of Initiating an Investigation (the "Report of 7 January 1998") that there was sufficient evidence of dumping to justify initiating an investigation.⁶ On that same date, the CNCE determined in Record No. 405 that there was not sufficient evidence of injury or threat of injury to justify the initiation of an investigation.⁷ On 17 February 1998, CEPA presented new and updated information to the Secretariat for Industry, Trade and Mining (the "SICyM").⁸ On 18 June 1998, the General Directorate for Legal Affairs (the "DGAJ") of the Ministry of the Economy and Public Works and Services (the "MEyOSP"), at the request of the then Under-Secretariat for Foreign Trade, determined that "... in view of the fact that the information submitted by ... CEPA ... was not evaluated by the National Foreign Trade Commission when ruling on injury to the domestic industry in Record No. 405/98, this Directorate-General considers that before proceeding any further, the said National Commission should be asked to intervene once again in order to rule on the items submitted ...".⁹ Following an examination of the new evidence submitted by CEPA, the CNCE determined in Record No. 464 of 22 September 1998 that there was sufficient evidence of threat of injury to justify the initiation of the investigation.¹⁰

2.4   On 20 January 1999, the Secretary for Industry, Trade and Mining (the "Secretary") decided to initiate the anti-dumping investigation concerning poultry from Brazil.¹¹ A Notice of Initiation of the anti-dumping investigation was published in the Official Bulletin on 25 January 1999.

2.5   The CNCE and the DCD sent, on 10 and 16 February 1999, respectively, letters to five Brazilian exporters (i.e., Sadia S.A. ("Sadia"), Avipal S.A. Avicultura e Agropecuaria ("Avipal"), Frigorífico Nicolini Ltda. ("Nicolini"), Seara Alimentos S.A. ("Seara"), and Frangosul S.A. Agro Avícola Industrial ("Frangosul")) *inter alia* notifying them of the initiation of the investigation.¹²

2.6   On 28 June 1999, the CNCE issued its preliminary affirmative injury determination.¹³ On 6 August 1999, the DCD issued its preliminary affirmative dumping determination.¹⁴ On 20 August 1999, the SSCE issued its preliminary affirmative determination on causal link between the allegedly dumped imports and the injury to the domestic industry.¹⁵ No provisional measures were imposed.

2.7   On 15 September 1999, various Brazilian exporters, namely Cooperativa Central de Laticínios do Paraná ("CCLP"), Cooperativa Central Oeste Catarinense

---

[5]   Exhibit BRA-1.
[6]   Exhibit BRA-2.
[7]   Exhibit BRA-3.
[8]   Exhibit BRA-4.
[9]   Exhibit BRA-5.
[10] Exhibit BRA-6.
[11] Exhibit BRA-7.
[12] Exhibits BRA-8 and BRA-9.
[13] Exhibit BRA-10.
[14] Exhibit BRA-11.
[15] Exhibit BRA-12.

Ltda. ("Catarinense"), Chapecó Cia. Industrial ("Chapecó"), Cia. Minuano de Alimentos ("Minuano"), Perdigão Agroindustrial ("Perdigão"), and Comaves Industria e Comércio de Alimentos Ltda. ("Comaves"), were contacted by the DCD, and were provided with the same questionnaire sent by the DCD to other exporters on 16 February 1999.[16]

2.8 On 23 December 1999, the CNCE issued its final affirmative injury determination.[17] The DCD issued its final affirmative dumping determination on 23 June 2000.[18] The dumping margins found for Sadia, Avipal and all other exporters were 14.91 per cent, 15.48 per cent and 8.19 per cent, respectively. No dumping margin was found with regard to Nicolini and Seara. On 17 July 2000, the SSICM issued its final affirmative determination of causal link between the dumped imports and the injury to the domestic industry.[19]

2.9 Based upon the final dumping, injury and causal link determinations, the Ministry of Economics (the "ME"), formerly the MEyOSP, issued Resolution No. 574 of 21 July 2000, imposing definitive anti-dumping measures on imports of poultry from Brazil for a period of three years.[20] Such measures took the form of specific anti-dumping duties to be collected as the absolute difference between the f.o.b. price invoiced in any one shipment and a designated "minimum export price" also fixed in f.o.b. terms, to be applied whenever the former price was lower than the latter. A "minimum export price" of US$0.92 per kilogram was established for Sadia, and US$0.98 per kilogram for Avipal and all other exporters. No measures were imposed on the Brazilian exporters Nicolini and Seara because they were found not to be exporting poultry at dumped prices. Resolution No. 574 was published in the Official Bulletin of 24 July 2000.

2.10 On 30 August 2000, in conformity with Article 2 of the MERCOSUR Protocol of Brasilia, Brazil requested the initiation of direct negotiations with Argentina on Resolution No. 574. On 24 January 2001, Brazil gave notice of its intention to initiate the arbitral proceedings provided for in Article 7 of the Protocol of Brasilia. A MERCOSUR Ad Hoc Arbitral Tribunal made its award on 21 May 2001. In accordance with Article 22 of the Protocol of Brasilia, following the award, the Arbitral Tribunal issued a clarification thereof on 18 June 2001.

III. PARTIES' REQUESTS FOR FINDINGS AND RECOMMENDATIONS

A. Brazil

3.1 In its first written submission, Brazil requested that the Panel:

(a) find that Argentina has acted inconsistently with the *AD Agreement* as per the claims below:

- Petitioner's application presented a calculation to adjust normal value in view of alleged physical characteristic differences between poultry sold to Argentina and poultry sold in Brazil. The application did not offer relevant evidence of such

---

[16] Exhibit BRA-13.
[17] Exhibit BRA-14.
[18] Exhibit BRA-15.
[19] Exhibit BRA-16.
[20] Exhibit BRA-17.

differences contrary to the requirement set out in Article 5.2 (Claim 1). By accepting petitioner's adjustment calculation, Argentina failed to examine the accuracy and adequacy of the evidence presented in the application pursuant to Article 5.3 (Claim 2), and to reject the application as provided in Article 5.8 (Claim 3);

- Argentina acted inconsistently with Article 5.3 (Claim 4) by establishing export prices based only on export transactions with prices below normal value;

- Petitioner's application presented export price and normal value data for different periods. Specifically, the application presented normal value data for only one day in 1997 (30 June 1997), which cannot be considered relevant evidence to establish normal value pursuant to Article 5.2 (Claim 5). By calculating a dumping margin by making a comparison between export price and normal value in respect of sales that were not made at as nearly as possible the same time and by establishing normal value for only one day in 1997, Argentina failed to examine the accuracy and adequacy of the evidence provided in the application as required by Article 5.3 (Claim 6), and to reject the application pursuant to Article 5.8 (Claim 7);

- By comparing different periods of data collected for dumping and injury, Argentina incorrectly examined the evidence provided in the application, violating Article 5.3 (Claim 8);

- Argentina has acted inconsistently with Article 5.7 (Claim 9) by not considering, in the determination whether or not to initiate the investigation, the data collected for dumping simultaneously with the data collected for injury;

- Argentina failed to notify seven Brazilian exporters when it was satisfied that there was sufficient evidence to justify the initiation of the anti-dumping investigation. By not notifying these exporters when the investigation was initiated, Argentina acted inconsistently with Article 12.1 (Claim 10);

- Argentina failed to give the seven Brazilian exporters at least 30 days to reply to the dumping questionnaires provided by the DCD in a *prima facie* violation of Article 6.1.1 (Claim 11). Moreover, the CNCE never notified these seven exporters and never provided them with the injury questionnaire;

- Argentina also failed to promptly make available to the seven Brazilian exporters evidence presented in writing by the other interested parties involved in the investigation, in violation of Article 6.1.2 (Claim 12);

- By failing to give the seven exporters the required time to respond to the questionnaires and not promptly making available to these exporters the evidence presented in writing by the other interested parties involved in the investigation,

Argentina did not give these exporters full opportunity for the defence of their interests as required by Article 6.2 (Claim 13);

- Argentina acted inconsistently with Article 6.1.3 (Claim 14) by not providing the text of the written application to the Brazilian exporters and to the Government of Brazil as soon as the investigation was initiated;
- Argentina acted inconsistently with Article 6.8 and Annex II (Claim 15) by disregarding the responses submitted by Brazilian exporters with respect to the description of the product sold to Argentina and in Brazil, and resorting to the normal value adjustment calculation provided by petitioner in the application;
- Argentina acted inconsistently with Article 12.2.2 (Claim 16) by failing to adequately explain in the final determination its decision to disregard the information provided by the exporters regarding the product description and to use instead the normal value adjustment proposed by petitioner;
- Argentina acted inconsistently with Article 6.8 and Annex II (Claim 17) by disregarding the export price data provided by the Brazilian exporters, and resorting to the export price information provided by the Argentinean Livestock Directorate of the Secretariat for Agriculture, Livestock, Fisheries and Food;
- Argentina acted inconsistently with Article 12.2.2 (Claim 18) by failing to adequately explain in the final determination its decision to disregard the export price data provided by the Brazilian exporters, and to resort to the export price data provided by the Argentinean Livestock Directorate of the Secretariat for Agriculture, Livestock, Fisheries and Food;
- Argentina acted inconsistently with Article 6.8 and Annex II (Claim 19) by disregarding all normal value information submitted by two Brazilian exporters, and resorting to the information provided by petitioner;
- Argentina acted inconsistently with Article 12.2.2 (Claim 20) by failing to adequately explain in the final determination its decision to disregard all normal value information submitted by two Brazilian exporters, and to resort to the information provided by petitioner;
- Argentina failed to inform the Brazilian exporters of the essential facts under consideration which formed the basis for the decision whether to apply definitive measures, thereby preventing the Brazilian exporters from adequately defending their interests, contrary to the requirement set forth in Article 6.9 (Claim 21);
- Argentina failed to establish individual margins of dumping for two Brazilian exporters, as required by Article 6.10 (Claim 22);

- Argentina acted inconsistently with Article 2.4 (Claim 23) by not making due allowance for differences in freight in the normal value established for two Brazilian exporters;

- Argentina acted inconsistently with Article 2.4 (Claim 24) by not making due allowance for differences in taxation, freight and financial cost in the normal value established for all other exporters;

- Argentina acted inconsistently with Article 2.4 (Claim 25) by incorrectly making allowances to normal value based on alleged physical characteristic differences between the product sold in Brazil and Argentina;

- Argentina acted inconsistently with Article 2.4 (Claim 26) by imposing an unreasonable burden of proof on three Brazilian exporters by not determining the dumping period of investigation and, thus, allowing these exporters to submit dumping information for the years 1996 through 1999, when the dumping period of investigation was later determined as from January 1998 through January 1999;

- Argentina acted inconsistently with Article 2.4.2 (Claim 27) by establishing a dumping margin based on an incorrect comparison between the export price and the normal value for two Brazilian exporters. Argentina established normal value based only on internal market transactions for which invoices were presented, instead of determining normal value based on all the reported transactions in the internal market for the period. The DCD established the margins of dumping for these two Brazilian exporters on the basis of a comparison of a weighted average statistical sample of normal value with a weighted average of prices of all comparable export transactions;

- Argentina has acted inconsistently with Article 9.2 (Claim 28) and Article 9.3 (Claim 29) by imposing a variable antidumping duty that can exceed the margin of dumping established in the final determination;

- Argentina acted inconsistently with Article 12.2.2 (Claim 30) by failing to provide how the "minimum export price" was established in the determination to impose definitive antidumping duties;

- Argentina acted inconsistently with Article 5.8 (Claim 31) by failing to reject the application and promptly terminate the investigation, as soon as the CNCE determined in Record No. 405 that there was insufficient evidence of injury or threat of injury to justify the initiation of the investigation;

- By using different periods to evaluate the relevant economic factors and indices listed in Article 3.4, Argentina failed to make a final injury determination based on positive evidence and involving an objective examination as provided for in Articles 3.1, 3.4 and 3.5 (Claim 32);

- Argentina acted inconsistently with Article 12.2.2 (Claim 33) by failing to explain in the final determination why the CNCE examined the relevant economic factors and indices listed in Article 3.4 based on different periods;

- The injury analysis in the final determination did not exclude the imports of two Brazilian exporters, even though the DCD considered that these were not "dumped imports". By not excluding the imports of these two Brazilian exporters from the "dumped imports", the CNCE did not properly consider the volume of the "dumped imports", the effect of the "dumped imports" on prices, and the impact of the "dumped imports" on the domestic industry, as provided for in Articles 3.2 (Claim 34) and 3.4 (Claim 36). The flawed evaluation of the "dumped imports" indicates that the final injury determination was not based on positive evidence and did not involve an objective examination as required by Article 3.1 (Claim 35);

- By not excluding the imports from these two Brazilian exporters from the "dumped imports", Argentina failed to properly consider injury as prescribed in Article 3.1, and, consequently, did not properly demonstrate the causal link between the "dumped imports" and the injury to the domestic industry as provided for in Article 3.5 (Claim 37);

- Argentina acted inconsistently with Articles 3.4 (Claim 38) and 3.1 (Claim 39) by failing to evaluate all the relevant economic factors and indices listed in Article 3.4;

- Argentina acted inconsistently with Article 12.2.2 (Claim 40) by failing to adequately provide and consider in the final determination the evaluation of all relevant economic factors and indices listed in Article 3.4;

- Argentina has acted inconsistently with Article 4.1 (Claim 41) by considering that 46 per cent constituted the major proportion of the total domestic production of poultry in Argentina and, thus, qualified as the domestic industry; and

- By determining dumping, injury and causal link inconsistently with the provisions of the *AD Agreement*, Argentina has acted inconsistently with Article VI of *GATT 1994* and Article 1 of the *AD Agreement*.

(b) recommend that the DSB request Argentina to bring these actions into conformity with *GATT 1994* and the *AD Agreement*;

(c) suggest ways in which Argentina could implement the Panel's recommendations, as provided in Article 19.1 of the *DSU*; and

(d) suggest that, in light of the numerous outcome-decisive violations of the *AD Agreement* that Argentina immediately repeal Resolution

No. 574/2000 imposing definitive anti-dumping duties on eviscerated poultry from Brazil.[21]

B. *Argentina*

3.2 In its first written submission, Argentina requested that the Panel:

(a) refrain from ruling on the forty-one claims of inconsistency with various provisions of the *AD Agreement* submitted by Brazil.

If the Panel should decide not to accede to the above request, Argentina requested that the Panel:

(b) reject Brazil's claims that Resolution No. 574/2000 of the Ministry of the Economy of Argentina is inconsistent with:

- Articles 5.2, 5.3, 5.7 and 5.8 of the *AD Agreement*;
- Article 12.1 of the *AD Agreement*;
- Articles 6.1.1, 6.1.2, 6.1.3, 6.2 and 6.8, and paragraphs 3, 5, 6 and 7 of Annex II, and Articles 6.9 and 6.10 of the *AD Agreement*;
- Articles 2.4 and 2.4.2 of the *AD Agreement*;
- Articles 3.1, 3.2, 3.4 and 3.5 of the *AD Agreement*;
- Article 4.1 of the *AD Agreement*;
- Articles 9.2 and 9.3 of the *AD Agreement*;
- Article 12.2.2 of the *AD Agreement*.

(c) reject the request for the immediate repeal of Resolution No. 574/2000 imposing definitive anti-dumping duties.[22]

IV. ARGUMENTS OF THE PARTIES

4.1 The arguments of the parties, as contained in their submissions to the Panel, are attached as Annexes (see List of Annexes, page vi).

4.2 The parties' answers to questions both from the Panel and from the other party, and their comments on each other's answers, are also attached as Annexes (see List of Annexes, page vi).

V. ARGUMENTS OF THE THIRD PARTIES

5.1 The arguments of the third parties, Canada, Chile, the European Communities, Guatemala, Paraguay and the United States, are set out in their submissions to the Panel and are attached to this Report as Annexes. The third parties' answers to the Panel's questions are also attached as Annexes (see List of Annexes, page vi).

---

[21] Brazil's first written submission, paras. 549 and 550.
[22] Argentina's first written submission, para. 322.

VI. INTERIM REVIEW

6.1   The Panel issued the draft descriptive (factual and argument) sections of its report to the parties on 20 December 2002 in accordance with Article 15.1 of the DSU. Both parties offered written comments on the draft descriptive sections on 13 January 2003. The Panel noted all these comments and amended the draft descriptive part where appropriate. The Panel issued its Interim Report to the parties on 25 February 2003 in accordance with Article 15.2 of the DSU. On 11 March 2003, both parties requested that the Panel review precise aspects of the Interim Report. Neither of the parties requested an interim review meeting. On 18 March 2003, both parties submitted written comments on the other party's written requests for interim review. The Panel carefully reviewed the arguments made, and addresses them below, in accordance with Article 15.3 of the DSU.[23]

A.   *Previous Mercosur Proceedings*

6.2   Argentina asked the Panel to include a reference to the prior MERCOSUR proceedings in Section II (Factual Aspects) of the Report. Brazil asked the Panel to reject this request. Having considered carefully the arguments of the parties, we have included a reference to the prior MERCOSUR proceedings in Section II (Factual Aspects) of the Report.

6.3   Concerning paragraphs 7.35 and 7.36 of the Interim Report (paras 7.35 and 7.36 of the final Report), Argentina referred to the Appellate Body report in *United States - Tax Treatment for "Foreign Sales Corporations"*[24] to invoke a "principle of good faith with respect to the objective presentation of the facts of a dispute".[25] We note that the Appellate Body in that case was referring to the requirement for both complaining and responding Members "to comply with the requirements of the *DSU* (and related requirements in other covered agreements) in good faith".[26] However, since Argentina has not argued that Brazil failed to comply with any requirements of the *DSU* (or related requirements in other covered agreements) in bringing these proceedings, good faith compliance *with those requirements* is not an issue in the present case. The Appellate Body report in *US - FSC* is therefore not relevant in the present case.

6.4   Argentina made a number of comments regarding paragraphs 7.38 and 7.39 (paras. 7.38 and 7.39 of the final Report). However, we saw nothing in Argentina's comments that caused us to make any changes to the Report.

6.5   In light of an issue raised by Argentina, we have deleted footnote 52 of the Interim Report.

6.6   Concerning para. 7.41 of the Interim Report (para. 7.41 of the final Report), Argentina asserted that the MERCOSUR ruling should be taken into account "for the purposes of *interpretation* of the current dispute" (emphasis in original). However, Argentina still failed to point to any element of the MERCOSUR ruling that would

---

[23] Section VI of this Report entitled "Interim Review" therefore forms part of the findings of the final panel report, in accordance with Article 15.3 of the DSU.
[24] Appellate Body Report, *United States - Tax Treatment for "Foreign Sales Corporations"* ("*US - FSC*"), WT/DS108/AB/R, adopted 20 March 2000, DSR 2000:III, 1619.
[25] Argentina's comments to the Interim Report of the Panel, para. 5.
[26] *US - FSC, supra*, note 24, para. 166.

require the Panel to interpret specific provisions of the WTO agreements in a particular way. Argentina effectively wanted the Panel to "interpret" the WTO agreements in such a way that it follows the MERCOSUR ruling and finds against Brazil. This, however, would go beyond the mere interpretation of specific WTO provisions: it would be tantamount to requiring the Panel to rule in a particular way. This argument was already addressed in para. 7.41 of the Interim Report.

B. Claim 10

6.7 Brazil made a number of comments regarding the scope of the Panel's findings under this Claim. In particular, Brazil asserted that our findings should include Catarinense. We have amended our findings to resolve the issues raised by these comments.

C. Claim 11

6.8 Brazil asserts that the Panel erred by stating in the Interim Report that Brazil initially claimed that Penabranca was notified by the DCD on 15 September 1999 and that only at a subsequent stage did Brazil assert that there was no evidence on the record indicating that the DCD ever contacted or notified the exporter Penabranca of the investigation. Brazil refers to footnotes 18 and 78 of Brazil's first written submission which provide that "from the documents of the investigation to which Brazil had access to, Brazil was not able to find the DCD's notification to the Brazilian exporter Penabranca". As a result, we made changes to our characterization of Brazil's presentation of evidence regarding Penabranca.

6.9 Argentina disagrees with certain views expressed by the Panel in para. 7.143 of the Interim Report. First, we understand Argentina to argue that the requests for information sent to certain Brazilian exporters on 15 September 1999 cannot be considered to be "questionnaire[s]" within the meaning of Article 6.1.1 of the *AD Agreement*. Although we slightly amended para. 7.143 of the Interim Report, this does not affect our conclusion that those requests were "questionnaires" within the meaning of Article 6.1.1. We also understand Argentina to argue that it never stated "that the total time-period for the [reply of] questionnaire responses was 30 days including the extension."[27] As a result, we made changes in respect of paras. 7.144 and 7.145 of the Interim Report. The abovementioned changes resulted in the bulk of paras 7.143, 7.144 and 7.145 of the Interim Report being deleted. The remnants of these paragraphs are set forth in para. 7.140 of the final Report.

D. Claim 13

6.10 Brazil identified an inconsistency in the Interim Report between the scope of the Panel's Article 6.2 findings and the Panel's treatment of Penabranca under other claims. We have addressed this inconsistency by modifying the Panel's treatment of Penabranca in Claims 10, 11 and 12.

6.11 Brazil also raised general concerns regarding the Panel's treatment of one of its Article 6.2 claims. Upon close inspection of Brazil's Request for Establishment of

---

[27] Argentina's comments to the Interim Report of the Panel, para. 17.

a panel, we find that the specific Article 6.2 claim at issue falls outside our terms of reference. We have modified our findings accordingly.

E. Claim 17

6.12 Argentina points to an inconsistency in the Panel's review of the DCD's treatment of data submitted by Catarinense in the context of Claims 17 and 19 (paras. 7.189 and 7.190 of the Interim Report / paras 7.187 and 7.188 of the final Report). Argentina asserts that, to the extent that the Panel found that the DCD was entitled to reject Catarinense's normal value data because it had failed to comply with an accreditation obligation, the Panel should also find that the DCD was entitled to reject Catarinense's export price data for the same reason. Brazil, on the other hand, requests us to affirm the conclusion in para. 7.190 of the Interim Report (para. 7.188 of the final Report).

6.13 We have examined carefully Argentina's comments, and agree that Catarinense's failure to comply with the relevant accreditation obligation should cause us to reject both Claims 17 and 19 regarding that exporter. We have amended our findings regarding Claim 17 accordingly (see para. 7.184 of the final Report).

6.14 Brazil requested us to verify whether the investigating authority had requested Catarinense to provide the information to have authorized legal status / accreditation. We consider that the correspondence referred to by Brazil in Exhibit BRA-27 shows that the DCD informed Catarinense of the need to comply with certain domestic procedures set forth in Law No. 19,549 and Decrees No. 1759/72 and 1883/91.[28] Brazil further asserts that Argentina's argument that Catarinense's export data was disregarded because of lack of accreditation constitutes *ex post* rationalization.[29] We do not agree with Brazil. In this regard, we note that the Report of 4 January 2000[30] and the Final Affirmative Dumping Determination[31] contain statements that the investigating authority informed Catarinense of the requirements under Law 19,549 and Decrees 1759/72 and 1883/91 with respect to submissions to the Administration.

6.15 Brazil argues that, by using the export price found for all other exporters instead of the individual export price found for Catarinense, the authority failed to use special circumspection in basing its export price findings on a secondary source of information. We note that Argentina did not determine an individual margin of dumping for Catarinense (contrary to Article 6.10 of the *AD Agreement* (Claim 22)). Since Argentina was not entitled to use an "all other exporters" rate for Catarinense,

---

[28] Brazil also claimed that Catarinense was not informed that this was the reason why its questionnaire response was being rejected, contrary to para. 6 of Annex II. We note, however, that Brazil did not invoke Annex II, para. 6, in the context of Claim 17 during the Panel proceedings (see paras 282 - 290 of Brazil's first written submission).

[29] We understand Brazil to make such request with respect to Claims 17 and 19. (Brazil's comments to Argentina's request for review of the Interim Report, para. 32) We consider that this is a comment which Brazil should have raised in its own request for review of the Interim Report, which Brazil did not do. We consider that for this reason alone we are precluded from examining it. In any case, we note that in para. 6.14 *supra* we state that the Report of 4 January 2000 and the Final Affirmative Dumping Determination contain statements that the investigating authority informed Catarinense of the requirements under Law 19,549 and Decrees 1759/72 and 1883/91 with respect to submissions to the Administration.

[30] Exhibit BRA-28, p. 2795.

[31] Exhibit BRA-15, p. 3025.

we see no need to consider whether or not Argentina exercised special circumspection in doing so.

F. Claim 21

6.16 Brazil requests the Panel to reverse its findings in para. 7.231 of the Interim Report (para. 7.229 of the final Report). Brazil bases such request on the fact that a party needs to know what information is not ultimately going to be used in the final determination by the investigating authority in order to provide reasons and arguments in its defence.[32] However, we see nothing in Brazil's comments that would cause us to change our interpretation of the plain meaning of Article 6.9 of the *AD Agreement*.

G. Claim 22

6.17 Argentina asserts that none of the paragraphs of Annex II to the *AD Agreement* establishes an obligation to determine an individual margin of dumping in cases in which the exporters have not cooperated in the investigation. For this reason, Argentina asserts that, when an investigating authority must resort to applying the rules of Annex II owing to lack of cooperation on the part of the interested party, the general rule laid down by Article 6.10 of the *AD Agreement* no longer applies. In particular, Argentina asserts that the general rule imposed by Article 6.10 does not apply to Catarinense, an exporter which was found by the Panel not to have accredited legal status in the context of the investigation before the Argentine authorities. With respect to Argentina's comments, Brazil asserts that the fact that an exporter has not submitted the relevant and appropriate information to establish normal value and export price does not exclude the authority's obligation under Article 6.10 to calculate an individual margin of dumping.

6.18 We fully addressed the relationship between Articles 6.10, on the one hand, and 6.8 and Annex II to the *AD Agreement*, on the other, in paras. 7.217 and 7.218 of the Interim Report (paras. 7.215 and 7.216 of the final Report). We see nothing in Argentina's comments that would cause us to amend our findings and conclusion with respect to this claim.

H. Claim 27

6.19 Argentina made a number of comments regarding the Panel's findings under Claim 27. In short, Argentina accepts the Panel's finding "with respect to the obligation to consider all of the transactions carried out in the ordinary course of trade to calculate the normal value", but challenges the Panel's finding of violation. Argentina submits that all the relevant domestic transactions are considered if a statistically valid sample is used.

6.20 Although there may be circumstances where an investigating authority may find it useful to use statistically valid samples of domestic sales transactions for the purpose of establishing normal value, such sampling is not envisaged by the plain meaning of Article 2.4.2, read in light of Article 2.2.1. Accordingly, we see no reason to change our findings on this matter.

---

[32] Brazil's comments to the Interim Report of the Panel, para. 44.

I. Claims 28 - 30

6.21 With respect to Claims 28 - 30, Brazil stated that it was not claiming that variable anti-dumping duties were *per se* inconsistent with Articles 9.2 and 9.3 of the *AD Agreement*. We have amended our report accordingly.

6.22 Brazil also made other arguments in support of its Claims 28 - 30. While these additional arguments resulted in some minor changes to the Panel's reasoning, the findings and conclusions of the Panel remain unchanged.

6.23 We note that Brazil seeks to suggest that our findings would enable a Member to "calculate a dumping margin in the investigation and apply any duty it saw fit".[33] This is plainly not the case, since the amount of duty to be collected must never exceed the relevant margin of dumping. The fact that the Panel finds that variable anti-dumping duties need not be limited to the margin of dumping established in the investigation does not mean that a Member may apply any variable anti-dumping duty it sees fit.

VII. FINDINGS

7.1 This case raises issues concerning the initiation of the anti-dumping investigation on poultry from Brazil, the conduct of that investigation, and the imposition of final measures. Before addressing Brazil's claims, we shall first examine two preliminary issues raised in these proceedings, and then consider a number of general issues relevant to these proceedings.

A. Preliminary Issues

7.2 Argentina has raised two preliminary issues.[34] The first concerns the disclosure of written statements under Article 18.2 of the *DSU*. The second concerns earlier MERCOSUR dispute settlement proceedings regarding the anti-dumping measure at issue.

1. Disclosure of Written Statements - Article 18.2 of the DSU

(a) Arguments of the Parties / Third Parties

7.3 By letter dated 8 August 2002, Brazil informed the Panel that it had received a request from a non-party Member for a non-confidential summary of the information contained in its submission that could be disclosed to the public. Brazil informed the Panel that it had classified as non-confidential the volume containing the text of its first submission, while the four volumes containing the exhibits to the first submission would be treated as confidential. Brazil stated that it would make the first (non-confidential) volume of its first written submission available to the public,

---

[33] Brazil's comments to the Interim Report of the Panel, para. 73.
[34] Argentina could be understood to have raised an additional preliminary issue, concerning standard of review, in paras. 9-15 of Section II.1 of its first written submission. Unlike the two preliminary issues which we do address, however, there is no request for a ruling on that additional issue in the pleadings set forth in Section IV of Argentina's submission (Section IV only requests a ruling in respect of paras. 23-25 of Section II, which do not pertain to the issue raised in Section II.1). Accordingly, we consider that Argentina has not requested any ruling in respect of the comments on standard of review set forth in paras. 9-15 of Section II.1 of its first written submission.

after providing Argentina an opportunity to indicate whether that volume should be revised to exclude any information deemed to be confidential.

7.4   By letter dated 15 August, Argentina objected to Brazil's decision to make the entirety of its first written submission (excluding exhibits) available to the public. Argentina submitted that a Member is only entitled by Article 18.2 of the *DSU* to disclose written statements of its positions. It is not entitled to disclose the entirety of its written submissions to the panel, since such submissions should remain confidential. According to Argentina, Article 18.2 of the *DSU* draws a clear distinction between "written submissions" and position "statements". Argentina did not allege that any of the information that Brazil proposed to make available was confidential.

7.5   On 21 August 2002, Brazil informed the Panel that it had made its first written submission (excluding those volumes containing exhibits) available to the public. Brazil noted that Argentina had not raised any issues regarding the confidentiality of information that Brazil had initially proposed to make available. Regarding the interpretation of Article 18.2 of the *DSU*, Brazil asserted *inter alia* that the *DSU* does not define the limit or scope, length, shape, form, or content of "statements" that may be disclosed by a party to a dispute. Brazil asserted that in the present case the relevant "statements" were identical to Brazil's first written submission minus exhibits.

7.6   On 23 August 2002, Canada submitted that Argentina's interpretation of Article 18.2 of the *DSU* was inconsistent with the spirit of transparency informing the operations of the WTO and the dispute settlement mechanism. Canada also asserted *inter alia* that Argentina's distinction between "written submission" and "statement" was formalistic, since a Member may consider that the most authoritative "statement" of its position in a WTO dispute was to be found in its written submissions.

7.7   On 27 August 2002, Argentina asserted that "if the Panel understands that the terms 'written submissions' and 'statements' in Article 18.2 of the *DSU* have the same meaning, Argentina would be ready to accept such interpretation". On the same date, Argentina asked the Panel to express its "view" on this matter.

7.8   On 9 September 2002, in its third party submission, the United States requested that the Panel decline to provide views on the proper interpretation of Article 18.2 of the *DSU*. The United States argued *inter alia* that Article 18.2 of the *DSU* falls outside the Panel's terms of reference, and that the Panel would effectively be providing an interpretation of that provision, contrary to the exclusive authority of the Ministerial Conference and General Council under Article IX:2 of the *Marrakesh Agreement Establishing the World Trade Organization* ("*WTO Agreement*") to interpret that Agreement.

7.9   On 26 September 2002, during the Panel's first substantive meeting with the parties, Argentina stated that it did not oppose Brazil's right to make its first written submission available to the public. However, Argentina considered that Brazil should not have made its first written submission available to the public so early in the Panel proceedings. Argentina asserted that, consistent with paragraph 11 of the Panel's working procedures (whereby the parties' submissions shall be included in the Panel report), Brazil's first written submission should only have been made public once the Panel's report was published.

7.10 Following Argentina's statement during the Panel's first substantive meeting with the parties, the Panel put the following question to Argentina:

> "Argentina stated at this morning's meeting that it was not opposed, as a matter of principle, to Brazil having made its first written submission available to the public. Instead, Argentina was concerned with the timing of Brazil's action. Does this mean that Argentina accepts that a Member may make its written submissions to a panel available to the public at some point in time without infringing Article 18.2 of the DSU? Would Brazil violate DSU Article 18.2 if it made its written submissions available to the public after the Panel issued its final report?"

7.11 Argentina replied "Yes, following the provisions of the Article 18.2 of the DSU" to the first part of the Panel's question, and "No" to the second part thereof.[35]

(b) Evaluation by the Panel

7.12 Before addressing the substance of the preliminary issue raised by Argentina, we shall first examine the US argument that we should decline to rule on the matter raised by Argentina. By virtue of Article 1.1 of the *DSU*, the provisions of the *DSU* apply to all WTO dispute settlement proceedings, subject to certain special or additional rules and procedures on dispute settlement identified in Appendix 2 to the *DSU*. The provisions of the *DSU* therefore apply in all cases, whether or not they are mentioned in a Member's request for establishment of a panel. Indeed, we are not being asked to rule on whether a measure identified in the request for establishment is consistent with Article 18.2 of the *DSU*. Rather, we are being asked to make such rulings in respect of Article 18.2 of the *DSU* as are necessary to manage procedural aspects of these proceedings. By ruling in respect of Article 18.2 of the *DSU*, we are simply acting in conformity with Article 1.1 of the *DSU*.[36] We are not purporting to make an interpretation within the meaning of Article IX:2 of the *WTO Agreement*. Accordingly, we reject the US argument that the Panel should decline to rule on the matter raised by Argentina.

7.13 This issue concerns Article 18.2 of the *DSU*, which provides that:

> "Written submissions to the panel or the Appellate Body shall be treated as confidential, but shall be made available to the parties to the dispute. Nothing in this Understanding shall preclude a party to a dispute from disclosing statements of its own positions to the public. Members shall treat as confidential information submitted by another Member to the panel or the Appellate Body which that Member has designated as confidential. A party to a dispute shall also, upon request of a Member, provide a non-confidential summary of the

---

[35] Argentina replied by fax on 22 October 2002.
[36] We note that other panels have similarly made rulings on procedural matters under the *DSU*. For example, the panel in *US - FSC (Article 21.5 - EC)* ruled on third party access to rebuttal submissions in light of Article 10.3 of the *DSU* (Panel Report, *United States - Tax Treatment for "Foreign Sales Corporations" - Recourse to Article 21.5 of the DSU by the European Communities ("US - FSC (Article 21.5 - EC)"*), WT/DS108/RW, adopted 29 January 2002, Section VI.A, DSR 2002:I, 119.). Although the substance of that panel's ruling was reversed by the Appellate Body, the ability of the panel to make rulings in respect of Article 10.3 of the *DSU* was not challenged. (Appellate Body Report, *US - FSC (Article 21.5 - EC)*, WT/DS108/AB/RW, adopted 29 January 2002, DSR 2002:I, 55, para. 252)

information contained in its written submissions that could be disclosed to the public."

7.14   On substance, we agree with Canada that Argentina's interpretation[37] of Article 18.2 of the *DSU* results in a formalistic distinction between the terms "written submission" and "statement". In doing so, Argentina negates that a party's written submissions to a panel necessarily contain statements of that party's positions. In our view, the first two sentences of Article 18.2 of the *DSU* should not be read in formalistic isolation of one another. Read together, and in context of one another, the first two sentences of Article 18.2 of the *DSU* mean that while one party shall not disclose the submissions of another party, each party is entitled to disclose statements of its own positions, subject to the confidentiality requirement set forth in the third sentence of Article 18.2 of the *DSU*. We recall that a party's written submissions to a panel necessarily contain statements of that party's positions. In our view, therefore, disclosing submissions to a panel is one way for a party to disclose statements of its positions. If a party chooses to make public the totality of the statements of its own position contained in its written submission, it is entitled to do so, provided the confidentiality requirement of the third sentence of Article 18.2 of the *DSU* is respected. Since Argentina has not argued that Brazil violated its confidentiality obligation, we do not consider that Brazil's decision to disclose the entirety of the statements of position contained in its first written submission to the Panel (excluding exhibits) was inconsistent with Article 18.2 of the *DSU*.[38]

7.15   Furthermore, we note that, by the time of our first substantive meeting with the parties, Argentina was no longer arguing that Brazil was not entitled to make the entirety of its written submissions to the Panel available to the public during the Panel proceedings. Implicitly, therefore, Argentina ultimately agreed that Brazil was entitled to make its written submission available to the public pursuant to Article 18.2 of the *DSU*. Although Argentina argued that Brazil should not have done so until after publication of the Panel's report, we find no basis for this argument in Article 18.2 of the *DSU*. Article 18.2 sets no temporal limits on Members' rights and obligations under that provision. Nor do we find any basis for this argument in paragraph 11 of the Panel's Working Procedures, which concerns the preparation of the descriptive part of the Panel's report.[39] We see nothing in this provision which would impose any limits on rights accruing to Members under Article 18.2 of the *DSU*.

---

[37]   We are referring to the arguments set forth in Argentina's submission of 15 August 2002.

[38]   In support of its position, Brazil also relied on the last sentence of Article 18.2 of the *DSU*. Since we reject the preliminary issue raised by Argentina on the basis of the first two sentences of Article 18.2 of the *DSU*, there is no need for us to consider arguments pertaining to the last sentence of that provision.

[39]   Paragraph 11 of the Panel's Working Procedures provides that "[t]he descriptive part of the Panel's report will include the procedural and factual background to the present dispute. There will be no description of the main arguments of the parties and third parties as such. Instead, the Panel will attach the parties' submissions (including first and second written submissions, written versions of the first and second oral statements, and each parties' replies to questions from the other party and from the Panel) to its report. Upon request of a party, specific portions of a submission designated by that party as confidential at the time of its submission will not be included in the submission attached to the Panel's report."

7.16   In conclusion, we do not consider that Brazil's decision to disclose the entirety of the statements of position contained in its first written submission to the Panel (excluding exhibits) was inconsistent with Article 18.2 of the *DSU*.

2.   Previous Mercosur Proceedings

7.17   Argentina has raised a preliminary issue concerning the fact that, prior to bringing WTO dispute settlement proceedings against Argentina's anti-dumping measure, Brazil had challenged that measure before a MERCOSUR Ad Hoc Arbitral Tribunal. Argentina requests that, in light of the prior MERCOSUR proceedings, the Panel refrain from ruling on the claims raised by Brazil in the present WTO dispute settlement proceedings. In the alternative, Argentina asserts that the Panel should be bound by the ruling of the MERCOSUR Tribunal.

(a)   Arguments of the Parties / Third Parties

7.18   Argentina considers that Brazil's conduct in bringing the dispute successively before different fora, first MERCOSUR and then the WTO, constitutes a legal approach that is contrary to the principle of good faith and which, in the case at issue, warrants invocation of the principle of estoppel. Argentina is not invoking the principle of *res judicata*. In the alternative, Argentina submits that in view of the relevant rule of international law applicable in the relations between parties pursuant to Article 31.3(c) of the *Vienna Convention on the Law of Treaties* ("*Vienna Convention*"),[40] in the light of Article 3.2 of the *DSU* the Panel cannot disregard, in its consideration and substantiation of the present case brought by Brazil, the precedents set by the proceedings in the framework of MERCOSUR.

7.19   Argentina asserts that, in the framework of MERCOSUR, it is a standing practice for all parties - including Brazil - to accept the obligations deriving from the legislative framework in force, including the MERCOSUR Treaty of Asunción and the Protocol of Brasilia. In Argentina's view, a State party is not acting in good faith if it first has recourse to the mechanism of the integration process to settle its dispute with another State party and then, dissatisfied with the outcome, files the same complaint within a different framework, making matters worse by omitting any reference to the previous procedure and its outcome.

7.20   Argentina asserts that the essential elements of estoppel are "(i) a statement of fact which is clear and unambiguous; (ii) this statement must be voluntary, unconditional, and authorized; (iii) there must be reliance in good faith upon the statement ... to the advantage of the party making the statement".[41] Argentina submits that Brazil's previous conduct with respect to the acceptance of awards, confirmed by the signature of the Protocol of Olivos, invalidates the complaint against Argentina that Brazil is now trying to substantiate on the basis of the *DSU*. Argentina submits that there is no provision or rule that prohibits a WTO panel from examining, and where it deems appropriate applying, the principle of estoppel. Argentina asserts that estoppel is a principle of international law and, according to the Appellate Body in *US - Gasoline*, there is "a measure of recognition that the *General Agreement* is not to be read in clinical isolation from public international

---

[40]   Done at Vienna, 23 May 1969, 1155 U.N.T.S. 331; 8 International Legal Materials 679.
[41]   I. Brownlie, *Principles of Public International Law* (Clarendon Press, 1990), p. 641.

law."[42] Argentina asserts that WTO panels are called upon to apply public international law to settle the disputes brought before them, and that previous panels have addressed the principle of estoppel.

7.21   Argentina's alternative argument is based on Article 31.3(c) of the *Vienna Convention*. Argentina submits that Article 3.2 of the *DSU* provides a rule of interpretation for the Panel, and WTO legal practice has confirmed that rule by referring to Articles 31 and 32 of the *Vienna Convention*. Argentina asserts that, in accordance with Article 31.3(c) of the *Vienna Convention*, the interpretation of a treaty must take account of all relevant rules of international law applicable between the parties at the time of implementation. In Argentina's view, the regulatory framework of MERCOSUR and the legal consequences deriving from the implementation of the Protocol of Brasilia by the Ad Hoc Arbitral Tribunal in the case at issue are relevant rules of public international law within the meaning of Article 31.3(c) of the *Vienna Convention*, such that the Panel is bound by earlier MERCOSUR rulings regarding the measure at issue.

7.22   Brazil submits that the principle of estoppel is not applicable in the present case, in part because the dispute before the MERCOSUR Tribunal was grounded on a different legal basis from the dispute before this Panel. In any event, Brazil asserts that the principle of estoppel means that "a party is prevented by his own acts from claiming a right to the detriment of other party who was entitled to rely on such conduct and has acted accordingly."[43] As noted by the panel in *EEC (Member States) - Bananas I*, "estoppel could only result from the express, or in exceptional cases implied, consent of such parties or of the CONTRACTING PARTIES".[44] According to Brazil, the simple fact that it had brought a similar dispute to the MERCOSUR Tribunal does not represent that Brazil has consented not to bring the current dispute before the WTO, especially when the dispute before this Panel is based on a different legal basis than the dispute brought before the MERCOSUR Tribunal. Brazil asserts that the MERCOSUR Protocol of Olivos on Dispute Settlement, signed on 18 February 2002, cannot be raised here as an implicit or express consent by Brazil to refrain from bringing the present case to the WTO dispute settlement, again because the object of the earlier MERCOSUR proceedings was different from the object of the present WTO proceedings. Furthermore, the Protocol of Olivos does not apply to disputes that have already been concluded under the Protocol of Brasilia.

7.23   Regarding Argentina's reference to Article 3.2 of the *DSU*, Brazil asserts that Article 3.2 deals exclusively with the clarification of the existing provisions of the WTO agreements and does not provide that a previous ruling by an international tribunal constrains a WTO panel's interpretation of a WTO agreement. In fact, Article 3.2 requires a WTO panel to consider a claim brought by a Member with respect to a violation of a covered agreement in order to preserve that Member's rights under that agreement.

7.24   Furthermore, Brazil notes that contrary to Argentina's allegations, Brazil has not engaged in an abusive exercise of its rights under the WTO agreements[45], nor has

---

[42]   Appellate Body Report, *United States - Standards for Reformulated and Conventional Gasoline* ("*US - Gasoline*"), WT/DS2/AB/R, adopted 20 May 1996, p. 20, DSR 1996:I, 3, at 29.
[43]   *Black's Law Dictionary* (West Publishing Co., 1990), p. 551.
[44]   Panel Report, *EEC - Member States' Import Regimes for Bananas* ("*EEC (Member States) - Bananas I*"), 3 June 1993, unadopted, DS32/R.
[45]   Argentina's first written submission, para. 23.

its conduct been contrary to good faith by not mentioning in the first submission the ruling by the MERCOSUR Tribunal.[46] Brazil did not refer to that ruling simply because it believed that it had no relevance to this case, since the claims currently before the Panel are not the same as the claims that were before the MERCOSUR Tribunal.

7.25   Chile, as a third party, asserts that Brazil is entitled to bring the present case before the WTO because the issues raised are different from the issues previously raised in MERCOSUR dispute settlement proceedings.

7.26   The European Communities, as a third party, asserts that Article 3.2 of the *DSU* is not relevant to these proceedings, since it is concerned exclusively with the interpretation of the WTO agreements, and not with the sources of WTO law. The European Communities submits that it is difficult to see how the interpretation of the provisions of MERCOSUR law made by the Ad Hoc Arbitral Tribunal could become relevant, in accordance with the rules laid down in Articles 31 and 32 of the *Vienna Convention*, for the interpretation of the provisions of the *AD Agreement* at issue in this dispute.

7.27   The European Communities does not consider it necessary to take a position on the issue of whether a Member would abuse its right to a panel under the *DSU* and, hence, act inconsistently with Article 3.10 if it were to request the establishment of a panel in violation of the principle of estoppel.[47] Indeed, this Panel need not reach this issue because, in any event, Brazil's conduct is not contrary to that principle. As noted by the panel in *EEC (Member States) - Bananas I*, estoppel can only "result from the express, or in exceptional cases implied consent of the complaining parties".[48] The facts alleged by Argentina are not sufficient to conclude that Brazil has "consented", whether explicitly or implicitly, not to bring this dispute before the WTO. The Protocol of Brasilia contains no provision which limits in any manner the right of the parties to request a panel under the WTO agreements with respect to a measure that has already been the subject of a dispute under that Protocol.[49] Thus, the

---

[46]   *Ibid.*, para. 16.

[47]   The European Communities notes that the panel in *India - Autos* suggested that a Member may be estopped from requesting the establishment of a panel with respect to a matter which has been the subject of a mutually agreed solution. (Panel Report, *India - Measures Affecting the Automotive Sector* ("*India - Autos*"), WT/DS146/R, WT/DS175/R and Corr.1, adopted 5 April 2002, footnote 364)

[48]   Panel Report, *EEC (Member States) - Bananas I*, *supra*, note 44, para 361. See also Panel Report, *Guatemala - Definitive Anti-Dumping Measures on Grey Portland Cement from Mexico* ("*Guatemala - Cement II*"), WT/DS156/R, adopted 17 November 2000, DSR 2000:XI, 5295, footnote 791: "it is clear that not any silence can be considered to constitute consent".

[49]   Unlike the more recent Protocol of Olivos on Dispute Settlement, which provides in its Article 1.2 that:

> "Las controversias comprendidas en el ámbito de aplicación del presente Protocolo que puedan también ser sometidas al sistema de solución de controversias de la Organización Mundial de Comercio o de otros esquemas preferenciales de comercio de que sean parte individualmente los Estados Partes del MERCOSUR, podrán someterse a uno u otro foro a elección de la parte demandante. Sin perjuicio de ello, las partes en la controversia podrán, de común acuerdo, convenir el foro.
> Una vez iniciado un procedimiento de solución de controversias de acuerdo al párrafo anterior, ninguna de las partes podrá recurrir a los mecanismos establecidos en los otros foros respecto del mismo objeto ..."

The Protocol of Olivos was signed on 18 February 2002 and has not entered into force yet. According to the European Communities, the question might be raised whether the request for the establishment of the panel made by Brazil on 25 February 2002, i.e., after the signature of the

mere fact that Brazil requested first the establishment of an Ad Hoc Arbitral Tribunal under the Protocol of Brasilia does not amount to a renunciation by Brazil to bring a dispute settlement action under the WTO agreements. Similarly, the mere fact that Brazil did not consider it necessary to take dispute settlement action under the WTO agreements following the arbitration rulings issued in a number of other cases cited by Argentina cannot be construed as an implicit renunciation by Brazil to its right under the WTO agreements to take such action in this case.

7.28 Paraguay, as a third party, considers that, in accordance with the general principles of public international law, this case is *res judicata* because it has already been brought under the dispute settlement procedure established within the framework of MERCOSUR, and under the Brasilia Protocol in particular. In this regard, Article 21[50] of the Brasilia Protocol clearly establishes the unappealable and binding nature of awards rendered by the Ad Hoc Arbitral Tribunal, which are deemed to be *res judicata* - a principle that should prevail in addressing this case.

7.29 Paraguay also refers to the MERCOSUR Protocol of Olivos which, although not yet in force, allows MERCOSUR members to choose the forum in which they wish disputes to be settled, with the restriction constituted by the exclusion clause, which stipulates that once a procedure has been initiated in one forum, this precludes resorting to any of the other forums provided for in the Protocol.

7.30 The United States, as a third party, asserts that the MERCOSUR dispute settlement rules are not within the Panel's terms of reference. Article 7.1 of the *DSU* makes quite clear that a Panel's role in a dispute is to make findings in light of the relevant provisions of the "covered agreements" at issue. The Protocol of Brasilia is not a covered agreement, and Argentina has not claimed that Brazil's actions with respect to the Protocol breach any provision of a covered agreement. Rather, Argentina's claim appears to be that Brazil's actions could be considered to be inconsistent with the terms of the Protocol. A claim of a breach of the Protocol is not within this Panel's terms of reference, and there are no grounds for the Panel to consider this matter. Argentina may, however, be able to pursue that claim under the MERCOSUR dispute settlement system.

7.31 Furthermore, the United States submits that Argentina's reliance on the principle of estoppel appears to relate to Brazil's obligations under MERCOSUR rather than to any provision of the *DSU* or the other covered agreements. As a result, the matter is not within the Panel's terms of reference and the Panel has no basis for making the requested finding. The United States also disagrees with Argentina that the Panel may apply what Argentina calls the principle of estoppel. The fact that Argentina cites to no textual basis for its request reflects the fact that Members have not consented to provide for the application of any such principle of estoppel in

---

Protocol of Olivos, was consistent with Brazil's obligation under Article 18 of the *Vienna Convention* not to defeat the object and purpose of a signed treaty prior to its entry into force. However, Article 50 of the Protocol of Olivos appears to suggest that it does not apply to disputes already decided in accordance with the Protocol of Brasilia.

[50] Article 21 reads as follows:
"1. The decisions of the Arbitral Tribunal cannot be appealed, and are binding on the State Parties to the controversies from the moment the respective notification is received and will be deemed by them to have the effect of res judicata.
2. The decisions should be complied with within a time-limit of fifteen (15) days, unless the Arbitral Tribunal fixes a different time-limit."

WTO dispute settlement. The term estoppel appears nowhere in the text nor does Argentina cite to any provision which in substance provides Argentina the type of defence it asserts. The United States also notes that the lack of any textual basis is reflected in the fact that no panel to date has applied a principle of estoppel. Moreover, there is no basis for attempting to import into WTO dispute settlement proceedings legal concepts with no grounding in the *DSU*. The lack of any textual basis is further emphasized by the lack of consistent description of the concept when panels have had occasion to discuss estoppel in the past. In *EEC (Member States) - Bananas I*, for example, the panel stated that estoppel can only "result from the express, or in exceptional cases implied, consent of the complaining parties."[51] In *EC - Asbestos* and *Guatemala - Cement II*, by contrast, the panels stated that estoppel is relevant when a party "reasonably relies" on the assurances of another party, and then suffers negative consequences resulting from a change in the other party's position.[52] According to the US, these inconsistencies illustrate the dangers of seeking to identify purportedly agreed-upon legal concepts beyond the only source all Members *have* agreed to - the text of the *DSU* itself.

7.32   Finally, the United States asserts that Argentina's citation of Article 3.2 of the *DSU* in support of its position is misplaced. By its plain terms, Article 3.2 is limited to the rules of *interpretation* used to clarify the existing provisions of the WTO agreements. Argentina's request that the Panel refuse to consider Brazil's claims does not present an issue of the proper interpretation of a provision of the WTO agreements.

(b)   Evaluation by the Panel

7.33   This preliminary issue concerns the principles of good faith and estoppel. It also relates to Article 3.2 of the *DSU* and Article 31.3(c) of the *Vienna Convention*.[53]

7.34   Argentina asserts that Brazil failed to act in good faith by first challenging Argentina's anti-dumping measure before a MERCOSUR Ad Hoc Tribunal and then, having lost that case, initiating WTO dispute settlement proceedings against the same measure. For the following reasons, however, we find that the preconditions for a finding that Brazil failed to act in good faith are not met.

7.35   The Appellate Body recently stated in *US - Offset Act (Byrd Amendment)* that "there is a basis for a dispute settlement panel to determine, in an appropriate case, whether a Member has not acted in good faith."[54] There are circumstances, therefore, in which a panel could find that a Member had failed to act in good faith. It is clear to

---

[51]   See Third Party Submission of the European Communities, citing Panel Report, *EEC (Member States) - Bananas I*, *supra*, note 44, para. 361.

[52]   The United States refers to the Panel Report, *European Communities - Measures Affecting Asbestos and Asbestos-Containing Products* ("*EC - Asbestos*"), WT/DS135/R and Add.1, adopted 5 April 2001, as modified by the Appellate Body Report, WT/DS135/AB/R, DSR 2001:VIII, 3305, para. 8.60 (citations omitted); Panel Report, *Guatemala - Cement II*, *supra*, note 48, paras. 8.23-24. The United States asserts that one could also argue that these panels are describing the concept of "detrimental reliance."

[53]   Argentina has made it clear that it is not invoking the principle of *res judicata*. Even though Paraguay considers this principle relevant to these proceedings, Paraguay, as a third party, does not have the right to determine the scope of any preliminary issues to be examined by us.

[54]   Appellate Body Report, *United States - Continued Dumping and Subsidy Offset Act of 2000* ("*US - Offset Act (Byrd Amendment)*"), WT/DS217/AB/R, WT/DS234/AB/R, adopted 27 January 2003, para. 297.

us, however, that such findings should not be made lightly. In *US - Offset Act (Byrd Amendment)* the Appellate Body found that:

> "Nothing, however, in the covered agreements supports the conclusion that simply because a WTO Member is found to have violated a substantive treaty provision, it has therefore not acted in good faith. In our view, it would be necessary to prove more than mere violation to support such a conclusion."[55]

7.36 On the basis of the abovementioned Appellate Body finding, we consider that two conditions must be satisfied before a Member may be found to have failed to act in good faith. First, the Member must have violated a substantive provision of the WTO agreements. Second, there must be something "more than mere violation". With regard to the first condition, Argentina has not alleged that Brazil violated any substantive provision of the WTO agreements in bringing the present case. Thus, even without examining the second condition, there is no basis for us to find that Brazil violated the principle of good faith in bringing the present proceedings before the WTO.

7.37 Argentina has also argued that Brazil is estopped from pursuing the present WTO dispute settlement proceedings. Argentina asserts that the principle of estoppel applies in circumstances where (i) a statement of fact which is clear and unambiguous, and which (ii) is voluntary, unconditional, and authorized, is (iii) relied on in good faith. We asked Argentina to explain exactly how it considers that these three conditions are satisfied in this case. In particular, we asked Argentina to identify the relevant "statement of fact" made by Brazil, and to describe how Argentina had relied on it in good faith.[56] Argentina replied:

> "Firstly, Argentina considers that Brazil's conduct in successively filing its case and activating dispute settlement proceedings in different fora, first in MERCOSUR and then in the WTO - particularly in view of the precedents described in Argentina's first written submission[1], i.e. recourse to the dispute settlement mechanism under the Protocol of Brasilia to settle conflicts with other MERCOSUR States parties and compliance with the content and scope of the arbitral awards in all of the disputes - provides statements of fact which meet the requirement of being clear, unambiguous, voluntary, unconditional and authorized, the essential elements of estoppel under the definition provided in paragraph 13 of Argentina's submission.
>
> In paragraph 20 of its rebuttal submission[2], Argentina sets out the elements which are present in the current dispute brought by Brazil before the WTO. Among these elements, the last sentence of subparagraph (iii) of paragraph 20 states that: "Consequently Brazil's previous conduct with respect to the acceptance of awards, confirmed by the signature of the Protocol of Olivos, invalidates the complaint against Argentina that Brazil is now trying to substantiate on the basis of the DSU."

---

[55] *Ibid.*, para. 298.
[56] Question 66 from the Panel reads: "Regarding para. 13 of Argentina's second submission ("ASS"), what was the "statement of fact" (point I) allegedly made by Brazil? Please explain how Argentina relied in good faith upon that alleged statement (point III)".

Moreover, the fact that Brazil signed the Protocol of Olivos on 18 February 2002 - by which it expressly accepted the choice of forum clause - and then, seven days later, on 25 February 2002, requested the establishment of a Panel in the current dispute,

displays a clear contradiction in its conduct, in which Argentina had had full confidence, both countries being member States of MERCOSUR; and Argentina is now suffering the negative impact of this change of position.[3] This fact was also raised in the submissions of the EC[4] and Paraguay[5] as third parties."[57]

---

[1] First written submission of Argentina, 29 August 2002, paragraphs 18-22 and corresponding footnotes.

[2] Rebuttal of Argentina, 17 October 2002, paragraph 20.

[3] In fact, Argentina has already approved the Protocol of Olivos. On 9 October 2002, the National Congress adopted the Protocol of Olivos by Law 25,663, promulgated by the Executive through Decree 2091/02 of 18 October 2002 and published in Official Bulletin of the Republic of Argentina No. 30,008 of 21 October 2002.

[4] Third party submission of the European Communities, 9 September 2002, paragraph 17 and footnote 17.

[5] Third party submission of Paraguay, 9 September 2002, paragraph 8.

7.38 We do not consider Argentina's response sufficient to establish that the three conditions it identified for the application of the principle of estoppel are fulfilled in the present case.[58] Regarding the first condition identified by Argentina, we do not consider that Brazil has made a clear and unambiguous statement to the effect that, having brought a case under the MERCOSUR dispute settlement framework, it would not subsequently resort to WTO dispute settlement proceedings. In this regard, we note that the panel in *EEC (Member States) - Bananas I* found that estoppel can only "result from the express, or in exceptional cases implied consent of the complaining parties".[59] We agree. There is no evidence on the record that Brazil made an express statement that it would not bring WTO dispute settlement proceedings in respect of measures previously challenged through MERCOSUR. Nor does the record indicate exceptional circumstances requiring us to imply any such statement. In particular, the fact that Brazil chose not to invoke its WTO dispute settlement rights after previous MERCOSUR dispute settlement proceedings does not, in our view, mean that Brazil implicitly waived its rights under the *DSU*. This is especially because the Protocol of Brasilia, under which previous MERCOSUR cases

---

[57] Argentina's reply to Question 66 from the Panel.

[58] The United States has argued that there is no basis for a WTO panel to apply the principle of estoppel. Since we find that the conditions identified by Argentina for the application of the principle of estoppel are not present, we do not consider it necessary to determine whether or not we would have had the authority to apply the principle of estoppel if the relevant conditions had been satisfied. Nor do we consider it necessary to determine whether the three conditions proposed by Argentina are sufficient for the application of that proposal.

[59] Panel Report, *EEC (Member States) - Bananas I*, *supra*, note 44, para 361. See also Panel Report, *Guatemala - Cement II*, *supra*, note 48, footnote 791: "it is clear that not any silence can be considered to constitute consent".

had been brought by Brazil, imposes no restrictions on Brazil's right to bring subsequent WTO dispute settlement proceedings in respect of the same measure. We note that Brazil signed the Protocol of Olivos in February 2002. Article 1 of the Protocol of Olivos provides that once a party decides to bring a case under either the MERCOSUR or WTO dispute settlement forums, that party may not bring a subsequent case regarding the same subject-matter in the other forum. The Protocol of Olivos, however, does not change our assessment, since that Protocol has not yet entered into force, and in any event it does not apply in respect of disputes already decided in accordance with the MERCOSUR Protocol of Brasilia.[60] Indeed, the fact that parties to MERCOSUR saw the need to introduce the Protocol of Olivos suggests to us that they recognised that (in the absence of such Protocol) a MERCOSUR dispute settlement proceeding could be followed by a WTO dispute settlement proceeding in respect of the same measure.

7.39   Regarding the third condition, we note that Argentina failed to quote the entirety of the relevant author's text. Quoted in full, the third condition reads "there must be reliance in good faith upon the statement either to the detriment of the party so relying on the statement or to the advantage of the party making the statement".[61] Citing the same author, another panel has asserted that "[e]stoppel is premised on the view that where one party has been induced to act in reliance on the assurances of another party, in such a way that it would be prejudiced were the other party later to change its position, such a change in position is 'estopped', that is precluded".[62] In our view, merely being inconvenienced by alleged statements by Brazil is not sufficient for Argentina to demonstrate that it was induced to *act* in reliance of such alleged statements. There is nothing on the record to suggest to us that Argentina actively relied in good faith on any statement made by Brazil, either to the advantage of Brazil or to the disadvantage of Argentina. There is nothing on the record to suggest that Argentina would have acted any differently had Brazil not made the alleged statement that it would not bring the present WTO dispute settlement proceedings. In its abovementioned response to Question 66, which was specifically addressing this issue, Argentina simply stated that it "is now suffering the negative impact of [Brazil's] change of position" (regarding its earlier practice of not pursuing WTO cases following MERCOSUR rulings in respect of the same subject-matter), without explaining further the nature of that "negative impact". Argentina's vague assertion regarding "negative impact" is not sufficient to demonstrate that it was induced to act in reliance on the alleged statement by Brazil, and that it is now suffering the negative consequences of the alleged change in Brazil's position. For these reasons, we reject Argentina's claim that Brazil is estopped from pursuing the present WTO dispute settlement proceedings.

7.40   Argentina argues in the alternative that if the Panel finds that Brazil is entitled to bring the present WTO dispute settlement proceedings, then the Panel is bound by the earlier MERCOSUR ruling on the measure at issue in this case. Argentina asserts that the earlier MERCOSUR ruling is part of the normative framework to be applied by the Panel as a result of Article 31.3(c) of the *Vienna Convention*, whereby

---

[60] Article 50 of the Protocol of Olivos provides that "disputes underway initiated in accordance with the Protocol of Brasilia will continue to be exclusively governed by that Protocol until the dispute has been concluded".

[61] See footnote 41 *supra*.

[62] Panel Report, *Guatemala - Cement II*, *supra*, note 48 , para. 8.23.

"relevant rules of international law applicable in the relations between the parties" shall be taken into account for the purpose of treaty interpretation. Argentina asserts that the provisions of the *Vienna Convention* are applicable in the present proceedings by virtue of Article 3.2 of the *DSU*, which provides that the WTO dispute settlement system serves to clarify the existing provisions of the covered agreements "in accordance with customary rules of interpretation of public international law".

7.41   We note that Article 3.2 of the *DSU* is concerned with international rules of treaty *interpretation*. Article 31.3(c) of the *Vienna Convention* is similarly concerned with treaty *interpretation*. However, Argentina has not sought to rely on any law providing that, in respect of relations between Argentina and Brazil, the WTO agreements should be *interpreted* in a particular way. In particular, Argentina has not relied on any statement or finding in the MERCOSUR Tribunal ruling to suggest that we should interpret specific provisions of the WTO agreements in a particular way. Rather than concerning itself with the interpretation of the WTO agreements, Argentina actually argues that the earlier MERCOSUR Tribunal ruling requires us to *rule* in a particular way. In other words, Argentina would have us *apply* the relevant WTO provisions in a particular way, rather than *interpret* them in a particular way. However, there is no basis in Article 3.2 of the *DSU*, or any other provision, to suggest that we are bound to rule in a particular way, or apply the relevant WTO provisions in a particular way. We note that we are not even bound to follow rulings contained in adopted WTO panel reports[63], so we see no reason at all why we should be bound by the rulings of non-WTO dispute settlement bodies. Accordingly, we reject Argentina's alternative arguments regarding Article 31.3(c) of the *Vienna Convention*.[64]

7.42   In light of the above, we decline Argentina's request that, in light of the prior MERCOSUR proceedings, the Panel refrain from ruling on the claims raised by Brazil in the present WTO dispute settlement proceedings. We also decline Argentina's alternative request that we consider ourselves bound by the ruling of the MERCOSUR Tribunal.

B.   General Issues

1.   Standard of Review

7.43   Article 17.6 of the *AD Agreement* sets forth the special standard of review applicable to anti-dumping disputes. With regard to factual issues, Article 17.6(i) provides:

> "in its assessment of the facts of the matter, the panel shall determine whether the **authorities' establishment of the facts was proper** and whether their **evaluation of those facts was unbiased and objective**.

---

[63] See Appellate Body Report, *Japan - Taxes on Alcoholic Beverages* ("*Japan - Alcoholic Beverages II*"), WT/DS8/AB/R, WT/DS10/AB/R, WT/DS11/AB/R, adopted 1 November 1996, p. 14, DSR 1996:I, 97, at 125.

[64] Even if Argentina had relied on the MERCOSUR Tribunal ruling to argue that particular provisions of the WTO Agreement should be interpreted in a particular way, it is not entirely clear that Article 31.3(c) of the *Vienna Convention* would apply. In particular, it is not clear to us that a rule applicable between only several WTO Members would constitute a relevant rule of international law applicable in the relations between the "parties".

If the establishment of the facts was proper and the evaluation was unbiased and objective, even though the panel might have reached a different conclusion, the evaluation shall not be overturned;" (emphasis added)

7.44   Assuming that we conclude that the establishment of the facts with regard to a particular claim in this case was proper, we then may consider whether, based on the evidence before the Argentine authorities at the time of the determination, an unbiased and objective investigating authority evaluating that evidence could have reached the conclusions that the Argentine authorities reached on the matter in question.[65]

7.45   Article 17.6(i) requires us to assess the facts to determine whether the investigating authorities' own establishment of the facts was proper, and to assess the investigating authorities' own evaluation of those facts to determine if it was unbiased and objective. What is clear from this is that we are precluded from establishing facts and evaluating them for ourselves - that is, we may not engage in *de novo* review. However, this does not limit our examination of the matters in dispute, but only the manner in which we conduct that examination. In this regard, we keep in mind that Article 17.5(ii) of the *AD Agreement* establishes that we are to examine the matter based upon "the facts made available in conformity with appropriate domestic procedures to the authorities of the importing Member."

7.46   With respect to questions of the interpretation of the *AD Agreement*, Article 17.6(ii) provides:

"the panel shall interpret the relevant provisions of the Agreement in accordance with customary rules of interpretation of public international law. Where the panel finds that a relevant provision of the **Agreement admits of more than one permissible interpretation**, the panel shall find the authorities' measure to be in **conformity with the Agreement if it rests upon one of those permissible interpretations**." (emphasis added)

7.47   Article 17.6(ii) requires us to apply the customary rules of interpretation of treaties, which are reflected in Articles 31-32 of the *Vienna Convention*. Article 31 of the *Vienna Convention* provides that a treaty shall be interpreted in accordance with the ordinary meaning to be given to the terms of the treaty in their context and in light of its object and purpose. This is no different from the task of all panels in interpreting the text of the WTO agreements pursuant to Article 3.2 of the *DSU*. What Article 17.6(ii) of the *AD Agreement* adds is an instruction that, if this process of treaty interpretation leads us to the conclusion that the interpretation of the provision in question put forward by the defending party is permissible, we shall find the measure in conformity if it is based on that permissible interpretation.

7.48   Finally, as mentioned below, Argentina has presented arguments before us in support of the investigating authorities' decisions which we could not find on the record of the investigation before us. This raises the question of whether *ex post*

---

[65] We note that this is the same standard as that applied by the panels in *United States - Anti-Dumping Measures on Stainless Steel Plate in Coils and Stainless Steel Sheet and Strip from Korea* ("*US - Stainless Steel*"), WT/DS179/R, adopted 1 February 2001, DSR 2001:IV, 1295; and *Mexico - Anti-Dumping Investigation of High Fructose Corn Syrup*, ("*Mexico - Corn Syrup*"), WT/DS132/R and Corr.1, adopted 24 February 2000, DSR 2000:III, 1345.

rationalization should be taken into account in order to assess Argentina's compliance with the provisions of the *AD Agreement*. We note that the *Argentina - Ceramic Tiles* panel expressed its view that:

> "Under Article 17.6 of the AD Agreement we are to determine whether the DCD established the facts properly and whether the evaluation performed by the DCD was unbiased and objective. In other words, we are asked to review the evaluation of the DCD *made at the time of the determination* as set forth in a public notice or in any other document of a public or confidential nature. We do not believe that, as a panel reviewing the evaluation of the investigating authority, we are to take into consideration any arguments and reasons that did not form part of the evaluation process of the investigating authority, but instead are *ex post facto* justifications which were not provided at the time the determination was made."[66] (emphasis in original, footnote not included)

7.49 We agree with the approach followed by that panel. Thus, we do not believe that, as a panel reviewing the evaluation of the investigating authority, we are to take into consideration any arguments and reasons that are not demonstrated to have formed part of the evaluation process of the investigating authority.

2. Burden of Proof

7.50 In WTO dispute settlement proceedings, the burden of proof rests with the party that asserts the affirmative of a particular claim or defence.[67] The complaining party must therefore make a *prima facie* case of violation of the relevant provisions of the WTO agreements, which the respondent must refute.[68] In these Panel proceedings, we thus observe that it is for Brazil, which has challenged the consistency of Argentina's measure, to bear the burden of demonstrating that the measure is not consistent with the relevant provisions of the *AD Agreement*. We also note, however, that it is generally for each party asserting a fact, whether complainant or respondent, to provide proof thereof.[69] In this respect, therefore, it is also for Argentina to provide evidence for the facts which it asserts. We also recall

---

[66] Panel Report, *Argentina - Definitive Anti-Dumping Measures on Imports of Ceramic Floor Tiles from Italy* ("*Argentina - Ceramic Tiles*"), WT/DS189/R, adopted 5 November 2001, DSR 2001:XII, 6241, para. 6.27.

[67] Appellate Body Report, *United States - Measure Affecting Imports of Woven Wool Shirts and Blouses from India* ("*US - Wool Shirts and Blouses*"), WT/DS33/AB/R and Corr.1, adopted 23 May 1997, DSR 1997:I, 323, p. 337 *et seq*.

[68] We note the statement of the Appellate Body in *Korea - Dairy* that: "We find no provision in the DSU or in the Agreement on Safeguards that requires a Panel to make an explicit ruling on whether the complainant has established a prima facie case of violation before a panel may proceed to examine the respondent's defence and evidence." (Appellate Body Report, *Korea - Definitive Safeguard Measure on Imports of Certain Dairy Products* ("*Korea - Dairy*"), WT/DS98/AB/R, adopted 12 January 2000, DSR 2000:I, 3, para. 145) The Appellate Body confirmed this view in *Thailand - Anti-Dumping Duties on Angles, Shapes and Sections of Iron or Non-Alloy Steel and H-Beams from Poland* ("*Thailand - H-Beams*"), WT/DS122/AB/R, adopted 5 April 2001, DSR 2001:VII, 2701, para. 134: "In our view a panel is not required to make a separate and specific finding in each and every instance that a party has met its burden of proof in respect of a particular claim, or that a party has rebutted a prima facie case."

[69] See footnote 67, *supra*.

that a *prima facie* case is one which, in the absence of effective refutation by the other party, requires a panel, as a matter of law, to rule in favour of the party presenting the *prima facie* case. The role of the Panel is not to make the case for either party, but it may pose questions to the parties "in order to clarify and distil the legal arguments".[70] In addition, we consider that both parties generally have a duty to cooperate in the proceedings in order to assist us in fulfilling our mandate, through the provision of relevant information.[71] We must draw inferences on the basis of all of the relevant facts of record, including, for example, where a party refuses to provide relevant information.[72]

C. Claims Concerning the Initiation of the Investigation / Alleged Procedural Violations During the Course of the Investigation

1. Sufficiency of Evidence to Justify Initiation of the Investigation - Claims 2, 4, 6 and 8

7.51 These claims concern the investigating authority's decision that there was sufficient evidence under Article 5.3 of the *AD Agreement* to justify initiating an investigation on imports of poultry from Brazil. Since the investigating authority's decision to initiate was based on the information contained in the application, Brazil's claims are concerned with the investigating authority's treatment of information contained in that application.

(a) Arguments of the Parties

(i) Claim 2

7.52 Brazil claims that there was not sufficient evidence for the investigating authority to have made an adjustment to normal value to reflect alleged differences in physical characteristics between the poultry sold in Argentina and Brazil respectively. Brazil asserts that there was not sufficient evidence to support the applicant's claim that poultry sold in Brazil differed from that sold in Argentina because the former included head and feet whereas the latter did not. Brazil also argues that the applicant did not demonstrate that the alleged difference in physical characteristics affected price comparability. Finally, Brazil asserts that there was no evidence to support the accuracy and adequacy of the yield rates used by the investigating authority at the time of initiation to calculate the amount of the adjustment for the alleged differences in physical characteristics.

7.53 Argentina rejects Brazil's claim on the basis of the finding of the panel in *Guatemala - Cement I*[73] that "the quantum and quality of evidence to be required of an investigating authority prior to initiation of an investigation would necessarily

---

[70] Appellate Body Report, *Thailand - H-Beams, supra*, note 68, para. 136.
[71] Appellate Body Report, *Canada - Measures Affecting the Export of Civilian Aircraft ("Canada - Aircraft")*, WT/DS70/AB/R, adopted 20 August 1999, DSR 1999:III, 1377, para. 190.
[72] *Ibid.*, para. 203; Appellate Body Report, *United States - Definitive Safeguard Measures on Imports of Wheat Gluten from the European Communities ("US - Wheat Gluten")*, WT/DS166/AB/R, adopted 19 January 2001, DSR 2001:II, 717, paras. 173-174.
[73] Panel Report, *Guatemala - Anti-Dumping Investigation Regarding Portland Cement from Mexico ("Guatemala - Cement I")*, WT/DS60/R, adopted 25 November 1998, as modified by the Appellate Body Report, WT/DS60/AB/R, DSR 1998:IX, 3797.

have to be less than that required of that authority at the time of making a final determination". Argentina asserts that the investigating authority made the adjustment on the basis of evidence submitted by the applicant in the form of information published by JOX Assessoria Agropecuaria S/C Ltda. ("JOX"), a Brazilian consulting firm specialized in the farming sector, regarding sales of poultry in São Paulo. According to Argentina, the JOX information indicated that chilled poultry was sold in São Paulo with head and feet. Argentina states that JOX is a specialized publication reflecting the state of the São Paulo market, and that São Paulo is a large urban centre which reflects domestic consumption patterns throughout Brazil.

(ii) Claim 4

7.54 Brazil claims that the investigating authority excluded export prices that were above the normal value, and established the export price for purposes of initiation based only on those transactions that were below the normal value. In the view of Brazil, by doing so, the investigating authority incorrectly established the export price and, consequently, made a skewed comparison of the export price with the normal value, in establishing the margin of dumping. Brazil asserts that an investigating authority should decide whether or not to initiate on the basis of all the evidence presented in the application. Brazil argues that, under Article 2.4.2 of the *AD Agreement*, investigating authorities are required to compare the weighted average normal value with the weighted average of prices of all comparable export transactions, and not only those export transactions for which prices are below the normal value. The methodology used by the investigating authority resulted in the establishment of an incorrect export price and in an unfair comparison between the export price and the normal value, contrary to the requirements in Articles 2.4 and 2.4.2. Finally, Brazil asserts that Argentina's decision to initiate the investigation pursuant to this method was based on a biased and non-objective evaluation of the facts before it.

7.55 Argentina asserts that the investigating authority analysed the import transactions in an attempt to determine which of them corresponded closest to the product under investigation. Argentina asserts that the investigating authority did so for the sole purpose of calculating the most appropriate and comparable export price possible at the pre-initiation stage. In other words, Argentina claims that it only excluded those export transactions which were not "like" the product under investigation. Furthermore, Argentina asserts that the investigating authority worked out an average of the appropriate transactions, without in fact making any selection which might distort the difference between the export price and the normal value. According to Argentina, the Report of 7 January 1998 contains the margins of dumping established on the basis of the average price of export transactions to Argentina involving the product under investigation.

(iii) Claim 6

7.56 Brazil asserts that the Argentine authorities determined normal value for the purpose of initiation on the basis of information for one day only, while export price data covered several months. Brazil argues that Article 5.3, read in conjunction with Article 2.4, requires that a fair comparison be made between the export price and the normal value in respect of sales made at as nearly as possible the same time. Brazil asserts that, had the investigating authority examined the accuracy and adequacy of the evidence provided in the application, it would have required the petitioner to provide normal value data for the entire period under analysis in order to correctly make a fair comparison with export prices for the same period. In addition, Brazil asserts that the investigating authority went beyond the scope of the data provided in the application and extended the period for the export transactions, in order to establish the export price. This, in the view of Brazil, clearly indicates that the investigating authority did not rely on the information provided in the application to determine that there was sufficient evidence of dumping to justify the initiation of the investigation. Brazil concludes that, by not accurately examining the evidence in the application and by adding export price information not provided in the application to determine the initiation of the investigation, Argentina acted inconsistently with Article 5.3 of the *AD Agreement*.

7.57 Argentina asserts that Article 5.3 does not impose any requirements in respect of the time-periods for which export price and normal value data must be available. Argentina alleges that the investigating authority acted consistently with Article 2.4. Argentina contends that the basis for comparison was established in the light of the evidence reasonably available to the applicant and submitted in the application. Argentina argues that the investigating authority should not be expected to meet a standard in respect of the examination required by Article 5.3 similar to the standard required once the investigation has been initiated.

(iv)   Claim 8

7.58 Brazil argues that, due to the different data collection periods for dumping and injury used in the application, the investigating authority could not have found that there was sufficient evidence of causal link between the dumped imports on June 1997 and the threat of injury on June 1998. Brazil argues that, in order to verify that there was threat of injury from dumped imports, the dumping data collected and analyzed should have been extended until June 1998.

7.59 Argentina argues that the investigating authority should not be expected to meet a standard in respect of the examination required by Article 5.3 similar to the standard required once the investigation has been initiated.

(b)   Evaluation by the Panel

7.60 These claims raise the issue of whether or not the investigating authority complied with the requirements of Article 5.3 of the *AD Agreement,* as interpreted in light of Article 2, when deciding to initiate its investigation on the basis of the information contained in the application. In addressing this issue, we shall adopt an approach similar to that of previous panels which have examined claims under Article 5.3 of the *AD Agreement*.[74] Thus, in accordance with our standard of review, we shall determine whether or not an objective and unbiased investigating authority, looking at the facts before it, could properly have determined that there was sufficient evidence of dumping, injury and causal link to justify the initiation of an anti-dumping investigation. In making this determination, Article 5.3 requires the investigating authority to examine the accuracy and adequacy of the evidence in the

---

[74] Panel Report, *Mexico - Corn Syrup, supra*, note 65, paras. 7.91-7.110; Panel Report, *Guatemala - Cement II, supra*, note 48, paras. 8.29-8.58.

application. Clearly, the accuracy and adequacy of the evidence is relevant to the investigating authority's determination whether there is sufficient evidence to justify the initiation of an investigation. However, it is not merely the fact of the accuracy and adequacy of the evidence *per se* which is the legal standard under Article 5.3, but the *sufficiency* of that evidence. In analysing the sufficiency of evidence, we agree with a previous panel that statements and assertions unsubstantiated by any evidence do not constitute sufficient evidence within the meaning of Article 5.3.[75]

7.61   Although Brazil's claims are based on Article 5.3 of the *AD Agreement*, they also raise issues regarding the relationship between Article 5.3 and other provisions of the *AD Agreement*, especially Article 2 thereof.[76] We note that this issue was addressed by the panel in *Guatemala - Cement II* in the following terms:

> "although there is no express reference to evidence of dumping in Article 5.3, evidence on the three elements necessary for the imposition of an anti-dumping measure may be inferred into Article 5.3 by way of Article 5.2. In other words, Article 5.2 requires that the application contain sufficient evidence on dumping, injury and causation, while Article 5.3 requires the investigating authority to satisfy itself as to the accuracy and adequacy of the evidence to determine that it is sufficient to justify initiation. Thus, reading Article 5.3 in the context of Article 5.2, the evidence mentioned in Article 5.3 must be evidence of dumping, injury and causation. We further observe that the only clarification of the term "dumping" in the AD Agreement is that contained in Article 2. In consequence, in order to determine that there is sufficient evidence of dumping, the investigating authority cannot entirely disregard the elements that configure the existence of this practice as outlined in Article 2. This analysis is done not with a view to making a determination that Article 2 has been violated through the initiation of an investigation, but rather to provide guidance in our review of the Ministry's determination that there was sufficient evidence of dumping to warrant an investigation. We do not of course mean to suggest that an investigating authority must have before it at the time it initiates an investigation evidence of dumping within the meaning of Article 2 of the quantity and quality that would be necessary to support a preliminary or final determination. An anti-dumping investigation is a process where certainty on the existence of all the elements necessary in order to adopt a measure is reached gradually as the investigation moves forward. However, the evidence must be such that an unbiased and objective investigating authority could determine that there was sufficient evidence of dumping within the meaning of Article 2 to justify initiation of an investigation.[794],[77]
>
> ---
> [794] On this question we concur fully with the reasoning of the *Guatemala - Cement I* panel when they state that:

---
[75] Panel Report, *Guatemala - Cement II*, *supra*, note 48, paras. 8.51-8.53.
[76] Brazil's first written submission, paras. 102-104 (Claim 4); para. 132 (Claim 6); and paras. 149 and 155 (Claim 8).
[77] Panel Report, *Guatemala - Cement II*, *supra*, note 48, para. 8.35.

"In our view, the reference in Article 5.2 to "dumping" must be read as a reference to dumping as it is defined in Article 2. This does not, of course, mean that the evidence provided in the application must be of the quantity and quality that would be necessary to make a preliminary or final determination of dumping. However, evidence of the relevant **type** is, in our view, required in a case such as this one where it is obvious on the face of the application that the normal value and export price alleged in the application will require adjustments in order to effectuate a fair comparison. At a minimum, there should be some recognition that a fair comparison will require such adjustments." *Guatemala - Cement I*, WT/DS60/R, para. 7.64 (emphasis in original)

7.62   We fully agree with the findings of that panel, and shall follow the same approach in the present case. In order to determine whether there is sufficient evidence of dumping, an investigating authority cannot entirely disregard the elements that configure the existence of that practice as outlined in Article 2. We do not of course mean to suggest that an investigating authority must have before it at the time it initiates an investigation evidence of dumping within the meaning of Article 2 of the *quantity* and *quality* that would be necessary to support a preliminary or final determination. However, the evidence must be such that an unbiased and objective investigating authority could determine that there was sufficient evidence of dumping within the meaning of Article 2 to justify initiation of an investigation.

7.63   With these considerations in mind, we now turn to the examination of the claims put forward by Brazil.

(i)   Claim 2

7.64   The primary issue raised by Claim 2 is whether or not there was sufficient evidence before the investigating authority at the time of initiation to warrant an adjustment for differences in physical characteristics between the eviscerated poultry sold in Argentina and that sold in Brazil. This issue goes to the heart of the claim that there was insufficient evidence to justify initiation, since the investigating authority would not have found dumping had it not made the adjustment for the alleged differences in physical characteristics. Brazil's claim also challenges the investigating authority's conclusion regarding the amount of the adjustment made.

7.65   We recall that, in order to determine whether there is sufficient evidence of dumping, the investigating authority cannot entirely disregard the elements that configure the existence of this practice as outlined in Article 2. In a claim concerning adjustments, paragraph 4 of Article 2 is of particular relevance. Article 2.4 provides in relevant part:

"A fair comparison shall be made between the export price and the normal value. This comparison shall be made at the same level of trade, normally at the ex-factory level, and in respect of sales made at as nearly as possible the same time. Due allowance shall be made in each case, on its merits, for differences which affect price comparability, including differences in (...) physical characteristics..."

7.66   We further note that the issue before us is not whether Argentina was *required* to make an adjustment for differences in physical characteristics in deciding to initiate, but whether it was *entitled* to do so.

7.67   We turn now to the examination of Brazil's first argument. Brazil claims that the normal value data contained in the application only related to sales in São Paulo. According to Brazil, even if that data indicated that poultry was sold in São Paulo with head and feet, that did not mean that poultry was sold throughout Brazil with head and feet. Argentina asserts that São Paulo is a large urban centre, and that sales in São Paulo are therefore representative of consumption patterns throughout Brazil. Brazil does not deny that São Paulo is a large urban centre. We recall that, at the time of initiation, an investigating authority is not required to possess evidence of dumping of the quantity (or quality) that it would need to support a preliminary or final determination. In our view, it is sufficient for an investigating authority to base its decision to initiate on evidence concerning domestic sales in a major market of the exporting country subject to the investigation, without necessarily having data for sales throughout that country.

7.68   Brazil also argues that the investigating authority incorrectly accepted a statement by JOX (attached to the application) as evidence that poultry sold in São Paulo contained head and feet. We have examined the relevant statement, and find that it clearly indicates that the JOX domestic price data provided by the applicant, and relied on by the investigating authority at the time of initiation, concerned poultry sold in São Paulo with head and feet. Since Brazil has not disputed Argentina's assertion that JOX was a specialized publication reflecting the state of the São Paulo market, we see no reason why the investigating authority was not entitled to rely on the JOX statement.

7.69   Brazil further argues that the investigating authority did not have sufficient evidence that the alleged differences in physical characteristics affected price comparability. This issue is closely linked to Brazil's claim against the amount of the adjustment made by the investigating authority. In light of our finding on that claim below, we do not consider it necessary to rule on Brazil's argument concerning the lack of evidence on price comparability.

7.70   Regarding the amount of the adjustment, Brazil notes that the 9.09 per cent adjustment made by the investigating authority at the time of initiation was calculated on the basis of yield rates[78] set forth in the application. The applicant stated that the yield rate for poultry sold (with head and feet) in Brazil was 88 per cent, whereas the yield rate for poultry sold in Argentina (without head and feet) was 80 per cent. Brazil asserts that the applicant failed to submit any evidence in support of those yield rates. In response to Question 5 from the Panel, Argentina stated that the evidence supporting the use of 88 and 80 per cent yield rates was contained in a JOX report included in the application.[79] However, upon close examination we find

---

[78]   The yield rate refers to the amount of eviscerated poultry obtained from live poultry. According to the applicant, out of 1 kg of live poultry sold in Brazil (including head and feet), 880 gm of eviscerated poultry is obtained (including giblets (heart, stomach, neck and liver), head and feet). This amounts to a yield rate of 88 per cent. According to the applicant, the yield rate for poultry exported to Argentina was less, because sales to Argentina did not include head and feet. Thus, out of 1 kg of live poultry exported to Argentina, only 800 gm of eviscerated poultry (including giblets, but no head or feet) is obtained. This gives a yield rate of 80 per cent for poultry exported to Argentina.

[79]   It appeared from Argentina's reply to Question 6 of the Panel that supporting information for the adjustment could be found in a publication by Aves & Ovos, included in the application. However, in its reply to Question 68 of the Panel, Argentina asserts that that publication does not provide any information with respect to the 9.09 per cent adjustment carried out. We also take into account the following reply of Argentina:

that the relevant JOX report does not contain any such evidence. Indeed, the JOX report makes no reference to yield rates whatsoever.

7.71   In response to an additional question from the Panel, Argentina asserted that:

"The adjustment made by the implementing authority for the differences between the poultry sold in Brazil and poultry sold in Argentina was included by the applicant when submitting the application, and applied by the authority as from the initiation of the investigation on the understanding that the said information was what was reasonably available to the applicant, that it was reasonable and that the implementing authority did not have knowledge of any elements to suggest that it should not be considered. Having evaluated the said information, the authority did not consider that it was necessary to request additional information in that respect in view of the standards applicable to the information to be considered at that stage of the investigation."[80]

7.72   This suggests that, according to Argentina, the investigating authority was entitled to make an adjustment on the basis of the yield rate information included in the application simply because the information "was reasonable and ... the implementing authority did not have knowledge of any elements to suggest that it should not be considered." We cannot accept this approach because, as we noted above, statements and assertions unsubstantiated by any evidence do not constitute sufficient evidence within the meaning of Article 5.3. In light of the lack of evidence to support the yield rates included in the application, and consequently the adjustment to be made, we fail to see how an unbiased and objective investigating authority could have considered the yield rate information available at the time of initiation adequate to support a 9.09 per cent adjustment to normal value.

7.73   In light of the above, we find that the investigating authority did not have adequate information at the time of initiation to make an adjustment to normal value of 9.09 per cent. Accordingly, although we have rejected Brazil's arguments regarding the adequacy of the evidence concerning the need for an adjustment to normal value to reflect differences in physical characteristics between the poultry sold in Brazil and Argentina respectively, we uphold Brazil's claim regarding the adequacy of the information concerning the amount of that adjustment. We therefore find that Argentina violated Article 5.3 of the *AD Agreement* by determining that it had sufficient evidence of dumping to initiate an investigation, because its determination of dumping was based on an adjustment to normal value for which it did not have adequate evidence.[81]

"as far as normal value is concerned, the evidence considered was the JOX publication of 30 June 1997 accompanying the application, there being no additional requests by the implementing authority in that respect." (Argentina's reply to Question 9 of the Panel)

This statement confirms our finding that the APCDS did not have at the time of initiation any other evidence supporting the application other than that examined by us. We recall that we examined the application and did not find any evidence in it supporting the alleged yield rates of eviscerated poultry.

[80]   Argentina's reply to Question 11(a) of the Panel.

[81]   We note Brazil's assertion that there would have been no margin of dumping had the relevant adjustment not been made. (Brazil's reply to Question 3 of the Panel)

(ii) Claim 4

7.74 Brazil asserts that the investigating authority only took into account export prices less than normal value when calculating the margin of dumping for the purpose of initiation. Brazil submits that this methodology was not in conformity with Article 5.3, read in conjunction with Article 2.4.2 of the *AD Agreement*.

7.75 At the time of initiation, the APCDS calculated four margins of dumping.[82] In its first written submission, Argentina stated that the decision to initiate was based on the second margin of dumping calculated by the APCDS, and that the three remaining margins were used for additional analysis.[83] In response to part of Question 18 from the Panel, Argentina stated that "[t]he period used to determine the f.o.b. export price in this case was January to June 1997 and August 1997." Since this was the period covered by the second margin of dumping calculated by the APCDS, this would confirm Argentina's statement that the decision to initiate was based on the second of the four margins calculated by the APCDS. Accordingly, for the purpose of analysing Brazil's claim, we shall focus on the second margin of dumping calculated by the APCDS, since this was the margin on which the decision to initiate the investigation was based.

7.76 The starting point for the APCDS calculation of the second margin of dumping was the totality of export transactions recorded in official import statistics for the period January to June 1997 and August 1997. As a first step, the investigating authority discarded export transactions which did not concern products "like" the product under investigation.[84] Second, the investigating authority excluded those export transactions with a price that was higher than or equal to the normal value (USD/Kg. 1.044).[85] Third, a weighted average export price was calculated using only those transactions with a price lower than the normal value. Accordingly, the weighted average export price was not based on the totality of comparable export transactions.

7.77 In examining the compatibility of this methodology with Article 5.3, read in light of Article 2.4.2, we note the following statement by the Appellate Body in *EC - Bed Linen*:

> "By 'zeroing' the 'negative dumping margins', the European Communities, therefore, did *not* take fully into account the entirety of the prices of *some* export transactions, namely, those export transactions involving models of cotton-type bed linen where 'negative dumping margins' were found. Instead, the European Communities treated those export prices as if they were less than what they were. This, in turn, inflated the result from the calculation of the margin of dumping. Thus, the European Communities did *not* establish 'the existence of margins of dumping' for cotton-type bed linen on the basis of a comparison of the weighted average normal value with the weighted average of prices of *all* comparable export transactions - that is, for *all* transactions involving *all* models or types of the product under investigation. Furthermore, we are also of the view that a

---

[82] Exhibit BRA-2, p. 12 and 13.
[83] Argentina's first written submission, para. 80.
[84] Argentina's reply to Question 19 of the Panel.
[85] Argentina's reply to Question 11(b) of the Panel.

comparison between export price and normal value that does *not* take fully into account the prices of *all* comparable export transactions - such as the practice of 'zeroing' at issue in this dispute - is *not* a 'fair comparison' between export price and normal value, as required by Article 2.4 and by Article 2.4.2."[86] (emphasis in original)

7.78   We agree with the Appellate Body's analysis. We note that the Appellate Body was primarily addressing the practice of "zeroing". The practice adopted by Argentina in the present case is more egregious than zeroing, because it does not merely fix the value of comparisons involving certain export transactions at zero, but totally excludes certain export prices from the weighted average, so that the weighted average export price used by the investigating authority is even lower than it would be through zeroing. We are in no doubt that, if zeroing is inconsistent with Article 2.4.2, then Argentina's practice of totally disregarding certain export transactions would also be inconsistent with Article 2.4.2 because it does not compare the weighted average normal value with the weighted average of prices of *all* comparable export transactions. In our view, the use of such a practice would not allow an objective and impartial investigating authority to properly conclude that there was sufficient evidence of dumping to justify the initiation of an investigation.

7.79   Argentina asserts that the methodology used by the APCDS has also been used by other WTO Members.[87] Even assuming for the sake of argument that Argentina is correct, this argument is nevertheless irrelevant. In this dispute, we must determine the conformity of Argentina's methodology (and not that of other WTO Members) in light of the relevant provisions of the *AD Agreement*.

7.80   Argentina also argues that "[w]hat is required [at the time of initiation] is the knowledge that there have been transactions involving dumping which justify, from that point of view, the initiation of an investigation."[88] We understand Argentina to argue that, in order to initiate, an investigating authority need only satisfy itself that there has been some dumping, in the sense that certain transactions were dumped. We disagree. We recall that, "in order to determine whether or not there is sufficient evidence of dumping for the purpose of initiation, an investigating authority cannot entirely disregard the elements that configure the existence of [dumping] outlined in Article 2".[89] A determination of dumping should be made in respect of the product as a whole, for a given period, and not for individual transactions concerning that product. An investigating authority therefore cannot disregard export transactions at the time of initiation simply because they are equal to or greater than normal value. Disregarding such transactions does not provide a proper basis for determining whether or not there is sufficient evidence of dumping to justify initiation.

7.81   In light of the above, we find that Argentina violated Article 5.3 of the *AD Agreement* by initiating its investigation without a proper basis to conclude that there was sufficient evidence of dumping to justify initiation.

---

[86] Appellate Body Report, *European Communities - Anti-Dumping Duties on Imports of Cotton-Type Bed Linen from India* ("*EC - Bed Linen*"), WT/DS141/AB/R, adopted 12 March 2001, para. 55.
[87] See footnote 85, *supra*.
[88] *Ibid.*
[89] Panel Report, *Guatemala - Cement II*, *supra*, note 48, para. 8.35.

(iii) Claim 6

7.82 The APCDS established the normal value on the basis of a JOX publication setting forth the prices of poultry for one day - 30 June 1997 - while the export price covered a period of several months in 1997.[90] The issue before us is whether a comparison between a normal value for one day and an export price for a period of several months constitutes a proper basis for determining whether or not there is sufficient evidence of dumping to justify the initiation of an investigation.

7.83 We recall that, in order to determine that there is sufficient evidence of dumping, the investigating authority cannot entirely disregard the elements that configure the existence of that practice as outlined in Article 2. In particular, we note that Article 2.4 requires that a fair comparison be made between the export price and the normal value in respect of sales "made at as nearly as possible the same time". In interpreting the term "made at as nearly as possible the same time" in the context of Article 2.4, we consider it useful to refer to the following finding of the *US - Stainless Steel* panel:

> "we consider that, in the context of weighted average to weighted average comparisons, the requirement that a comparison be made between sales made at as nearly as possible the same time requires *as a general matter* that the periods on the basis of which the weighted average normal value and the weighted average export price are calculated must be the same." (emphasis in original)[91]

7.84 The above finding concerns a definitive determination of a margin of dumping, while the present claim concerns a pre-initiation determination of sufficient evidence of dumping. At the time of initiation an investigating authority does not need to be in possession of the same quantity and quality of evidence that would be necessary to support a preliminary or final determination of dumping. However, since evidence of the same *type* is required upon initiation as for a preliminary or final determination, in our view there should be a substantial degree of overlap in the periods considered in order for the comparison of normal value and export price to be fair within the meaning of Article 2.4. We consider however that Article 5.3, read in light of Article 2.4, cannot be interpreted to require that data on normal value and export price cover identical periods of time. Otherwise, the quantity of evidence of dumping required upon initiation would be the same as that required for a preliminary or final determination of dumping. Thus, we consider that an investigating authority might comply with the requirements in Article 5.3 even though the periods chosen for the comparison of a weighted average normal value and a weighted average export price are not identical.

7.85 For a product such as eviscerated poultry, in respect of which there are many transactions taking place on a daily basis, we are not persuaded that domestic sales data for one day provides sufficient overlap with export price data for several months

---

[90] We note that the APCDS calculated four different margins of dumping based on *four* different export prices. We also observe that the determination of the existence of sufficient evidence on dumping was based on a comparison between the normal value for 30 June 1997 and the export price for the period January to June 1997 and August 1997, as discussed in para. 7.75 *supra*. Bearing this in mind, under this claim we will examine whether a comparison between information on normal value for 30 June 1997 and data for export price for January to June 1997 and August 1997 meets the requirements of Article 2.4 of the *AD Agreement*.

[91] Panel Report, *US - Stainless Steel*, *supra*, note 65, para. 6.121.

for the purpose of Article 5.3. Argentina asserts that the domestic price for one day was indicative of the trend in prices of poultry sold in São Paulo over a longer period of time. If that had been true, the use of normal value for one day may well have been consistent with Article 5.3. However, Argentina has not pointed to any evidence in the record suggesting that the investigating authority actually considered normal value evidence for one day to be indicative of the trend in domestic poultry prices. Furthermore, we note that the evidence relied on by Argentina (to claim that price data for one day was indicative of a trend in prices) related to live, and not eviscerated, poultry.[92] Although Argentina argued in these proceedings that stability in the pricing of an input (live poultry) would result in stability in the pricing of the finished product (eviscerated poultry), it has failed to identify any evidence to suggest that, at the time of initiation, the investigating authority considered that stable pricing for live poultry would lead to stable pricing for eviscerated poultry. Accordingly, Argentina's argument must be rejected.

7.86   We therefore uphold Brazil's claim that Argentina violated Article 5.3 of the *AD Agreement* by initiating the investigation without sufficient evidence of dumping to justify initiation.

(iv)   Claim 8

7.87   Brazil argues that the periods used for the purpose of the dumping and injury determinations at the time of initiation did not coincide and, hence, a causal link could not have properly been established.

7.88   We are of the view that it would only be necessary for us to examine this claim if the investigating authority had had sufficient evidence of dumping and injury - the two elements needed to carry out the causal link determination - to justify the initiation of the investigation against eviscerated poultry from Brazil. However, we recall that in our view the investigating authority did not have sufficient evidence of dumping to justify the initiation of that investigation. Having reached this conclusion, it is not necessary for us to examine Brazil's claim concerning causation.

(c)   Conclusion

7.89   For the reasons set forth above, we find that Argentina acted inconsistently with Article 5.3 of the *AD Agreement* by determining that there was sufficient evidence of dumping to justify the initiation of an investigation.

2.   *Sufficiency of the Application - Claims 1 and 5*

(a)   Arguments of the Parties

(i)   Claim 1

7.90   Brazil asserts that Argentina violated Article 5.2 of the *AD Agreement* by initiating its investigation on the basis of an application that did not meet the

---

[92]   See Argentina's reply to Question 12 of the Panel: "the right-hand margin of the text [of the Report of JOX of 30 June 1997] contains CEPA's translation of the following words: " ... production on the parallel market within São Paulo is sharply lower, *so that the price remains on very firm ground...*". In other words, the quotation did not vary much, but rather remained stable." (emphasis added)

requirements of that provision. Brazil asserts that Article 5.2 requires that an application include "evidence" of dumping, injury and the causal relationship between the dumped imports and the alleged injury. Brazil further asserts that an allegation or information provided in the application, without supporting documentation, does not qualify as evidence under Article 5.2. In the view of Brazil, the application which led to the initiation of the investigation against eviscerated poultry from Brazil did not contain evidence to support an adjustment for physical characteristics claimed by the applicant. Brazil acknowledges that the application contained a JOX report dated 30 June 1997, which allegedly supported the applicant's request for an adjustment. Brazil identifies several problems with the JOX report. Brazil argues that that report does not constitute evidence that justifies the adjustment. Brazil also asserts that no evidence was presented showing that price comparability would be affected and that the yield rate proposed by the petitioner was justified.

7.91   Argentina asserts that the applicant provided all of the necessary evidence with respect to the normal value and the export price as well as the relevant evidence for the adjustments needed in order to make a fair comparison between the normal value and the export value. Argentina also asserts that the applicant supplied, with its application, the documentation that was available to it. Argentina also contends that the applicant for the initiation of an investigation is not required to prove beyond all doubt the existence of dumping, injury and causal link, since the final determination of these elements is the responsibility of the investigating authority. With regard to the adjustment issue, Argentina asserts that the applicant submitted the JOX report with information regarding domestic prices of eviscerated poultry in Brazil. In the view of Argentina, the evidence provided is a representative value taken from a specialized publication for a given period. Bearing in mind that the JOX report mentioned that eviscerated poultry was sold in Brazil with head and feet and that poultry exported to Argentina did not contain head and feet, Argentina concluded that it was necessary to make an adjustment for physical characteristic differences.

7.92   Brazil agrees with Argentina that the quantum and quality of evidence required prior to initiation has to be necessarily less than that required for a final determination. However, Brazil asserts that relevant evidence of the "type" needed to justify initiation is the same as that needed to make a preliminary or final determination of dumping, although the quality and quantity is less.

(ii)   Claim 5

7.93   Brazil argues that the data presented by the petitioner in the application, and used to calculate the dumping margin, was inconsistent with Article 5.2 in two ways. First, Brazil asserts that, because the normal value and the export price information provided were for transactions which were not made at as nearly as possible the same time, the application failed to include sufficient evidence of dumping as required in Article 5.2. Because in the view of Brazil the timing of the sales transactions may have implications in respect of the comparability of prices of export and home market transactions, it argues that the establishment of normal value based on one single day (30 June 1997) cannot be used as a parameter for a fair comparison with the export price determined for two periods of time with more than thirty days each (one for January through June 1997 and the other for August 1997), neither of which included the one day used to establish the normal value. Second, Brazil argues that normal value information for all of 1996 and 1997 was reasonably available to the petitioner in view of the fact that on 26 July 1999 it provided updated information on normal value for the period 1998 through January 1999.

7.94   Apart from the general comments referred to in para. 7.91 *supra*, Argentina asserts that Article 5.2 does not require the applicant to provide evidence of normal value in respect of the entire period for which evidence of export value was provided. In the view of Argentina, it is clear and reasonable that the quantity and quality of information available to the applicant on prices in the market of the exporting country should not be the same as for the export price.

(b)   Evaluation by the Panel

7.95   We recall that we have concluded that the APCDS's determination that there was sufficient evidence of dumping to justify the initiation of an investigation was inconsistent with Article 5.3. For this reason, we do not consider it necessary to rule on Brazil's Article 5.2 claims regarding the sufficiency of the application.

7.96   Although we do not consider it necessary to make findings on Brazil's Article 5.2 claims, we do note that the parties' submissions raised the issue of the extent - if any - to which Article 5.2 imposes obligations on Members, as opposed to applicants. We therefore asked the parties for their views on this matter. Brazil replied:

> "Article 5.2 of the Anti-Dumping Agreement requires an application to include evidence of dumping, injury and causal link. Specifically, the application must contain information required in items (i) through (iv) of Article 5.2. We cannot presume from the language in Article 5.2 that these obligations are imposed on the applicant. Relevant part of Article 5.2 provides that:
>
>> "(...) Simple assertion, unsubstantiated by relevant evidence, cannot be *considered* sufficient to meet the requirements of this paragraph.(...)". (emphasis added)
>
> The ***consideration*** of sufficient evidence to meet the requirements of the paragraph in Article 5.2 is made by the investigating authority and not by the applicant. After all, the applicant is not the one to consider whether the evidence it submitted in the application is sufficient to meet the requirements of Article 5.2.
>
> Furthermore, the WTO and its Agreements provide for obligations and rights of ***Members*** of the WTO. Consequently, the Anti-Dumping Agreement also imposes obligations on ***Members*** of the WTO and not on specific interested parties in an investigation. We cannot, therefore, infer that the obligations under Article 5.2 are obligations of the applicant and not the investigating authority.
>
> Under Article 5.2 of the Agreement, the investigating authority must check the application to see whether the information required by that Article is present in the application. In order for an investigating authority to accept an application it must ***consider*** whether information and evidence in the application is sufficient to meet the requirements set forth in items (i) through (iv) of Article 5.2. At a subsequent stage, and once the application has be considered and accepted by the authority as meeting the requirements in Article 5.2,

Article 5.3 of the Agreement imposes another obligation on the investigating authority. This obligation is the examination of the accuracy and adequacy of the evidence provided in the application to determine whether it is sufficient to justify the initiation of the investigation."[93] (emphasis in original)

7.97 Argentina replied:

"It is Argentina's understanding that the Agreement imposes obligations on Members. In principle, Article 5.2 imposes an obligation on Members with respect to the information that is required to be provided with the application for the initiation of an investigation. In other words, Article 5.2 lays down the requirements governing what the sector wishing to file an application for the initiation of an investigation must provide with its application."[94]

7.98 Thus, both parties agree that Article 5.2 imposes obligations on Members. Without ruling on this matter, we do not exclude the possibility that Article 5.2 could oblige Members to verify that applications contain evidence, and not mere assertion, of dumping, injury, and causal link. In particular, in cases where applicants propose adjustments to normal value, Article 5.2 could oblige Members to verify that such adjustments are supported by evidence, rather than mere assertion. A consequence of this obligation may be that applications not meeting the requirements of Article 5.2 are rejected. Although Members may choose to correct any deficiencies in an application,[95] they are not obliged to do so.

3. Failure to Reject the Application - Claims 3, 7 and 31

7.99 These claims are made under Article 5.8 of the *AD Agreement*. Claims 3 and 7 concern the issue of whether or not the application should have been rejected for lack of sufficient evidence of dumping. Claim 31 concerns the issue of whether or not the application should have been rejected for lack of sufficient evidence of injury.

(a) Arguments of the Parties

(i) Claims 3 and 7

7.100 In Claims 3 and 7, Brazil contends that the application contained no substantial evidence to support the APCDS's adjustment for differences in physical characteristics, or the yield rate used to make that adjustment. Nor did it contain sufficient evidence to establish normal value. In view of that, Brazil argues that the application should have been rejected because there was insufficient evidence of dumping to justify proceeding with the investigation. According to Brazil, failure to reject the application constituted a violation of Article 5.8 of the *AD Agreement*.

7.101 Argentina asserts that, since the applicant had provided all of the documentation available to it and the documentation was examined for accuracy and adequacy by the investigating authority, there was no reason for the implementing authority to reject the application.

---

[93] Brazil's reply to Question 2 of the Panel.
[94] Argentina's reply to Question 2 of the Panel.
[95] Panel Report, "*Guatemala - Cement I, supra*, note 73, para. 7.53.

(ii) Claim 31

7.102 Brazil asserts that the CNCE issued a determination (Record No. 405) dated 7 January 1998 to the effect that the application contained insufficient evidence of injury to justify the initiation of an investigation. Brazil submits that, in accordance with Article 5.8 of the *AD Agreement*, the application should have been rejected at that time, because that was the point when the investigating authority was "satisfied" that there was not sufficient evidence of injury to justify proceeding with the case.

7.103 Argentina asserts that, following the CNCE determination contained in Record No. 405, the applicant submitted new evidence. Argentina points to Article 60 of the Regulations to the National Law on Administrative Procedures which stipulates that the competent body shall intervene once again in proceedings if any new developments occur or come to its knowledge. Argentina also points to an opinion from the Legal Department of the MEyOSP which stated that, before proceeding any further, the Secretary should ask the CNCE to intervene once again in order to rule on the sufficiency (from the perspective of injury) of the new information submitted by the applicant. In light of the above, Argentina concludes that the Argentine authorities would not have acted in conformity with internal law if they had rejected the application following the CNCE determination in Record No. 405 and, hence, had not examined the new evidence submitted by the applicant on 17 February 1998. In addition, Argentina asserts that, apart from being contrary to domestic administrative law, the rejection of the application and closing of the file in January 1998 (pursuant to the conclusions set forth in Record No. 405) would have adversely affected the individual rights of the applicant with all of the administrative consequences that such an act would entail.

(b) Evaluation by the Panel

7.104 We begin by analysing Claim 31.

(i) Claim 31

7.105 In order to resolve Claim 31, we must determine whether, following CNCE's 7 January 1998 conclusion in Record No. 405 that there was not sufficient evidence of injury to justify the initiation of the investigation, the application should have been rejected.

7.106 Article 5.8 of the *AD Agreement* reads in relevant part as follows:

> "An application under paragraph 1 shall be rejected and an investigation shall be terminated promptly as soon as the authorities concerned are satisfied that there is not sufficient evidence of either dumping or of injury to justify proceeding with the case."

7.107 Argentina operates a bifurcated anti-dumping system, as explained in more detail in para. 7.122 *infra*. Thus, while the DCD (formerly the APCDS) investigates issues of dumping, the CNCE investigates issues of injury. This division of labour applies both at the time of the (pre-initiation) review of the application, and during any subsequent investigation. Although only the Secretary has the authority to decide whether or not to initiate an investigation,[96] the Secretary cannot decide to initiate an investigation if either the CNCE or the DCD/APCDS have found that there is

---

[96] Argentina's reply to Question 70 of the Panel.

insufficient evidence of injury or dumping, respectively, to justify the initiation of an investigation. In the case at hand, the CNCE issued Record No. 405 on 7 January 1998 to the effect that the application did not contain sufficient evidence of injury to justify the initiation of an investigation.[97] The CNCE's determination was received by the Secretary on 9 January 1998.[98] We recall that, faced with a negative assessment of the application by the CNCE, the Secretary is precluded from initiating an investigation. Accordingly, from the time that the Secretary received the CNCE's negative assessment of the application, the Secretary should have been satisfied that there was not sufficient evidence on injury to justify proceeding with the case.[99] Thus, in accordance with Article 5.8, the Secretary should have rejected the application "as soon as" it received CNCE Record No. 405 dated 7 January 1998. Rather than doing so, however, the Secretary kept the file open, subsequently deciding to initiate the investigation following the submission of additional information by the applicant. The Secretary therefore failed to meet the requirements of Article 5.8 of the *AD Agreement*.

7.108 Argentina argues that rejection of the application "as soon as" the CNCE's negative assessment was received would have been contrary to domestic administrative law, and would have adversely affected the individual rights of the applicant, with all of the administrative consequences that such an act would entail.[100] This does not affect our conclusion that Argentina acted inconsistently with Article 5.8 in this case. We consider that a WTO Member's domestic law does not excuse that Member from fulfilling its obligations under the WTO agreements. In acceding to the WTO, Argentina undertook to be bound by the rules contained in the *AD Agreement*, and our mandate is to review Argentina's compliance with those rules. Any failure to respect Article 5.8 may not be justified on the basis of inconsistent provisions of domestic law. Article XVI:4 of the *WTO Agreement* explicitly provides that each Member "shall ensure the conformity of its laws, regulations and administrative procedures with its obligations as provided in the annexed Agreements". We note that a similar view was expressed by the *Guatemala - Cement II* panel.[101] Regarding Argentina's comment that rejection of the application in January 1998 would have adversely affected the individual rights of the applicant, we note that there is nothing in the *AD Agreement* that would have prevented the applicant from filing an additional application after rejection of its original application. For this reason, we reject the argument that the individual rights of the applicant would have been negatively affected by the rejection of the application in January 1998.

7.109 In light of the above, we find that, by failing to reject the application "as soon as" the negative assessment from the CNCE was received, the Secretary violated Article 5.8 of the *AD Agreement*.

---

[97] Exhibit BRA-3.
[98] See *supra*, note 96.
[99] There is no evidence on the record that the Secretary sought additional information from the applicant at this stage, or even that the Secretary would have had the authority to do so.
[100] Argentina's reply to Question 16 of the Panel.
[101] Panel Report, *Guatemala - Cement II*, *supra*, note 48, para. 8.83.

(ii) Claims 3 and 7

7.110 Brazil's Claims 3 and 7 are dependent on a finding of violation under Claims 1, 2, 5 and 6. In other words, Brazil asserts that, if the investigating authorities' treatment of the application and decision to initiate constitute violations of Articles 5.2 and 5.3 of the *AD Agreement*, then it should never have initiated the investigation in the first place, and should instead have rejected the application in accordance with Article 5.8.

7.111 We recall that we have concluded in para. 7.89 *supra* that Argentina violated Article 5.3 of the *AD Agreement* by determining that there was sufficient evidence of dumping to justify the initiation of an investigation. Since the factual basis for Claims 3 and 7 is identical to that for Claims 2 and 6, and since we have already found that those factual circumstances constitute a violation of Article 5.3, it is not necessary to address Brazil's Claims 3 and 7.

(c) Conclusion

7.112 In light of the above, we find that Argentina acted inconsistently with its obligations under Article 5.8 in failing to reject the application "as soon as" the Secretary received the CNCE's negative assessment (in the form of record No. 405) on 9 January 1998.

4. *Simultaneous Examination of the Evidence and Failure to Reject the Application - Claim 9*

(a) Arguments of the Parties / Third Parties

7.113 Brazil asserts that the time-periods covered by data used for the purpose of examining whether there was sufficient evidence of dumping and injury to justify the initiation of the investigation were different. Brazil alleges that while the period covered to establish sufficient evidence of dumping included portions of 1996 and 1997, the period taken into account to establish sufficient evidence of injury ended in June 1998. In the view of Brazil, the use of different data collection periods for dumping and injury in the decision to initiate the investigation was inconsistent with Article 5.7 of the *AD Agreement* in two ways. First, Brazil asserts that the collection period for dumping should have been extended to include all of the period considered for injury purposes, i.e., until June 1998. In the view of Brazil, the fact that different periods were considered indicates that the dumping and injury evidence was not considered simultaneously in the decision whether or not to initiate the investigation. Second, Brazil asserts that Argentina failed to comply with Article 5.7 by not considering the evidence of both dumping and injury simultaneously in the same decision to initiate the investigation. Brazil argues that the APCDS determined that there was sufficient evidence of dumping in its report of 7 January 1998. Brazil asserts that the CNCE determined that there was sufficient evidence of threat of injury to justify the initiation on 22 September 1998, following its review of additional information submitted by the applicant. In the view of Brazil, this shows that the evidence of injury was considered more than eight months after the dumping evidence, in breach of Article 5.7 of the *AD Agreement*. Brazil argues that, for Argentina to have met the requirement in Article 5.7, a new dumping determination taking into account the additional dumping information presented by the applicant on

17 February 1998 should have occurred on 22 September 1998, the date when the CNCE decided that there was sufficient evidence of threat of material injury.

7.114   Argentina argues that the fact that the dates of the reports in which the APCDS and the CNCE found sufficient evidence of dumping and threat of injury are different does not mean that, at the moment of deciding on the initiation of the investigation, the Argentine authorities did not consider simultaneously the evidence of dumping and injury.

7.115   The United States, as a third party, argues that Brazil's argument is based on a misinterpretation of the term "simultaneously" as this term is used in Article 5.7. In the view of the United States, when viewed in context, the term "simultaneously" in Article 5.7 is linked to the term "considered", not the term "evidence". Thus, in the view of the United States, the obligation in Article 5.7 is to consider the evidence of dumping and injury simultaneously (for example, in concurrent investigations), not to consider evidence of dumping and injury collected from simultaneous (or identical) time-periods.

(b)   Evaluation by the Panel

7.116   The issue before us is whether Argentina violated Article 5.7 by not considering simultaneously evidence of both dumping and injury in the decision whether or not to initiate an investigation. Brazil raises two main arguments in support of its claim. First, the periods covered by data used to determine whether there was sufficient evidence of dumping and injury to justify the initiation of the anti-dumping investigation were different. Second, Brazil argues that the requirement of Article 5.7 could not have been met because the Argentine authorities considered evidence of injury and dumping at different times.

7.117   Article 5.7 provides in relevant part:

"The evidence of both dumping and injury shall be considered simultaneously *(a)* in the decision whether or not to initiate an investigation…"

7.118   In our view, Article 5.7 imposes a procedural obligation on the investigating authority to examine the evidence before it of dumping and injury simultaneously, rather than sequentially, *inter alia* in the decision whether or not to initiate an investigation. We are of the view that Article 5.7 is not concerned with the substance of the decision to initiate an investigation, which is dealt with in Article 5.3 of the *AD Agreement*. We note that a previous panel has expressed a similar view on this matter.[102]

7.119   We turn to Brazil's first argument. Brazil asserts that the periods covered by data used to determine whether there was sufficient evidence of dumping and injury to justify the initiation of the investigation were different. In other words, Brazil seems to argue that Article 5.7 requires a Member to ensure that its investigating authorities consider evidence of dumping and injury from simultaneous time-periods. We disagree with Brazil's interpretation. Consistent with our view expressed in

---

[102] The panel in *Guatemala - Cement II* expressed its view that "Article 5.7 requires the investigating authority to examine the evidence before it on dumping and injury simultaneously, rather than sequentially" and that "the fulfilment of this requirement is [not] conditioned in any way on the *substantive nature* of that evidence." (emphasis added) (Panel Report, *Guatemala - Cement II*, *supra*, note 48, para. 8.67)

para. 7.118 *supra*, we recall that Article 5.7 imposes only a procedural obligation on the part of the authorities of the importing Member. We do not consider that Article 5.7 imposes obligations of a substantive nature. In essence, Brazil argues that evidence of dumping and injury must cover simultaneous periods. We consider that this argument concerns the substantive nature of the evidence considered by the authorities in the decision whether or not to initiate an investigation, rather than the timing of the consideration itself. Brazil's argument therefore falls outside the scope of the obligation contained in Article 5.7. We therefore reject Brazil's first argument.

7.120 The second argument put forward by Brazil is that the requirement of Article 5.7 could not have been met because the Argentine authorities considered evidence of injury and dumping at different times. We recall that the CNCE initially found in January 1998 that the application did not contain sufficient evidence of injury, whereas the APCDS found that it did contain sufficient evidence of dumping. As a result of the CNCE's determination, the applicant submitted additional, updated evidence of both dumping and injury in February 1998. While the Secretary referred the additional, updated evidence of injury to the CNCE, it did not refer the additional, updated evidence of dumping to the APCDS. Thus, when the CNCE found in September 1998 that the additional, updated evidence of injury was sufficient to justify initiation, that finding was based on more recent data than the ACPDS's January 1998 determination (based on dumping data contained in the original application) that there was sufficient evidence of dumping. Since Brazil's argument concerns the timing of the consideration of evidence of dumping and injury, it is in principle covered by the scope of the procedural obligation contained in Article 5.7. We must now determine whether or not Argentina complied with that obligation. In addressing this issue, we shall first determine what constitutes "the decision whether or not to initiate an investigation", and then examine whether evidence of dumping and injury was simultaneously considered in that decision.

7.121 Brazil argues that there were in fact two decisions for the purposes of Article 5.7: one by the APCDS in January 1998, and another by the CNCE in September 1998. Argentina argues that there was only one decision whether or not to initiate the investigation, and that it was taken by the Secretary on 20 January 1999.[103] Argentina acknowledges that this decision is based on the determinations on dumping and injury received by the Secretary from the APCDS and the CNCE, respectively. At the outset, we consider that "the decision whether or not to initiate an investigation" must be a decision that occurs before, or at the same time as, the moment of initiation of an investigation, because the purpose of the decision is to determine whether or not to initiate an investigation. We further note that Article 5.7 uses the term "decision" in singular form rather than plural. We believe that this means that there is normally one decision in which the relevant authority of the importing Member determines whether or not to initiate an investigation. We consider that it is *only* in this decision, and *not* in other decisions, that the relevant investigating authority must simultaneously consider the evidence of dumping and injury.

7.122 Having said that, we must examine the relevant facts of the present dispute. Brazil's argument is that the requirement of Article 5.7 could not have been met because the Argentine authorities considered evidence of injury and dumping at different times. In order to understand how the Argentine system works, we posed

---

[103] Exhibit BRA-7.

various questions to Argentina.[104] Argentina explained that it has a bifurcated system, in which the APCDS - currently the DCD - and the CNCE examine dumping and injury, respectively. Consistent with this separation, at the pre-initiation stage those two agencies examine separately the evidence available and determine whether there is sufficient evidence of dumping and injury, respectively, to justify the initiation of an investigation. These separate determinations are sent by both agencies to the authority in charge of deciding whether or not to initiate an investigation, which is the Secretary. Taking into account the explanations received from the parties, it is clear to us that the Secretary is the authority entitled to decide whether or not to initiate an anti-dumping investigation in Argentina. In this regard, we note that Article 37 of Decree No. 2121/94 provides in relevant part "the Under-Secretariat for Foreign Trade and the National Commission for Foreign Trade (...) shall submit their conclusions to the Secretary for Foreign Trade for a decision on the opening of the investigation to be taken...".[105] Brazil acknowledges that "the MEOSP [is] the authority that issued the decision to initiate the investigation."[106] If the MEyOSP - through the Secretary - is the authority entrusted to decide whether or not to initiate an investigation, then it is with respect to the Secretary's decision whether or not to initiate an investigation against poultry from Brazil that the evidence of dumping and injury should have been considered simultaneously. Brazil's argument that the requirement of Article 5.7 could not have been met because the APCDS and the CNCE considered evidence of injury and dumping at different times must therefore be rejected, because the APCDS and CNCE's determinations were not subject to the requirements of Article 5.7. Provided the Secretary, who is the relevant authority, considered the evidence of dumping and injury simultaneously in his decision to initiate, the requirement of Article 5.7 is met. Brazil has not argued that the Secretary failed to meet this requirement.

7.123 Finally, Brazil argued that, for Argentina to have met the requirement in Article 5.7, a new dumping determination taking into account the updated information presented by the applicant in February 1998 should have been made on 22 September 1998 (which was the date on which the CNCE issued its determination regarding the additional injury data submitted by the applicant in February 1998).[107] We do not agree with Brazil. We recall that Article 5.7 does not impose obligations of a substantive nature. To the extent that this argument concerns the substance of the decision, it must therefore be rejected. Nevertheless, even if that argument were of a procedural nature, we recall that the Secretary is *the* authority entrusted to decide whether or not to initiate an investigation and hence it is the Secretary's decision - and not that of the CNCE or the APCDS - that must be considered the "decision whether or not to initiate an investigation" within the meaning of Article 5.7. In light of the above, we find that Argentina did not violate Article 5.7 of the *AD Agreement* simply because the APCDS and CNCE determinations on dumping and injury, respectively, were issued at different times.

---

[104] Questions 15, 22 and 23.
[105] Document notified by Argentina and available in the WTO website (http://www.wto.org) under reference G/ADP/N/1/ARG/1 / G/SCM/N/1/ARG/1.
[106] Brazil's reply to Question 22 by the Panel.
[107] *Ibid.*

Report of the Panel

(c) Conclusion

7.124 For the foregoing reasons, we reject Brazil's claim that Argentina acted inconsistently with Article 5.7 by not considering, in the decision whether or not to initiate the investigation, the evidence of dumping and injury simultaneously.

5. *Failure to Notify Known Exporters - Claim 10*

(a) Arguments of the Parties

7.125 Brazil asserts that Article 12.1 requires that, in addition to a public notice, a notification (to certain interested parties and the exporting Member) be given when the authorities are satisfied that there is sufficient evidence to justify the initiation of an investigation. The public notice was given when Resolution No. 11 was issued announcing the initiation of the investigation on 25 January 1999. Brazil asserts that it was notified of the initiation on 1 February 1999. Five Brazilian exporters (Avipal, Frangosul, Nicolini, Sadia, and Seara) were also notified of the initiation through communications from the CNCE and the DCD dated 10 and 16 February 1999, respectively. Brazil asserts that another group of seven exporters (Catarinense, CCLP, Chapecó, Comaves, Minuano, Penabranca and Perdigão) were only notified of the initiation of the investigation in September 1999, even though at least five of those seven exporters were known to the CNCE and the APCDS in January 1999. In this regard, Brazil notes that the Report of 7 January 1999 listed ten Brazilian exporters, including Catarinense, Chapecó, Comaves, Minuano and Perdigão. Brazil argues that the September 1999 notification to these seven exporters did not comply with the requirement under Article 12.1 because it was not made "when the authorities [were] satisfied that there [was] sufficient evidence to justify the initiation of an anti-dumping investigation".

7.126 Argentina asserts that Resolution No. 11 initiating the investigation was published in the Official Bulletin on 25 January 1999. Argentina asserts that it notified Brazil of the initiation of the investigation through a Note dated 1 February 1999 addressed to the Mission of Brazil in Argentina. In this communication, Argentina requested the cooperation of the Brazilian authorities "in identifying the interested producers/exporters in that investigation." Argentina asserts that the DCD notified the exporters Avipal, Frangosul, Nicolini, Sadia and Seara of the initiation of the investigation on 16 February 1999. Argentina asserts further that, through the questionnaire response of an importer dated 21 April 1999, it learned of the interest of seven other Brazilian exporters in the investigation. These exporters were Catarinense, CCLP, Chapecó, Comaves, Minuano, Penabranca and Perdigão. Argentina asserts that the importer requested that the Argentine authorities contact those exporters. As a result of this request, the DCD contacted Catarinense, CCLP, Chapecó, Comaves, Minuano and Perdigão on 15 September 1999 and requested information from them. Argentina argues that the investigating authority satisfied the Article 12.1 requirement of public notice and notification to interested parties (exporter or foreign producer) known to have an interest, such as the Government of Brazil, and that it would have been impossible to notify parties whose interest in the investigation was not known. Argentina asserts that it requested the assistance of the Government of Brazil in informing potential interested parties of the initiation of the investigation. Argentina argues that notification must be given to those parties that are considered interested within the meaning of Article 6.11, and that are known and identified in such a way as to make such notification possible and identified as interested parties. Regarding Brazil's statement that Argentina implicitly acknowledged that it knew of certain exporters by listing them in the Report of 7 January 1998, Argentina stated that those exporters had not been sufficiently identified to allow the relevant questionnaires to be sent to them.

7.127 Brazil asserts that Article 12.1 imposes the obligation to notify interested parties on the investigating authorities of the importing Member, and not the authorities of the exporting Member. Brazil notes that Argentina tries to share this obligation with Brazil when it states that it notified the Brazilian authorities and requested their cooperation to identify the producers and exporters. Brazil asserts that it never received any communication from the Argentine authorities requesting such information concerning the five specific exporters identified in the Report of 7 January 1998. Brazil further argues that Argentina's argument that the authority must notify only those parties that consider themselves interested in the investigation, within the meaning of Article 6.1.1, is untenable. Brazil asks how a party can present itself as an interested party if it does not even know that an investigation has been initiated? In the view of Brazil, that is exactly why Article 12.1 requires the authority to notify interested parties known to them.

(b) Evaluation by the Panel

7.128 The issue before us is whether or not Argentina complied with its notification obligations under Article 12.1 of the *AD Agreement* in respect of Catarinense, CCLP, Chapecó, Comaves, Minuano, Penabranca and Perdigão. As always, we start with the relevant provision in the *AD Agreement*, which in this case is Article 12.1. This provides in relevant part:

> "When the authorities are satisfied that there is sufficient evidence to justify the initiation of an anti-dumping investigation pursuant to Article 5, the Member or Members the products of which are subject to such investigation and other interested parties known to the investigating authorities to have an interest therein shall be notified..."

7.129 Article 12.1 requires the authorities of the importing Member to notify the initiation of an investigation to the WTO Member or Members the products of which are subject to such investigation. Article 12.1 also requires those authorities to notify "other interested parties known to the investigating authorities to have an interest" in the investigation. As far as the timing of the notification is concerned, Article 12.1 provides that the notification shall take place when the authorities of the importing Member are satisfied that there is sufficient evidence to justify the initiation of an anti-dumping investigation pursuant to Article 5.

7.130 In addressing this issue, we must first establish whether or not the relevant exporters were "interested parties" in the meaning of Article 12.1. If they were, we must then examine whether or not their interest was known to the investigating authority.

7.131 The phrase "interested parties" is defined in Article 6.11 of the *AD Agreement*. We consider that it is appropriate to be guided by the definition set forth in Article 6.11 since that definition is expressly provided for the purposes of the *AD Agreement* as a whole, including therefore Article 12.1. According to Article 6.11(i), exporters or foreign producers of a product subject to investigation constitute "interested parties". In an attachment to CEPA's application of 2 September 1997, a

Report of the Panel

table sourced from the Associação Paulista de Avicultura listed Catarinense, CCLP, Chapecó, Comaves, Minuano, Penabranca and Perdigão as exporters to Argentina of whole poultry.[108] Accordingly, based on the evidence before it at the time of initiation, there is a *prima facie* case that those exporters were "interested parties" within the meaning of Article 6.11 and, therefore, Article 12.1. By definition, "interested parties" necessarily have an interest in the investigation. The evidence before the investigating authority at the time of initiation further establishes *prima facie* that those exporters' interest was known to the investigating authority, since those exporters were expressly identified in that evidence. There is therefore *prima facie* evidence that those exporters were "interested parties known to the investigating authorities to have an interest" in the investigation. Accordingly, there is a *prima facie* case that those exporters should have been notified in accordance with Article 12.1.

7.132 Argentina asserts that it was not able to notify those exporters because the requisite contact details were not available to its authorities. In support, Argentina refers to a letter dated 1 February 1999 to the Brazilian Embassy in Argentina, in which the authorities requested Brazil's cooperation "in identifying the interested producers/exporters in this investigation and providing them with the attached requests for information, in order that they should supply the Argentine Government with the details requested on the product under investigation".[109] In our view, this letter does not support Argentina's argument that it could not make an Article 12.1 notification to the above-mentioned exporters because it did not have the requisite contact details. Instead, this letter demonstrates to us that the Argentine authorities failed to treat the above-mentioned exporters as "known ... to have an interest" in the investigation. If it had treated them thus, the letter would have specifically identified those exporters, and specifically requested contact details for them. Instead, the letter contained only a general request for assistance, without any reference to the specific exporters at issue. We accept that there may be circumstances in which an investigating authority may not have sufficient information to allow it to notify all interested parties known to have an interest in an investigation. In this sense, the fact that an exporter is "known" by the investigating authority to have an interest in an investigation does not necessarily mean that sufficient details concerning the exporter are "known" to the investigating authority such that it may make the Article 12.1 notification. In other words, knowledge of an exporter's interest in an investigation does not necessarily imply knowledge of contact details regarding that exporter. In such circumstances, however, we consider that the nature of the Article 12.1 notification obligation is such that the investigating authority should make all reasonable efforts to obtain the requisite contact details. Sending a letter with only a very general request for assistance, without specifying the exporters for which contact details are required, does not satisfy the need to make all reasonable efforts.

7.133 Argentina also submits that "the initiation of an investigation is a general administrative procedure and published as such in the Official Journal, which constitutes sufficient notification of general scope".[110] In other words, Argentina suggests that, by fulfilling the requirement to publish a notice of initiation of an investigation, it has fulfilled the obligation to notify. We do not agree. Article 12.1

---

[108] Exhibit BRA-1, p. 190.
[109] Exhibit ARG-III, p. 729-730.
[110] Argentina's first written submission, para. 167.

clearly imposes two separate obligations, one to notify and another to give public notice. These separate obligations must both be fulfilled in any given investigation. We therefore reject Argentina's argument.

7.134 We have concluded that Catarinense, CCLP, Chapecó, Comaves, Minuano, Penabranca and Perdigão should have been notified in accordance with Article 12.1. Although questionnaires were sent to some of these exporters on 15 September 1999, we do not understand Argentina to argue that this communication constitutes notification for the purpose of Article 12.1. In any event, we are of the view that a communication made approximately eight months after initiation would not satisfy the requirements of Article 12.1. Article 12.1 provides that notification must be made "when" the authorities are satisfied that there is sufficient evidence to justify initiation. The word "when" is defined *inter alia* as "as soon as".[111] Thus, Article 12.1 requires notification *as soon as* the authorities are satisfied that there is sufficient evidence to justify initiation. A notification made approximately 8 months after initiation clearly does not satisfy this requirement of expediency.

(c) Conclusion

7.135 In light of the above, we conclude that Argentina violated Article 12.1 of the *AD Agreement* by failing to notify Catarinense, CCLP, Chapecó, Comaves, Minuano, Penabranca and Perdigão of the initiation of the investigation.

6. *Failure to Give 30 Days to Reply to the Questionnaire / Failure to Provide the Injury Questionnaire - Claim 11*

(a) Arguments of the Parties

7.136 Brazil alleges that Argentina violated Article 6.1.1 of the *AD Agreement* because (i) the investigating authority gave CCLP, Catarinense, Chapecó, Comaves, Minuano, Perdigão and Penabranca only 20 days to reply to the questionnaire and (ii) these exporters never received the injury questionnaire issued by the CNCE.

7.137 Argentina acknowledges that the DCD contacted certain Brazilian exporters on 15 September 1999.[112] In these communications, the DCD requested those Brazilian exporters to submit evidence on, *inter alia*, sales prices in the domestic market, export prices and costs.[113] Argentina asserts that the DCD sent the questionnaire forms for the sole purpose of responding adequately to the general requirements and enabling exporters to attach any other information that they considered important.[114] According to Argentina, only one of those seven exporters, Catarinense, provided a reply to the questionnaire. Argentina alleges that it not only granted the Brazilian exporters a period of more than 30 days to reply to the questionnaires, but also acceded to their requests for extension by granting them whenever practicable.[115]

---

[111] *The Concise Oxford Dictionary of Current English* (Clarendon Press, 1995), p. 1595.
[112] Argentina's first written submission, paras. 127, 133, and 134.
[113] Argentina's reply to Question 28 of the Panel.
[114] *Ibid.*
[115] Argentina's first written submission, para. 134.

(b) Evaluation by the Panel

7.138 This claim concerns communications allegedly sent to the following seven exporters: CCLP, Catarinense, Chapecó, Comaves, Minuano, Penabranca and Perdigão. There are two issues before us. First, we will have to determine whether the DCD failed to give certain specific Brazilian exporters 30 days to reply to the dumping questionnaire it sent to them.[116] The second issue before us concerns whether the CNCE's injury questionnaire should also have been sent to the seven exporters identified by Brazil.

7.139 We start our analysis of the first issue by examining the text of Article 6.1.1 of the *AD Agreement*:

> "Exporters or foreign producers receiving questionnaires used in an anti-dumping investigation shall be given at least 30 days for reply. Due consideration should be given to any request for an extension of the 30-day period and, upon cause shown, such an extension should be granted whenever practicable." (footnote in original omitted)

7.140 On its face, Article 6.1.1 is straightforward. In accordance with the first sentence of that provision, exporters or foreign producers receiving questionnaires used in an anti-dumping investigation must be given *at least* 30 days for reply. Since the second sentence of Article 6.1.1 envisages extensions of the 30-day period provided for in the first sentence of Article 6.1.1, that 30-day period is an absolute minimum that must be granted to exporters from the outset. In other words, any extension is in addition to the initial (minimum) 30-day period provided for in the first sentence.

7.141 Brazil claims that the requests for information that Catarinense, CCLP, Chapecó, Comaves, Minuano and Perdigão received on 15 September 1999 constitute questionnaires falling within the scope of Article 6.1.1, and that there was a violation of that provision because the exporters were only provided 20 days to respond to those questionnaires. Argentina does not deny that on 15 September 1999 it requested information from those exporters. According to Argentina, the information requested "consisted, *inter alia*, of sales prices in the domestic market, export prices and costs."[117] Nor does Argentina deny that it sent those exporters a copy of the questionnaire sent out to other exporters / foreign producers at the beginning of its investigation. Argentina asserts that it did so "for the sole purpose of responding adequately to the general requirements and enabling exporters to attach any other information that they considered important."[118] Only one of the exporters contacted on 15 September 1999 responded to the DCD's request for information. That exporter did so by responding to the 11 sections of the questionnaire attached to

---

[116] With respect to Penabranca, Brazil asserted that this exporter was notified by the DCD on 15 September 1999 and was given 20 days to reply to the questionnaire. However, Brazil asserted that from the documents of the investigation to which it had access, it was unable to find the DCD's notification to Penabranca. Brazil therefore failed to provide copies of any documentation sent by the Argentine authorities to Penabranca. We recall that, being the complainant, Brazil is obliged to present a *prima facie* case of violation. Brazil has not shown us - nor referred us to - any document on the record which proves that Penabranca was given only 20 days to reply to the questionnaire. Thus, we consider that Brazil has not presented a *prima facie* case that the DCD failed to give Penabranca at least 30 days to respond to the DCD's dumping questionnaire.

[117] Argentina's reply to Question 28 of the Panel.

[118] Argentina's reply to Question 28 of the Panel. See also Exhibit BRA-13, and Sections VII.3.1 to VII.3.6 of Exhibit BRA-15.

the DCD's request for information. That exporter therefore clearly understood that it had been asked to respond to the DCD's questionnaire. In these circumstances, we consider that the requests for information sent to Brazilian exporters on 15 September 1999 were in the form of "questionnaire[s]" within the meaning of Article 6.1.1 of the *AD Agreement*.

7.142 With respect to the time given to CCLP, Catarinense, Chapecó, Comaves, Minuano, and Perdigão to reply to the questionnaires, we should note that there is some uncertainty regarding Argentina's argument on this issue. On the one hand, in response to Question 31 from the Panel, Argentina stated that "[e]xporters have a right to the 30 days, and the 30 days are granted. The alternative examined by the Panel of initially granting a lesser period and then increasing the number of days to 30 does not reflect the system applied by Argentina. What the Argentine authority stated was that in addition to the 30 days, it granted the requested extensions. It is understood that the time-limits granted for responding to the requests should be in keeping with the nature and complexity of those requests. Thus, the initial 30-day period for replying in full to the basic investigation questionnaire at the outset is appropriate." On the other hand, the communications sent to those Brazilian exporters show that they were given 20 days to send their replies to the investigating authority.[119] This has not been denied by Argentina. Based on the facts before us, we are therefore in no doubt that the DCD only allowed an initial period of 20 days for the relevant questionnaire responses.

7.143 Argentina also argues that the period allowed for the relevant questionnaire responses was sufficient for the purpose of Article 6.1.1 because only one of the exporters contacted by the DCD on 15 September 1999 (i.e., Catarinense) replied to the questionnaire; the others either did not export the product concerned to Argentina (i.e., CCLP and Chapecó) or did not show an interest in the investigation and did not submit any information (i.e., Comaves, Minuano, and Perdigão).[120] We fail to see the relevance of this fact. The requirement in the first sentence of Article 6.1.1 is that exporters or producers shall be given at least 30 days to reply to the questionnaire, irrespective of whether or not they actually choose to do so.

7.144 Since the DCD failed to allow the exporters contacted on 15 September 1999 an initial period of at least 30 days to respond to the questionnaires sent by the DCD, Argentina failed to comply with the requirement set forth in the first sentence of Article 6.1.1.

7.145 The second question before us is whether or not Article 6.1.1 of the *AD Agreement* required the CNCE to send its injury questionnaire to the seven exporters identified by Brazil.[121] We read the first sentence of Article 6.1.1 to mean that *if* questionnaires are sent to exporters or foreign producers, they shall be given at least 30 days for reply. The first sentence of that Article does not, however, address *which* questionnaires should be sent to exporters or foreign producers. Accordingly, the

---

[119] Exhibit BRA-13.

[120] Argentina's first written submission, para. 133 and Argentina's second oral statement, para. 41.

[121] We note that, in para. 212 of its first written submission, Brazil asserts that '[t]he CNCE never notified these seven exporters of the investigation...' However, we do not understand that Brazil is claiming that Argentina acted in violation of Article 6.1.1 of the *AD Agreement* on the basis that the CNCE never notified the initiation of the investigation to those seven exporters. In our view, any such claim would be unfounded as Article 6.1.1 is clearly not a provision concerned with the notification of the initiation of an investigation.

failure to send a particular questionnaire to exporters or foreign producers does not constitute a violation of Article 6.1.1.

7.146 Finally, Argentina asserts that Brazil did not challenge in the course of the investigation the circumstances which form the basis of the claim before us.[122] However, the fact that an argument was not raised in the context of the investigation, in particular an argument relating to a violation of a procedural provision in the *AD Agreement*, does not preclude a party from raising it at a later stage in a WTO panel proceeding.[123] We note that Argentina has not argued that this issue is not properly before us, or that it falls outside our terms of reference.

(c) Conclusion

7.147 In light of the foregoing, we conclude that Argentina violated Article 6.1.1 of the *AD Agreement* because it failed to give Catarinense, CCLP, Chapecó, Comaves, Minuano, and Perdigão at least 30 days to reply to the DCD's dumping questionnaire. We further conclude that Argentina did not violate Article 6.1.1 of the *AD Agreement* by not sending the CNCE's injury questionnaire to the exporters identified by Brazil.

7. *Failure to Make Evidence Available Promptly to Certain Brazilian Exporters - Claim 12*

(a) Arguments of the Parties

7.148 Brazil alleges that, because the DCD and the CNCE did not inform Catarinense, CCLP, Comaves, Chapecó, Minuano, Penabranca and Perdigão of the initiation of the investigation and of the need to submit responses, those seven exporters did not have evidence that was presented in writing by other interested parties made promptly available to them. In the view of Brazil, evidence could not be made readily or immediately available to these exporters if they were notified to participate eight months after the investigation had been initiated and after a preliminary determination of dumping, injury and causal link had been made. Brazil further argues that companies that are aware of an ongoing investigation qualify as "interested parties participating in the investigation", even if they do not show an interest in the investigation. Brazil asserts that Catarinense, CCLP, Comaves, Chapecó, Minuano, Perdigão and Penabranca were *not* aware of the ongoing investigation until they were notified by the authorities, eight months after it had been initiated.

7.149 Argentina replies that the DCD and the CNCE met the requirement in Article 6.1.2 because they promptly made available to the interested parties participating in the investigation evidence presented in writing by other interested parties. Argentina

---

[122] Argentina's first written submission, para. 136 and Argentina's second oral statement, para. 44.
[123] In this regard, we note that an argument similar to that raised by Argentina before us was examined by two GATT panels, namely *US - Norwegian Salmon AD* and *US - Norwegian Salmon CVD*. In both cases, the panels did not find any basis to refuse to consider a claim by a signatory in dispute settlement merely because the subject matter of the claim had not been raised before the investigating authorities under domestic law. (Panel Report, *Imposition of Anti-Dumping Duties on Imports of Fresh and Chilled Atlantic Salmon from Norway* ("*US - Norwegian Salmon AD*"), adopted 27 April 1994, BISD 41S/I/229, para. 349 and Panel Report, *Imposition of Countervailing Duties on Imports of Fresh and Chilled Atlantic Salmon from Norway* ("*US - Norwegian Salmon CVD*"), adopted 28 April 1994, BISD 41S/II/576, paras. 218)

asserts that the DCD and the CNCE could hardly have made available evidence presented in writing by the other interested parties participating in the investigation to the seven Brazilian exporters if those exporters were not part of the investigation. Argentina's obligation was to make available promptly to the other interested parties participating in the investigation evidence presented in writing by one interested party, which Argentina asserts the DCD and the CNCE did.

(b) Evaluation by the Panel

7.150 The issue before us is whether the investigating authorities were required to make available evidence presented by other interested parties to Catarinense, CCLP, Comaves, Chapecó, Minuano, Penabranca and Perdigão.

7.151 Article 6.1.2 of the *AD Agreement* reads as follows:

"Subject to the requirement to protect confidential information, evidence presented in writing by one interested party shall be made available promptly to other interested parties *participating* in the investigation." (emphasis added)

7.152 We understand Article 6.1.2 to impose an obligation on investigating authorities to make evidence available promptly to other interested parties participating in the investigation.

7.153 We note that Article 6.1.2 does not refer to "interested parties" but to "interested parties participating in the investigation." Thus, the term "interested parties" is qualified by the term "participating".[124] In our view, had the drafters intended to extend the obligation imposed by Article 6.1.2 to all interested parties as defined in Article 6.11 of the *AD Agreement*, they would not have included the term "participating". We must first determine what the ordinary meaning of the term "participating" is. We note that Article 6.1.2 uses the term "parties participating in the investigation." The ordinary meaning of the term "participate" is "share or take part (in)".[125] This definition of the term "participating" suggests to us that, in order to participate in an investigation, a party must undertake some action.[126] In our view, the mere knowledge by an interested party of an ongoing investigation does not make that party an interested party "participating in the investigation" within the meaning of Article 6.1.2 unless it actively takes part in the investigation. Thus, we have to examine in light of the record before us whether the exporters identified by Brazil were actively taking part in the investigation. In this regard, Brazil asserts that those exporters were not even aware of the investigation until they were contacted by the DCD on 15 September 1999.[127] We consider that, if they were not even aware of the

---

[124] Bearing in mind the text of Article 6.1.2, we cannot agree with an interpretation of Article 6.1.2 which ignores the term "participating in the investigation."

[125] *The Concise Oxford Dictionary of Current English* (Clarendon Press, 1995), p. 996.

[126] For the purposes of Article 6.1.2, we are of the view that the term "interested parties" should be interpreted in light of Article 6.11 of the *AD Agreement*. Thus, we find that the term "interested parties" in Article 6.1.2 includes "an exporter or foreign producer (...) of a product subject to investigation", such as the Brazilian exporters Catarinense, CCLP, Comaves, Chapecó, Minuano, Penabranca and Perdigão.

[127] "Brazil reaffirms that the Brazilian exporters CCLP, Catarinense, Chapecó, Minuano, Perdigão, Comaves and PenaBranca were ***not aware*** of the ongoing investigation until they were notified by the authorities, eight months after it had been initiated." (emphasis in original) (Brazil's reply to Question 32 of the Panel) We recall that Brazil has failed to produce any evidence that Penabranca

investigation, they could not possibly have participated in that investigation within the meaning of Article 6.1.2 of the *AD Agreement*.[128] Since the relevant exporters were not "participating" in the investigation, the investigating authority was not required to promptly make evidence presented in writing by other interested parties available to them.

(c)   Conclusion

7.154 For the foregoing reasons, we reject Brazil's claim that Argentina violated Article 6.1.2 by failing to promptly make available to Catarinense, CCLP, Comaves, Chapecó, Minuano, Penabranca and Perdigão evidence presented in writing by other interested parties involved in the investigation.

8.   *Interested Party's Right to Defend Its Interests - Claim 13*

(a)   Arguments of the Parties

7.155 Brazil argues that Catarinense, CCLP, Comaves, Chapecó, Minuano, Penabranca and Perdigão did not have a full opportunity to defend their interests in violation of Article 6.2 of the *AD Agreement*. Brazil asserts that those exporters were only given 20 days to reply to the questionnaire, in breach of Article 6.1.1. Brazil further asserts that the CNCE did not notify those exporters of the initiation of the investigation, nor provide them with injury questionnaires. Finally, Brazil argues that, since those exporters were not notified of the investigation and of the need to submit replies to the questionnaire until eight months after the initiation of the investigation, evidence presented by other interested parties was not made available promptly to them.

7.156 Argentina replies that, once the investigation had started, Argentina made available the documentation relating to the proceedings at issue to interested parties such as the exporters and the Brazilian authorities. Argentina asserts that authorized interested parties could consult the file and obtain a copy thereof at all times. Any other party that considered itself as having an interest therein could present itself at the offices of the investigating authority with a request to consult the file. Regarding the issue of sending the notification of the initiation to certain exporters on 15 September 1999, Argentina argues that the obligation to give public notice and to notify the interested parties applies only to parties known to have an interest in the investigation. Argentina asserts that it would have been impossible to notify parties

---

was contacted by the DCD on 15 September 1999 (see note 116 above). However, this is not relevant to the issue of whether or not Penabranca was participating in the investigation.

[128] Brazil argues that, if an investigating authority fails to notify a foreign producer or an exporter of the initiation of the investigation, the requirement set forth in Article 6.1.2 cannot possibly be met. We disagree, since the beneficiaries of the obligation in Article 6.1.2 are different from the beneficiaries of the obligation in Article 12.1. Whereas Article 6.1.2 applies in respect of interested parties "participating in the investigation", Article 12.1 applies in respect of interested parties "known to the investigating authorities to have an interest" in the investigation. Thus, a violation of Article 12.1 does not automatically entail a violation of Article 6.1.2. The fact that interested parties were not participating in the investigation because they were not notified of the initiation of the investigation does not change the fact that the beneficiaries of the obligations in Articles 12.1 and 6.1.2 are different. We consider that the Brazilian exporters were not aware of the investigation because they had not been notified in accordance with Article 12.1 of the *AD Agreement*. We recall that separate findings have been reached under Claim 10 in para. 7.135 *supra* with respect to this matter.

whose interest therein was not known. In this regard, Argentina asserts that the investigating authority notified the Government of Brazil of the initiation of the investigation and requested its cooperation in order to identify the interested producers/exporters. Argentina asserts that the Brazilian authorities did not inform the investigating authority of the alleged interest of the exporters which were notified on 15 September 1999 and whose right of defence was, according to Brazil, impaired. Argentina concludes that the way in which the investigating authorities provided access to the proceedings for interested parties clearly did not in any way impair the right of access to the records and even less the right of defence.

(b) Evaluation by the Panel

7.157 Brazil has raised three claims under Article 6.2 of the *AD Agreement*. One claim concerns the alleged failure by the CNCE to notify certain exporters and provide them with the injury questionnaire sent to other exporters. Upon close examination, we find that there is no reference to this claim in Brazil's Request for Establishment of this Panel.[129] Accordingly, this claim falls outside our terms of reference.

7.158 With regard to the two Article 6.2 claims that are within our terms of reference, the issue before us is whether Catarinense, CCLP, Comaves, Chapecó, Minuano, Penabranca and Perdigão did not have a full opportunity for the defence of their interests because (a) the DCD did not give them at least 30 days to reply to the dumping questionnaire, and (b) the DCD and the CNCE did not make available promptly to them evidence presented by other interested parties.

7.159 Article 6.2 of the *AD Agreement* provides in relevant part:

"Throughout the anti-dumping investigation all interested parties shall have a full opportunity for the defence of their interests."

7.160 The parties agree that, while Article 6.2 clearly imposes a general duty on investigating authorities to ensure that interested parties have a full opportunity throughout an anti-dumping investigation for the defence of their interests, it provides no specific guidance as to what steps investigating authorities must take in practice.[130] We agree.[131] We also agree with previous panels[132] and the Appellate

---

[129] The relevant part of Brazil's Request for Establishment (document WT/DS241/3, Section B.4) provides:

"The DCD failed to give the legally required time for some of the exporters to respond to the questionnaires. The DCD also failed to promptly make available to these Brazilian exporters, evidence presented in writing by other interested parties. By not giving these exporters sufficient time to respond to the questionnaires and by not promptly making available the evidence presented by other interested parties, the DCD did not give these exporters full opportunity to defend their interests in this investigation, thereby violating **Articles 6.1.1, 6.1.2 and 6.2**." (emphasis in original)

[130] Brazil's first written submission, para. 222 and Argentina's first written submission, para. 150.

[131] We note that a similar view was expressed by the *Guatemala - Cement II* panel. (Panel Report, *Guatemala - Cement II, supra*, note 48, para. 8.162)

[132] See e.g., Panel Report, *Guatemala - Cement II, supra*, note 48, para. 8.162 and Panel Report, *United States - Anti-Dumping Act of 1916 - Complaint by the European Communities* ("*US - 1916 Act (EC)*"), WT/DS136/R and Corr.1, adopted 26 September 2000, as upheld by the Appellate Body Report, WT/DS136/AB/R, WT/DS162/AB/R, DSR 2000:X, 4593, para. 6.76.

Body[133] in that we do not consider it necessary for us to address claims under Article 6.2 when we have already made findings concerning the conduct allegedly violating Article 6.2 under other, more specific provisions of the *AD Agreement*.

7.161 Accordingly, we shall only consider Brazil's claims under Article 6.2 to the extent that we have not made findings regarding the factual situation at issue under other provisions of the *AD Agreement* which specifically address that situation. Regarding Brazil's argument that the DCD did not give CCLP, Catarinense, Chapecó, Comaves, Minuano, Penabranca and Perdigão at least 30 days to reply the dumping questionnaire, we recall that we made findings under Article 6.1.1.[134] We have also made findings regarding Brazil's contention that the DCD and the CNCE did not make available promptly to Catarinense, CCLP, Comaves, Chapecó, Minuano, Penabranca and Perdigão evidence presented by other interested parties under Article 6.1.2.[135] Accordingly, we have already made findings regarding the factual situations forming the basis of Brazil's Article 6.2 claims under other provisions of the *AD Agreement* which specifically address those factual situations.

(c) Conclusion

7.162 For the foregoing reasons, we consider that it is not necessary for us to make separate findings with respect to Brazil's Article 6.2 claims.

9. *Failure to Provide the Full Text of the Written Application in a Timely Manner - Claim 14*

(a) Arguments of the Parties

7.163 Brazil argues that the investigating authority failed to provide the text of the application to the exporters and to the Government of Brazil, thus making it impossible for the exporters to prepare arguments in the defence of their interests and to devise a strategy to defend against the allegations made by petitioner in the application. Brazil argues that the requirement under Article 6.1.3 of the *AD Agreement* with respect to known exporters and authorities of the exporting Member cannot be met by simply making the application available to the exporters and to the authorities of the exporting Member. In the view of Brazil, that requirement can only be met if the investigating authority *actively* provides the full text of the written application to the exporting Member and to the exporters involved in the investigation. Brazil asserts that its interpretation of the obligation imposed by Article 6.1.3 is confirmed by the fact that the same provision requires that the text of the application be "made available" to "other interested parties involved." In the view of Brazil, if the requirement imposed on the investigating authority was to be understood as being the same for the exporters and exporting Member as that for

---

[133] The Appellate Body stated in *EC - Bananas III (Ecuador)* that "[a]lthough Article X:3(a) of the GATT 1994 and Article 1.3 of the *Licensing Agreement* both apply, the Panel, in our view, should have applied the *Licensing Agreement* first, since this agreement deals specifically, and in detail, with the administration of import licensing procedures." (Appellate Body Report, *European Communities - Regime for the Importation, Sale and Distribution of Bananas - Complaint by Ecuador* ("*EC - Bananas III (Ecuador)*"), WT/DS27/AB/R, adopted 25 September 1997, DSR 1997:III, 1085, para. 204).

[134] See paras. 7.138-7.146 *supra*.

[135] See paras. 7.150-7.153 *supra*.

other interested parties, there would be no need for the use of different language in Article 6.1.3 of the *AD Agreement*. Brazil also argues that, even if "provide" had to be interpreted as "make available", the investigating authority would have violated Article 6.1.3 because the notification that the full text of the written application was available was not sent "as soon as an investigation has been initiated."

7.164 Argentina replies that Article 6.1.3 does not require an investigating authority "enviar", i.e., to "send", the full text of the application but "facilitar", i.e., to "provide", it to the known exporters and to the authorities of the exporting Member. Argentina asserts that, once the investigation was initiated, it made the records of the proceedings available to authorized interested parties. In so doing, Argentina states that it met the requirement set forth in Article 6.1.3. Argentina asserts that, considering that the Brazilian authorities were notified on 1 February 1999 and the notice of initiation of the investigation against poultry from Brazil was published in the Official Bulletin on 25 January 1999, the notification to the Government of Brazil took place five working days after the date of initiation of the investigation.

7.165 Brazil asserts that the word "facilitar" in the Spanish version of Article 6.1.3 of the *AD Agreement* should be understood to mean "proporcionar o entregar", a definition which is entirely compatible with that of the verb to "provide" in the English version of the *AD Agreement*.

(b) Evaluation by the Panel

7.166 The issue before us concerns the interpretation of the obligation imposed by the term "provide" in the first sentence of Article 6.1.3.

7.167 The text of Article 6.1.3 reads as follows:

"As soon as an investigation has been initiated, the authorities shall provide the full text of the written application received under paragraph 1 of Article 5 to the known exporters and to the authorities of the exporting Member and shall make it available, upon request, to other interested parties involved. Due regard shall be paid to the requirement for the protection of confidential information, as provided for in paragraph 5." (footnote in original omitted)

7.168 The obligation in Article 6.1.3 is clear. Subject to the proviso of protection of confidential information, investigating authorities must *provide* the text of the written application to the known exporters and to the authorities of the exporting Member. They must also *make it available*, upon request, to other interested parties. This obligation applies as soon as the investigation has been initiated.

7.169 Argentina is of the view that it satisfied its "obligation [under Article 6.1.3 of the *AD Agreement*] by making the records of the proceedings available to authorized interested parties."[136] In the view of Argentina, the term "*facilitar*" means "to permit access to a thing or element that is of interest to the other party".[137] In other words, in the view of Argentina the verb to "provide" in Article 6.1.3 has the meaning of permitting access to a thing or element that is of interest to the other party. We note that the term "provide" is defined as, *inter alia*, "supply; furnish".[138] "Provide" might consequently be understood as supply or furnish the text of the application. Bearing

---

[136] Argentina's first written submission, paras. 164 and 165.
[137] Reply of Argentina to Question 37 of the Panel.
[138] *The Concise Oxford Dictionary of Current English* (Clarendon Press, 1995), p. 1102.

Report of the Panel

this definition in mind, we consider that the term "provide" would require a positive action on the part of the investigating authority akin to that of furnishing or supplying something (i.e., the full text of the application) to someone (i.e., known exporters and authorities of the exporting Member). Therefore, we cannot agree with Argentina that the term "provide" in the English text of the *AD Agreement* or "facilitar" in its Spanish text can be interpreted as meaning "permitting access". In our view, an investigating authority cannot comply with the obligation to "provide the (…) application (…) to the known exporters and to the authorities of the exporting Member" simply by permitting them access to that application.

7.170 Our interpretation is confirmed by the words chosen by the drafters of Article 6.1.3. In this regard, we note that Article 6.1.3 provides for two different obligations, depending on the party concerned. Article 6.1.3 provides that the full text of the written application must be *provided* to the known exporters and to the authorities of the exporting Member. With respect to other interested parties involved, that provision imposes the obligation on the investigating authority to *make the application available* to those other interested parties. In our view, with the use of different verbs in the first sentence of Article 6.1.3, "provide" on the one hand and "make available" on the other, the drafters intended to impose different obligations on investigating authorities depending on the party concerned. The first obligation requires a positive action on the part of the investigating authority, while the second envisages only a passive act.

7.171 Argentina argues further that it understands the term "facilitar" in the Spanish text of Article 6.1.3, on the basis of the accepted meaning in Spanish, as meaning to permit access to a thing or element that is of interest to the other party.[139] "Facilitar" is defined *inter alia* as "proporcionar o entregar", i.e. to "give".[140] The term "facilitar" in the Spanish text might therefore be understood to require giving the full text of the written application to the known exporters and to the authorities of the exporting Member. This is consistent with our conclusion of the meaning of the term "provide" in the English text of the *AD Agreement*. This conclusion is again confirmed by the choice of the words of the drafters in the Spanish text of Article 6.1.3. We found that the obligation imposed on the investigating authority with respect to known exporters and the authorities of the exporting countries is to "facilitar" the full text of the application. By contrast, regarding other interested parties involved, Article 6.1.3 provides that "las autoridades lo [el texto completo de la solicitud escrita] pondrán a disposición de las otras partes interesadas intervinientes que lo soliciten", i.e., the authorities shall make it [the full text of the application] available, upon request, to other interested parties involved. An analysis of the Spanish text of Article 6.1.3 therefore does not support Argentina's position. For this reason, the argument of Argentina must fail.

7.172 We must next examine whether Argentina actively "provided" the full text of the application to the known exporters and the Brazilian authorities. Brazil asserts that the investigating authority never provided known Brazilian exporters and the Brazilian authorities the full text of the application.[141] Argentina asserts that "[t]he Argentine authorities satisfied that obligation by making *the records of the*

---

[139] Argentina's reply to Question 37 of the Panel.
[140] *Diccionario de la Lengua Española* (Espasa Calpe, 1992), p. 943.
[141] Brazil's first written submission, para. 230. See also, Brazil's replies to Questions 34, 35 and 36 from the Panel.

proceedings available to authorized interested parties."[142] Through this statement, Argentina acknowledges that the investigating authority merely made the full text of the written application available to the known exporters and to the Brazilian authorities. This, however, does not meet the requirement to actively "provide" the written application in the sense of Article 6.1.3. Finally, we examined the record of the investigation as presented to us.[143] We found no indication that the Argentine authorities provided the text of the application to known exporters and the authorities of Brazil. We consider therefore that Argentina did not provide the full text of the application to the known Brazilian exporters and to the authorities of the exporting Member.

(c) Conclusion

7.173 Having determined that Argentina did not actively provide the full text of the written application to known Brazilian exporters and to the Brazilian authorities, we find that Argentina acted inconsistently with its obligation under Article 6.1.3 of the *AD Agreement*.

10. Use of Facts Available - Claims 15, 17 and 19

7.174 These claims concern the DCD's use of "facts available" within the meaning of Article 6.8 of the *AD Agreement*, and relate to the DCD's rejection of certain data submitted by exporters.

(a) Arguments of the Parties

(i) Claim 15

7.175 Brazil challenges the DCD's determination that there were differences in the physical characteristics of poultry sold in Brazil and Argentina respectively, despite Avipal, Frangosul and Sadia informing the DCD through their questionnaire

---

[142] Argentina's first written submission, para. 164. In the same vein, para. 165 reads as follows:
'Once the investigation had started, Argentina *made available to the interested parties - inter alia* the exporters, importers and the authorities of the country concerned - the documentation relating to the proceedings at issue. Authorized interested parties could thus consult the file and obtain a copy thereof at all times, that is, not only of the application itself but also of all the other records on file.'
(emphasis added)

[143] In particular, we examined a communication dated 1 February 1999 sent by the DCD to the Mission of Brazil in Argentina (Exhibit ARG-III) as well as communications sent by the CNCE and the DCD to the Brazilian exporters Avipal, Frangosul, Nicolini, Sadia and Seara on 10 and 16 February 1999, respectively (Exhibits BRA-8 and BRA-9). Even if these communications had enclosed the full text of the written application, which they did not, Argentina would have been found to have acted in violation of Article 6.1.3 of the *AD Agreement* because, with regard to *those five known exporters*, Argentina would have failed to provide the full text of the application as soon as the investigation had been initiated, as mandated by Article 6.1.3 of the *AD Agreement*. We note that the communications were sent more than *15 days* after the publication of the initiation of the investigation in the Official Bulletin (25 January 1999). We agree with the view expressed by the *Guatemala - Cement II* panel that:
"given the nature of the obligation in Article 6.1.3 [the] sending (...) of the application even 8 days after the initiation of investigation is not adequate to fulfil the requirement that it be done "as soon as an investigation has been initiated.""
(Panel Report, *Guatemala - Cement II*, *supra*, note 48, para. 8.104)

responses that poultry sold to Argentina was identical to the poultry sold in Brazil. Brazil asserts that Catarinense only reported a difference in respect of broiler poultry, in the sense that its broiler poultry sold in Argentina did not contain head and feet, while its broiler poultry sold in Brazil contained head but not feet. Brazil asserts that the relevant information was submitted by the exporters within a reasonable period and that the DCD did not question the exporters on that information. Brazil alleges that the questionnaire did not specify that information on the product description required supporting documentation. In addition, Brazil asserts that, throughout the investigation, the DCD never requested any supporting information in order to verify the product description reported by those exporters.

7.176 Argentina asserts that it based its findings on all information which was verifiable and appropriately submitted. Argentina acknowledges that the exporters and the Brazilian authorities commented on the justification of the adjustment for physical characteristic differences. However, Argentina asserts that those arguments were unsubstantiated by technical data. Argentina also contends that the appropriateness of the adjustment is further demonstrated by the fact that those comments do not question the need for such adjustment. Argentina also acknowledges that the DCD received comments concerning the incidence of freezing and/or chilling at the time of determining the normal value for the product concerned. However, Argentina alleges that those comments were not supported with evidence either.

7.177 Brazil refers to the *Argentina - Ceramic Tiles* panel finding that an investigating authority may not disregard information and resort to facts available on the grounds that a party has failed to provide sufficient supporting documentation in respect of information provided unless the investigating authority has clearly requested that the party provide such supporting documentation. Reading the general instructions in the questionnaire, Brazil does not believe that the DCD provided sufficient information on the precise supporting documentation that it expected to receive from the exporters regarding product description / product differences. Brazil also asserts that submitting supporting documentation for all the information provided in the questionnaire response would impose an unreasonable burden on the exporters and make it impossible for them to reply within the 30-day period.

(ii) Claim 17

7.178 This claim concerns the DCD's rejection of export price data reported by four exporters. Brazil asserts that Avipal, Catarinense, Frangosul and Sadia submitted information on export price in their questionnaire responses. Brazil contends that the last two companies submitted export price data for individual export transactions, with respective invoices. In so doing, Brazil argues that the four exporters have provided information to the best of their abilities and have never refused to cooperate with the investigating authority. In spite of the above, Brazil asserts that information on export prices submitted by those exporters was rejected and information from the Secretariat for Agriculture, Fisheries and Food was used instead as a source to determine their export prices.

7.179 Argentina states that each time the parties supplied the information in the prescribed timely and appropriate fashion, the information was used. Argentina further asserts that the DCD had to resort to other sources of information in cases where any aspect of those requirements had not been met. With respect to

Catarinense and Frangosul, Argentina asserts that the information was not used simply because, in Frangosul's case, the data provided was insufficient and was submitted after the deadline that would have permitted its use had expired[144] and, in Catarinense's case, because the data was insufficient.[145]

7.180 According to Brazil, Argentina "explains, for the first time, that the information provided by Frangosul and Catarinense was not used simply because in Frangosul's case the information submitted was insufficient and outside the deadline, and in the case of Catarinense because the information was considered insufficient." Brazil also asserts that this explanation given by Argentina seems to contradict Argentina's own response that Frangosul provided supporting documentation for the export prices reported in the investigation.

(iii) Claim 19

7.181 This claim concerns the DCD's decision not to use normal value submitted by two exporters. Brazil asserts that information required in order to determine normal value was submitted by Catarinense and Frangosul. However, it was not used by the DCD. To the extent that Argentina may argue that the information was not received within the deadlines established by the authority, Brazil asserts that a reasonable period will not be commensurate with the pre-established deadlines if the investigating authority has not acted in a reasonable, objective and impartial manner. In this regard, Brazil asserts that Frangosul was subject to 'an excessive burden' in having to present dumping data from 1996 to 1999. Brazil also notes that Frangosul invited the investigating authority to verify the information in its response. Brazil contends that the late reply to the questionnaire by Catarinense was due to the fact that it was notified of the existence of the investigation approximately eight months after its initiation. Brazil also takes issue with the fact that the normal value used instead was for chilled poultry *with* head and feet. This in the view of Brazil was wrong because Catarinense and Frangosul had reported to have sold the product in the domestic market *without* head and feet.

7.182 Argentina asserts that the DCD analysed and examined all the information before it that was consistent with the principles enshrined in the *AD Agreement*, i.e., information that was properly provided within the required time-frame and was accompanied by proper evidence. Argentina alleges that, as was pointed out in the Final Affirmative Dumping Determination, the data received from Catarinense was presented on aggregate basis, without any supporting documentation. Moreover, Argentina asserts that Catarinense did not have authorized legal status. Regarding Frangosul, Argentina asserts that this exporter never presented any supporting documentation for domestic sales and that its final submission arrived beyond the deadline for analysing the information.

(b) Evaluation by the Panel

(i) Claim 15

7.183 We note that the facts relating to Claim 15 are substantially identical to those which form the basis of our finding in respect of Claim 25. Since we concluded

---

[144] Argentina's first written submission, paras. 187-200.
[145] *Ibid.*, para. 203.

under Claim 25 that those facts gave rise to a violation of Article 2.4 of the *AD Agreement*, it is not necessary for us to rule on those same facts in the context of Claim 15.

(ii) Claim 17

7.184 The issue before us is whether the DCD was entitled to disregard export price data submitted by Avipal, Catarinense, Frangosul and Sadia. With respect to Catarinense, we find at paras. 7.190-7.193 below that the DCD was entitled to reject normal value data submitted by that exporter because it had failed to comply with an accreditation obligation. For the same reason, we find that the DCD was also entitled to reject the export price data submitted by that exporter. We therefore reject Brazil's Claim 17 in respect of Catarinense.

7.185 With regard to the DCD's treatment of the export price data submitted by Avipal, Frangosul and Sadia, we first note that Article 6.8 of the *AD Agreement* governs the use by an investigating authority in an anti-dumping investigation of the "facts available". That Article provides as follows:

> "In case any interested party refuses access to, or otherwise does not provide, necessary information within a reasonable period or significantly impedes the investigation, preliminary and final determinations, affirmative or negative, may be made on the basis of facts available. The provisions of Annex II shall be observed in the application of this paragraph."

7.186 Paragraphs 5 and 7 of Annex II to the *AD Agreement* are also relevant to our examination of this claim. They provide as follows:

> "5. Even though the information provided may not be ideal in all respects, this should not justify the authorities from disregarding it, provided the interested party has acted to the best of its ability.
>
> (...)
>
> 7. If the authorities have to base their findings, including those with respect to normal value, on information from a secondary source, including the information supplied in the application for the initiation of the investigation, they should do so with special circumspection. In such cases, the authorities should, where practicable, check the information from other independent sources at their disposal, such as published price lists, official import statistics and customs returns, and from the information obtained from other interested parties during the investigation. It is clear, however, that if an interested party does not cooperate and thus relevant information is being withheld from the authorities, this situation could lead to a result which is less favourable to the party than if the party did cooperate."

7.187 In examining the record before us, we find that Avipal, Frangosul and Sadia did submit information on export prices.[146] Argentina asserts that it was justified in disregarding information which was not submitted in a timely manner, or in the

---

[146] Exhibit BRA-15, Sections V.3.1 (Sadia), V.3.2 (Avipal), V.3.5 (Frangosul) and VII.3.2 (Catarinense).

appropriate fashion.¹⁴⁷ Argentina also argued during these proceedings that "[t]he implementing authority obviously cannot examine claims put forward by the parties without supporting documentation that can be verified."¹⁴⁸ We asked Argentina to prove that the investigating authority based its rejection of the relevant export price data on these reasons. Argentina replied that the explanation could be found in the Report of 4 January 2000 and in the Final Affirmative Dumping Determination, without pointing to any particular statement therein.¹⁴⁹ We therefore examined these documents, in particular Sections V.3 (Submissions made by Foreign Companies), VII.3 (Analysis of the Submissions made by Brazilian Exporting Companies after the Initiation of the Investigation) and VIII.2 (Elements for the Determination of the f.o.b. Export Price) thereof. We could not find in any of those sections references to any of the reasons provided by Argentina which could justify the DCD's decision to disregard the export price data received from Avipal, Frangosul and Sadia.¹⁵⁰ In light of these circumstances, we consider that Argentina's arguments concerning the reasons why the DCD rejected the export price data submitted by Avipal, Frangosul and Sadia constitute *ex post* rationalization which we should not take into account for the purpose of determining whether the Argentine authorities complied with their obligations under Article 6.8.¹⁵¹

7.188   In light of the above, we uphold Brazil's claim that Argentina violated Article 6.8 in rejecting the export price data submitted by Avipal, Frangosul and Sadia.

(iii)   Claim 19

7.189   This claim concerns the DCD's rejection of normal value data submitted by Catarinense and Frangosul.

---

¹⁴⁷ We note that, in particular, Argentina asserts that Frangosul's export data was insufficient and was submitted after the deadline.
¹⁴⁸ Argentina's first written submission, para. 178. See also Argentina's second written submission, paras. 54-56.
¹⁴⁹ Argentina's reply to Question 40 of the Panel.
¹⁵⁰ The only reason that we could find in the Final Affirmative Dumping Determination for the rejection of the exporters' data and the use of data provided by the Livestock Directorate of the Secretariat for Agriculture, Livestock, Fisheries and Food instead is that the DCD considered it appropriate to determine the f.o.b. export price based on information from the Livestock Directorate because it came from the most detailed and complete source. (Exhibit BRA-15, Section VIII.2.3) We do not consider that such a justification or reasoning provided by the DCD is sufficient to meet the requirements of Article 6.8. In particular, such reasoning does not indicate that the relevant exporters significantly impeded the investigation. Nor does it indicate that the relevant exporters refused access to, or otherwise did not provide, necessary information within a reasonable period.
¹⁵¹ In the same vein, we note that the panel in *Argentina - Ceramic Tiles* found when examining a claim raised under Article 6.8:

"(…) Under Article 17.6 of the AD Agreement we are to determine whether the DCD established the facts properly and whether the evaluation performed by the DCD was unbiased and objective. In other words, we are asked to review the evaluation of the DCD *made at the time of the determination* as set forth in a public notice or in any other document of a public or confidential nature. We do not believe that, as a panel reviewing the evaluation of the investigating authority, we are to take into consideration any arguments and reasons that did not form part of the evaluation process of the investigating authority, but instead are *ex post facto* justifications which were not provided at the time the determination was made." (emphasis in original, footnote not included) (Panel Report, *Argentina - Ceramic Tiles*, *supra*, note 66, para. 6.27)

Catarinense

7.190 Based on the record before us, we note that Catarinense was contacted by the DCD on 15 September 1999. Argentina acknowledges that it sent Catarinense a copy of the original questionnaire, to which Catarinense replied on 3 November 1999. Brazil asserts that information on normal value submitted by Catarinense should have been used as a basis for the determination of the normal value for this exporter. Argentina argues that the DCD was justified in disregarding data submitted by Catarinense because (a) this exporter had not accredited itself in accordance with domestic legislation,[152] and (b) information on domestic prices was submitted in aggregated form and without supporting documentation.[153]

7.191 We will examine first Argentina's argument that Catarinense had not accredited itself in accordance with domestic legislation. Argentina argues that, in accordance with Law No. 19,549 on Administrative Procedures, a company must have authorized legal status in order to appear before the DCD.[154] We note that the DCD informed that exporter that it had to have authorized legal status in conformity with Law No. 19,549 on 8 November 1999.[155] There is no evidence on the record to suggest that Catarinense pursued this matter with the DCD, or made any other attempt to comply with the accreditation obligation. The issue before us is therefore whether the DCD was justified in disregarding data submitted by Catarinense on the basis that it did not have authorized legal status. We do not find any provision in the *AD Agreement* which expressly disallows an investigating authority from imposing basic procedural requirements such as accreditation. We observe that paragraph 3 of Annex II to the *AD Agreement* provides that "[a]ll information which is (…) appropriately submitted so that it can be used in the investigation without undue difficulties (…) should be taken into account when determinations are made." We consider that the reference to the terms "appropriately submitted" is designed to cover *inter alia* information which is submitted in accordance with relevant procedural provisions of WTO Members' domestic laws. In our view, paragraph 3 of Annex II to the *AD Agreement* can be interpreted to mean that information not "appropriately submitted" in accordance with relevant procedural provisions of WTO Members' domestic laws may be disregarded. In the circumstances of this case, we consider that information submitted by Catarinense was not "appropriately submitted" within the meaning of paragraph 3 of Annex II to the *AD Agreement* because Catarinense had not complied with Argentina's accreditation requirements. Accordingly, the DCD was entitled to reject that information.

7.192 Citing a finding of the *Guatemala - Cement II* panel, Brazil argues that the DCD did not act in a reasonable, objective and impartial manner with respect to Catarinense. We disagree, since the DCD explicitly reminded Catarinense of the need to comply with the accreditation requirement. Brazil also refers to paragraphs 5 and 7 of Annex II to the *AD Agreement* in support of its claim. However, we fail to see how Catarinense could be said to have "acted to the best of its ability" (Annex II, paragraph 5), since it failed to respond in any way to the DCD's letter of 8 November 1999. Nor do we see the relevance of paragraph 7 of Annex II, since Brazil has failed to explain how the exercise of "special circumspection" by the DCD would have

---

[152] Argentina's first written submission, para. 202.
[153] *Ibid.*, para. 189.
[154] Exhibits ARG-XIII and BRA-28, p. 2795.
[155] Exhibit ARG-XIII.

remedied the fact that Catarinense failed to comply with Argentina's accreditation requirement.

7.193 Nor can we agree with Brazil that normal value data provided by Catarinense was more accurate than the normal value data provided by the applicant on account of the particular product characteristics. In our view, once data from the exporter cannot be used in accordance with Article 6.8 and Annex II to the *AD Agreement*, an investigating authority is entitled to use information from other sources, including the applicant. The fact that, as argued by Brazil, information supplied by the applicant on normal value concerns a product (poultry with head and feet) which is not identical to that exported by Catarinense (poultry without head and feet) in our view does not impede the investigating authority's use of the applicant's information as long as a fair comparison is made. Brazil has not argued under this claim that the comparison was not fair. For this reason, we must reject Brazil's argument.

Frangosul

7.194 We note that Frangosul was first contacted by the DCD on 16 February 1999. This exporter submitted a reply to the questionnaire on 27 April 1999, after the deadline initially provided by the DCD. With respect to normal value, Frangosul submitted information on sales in the domestic market corresponding to years 1996, 1997, 1998 and the first three months of 1999, reported on a monthly basis.[156] On 12 July 1999, the DCD requested documentation supporting sales made in the domestic market. On 19 August 1999, Frangosul replied that it was not possible to send copies of all invoices. Frangosul referred to the list of invoices already provided in its questionnaire response. On 12 October 1999, the DCD requested Frangosul to submit a list of invoices covering all transactions in the domestic market during the period of investigation.[157] In this communication, it is stated that the list of invoices submitted in the questionnaire response was incomplete. Frangosul failed to respond within the applicable deadline.[158] On 18 November 1999, the DCD renewed its request.[159] The required list was submitted by Frangosul on 30 December 1999, outside the second deadline established in DCD's communication of 18 November 1999.[160]

7.195 Brazil asserts that Frangosul did submit the information "within a reasonable period". In support of its claim, Brazil cites the following portion of the *US - Hot-Rolled Steel* panel report:

> "The AD Agreement establishes that facts available may be used if necessary information is not provided within a reasonable period. What is a "reasonable period" will not, in all instances be commensurate with pre-established deadlines set out in general regulations. We recognize that in the interest of orderly administration investigating authorities do, and indeed must establish deadlines.

---

[156] There is no indication that, at that point in time, Frangosul informed the DCD that the high number of invoices impeded it to submit more detailed information and supporting documentation.

[157] Argentina's first written submission, para. 197 and Brazil's reply to Question 41 of the Panel.

[158] We note Argentina's argument that, in the absence of a specific deadline being contained in the communication sent to Frangosul, the general deadline provided for in Law No. 19,549 applies. Thus, the deadline for the submission of the information requested through that communication was 10 days.

[159] See *supra* note 157.

[160] Exhibit ARG-XXX.

However, a rigid adherence to such deadlines does not in all cases suffice as the basis for a conclusion that information was not submitted within a reasonable period and consequently that facts available may be applied."[161]

7.196 In light of this report, Brazil asserts that "Article 6.8 suggests a degree of flexibility by authorities that involves consideration of *all* of the circumstances of a particular case." (emphasis in original)[162] We agree with Brazil. However, in examining the facts in this case we are of the view that Frangosul did not submit "the necessary information within a reasonable period".[163] First, we note that there is no indication on the record that Frangosul informed the DCD of the difficulties of submitting documentary evidence regarding all domestic transactions until approximately seven months after the initiation of the investigation (19 August 1999). Other exporters, namely Avipal, Nicolini, Sadia and Seara, instead informed the investigating authority of such difficulties much earlier in the investigation.[164] We consider that Frangosul could and should have been aware of that problem much before 19 August 1999, and hence should have informed the DCD much before that date. Brazil argues that what is a "reasonable period" for the submission of data to an investigating authority will not, in all instances, be commensurate with pre-established deadlines set out in general regulations. We agree. However, we recall that the *AD Agreement* imposes a deadline for the conclusion of an investigation in Article 5.10. We consider that, if an investigation is to be completed in conformity with the timeframe provided for in Article 5.10, deadlines are indeed necessary, as recognized by the *US - Hot-Rolled Steel* panel. In the case at stake, we note that a complete list of all domestic sales transactions was requested on 12 October 1999. As no reply was received within the deadline provided, the DCD sent a reminder on 18 November 1999. Again, we note that the response was not provided within the second deadline set by the DCD. As Brazil acknowledges, the response to the 12 October request was finally submitted to the DCD on 30 December 1999,[165] i.e., more than two months after that list had been requested. Brazil asserts before us that "Frangosul had to go back and collect specific information for the period January 1998 through January 1999, which sometimes meant manually having to search the many invoices (over 320.000) to find the information requested by the authority." To the extent that Brazil's argument is that, following the DCD's request of 12 October 1999, Frangosul had informed the DCD that it could not submit the data requested by that authority due to the large number of domestic sales transactions involved, we consider that Brazil's argument shall be rejected because we have not found any indication on the record before us that Frangosul made that argument in response to

---

[161] Panel Report, *United States - Anti-Dumping Measures on Certain Hot-Rolled Steel Products from Japan* ("*US - Hot-Rolled Steel*"), WT/DS184/R, adopted 23 August 2001 as modified by the Appellate Body Report, WT/DS184/AB/R, DSR 2001:X, 4769, at para. 7.54. The Appellate Body upheld the Panel's findings with respect to Article 6.8 and Annex II of the *AD Agreement*. (Appellate Body Report, *US - Hot-Rolled Steel*, WT/DS184/AB/R, adopted 23 August 2001, DSR 2001:X, 4697, para. 240)
[162] Brazil's reply to Question 41 of the Panel.
[163] We note that Brazil has not argued before us that the information requested by the DCD was not "necessary" within the meaning of Article 6.8. We consider that it was, as the determination of the normal value depended on it.
[164] Exhibit BRA-28, ps. 2773 (Sadia), 2777 (Avipal), 2781 (Nicolini) and 2783 (Seara).
[165] See *supra,* note 162.

the DCD's request of 12 October. However, we note that an argument similar to that raised by Brazil before us is contained in a Frangosul communication sent in response to a DCD request dated 12 July 1999 in which the investigating authority requested Frangosul to submit "*supporting documentation* for all the sales transactions in the domestic market...".[166] (emphasis added) Taking this into account, we consider that the statement of Frangosul referred to by Brazil relates to another (previous) request of the DCD regarding the submission of *supporting documentation*, and not the DCD's 12 October request for a list of domestic sales transactions. This conclusion is bolstered by the fact that the statement referred to by Brazil is contained in a document which predates the DCD's request of 12 October 1999. Hence, we consider that the argument presented by Brazil before us does not justify Frangosul's belated submission of the list of domestic sales transactions. As Brazil has not presented any other justification for that belated submission, and bearing in mind all the circumstances of this particular case, we are of the view that Frangosul did not submit necessary information within a "reasonable period" as set forth in Article 6.8. For the same reasons, we find that the information was not supplied "in a timely fashion" within the meaning of paragraph 3 of Annex II.

7.197 As in the case of Catarinense, Brazil refers to paragraphs 5 and 7 of Annex II in support of its claim. Bearing in mind the facts as described in para. 7.196 *supra*, in particular Frangosul's belated reply to the DCD's request of 12 October 1999, we cannot consider that Frangosul acted to the best of its ability in the sense of Annex II, paragraph 5. Nor do we see how "special circumspection" in the sense of Annex II, paragraph 7, would have required the DCD to accept Frangosul's normal value data given the circumstances set forth above. Brazil argues that the normal value data provided by Frangosul was more accurate than the normal value data provided by the applicant on account of the particular product characteristics. An identical argument has been examined in para. 7.193 *supra* concerning Catarinense. For the reasons set forth in that paragraph, we also reject this argument.

(c) Conclusion

7.198 For the foregoing reasons, we uphold Brazil's Claim 17 that Argentina violated Article 6.8 in rejecting the export price data submitted by Avipal, Frangosul and Sadia. We reject Brazil's Claim 19 that Argentina violated Article 6.8, and paragraphs 3, 5 and 7 of Annex II to the *AD Agreement* by not using the normal value data reported by Catarinense and Frangosul. We make no findings in respect of Brazil's Claim 15.

11. *Failure to Provide a Public Notice of Conclusion of an Investigation - Claims 16, 18 and 20*

7.199 These claims raise issues under Article 12.2.2 of the *AD Agreement*. They concern alleged omissions from Argentina's public notice of conclusion of the investigation.

---

[166] *Ibid.*

Report of the Panel

(a) Arguments of the Parties

(i) Claim 16

7.200 According to Brazil, Article 12.2.2 mandates that a public notice of conclusion of the investigation contain, or otherwise make available through a separate report, all relevant information on matters of fact and law and reasons which have led to the imposition of final measures. In the view of Brazil, the established margins of dumping as well as a full explanation of the reasons for the methodology used in their establishment and comparison of normal value and export price are considered as relevant information. In spite of this obligation, Brazil asserts that the DCD provided no explanation of why it made an adjustment to normal value for differences in the physical characteristics of poultry sold in Brazil and that sold in Argentina, even though the product description provided by certain exporters indicated that such differences did not exist.

7.201 Argentina argues that the Report of 4 January 2000 and the Final Affirmative Dumping Determination, "throughout the text and under different headings," dealt in detail with each of the exporters' submissions in order to reach a reasoned conclusion as to the investigating authority's motives for excluding submissions that lacked sufficient supporting documentation or were made after the deadline had expired.

(ii) Claim 18

7.202 Brazil asserts that, contrary to Article 12.2.2, the public notice of conclusion contained no explanation of why the investigating authority did not establish export price based on the information provided by Sadia, Avipal, Frangosul and Catarinense.

7.203 As in the case of Claim 16, Argentina argues that the Report of 4 January 2000 and the Final Affirmative Dumping Determination, "throughout the text and under different headings," dealt in detail with each of the exporters' submissions in order to reach a reasoned conclusion as to the investigating authority's motives for excluding submissions that lacked sufficient supporting documentation or were made after the deadline had expired.

(iii) Claim 20

7.204 Brazil claims that the public notice of conclusion did not adequately explain why the DCD did not use normal value submitted by Frangosul and Catarinense.

7.205 Similar to Claim 16, Argentina argues that the Report of 4 January 2000 and the Final Affirmative Dumping Determination, "throughout the text and under different headings," dealt in detail with each of the exporters' submissions in order to reach a reasoned conclusion as to the investigating authority's motives for excluding submissions that lacked sufficient supporting documentation or were made after the deadline had expired.

(b) Evaluation by the Panel

7.206 In examining similar claims, the *Guatemala - Cement II* panel expressed its view that:

> "the issue of Guatemala's compliance with the transparency obligations deriving from its decision to impose definitive anti-

dumping measures on imports of cement from Mexico would only be relevant if the decision to impose the measure itself had been consistent with the AD Agreement. Therefore, having found that Guatemala infringed the substantive provisions of the AD Agreement in their decision to impose an anti-dumping measure in this case, we consider that it is not necessary for us to rule on whether Guatemala complied with its transparency obligations under Article 12.2 and 12.2.2 with respect to the imposition of a measure already found not to be consistent with Guatemala's WTO obligations."[167]

7.207 We agree with that panel. In our view, it is not necessary to determine whether a Member complied with the transparency requirements of Article 12.2.2 in imposing an anti-dumping measure if that measure has already been found to violate various substantive provisions of the *AD Agreement*. Since we have already found that Argentina's anti-dumping measure is inconsistent with various substantive provisions of the *AD Agreement*, it is not necessary for us to determine whether or not Argentina complied with the transparency requirements of Article 12.2.2 in imposing that measure.

(c) Conclusion

7.208 For the foregoing reasons, we do not consider it necessary to make any findings on Claims 16, 18 and 20.

12. *Calculation of an Individual Margin of Dumping - Claim 22*

(a) Arguments of the Parties

7.209 Brazil asserts that the investigating authority did not calculate individual dumping margins for Catarinense and Frangosul in spite of the fact that these companies submitted data on normal value and export price within a reasonable period of time. Brazil asserts that the investigating authority did not provide an explanation, either in the final determination or in any other document on the record of the investigation, as to why, in this case, it did not determine an individual dumping margin for Catarinense and Frangosul. In the view of Brazil, by failing to determine an individual margin of dumping for those two exporters, and by applying instead the dumping rate for "all others", Argentina acted inconsistently with the general rule set forth in Article 6.10 of the *AD Agreement*.

7.210 Argentina disagrees with Brazil's presentation of the facts. With respect to Catarinense, Argentina submits that, as stated in the Final Affirmative Dumping Determination, the data received from the exporter was presented on an aggregate basis, without any supporting documentation. According to Argentina, Catarinense failed to provide information on sales in the Brazilian market. Argentina asserts that the only supporting documentation that Catarinense submitted was a list of invoices for exports to Argentina. In the case of Frangosul, Argentina asserts that several notifications were sent to the exporter with a request to provide the lists of *Notas fiscales* (invoices), in order to establish a statistical sample. Argentina asserts that a reminder was sent to the exporter on 18 November 1999. According to Argentina,

---

[167] Panel Report, *Guatemala - Cement II, supra*, note 48, para. 8.291.

Report of the Panel

two diskettes containing data with respect to domestic sales, without supporting documentation, arrived after the expiry of the deadline. Argentina notes that, in the Final Affirmative Dumping Determination, the DCD stated that:

> "Finally, we stress that in the case of the companies Catarinense Limitada, Frangosul, Comave [sic], Da Granja Agroi, Sadia Concordia, Minuano De Alimentos, Acaua Industria, Felipe Avicola, Agroi, Veneto, Chapeco and Litoral Alimen [sic], the implementing authority did not have sufficient additional information or supporting documentation to enable it to reach an individual final determination of the margin of dumping."[168]

7.211 Brazil notes that the DCD also disregarded the export price data submitted by the exporters Sadia and Avipal. Nevertheless, it still calculated individual margins of dumping for those two exporters. Brazil fails to see the reason why the DCD proceeded differently with respect to the information provided by Frangosul and Catarinense. Brazil further asserts that the fact that an exporter has not submitted the relevant and appropriate information to establish normal value and export price does not exclude the authority's obligation under Article 6.10 to calculate an individual margin of dumping for that exporter.[169]

(b) Evaluation by the Panel

7.212 The issue before us is whether, in light of the facts in this dispute, Article 6.10 of the *AD Agreement* required the DCD to determine separate dumping margins for the exporters Catarinense and Frangosul.

7.213 Article 6.10 provides in relevant part:

> "The authorities *shall, as a rule, determine an individual margin of dumping for each known exporter or producer concerned* of the product under investigation." (emphasis added)

7.214 We agree with the view expressed by the *Argentina - Ceramic Tiles* panel that Article 6.10, first sentence, imposes a general obligation on investigating authorities to calculate individual margins of dumping for each known exporter or producer concerned of the product under investigation.[170]

7.215 Argentina argues that, for the requirement of Article 6.10 to apply, the exporter or producer concerned should supply the documentation needed to determine an individual margin of dumping.[171] We see no such obligation in the text of Article 6.10. In our view, Article 6.10 is purely procedural in nature, in the sense that it imposes a procedural obligation on the investigating agency to determine individual margins of dumping for each known exporter or producer concerned of the product under investigation. Article 6.10 is *not* concerned with substantive issues concerning the determination of individual margins, such as the availability of the relevant data. Such issues are addressed by provisions such as Articles 2 and 6.8 of the *AD Agreement*. In this regard, we note that the *Argentina - Ceramic Tiles* panel found that:

---

[168] Argentina's reply to Question 44 of the Panel and Exhibit BRA-15.
[169] Brazil's second oral statement, para. 59 and Brazil's reply to Question 90 of the Panel.
[170] Panel Report, *Argentina - Ceramic Tiles, supra*, note 66, para. 6.89.
[171] Argentina's reply to Question 97 of the Panel.

"the provisions of Article 2 concerning the determination of dumping and Article 6.8 AD Agreement concerning facts available are intended to allow the investigating authority to complete the data with regard to a particular exporter in order to determine a dumping margin in case the information provided is unreliable or necessary information is simply not provided. It is precisely because of Articles 2 and 6.8, among others, that it will remain possible to determine an individual margin of dumping for each exporter on the basis of facts."[172]

7.216 We agree. The fact that an investigating authority does not receive any information from an exporter, or only receives partial information, or information that is not usable or is unreliable, should not prevent the calculation of an individual margin of dumping for that exporter, since the substantive provisions in the *AD Agreement* referred to in para. 7.215 *supra* expressly allow investigating authorities to complete the data with regard to a particular exporter in order to determine a dumping margin in case the information provided is unreliable or necessary information is simply not provided. We therefore reject Argentina's argument that "a condition for the determination of an individual margin of dumping for each exporter is that the exporter should (…) supply the documentation needed to reach such a determination."[173]

(c) Conclusion

7.217 In light of the above, we conclude that Argentina violated Article 6.10 of the *AD Agreement* by not determining an individual margin of dumping for Catarinense and Frangosul.

13. *Essential Facts - Claim 21*

(a) Arguments of the Parties / Third Parties

7.218 Brazil claims that Argentina violated Article 6.9 of the *AD Agreement* by failing to inform all interested parties of the essential facts under consideration which formed the basis of the decision that a definitive anti-dumping duty should be applied. In particular, Brazil argues that the investigating authority failed to inform interested parties that certain domestic and export sales price data was not going to be used for the purpose of establishing normal value and export price. Brazil also asserts that the investigating authority failed to inform interested parties of the reasons why that information was not used.

7.219 Argentina asserts that, through the DCD's Report of 4 January 2000, the investigating authority informed the parties of all the essential facts on which it intended to base its final decision.

7.220 The European Communities, as a third party, does not take a position on whether, under the facts of this case, the measure is consistent with Article 6.9 of the *AD Agreement*. The European Communities argues that Article 6.9 entails a positive action by the investigating authorities, and requires the authorities to actively disclose those essential facts on which the decision whether to apply definitive measures is based. Referring to the *Guatemala - Cement II* panel, the European

---

[172] Panel Report, *Argentina - Ceramic Tiles*, *supra*, note 66, footnote 96.
[173] See *supra*, note 171.

Communities asserts that mere access to the file is not sufficient, unless the file contains a disclosure document specifically prepared by the authorities which clearly identifies the "essential facts".

(b) Evaluation by the Panel

7.221 This claim raises the issue of whether certain alleged "essential facts" identified by Brazil should have been disclosed to interested parties pursuant to Article 6.9 of the *AD Agreement*.

7.222 Article 6.9 of the *AD Agreement* reads as follows:

"The authorities shall, before a final determination is made, inform all interested parties of the essential facts under consideration which form the basis for the decision whether to apply definitive measures. Such disclosure should take place in sufficient time for the parties to defend their interests."

7.223 The first sentence of Article 6.9 therefore imposes the obligation on investigating authorities to inform interested parties of the essential *facts* which form the basis *for the decision whether to apply definitive measures*. We emphasise that the Article 6.9 obligation applies only in respect of (1) "essential facts" which (2) form the basis for the decision whether to apply definitive measures. In our view, facts which do not form the basis for the decision whether to apply definitive measures cannot be considered to be "essential facts" within the meaning of Article 6.9 of the *AD Agreement*.[174]

7.224 Brazil claims that Argentina violated Article 6.9 by failing to inform interested parties of the "essential fact" that certain normal value and export price data reported by the exporters was not going to be used in the final determination. In our view, however, the fact that certain normal value or export price data is not going to be relied on in making a final determination is not a fact which forms the basis for *the decision whether to apply definitive measures*. While we accept that the normal value and export price data *ultimately used in the final determination* are essential facts which form the basis for the decision whether to apply definitive measures, the fact that certain normal value and export price data is not going to be used is not. In this regard, the fact that interested parties may not have been informed that certain normal value and export price data was not going to be used in the final determination should perhaps have been addressed by Brazil in the context of Article 6.8 of the *AD Agreement*.

7.225 Brazil also claims that Argentina violated Article 6.9 by failing to inform interested parties of the *reasons* why the investigating authority failed to use certain domestic and export sales price data reported by exporters. In our view, however, the failure to inform an interested party of a *reason* does not equate to failure to inform an interested party of an essential *fact*. The word "fact" is defined *inter alia* as "a thing that is known to have occurred, to exist or to be true", whereas a "reason" is a

---

[174] In examining this issue, we took into account, and agree with, the following finding of the *Guatemala - Cement II* panel:

"An interested party will not know whether a particular fact is "important" or not unless the investigating authority has explicitly identified it as one of the "essential facts" which form the basis of the authority's decision whether to impose definitive measures." (Panel Report, *Guatemala - Cement II*, *supra*, note 48, para. 8.229)

"motive, cause or justification".[175] We do not believe that the ordinary meaning of the word "fact" would support a conclusion that Article 6.9, when using the term "fact", refers not only to "facts" in the sense of "things which are known to have occurred, to exist or to be true", but also to "motives, causes or justifications".

7.226 Brazil asserted in response to Question 95 from the Panel that:

> "It is important to note that the term "facts" is also present in Article 17.6(i) of the Agreement. According to Article 17.6(i), "in its assessment of the *facts* of the matter, the panel shall determine whether the authorities' establishment of the *facts* was proper and whether their evaluation of those *facts* was unbiased and objective (...)". Under that Article, "facts" is not merely the data established and evaluated by the authority but also the reasoning supporting a certain conclusion in establishing a fact.
>
> Accordingly, we understand that in Article 6.9 the phrase "essential facts" covers the data collected *and* the reasoning supporting a certain conclusion made by an authority in establishing the facts. The conclusion made by an authority relates to the authority's establishment of the facts. For example, it is not sufficient for an authority to simply state that it has disregarded the normal value submitted by a certain exporter based on Article 6.8 of the Agreement. The authority must inform the reasons why certain information was disregarded pursuant to Article 6.8." (emphasis in original)

7.227 We do not consider that this response supports Brazil's claim. First, Article 17.6(i) of the *AD Agreement* distinguishes between (1) the establishment of facts and (2) the evaluation of facts. In our view, a reason is part of the evaluation of a fact, and not the fact itself. Second, we agree with Brazil that an investigating authority must inform interested parties why certain information is disregarded. However, as Brazil itself notes in the last two sentences cited above, that obligation is found in Article 6.8 (through Annex II, para. 6),[176] and not in Article 6.9.

7.228 Brazil also relies on the *Argentina - Ceramic Tiles* panel in support of its claim.[177] We consider that our conclusion is entirely compatible with the finding of the *Argentina - Ceramic Tiles* panel. In our view, that panel concluded that *factual information* - rather than reasoning - represents the "essential facts" which form the basis for the decision whether to apply definitive measures. In particular, that panel found that "petitioner and secondary source information, rather than exporters' information, represented (with respect to the existence of dumping) the essential facts which formed the basis for the decision whether to apply definitive measures".[178]

---

[175] *The Concise Oxford Dictionary of Current English* (Clarendon Press, 1995), p. 482.

[176] Para. 6 of Annex II provides as follows:
"If evidence or information is not accepted, the supplying party should be informed forthwith of the reasons therefor, and should have an opportunity to provide further explanations within a reasonable period, due account being taken of the time-limits of the investigation. If the explanations are considered by the authorities as not being satisfactory, the reasons for the rejection of such evidence or information should be given in any published determinations."

[177] Brazil's first written submission, paras. 346-348.

[178] Panel Report, *Argentina - Ceramic Tiles*, *supra*, note 66, para. 6.127.

This shows clearly that that panel defined "essential facts" in terms of factual information, rather than reasoning.

7.229 We recall that the scope of the obligation set forth in Article 6.9 is limited to (1) "essential facts" which (2) form the basis for the decision whether to apply definitive measures. Since some of the elements identified by Brazil are not "essential facts", and the remainder are facts which do not "form the basis for the decision whether to apply definitive measures", we reject Brazil's claim that Argentina failed to inform interested parties of "the essential facts under consideration which form the basis for the decision whether to apply definitive measures".

(c) Conclusion

7.230 In light of the foregoing, we reject Brazil's claim that Argentina has violated Article 6.9 of the *AD Agreement*.

D. *Conduct of the Investigation and Final Affirmative Determination*

1. *Failure to Make an Adjustment for Freight Costs - Claim 23*

(a) Arguments of the Parties

7.231 Brazil's Claim 23 concerns the DCD's failure to make freight cost adjustments to the normal value of both Sadia and Avipal. Brazil claims that Argentina violated Article 2.4 of the *AD Agreement* because the DCD failed to adjust Sadia and Avipal's normal value for freight costs reported by those exporters. Brazil asserts that the freight cost adjustment was claimed by Sadia in Annex VIII, Section C of its questionnaire response of 20 April 1999. Brazil asserts that Avipal claimed a freight cost adjustment in its supplementary questionnaire response dated 21 December 1999.

7.232 Argentina asserts that the DCD did not make the freight adjustment requested by Sadia because the adjustment was not sufficiently proven. In particular, freight costs were not stipulated in the sample invoices submitted by the exporter, nor otherwise properly documented. Instead, Sadia merely submitted a figure representing average freight costs over an extended period of time, rather than transaction-by-transaction freight costs. In this regard, Argentina provided the following response to Question 81 from the Panel:

> "Argentina reaffirms what it said in paragraphs 210 and 211 of its first written submission. Indeed, Sadia replied to the questionnaire item concerning internal freight, but never provided any supporting documentation for that item. Nor do the invoices submitted provide any indication of the percentage and/or amount of the adjustment to be made.
>
> In other words, although in Annex X Sadia provided a US$/Ton value to be discounted for freight, and also did so in Annex VIII - Sales in the domestic market - these values were presented in annualized form without any supporting documentation that would have enabled the authority to verify whether they corresponded to the reality and hence carry out the said adjustment.

In this connection, a "*nota fiscal*" (invoice) from SADIA has been provided showing clearly that the box corresponding to cost of freight does not contain any figure at all. And the box corresponding to "*frete por conta*" contains the indication "1", which corresponds to "*emitente*".

The kind of supporting documentation to which we refer in this case would be, for example, a contract between Sadia and a shipping company or any other documentation from the company which clearly indicates the amount to be discounted for freight. We insist that the "*notas fiscales*", which did not reveal the indicative amount of the requested adjustment, were the only documentation on hand.

(...)"

7.233 Argentina asserts that Avipal's request for a freight cost adjustment was made too late in the proceedings, was not accompanied by supporting documentation, and was not provided with the proper Spanish translation.

(b) Evaluation by the Panel

7.234 Brazil's claim concerns the DCD's failure to make freight cost adjustments to the normal value of both Sadia and Avipal. Brazil's claim is based on Article 2.4 of the *AD Agreement*, which provides in relevant part that:

"A fair comparison shall be made between the export price and the normal value. This comparison shall be made at the same level of trade, normally at the ex-factory level, and in respect of sales made at as nearly as possible the same time. Due allowance shall be made in each case, on its merits, for differences which affect price comparability, including differences in conditions and terms of sale, taxation, levels of trade, quantities, physical characteristics, and any other differences which are also demonstrated to affect price comparability." (footnote omitted)

7.235 As noted by the panel in *Argentina - Ceramic Tiles*, "Article 2.4 places the obligation on the investigating authority to make due allowance, in each case on its merits, for differences which affect price comparability...".[179] Argentina has not argued that it would not have been appropriate in principle to make the adjustment for freight costs. This is entirely reasonable, since it seems to us that under normal circumstances there is an obvious inconsistency with Article 2.4 if an investigating authority compares f.o.b. export prices with "delivered" domestic prices, because such a comparison would not be made at the same level of trade. We shall now examine the reasons why, according to Argentina, the DCD was entitled not to make the freight cost adjustment.

7.236 Regarding Sadia, Argentina asserts that it was entitled not to adjust for freight costs because Sadia reported its freight costs on an annualized basis, without supporting documentation. We see nothing in the DCD's questionnaire that would exclude specific forms of reporting, including "annualization". Nor has Argentina identified anything in the questionnaire that would exclude such reporting. Since the questionnaire did not exclude "annualized" reporting, and since there is nothing on

---

[179] *Ibid.*, para. 6.113.

the record to explain why "annualized" reporting might be considered unreasonable, the fact that Sadia reported freight costs on an "annualized" basis is not sufficient reason for the DCD not to make any freight cost adjustment.

7.237 Regarding Argentina's argument that Sadia failed to submit supporting documentation for any freight cost adjustment, the Panel asked Argentina to "indicate precisely (page number, paragraph number, line number) where the investigating authority explained the reason for rejecting Sadia's request in its final determination, or in any other document prepared by the investigating authority at the time of its determination".[180] Argentina replied that "[t]he relevant explanation can be found in Section VIII.1.3.3.1 of the Report on Action Taken. In that report, the DCD identified the information that it would use for the determination of normal value, which did not include any adjustment for freight." In reviewing the relevant section of the DCD's final determination, we find no reference to Sadia's alleged failure to provide supporting documentation. Argentina's explanation is therefore *ex post* rationalization which we are bound to ignore in examining this claim. Although Argentina's reply to Question 82 seems to suggest that the absence of documentary evidence should be inferred from the fact that the DCD failed to make the freight cost adjustment requested by Sadia, there is no basis for us to make any such inference. There could be a any number of reasons why the DCD failed to make the adjustment requested by Sadia, and the purpose of this claim is to determine whether or not the DCD was entitled to do so.

7.238 In any event, we note that in response to Question 81 from the Panel, Argentina acknowledged[181] that at least one sales invoice supplied by Sadia referred to freight charged to "*emitente*", i.e., the supplier.[182] Thus, Sadia had supplied some documentary evidence in support of its request for a freight cost adjustment, since the relevant invoice clearly indicated that freight costs were incurred by the supplier, i.e., Sadia, and not the customer. In light of the requirement in Article 2.4 that investigating authorities make due allowance, in each case on its merits, for differences which affect price comparability, we consider that this documentary evidence should have caused the DCD to seek further clarification from Sadia on this issue. The documentary evidence was in any event sufficient to prevent the DCD from concluding that Sadia had failed to provide any supporting evidence for its freight cost adjustment. On the contrary, there was documentary evidence on the record indicating that Sadia did incur freight costs in respect of domestic sales. We are therefore not persuaded by Argentina's justification for not accepting Sadia's request for a freight cost adjustment.

7.239 Regarding Avipal, Argentina submits that its request for a freight cost adjustment was rejected because it was not supported by documentary evidence, was not fully translated into Spanish, and was tardy. Concerning the issues of translation and tardiness, we find no reference to such considerations in the DCD's final determination. Nor has Argentina provided us with any evidence from the time of the DCD's determination to suggest that such factors caused the DCD to reject Avipal's request for a freight cost adjustment. In the absence of such evidence, Argentina's arguments concerning translation and tardiness constitute *ex post* rationalization, and therefore provide no basis for us to decide on the issue before us. Concerning the

---

[180] Question 82 from the Panel.
[181] See para. 7.232 *supra*.
[182] See Exhibit BRA-29, p. 6.

absence of supporting documentation, we note that the first paragraph of page 65 of the Final Affirmative Dumping Determination indicates that the DCD only made those adjustments which it could verify. We understand this to be an assertion by the DCD that it would only make those adjustments for which it had supporting documentation. In examining the substance of Brazil's claim, we find that there is nothing on the record to suggest that Avipal had supplied any documentary evidence in support of its request for a freight cost adjustment. There is therefore a clear distinction between the factual circumstances surrounding the freight cost adjustment requests made by Sadia and Avipal.[183] Accordingly, we find that the DCD was entitled to reject the freight cost adjustment requested by Avipal.

(c) Conclusion

7.240 To conclude, we find that the DCD acted in violation of Article 2.4 of the *AD Agreement* by failing to make the freight cost adjustment to normal value requested by Sadia.

2. *Failure to Make Various Adjustments for Differences Reported by JOX - Claim 24*

(a) Arguments of the Parties

7.241 This claim concerns the DCD's use of domestic sales data obtained from JOX for the purpose of establishing normal value for certain Brazilian exporters. Brazil claims that Argentina violated Article 2.4 of the *AD Agreement* because the DCD compared the JOX data (normal value) with export price without adjusting for differences reported by JOX in respect of tax, finance costs, sales commission and freight costs.

7.242 During the course of these proceedings, Argentina made two arguments in defence of the DCD's decision not to make the requested adjustments to normal value. First, Argentina asserted that the JOX domestic sales data was not adjusted to ensure that normal value and export price were compared at the same level of trade. If the adjustments had been made, the comparison would have been - improperly - between an ex-factory price for the normal value and an f.o.b. export price, because there was no identical information on the deductions to be made from the export price of the goods. Second, Argentina submitted that details of the relevant adjustments were submitted by JOX in Portuguese, whereas the Law No. 19,549 on Administrative Procedures and Article 28 of Implementing Decree No. 1759/72 provide that foreign-language submissions to the investigating authority must be translated into Spanish by a registered translator.

7.243 Regarding Argentina's level-of-trade argument, Brazil asserts that even the use of an f.o.b. normal value (i.e., at the same level of trade as the f.o.b. export price) would have required adjustments / deductions for differences in tax and finance costs, because the f.o.b. export price does not include taxes and finance costs.[184]

---

[183] Furthermore, Avipal's request was made very late in the proceedings, on 21 December 1999 (even though its initial questionnaire response was submitted in April 1999), thereby limiting the time available for the DCD to revert to Avipal on this issue.

[184] See Brazil's reply to Question 93 from the Panel.

7.244 Regarding the submission of data by JOX in Portuguese, Brazil asserts that the relevant information was submitted by JOX in response to a request made by the DCD, and *not* by the Brazilian exporters or petitioner.[185] JOX is a private entity, not related to the Brazilian Government or any of the Brazilian exporters subject to the investigation. Thus, JOX did not constitute an "interested part[y]" within the meaning of Article 6.11 of the *AD Agreement*, and was therefore under no obligation to respond to the Argentinean authorities, much less to provide a translation of its response in Spanish.

(b) Evaluation by the Panel

7.245 As noted above, Argentina has submitted two arguments (i.e., level of trade and language) in support of the DCD's decision not to make certain adjustments to the JOX data used to establish normal value for certain exporters. There is no evidence before us to suggest that the first argument, concerning level of trade, was relied on by the DCD at the time of its decision. That argument therefore constitutes *ex post* rationalization which we are unable to consider.

7.246 Regarding the choice of language by JOX, we note that the JOX data first became relevant to the investigation because it was relied on by the applicant for the purpose of establishing normal value in its application. The DCD subsequently had recourse to the JOX data for the purpose of establishing normal value for certain exporters when it determined that those exporters had not submitted domestic sales data sufficient for the purpose of establishing normal value. The DCD requested clarification from JOX regarding the possible need for adjustments on 25 June 1999. Although the official language of the DCD's investigation was Spanish, JOX replied to the DCD in Portuguese (reply received by the DCD on 3 August 1999). JOX informed the DCD that the JOX domestic sales data available to the DCD included various sales taxes (14.65 per cent in total), finance costs (depending on sales terms), sales commissions (0.5 to 1 per cent) and freight costs (depending on geographic location).

7.247 We note, therefore, that JOX only presented details regarding adjustments to the relevant sales data in response to a request from the DCD. JOX did not have any interest in the proceedings. There is nothing on the record before us to suggest that JOX was an "interested part[y]" within the meaning of Article 6.11 of the *AD Agreement*. Nor is there any evidence that JOX sought to participate in the DCD's investigation as an interested party. In such circumstances, we fail to see why Brazilian exporters should be penalized (because the non-adjusted normal value would have led to a higher margin of dumping) by JOX's failure to submit the relevant information in Spanish, or by the DCD's failure to procure its own translation of that information. The DCD was seeking the information from JOX because the DCD was going to use the JOX data as the basis for normal value, and because it was aware of the likely need to make adjustments to the JOX data. The fact that JOX, which was not an interested party, and not itself taking part in the investigation, failed to respond in Spanish does not absolve the DCD from its obligations under Article 2.4. To the extent that the DCD was seeking clarification from JOX for its own purposes, we consider that the onus was on the DCD to procure its own Spanish translation of JOX's submission.

---

[185] See Brazil's comments on Argentina's reply to Question 85 from the Panel.

7.248 We also note that, as demonstrated *inter alia* in respect of Claim 25 below, the DCD relied in part on the same JOX document - in Portuguese - to increase normal value to reflect alleged differences in the physical characteristics of poultry sold in Brazil and that sold in Argentina.[186] To the extent that the DCD was able to rely on JOX's Portuguese document to make an upward adjustment to normal value, we see no reason why the DCD was similarly not able to rely on the *same* JOX document to make other, downward adjustments to normal value. Such conduct is not indicative of the actions of an objective and impartial investigating authority.

(c) Conclusion

7.249 In light of the above, we find that the Argentine investigating authority violated Article 2.4 of the *AD Agreement* by failing to make adjustments when comparing the export price with normal value established on the basis of JOX domestic sales data.

3. *Differences in Physical Characteristics Justifying an Adjustment - Claim 25*

7.250 This claim concerns a 9.09 per cent upward adjustment of normal value made by the DCD to reflect alleged differences in the physical characteristics of poultry sold in Brazil and poultry exported to Argentina. The DCD found that poultry was sold in Brazil with head and feet, whereas poultry was exported to Argentina without head and feet. The DCD concluded that the yield rate (per kg) for poultry sold in Brazil was therefore higher than that for poultry exported to Argentina. Since the alleged difference in yield rates was 9.09 per cent, the DCD increased normal value by that margin.

(a) Arguments of the Parties

7.251 Brazil claims that the 9.09 per cent adjustment was inconsistent with Article 2.4 of the *AD Agreement* because, for the most part, there is no difference between poultry sold in Brazil and poultry exported to Argentina. According to Brazil, most exporters / producers sell in both markets eviscerated poultry without head and feet. Brazil submits that this fact was evident from the questionnaire responses submitted by exporters: Sadia, Avipal and Frangosul indicated in their questionnaire responses that they sold the same poultry in Argentina and Brazil, whereas Catarinense reported differences in respect of broiler (but not griller) poultry only. Catarinense reported that broilers were sold in Brazil without the feet but with the head, whereas broilers exported to Argentina had neither head nor feet.

7.252 Argentina asserts that the Brazilian exporters did not expressly deny the need for an adjustment for differences in physical characteristics during the investigation (although Argentina acknowledges that the exporters criticized the amount of the adjustment). Argentina also asserts that it received evidence from JOX to the effect that poultry was sold with head and feet in Brazil. In particular, a note from JOX received on 3 August 1999 reads: "Except otherwise stated, refrigerated chicken sold

---

[186] The DCD also relied on a second JOX document submitted by the applicant, which had been translated from Portuguese into Spanish.

Report of the Panel

in São Paulo includes feet and head. The price of (refrigerated chicken without feet and head) should be 10 per cent higher".[187]

(b) Evaluation by the Panel

7.253 This claim concerns the DCD's decision to increase all exporters' normal values by 9.09 per cent to reflect alleged differences in the physical characteristics of poultry sold in Brazil and Argentina respectively.[188] Since Brazil does not dispute that such an adjustment would have been necessary if indeed there had been differences between poultry sold in Brazil and Argentina respectively, we shall resolve this issue by examining whether or not the DCD properly found that such differences existed.

7.254 As a starting-point, we note that the DCD's record contained evidence to the effect that there were differences between poultry sold in Brazil and poultry exported to Argentina. The DCD was in possession of a document from JOX (received 3 August 1999) indicating that certain poultry sold in Brazil included head and feet.[189] In that document, JOX stated that "[e]xcept otherwise stated, refrigerated chicken sold in Sao Paulo includes feet and head".

7.255 However, there was also evidence on the record indicating that at least certain exporters sold an identical product in both Brazil and Argentina. In particular, Section A, Annex II, of Sadia's questionnaire responses (i.e., both the original and supplemental responses) described the product sold in both Brazil and Argentina in identical terms (namely "whole poultry with giblets").[190] The product description in the equivalent section of Avipal's questionnaire response[191] also did not distinguish between domestic and export sales. Both these exporters' questionnaire responses suggested, therefore, that they sold the same product in both Brazil and Argentina.

7.256 Section A, Annex II, of Frangosul's original questionnaire response also drew no distinction between domestic and export products.[192] Furthermore, Frangosul's supplementary questionnaire response included a product brochure stating that both broiler and griller poultry did not contain head or feet. Thus, Frangosul's questionnaire response not only indicated that it sold the same products in Brazil and Argentina, but also demonstrated that those products did not include head and feet.

7.257 Only one exporter, Catarinense, reported any difference between the products sold in Brazil and Argentina. Catarinense's questionnaire response reported that broilers sold in Brazil included head but not feet, whereas broilers exported to Argentina contained neither head nor feet.

7.258 Furthermore, we note that the Government of Brazil objected to the DCD's adjustment for differences in physical characteristics in a letter dated 19 January 2000.[193] Brazil stated that the adjustment was "absurd", since poultry was sold in the same condition in Brazil as it was in Argentina.

---

[187] Exhibit BRA-32.
[188] Unlike the similar claim under Article 5.3 (Claim 2), Brazil's Claim 25 only challenges the need for - but not the amount of - the adjustment made by the DCD during the course of the investigation.
[189] See *supra*, note 187.
[190] Exhibit BRA-22.
[191] Exhibit BRA-23.
[192] Exhibit BRA-24.
[193] Letter from the Brazilian Embassy in Buenos Aires to the Argentine authorities (Exhibit BRA-39).

7.259 In light of the above, we are of the view that the record did not provide sufficient basis for the DCD to conclude that there were differences in the physical characteristics of all poultry sold in Brazil and Argentina respectively. Only one exporter's questionnaire response suggested that some form of adjustment may be necessary. Other exporters' questionnaire responses indicated that the same product was sold in both Brazil and Argentina. Despite the possibility of an adjustment alluded to in the above-mentioned JOX document, the substance of the exporters' questionnaire responses, and the observations of the Government of Brazil, should have precluded an objective and impartial investigating authority from concluding, on the basis of the JOX document alone, that there were differences in the physical characteristics of poultry sold in Brazil and Argentina respectively. At the very least, the conflicting evidence should have caused the DCD to pursue this matter further with the exporters.

(c) Conclusion

7.260 For the above reasons, we find that the DCD violated Article 2.4 of the *AD Agreement* by increasing all exporters' normal values by 9.09 per cent to reflect alleged differences in the physical characteristics of poultry sold in Brazil and Argentina.

4. *Period of Collection of Dumping Data - Claim 26*

(a) Arguments of the Parties / Third Parties

7.261 Brazil asserts that the DCD violated Article 2.4 of the *AD Agreement* because it did not inform exporters of the period of investigation for dumping until nine months after initiation of the investigation, during which time exporters were faced with the unreasonable burden of submitting domestic and export sales data for 1996-1998 and the months of 1999 for which data was available.

7.262 Argentina asserts that the *AD Agreement* does not regulate the period for which dumping data may be collected. Argentina denies that the DCD imposed an unreasonable burden on exporters by requesting an excessive amount of data. Indeed, Argentina submits that it calculated normal value on the basis of a limited sample of invoices precisely so that exporters would not need to produce a large volume of invoices.

7.263 The European Communities submits that Brazil's claim is not covered by the scope of Article 2.4 of the *AD Agreement*. The European Communities asserts that, as recently recalled by the panel report in *Egypt - Steel Rebar,* Article 2.4 is concerned exclusively with the comparison between the normal value and the export price.[194] It does not apply to the determination of the normal value and the export price. The European Communities suggests that the relevant provisions of the *AD Agreement* for examining the issue raised by Brazil are Article 6.1 and the first paragraph of Annex II.

---

[194] Panel Report, *Egypt - Definitive Anti-Dumping Measures on Steel Rebar from Turkey* ("*Egypt - Steel Rebar*"), WT/DS211/R, adopted 1 October 2002, para. 7.335.

Report of the Panel

(b) Evaluation by the Panel

7.264 This claim concerns the fixing of the period of investigation by the investigating authority. It does not concern the comparison between normal value and export price. We recall the finding by the panel in *Egypt - Steel Rebar* that:

"In short, Article 2.4 in its entirety, including its burden of proof requirement, has to do with ensuring a fair comparison, through various adjustments as appropriate, of export price and normal value."[195]

7.265 The report of the *Egypt - Steel Rebar* panel was adopted during the course of these Panel proceedings. We agree with that panel's finding that Article 2.4 imposes obligations in respect of the comparison between normal value and export price. In our view, Article 2.4 does not impose obligations in respect of the fixing of the period of investigation by the investigating authority, which is the object of Brazil's Claim 26.

(c) Conclusion

7.266 In light of the above, we reject Brazil's Claim 26.

5. *Sampling of Domestic Sales Transactions - Claim 27*

7.267 This claim concerns the comparison methodology used by the DCD to calculate margins of dumping for Sadia and Avipal.

(a) Arguments of the Parties

7.268 Brazil claims that the DCD acted in violation of Article 2.4.2 because, although Sadia and Avipal reported all relevant domestic sales transactions, the DCD did not take into account all domestic sales when comparing the weighted average normal value with the weighted average export price. In other words, Brazil claims that the DCD violated Article 2.4.2 by comparing the weighted average export price with only a weighted average statistical sample of normal value.

7.269 Argentina asserts that the sample of domestic sales transactions used by the DCD for the purpose of establishing a weighted average normal value was statistically valid, and based on documentation provided by the exporters.

(b) Evaluation by the Panel

7.270 Article 2.4.2 provides that:

"Subject to the provisions governing fair comparison in paragraph 4, the existence of margins of dumping during the investigation phase shall normally be established on the basis of a comparison of a weighted average normal value with a weighted average of prices of all comparable export transactions or by a comparison of normal value and export prices on a transaction-to-transaction basis. A normal value established on a weighted average basis may be compared to prices of individual export transactions if the authorities find a pattern of export prices which differ significantly among different purchasers, regions

---

[195] *Ibid.*

or time periods, and if an explanation is provided as to why such differences cannot be taken into account appropriately by the use of a weighted average-to-weighted average or transaction-to-transaction comparison."

7.271 Article 2.4.2 provides that an investigating authority should normally calculate a margin of dumping by comparing normal value and export price either on a weighted average basis, or transaction-to-transaction. In the event that a weighted average comparison is used, Article 2.4.2 provides for the comparison of "a weighted average normal value" with a weighted average of prices of all comparable export transactions. Brazil claims that Argentina violated Article 2.4.2 because, instead of calculating weighted average normal values for Sadia and Avipal on the basis of all of those exporters' domestic sales transactions, the DCD calculated weighted averages of a statistical sample of the domestic transactions reported by them. This raises the issue of whether or not a Member must include all domestic sales transactions when establishing "a weighted average normal value" for the purpose of Article 2.4.2.[196]

7.272 In examining what is meant by "a weighted average normal value", we attach particular importance to the meaning of the term "normal value". We note that Article 2.1 of the *AD Agreement* refers to normal value as "the comparable price, in the ordinary course of trade, for the like product when destined for consumption in the exporting country". Article 2.1 therefore defines normal value in terms of domestic sales transactions in the exporting Member (although Article 2.2 provides that alternative methods to establish normal value may be used in certain circumstances).[197] Article 2.1 does not specify, however, whether or not all domestic sales transactions need be included. This issue is addressed by Article 2.2.1, which sets out the conditions to be met before domestic sales may be treated as not in "the ordinary course of trade", and therefore excluded for the purpose of establishing normal value in accordance with Article 2.1. Article 2.2.1 states that domestic sales "may be disregarded in determining normal value only if" the relevant conditions are met. We understand these provisions to mean that there are only specific circumstances in which domestic sales transactions may be excluded from normal value. We consider that these provisions constitute relevant context for interpreting the phrase "a weighted average normal value", since they indicate that "a weighted average normal value" is a weighted average of *all* domestic sales other than those which may be disregarded pursuant to Article 2.2.1 of the *AD Agreement*.

7.273 We do not consider that our interpretation is undermined by the fact that Article 2.4.2 refers to *a* weighted average normal value, and not *the* weighted average normal value. In our view, use of the word "a" simply means that there are

---

[196] We note that the panel in *Egypt - Steel Rebar* found that Article 2.4 "has to do with ensuring a fair comparison (...) of export price and normal value. Thus, we find that it does not apply to the investigating authority's establishment of normal value as such..." (see footnote 194 *supra*). Although we examine the present issue in light of the provisions of Article 2 governing the establishment of normal value, we are not examining the establishment of normal value *per se*. Rather, we are examining the weighted average normal value established by the investigating authority for the purpose of comparison with the weighted average export price.

[197] These methods are not relevant in the present proceedings, since the DCD established normal value on the basis of domestic sales transactions.

various ways of establishing a weighted average.[198] It does not mean that there are various ways of establishing normal value.

7.274 Nor do we consider that our interpretation is undermined simply by the fact that Article 2.4.2 does not refer to weighted average normal value in terms of *all* domestic transactions, whereas for the purpose of weighted average export price Article 2.4.2 specifies that prices of *all* comparable export transactions shall be included. We believe that the strict rules in Article 2 regarding the determination of normal value require that, in the usual case,[199] normal value should be established by reference to all domestic sales of the like product in the ordinary course of trade. There would be no need to stipulate the circumstances in which domestic transactions may be excluded from normal value if there were no general obligation to otherwise include all domestic transactions in normal value.

7.275 In the present case, the DCD established weighted average normal values on the basis of statistical samples of domestic sales transactions. The DCD did not establish weighted average normal values on the basis of all domestic sales transactions other than those it was entitled to exclude under Article 2.2.1.

(c) Conclusion

7.276 In light of the above, we find that the DCD acted in violation of Article 2.4.2 by failing to compare the weighted average export price with a proper weighted average normal value.

6. *Injury Determination - Claim 32*

7.277 This claim concerns the consistency of the CNCE's injury determination with Articles 3.1, 3.4 and 3.5 of the *AD Agreement*.

(a) Arguments of the Parties

7.278 Brazil claims that the CNCE's injury determination was inconsistent with Article 3.1 of the *AD Agreement* because it reviewed certain injury factors on the basis of January 96 - December 98 data, but other injury factors on the basis of January 96 - June 99 data. In other words, some injury factors were analysed in light of 1999 data, whereas others were not. Brazil submits that a violation of Article 3.1 necessarily gives rise to a violation of Articles 3.4 and 3.5. Brazil also argues that Argentina violated Article 3.5 because the period of review for dumping ended in January 1999, whereas the period of review for injury ended in June 1999. According to Brazil, the investigating authority should not have attributed injury found to exist in June 1999 to dumped imports from January 1999.

7.279 Argentina asserts that the CNCE took 1999 injury data into account because the investigation was initiated on the basis of a threat of injury, and an investigation of an alleged threat of injury requires the examination of the most recent data possible. Argentina also asserts that the existence of a voluntary agreement between "the parties" between October 1998 and March 1999 meant that it was necessary to

---

[198] "Weighted average" is defined as "an average in taking which each component is multiplied by a factor chosen to give it its proper importance" (http://www.oed.com). The weighted average may vary, therefore, depending on the factor chosen.

[199] That is to say, in the case where normal value is based on domestic transactions.

analyse imports without the effects produced by that agreement, so the analysis was extended until June 1999.

7.280 In addition, Argentina provided the following response to Question 87 from the Panel:

> "Lines 1 to 6 in the second paragraph of Section V (State of the Domestic Industry) of Record No. 576 of 23 December 1999, which appears in CNCE File No. 43/1997 (folio 7313), clearly state that:
>
>> "The 'period under analysis' corresponds to the period from January 1996 to December 1998. For certain variables, such as domestic production, prices, imports, national exports and apparent consumption, data is included for the first half of 1999. Data for 1995 is provided for reference purposes. Variations for the first half of 1999 are against the same period for the previous year." (emphasis added)
>
> Nevertheless, Argentina reiterates what it stated in its two previous submissions, and for a better understanding of the overall context, we repeat our reply that:
>
>> "First of all, there is no obligation to analyse any indicator outside the period established by the authorities as the investigation period.
>>
>> In accordance with international practice in certain countries, Argentina considered a number of variables accessible to the public in order to double check the trends observed during the investigation period. If we were to insist on the constant updating of all indicators during the investigation, as Brazil seems to suggest in this case, the investigation would be endless. We repeat that this is not the objective of the AD Agreement, nor is it the practice of those countries which, like Argentina, examine certain relevant indicators of reference data."
>
> It should be noted that the determination of threat of injury was based on the period from January 1996 to December 1998, and the other data, as stated in previous replies and in the Record in question, was used for reference purposes."[200]

7.281 Brazil provided the following comments on Argentina's response:

> "In responding to the Panel's question, Argentina fails to provide where the investigating authority *explained* why it looked at 1999 data for only certain injury factors and not others. The passage referred to by Argentina clearly states that the data corresponding to the year 1995 is used by way of reference. However, that same passage does ***not*** provide that the data corresponding to the first semester of 1999 is used by way of reference. What that passage provides is that the data for the variables national production, prices, imports, national exports and apparent consumption corresponding to the first semester of 1999 were included in the period of injury analysis. Had the authority

---

[200] See Argentina's reply to Question 87 of the Panel.

Report of the Panel

intended to use the data for the first semester of 1999 merely as reference, the authority would have clearly stated this in the final determination, just as it did with the data for the year 1995. In this investigation, the Argentinean authority considered a certain period of injury analysis for the factors production, prices, imports, exports and apparent consumption and considered another period of injury analysis for the remaining Article 3.4 factors." (emphasis in original, footnotes omitted)[201]

(b) Evaluation by the Panel

7.282 Articles 3.1, 3.4 and 3.5 provide that:

"3.1 A determination of injury for purposes of Article VI of GATT 1994 shall be based on positive evidence and involve an objective examination of both *(a)* the volume of the dumped imports and the effect of the dumped imports on prices in the domestic market for like products, and *(b)* the consequent impact of these imports on domestic producers of such products.

3.4 The examination of the impact of the dumped imports on the domestic industry concerned shall include an evaluation of all relevant economic factors and indices having a bearing on the state of the industry, including actual and potential decline in sales, profits, output, market share, productivity, return on investments, or utilization of capacity; factors affecting domestic prices; the magnitude of the margin of dumping; actual and potential negative effects on cash flow, inventories, employment, wages, growth, ability to raise capital or investments. This list is not exhaustive, nor can one or several of these factors necessarily give decisive guidance.

3.5 It must be demonstrated that the dumped imports are, through the effects of dumping, as set forth in paragraphs 2 and 4, causing injury within the meaning of this Agreement. The demonstration of a causal relationship between the dumped imports and the injury to the domestic industry shall be based on an examination of all relevant evidence before the authorities. The authorities shall also examine any known factors other than the dumped imports which at the same time are injuring the domestic industry, and the injuries caused by these other factors must not be attributed to the dumped imports. Factors which may be relevant in this respect include, *inter alia*, the volume and prices of imports not sold at dumping prices, contraction in demand or changes in the patterns of consumption, trade restrictive practices of and competition between the foreign and domestic producers, developments in technology and the export performance and productivity of the domestic industry."

7.283 Argentina does not deny that the CNCE only reviewed 1999 data for certain injury factors. Article 3.1 requires an "objective" examination of injury. In our view, there is a *prima facie* case that an investigating authority fails to conduct an "objective" examination if it examines different injury factors using different periods.

---

[201] See Brazil's comments to Argentina's reply to Question 87 of the Panel.

Such a *prima facie* case may be rebutted if the investigating authority demonstrates that the use of different periods is justifiable on the basis of objective grounds (because, for example, data for more recent periods was not available for certain injury factors). Since the CNCE only examined 1999 data for certain injury factors, we find *prima facie* that the CNCE failed to conduct an objective examination of injury. We shall now consider whether or not Argentina has rebutted that *prima facie* case.

7.284 Argentina asserted in reply to Panel Question 87 that 1999 data was used for certain injury factors to "double check the trends". However, although the final determination refers to *1995* data being used for "reference purposes", it does not refer to *1999* data being used for this purpose. Argentina also argued before the Panel that the CNCE needed to review 1999 data because it was examining the existence of a threat of injury. However, there is nothing in the CNCE's final determination, or any evidence on the record, to suggest that these explanations constitute anything other than *ex post* rationalization which we are precluded from taking into consideration. In any event, even if there were good reasons for the CNCE to review injury data for 1999, this does not explain why the CNCE considered 1999 data for certain injury factors only, and not all of them. Argentina has failed to provide any justification as to why 1999 data was only used for certain, but not all, injury factors. Although Argentina's response to Question 87 from the Panel could perhaps be understood to mean that 1999 data was only available for certain injury factors ("Argentina considered a number of variables accessible to the public"), no such explanation was contained in the CNCE's final injury determination, or in any other document on the record before us. Furthermore, the fact that 1999 data for the remaining injury factors may not have been available to the *public* does not necessarily mean that such data was not available to the *investigating authority*. Accordingly, Argentina has failed to rebut the presumption that the CNCE conducted a subjective examination of the relevant injury factors.

7.285 In light of the above, we find that the CNCE acted inconsistently with Article 3.1 of the *AD Agreement* by only examining 1999 data for certain injury factors.

7.286 Brazil asserts that the abovementioned violation of Article 3.1 would also constitute a violation of Articles 3.4 and 3.5. In this respect, Brazil appears to consider that Articles 3.4 and 3.5 also require investigating authorities to conduct an objective examination of injury and causation. That part of Brazil's Claim 32 concerning an alleged violation of Article 3.4 is based on exactly the same facts underpinning our finding of violation of Article 3.1. According to the logic of Brazil's claim, therefore, if Argentina were to bring its measure into conformity with Article 3.1, it would also bring its measure into conformity with Article 3.4. Accordingly, there is no need for us to examine that part of Claim 32 concerning Article 3.4 of the *AD Agreement*.

7.287 That part of Claim 32 concerning Article 3.5 is not based on the same facts as Brazil's arguments concerning Articles 3.1 and 3.4. It is therefore necessary for us to address Brazil's arguments concerning Article 3.5. Brazil's arguments relate to the fact that the periods of review used for the separate dumping and injury determinations did not end at the same point in time. We note, however, that there is nothing in the *AD Agreement* to suggest that the periods of review for dumping and injury must necessarily end at the same point in time. Indeed, since there may be a time-lag between the entry of dumped imports and the injury caused by them, it may not be appropriate to use identical periods of review for the dumping and injury analyses in all cases. Furthermore, we note that the issue of periods of review has been examined by the Anti-Dumping Committee. It has issued a recommendation to the effect that, as a general rule, "the period of data collection for injury investigations normally should be at least three years, unless a party from whom data is being gathered has existed for a lesser period, **and should include the entirety of the period of data collection for the dumping investigation**" (emphasis added).[202] It would appear, therefore, that the period of review for injury need only "include" the entirety of the period of review for dumping. There is nothing in the Anti-Dumping Committee's recommendation to suggest that it should not exceed (in the sense of including more recent data) the period of review for dumping.[203]

(c) Conclusion

7.288 For the above reasons, we uphold Brazil's Claim 32 in respect of the violation of Article 3.1 of the *AD Agreement*. We make no findings in respect of Article 3.4, and we reject that part of Brazil's Claim 32 based on Article 3.5 of the *AD Agreement*.

7. *Failure to Explain Why the CNCE Examined 1999 Data for Certain Injury Factors but Not Others - Claim 33*

7.289 Brazil's Claim 33, concerning Article 12.2.2 of the *AD Agreement*, is based on the same factual circumstances as the preceding Claim 32.

(a) Arguments of the Parties

7.290 Brazil submits that Argentina violated Article 12.2.2 of the *AD Agreement* because the CNCE's final determination on injury did not explain why the CNCE examined 1999 data for certain injury factors but not for others.

7.291 Argentina submits that all relevant information was made public through published resolutions, and was available in the record to interested parties.

(b) Evaluation by the Panel

7.292 In essence, Brazil claims that a violation of Article 12.2.2 follows automatically from the abovementioned violation of Article 3.1 (Claim 32). In other words, just as the CNCE violated Article 3.1 by failing to explain why it considered 1999 data for some factors but not for others, so the absence of any such explanation in the final determination constitutes a violation of Article 12.2.2 of the *AD Agreement*.

7.293 We note that two adopted panel reports have already examined the application of the procedural provisions of Article 12.2.2 to factual circumstances which have already been found to be in violation of substantive provisions of the *AD*

---

[202] Recommendation concerning the periods of data collection for anti-dumping investigations, G/ADP/6, adopted by the Committee on Anti-Dumping Practices on 5 May 2000.
[203] We note that even when different periods of review are applied in respect of dumping and injury, there is still an obligation under Article 3.5 to establish a causal link between the injury and dumped imports.

Agreement.[204] Those panels found that it was not necessary to make findings under Article 12.2.2 in such circumstances. We agree with those panels. If the CNCE's injury determination was substantively inconsistent with the relevant legal obligations, the adequacy of the public notice of the CNCE's findings on injury is immaterial.

(c) Conclusion

7.294 For the above reasons, we do not consider it necessary to examine Brazil's Claim 33.

8. *Failure to Exclude the Effect of Non-Dumped Imports in the Injury Determination - Claims 34 - 37*

7.295 These claims concern the meaning of the term "dumped imports" in Articles 3.1, 3.2, 3.4 and 3.5 of the *AD Agreement*.

(a) Arguments of the Parties / Third Parties

7.296 Brazil claims that Argentina violated Articles 3.1, 3.2, 3.4 and 3.5 of the *AD Agreement* by including the effect of non-dumped imports in its injury determination. These non-dumped imports were exported / produced by Nicolini and Seara, which were found by the DCD not to be dumping. According to Brazil, Article 3 only allows Members to take into account the injurious effects of dumped imports.

7.297 Argentina submits that, when analysing causal link, the CNCE did take into account the fact that imports from Nicolini and Seara were not dumped. The average f.o.b. prices of these enterprises were substantially higher than the prices of other exports found to have dumped. Furthermore, the volume of imports from Nicolini and Seara came nowhere close to the levels reached by the majority of exports from Brazil throughout the period analysed by the CNCE. The CNCE found that price was the decisive factor on the market, and that the decrease in domestic prices throughout the period of investigation was caused by the price of dumped imports. Had the CNCE excluded imports from Nicolini and Seara, the average f.o.b. price of imports taken into account by the CNCE would have been even lower, thereby accentuating the causal link between imports and injury to the domestic industry. In this regard, Argentina submitted evidence to the Panel showing that in 1997 and 1998 the average f.o.b. prices of imports from Nicolini and Seara were 13 per cent higher than the other imports investigated. In addition, the fact that imports from Nicolini and Seara did not have the major share in any year during the period investigated by the CNCE implied that no radical changes could be expected in the volume and share of the other imports investigated. Imports from exporters / producers found to have dumped represented the majority of imports, rising in 1998 to almost 40,000 tonnes compared with 56,000 tonnes for total imports from Brazil, and with the volume of dumped imports increasing more rapidly than the volume of total imports in 1998.

---

[204] Panel Report, *Guatemala - Cement II*, *supra*, note 48, para. 8.291 and Panel Report, *European Communities - Anti-Dumping Duties on Imports of Cotton-Type Bed Linen from India* ("*EC - Bed Linen*"), WT/DS141/R, adopted 12 March 2001, as modified by the Appellate Body Report, WT/DS141/AB/R, DSR 2001:VI, 2077, para. 6.259.

Consequently, the share of dumped imports in apparent consumption rose, displacing domestic sales of the like domestic product.

7.298 The European Communities opposed Brazil's interpretation of Article 3. The European Communities suggested that an anti-dumping investigation is country-specific, rather than exporter-specific, so that once certain imports from an exporting country are found to be dumped, an investigating authority is entitled to treat all imports from that country as dumped.

(b) Evaluation by the Panel

7.299 Brazil's claims are based on Articles 3.1, 3.2, 3.4 and 3.5 of the *AD Agreement*. Brazil asserts that the CNCE violated these provisions by including the effects of non-dumped imports (i.e., imports from exporters / foreign producers found by the DCD not to have dumped) in its injury analysis. In examining these claims, we must first determine whether or not the term "dumped imports" in the relevant provisions of Article 3 of the *AD Agreement* excludes imports from producers / exporters found not to have dumped. If it does, we must determine whether or not the CNCE excluded non-dumped imports from Nicolini and Seara when making its final determination on injury.

7.300 We consider that a determination of dumping is made with reference to a product from a particular producer/exporter. If a particular producer/exporter has been found not to have dumped, then we see no basis for including that producer/exporter's imports in the category of "dumped imports". We note that the term "dumped imports" was interpreted by the panel in *EC - Bed Linen*, and by the subsequent panel reviewing India's recourse to Article 21.5 of the *DSU* regarding the EC's implementation of the results of the original proceeding.

7.301 The *EC - Bed Linen* panel found that "all imports from any producer/exporter found to be dumping may be considered as dumped imports for purposes of injury analysis".[205] Although this finding does not resolve the issue of whether imports from producers / exporters found *not* to be dumping may be considered as "dumped imports", that panel observed that

> "It is possible that a calculation conducted consistently with the AD Agreement would lead to the conclusion that one or another Indian producer should be attributed a zero or *de minimis* margin of dumping. In such a case, it is our view that the imports attributable to such a producer/exporter may not be considered as "dumped" for purposes of injury analysis."[206]

7.302 In the implementation proceedings under Article 21.5 of the *DSU*, the panel "agree[d] fully"[207] with the preceding observation of the *EC - Bed Linen* panel, and in turn found that:

> "the question of which imports are to be considered dumped is readily answered - 'dumped imports' are all imports attributable to producers

---

[205] *Ibid.*, para. 6.137.
[206] *Ibid.*, para. 6.138.
[207] Panel Report, *European Communities - Anti-Dumping Duties on Imports of Cotton-Type Bed Linen from India - Recourse to Article 21.5 of the DSU by India ("EC - Bed Linen (Article 21.5 - India)")*, WT/DS141/RW, 29 November 2002 (reports of the panel and Appellate Body not yet adopted), para. 6.131.

or exporters for which a margin of dumping greater than *de minimis* is calculated. This was the decision of the original Panel in this dispute, rejecting the argument that the imports attributable to a single producer found to be dumping should be divided into two categories - 'dumped' and 'not-dumped' sales transactions."[208]

7.303 We agree with the findings of the *EC - Bed Linen* and the *EC - Bed Linen (Article 21.5 - India)* panels, and with the abovementioned observation by the *EC - Bed Linen* panel. On the basis of the ordinary meaning of the text, we find that the term "dumped imports" refers to all imports attributable to producers or exporters for which a margin of dumping greater than *de minimis* has been calculated. The term "dumped imports" excludes imports from producers / exporters found in the course of the investigation not to have dumped.

7.304 We recall that the DCD found that imports from Nicolini and Seara were not dumped. Our finding regarding the meaning of the term "dumped imports" therefore means that the CNCE should have excluded imports from Nicolini and Seara when examining the potentially injurious effects of "dumped imports" on the domestic industry. We shall now examine whether or not the CNCE did so.

7.305 There is nothing on the record before us or in the CNCE's final injury determination to suggest that the CNCE excluded imports from Nicolini and Seara from its injury analysis. Indeed, it would have been unlikely that CNCE could have excluded Nicolini and Seara's imports (by virtue of their being non-dumped) since the CNCE's injury determination preceded by six months the DCD's determination that Nicolini and Seara were not dumping. In other words, the CNCE could not have excluded imports from Nicolini and Seara from its injury analysis, since it did not know at the time of its injury analysis that imports from those exporters / producers were not dumped.

7.306 Furthermore, Argentina has not argued that imports from Nicolini and Seara were excluded from the CNCE's injury analysis. Rather, Argentina has focused on the effects of the inclusion of Nicolini and Seara imports in the CNCE's injury analysis, suggesting that the finding of injury would have been aggravated had those imports been excluded because the average f.o.b. price of imports would have decreased. While Argentina made arguments to the Panel regarding average f.o.b. import prices excluding imports from Nicolini and Seara, it failed to identify anything in the record to the effect that the CNCE considered such arguments during its injury analysis. The same is true of Argentina's arguments to the Panel regarding the Nicolini and Seara's share of total imports. Thus, even if such arguments were relevant for the purpose of determining whether or not relevant imports from Nicolini and Seara were excluded from the CNCE's injury analysis - a fact of which we are not at all convinced - such arguments constitute *ex post* rationalization which we are bound not to consider. In any event, we consider that, consistent with a proper interpretation of the term "dumped imports", imports from Nicolini and Seara should have been excluded outright from the CNCE's injury analysis. It is clear from the record that CNCE failed to do this.

---

[208] Panel Report, *EC - Bed Linen (Article 21.5 - India)*, *supra*, note 207, para. 6.133.

(c) Conclusion

7.307 In light of the above, we find that the CNCE violated Articles 3.1, 3.2, 3.4 and 3.5 of the *AD Agreement* by including imports from Nicolini and Seara in its injury analysis, even though such imports had been found by the DCD to be non-dumped.

9. *Failure to Examine Each of the Injury Factors and Indices Having a Bearing on the State of the Domestic Industry - Claims 38 - 40*

7.308 These claims concern the issue of whether or not the CNCE examined each of the injury factors set forth in Article 3.4 of the *AD Agreement*. Brazil submits that the CNCE failed to do so, thereby violating Articles 3.1, 3.4 and 12.2.2 of the *AD Agreement*.

(a) Arguments of the Parties / Third Parties

7.309 Brazil submits that the CNCE violated Articles 3.1 and 3.4 of the *AD Agreement* by failing to examine each of the injury factors and indices having a bearing on the state of the domestic industry set forth in Article 3.4. In particular, Brazil asserts that the CNCE failed to examine actual and potential decline in productivity, factors affecting domestic prices, the magnitude of the margin of dumping, actual and potential negative effects on cash flow, growth, the ability to raise capital or investments. Brazil further asserts that failure to address each of the Article 3.4 injury factors also constitutes a violation of the public notice requirement set forth in Article 12.2.2 because not all of the Article 3.4 injury factors were referred to or evaluated in the CNCE's injury determination.

7.310 Argentina submits that the CNCE did evaluate the injury factors identified by Brazil. Argentina refers to the inclusion of factors relating to productivity in the CNCE's injury determination, and provides a summary of the characteristics of the Argentine poultry market, of factors affecting domestic prices, and the effects of the margin of dumping. Argentina also explains why the CNCE did not need to analyse cash flow and the ability to raise capital, claiming that it correctly focused on liquidity and the "break-even point" instead.

7.311 The United States asserts that a violation of Article 3.4 would not necessarily constitute a violation of Article 12.2.2, since Article 12.2.2 only requires publication of findings and conclusions on issues of fact and law considered material by the investigating authorities. Thus, if certain Article 3.4 factors are not material to a given case, they need not be included in the Article 12.2.2 publication, as long as the lack of materiality is at least implicitly apparent from the final determination.

(b) Evaluation by the Panel

7.312 We shall first examine Brazil's Claim 38, concerning the application of Article 3.4 of the *AD Agreement*. We shall then examine Claims 39 and 40, concerning Articles 3.1 and 12.2.2, respectively.

7.313 Article 3.4 of the *AD Agreement* provides that:

"The examination of the impact of the dumped imports on the domestic industry concerned shall include an evaluation of all relevant economic factors and indices having a bearing on the state of the industry, including actual and potential decline in sales, profits, output, market share, productivity, return on investments, or utilization of capacity; factors affecting domestic prices; the magnitude of the margin of dumping; actual and potential negative effects on cash flow, inventories, employment, wages, growth, ability to raise capital or investments. This list is not exhaustive, nor can one or several of these factors necessarily give decisive guidance."

7.314 It is well-established in WTO dispute settlement proceedings that an investigating authority must analyse each of the factors enumerated in Article 3.4. We note that both the *EC - Bed Linen* panel, and the *Mexico - Corn Syrup* panel to which it referred, have found that Article 3.4 is a mandatory provision, that every Article 3.4 factor must be considered, and that the nature of the investigating authority's consideration must be apparent.[209] We agree, and shall now examine whether or not the CNCE complied with these requirements in respect of the specific Article 3.4 factors identified by Brazil, namely actual and potential decline in productivity, factors affecting domestic prices, the magnitude of the margin of dumping, actual and potential negative effects on cash flow, growth, and the ability to raise capital or investments.

(i) Productivity

7.315 Argentina asserts that the CNCE made a number of considerations regarding productivity, including the following statement in the CNCE's final injury determination:

"Generally speaking, the relative stability of the number of employees in spite of the increases in production would indicate higher physical labour productivity, probably due to the above-mentioned introduction of new technology."[210]

7.316 In our view, this statement is sufficient to demonstrate that the CNCE considered productivity, and found that productivity increased as a result of the introduction of new technology. This statement alone, therefore, is sufficient for the purposes of Article 3.4 of the *AD Agreement*.[211] Accordingly, we reject Brazil's claim that the CNCE failed to consider productivity.

(ii) Factors Affecting Domestic Prices

7.317 Argentina asserts that the CNCE considered factors affecting domestic prices by analysing the trend in the price index for substitute products, mainly red meat, as well as the general level of activity and price indexes in the most important relevant sectors. In this regard, Argentina provided the following response to part of Question 59 from the Panel:

---

[209] See Panel Report, *EC - Bed Linen, supra,* note 204, para. 6.159, and Panel Report, *Mexico - Corn Syrup, supra,* note 65, para. 7.128.
[210] Exhibit BRA-14, Record No. 576, page 13.
[211] For this reason, we do not consider it necessary to conduct a detailed examination of the other instances in which Argentina claims that the CNCE considered productivity. We note, however, that in some instances Argentina has pointed to CNCE statements on production, which is not the same as productivity.

"Regarding the fact that Brazil fails to find an evaluation of other factors affecting the price of whole eviscerated poultry during the investigation period, we note that this evaluation appears both in CNCE Record No. 576 and in the Technical Report. Indeed, regarding the evolution of the price of a substitute product - red meat - the said Record states the following: "An econometric exercise was conducted which showed that for the period from January 1995 to June 1999, the price of the product on the domestic market depended on the volume of imports for the previous month, the price of the imported product and the price of bovine meat. The inclusion of the price of maize in the mentioned model did not produce satisfactory results, indicating that the considerable variability of the price of whole eviscerated poultry does not coincide with the price of maize. Nevertheless, both variables showed similar patterns ... " [Record No. 576, pages 24 and 25]. This analysis was based on the elements set forth in the Technical Report at folios 7371/2 and 7491/507. CNCE Record No. 576 also refers to the analysis of the evolution of the general level of activity, stating that "[t]he economic recession did not particularly affect the consumption of whole eviscerated poultry, which continued to increase (in 1998 it increased by 14 per cent)." [Record No. 576, page 25] Finally, with respect to relative prices, CNCE Record No. 576 states that "...with regard to the price of industrial goods taken as a whole and of bovine meat - represented respectively by the Wholesale Industrial Price Index for Manufactured Goods and the simple average of the consumer price indices for fresh bovine meat, front and hind cuts - followed the same trend as the sales revenue described above, although in the case of bovine meat, the annual variations reflected a stronger decrease in 1998 as a result of the increase in the price of bovine meat recorded that year." [Record No. 576, page 14] The above analysis was supported by the information provided in the Technical Report, in particular Table No. 16 at folio 7474 and the description at folio 7410. Regarding Table No. 16 of the Technical Report, Argentina notes that according to Brazil it contains only the average sales revenue for poultry, when in fact it also provides the relative prices mentioned above."[212]

7.318 In addition, Argentina provided the following response to Question 88 from the Panel regarding Table 16 of Record No. 576:

"Table No. 16, which belongs to Technical Report GEGE/1TDF No. 03/99 and is an integral part of Record No. 576, provides the average sales revenue for one kilogram of eviscerated poultry, fresh or chilled, and the relative prices of the comparable product, with regard to the price of industrial goods taken as a whole and of bovine meat - represented respectively by the Wholesale Industrial Price Index for Manufactured Goods and the simple average of the consumer price indices for fresh bovine meat, front and hind cuts.

---

[212] See Argentina's reply to Question 59 of the Panel.

The comparison made with respect to the Wholesale Industrial Price Index for Manufactured Goods was based on the need to assess whether the price of the product in question was following the same trend as the other manufactured goods.

With regard to the second index, Argentina has traditionally been a consumer of red meat, so that it was considered appropriate to use this index to analyse the impact of variations in that product on poultry meat as from a certain degree of substitution between bovine meat and poultry meat.

As can be seen from the table, the two relative prices analysed followed the same trend as average sales revenue for the product in question, although in the case of the price in relation to the simple average for bovine meat the annual variations reflected a stronger decrease in 1998 as a result of the increase in the price of bovine meat recorded that year. Indeed, as indicated in the Market Chapter of Technical Report GEGE/ITDF No. 03/99, Section VI.5 (Recent evolution of the market), folio 7371, paragraph 3: "During 1998 there was a further increase in the demand for poultry as a result of the substitution effect following the sharp increases in the price of bovine meat, which reached its peak in the middle of 1998. No decline in the consumption of poultry was recorded following the subsequent fall in the price of bovine meat. This because the market perception is that the price of poultry is so low that it is even pushing the price of bovine meat downwards".

Consequently Article 3.4 was clearly taken into consideration where it provides that "[t]he examination of the impact of the dumped imports on the domestic industry concerned shall include an evaluation of all relevant economic factors and indices having a bearing on the state of the industry, including ... factors affecting domestic prices ...".[213]

7.319   In our view, the above extracts from the CNCE's final determination on injury (Record No. 576 and the accompanying Technical Report) clearly indicate that the CNCE did consider factors affecting domestic prices, by considering the trend in poultry prices relative to the trend in the price of substitute products. Accordingly, we reject Brazil's claim that the CNCE failed to consider factors affecting domestic prices.

(iii)   Magnitude of the Margin of Dumping

7.320   The only arguments made by Argentina concerning the CNCE's consideration of the magnitude of the margin of dumping for the purpose of Article 3.4 of the *AD Agreement* are contained in the following two paragraphs taken from Argentina's first written submission:

"In a situation where, in addition to the factors already explained regarding the characteristics of the Argentine market, there is a fixed exchange rate and a recession, the impact of unfair practices such as dumping can be felt all the more strongly, even with relatively small

---

[213] See Argentina's reply to Question 88 of the Panel.

margins. This is particularly true when commodities are the reference product and the price variable is the essential factor in competition.

Consequently, bearing in mind the above explanations concerning Brazil's potential to generate surpluses under conditions of unfair competition, margins of 8-14 per cent are significant and were evaluated thus by the investigating authority because of their potential impact on Argentine production."[214]

7.321 We note that Argentina has failed to indicate where such arguments are set forth in the CNCE's Record No. 576, or to point us to any other document in which the CNCE is alleged to have considered such arguments. Such arguments therefore constitute *ex post* rationalization which we are precluded from taking into account. In any event, we note that Argentina's reference to dumping margins of 8 - 14 per cent concerns the margins calculated by the applicant in its application. They are not the margins calculated by the DCD during the investigation. Furthermore, the CNCE completed its injury analysis (on 23 December 1999) six months before the DCD completed its dumping investigation (on 23 June 2000), so we do not see how the CNCE could have taken the magnitude of the margin of dumping into account in its injury analysis.

7.322 For the above reasons, we uphold Brazil's claim that Argentina violated Article 3.4 of the *AD Agreement* because the CNCE failed to consider the magnitude of the margin of dumping in its analysis of the impact of the dumped imports on the domestic industry.

        (iv) Actual and Potential Negative Effects on Cash Flow, Growth, Ability to Raise Capital, or Investments

7.323 Argentina's most detailed arguments concerning the CNCE's alleged analysis of cash flow, growth, the ability to raise capital and investments were contained in its first written submission:

"A few words, to begin with, on the terms of financing for companies in Argentina, where the capital market has never been an important source, apart from occasional exceptions such as occurred in the 1990s, a fact which is to a large extent reflected in the accounting legislation.

At the legislative level, pursuant to Article 299 of Law No. 19550, companies are obliged to submit a "Statement of the Origin and Utilization of Funds" which, unlike the cash flow statement within the strict meaning of financial accounting, is not a detailed breakdown of the cash flow situation but simply a synthetic description of the elements that have led to increases or decreases in funds. These headings, therefore, in no way allow any conclusions to be drawn regarding cash flow trends.

Taking account of the above, the indicators which make it possible to undertake such an analysis in terms of the reference variable would be

---

[214] See Argentina's first written submission, paras. 294-295.

liquidity and the breakeven point, which were analysed in a consistent manner in the Technical Report attached to Record No. 576.

Lastly, in relation to paragraph 296 above and the financing mechanisms in this sector, none of the applicants is quoted on the stock exchange or has utilized the capital market, so that irrespective of the rules in force, the cash-flow analysis requirement is not relevant and cannot be met."[215]

7.324 Argentina therefore argues that, because of the particular statutory and market circumstances in which Argentine poultry producers operate, certain Article 3.4 factors were not relevant to the state of the domestic industry. However, we find no reference to this explanation in any of the documentation prepared by or for CNCE (i.e., neither in the CNCE's final injury determination nor in the Technical Report attached thereto). For this reason, we are bound to treat these arguments as *ex post* rationalization that we are precluded from taking into account. Leaving such arguments aside, there is nothing on the record to suggest to us that the CNCE considered cash flow, growth, ability to raise capital, or investments. Furthermore, we recall that both the *Mexico - Corn Syrup* and *EC - Bed Linen* panels found that that "while the authorities may determine that some factors are not relevant or do not weigh significantly in the decision, the authorities may not simply disregard such factors, but must explain their conclusion as to the lack of relevance or significance of such factors."[216] We agree with that finding, and note that there is nothing on the record to suggest that the CNCE excluded those factors because it had found that such factors were not relevant or did not weigh significantly in its decision on injury. We therefore find that the CNCE failed to consider these factors, in violation of Article 3.4 of the *AD Agreement*.

7.325 In Claim 39, Brazil argues that our finding in the preceding paragraph that Argentina violated Article 3.4 should necessarily lead us to conclude that Argentina also violated Article 3.1 of the *AD Agreement*. Argentina does not respond to this argument. In our view, there is an obvious connection between paragraphs 1 and 4 of Article 3. Article 3.1(b) requires "an objective examination of ... the consequent impact of the[] imports on domestic producers" of the relevant products. Article 3.4 provides that "[t]he examination of the impact of the dumped imports on the domestic industry concerned shall include an evaluation of all relevant economic factors and indices having a bearing on the state of the industry ...". We consider that "[t]he examination of the impact of dumped imports" referred to in Article 3.4 is precisely the same "objective examination of ... the consequent impact of the[] imports" referred to in Article 3.1(b). Thus, to the extent that a Member failed to conduct a proper "examination of the impact of dumped imports" for the purpose of Article 3.4, that Member also failed to conduct an "objective examination of ... the consequent impact of the[] imports" within the meaning of Article 3.1(b). Accordingly, since we have found that Argentina violated Article 3.4 of the *AD Agreement*, we also find that Argentina violated Article 3.1(b) thereof.

7.326 Brazil further claims (Claim 40) that a violation of Article 3.4 would automatically violate the procedural requirements of Article 12.2.2. As noted above

---

[215] *Ibid.*, paras. 296-299.
[216] See Panel Report, *EC - Bed Linen, supra,* note 204, para. 6.162, and Panel Report, *Mexico - Corn Syrup, supra,* note 65, para. 7.129.

Report of the Panel

in respect of Claim 33, once the CNCE's injury determination is found to be inconsistent with the relevant legal requirements, findings concerning the adequacy of the CNCE's notice become immaterial.[217] Accordingly, it is neither necessary nor appropriate for us to examine this claim.

(c) Conclusion

7.327 For the above reasons, we find that Argentina violated Articles 3.1(b) and 3.4 by failing to evaluate all of the economic factors and indices enumerated in Article 3.4 of the *AD Agreement*. We do not consider it necessary to address Brazil's Claim 40.

10. Domestic Industry - Claim 41

7.328 This claim concerns the definition of the term "domestic industry" contained in Article 4.1 of the *AD Agreement*.

(a) Arguments of the Parties / Third Parties

7.329 Brazil notes that Article 4.1 defines the term "domestic industry" as referring to the domestic producers as a whole of the like products or to those of them whose collective output of the products constitutes "a major proportion" of the total domestic production of those products. Brazil submits that the reference in Article 4.1 to "a major proportion" means "the majority", or the greater part in relation to the whole (i.e., 50+ per cent). Brazil submits that Argentina violated Article 4.1 because the CNCE defined the domestic industry as - and collected injury data for - those producers whose collective output constitutes 46 per cent - and therefore less than the majority - of total domestic production.

7.330 Argentina argues that Article 4.1 deliberately failed to define exactly what is meant by "a major proportion". Argentina denies that "a major proportion" must be greater than 50 per cent, and notes that the practice of other Members supports Argentina's interpretation.

7.331 The United States asserts that Article 4.1 merely contains a definition of "domestic industry", and does not impose any obligation on Members. The United States also asserts that "a major proportion" does not necessarily mean "the majority", but may also mean "unusually important, serious, or significant". The United States further argues that the drafters of the *AD Agreement* were quite explicit when they intended to impose a majority requirement for a particular obligation, such as the 50 per cent standing requirement in Article 5.4.

7.332 According to the European Communities, the phrase "major proportion" does not mean the majority of the domestic production, but rather an important part thereof, which may be less than 50 per cent. The European Communities relies on the same definition of "major proportion" as does the United States. The European Communities also notes that Article 4.1 refers to "a" major proportion, and not "the" major proportion, suggesting that there may be more than one major proportion.

7.333 The European Communities further asserts that its interpretation is supported by Article 5.4, which provides that an investigation shall not be initiated unless the

---

[217] See para. 7.293 *supra*.

authorities determine that the application has been made "by or on behalf of the domestic industry". Article 5.4 goes on to state that:

> "[t]he application shall be considered to have been made 'by or on behalf of the domestic industry' if it is supported by those domestic producers whose collective output constitutes more than 50 per cent of the total production of the like product produced by that portion of the domestic industry expressing either support for or opposition to the application. However, no investigation shall be initiated when domestic producers expressly supporting the application account for less than 25 per cent of the total production of the like product produced by the domestic industry."

7.334 The European Communities asserts that, in accordance with Article 5.4, an application may be considered to have been made "on behalf of the domestic industry" even if the producers which support it represent less than 50 per cent of the domestic production. The term "domestic industry" has the same meaning throughout the *AD Agreement*. If a number of producers which accounts for less than 50 per cent of the domestic production may, in certain circumstances, be considered to constitute "a major proportion" of the domestic production for the purposes of Article 5.4, then the same should be true also for the purposes of the other provisions of the *AD Agreement*. Moreover, it would be illogical to allow the opening of an investigation on the basis of an application filed by producers which represent less than 50 per cent of the domestic production only to conclude subsequently that the injury suffered by those producers does not, by reason of the percentage of the domestic production accounted by those producers, amount to injury to the "domestic industry".

7.335 The European Communities also argues that, even if "a major proportion" does mean the majority (i.e., 50+ per cent), this does not necessarily mean that an investigating authority's injury determination must evaluate data concerning the majority of domestic producers. In the first place, if a domestic producer which is part of the domestic industry fails to co-operate in the investigation, as indeed happened in the case under consideration, the authorities may, in accordance with the provisions of Article 6.8 and Annex II, resort to "facts available" in order to establish whether such producer has been injured. For that purpose, the relevant "facts available" may include the data collected from other producers which have co-operated in the investigation. Second, when assessing the state of the domestic industry, the authorities may resort to sampling techniques. In other words, the investigating authorities may consider that data for some domestic producers are representative of the state of the whole of the domestic industry. The possibility to use sampling techniques is expressly envisaged in Article 6.10 with respect to the dumping determination. There is no reason why similar sampling techniques should not be allowed also for the purposes of the injury determination, subject to the general requirement of Article 3.1 that the determination of injury must be based on "positive evidence" and involve an "objective examination" of the relevant facts.

7.336 Brazil rejects the US argument that Article 4.1 does not impose any obligation on Members. Brazil submits that Article 4.1 requires Members to interpret the term "domestic industry" consistently with the definition set forth in that provision. Brazil also rejects the EC argument concerning the Article 5.4 standing requirements, on the basis that nothing in Article 5.4 equates "producers expressly supporting the application" to the "domestic industry".

(b) Evaluation by the Panel

7.337 Article 4.1 provides in relevant part:

"For the purposes of this Agreement, the term "domestic industry" shall be interpreted as referring to the domestic producers as a whole of the like products or to those of them whose collective output of the products constitutes a major proportion of the total domestic production of those products …"

7.338 We must first determine whether or not Article 4.1 imposes any obligation on Members, i.e., whether or not Argentina could be found to have acted inconsistently with Article 4.1 (as opposed to any other provision of the *AD Agreement*) by using a definition of "domestic industry" other than that prescribed by Article 4.1. We note that Article 4.1 provides that the term "domestic industry" "shall" be interpreted in a specific manner. In our view, this imposes an express obligation on Members to interpret the term "domestic industry" in that specified manner. Thus, if a Member were to interpret the term differently in the context of an anti-dumping investigation, that Member would violate the obligation set forth in Article 4.1.

7.339 Having found that Article 4.1 does contain an obligation that Argentina could potentially have violated, we must now determine whether or not it did so by defining the "domestic industry" as producers of 46 per cent of total domestic production. In particular, we must consider whether or not the phrase "a major proportion" means that the "domestic industry" must include domestic producers whose collective output constitutes the majority, i.e., 50+ per cent, of domestic total production.[218]

7.340 Regarding the ordinary meaning of the phrase "major proportion", Brazil asserts that the term "major proportion" is synonymous with "major part", which in turn is defined as "the majority".[219] Brazil submits that "the majority" is understood to mean "the greater number or part". Brazil submits that 46 per cent of total domestic production cannot be considered as the greater part of 100 per cent of total domestic production. The European Communities and the United States assert that the word "major" does not necessarily mean "majority", but may also mean "unusually important, serious, or significant".[220,221]

---

[218] We note that this claim is not concerned with the issue of whether an investigating authority may immediately define the "domestic industry" in terms of domestic producers "whose collective output of the products constitutes a major proportion of the total domestic production", without first seeking to include in the "domestic industry" all domestic producers as a whole of like products.

[219] Brazil relies on *The Concise Oxford Dictionary of Current English* (Clarendon Press, 1995).

[220] *The New Shorter Oxford English Dictionary* (Clarendon Press, 1993).

[221] The EC also argued that its interpretation was supported by Article 5.4 of the *AD Agreement*. We are not convinced by this argument, because the Article 5.4 standard relates to the standing of applicants, and not the definition of the domestic industry. Furthermore, Article 5.4 does not mean that the application is necessarily filed "by" the domestic industry if it is supported by domestic producers accounting for 25 per cent of domestic production. In such a case, one cannot exclude the possibility that the application was merely filed "on behalf of" - rather than "by" - the domestic industry. It is illogical to suggest that an application could have been filed both "by" and "on behalf of" a single domestic industry. Thus, domestic producers accounting for 25 per cent of domestic production do not necessarily constitute the "domestic industry", contrary to the view expressed by the EC.

7.341 In considering these different dictionary definitions, we note that the word "major" is also defined as "important, serious, or significant".[222] Accordingly, an interpretation that defines the domestic industry in terms of domestic producers of an important, serious or significant proportion of total domestic production is permissible.[223] Indeed, this approach is entirely consistent with the Spanish version of Article 4.1, which refers to producers representing "una proporción importante" of domestic production. Furthermore, Article 4.1 does not define the "domestic industry" in terms of producers of *the* major proportion of total domestic production. Instead, Article 4.1 refers to producers of *a* major proportion of total domestic production. If Article 4.1 had referred to *the* major proportion, the requirement would clearly have been to define the "domestic industry" as producers constituting 50+ per cent of total domestic production.[224] However, the reference to *a* major proportion suggests that there may be more than one "major proportion" for the purpose of defining "domestic industry". In the event of multiple "major proportions", it is inconceivable that each individual "major proportion" could - or must - exceed 50 per cent. This therefore supports our finding that it is permissible to define the "domestic industry" in terms of domestic producers of an important, serious or significant proportion of total domestic production. For these reasons, we find that Article 4.1 of the *AD Agreement* does not require Members to define the "domestic industry" in terms of domestic producers representing the majority, or 50+ per cent, of total domestic production.

7.342 There is nothing on the record to suggest that, in the circumstances of this case, 46 per cent of total domestic production is not an important, serious or significant proportion of total domestic production. Accordingly, we reject Brazil's claim that Argentina violated Article 4.1 of the *AD Agreement* by defining "domestic industry" in terms of domestic producers representing 46 per cent of total domestic production.

7.343 Finally, Brazil has argued that if the *AD Agreement* provides no specific benchmark for what would constitute a major proportion of total domestic production, then the investigating authorities are under the obligation to expressly elucidate how they found that a percentage lower than 50 per cent could be considered a major proportion.[225] However, we see no basis for any such obligation in Article 4.1 of the *AD Agreement*.

(c) Conclusion

7.344 In light of the above, we conclude that Argentina did not violate Article 4.1 by defining domestic industry in terms of domestic producers accounting for 46 per cent of total domestic production.

---

[222] *The Concise Oxford Dictionary of Current English* (Clarendon Press, 1995), p. 822.
[223] We recall that, in accordance with Article 17.6(ii) of the *AD Agreement*, if an interpretation is "permissible", then we are compelled to accept it.
[224] If Article 4.1 had referred to "the" major proportion, we may have been required to accept Brazil's interpretation of Article 4.1.
[225] Brazil's first oral statement, para. 87.

Report of the Panel

11. Imposition of Variable Duties - Claims 28 - 30

7.345 The present case concerns the imposition through Resolution No. 574/2000 of variable anti-dumping duties on poultry from Brazil. Claims 28-30 are concerned primarily with the consistency of variable anti-dumping duties with Article 9 of the *AD Agreement*.

(a) Arguments of the Parties / Third Parties

7.346 Brazil claims that Argentina violated Articles 9.2 and 9.3 by imposing a variable anti-dumping duty that can exceed the margin of dumping established by the DCD during its investigation, and that can therefore be collected in "inappropriate" amounts (Claims 28 and 29). This is because the duty is based on the difference between the invoiced f.o.b. price and a "minimum export price" calculated for each exporter found to have dumped and, depending on the amount of the invoiced f.o.b. price for a given import transaction, this difference (and therefore the resultant duty) can sometimes exceed the margin of dumping calculated for the relevant exporter during the investigation. Brazil submits that anti-dumping duties shall not exceed the margin of dumping established during the investigation (in accordance with Article 2 of the *AD Agreement*). Brazil's argument is based on the reference in Article 9.3 to "the margin of dumping as established under Article 2". Brazil asserts that the only provision of Article 2 concerning the establishment of a margin of dumping is Article 2.4.2, which refers to the margin of dumping established "during the investigation phase". According to Brazil, therefore, the "margin of dumping" referred to in Article 9.3 must be the margin of dumping established "during the investigation phase". According to Brazil, the "minimum export price" determined in Resolution No. 574/2000 does not qualify as a dumping margin established under Article 2, since it does not reflect the normal value and export price as provided by the exporters and examined by the investigating authority in the investigation. Brazil asserts that a Member may not assume that the normal value established during the investigation remains unchanged at some future point in time when duties are collected. Brazil submits that market circumstances leading to a change in export price are also likely to lead to a change in normal value. Brazil also asserts that Argentina violated Article 12.2.2 because it failed to explain in its decision to impose an anti-dumping duty how and why it established the "minimum export prices" (Claim 30).

7.347 Argentina submits that the *AD Agreement* does not regulate the type of anti-dumping duties that Members may impose. Argentina asserts that Members have in practice imposed three different types of duty: fixed *ad valorem* duties, fixed specific duties, and variable duties. Argentina asserts that, when duties are imposed prospectively (as Argentina has done), Article 9.3.2 provides for the refund of duties collected in excess of the margin of dumping. Argentina notes that no refund has been requested by Brazilian exporters, so no duty has been collected in excess of the margin of dumping. Argentina also asserts that it imposed a variable duty precisely to ensure that the amount of duty would not exceed the margin of dumping: if export prices became aligned with normal value, no duty would be collected. Argentina further submits that even the use of fixed *ad valorem* duties - which Brazil would have had Argentina impose - can sometimes cause duties to exceed the margin of dumping, because the actual margin of dumping may be lower than that established during the investigation. Argentina asserts that it complied with Article 12.2.2

because the various published determinations referred to submissions made by exporters, and because all essential facts were disclosed to interested parties.

7.348 Canada would have the Panel reject Brazil's claim. Regarding the relationship between Articles 9.2 and 9.3, Canada asserts that an amount of duty permitted under Article 9.3 is "appropriate" for the purpose of Article 9.2. Canada rejects Brazil's argument that a duty must not exceed the margin of dumping established during the investigation. According to Canada, nothing limits the relevant margin of dumping to a static amount found during the period of investigation. Canada asserts that Brazil's approach would undermine the object and purpose of the *AD Agreement* and *GATT* Article VI, which is to provide a mechanism to address unfair trade situations where products are sold at prices below their normal value. In particular, Brazil's approach would allow exporters to dump (after imposition of an anti-dumping measure) at even greater margins than they did during the course of the investigation, without the importing Member being able to impose a level of duty in excess of the margin of dumping found during the investigation. Canada asserts that this undermining of the object and purpose of the *AD Agreement* and *GATT* Article VI would be prevented if Members were entitled to impose duties commensurate with the margin of dumping prevailing at the time the duties are collected. According to Canada, while Members may choose to apply a rate of duty equal to the margin of dumping found in the original investigation, nothing in Article 9.3 compels them to do so.

7.349 The European Communities asserts that the margin of dumping referred to in Article 9.3 need not necessarily be that calculated during the investigation. The European Communities notes that Article 9.3 permits the collection of duties on a retrospective basis, which necessarily entails the calculation of a margin of dumping outside the original period of investigation. The European Communities submits that Brazil's claim would mean that the application of variable anti-dumping duties, or the application of any kind of specific duties, is *per se* inconsistent with Article 9.2. The European Communities disagrees with Brazil since, with the exception of checking for a *de minimis* margin of dumping under Article 5.8, the *AD Agreement* does not require that dumping margins be expressed as a percentage of the export price. Nor does it prescribe any particular type of duties.

7.350 The European Communities submits that the collection of variable duties equal to the difference between the normal value established for the investigation period and the export prices of the shipments made after the imposition of the duties is expressly contemplated in Article 9.4 of the *AD Agreement*. Article 9.4 (ii) lays down rules to calculate the "all-others" rate where the duties applied to the exporters included in the sample are calculated on the basis of prospective normal values. It presupposes, therefore, that the use of such prospective normal values is not inconsistent *per se* with the *AD Agreement*, including with Articles 9.2 and 9.3.

(b) Evaluation by the Panel

7.351 We shall first consider Brazil's Claims 28 and 29, which are based on paragraphs 2 and 3 of Article 9 of the *AD Agreement*, respectively. According to those provisions:

> "9.2 When an anti-dumping duty is imposed in respect of any product, such anti-dumping duty shall be collected in the appropriate amounts in each case, on a non-discriminatory basis on imports of such product from all sources found to be dumped and causing injury,

Report of the Panel

except as to imports from those sources from which price undertakings under the terms of this Agreement have been accepted. (…)

9.3 The amount of the anti-dumping duty shall not exceed the margin of dumping as established under Article 2."

7.352 Sub-paragraphs 1 - 3 of Article 9.3 provide that:

"9.3.1 When the amount of the anti-dumping duty is assessed on a retrospective basis, the determination of the final liability for payment of anti-dumping duties shall take place as soon as possible, normally within 12 months, and in no case more than 18 months, after the date on which a request for a final assessment of the amount of the anti-dumping duty has been made. Any refund shall be made promptly and normally in not more than 90 days following the determination of final liability made pursuant to this sub-paragraph. In any case, where a refund is not made within 90 days, the authorities shall provide an explanation if so requested.

9.3.2 When the amount of the anti-dumping duty is assessed on a prospective basis, provision shall be made for a prompt refund, upon request, of any duty paid in excess of the margin of dumping. A refund of any such duty paid in excess of the actual margin of dumping shall normally take place within 12 months, and in no case more than 18 months, after the date on which a request for a refund, duly supported by evidence, has been made by an importer of the product subject to the anti-dumping duty. The refund authorized should normally be made within 90 days of the above-noted decision.

9.3.3 In determining whether and to what extent a reimbursement should be made when the export price is constructed in accordance with paragraph 3 of Article 2, authorities should take account of any change in normal value, any change in costs incurred between importation and resale, and any movement in the resale price which is duly reflected in subsequent selling prices, and should calculate the export price with no deduction for the amount of anti-dumping duties paid when conclusive evidence of the above is provided." (footnote omitted)

7.353 In examining Brazil's claims, we also consider it necessary to have regard to Article 9.4 of the *AD Agreement*, which provides that:

"9.4 When the authorities have limited their examination in accordance with the second sentence of paragraph 10 of Article 6, any anti-dumping duty applied to imports from exporters or producers not included in the examination shall not exceed:

(i) the weighted average margin of dumping established with respect to the selected exporters or producers or,

(ii) where the liability for payment of anti-dumping duties is calculated on the basis of a prospective normal value, the difference between the weighted average normal value of the selected exporters or producers and the export prices of exporters or producers not individually examined, provided that the authorities shall disregard for the purpose of this paragraph any zero and *de minimis* margins and margins established under the circumstances referred to in paragraph 8 of Article 6. The authorities shall apply individual duties or normal values to imports from any exporter or producer not included in the examination who has provided the necessary information during the course of the investigation, as provided for in subparagraph 10.2 of Article 6."

7.354   We begin by examining Brazil's claim that the variable anti-dumping duties at issue are inconsistent with Article 9.3 because they are collected by reference to a margin of dumping established *at the time of collection* (i.e., the difference between a "minimum export price", or reference normal value, and actual export price). Brazil claims that duties must not exceed the margin of dumping established *during the investigation*. Brazil asserts that "[f]rom the moment the anti-dumping duty is imposed until a review of the imposition of that duty is made, the only margin of dumping available, calculated pursuant to Article 2, is the margin assessed in the investigation, found in the final determination, and informed to all interested parties through a public notice, as provided in Article 12.2 of the *AD Agreement*."[226]

7.355   In addressing this claim, we note that nothing in the *AD Agreement* explicitly identifies the form that anti-dumping duties must take. In particular, nothing in the *AD Agreement* explicitly prohibits the use of variable anti-dumping duties. Brazil's Claim 29 is based on Article 9.3 of the *AD Agreement*. As the title of Article 9 of the *AD Agreement* suggests, Article 9.3 is a provision concerning the imposition and collection of anti-dumping duties. Article 9.3 provides that a duty may not be collected in excess of the margin of dumping as established under Article 2. The modalities for ensuring compliance with this obligation are set forth in sub-paragraphs 1, 2 and 3 of Article 9.3, each of which addresses duty assessment and the reimbursement of excess duties. The primary focus of Article 9.3, read together with sub-paragraphs 1-3, is to ensure that final anti-dumping duties shall not be assessed in excess of the relevant margin of dumping, and to provide for duty refund in cases where excessive anti-dumping duties would otherwise be collected. Our understanding that Article 9.3 is concerned primarily with duty assessment is confirmed by the fact that the broadly equivalent provision in the *SCM Agreement* (i.e., Article 19.4) refers to the "lev[ying]" of duties, and footnote 51 to that provision states that "'levy' shall mean the definitive or final legal **assessment or collection** of a duty or tax" (emphasis added).[227] When viewed in this light, it is not obvious that - as Brazil effectively argues - Article 9.3 prohibits variable anti-dumping duties by ensuring that anti-dumping duties do not exceed the margin of dumping established during "the investigation phase" pursuant to Article 2.4.2. Neither the ordinary meaning of Article 9.3, nor its context (i.e., sub-paragraphs 1-3), supports that view. If Article 9.3 were designed to prohibit the use of variable customs duties, presumably that prohibition would have been clearly spelled out.

---

[226]   Brazil's second written submission, para. 127.

[227]   The Tokyo Round *AD Agreement* is also instructive, since Article 8.3 of that Agreement stated "[t]he amount of the anti-dumping duty must not exceed the margin of dumping as established under Article 2. **Therefore**, if subsequent to the application of the anti-dumping duty it is found that the duty so collected exceeds the actual dumping margin, the amount in excess of the margin shall be reimbursed as quickly as possible" (emphasis added). This provision clearly demonstrates that the general requirement that anti-dumping duties shall not exceed the margin of dumping is concerned with duty assessment.

Report of the Panel

7.356 Brazil relies on Article 2.4.2 of the *AD Agreement* to support its argument that anti-dumping duties may not exceed the margin of dumping established during the investigation. Article 2.4.2 provides in relevant part that "the existence of margins of dumping during the investigation phase shall normally be established on the basis of a comparison of a weighted average normal value with a weighted average of prices of all comparable export transactions or by comparison of normal value and export prices on a transaction-to-transaction basis." Brazil asserts that because Article 9.3 refers to the margin of dumping "as established under Article 2", and because the only provision of Article 2 governing the establishment of a margin of dumping is the abovementioned extract from Article 2.4.2, which refers to the "investigation phase", the margin of dumping relevant for the purpose of Article 9.3 is that established "during the investigation phase". Brazil submits that the margin of dumping is established based on the information collected and examined during the investigation and, in that sense, dumping margins are restricted to the investigation period, as set out in Article 2.4.2 of the *AD Agreement*.

7.357 We consider that Brazil's principal argument misinterprets the reference to "margin of dumping" in Article 9.3. Based on that language, Brazil focuses entirely on Article 2.4.2, and the reference to the "investigation phase" in that provision. However, Article 9.3 does not refer to the margin of dumping established "under Article 2.4.2", but to the margin of dumping established "under Article 2". In our view, this means simply that, when ensuring that the amount of the duty does not exceed the margin of dumping, a Member should have reference to the methodology set out in Article 2. This is entirely consistent with the introductory clause of Article 2, which sets forth a definition of dumping "for the purpose of this Agreement ...". In fact, it would not be possible to establish a margin of dumping without reference to the various elements of Article 2. For example, it would not be possible to establish a margin of dumping without determining normal value, as provided in Article 2.2, or without making relevant adjustments to ensure a fair comparison, as provided in Article 2.4. Thus, the fact that Article 2.4.2, uniquely among the provisions of Article 2, relates to the establishment of the margin of dumping "during the investigation phase" is not determinative of the issue before us, since other provisions of Article 2 do not contain that limitation.[228]

7.358 Our view that Brazil misinterprets the reference to "margin of dumping" in Article 9.3 is supported by the fact that the first sentence of Article 8.3 of the Tokyo Round *AD Agreement* also referred to "the margin of dumping as established under Article 2", even though there was no equivalent of Article 2.4.2 of the *AD Agreement* in the Tokyo Round *AD Agreement*. Under the Tokyo Round *AD Agreement*, therefore, the reference to the "margin of dumping as established under Article 2" must have meant the provisions of Article 2 generally. We see no reason why the same does not remain true of the equivalent provision of the *AD Agreement*. If the

---

[228] Taken literally, Brazil's argument concerning Article 2.4.2 would mean that Article 2.4.2 is the only provision of Article 2 that applies in the context of Article 9.3. This is because Brazil notes that Article 9.3 refers to the "margin of dumping as established under Article 2", and that Article 2.4.2 is the only provision of Article 2 that refers to the establishment of a "margin of dumping". We cannot accept such an approach, however, since it would mean that the provisions of Article 2 governing sales not made in the ordinary course of trade and fair comparisons etc. would not apply in the context of Article 9.3. Although Brazil has asserted that its argument should not be understood in this way (Brazil's second written submission, para. 136), this is the inevitable result of Brazil attaching such prominence to the words "margin of dumping" in Article 9.3.

drafters of the *AD Agreement* had intended to refer exclusively to Article 2.4.2 in the context of Article 9.3, the latter provision would have stated that "the amount of the anti-dumping duty shall not exceed the margin of dumping as established under Article 2.4.2". This is not what Article 9.3 says.

7.359 Brazil's interpretation is also contradicted by the immediate context of Article 9.3. In particular, by interpreting Article 9.3 to mean that anti-dumping duties may not be collected in excess of the margin of dumping established during the initial investigation, Brazil misunderstands the significance of Article 9.4(ii) of the *AD Agreement*, which refers to circumstances "where the liability for payment of anti-dumping duties is calculated on the basis of a prospective normal value". In our view, Article 9.4(ii) is describing the use of variable anti-dumping duties, which are calculated by comparing actual (i.e., at the time of collection) export price with a prospective normal value. Since Article 9.4(ii) expressly envisages the imposition of variable anti-dumping duties, there is no basis for us to find that Argentina's recourse to variable duties (calculated on the basis of "minimum export prices" used as prospective normal values) is necessarily inconsistent with Article 9.3 of the *AD Agreement*.[229]

7.360 We note Brazil's argument that Article 9.4(ii) "refers to cases where duties are assessed on a retrospective basis".[230] However, we see no basis for concluding that *retrospective* duty assessment involves the use of a *prospective* normal value. To the contrary, retrospective duty assessment involves the use of an *actual* normal value established at the time of duty assessment.

7.361 Further contextual support for our approach to Article 9.3 is found in Article 9.3.1, which envisages the collection of anti-dumping duties on a retrospective basis. By definition, the retrospective collection of duties presupposes the calculation of dumping margins on the basis of information for individual shipments or for time-periods outside of the initial investigation period. Furthermore, in emphasising the importance of the margin of dumping established during the investigation, we consider that Brazil has diminished the contextual importance of the refund mechanism provided for in respect of prospective anti-dumping duties. The first sentence of Article 9.3.2 provides that "[w]hen the amount of the anti-dumping duty is assessed on a prospective basis, provision shall be made for a prompt refund, upon request, of any duty paid in excess of the margin of dumping. A refund of any such duty paid in excess of the **actual** margin of dumping shall normally take place within 12 months …" (emphasis added). Thus, Article 9.3.2 provides for a refund of anti-dumping duties collected in excess of the *actual* margin of dumping. The word "actual" is defined *inter alia* as "existing now; current". Accordingly, we understand that the Article 9.3.2 refund mechanism would include refunds of anti-dumping duties paid in excess of the margin of dumping prevailing at the time the duty is

---

[229] We note that the measure at issue calculates anti-dumping duty liability by comparing actual export price with a "minimum export price", which is slightly lower than the normal value established during the investigation. Accordingly, it may not be entirely appropriate to state that the Argentine collection mechanism involves the use of a prospective "normal value". It does, however, involve the use of a prospective reference price, which in our view is sufficient to bring it within the scope of Article 9.4(ii). To conclude otherwise would elevate form over substance, since it would mean that the collection of variable duties calculated by reference to a prospective normal value is permitted, whereas the collection of *lower* duties by reference to a reference price lower than the normal value established during the investigation is not.

[230] Brazil's second written submission, para. 149.

collected. This therefore further undermines Brazil's argument that the only margin of dumping relevant until such time that there is an Article 11.2 review is the margin established during the investigation. If the basis for duty *refund* is the margin of dumping prevailing at the time of duty collection, we see no reason why a Member should not use the same basis for duty *collection*. Brazil has noted that refunds do not imply modification of the duty, and are only available if requested by the importer.[231] While these points may be correct, they do not change the fact that the refund mechanism operates by reference to the margin of dumping prevailing at the time of duty collection. It is this aspect of the refund mechanism that renders it contextually relevant to the issue before us. Accordingly, we see no reason why it is not permissible[232] for a Member to levy anti-dumping duties on the basis of the actual margin of dumping prevailing at the time of duty collection.

7.362 Brazil also asserts that Argentina was not entitled to collect duties on the basis that the normal value calculated during the investigation remained constant thereafter, without considering any possible changes in the prices in the internal market. According to Brazil, it is not unlikely that changes in market conditions or exporter's improvement in productivity create a situation where the price of the product, in the internal market and the export market, is reduced. In other words, if there is a change in export price, there may also be a change in normal value. Again, we disagree. First, because we have already noted that Article 9.4(ii) refers to the use of a prospective normal value. Second, because even fixed *ad valorem* duties collected on a prospective basis are collected on the assumption that *both* normal value and export price (and therefore the margin of dumping) established in the investigation will not change. In any event, a properly designed variable duty system would include a refund mechanism consistent with Article 9.3.2, and would provide for an Article 11.2 changed circumstances review.

7.363 Finally, in support of its argument that the margin of dumping referred to in Article 9.3 is that established during the period of investigation, Brazil asked what would be the purpose of establishing a margin of dumping in the initial investigation if that margin did not circumscribe the amount of duties that could subsequently be collected.[233] Without intending to provide a comprehensive response to this question, we note that, in accordance with Article 5.8 of the *AD Agreement*, there shall be immediate termination of an investigation if the margin of dumping is *de minimis*. Accordingly, one of the principal reasons for establishing a margin of dumping in the investigation is to ensure compliance with Article 5.8.

7.364 For the above reasons, we find that the variable anti-dumping duties at issue are not inconsistent with Article 9.3 simply because they are collected by reference to a margin of dumping established *at the time of collection* (i.e., the difference between a "minimum export price", or reference normal value, and actual export price).[234] Since Brazil has not argued that any of the anti-dumping duties actually collected by the Argentine authorities exceeded the margin of dumping (prevailing at the time of duty collection), we reject Brazil's Claim 29.

---

[231] *Ibid.*, para. 141.
[232] We use this term with particular regard to the Article 17.6(ii) standard of review.
[233] Brazil's second written submission, para. 133.
[234] The scope of this finding is of course limited to the circumstances of the case at hand, which concerns initial duty imposition, and not Article 9.3.2 refund or Article 11 review proceedings.

7.365   Turning to Brazils' Claim 28, which is based on Article 9.2 of the *AD Agreement*, we note that Canada has asserted that an anti-dumping duty that is in conformity with Article 9.3 is necessarily "appropriate" within the meaning of Article 9.2. Brazil agrees with this approach, arguing that "a violation of Article 9.2 is entirely dependent on a violation of Article 9.3".[235] We note that Article 9.3 contains a specific obligation regarding the amount of anti-dumping duty to be imposed, whereas Article 9.2 employs far more general language in referring to the collection of duties in "appropriate" amounts. In particular, Article 9.2 provides no guidance on what an "appropriate" amount of duty may be in a given case. In the absence of any other guidance regarding the appropriateness of the amount of anti-dumping duties, it would appear reasonable to conclude that an anti-dumping duty meeting the requirements of Article 9.3 (i.e., not exceeding the margin of dumping) would be "appropriate" within the meaning of Article 9.2. Since we have already found that Argentina's variable anti-dumping duties are not inconsistent with Article 9.3, and since Brazil has not adduced any additional evidence to the effect that the amount of the anti-dumping duties was not "appropriate", we reject Brazil's Claim 28.

7.366   Brazil further claims (Claim 30) that Argentina violated Article 12.2.2 of the *AD Agreement* because Resolution No. 574/2000 failed to explain how Argentina calculated the "minimum export prices". In our view, once an anti-dumping measure is found to be inconsistent with the substantive provisions of the *AD Agreement*, findings concerning the adequacy of the DCD's notice become immaterial.[236] Accordingly, since we have found that Resolution No. 574/2000 is inconsistent with various substantive provisions of the *AD Agreement*, it is not necessary for us to examine this claim.

(c)   Conclusion

7.367   In light of the above, we conclude that Argentina did not violate Articles 9.2 and 9.3 of the *AD Agreement* by imposing variable anti-dumping duties. In addition, we conclude that it is not necessary for us to examine Brazil's Claim 30.

E.   *Violation of Article VI of GATT 1994 and Article 1 of the AD Agreement*

(a)   Arguments of the Parties

7.368   Brazil considers that Argentina has acted inconsistently with Article VI of the *GATT 1994* and Article 1 of the *AD Agreement*, which only permit anti-dumping measures to be applied under the circumstances provided for in Article VI and pursuant to investigations initiated and conducted in accordance with the *AD Agreement*. Brazil asserts that, because the claims set forth in Section 0 *supra* of this report indicate the violation of various provisions under the *AD Agreement*, Article VI of the *GATT 1994* and Article 1 of the *AD Agreement* are consequently violated.

---

[235]   Brazil's second written submission, para. 124.
[236]   See para. 7.293 *supra*.

Report of the Panel

(b) Evaluation by the Panel

7.369 In examining this issue, we note that a panel "need only address those issues which must be addressed in order to resolve the matter in issue in the dispute."[237] We note that Brazil's claims under Article 1 of the *AD Agreement*, and Article VI of *GATT 1994*, are dependent claims, in the sense that they depend entirely on findings that Argentina has violated other provisions of the *AD Agreement*. There would be no basis to Brazil's claims under Article 1 of the *AD Agreement*, and Article VI of *GATT 1994*, if Argentina were not found to have violated other provisions of the *AD Agreement*. In light of the dependent nature of Brazil's claims under Article 1 of the *AD Agreement*, and Article VI of *GATT 1994*, we see no useful purpose to deciding them.[238] In particular, deciding such dependent claims will provide no additional guidance as to the steps to be undertaken by Argentina in order to implement our recommendation regarding the violations on which they are dependent.

(c) Conclusion

7.370 In light of the foregoing, we consider it unnecessary to examine Brazil's claims under Article VI of the *GATT 1994* and Article 1 of the *AD Agreement*.

VIII. CONCLUSIONS AND RECOMMENDATION

A. Conclusions

8.1 In light of our findings above, we conclude that:

(a) Argentina has acted inconsistently with its obligations under:

(i) Article 5.3 of the *AD Agreement* by determining that there was sufficient evidence of dumping to initiate an investigation (Claims 2, 4 and 6);

(ii) Article 5.8 of the *AD Agreement* by failing to reject the application and promptly terminate the investigation, as soon as the authorities concerned were satisfied that there was not sufficient evidence of injury or threat thereof to justify the initiation of the investigation (Claim 31);

(iii) Article 12.1 of the *AD Agreement* by failing to notify several exporters known to the investigating authority to have an interest in the investigation when that authority was satisfied that there was sufficient evidence to justify the initiation of the anti-dumping investigation (Claim 10);

(iv) Article 6.1.1 of the *AD Agreement* by failing to give several exporters at least 30 days to reply to the dumping questionnaires provided by the investigating authority (Claim 11);

---

[237] Appellate Body Report, *US - Wool Shirts and Blouses*, *supra*, note 67, p. 19.
[238] We note that a similar approach was followed by the panels *Guatemala - Cement II* (Panel Report, *Guatemala - Cement II*, *supra*, note 48, para. 8.296) and *US - DRAMS* (Panel Report, *United States - Anti-Dumping Duty on Dynamic Random Access Memory Semiconductors (DRAMS) of One Megabit or Above from Korea* ("*US - DRAMS*"), WT/DS99/R, adopted 19 March 1999, DSR 1999:II, 521, para. 6.92).

(v) Article 6.1.3 of the *AD Agreement* by not providing the text of the written application to the known exporters and to the Government of Brazil as soon as the investigation was initiated (Claim 14);

(vi) Article 6.8 and Annex II of the *AD Agreement* by disregarding the export price data submitted by certain exporters (Claim 17);

(vii) Article 6.10 of the *AD Agreement* by failing to establish individual margins of dumping for two exporters (Claim 22);

(viii) Article 2.4 of the *AD Agreement* by not making due allowance for differences in freight costs in the normal value established for an exporter (Claim 23);

(ix) Article 2.4 of the *AD Agreement* by not making due allowance for differences in taxation, freight and financial costs in the normal value established for several exporters (Claim 24);

(x) Article 2.4 of the *AD Agreement* by increasing all exporters' normal values by 9.09 per cent to reflect alleged differences in the physical characteristics of poultry sold in Argentina and Brazil (Claim 25);

(xi) Article 2.4.2 of the *AD Agreement* by establishing a dumping margin for two exporters on the basis of an inaccurate weighted average normal value (Claim 27);

(xii) Article 3.1 of the *AD Agreement* by failing to make an objective examination of injury when using different periods to evaluate the relevant economic factors and indices listed in Article 3.4 (Claim 32);

(xiii) Articles 3.1, 3.2, 3.4 and 3.5 of the *AD Agreement* by including non-dumped imports from two exporters in its injury analysis (Claims 34-37); and

(xiv) Articles 3.1 and 3.4 of the *AD Agreement* by failing to evaluate all the relevant economic factors and indices listed in Article 3.4 (Claims 38 and 39).

(b) Argentina has not acted inconsistently with its obligations under:

(i) Article 5.7 of the *AD Agreement* by not considering simultaneously, in the determination whether or not to initiate the investigation, the evidence of both dumping and injury (Claim 9);

(ii) Article 6.1.2 of the *AD Agreement* in not making available promptly to certain Brazilian exporters evidence presented in writing by the other interested parties involved in the investigation (Claim 12);

(iii) Article 6.8 and Annex II of the *AD Agreement* by disregarding normal value data submitted by two exporters (Claim 19);

(iv) Article 6.9 of the *AD Agreement* by not informing the exporters of the essential facts under consideration which formed the basis for the decision whether to apply definitive measures (Claim 21);

(v) Article 2.4 of the *AD Agreement* in fixing the period of investigation for dumping (Claim 26);

(vi) Articles 9.2 and 9.3 of the *AD Agreement* by collecting variable anti-dumping duties on the basis of "minimum export prices" (Claims 28 and 29);

(vii) Article 4.1 of the *AD Agreement* by defining the domestic industry in terms of domestic producers accounting for 46 per cent of total domestic production of poultry in Argentina (Claim 41).

(c) We have concluded that it is not necessary for us to make findings in respect of Brazil's Claims 1, 3, 5, 7, 8, 13, 15, 16, 18, 20, 30, 33, and 40. We also consider it unnecessary to examine Brazil's claims under Article VI of the *GATT 1994* and Article 1 of the *AD Agreement*.

B. Nullification or Impairment

8.2 Under Article 3.8 of the *DSU*, in cases where there is infringement of the obligations assumed under a covered agreement, the action is considered *prima facie* to constitute a case of nullification or impairment of benefits under that agreement. Accordingly, we conclude that to the extent Argentina has acted inconsistently with the provisions of the *AD Agreement*, it has nullified or impaired benefits accruing to Brazil under that Agreement.

C. Recommendation

8.3 Brazil requests that we exercise our discretion under Article 19.1 of the *DSU* to suggest ways in which Argentina could implement our recommendation. Specifically, Brazil requests us to suggest that Argentina repeal Resolution No. 574/2000 imposing definitive anti-dumping measures on eviscerated poultry from Brazil "in light of the numerous outcome-decisive violations of the AD Agreement."[239]

8.4 In considering Brazil's request, we first recall that Article 19.1 of the *DSU* provides in relevant part that:

"When a Panel or the Appellate Body concludes that a measure is inconsistent with a covered agreement, it shall recommend that the Member concerned bring the measure into conformity with that agreement. In addition to its recommendations, the panel or Appellate Body *may suggest ways in which the Member concerned could implement the recommendations*". (emphasis added; footnotes omitted)

8.5 Therefore, by virtue of Article 19.1 of the *DSU*, panels have discretion ("may") to suggest ways in which a Member could implement the relevant recommendation. Clearly, however, a panel is not required to make a suggestion should it not deem it appropriate to do so.

---

[239] Brazil's first written submission, para. 550.

8.6   We have determined that Argentina has acted inconsistently with its obligations under the *AD Agreement* in its imposition of anti-dumping duties on imports of eviscerated poultry from Brazil. We have found these violations to be of a fundamental nature and pervasive.

8.7   In light of the nature and extent of the violations in this case, we do not perceive how Argentina could properly implement our recommendation without revoking the anti-dumping measure at issue in this dispute. Accordingly, we suggest that Argentina repeal Resolution No. 574/2000 imposing definitive anti-dumping measures on eviscerated poultry from Brazil.

ANNEX A

Brazil

	Contents	Page
Annex A-1	First Written Submission of Brazil	A-1851
Annex A-2	First Oral Statement of Brazil	A-1964
Annex A-3	Second Written Submission of Brazil	A-1978
Annex A-4	Replies of Brazil to Questions of the Panel - First Meeting	A-2008
Annex A-5	Second Oral Statement of Brazil	A-2040
Annex A-6	Replies of Brazil to Questions of the Panel - Second Meeting	A-2054
Annex A-7	Comments of Brazil on the Responses of Argentina to the Panel's and to Brazil's Questions - Second Meeting	A-2067

ANNEX A-1

FIRST WRITTEN SUBMISSION OF BRAZIL
(8 August 2002)

TABLE OF CONTENTS

		Page
I.	INTRODUCTION	A-1854
II.	PROCEDURAL BACKGROUND FOR DISPUTE SETTLEMENT IN THIS CASE	A-1858
III.	FACTUAL BACKGROUND	A-1859
IV.	LEGAL ARGUMENTS	A-1861
	A. Anti-Dumping Agreement Standard of Review	A-1861
	B. Initiation of the Anti-Dumping Investigation	A-1863
	1. Articles 5.2, 5.3, 5.7 and 5.8	A-1863
	(a) Facts	A-1864
	(i) Claim 1: Inconsistency with Article 5.2 of the Anti-Dumping Agreement	A-1870
	(ii) Claim 2: Inconsistency with Article 5.3 of the Anti-Dumping Agreement	A-1872
	(iii) Claim 3: Inconsistency with Article 5.8 of the Anti-Dumping Agreement	A-1877
	(iv) Claim 4: Inconsistency with Article 5.3 of the Anti-Dumping Agreement	A-1877

				Page
		(v)	Claim 5: Inconsistency with Article 5.2 of the Anti-Dumping Agreement	A-1880
		(vi)	Claim 6: Inconsistency with Article 5.3 of the Anti-Dumping Agreement	A-1882
		(vii)	Claim 7: Inconsistency with Article 5.8 of the Anti-Dumping Agreement	A-1884
		(viii)	Claim 8: Inconsistency with Article 5.3 of the Anti-Dumping Agreement	A-1884
		(ix)	Claim 9: Inconsistency with Article 5.7 of the Anti-Dumping Agreement	A-1887
		(x)	Claim 31: Inconsistency with Article 5.8 of the Anti-Dumping Agreement	A-1889

C. Conduct of the Anti-Dumping Investigation - Evidentiary and Public Notice Requirements A-1890

1. Article 12.1 .... A-1890

   (a) Facts A-1891

       (i) Claim 10: Inconsistency with Article 12.1 of the Anti-Dumping Agreement A-1891

2. Articles 6.1.1, 6.1.2, 6.1.3 and 6.2 .... A-1893

   (a) Facts A-1893

       (i) Claim 11: Inconsistency with Article 6.1.1 of the Anti-Dumping Agreement ... A-1894

       (ii) Claim 12: Inconsistency with Article 6.1.2 of the Anti-Dumping Agreement ... A-1895

       (iii) Claim 13: Inconsistency with Article 6.2 of the Anti-Dumping Agreement A-1896

       (iv) Claim 14: Inconsistency with Article 6.1.3 of the Anti-Dumping Agreement ... A-1896

3. Articles 6.8, 6.10, 12.2.2 and Annex II A-1899

   (a) Facts A-1900

       (i) Claim 15: Inconsistency with Article 6.8 and Annex II of the Anti-Dumping Agreement A-1903

       (ii) Claim 16: Inconsistency with Article 12.2.2 of the Anti-Dumping Agreement . A-1907

       (iii) Claim 17: Inconsistency with Article 6.8 and Annex II of the Anti-Dumping Agreement A-1909

       (iv) Claim 18: Inconsistency with Article 12.2.2 of the Anti-Dumping Agreement . A-1911

       (v) Claim 19: Inconsistency with Article 6.8 and Annex II of the Anti-Dumping Agreement A-1912

				Page
		(vi)	Claim 20: Inconsistency with Article 12.2.2 of the Anti-Dumping Agreement	A-1915
		(vii)	Claim 22: Inconsistency with Article 6.10 of the Anti-Dumping Agreement	A-1916
	4.	Article 6.9		A-1917
		(a)	Facts	A-1917
		(i)	Claim 21: Inconsistency with Article 6.9 of the Anti-Dumping Agreement	A-1920
D.	Conduct of the Anti-Dumping Investigation and Final Affirmative Determination			A-1922
	1.	Article 2.4 and 2.4.2		A-1922
		(a)	Facts	A-1923
		(i)	Claim 23: Inconsistency with Article 2.4 of the Anti-Dumping Agreement	A-1931
		(ii)	Claim 24: Inconsistency with Article 2.4 of the Anti-Dumping Agreement	A-1932
		(iii)	Claim 25: Inconsistency with Article 2.4 of the Anti-Dumping Agreement	A-1935
		(iv)	Claim 26: Inconsistency with Article 2.4 of the Anti-Dumping Agreement	A-1937
		(v)	Claim 27: Inconsistency with Article 2.4.2 of the Anti-Dumping Agreement	A-1938
	2.	Articles 3.1, 3.4, 3.5 and 12.2.2		A-1939
		(a)	Facts	A-1940
		(i)	Claim 32: Inconsistency with Articles 3.1, 3.4 and 3.5 of the Anti-Dumping Agreement	A-1940
		(ii)	Claim 33: Inconsistency with Article 12.2.2 of the Anti-Dumping Agreement	A-1941
	3.	Articles 3.1, 3.2, 3.4 and 3.5		A-1942
		(a)	Facts	A-1943
		(i)	Claim 34: Inconsistency with Article 3.2 of the Anti-Dumping Agreement	A-1943
		(ii)	Claim 35: Inconsistency with Article 3.1 of the Anti-Dumping Agreement	A-1945
		(iii)	Claim 36: Inconsistency with Article 3.4 of the Anti-Dumping Agreement	A-1945
		(iv)	Claim 37: Inconsistency with Article 3.5 of the Anti-Dumping Agreement	A-1947
	4.	Articles 3.1, 3.4 and 12.2.2		A-1948
		(a)	Facts	A-1948

Report of the Panel

				Page
		(i)	Claim 38: Inconsistency with Article 3.4 of the Anti-Dumping Agreement	A-1948
		(ii)	Claim 39: Inconsistency with Article 3.1 of the Anti-Dumping Agreement	A-1951
		(iii)	Claim 40: Inconsistency with Article 12.2.2 of the Anti-Dumping Agreement	A-1953
	5.	Article 4.1		A-1954
	(a)	Facts		A-1954
		(i)	Claim 41: Inconsistency with Article 4.1 of the Anti-Dumping Agreement	A-1955
E.	Imposition and Collection of Anti-Dumping Duties as a Result of the Anti-Dumping Investigation			A-1956
	1.	Articles 9.2, 9.3 and 12.2.2		A-1956
	(a)	Facts		A-1956
		(i)	Claim 28: Inconsistency with Article 9.2 of the Anti-Dumping Agreement	A-1958
		(ii)	Claim 29: Inconsistency with Article 9.3 of the Anti-Dumping Agreement	A-1959
		(iii)	Claim 30: Inconsistency with Article 12.2.2 of the Anti-Dumping Agreement	A-1960
V.	CONCLUSION AND REQUESTS			A-1961
A.	Conclusion			A-1961
B.	Requests			A-1962

I. INTRODUCTION

1. This submission sets forth Brazil's challenge to the imposition by Argentina of definitive anti-dumping measures on imports of poultry from Brazil, classified under Mercosul tariff line 0207.11.00 and 0207.12.00. Various actions related to the initiation, conduct and imposition of these definitive measures are inconsistent with Argentina's obligations under the General Agreement on Tariffs and Trade 1994 ("GATT 1994") and the Agreement on Implementation of Article VI of GATT 1994 ("Anti-Dumping Agreement").

2. The anti-dumping measures on poultry were imposed following an investigation and determinations made by the Comisión Nacional de Comercio Exterior ("CNCE") and the Dirección de Competencia Desleal ("DCD"). These two agencies share the responsibility for administering the anti-dumping law and investigation procedures in Argentina, with the DCD determining the existence of dumping and calculating dumping margins and the CNCE determining whether the domestic industry has been injured by the allegedly dumped imports.

3. The dumping investigation conducted by the DCD and the imposition of definitive measures have violated Articles 2, 5, 6, 9, 12 and Annex II of the Anti-Dumping Agreement. Brazil's claims, as set out in this submission, regarding the

dumping investigation and the imposition of definitive measures are summarized as follows:

- Petitioner's application presented a calculation to adjust normal value in view of alleged physical characteristic differences between poultry sold to Argentina and poultry sold in Brazil. The application did not offer relevant evidence of such differences contrary to the requirement set out in Article 5.2 **(Claim 1)**. By accepting petitioner's adjustment calculation, Argentina failed to examine the accuracy and adequacy of the evidence presented in the application pursuant to Article 5.3 **(Claim 2)**, and to reject the application as provided in Article 5.8 **(Claim 3)**.

- Argentina acted inconsistently with Article 5.3 **(Claim 4)** by establishing export prices based only on export transactions with prices below normal value.

- Petitioner's application presented export price and normal value data for different periods. Specifically, the application presented normal value data for only one day in 1997 (30 June 1997), which cannot be considered relevant evidence to establish normal value pursuant to Article 5.2 **(Claim 5)**. By calculating a dumping margin by making a comparison between export price and normal value in respect of sales that were not made at as nearly as possible the same time and by establishing normal value for only one day in 1997, Argentina failed to examine the accuracy and adequacy of the evidence provided in the application as required by Article 5.3 (Claim 6), and to reject the application pursuant to Article 5.8 (Claim 7).

- By comparing different periods of data collected for dumping and injury, Argentina incorrectly examined the evidence provided in the application, violating Article 5.3 (Claim 8).

- Argentina has acted inconsistently with Article 5.7 (Claim 9) by not considering, in the determination whether or not to initiate the investigation, the data collected for dumping simultaneously with the data collected for injury.

- Argentina failed to notify seven Brazilian exporters when it was satisfied that there was sufficient evidence to justify the initiation of the anti-dumping investigation. By not notifying these exporters when the investigation was initiated, Argentina acted inconsistently with Article 12.1 (Claim 10).

- Argentina failed to give the seven Brazilian exporters at least 30 days to reply to the dumping questionnaires provided by the DCD in a prima facie violation of Article 6.1.1 (Claim 11). Moreover, the CNCE never notified these seven exporters and never provided them with the injury questionnaire.

- Argentina also failed to promptly make available to the seven Brazilian exporters evidence presented in writing by the other interested parties involved in the investigation, in violation of Article 6.1.2 (Claim 12).

- By failing to give the seven exporters the required time to respond to the questionnaires and not promptly making available to these exporters the evidence presented in writing by the other interested parties involved in the investigation, Argentina did not give these exporters full opportunity for the defense of their interests as required by Article 6.2 (Claim 13).
- Argentina acted inconsistently with Article 6.1.3 (Claim 14) by not providing the text of the written application to the Brazilian exporters and to the Government of Brazil as soon as the investigation was initiated.
- Argentina acted inconsistently with Article 6.8 and Annex II (Claim 15) by disregarding the responses submitted by Brazilian exporters with respect to the description of the product sold to Argentina and in Brazil, and resorting to the normal value adjustment calculation provided by petitioner in the application.
- Argentina acted inconsistently with Article 12.2.2 (Claim 16) by failing to adequately explain in the final determination its decision to disregard the information provided by the exporters regarding the product description and to use instead the normal value adjustment proposed by petitioner.
- Argentina acted inconsistently with Article 6.8 and Annex II (Claim 17) by disregarding the export price data provided by the Brazilian exporters, and resorting to the export price information provided by the Argentinean agency the Dirección de Ganaderia, Secretaria de Agricultura, Ganaderia, Pesca y Alimentación ("Ganaderia").
- Argentina acted inconsistently with Article 12.2.2 (Claim 18) by failing to adequately explain in the final determination its decision to disregard the export price data provided by the Brazilian exporters, and to resort to the export price data provided by the Argentinean agency Ganaderia.
- Argentina acted inconsistently with Article 6.8 and Annex II (Claim 19) by disregarding all normal value information submitted by two Brazilian exporters, and resorting to the information provided by petitioner.
- Argentina acted inconsistently with Article 12.2.2 (Claim 20) by failing to adequately explain in the final determination its decision to disregard all normal value information submitted by two Brazilian exporters, and to resort to the information provided by petitioner.
- Argentina failed to inform the Brazilian exporters of the essential facts under consideration which formed the basis for the decision whether to apply definitive measures, thereby preventing the Brazilian exporters from adequately defending their interests, contrary to the requirement set forth in Article 6.9 (Claim 21).
- Argentina failed to establish individual margins of dumping for two Brazilian exporters, as required by Article 6.10 (Claim 22).

- Argentina acted inconsistently with Article 2.4 (Claim 23) by not making due allowance for differences in freight in the normal value established for two Brazilian exporters.

- Argentina acted inconsistently with Article 2.4 (Claim 24) by not making due allowance for differences in taxation, freight and financial cost in the normal value established for all other exporters.

- Argentina acted inconsistently with Article 2.4 (Claim 25) by incorrectly making allowances to normal value based on alleged physical characteristic differences between the product sold in Brazil and to Argentina.

- Argentina acted inconsistently with Article 2.4 (Claim 26) by imposing an unreasonable burden of proof on three Brazilian exporters by not determining the dumping period of investigation and, thus, allowing these exporters to submit dumping information for the years 1996 through 1999, when the dumping period of investigation was later determined as from January 1998 through January 1999.

- Argentina acted inconsistently with Article 2.4.2 (Claim 27) by establishing a dumping margin based on an incorrect comparison between the export price and the normal value for two Brazilian exporters. Argentina established normal value based only on internal market transactions for which invoices were presented, instead of determining normal value based on all the reported transactions in the internal market for the period. The DCD established the margins of dumping for these two Brazilian exporters on the basis of a comparison of a weighted average statistical sample of normal value with a weighted average of prices of all comparable export transactions.

- Argentina has acted inconsistently with Article 9.2 (Claim 28) and Article 9.3 (Claim 29) by imposing a variable anti-dumping duty that can exceed the margin of dumping established in the final determination.

- Argentina acted inconsistently with Article 12.2.2 (Claim 30) by failing to provide how the "minimum export price" was established in the determination to impose definitive anti-dumping duties.

4. The injury investigation and the final determination by the CNCE violated Articles 3, 4, 5 and 12 of the Anti-Dumping Agreement. Brazil's claims, as set out in this submission, regarding the injury investigation and the imposition of definitive measures are summarized as follows:

- Argentina acted inconsistently with Article 5.8 **(Claim 31)** by failing to reject the application and promptly terminate the investigation, as soon as the CNCE determined in Acta No. 405 that there was insufficient evidence of injury or threat of injury to justify the initiation of the investigation.

- By using different periods to evaluate the relevant economic factors and indices listed in Article 3.4, Argentina failed to make a final injury determination based on positive evidence and involving an objective examination as provided for in Article 3.1, 3.4 and 3.5 **(Claim 32)**.

- Argentina acted inconsistently with Article 12.2.2 **(Claim 33)** by failing to explain in the final determination why the CNCE examined the relevant economic factors and indices listed in Article 3.4 based on different periods.

- The injury analysis in the final determination did not exclude the imports of two Brazilian exporters, even though the DCD considered that these were not "dumped imports". By not excluding the imports of these two Brazilian exporters from the "dumped imports", the CNCE did not properly consider the volume of the "dumped imports", the effect of the "dumped imports" on prices, and the impact of the "dumped imports" on the domestic industry, as provided for in Articles 3.2 **(Claim 34)** and 3.4 **(Claim 36)**. The flawed evaluation of the "dumped imports" indicates that the final injury determination was not based on positive evidence and did not involve an objective examination as required by Article 3.1 **(Claim 35)**.

- By not excluding the imports from these two Brazilian exporters from the "dumped imports", Argentina failed to properly consider injury as prescribed in Article 3.1, and, consequently, did not properly demonstrate the causal link between the "dumped imports" and the injury to the domestic industry as provided for in Article 3.5 **(Claim 37)**.

- Argentina acted inconsistently with Articles 3.4 **(Claim 38)** and 3.1 **(Claim 39)** by failing to evaluate all the relevant economic factors and indices listed in Article 3.4.

- Argentina acted inconsistently with Article 12.2.2 **(Claim 40)** by failing to adequately provide and consider in the final determination the evaluation of all relevant economic factors and indices listed in Article 3.4.

- Argentina has acted inconsistently with Article 4.1 **(Claim 41)** by considering that 46 per cent constituted the major proportion of the total domestic production of poultry in Argentina and, thus, qualified as the domestic industry.

5. By determining dumping, injury and causal link inconsistently with the provisions of the Anti-Dumping Agreement, Argentina has acted inconsistently with Article VI of GATT 1994 and Article 1 of the Anti-Dumping Agreement.

6. In light of these violations by Argentina, which Brazil will demonstrate in detail in this submission, Brazil requests that the Panel issue the findings and recommendations set forth in Part IV of this submission.

II. PROCEDURAL BACKGROUND FOR DISPUTE SETTLEMENT IN THIS CASE

7. On 7 November 2001, the Government of Brazil requested consultations with the Government of Argentina pursuant to Article 4 of the Understanding on Rules and Procedures Governing the Settlement of Disputes ("DSU"), Article XXII of

GATT 1994, Article 17 of the Anti-Dumping Agreement, and Article 19 of the Agreement on Implementation of Article VII of GATT 1994 ("Agreement on Customs Valuation"), concerning the definitive anti-dumping measures on imports of poultry from Brazil.[1]

8. Consultations were held in Geneva on 10 December 2001. Even though consultations allowed a better understanding of the issue, they did not lead to a mutually agreed solution.

9. On 25 February 2002, the Government of Brazil requested the establishment of a panel pursuant to Article XXII of GATT 1994, Article 6 of the DSU, and Article 17 of the Anti-Dumping Agreement, and requested that the panel have standard terms as provided for in Article 7 of the DSU.[2]

10. At its 17 April 2002 meeting, the Dispute Settlement Body ("DSB") established a panel to examine the complaints of the Government of Brazil. The Panel was composed on 27 June 2002.[3]

11. The Panel's terms of reference, pursuant to Article 7 of the DSU, were set as follows:

> "To examine, in light of the relevant provisions of the covered agreements cited by Brazil in document WT/DS241/3, the matter referred by Brazil to the DSB in that document, and to make such findings as will assist the DSB in making the recommendations or in giving the rulings provided for in those agreements."

III. FACTUAL BACKGROUND

12. On 2 September 1997, the Centro de Empresas Procesadoras Avícolas ("CEPA")[4] filed an application for an anti-dumping investigation with the Subsecretaria de Comercio Exterior ("SSCE") alleging that imports of poultry from Brazil were being exported to Argentina at dumped prices and that these imports represented a threat of material injury to the domestic industry.[5] On 23 September 1997, the CNCE issued an opinion regarding the representativeness of the domestic industry and, on 21 October 1997, the SSCE accepted the application presented by CEPA.

13. On 7 January 1998, the Área de Prácticas Comerciales Desleales y Salvaguardias ("APCDS") concluded in its report regarding the viability of the initiation of the investigation that there was unfair trade practice in the form of dumping into the Argentinean market of poultry from Brazil.[6]

14. On 7 January 1998, the CNCE determined in Acta No. 405 that there was not sufficient evidence of injury or threat of injury to justify the initiation of an investigation. In that determination, the data considered was for the period January

---

[1] *Argentina - Definitive Anti-Dumping Duties on Poultry from Brazil: Request for Consultations by Brazil*, WT/DS241/1 (12 Nov. 2001).

[2] *Argentina - Definitive Anti-Dumping Duties on Poultry from Brazil: Request for the Establishment of a Panel by Brazil*, WT/DS241/3 (26 Feb. 2002).

[3] *Argentina - Definitive Anti-Dumping Duties on Poultry from Brazil: Constitution of the Panel Established at the Request of Brazil*, WT/DS241/4 (5 Jul. 2002).

[4] Throughout this submission CEPA is also referred to as the petitioner.

[5] *See*, Exhibit BRA-1.

[6] *See*, Exhibit BRA-2.

1994 through June 1997, taking into account data for the year 1993 as a reference year.[7]

15. More than one month after the CNCE determined that there was insufficient evidence of injury or threat of injury to justify the initiation of the investigation, CEPA presented on 17 February 1998 new and updated information to Secretaria de Industria Comercio y Minería ("SICM").[8] On 18 June 1998, the Dirección General de Asuntos Jurídicos ("DGAJ") sent letter to SSCE stating that the new and updated information presented by CEPA had not been examined when CNCE issued its determination in Acta No. 405 and, thus, DGAJ requested that the CNCE take into account the new information and provide a new determination.[9]

16. On 22 September 1998, the CNCE determined in Acta No. 464 that there was sufficient evidence of threat of injury to justify the initiation of the investigation. The new injury determination considered CEPA's updated information for the period January 1994 through June 1998, taking into account data for the year 1993 as a reference year.[10]

17. On 20 January 1999, the Ministerio de Economia y Obras y Serviços Publicos ("MEOSP") issued Resolution No. 11, a public notice announcing the initiation of the anti-dumping investigation on imports of poultry from Brazil.[11]

18. On 10 February 1999, the CNCE sent letters to the Brazilian exporters Sadia S.A. ("Sadia"), Avipal S.A. Avicultura e Agropecuaria ("Avipal"), Frigorífico Nicolini Ltda. ("Nicolini"), Seara Alimentos S.A. ("Seara"), and Frangosul S.A. Agro Avícola Industrial ("Frangosul") communicating of the initiation of the investigation and requesting that they provide responses to the questionnaires sent by the CNCE, which is separate from the one sent by the SSCE.[12] On 16 February 1999, the SSCE sent letters to the five Brazilian exporters inviting them to participate in a hearing on 25 February 1999 for consultations regarding the initiation of the dumping investigation and for receipt of the questionnaires.[13]

19. On 28 June 1999, the CNCE issued a preliminary affirmative injury determination.[14] On 6 August 1999, the DCD issued a preliminary affirmative dumping determination.[15] On 20 August 1999, the SSCE issued a preliminary affirmative determination on causal link between the alleged dumped imports and the injury caused by these imports on the domestic industry.[16] No provisional measures were imposed.

20. On 15 September 1999, the DCD sent letters to seven Brazilian exporters: Cooperativa Central de Laticínios do Paraná ("CCLP"), Cooperativa Central Oeste Catarinense Ltda. ("Catarinense"),[17] Chapecó Cia. Industrial ("Chapecó"), Cia.

---

[7] See, Exhibit BRA-3.
[8] See, Exhibit BRA-4.
[9] See, Exhibit BRA-5.
[10] See, Exhibit BRA-6.
[11] See, Exhibit BRA-7.
[12] See, Exhibit BRA-8.
[13] See, Exhibit BRA-9. From the documents of the investigation to which Brazil had access to, Brazil was not able to find the SSCE's notification of 16 February 1999 to the Brazilian exporter Sadia.
[14] See, Exhibit BRA-10.
[15] See, Exhibit BRA-11.
[16] See, Exhibit BRA-12.
[17] Catarinense is also known as Aurora.

Minuano de Alimentos ("Minuano"), Perdigão Agroindustrial ("Perdigão"), Comaves Industria e Comércio de Alimentos Ltda. ("Comaves"), and Pena Branca S.A. ("Pena Branca"),[18] that had not been notified of the investigation, inviting them to provide responses to the questionnaire.[19] In this letter, the DCD established, for the first time, the data collection period of the investigation from January 1998 through January 1999.

21. On 23 December 1999, the CNCE issued a final affirmative injury determination.[20] Six months after the final injury determination was issued, the DCD issued a final affirmative dumping determination on 23 June 2000.[21] On 17 July 2000, the SSCE issued a final affirmative determination of causal link between the alleged dumped imports and the injury caused by these imports on the domestic industry.[22]

22. Based upon the final dumping, injury and causal link determinations, the MEOSP issued Resolution No. 574 of 21 July 2000, imposing definitive dumping measures on imports of poultry from Brazil for a period of three years.[23] Such measures took the form of specific anti-dumping duties to be collected as the absolute difference between the FOB price invoiced in any one shipment and a designated "minimum export price" also fixed in FOB terms, to be applied whenever the former price is lower than the latter. The "minimum export price" established for each exporter was US$ 0,92 per kilogram for Sadia, US$ 0,98 per kilogram for Avipal, and US$ 0,98 per kilogram for all other exporters. The Brazilian exporters Nicolini and Seara did not have dumping measures applied since they were found not to be exporting poultry at dumped prices. The public notice also set forth the dumping margins found for Sadia (14.91 per cent), Avipal (15.48 per cent) and all other exporters (8.19 per cent

IV. LEGAL ARGUMENTS

A. Anti-Dumping Agreement Standard of Review

23. The standard of review to be applied by a Panel in examining disputes arising under the Anti-Dumping Agreement is set forth in Article 17.6 of that Agreement. More specifically, Article 17.6 addresses issues relative to the assessment of facts in an investigation and issues relative to the interpretation of the Anti-Dumping Agreement.

24. With regard to factual issues, Article 17.6(i) provides that:

"in its assessment of the facts of the matter, the panel shall determine whether the authorities' establishment of the facts was proper and whether their evaluation of those facts was unbiased and objective. If the establishment of the facts was proper and the evaluation was

---

[18] From the documents of the investigation to which Brazil had access to, Brazil was not able to find the DCD's notification to the Brazilian exporter Pena Branca.
[19] *See*, Exhibit BRA-13.
[20] *See*, Exhibit BRA-14.
[21] *See*, Exhibit BRA-15.
[22] *See*, Exhibit BRA-16.
[23] *See*, Exhibit BRA-17.

unbiased and objective, even though the panel might have reached a different conclusion, the evaluation shall not be overturned;"

25. Article 17.6(i) addresses the Panel's assessment of an authority's establishment and evaluation of the facts. It is a two part standard of review, instructing that the Panel: (1) determine whether the authorities establishment of the facts was proper; and, (2) whether their evaluation of those facts was unbiased and objective.

26. First, to assess whether the facts were properly established involves determining whether the investigating authorities collected relevant and reliable information concerning the issue to be decided. In this particular case, the Panel should first determine whether the Government of Argentina collected, evaluated, and processed facts during the investigation in a manner consistent with the rules provided under the Anti-Dumping Agreement, and, thus, established the facts in a "proper" manner.

27. Second, the Panel should determine whether the Government of Argentina evaluated those facts in an unbiased and objective manner. In this regard, the Panel should consider whether based on the evidence before the Argentinean investigating authorities at the time of the determination, an unbiased and objective investigating authority evaluating that evidence could have reached the conclusions that the Argentinean investigating authorities reached on the matter in question. In that context, the Panel should examine whether all the evidence was considered, including facts which might detract from the decision actually reached by the investigating authorities.

28. The Government of Brazil does not ask the Panel to determine whether another conclusion is possible from the facts that were made available to the Argentinean authorities in the underlying investigation. The factual arguments in this case go directly to the Argentinean Government's improper establishment of the facts and the non-objective and biased evaluation of the facts so as to favor the interests of the domestic industry in a manner inconsistent with the provisions of the Anti-Dumping Agreement.

29. With regard to issues of interpretation of the Anti-Dumping Agreement, Article 17.6(ii) provides that:

> "the panel shall interpret the relevant provisions of the Agreement in accordance with customary rules of interpretation of public international law. Where the panel finds that a relevant provision of the Agreement admits more than one permissible interpretation, the panel shall find the authorities' measure to be in conformity with the agreement if it rests upon one of those permissible interpretations."

30. The first sentence of this provision instructs the Panel to "interpret the relevant provisions of the Agreement in accordance with customary rules of interpretation of public international law". The Appellate Body has repeatedly instructed that Panels are to consider interpretation of the WTO Agreements, including the Anti-Dumping Agreement, in accordance with the principles set out in the Vienna Convention on the Law of Treaties ("Vienna Convention"). Thus, the Panel should first look at the ordinary meaning of the provision in question, in its context, and in light of its object and purpose. The Panel may consider, as supplementary means of interpretation, the preparatory work of the provision, that is, the negotiating history. The Panel should then evaluate whether the Argentinean

interpretation is one that is "permissible" in light of the customary rules of interpretation of international law. If that is not the case, the Panel should reject the interpretation, and the challenged action should be considered inconsistent with the Anti-Dumping Agreement.

31. The Government of Brazil contends that the Argentinean measures challenged in this case are not permissible under the interpretative rules of the Vienna Convention. The Government of Argentina has completely ignored certain legal standards or provisions under the Anti-Dumping Agreement, or acted inconsistently with the relevant provisions beyond any permissible legal interpretation. These aspects of Argentinean practice rest upon interpretation of the Anti-Dumping Agreement that do not reflect good faith and cannot be considered as permissible interpretations.

B. Initiation of the Anti-Dumping Investigation

1. Articles 5.2, 5.3, 5.7 and 5.8

32. Ten claims follow from the facts described below and the legal text of the Anti-Dumping Agreement:

Claim 1: Petitioner's application presented a calculation to adjust normal value based on alleged differences in the physical characteristics of poultry sold to Argentina and poultry sold in Brazil. According to petitioner, the poultry sold to Argentina do not include head and feet and the poultry sold in Brazil include head and feet. As a consequence of this difference, petitioner alleged that the yield rate of eviscerated poultry sold to Argentina is 80 per cent of the live poultry and the yield rate of eviscerated poultry sold in Brazil is 88 per cent of the live poultry. Petitioner presented a calculation where 9.09 per cent is to be applied to the normal value to compensate for the difference between the two products.

Violation of Article 5.2 is based on the fact that the application submitted by petitioner offered no evidence to support: (1) that the poultry sold in Brazil was physically different from the product sold to Argentina; (2) that such alleged physical differences affected price comparability; and (3) that the yield rate of poultry sold in Brazil and to Argentina, as alleged by petitioner in the application, was correct.

Claim 2: By accepting petitioner's calculation to adjust normal value, which was unsubstantiated by relevant evidence, Argentina failed to examine the accuracy and adequacy of the evidence presented in the application and to determine that there was insufficient evidence to justify the initiation, as required by Article 5.3.

Claim 3: Pursuant to claims 1 and 2, Argentina failed to reject the application based on insufficient evidence of dumping to justify proceeding with the case, as provided in Article 5.8.

Claim 4: Argentina acted inconsistently with Article 5.3 by establishing export prices based only on export transactions with prices below normal value.

Claim 5: Petitioner's application presented export price and normal value data based on different periods. Specifically, the application presented normal value for only one day in the period, 30 June 1997. The export price data presented in the application was for January through May 1997 and August 1997. The fact that the export price and normal value data presented in the application were not for sales made at as nearly as possible the same time and that the normal value presented in the application was for only one day in 1997 cannot be considered sufficient relevant evidence to meet the requirements of Article 5.2.

Claim 6: By calculating a dumping margin by making a comparison between export price and normal value in respect of sales that were not made at as nearly as possible the same time and by establishing normal value for only one day in 1997, Argentina failed to examine the accuracy and adequacy of the evidence presented in the application. Thus, Argentina acted inconsistently with Article 5.3 by determining that there was sufficient evidence to justify the initiation of the investigation.

Claim 7: Pursuant to claims 5 and 6, Argentina failed to reject the application based on insufficient evidence of dumping to justify proceeding with the case, as provided in Article 5.8.

Claim 8: For purposes of initiation, the data collected for the dumping analysis was from January through May 1997 and the data collected for the injury analysis was from January 1994 through June 1998. Argentina incorrectly examined the evidence provided in the application by not examining the additional dumping data submitted by petitioner for the period July 1997 through June 1998, and thus violated Article 5.3.

Claim 9: Argentina has acted inconsistently with Article 5.7 by not considering, in the determination whether or not to initiate the investigation, the data collected for dumping simultaneously with the data collected for injury.

Claim 31: Argentina acted inconsistently with Article 5.8 by failing to reject the application and promptly terminate the investigation, as soon as the CNCE determined in Acta No. 405 that there was insufficient evidence of material injury or threat of material injury to justify the initiation of the investigation.

(a) Facts

33. On 7 January 1998, the DCD issued a determination to initiate the dumping investigation on imports of poultry from Brazil.[24] In that determination, the DCD established normal value and export price as follows.

Normal Value

34. The DCD established normal value according to the information provided by petitioner in the application. Petitioner established normal value based on prices published by the Brazilian company JOX Assessoria Agropecuária S/C Ltda. ("JOX")[25] on 30 June 1997, for *chilled* poultry, with head and feet, for the São Paulo wholesale market. The normal value was, thus, established upon prices for only one day in 1997, June 30.[26]

35. The prices published by JOX, and used by Petitioner to establish the normal value were for: (1) fresh poultry sold in the São Paulo distribution market that varied from R$1,05 to R$1,12 (average of R$1,085); (2) fresh poultry sold in the São Paulo wholesale market that varied from R$1,00 to R$1,077 (average of R$1,0385); and,

---

[24] *See*, Exhibit BRA-2.
[25] JOX is a privately owned firm dedicated to providing support market information to the farming industry. JOX produces reports that follow the behaviour of the following markets: eggs, poultry, swine, bovine meat, soybean, and corn. The Brazilian Government and the Brazilian exporters subject to the investigation at issue have no association or participation in JOX.
[26] *See*, Pages 7 and 8 of Exhibit BRA-2.

(3) fresh poultry sold in the São Paulo greater wholesale that varied from R$0,98 to R$1,00 (average of R$0,99). The normal value was obtained by the simple average of these prices (RS$ 1,0378), which was converted into US dollars (US$ 0,957).[27]

36. The table below indicates how the DCD established the normal value:

Product	$Real	US$
Fresh Poultry Distribution	1,085	1,00
Fresh Poultry Wholesale	1,0385	0,958
Fresh Poultry Greater Wholesale	0,990	0,913
Average	1,0378	0,957

Source: Page 9 of Exhibit BRA-2.

Adjustment to Normal Value

37. Based on the price above, the DCD made an adjustment to normal value, proposed by petitioner, to account for differences in the physical characteristics of the product sold in Brazil and to Argentina.

38. According to the suggested adjustment, the average weight of the live poultry raised in Brazil is 2.250 kgs. Petitioner alleged, without presenting any evidence, that the yield of the product in Brazil is 88 per cent and, therefore, out of 1 kg of live poultry 880 gm of eviscerated poultry is obtained, with giblets (heart, stomach, neck and liver), and with head and feet. Petitioner also alleged that the yield of the product sold to Argentina differs from the yield obtained in Brazil. In Argentina the yield of the product is 80 per cent, considering that head and feet are discarded. Petitioner's conclusion was that out of a live poultry weighing 2.250 kgs, for every 1kg, 800 gm of eviscerated poultry is obtained that can actually be sold in the Argentinean market. According to petitioner, the yield rate difference occurs because poultry is sold to Argentina without head and feet while poultry is sold in Brazil with head and feet.[28]

39. Petitioner presented the following adjustment based on this allegation:

Weight of Live Poultry	Yield in Brazil	Eviscerated Poultry sold in Brazil	Yield in Argentina	Eviscerated Poultry Sold in Argentina	Difference
(A)	(B)	(C)=(A) x (B)	(D)	(E)=(A) x (D)	(F) = (C) - (E)
2.250 Kg	88%	1.980 Kg	80%	1.800 Kg	0.180 Kg

Source: Page 9 of Exhibit BRA-2.

40. Petitioner alleged that this yield difference represents 9.09 per cent less poultry that can be sold to Argentina and, therefore, an equivalent adjustment must be made to the normal value price.[29]

41. Petitioner's calculation, which was accepted and used by the DCD, was the following:

---

[27] See, Page 9 of Exhibit BRA-2.
[28] Ibid.
[29] Ibid.

Difference in Yield	Eviscerated Poultry in Brazil	Adjustment
(A)	(B)	(C) = (A) ÷ (B) x 100
0.180 Kg	1.980 Kg	9.09%

Source: Page 9 of Exhibit BRA-2.

42. In order to compare the prices of poultry sold in Brazil (normal value) with the prices of poultry sold to Argentina (export price), the DCD would have to add 9.09 per cent to the price of poultry sold in Brazil to compensate for the fact that poultry in Argentina is sold without head and feet, while poultry in Brazil is sold with head and feet. Petitioner presented no evidence to support this allegation.

43. Based on the proposed adjustment calculation, the DCD established a normal value of US$1.044 per kilogram according to the calculation below.

Normal Value of Poultry US$/kg	Adjustment	Adjustment to Normal Value of Poultry US$/kg	Adjusted Normal Value of Poultry US$/kg
(A)	(B)	(C) = (A) x (B)	(D) = (A) + (C)
0.957	9.09%	0.087	1.044

Source: Page 9 of Exhibit BRA-2.

Export Price

44. The DCD established the export price of the subject merchandise sold in Argentina based on data offered by petitioner for the period of January through May 1997 and August 1997.[30] The source for the export price information submitted by CEPA came from Sysdec and was exclusively for *frozen* poultry sold in Argentina, under Mercosul tariff line 0207.12.00,[31] as shown in the table below:

Period	Volume of Imports - Ton	Value of Imports - US$	Average US$/Ton
January 1997	1,688.01	1,856,202.30	1,099.64
February 1997	1,351.76	1,420,448.69	1,050.81
March 1997	2,091.13	2,220,081.50	1,061.67
April 1997	859.22	862,237.89	1,003.51
May 1997	40.00	40,600.00	1,015.00
Subtotal	6,030.12	6,399,570.38	1,061.27
August 1997	2,847.14	2,608,635.66	916.23
Total	**8,877.26**	**9,008,206.04**	**1,014.75**

Source: Page 10 of Exhibit BRA-2.

45. Out of the information presented by petitioner, the DCD considered that a significant portion of the imports of poultry from Brazil were entering at dumped prices, that is, at prices lower than the price of eviscerated poultry sold in the domestic market of Brazil (normal value).[32]

---

[30] *See*, Page 10 of Exhibit BRA-2.
[31] *See*, Exhibit BRA-1.
[32] *See*, Page 10 of Exhibit BRA-2.

46. The DCD considered that these export prices, below normal value, represented 34.24 per cent of the total volume of imports from January through May 1997 and 28.86 per cent of the total value for the same period.[33]

47. Without justification, the DCD presented a table indicating the export price for the period January through May 1997 for transactions for which the price was below the established normal value.[34]

Period	Volume - Tons	Value - US$	Weighted Average US$/Ton
January 1997	414.37	369,244.86	891.10
February 1997	376.99	307,233.77	814.97
March 1997	495.43	406,077.69	819.65
April 1997	738.21	723,892.40	980.60
May 1997	40.00	40,600.00	1,015.00
Total	2,065.00	1,847,048.72	894.45

Source: Page 11 of Exhibit BRA-2.

48. In the determination, the DCD explained that of the export prices presented for the month of August 1997, 97.97 per cent came into Argentina at prices below the normal value average.[35]

49. By adding the export transactions below normal value in the month of August 1997 to the imports of poultry below normal value for the period January through May 1997, the DCD concluded that 54.68 per cent of the volume (4,854.24 tons) and 48.74 per cent of the value (US$ 4,390,836.38) of imports of poultry from Brazil were coming in at dumped prices.[36]

Period	Tons	Portion of Total Imports	US$	Portion of Total Imports	Weighted Average US$/Ton
	(A)		(B)		(C)=(B)÷(A)
Jan-May & Aug 1997	4,854.24	54.68%	4,390,836.38	48.74%	904.54

Source: Page 11 of Exhibit BRA-2.

50. The DCD also used data provided by the Argentinean agency Delegación II - Unidad Informatica ("DUI") of the SSCE to establish the export price. The data provided by that agency was for the period of August through October 1996.[37]

51. Once again, the DCD considered that a significant portion of the imports for that period were entering at dumped prices, that is, at prices lower than the price of eviscerated poultry sold in the domestic market of Brazil (normal value).[38]

---

[33] Ibid.
[34] See, Page 11 of Exhibit BRA-2.
[35] Ibid.
[36] Ibid.
[37] See, Pages 11 and 12 of Exhibit BRA-2.
[38] See, Page 11 of Exhibit BRA-2.

52. According to the DCD, 26.62 per cent of the volume and 23.47 per cent of the value of eviscerated poultry imported from Brazil during the period of August through October 1996 was at dumped prices.[39]

Period	Tons	Portion of Total Imports	US$	Portion of Total Imports	Weighted Average US$/Ton
Aug-Oct 1996	1,207.915	26.62%	1,162,809.10	23.47%	962.66

Source: Page 12 of Exhibit BRA-2.

Dumping Margin

53. Based on the normal value presented by petitioner and the export price presented by petitioner and by the DUI, the DCD calculated two dumping margins.

54. The first margin considered the normal value as the price of chilled poultry, with head and feet, sold in the São Paulo wholesale market on *30 June 1997*. The aforementioned adjustment calculation, to account for the allegation that all poultry in Brazil was sold with head and feet, was made to this normal value. This margin considered export prices to be the prices of imports below normal value of frozen poultry from Brazil for the period of *August through October 1996*.[40]

Normal Value US$/Kg	Average FOB Price US$/Kg	Dumping Margin
(A)	(B)	(C)=(A)÷(B)
1.044	0.9627	8.45%

Source: Page 12 of Exhibit BRA-2.

55. The second margin considered normal value to be the price of chilled poultry, with head and feet, sold in the São Paulo wholesale market on *30 June 1997*. Again, the aforementioned adjustment calculation, to account for the allegation that all poultry in Brazil was sold with head and feet, was made to this normal value. For the second margin, the DCD established the export price as the price of imports below normal value of frozen poultry from Brazil for the period of *January through May 1997 and August 1997*.[41]

Normal Value US$/Kg	Average FOB Price US$/Kg	Dumping Margin
(A)	(B)	(C)=(A)÷(B)
1.044	0.904536	15.42%

Source: Page 12 of Exhibit BRA-2.

56. The determination to initiate the dumping investigation further provided other margin calculations, without explanation or purpose. One considered the lowest FOB export price in January 1997, as presented by petitioner, and the normal value established for 30 June 1997, as indicated above.[42] The other, considered the lowest

---

[39] See, Pages 11 and 12 of Exhibit BRA-2.
[40] See, Page 12 of Exhibit BRA-2.
[41] Ibid.
[42] See, Pages 12 and 13 of Exhibit BRA-2.

FOB export price in the months of August and September 1996, as presented by the DUI, and the normal value established for 30 June 1997.[43]

Normal Value US$/Kg	Lowest FOB Price in Jan. 1997 US$/Kg	Dumping Margin
(A)	(B)	(C)=(A)÷(B)
1.044	0.76512	36.45%

Source: Page 13 of Exhibit BRA-2.

Normal Value US$/Kg	Lowest FOB Price in Aug/Sept 1996 US$/Kg	Dumping Margin
(A)	(B)	(C)=(A)÷(B)
1.044	0.880	18.64%

Source: Page 13 of Exhibit BRA-2.

Injury

57. On 7 January 1998, the CNCE determined in Acta No. 405 that there was *not* sufficient evidence of injury or threat of injury to justify the initiation of an investigation.[44] The data collection period for the injury analysis was from January 1994 through June 1997, taking into account data for the year 1993 as a reference year.[45]

58. On 17 February 1998, more than one month after the CNCE determined that there was insufficient evidence of injury or threat of injury to justify the initiation of an investigation, CEPA presented new and updated injury information to SICM.[46] On 18 June 1998, the DGAJ sent a letter addressed to the SSCE stating that the new and updated information presented by CEPA had not been examined at the time the CNCE issued its determination in Acta No. 405. The DGAJ requested and directed the CNCE to take into account the new information and to provide a new determination.[47]

59. On 15 July 1998, the SSCE sent a letter addressed to the CNCE for the agency to examine and make a determination based on the new information presented by CEPA.[48] On 24 July 1998, the CNCE requested update of the information presented on February 17 1998, setting a deadline to submit the updated information by 10 August 1998.[49] On 14 August 1998, the CNCE sent a letter to CEPA granting an extension to present the requested information until 20 August 1998.[50] On 26 August 1998, the CNCE sent another letter to CEPA setting 2 September 1998 as the new deadline to present the information requested on their 24 July 1998 letter.[51] On 1 September 1998, CEPA presented the information requested by the CNCE.

---

[43] *See*, Page 13 of Exhibit BRA-2.
[44] *See*, Page 9 of Exhibit BRA-3.
[45] *See*, Page 5 of Exhibit BRA-3.
[46] *See*, Exhibit BRA-4.
[47] *See*, Exhibit BRA-5.
[48] *See*, Exhibit BRA-18.
[49] *Ibid.*
[50] *Ibid.*
[51] *Ibid.*

Report of the Panel

60. On 22 September 1998, the CNCE determined in Acta No. 464 that there was sufficient evidence of threat of injury to justify the initiation of the investigation.[52] The data collection period for the new injury analysis was from January 1994 through June 1998, taking into account data for the year 1993 as a reference year.[53]

(i) Claim 1: Inconsistency with Article 5.2 of the Anti-Dumping Agreement

Text of Article 5.2

61. Article 5.2 governs the contents of an application for initiation of an anti-dumping investigation. The subsequent paragraphs of Article 5.2 list certain specific information regarding a series of factors, which must be included in the application. The text of Article 5.2 of the Anti-Dumping Agreement provides in part that:

> "An application under paragraph 1 shall include evidence of (a) dumping, (b) injury within the meaning of Article VI of GATT 1994 as interpreted by this Agreement and (c) causal link between the dumped imports and the alleged injury. Simple assertion, unsubstantiated by relevant evidence, cannot be considered sufficient to meet the requirements of this paragraph. The application shall contain such information as is reasonably available to the applicant on the following:
>
> (...)
>
> (iii) information on prices at which the product in question is sold when destined for consumption in the domestic markets of the country or countries of origin or export (or, where appropriate, information on the prices at which the product is sold from the country or countries of origin or export to a third country or countries, or on the constructed value of the product) and information on export prices or, where appropriate, on the prices at which the product is first resold to an independent buyer in the territory of the importing Member;
>
> (iv) information on the evolution of the volume of the allegedly dumped imports, the effect of these imports on prices of the like product in the domestic market and the consequent impact of the imports on the domestic industry, as demonstrated by relevant factors and indices having a bearing on the state of the domestic industry, such as those listed in paragraphs 2 and 4 of Article 3."

Legal Argument Relative to Claim 1

62. The chapeau of Article 5.2 requires that an application must include "evidence" of dumping, injury, and the causal relationship between the two.

63. In order to evaluate what kind of information is considered as "evidence", which must be included in an application to initiate an investigation, we turn to the ordinary meaning of the term "evidence". "Evidence" is defined as "the available facts, circumstances, etc. supporting or otherwise a belief, proposition, etc., or

---

[52] *See*, Exhibit BRA-6.
[53] *See*, Page 8 of the "Actualización Informe Técnico Previo a la Apertura" in Exhibit BRA-6.

indicating whether or not a thing is true or valid".[54] More specifically, in a legal context, "evidence" is the "information given personally or drawn from a document etc. and tending to prove a fact or a proposition".[55]

64. From the above interpretation of the term, Brazil understands that an allegation or information provided in the application, without supporting documentation, does not qualify as "evidence". Our understanding comes from the language in Article 5.2 that further qualifies the type of information that is needed in an application. Article 5.2 provides that "simple assertion, unsubstantiated by *relevant evidence*, cannot be considered sufficient to meet the requirements of this paragraph".

65. Thus, an assertion or allegation made by petitioner in the application does not meet the requirement in Article 5.2 for a viable application. A proposition or allegation made by petitioner in an application *must* be accompanied by supporting documentation or information in order to qualify as "evidence". More specifically, Brazil believes that information drawn from a document tending to prove a fact or proposition is the type of information required in an application.

66. With respect to the dumping evidence, the application must include "evidence" on prices at which the product in question is sold when destined for consumption in the domestic markets of the country or countries of origin or export.

67. In the instant case, the application offered no "evidence" to support: (1) that the poultry sold in Brazil was physically different from the poultry sold to Argentina; (2) that the alleged physical characteristic differences affect price comparability; and, (3) the alleged yield rate difference presented by petitioner between the poultry sold in Brazil and to Argentina.

68. In the application, petitioner alleged that the poultry sold in Brazil is physically different from the poultry sold to Argentina. To support this allegation, petitioner attached a report by the Brazilian company JOX, where prices of a kilogram of chilled poultry in São Paulo could be identified. Petitioner further stated that these prices were in Real (Brazilian currency), occurred in three alternatives, and corresponded to prices of "poultry with feet, head and giblets", according to the fax provided by JOX and attached to the application.[56] Then, petitioner affirmed that this difference obligated a calculation to homogenize the comparisons between the prices of poultry sold to Argentina and in Brazil and attached an adjustment calculation.

69. The JOX price report was for chilled poultry sold in São Paulo for 30 June 1997. The fax provided by JOX contained the following explanation regarding its published price of poultry:

> "Pursuant to your letter of 30 July 1997, we inform you that the poultry quotations in our report refer to chilled poultry with head, feet and giblets."[57]

70. The information provided by JOX referred exclusively to prices of chilled poultry, sold in São Paulo, with head, feet and giblets, for one day in 1997. This information did not provide or affirm that all poultry sold in Brazil contain head and feet. It simply stated that the prices published by JOX are for chilled poultry with

---

[54] *The Concise Oxford Dictionary - Ninth Edition*, Oxford University Press, 1995, p. 467.
[55] Ibid.
[56] *See*, Exhibit BRA-1.
[57] Ibid.

head and feet. Petitioner did not demonstrate or provide evidence that all poultry sold in Brazil contains head, feet and giblets. Thus, the application did not include information or evidence of prices at which the product in question is sold when destined for consumption in Brazil.

71. In fact, JOX price publication referred only to *chilled* poultry and not to *frozen* poultry. The normal value information provided by petitioner in the application was for *chilled* poultry, while the information provided in the application to establish export price was for *frozen* poultry. Petitioner provided no explanation or evidence that frozen poultry was not sold in Brazil and that, thus, the prices for *chilled* poultry were the correct prices to be used in the establishment of normal value and in the fair comparison analysis. It is clear that the normal value information provided in the application lacked evidence as to the prices of *frozen* poultry in Brazil.

72. Furthermore and in accordance with petitioner's reasoning for the adjustment calculation, petitioner should have also suggested, and the investigating authority should have considered, an adjustment to compensate for the fact that the price of poultry used to establish normal value was different (*chilled* poultry) from the price of poultry used to establish the export price (*frozen* poultry). No such adjustment was presented and the investigating authority did not inquire about such differences.

73. Moreover, JOX price publication and its explanation of the prices published in its report did not mention whether poultry sold with and poultry sold without head and feet present price differences. No "evidence" was presented by petitioner to support that the alleged physical characteristic difference affects price comparability and, therefore, would warrant an adjustment in the price of poultry in Brazil (normal value). In the application, petitioner made a simple assertion, unsubstantiated by any "evidence", that the alleged physical characteristic differences affect price comparability and that the normal value should, thus, be adjusted.

74. Furthermore, petitioner attached an adjustment calculation to compensate for differences in the physical characteristics of the poultry sold to Argentina and in Brazil, which *assumed* that the yield rate of the eviscerated poultry sold in Brazil was 88 per cent of the live poultry and that the yield rate of the eviscerated poultry sold to Argentina was 80 per cent of the live poultry. Petitioner based its adjustment calculation on these figures without producing any "evidence" to support the alleged yield rate differences.

(ii) Claim 2: Inconsistency with Article 5.3 of the Anti-Dumping Agreement

Text of Article 5.3

75. Article 5.3 of the Anti-Dumping Agreement imposes an obligation on the investigating authority in initiating the investigation. Article 5.3 provides that:

"The authorities shall examine the accuracy and adequacy of the evidence provided in the application to determine whether there is sufficient evidence to justify the initiation of an investigation"

Legal Argument Relative to Claim 2

76. Based on Article 5.3, the investigating authorities must examine the accuracy and adequacy of the evidence provided in the application to determine whether that evidence is *sufficient* to justify the initiation of an investigation.

77. As mentioned above, the information provided by JOX referred exclusively to prices of chilled poultry, sold in São Paulo, with head, feet and giblets, for one day in 1997. Petitioner used this information as evidence to establish normal value, as if this information represented the overall price of poultry sold in Brazil. The information in the JOX price publication did not provide or affirm that all poultry sold in Brazil contains head, feet and giblets. Thus, the evidence presented did not correspond to prices at which the product in question was sold when destined for consumption in Brazil. Brazil considers that the price information provided by JOX was not sufficient evidence to make an adjustment to the price of poultry in Brazil and, thus, was not sufficient to justify the initiation of the investigation.

78. With respect to what constitutes "sufficient evidence" to justify the initiation of an anti-dumping investigation, Brazil agrees with the standard set by the Panel in *Mexico - HFCS*:

> "With respect to the question of whether the evidence may be deemed sufficient under the AD Agreement for purposes of initiation, we note the findings of the Panel in Guatemala - Cement, which took into account the reasoning of the Panel in United States - Softwood Lumber. We recognize that, because the Appellate Body reversed the Guatemala - Cement Panel's conclusion on the issue of whether the dispute was properly before it, that Panel's conclusions in this regard have no legal status. However, the Panel's report sets out a standard that we consider instructive in this case:
>
>> "7.54. What constitutes "sufficient evidence" to justify the initiation of an anti-dumping investigation is not defined in the ADP Agreement. In this case, of course, we are bound by the requirements of Article 17.6(i) of the ADP Agreement as the standard of review applicable to our examination of the Ministry's decision to initiate. Article 17.6(i) provides:
>>
>>> "in its assessment of the facts of the matter, the panel shall determine whether the authorities' establishment of the facts was proper and whether their evaluation of those facts was unbiased and objective. If the establishment of the facts was proper and the evaluation was unbiased and objective, even though the panel might have reached a different conclusion, the evaluation shall not be overturned"
>>
>> 7.55 The Panel in United States - Measures Affecting Imports of Softwood Lumber From Canada considered much the same questions as faces us here in a dispute challenging the self-initiation of a countervailing duty investigation, on the basis, inter alia, of allegedly insufficient evidence to warrant initiation. The Panel observed:

Report of the Panel

> "In analyzing further what was meant by the term "sufficient evidence", the Panel noted that the quantum and quality of evidence to be required of an investigating authority prior to initiation of an investigation would necessarily have to be less than that required of that authority at the time of making a final determination. At the same time, it appeared to the Panel that "sufficient evidence" clearly had to mean more than mere allegation or conjecture, and could not be taken to mean just "any evidence". In particular, there had to be factual basis to the decision of the national investigative authorities and this factual basis had to be susceptible to review under the Agreement. Whereas the quantum and quality of evidence required at the time of initiation was less than that required to establish, pursuant to investigation, the required elements of subsidy, subsidized imports, injury and causal link between subsidized imports and injury, the Panel was of the view that the evidence required at the time of initiation nonetheless had to be relevant to establishing these same Agreement elements."[58]

79. Even though the quantum and quality of evidence to be required of an investigating authority for purposes of initiating an investigation is less than that required of that authority to make a preliminary or final determination, the "sufficient evidence" needed to justify the initiation of an investigation has to be more than mere allegation.

80. In the present case, petitioner tried to make the explanation presented by JOX, that the price published in its report for *chilled* poultry with head and feet, into evidence that all poultry sold in Brazil is chilled and includes head and feet. The investigating authority incorrectly accepted the explanation provided by JOX as evidence that all poultry sold in Brazil is chilled and contains head and feet.

81. Petitioner also alleged that it was necessary to compensate this difference in physical characteristic and assumed such differences affect price comparability. The investigating authority accepted petitioner's allegation as true, even though no evidence was presented to support that the alleged physical differences affect price comparability.

82. From the allegation that the physical differences affect price comparability, petitioner presented a calculation to adjust normal value based on differences in yield rate of eviscerated poultry sold in those markets. Petitioner alleged that the yield rate of eviscerated poultry sold in Brazil is 88 per cent of the live poultry and that the yield rate of eviscerated poultry sold to Argentina is 80 per cent of the live poultry. The investigating authority accepted petitioner's calculation even though no evidence was presented to support these yield rates.

---

[58] Mexico - Anti-Dumping Investigation of High Fructose Corn Syrup (HFCS) from the United States, 28 January 2000, WT/DS132/R, at para. 7.94 (adopted on 21 November 2001) ("*Mexico - HFCS*"). The Panel's findings on the Claim related to Article 5.3 were not appealed.

83. In the instant case, Brazil does not request that the Panel evaluate anew the evidence and information before the investigating authorities at the time it decided to initiate. Rather, we agree with the Panel in *Guatemala - Cement I* that the Panel is to:

> "(...) examine whether the evidence relied on by the Ministry was sufficient, that is, whether an unbiased and objective investigating authority evaluating that evidence could properly have determined that sufficient evidence of dumping, injury and causal link existed to justify the initiation of an investigation."[59] (emphasis added)

84. In this case, the insufficient evidence presented or the lack of evidence thereof indicates that an unbiased and objective investigating authority would have found that petitioner's allegations in the application were not supported by sufficient evidence to justify the initiation of an investigation.

85. The Panel in *Guatemala - Cement I* further stated that:

> "In our view, in assessing whether there is sufficient evidence of dumping to justify the initiation, an investigating authority may not ignore the provisions of Article 2 of the ADP Agreement. Article 5.2 of the Agreement requires an application to include sufficient evidence of "dumping" and Article 5.3 requires a determination that there is "sufficient" evidence to justify the initiation. Article 2 of the ADP Agreement sets forth the technical elements of a calculation of dumping, including the requirements for determining normal value, export price, and adjustments required for a fair comparison. In our view, the reference in Article 5.2 to "dumping" must be read as a reference to dumping as it is defined in Article 2. This does not, of course, mean that the evidence provided in the application must be of the quantity and quality that would be necessary to make a preliminary or final determination of dumping. However, evidence of the relevant **type** is, in our view, required in a case such as this one where it is obvious on the face of the application that normal value and export price alleged in the application will require adjustments in order to effectuate a fair comparison. At a minimum, there should be some recognition that a fair comparison will require such adjustments"[60] (emphasis added by the Panel)

86. In order for the DCD to have accepted that an adjustment to normal value was warranted, it should have required that relevant evidence of the *type* of poultry sold in Brazil and to Argentina be presented in the application. In that respect, we again cite the Panel in *Guatemala - Cement I*:

> "(...)The subject matter, or **type**, of evidence needed to justify initiation is the same as that needed to make a preliminary or final

---

[59] *Guatemala - Anti-Dumping Investigation Regarding Portland Cement from Mexico*, 19 June 1998, WT/DS60/R, at para. 7.57 (adopted on 25 November 1998) ("*Guatemala - Cement I*") DSR 1998:IX, 3797. The Appellate Body reversed the Panel's conclusion in *Guatemala - Cement I* on the issue of whether the dispute was properly before it. *Guatemala - Anti-Dumping Investigation Regarding Portland Cement from Mexico*, 2 November 1998, WT/DS60/AB/R, at para. 90 (adopted on 25 November 1998) ("*AB - Guatemala - Cement I*") DSR 1998:IX, 3767.

[60] *Guatemala - Cement I*, DSR 1998:IX, 3797, at para. 7.64.

Report of the Panel

determination of dumping, although the quality and quantity is less. (...)"[61] (emphasis added by the Panel)

87. In the instant case, the JOX publication for prices of *chilled* poultry sold in São Paulo with head, feet and giblets for 30 June 1997 was not representative of normal value prices of *frozen* poultry sold in Brazil and, thus, did not qualify as the *type* of evidence needed to justify the initiation of an investigation. Furthermore, petitioner presented no evidence to support that the normal value price of poultry in Brazil was different from the export price of Brazilian poultry sold to Argentina. Petitioner's proposed adjustment to normal value price took into account a yield rate for eviscerated poultry sold in those markets that was not supported by any evidence. Based on these facts, Argentinean authorities failed to examine the accuracy and adequacy of the evidence provided in the application when they decided that there was sufficient evidence of normal value in the application to justify the initiation of an investigation.

88. In that sense, the Panel in *Guatemala - Cement II* provided an appropriate conclusion as to the imposition of Article 5.3 on investigating authorities:

> "We would like to emphasize that we do not expect investigating authorities at the initiation phase to ferret out all possible differences that might affect the comparability of prices in an application or perform or request complex adjustments to them. *We do however expect that, when from the face of an application it is obvious that there are substantial questions of comparability between the export and home market prices being compared, the investigating authority will at least acknowledge that differences in the prices generate questions with regards to their comparability, and either give some consideration as to the impact of those differences on the sufficiency of the evidence of dumping or seek such further evidence as might be necessary to do so.*"[62] (emphasis added)

89. In the present case, the investigating authority neither gave consideration as to the impact of the possible differences on the sufficiency of the evidence presented nor did it seek further evidence as it clearly was necessary to do so.

90. Furthermore, Article 5.3 requires that the investigating authority examine the accuracy and adequacy of the evidence that is, in fact, provided in the application. In the present case, *no evidence* was presented by petitioner to support the allegation: (1) that the alleged physical characteristic differences between the poultry sold to Argentina (without head and feet) and the poultry sold in Brazil (with head and feet) affect price comparability that would warrant an adjustment in the price of poultry in Brazil (normal value); and, (2) that the yield rate presented by petitioner and used to calculate the adjustment to normal value was accurate.

---

[61] *Guatemala - Cement I*, at para. 7.77.
[62] *Guatemala - Definitive Anti-Dumping Measures on Grey Portland Cement from Mexico*, 24 October 2000, WT/DS156/R, DSR 2000:XI, 5295, at para. 8.40 (adopted on 17 November 2000) ("*Guatemala - Cement II*").

(iii) Claim 3: Inconsistency with Article 5.8 of the Anti-Dumping Agreement

Text of Article 5.8

91. The relevant part of Article 5.8 of the Anti-Dumping Agreement sets forth that:

"An application under paragraph 1 shall be rejected and an investigation shall be terminated promptly as soon as the authorities concerned are satisfied that there is not sufficient evidence of either dumping or of injury to justify proceeding with the case (...)"

Legal Argument Relative to Claim 3

92. As stated under the legal arguments relative to claims 1 and 2, petitioner offered no substantial evidence in the application to support the allegation: (1) that there exists physical characteristic differences between the poultry sold to Argentina and the poultry sold in Brazil; (2) that the alleged physical characteristic differences affect price comparability; and, (3) that the yield rate difference alleged by petitioner to calculate the adjustment to normal value was accurate.

93. Petitioner based its allegation on the prices published by the Brazilian company JOX for chilled poultry, with head and feet, sold in the São Paulo wholesale market. The DCD accepted petitioner's alleged adjustment to normal value without examining the adequacy and accuracy of the evidence presented in the application. In fact, the investigating authority accepted petitioner's suggested calculation to normal value even though *no* evidence was presented to support the allegation that the physical differences between the product sold in Brazil and to Argentina affect price comparability and that the yield rate proposed by the petitioner and used in the adjustment calculation was accurate.

94. Pursuant to claims 1 and 2, by not having rejected the application due to insufficient evidence to justify proceeding with the case, Argentina has violated Article 5.8 of the Anti-Dumping Agreement.

(iv) Claim 4: Inconsistency with Article 5.3 of the Anti-Dumping Agreement

Text of Article 5.3

95. Article 5.3 of the Anti-Dumping Agreement provides that:

"The authorities shall examine the accuracy and adequacy of the evidence presented in the application to determine whether there is sufficient evidence to justify the initiation of an investigation."

Legal Argument Relative to Claim 4

96. In the determination to initiate the dumping investigation, the DCD calculated export price from the data offered by petitioner for the period of January through May 1997 and August 1997 and the data provided by the DUI for the period of August through October 1996.

Report of the Panel

97. From that data, the DCD considered that a significant portion of the imports of poultry from Brazil were entering at dumped prices, that is, at prices lower than the price of eviscerated poultry in the domestic market of Brazil (normal value). Without justification, the DCD excluded the export prices for the import transactions, which were above the normal value and established the export price for purposes of initiation based only on the transactions, which were below the normal value.

98. By doing so, the DCD incorrectly established the export price and, consequently, made a skewed comparison of the export price with the normal value, in establishing the margin of dumping.

99. According to Article 5.3, authorities must consider, based on the evidence presented in the application, whether there is sufficient evidence that indicates the existence of dumping and injury to the domestic industry that would justify the initiation of an investigation. Thus, to determine whether there is an indication of dumping and injury, authorities must base their determination on the evidence presented in the application.

100. By selecting certain export transactions from the total export transactions presented by petitioner in the application, authorities failed to examine the accuracy and adequacy of *all* the evidence that was presented in the application, pursuant to Article 5.3 of the Anti-Dumping Agreement.

101. Article 5.3 specifically requires the investigating authority to examine the "accuracy and adequacy *of the evidence presented in the application...*". In this claim, Brazil does not argue that Argentina failed to "examine" evidence outside the scope of the application. What is argued here is that Argentina was obligated, consistent with the Agreement, to base its determination on its assessment of the facts of the matter which were before it.

102. Furthermore, Article 5.3 requires authorities to examine the accuracy and adequacy of the evidence in the application in order to determine whether there is sufficient evidence of *dumping*, injury and causal link to justify the initiation of an investigation. Examination of the dumping evidence, as provided in Article 5.3, introduces the concept of "dumping" as defined in Article 2 of the Anti-Dumping Agreement.

103. In particular, Article 2.4 establishes how a fair comparison between export price and normal value is made and Article 2.4.2 provides for how margins of dumping must be established. Article 2.4.2 states in part that:

> "(...) the existence of margins of dumping during the investigation phase shall normally be established on the basis of a comparison of a weighted average normal value with a weighted average of prices of *all* comparable export transactions (...)" (emphasis added)

104. Under this method, authorities are required to compare the weighted average normal value with the weighted average of prices of *all* comparable export transactions, and not only those export transactions for which prices are below the normal value.

105. By excluding the export transactions, for which prices were at or above the normal value price, in determining whether there was sufficient evidence of *dumping*, the investigating authority adopted a method that would always result in a dumping margin. This method adopted by the Argentinean authorities resulted in the establishment of an incorrect export price and in an unfair comparison between the

export price and the normal value, contrary to the requirements in Articles 2.4 and 2.4.2.

106. Our understanding of Article 2.4.2 comes from the following reasoning by the Appellate Body in *AB - EC - Bed Linen*:

> "(...) Here, we emphasize that Article 2.4.2 speaks of "*all*" comparable export transactions. As explained above, when "zeroing", the European Communities counted as zero the "dumping margins" for those models where the "dumping margin" was "negative". As the Panel correctly noted, for those models, *the European Communities counted "the weighted average export price to be equal to the weighted average normal value ... despite the fact that it was, in reality, higher than the weighted average normal value."* By "zeroing" the "negative dumping margins", the European Communities, therefore, *did not take fully into account the entirety of the prices of some export transactions, namely, those export transactions involving models of cotton-type bed linen where "the negative dumping margins" were found. Instead, the European Communities treated those export prices as if they were less than what they were. This, in turn, inflated the result from the calculation of the margin of dumping.* Thus, the European Communities did not establish "the existence of margins of dumping" for cotton-type bed linen on the basis of a comparison of the weighted average normal value with the weighted average of prices of *all* comparable export transactions - that is, for *all* transactions involving *all* models or types of the product under investigation. Furthermore, *we are also of the view that a comparison between export price and normal value that does not take fully into account the prices of all comparable export transactions - such as the practice of "zeroing" at issue in this dispute - is not a "fair comparison" between export price and normal value, as required by Article 2.4 and Article 2.4.2."*[63] (emphasis added)

107. Similar to what happened in that case, here the Argentinean authorities, by excluding the export prices that were at or above the normal value, did not fully take into account the entirety of the prices of the export transactions and treated the excluded transactions as if they were less than what they really were. This method not only inflated the dumping margin but also disregarded the evidence presented in the application.

108. Argentina's decision to initiate the investigation pursuant to this method was based on a biased and non-objective evaluation of the facts before it, inconsistent with the standard in Article 17.6(i) of the Anti-Dumping Agreement.

109. Because the method adopted by the Argentinean authorities in the establishment of the export price, the comparison between export price and normal value and in the establishment of a dumping margin did not fully take into account the prices of *all* the comparable export transactions reported in the application, Argentina violated Article 5.3 of the Anti-Dumping Agreement.

---

[63] *European Communities - Anti-Dumping Duties on Imports of Cotton-Type Bed Linen from India*, 1 March 2001, WT/DS141/AB/R, DSR 2001:V, 2049, at para. 55 (adopted on 12 March 2001) ("*AB - EC - Bed Linen*").

(v) Claim 5: Inconsistency with Article 5.2 of the Anti-Dumping Agreement

Text of Article 5.2

110. Pertinent language of Article 5.2 provides that:

"An application under paragraph 1 shall include evidence of (a) dumping, (b) injury within the meaning of Article VI of GATT 1994 as interpreted by this Agreement and (c) causal link between the dumped imports and the alleged injury. Simple assertion, unsubstantiated by relevant evidence, cannot be considered sufficient to meet the requirements of this paragraph. The application shall contain such information as is reasonably available to the applicant on the following: (...)"

Legal Argument Relative to Claim 5

111. Petitioner presented in the application data with different periods for export price and normal value. Normal value was based on the price of chilled poultry, with head and feet, sold in the São Paulo wholesale market for only one day in 1997, June 30. Export price was based on the export price data from Sysdec statistics for the period January through May 1997 and August 1997. The data presented by petitioner in the application, and used to calculate a dumping margin, was inconsistent with Article 5.2 in at least two different ways.

112. First, because the normal value and export price information provided were for transactions which were *not* made at as nearly as possible the same time, the application failed to include sufficient evidence of "dumping" as required in Article 5.2.

113. Article 5.2 of the Anti-Dumping Agreement requires an application to include sufficient evidence of "dumping". The reference in Article 5.2 to "dumping" introduces the concept of "dumping" as defined in Article 2 of the Anti-Dumping Agreement. Article 2 is the provision that sets forth the technical elements of a calculation of dumping, including the requirements for determining normal value, export price, and adjustments required for a fair comparison. Article 2.1 of the Anti-Dumping Agreement provides the following definition of the term "dumping":

"For the purposes of this Agreement, a product is to be considered as being *dumped*, i.e. introduced into the commerce of another country at less than its normal value, if the *export price* of the product exported from one country to another *is less than the comparable price* in the ordinary course of trade, for the like product destined for the consumption in the exporting country". (emphasis added)

114. The succeeding provisions in Article 2 set forth, in detail, information and methodologies to be used in the determination of whether "dumping" exists. In particular, Article 2.4 of the Anti-Dumping Agreement sets out how a fair comparison between normal value and export price is to be made. The *chapeau* of Article 2.4 provides in part that:

"A fair comparison *shall* be made between the export price and the normal value. This comparison *shall* be made at the same level of trade, normally at the ex-factory level, and *in respect of sales made at as nearly as possible the same time. (...)*" (emphasis added)

115. Article 2.4 requires that a fair comparison be made "*in respect of sales made at as nearly as possible the same time.*" From the language in Article 2.4, it is clear that the timing of the sales transactions may have implications in respect of the comparability of prices of export and home market transactions.

116. In the instant case, the normal value presented in the application was for only one day in 1997 (June 30), while the export price data presented covered the prices of export transactions for a period of six months in 1997 (January through May 1997 and August 1997). The establishment of normal value based on one single day (30 June 1997) cannot be used as parameter for a fair comparison with the export price determined for two periods of time with more than 30-days each (one for January through May 1997 and the other for August 1997), none of which included the one day used to establish the normal value.

117. Because prices can vary for a certain period, a comparison between an average of the export prices for a much longer period with only one price for normal value cannot be considered a fair comparison. According to Article 2.4, for a fair comparison to occur and for "dumping" to be established, export price and normal value have to be compared "*in respect of sales made at as nearly as possible the same time*". In order to have complied with the "dumping" evidence requirement in Article 5.2, petitioner should have presented normal value information for an equivalent period of time as that presented for the export price data.

118. Furthermore, Article 2.4.2 of the Anti-Dumping Agreement provides the basis of comparison between normal value and export price in establishing the existence of "dumping" margins. Relevant part of Article 2.4.2 states that:

> "(...) the existence of margins of dumping (...) shall normally be established on the basis of a comparison of a weighted average normal value with a weighed average of prices of *all comparable* export transactions or by comparison of the normal value and export prices on a transaction-to-transaction basis". (emphasis added)

119. In order to understand the meaning of Article 2.4.2, the term "comparable" has to be defined. According to plain text interpretation, "comparable" means to "be able to be compared", "fit to be compared" or "worth comparing".[64] The term "compare" is defined as to "express similarities in", "estimate the similarity or dissimilarity of", or "be equal or equivalent to".[65]

120. Therefore, a fair comparison between export price and normal value must be made on the basis of comparable transactions, that is, transactions that are fit to be compared or equivalent transactions.

121. One cannot estimate similarity or dissimilarity or assess the relation between two elements if one does not establish the basis for such comparison. That basis is established in Article 2.4, which requires that the comparison be made "*in respect of sales made at as nearly as possible the same time*".

122. The determination of the normal value based on prices for one single day in 1997 cannot be used as basis for a fair comparison in the establishment of whether or not there exists a dumping margin.

---

[64] *The Concise Oxford Dictionary - Ninth Edition*, Oxford University Press, 1995, p. 269.
[65] *The Concise Oxford Dictionary - Ninth Edition*, Oxford University Press, 1995, p. 270.

123. Brazil understands that even though evidence provided in the application is not the same, in terms of quantity and quality, as that necessary to make a preliminary or final determination of dumping, evidence of the relevant *type* of information is required in a case where the normal value presented in the application is based on a single price for the year.

124. Second, Article 5.2 requires that the application contain normal value and export price information "as is reasonably available to the applicant". In that regard, Brazil understands that normal value information for all of 1996 and 1997 was reasonably available to the petitioner. However, petitioner only provided in the application normal value information for one day in 1997 (June 30). Brazil believes petitioner had access to normal value information for all of 1996 and 1997 in view of the fact that petitioner provided on 26 July 1999 updated information on normal value for the period 1998 through January 1999. That spreadsheet presented normal value price information for three days in each of the twelve months of 1998 and two days in January 1999.[66] The normal value information was accompanied by the respective daily JOX price publication.

125. This demonstrates that JOX poultry price publication was reasonably available to petitioner and that normal value information for all of 1996 and 1997 could have been submitted in the application, since that information too was reasonably available. However, petitioner decided to include only normal value information for one day in 1997, June 30.

126. By not providing in the application information that was reasonably available to petitioner, the requirement set forth in Article 5.2 was not satisfied.

(vi) Claim 6: Inconsistency with Article 5.3 of the Anti-Dumping Agreement

Text of Article 5.3

127. Article 5.3:

"The authorities shall examine the accuracy and adequacy of the evidence provided in the application to determine whether there is sufficient evidence to justify the initiation of an investigation"

Legal Argument Relative to Claim 6

128. Regarding Claim 6, under Article 5.3 of the Anti-Dumping Agreement, the Panel should first consider the requirements of Article 5.2 concerning the evidence and information that must be contained in the application for initiation of a dumping investigation.

129. As stated in Claim 5 of this submission, petitioner presented in the application data with different periods for export price and normal value. Normal value was based on the price of *chilled* poultry, with head and feet, sold in the São Paulo wholesale market for 30 June 1997, and export price was established for the period January through May 1997 and August 1997.

130. In the determination to initiate the dumping investigation, the DCD established normal value based on the normal value data presented in the application

---

[66] *See*, Exhibit BRA-19.

for chilled poultry, with head and feet, sold in the São Paulo wholesale market for 30 June 1997. The DCD established export price based on the data offered by petitioner for the period January through May 1997 and August 1997 and the export data provided by the Argentinean agency DUI for the period August through October 1996.

131. The DCD failed to examine the accuracy and adequacy of the evidence provided in the application when it found that there was sufficient evidence to establish normal value and, thus, the existence of dumping, to justify the initiation of the investigation.

132. First, in assessing whether there is sufficient evidence of "dumping" in the application to justify the initiation, the investigating authority may not ignore the provisions of Article 2 of the Anti-Dumping Agreement, which defines and provides for the determination of "dumping". In particular, Article 2.4 of the Anti-Dumping Agreement requires that a *fair comparison* be made between the export price and the normal value *in respect of sales made at as nearly as possible the same time*.

133. Had the DCD examined the accuracy and adequacy of the evidence provided in the application, it would have realized that the normal value data in the application was for only one day in 1997 (June 30) and that the export price data provided was for a period of six months in 1997 (January though May 1997 and August 1997). Because prices vary over a period of time, a fair comparison must be made in respect of sales made at as nearly as possible the same time. The normal value data submitted in the application was for a period that was not equivalent to the period of the export price data provided in the application.

134. Furthermore, the authorities went beyond the scope of the data provided in the application and extended the period for the export transactions, in order to establish the export price. In the determination to initiate the investigation, the DCD established the export price based on data covering a period of nine months (six months of data provided by petitioner and three months of data provided by the DUI). Thus, the normal value was established in accordance with the information presented in the application (price of chilled poultry on 30 June 1997) but the export price was established based on the information presented by petitioner (January through May 1997 and August 1997) *and* the information provided by the DUI (August through October 1996). This clearly indicates that the investigating authority did not rely on the information provided in the application to determine that there was sufficient evidence of "dumping" to justify the initiation of the investigation.

135. In addition, the authority determined that there was sufficient evidence of dumping based on export price and normal value information in respect of sales that were *not* made at as nearly as possible the same time.

136. Brazil understands that even though evidence provided in the application is not the same, in terms of quantity and quality, as that necessary to make a preliminary or final determination of dumping, evidence of the relevant *type* of information is required in a case where the normal value presented in the application is based on a single price for the year. If authorities had examined the accuracy and adequacy of the evidence provided in the application they would have required that petitioner provide prices of poultry for the entire period under analysis in order to correctly make a fair comparison with export prices for the same period.

137. Second, because petitioner presented normal value information for only one day in 1997, the evidence in the application did not fulfill the requirement of

Article 5.2 that petitioner include information in the application that is reasonably available to it. As indicated in the arguments relative to Claim 5, petitioner could have presented normal value information for all of 1996 and 1997 from the available JOX publication. However, petitioner only presented normal value information for one day in the period.

138. By not accurately examining the evidence in the application and by adding export price information not provided in the application to determine the initiation of the investigation, the DCD acted inconsistently with Article 5.3 of the Anti-Dumping Agreement.

(vii) Claim 7: Inconsistency with Article 5.8 of the Anti-Dumping Agreement

Text of Article 5.8

139. Article 5.8 of the Anti-Dumping Agreement sets forth that:

"An application under paragraph 1 shall be rejected and an investigation shall be terminated promptly as soon as the authorities concerned are satisfied that there is not sufficient evidence of either dumping or of injury to justify proceeding with the case (...)"

Legal Argument Relative to Claim 7

140. Pursuant to claims 5 and 6 above, petitioner presented in the application insufficient evidence to establish normal value. This evidence was necessary to indicate the existence of dumping. Based on the insufficient normal value evidence presented by petitioner, the DCD incorrectly decided to initiate the investigation without examining the accuracy and adequacy of the evidence presented in the application.

141. In view of the lack of evidence to support the normal value alleged by petitioner in the application, the DCD failed to reject the application and, thus, violated Article 5.8 of the Anti-Dumping Agreement.

(viii) Claim 8: Inconsistency with Article 5.3 of the Anti-Dumping Agreement

Text of Article 5.3

142. Article 5.3:

"The authorities shall examine the accuracy and adequacy of the evidence provided in the application to determine whether there is sufficient evidence to justify the initiation of an investigation"

Legal Argument Relative to Claim 8

143. The dumping found in the determination to initiate the investigation was based on: (1) the price of poultry sold in Brazil on 30 June 1997 (normal value); and, (2) the price of imports of poultry into Argentina from Brazil for the period August through October 1996, January through May 1997 and August 1997 (export price).

144. The injury found in the determination to initiate the investigation was based on data for the period January 1994 through June 1998.

145. Regarding the data collection period for injury, the CNCE first examined injury in Acta No. 405 based on the data collected for the period January 1994 through June 1997. Based on the data for that period, Acta No. 405 did not find sufficient evidence of injury or threat of injury to the domestic industry. When the CNCE rectified its determination in Acta No. 464, the data collection period for the injury analysis was extended by one year and went from January 1994 through June 1998. Acta No. 464 found sufficient evidence of *threat* of injury to justify the initiation of the investigation.

146. In the causal link determination to initiate the investigation, the SICM explained that the APCDS based its dumping determination on elements included in the application that originally corresponded to information for the period of January through June 1997.[67] The SICM further pointed out that subsequent to the dumping determination, petitioner provided additional, updated information including data for all of 1997 and the first semester of 1998.[68] However, the additional data was submitted by petitioner[69] on 17 February 1998, more than one month after the APCDS determined the existence of dumping on 7 January 1998.[70] The dumping determination to initiate the investigation was never updated to take into account petitioner's new information.

147. The different data collection periods for dumping and injury considered by the investigative authorities in the decision to initiate indicate that the Argentinean authorities failed to examine the accuracy and adequacy of the *evidence provided in the application* in its determination that there was *sufficient evidence of causal link* to justify the initiation of the investigation.

148. Article 5.3 of the Anti-Dumping agreement requires authorities to examine the accuracy and adequacy of the *evidence provided in the application,* in order to determine whether there is sufficient evidence to justify the initiation of an investigation. Clearly, from the facts stated above, the APCDS did not consider petitioner's new information submitted on 17 February 1998 and, accordingly, did not update its dumping determination to initiate the investigation. Thus, the investigative authorities failed to examine the accuracy and adequacy of the *evidence provided in the application.*

149. Article 5.3 also refers to the sufficient "evidence" (in the application) that is needed to justify the initiation of an investigation. The "evidence" mentioned in Article 5.3 is that provided in Article 5.2, which states that:

> "An application (...) shall include *evidence* of (a) dumping, (b) injury (...) and (c) a *causal link* between the dumped imports and the alleged injury. (...)" (emphasis added)

150. Because the APCDS did not update its dumping determination to initiate the investigation with the new information provided by petitioner on 17 February 1998, the SICM could not have found that there was *sufficient evidence of causal link* between the dumped imports on June 1997 and the threat of injury on June 1998.

---

[67] *See,* Page 2 of Exhibit BRA-20.
[68] *See,* Page 4 of Exhibit BRA-20.
[69] *See,* Exhibit BRA-4.
[70] *See,* Exhibit BRA-2.

151. In Acta No. 405, the CNCE did not find sufficient evidence of injury or threat of injury to the domestic industry for the period January 1994 through June 1997. Since Acta No. 405 found that there was not sufficient evidence of injury or threat of injury, it is fair to assume that the dumping found by the APCDS, for the period of January through June of 1997, was not causing injury or threat of injury to the domestic industry on June 1997.

152. The new information provided by petitioner on 17 February 1998 was the basis for the CNCE's new injury determination in Acta No. 464. Based on the data collection period of January 1994 through June 1998, Acta No. 464 found sufficient evidence of *threat* of injury to justify the initiation of the investigation. However, the dumping determination had not been updated with the new information provided by petitioner.

153. By not considering the new information provided by petitioner in the dumping analysis, how could the APCDS determine that, in fact, there was dumping? Furthermore, if the dumping found for the period January through June 1997 was not causing injury or threat of injury to the domestic industry on June 1997, how could the SICM determine that the dumping found for the period January through June 1997 was causing *threat* of injury on June 1998?

154. In order to verify that there was *threat* of injury from the imports at dumped prices, the dumping data collected and analyzed would also have to have been extended until June 1998. The DCD did not examine whether there was dumping in the second semester of 1997 and/or the first semester of 1998.

155. For that purpose, Article 3.7 of the Anti-Dumping Agreement provides a good basis for what facts and circumstances are needed in regarding the existence of *threat* of material injury.

> "A determination of a threat of material injury shall be based on facts and not merely on allegation, conjecture or remote possibility. The change in circumstances which would create a situation in which the dumping would cause injury must be clearly foreseen and imminent."

156. More specifically, Article 3.7 indicates that the change in circumstances, which would create a situation in which the dumping would cause injury, must be clearly foreseen and imminent. Footnote 10 of Article 3.7 provides as example "convincing reason to believe that there will be in the near future substantially increased importation of the product at dumped prices."

157. In the present case, Acta No. 405 established that until June 1997 there was no sufficient evidence of injury or threat of injury. From June 1997 until June 1998, there was no foreseen and imminent change in circumstances that created a situation in which the dumped imports in June 1997 were causing *threat* of injury to the domestic industry in June 1998 (end of the data collection period for the injury analysis).

158. Contrary to Article 5.3, the DCD and the SICM failed to examine the accuracy and adequacy of the *evidence provided in the application* by not examining the additional dumping data submitted by petitioner for the period July 1997 through June 1998. By comparing different periods for dumping and injury, the SICM failed to make an accurate and adequate examination of the *causal link evidence* provided in the application.

(ix) Claim 9: Inconsistency with Article 5.7 of the Anti-Dumping Agreement

Text of Article 5.7

159. Articles 5.7 of the Anti-Dumping Agreement sets forth that:

"The evidence of both dumping and injury shall be considered simultaneously (a) in the decision whether or not to initiate an investigation, and (b) thereafter, during the course of the investigation, starting on a date no later than the earliest date on which in accordance with the provisions of the Agreement provisional measures may be applied."

Legal Argument Relative to Claim 9

160. The data collection period for dumping was established by the DCD as 30 June 1997 for normal value, and August through October 1996, January through May 1997 and August 1997 for export price. The data collection period for injury was established by the CNCE from January 1994 through June 1998.

161. With respect to the data collection period for injury, the CNCE first examined injury in Acta No. 405 based on the data collected for the period January 1994 through June 1997. Based on the data for that period, Acta No. 405 did not find sufficient evidence of injury or threat of injury to the domestic industry. When the CNCE rectified its determination in Acta No. 464, the data collection period for the injury analysis was extended by one year and went from January 1994 through June 1998. Acta No. 464 found sufficient evidence of *threat* of injury to justify the initiation of an investigation.

162. In the causal link determination to initiate the investigation, the SICM explained that the APCDS based its dumping determination on elements included in the application that originally corresponded to information for the period of January through June 1997. The SICM further pointed out that subsequent to the dumping determination, petitioner provided additional, updated information including data for all of 1997 and the first semester of 1998. However, the additional data was submitted by petitioner on 17 February 1998, more than one month after the APCDS determined the existence of dumping on 7 January 1998. The dumping determination to initiate the investigation was never updated to take into account petitioner's new information.

163. The different data collection periods for dumping and injury considered by the Argentinean authorities in the decision to initiate the investigation was inconsistent with Article 5.7 in at least two different ways.

164. First, and as shown above, the data collected for the dumping analysis went only until June 1997. The CNCE determined that there was sufficient evidence of *threat* of injury from the injury data collected until June 1998.

165. CNCE's Acta No. 405 established that there was no material injury or threat of material injury to the domestic industry for the period January 1994 through June 1997. Thus, the dumping found on June 1997 was not causing injury or threat of injury on June 1997. In order to verify that there was *threat* of injury on June 1998 from the imports at dumped prices, the data collection period for the dumping analysis would also have to have been extended until June 1998.

Report of the Panel

166. The CNCE's new injury determination in Acta No. 464 found *threat* of injury to the domestic industry based on the new data presented by petitioner for the second semester of 1997 and the first semester of 1998. The dumping period, which was examined by the DCD for purposes of the initiation, did not consider petitioner's new information provided on 17 February 1998 and only took into account prices until June 1997.

167. From the facts above, how could the SICM have found threat of injury on June 1998 if the dumped imports on June 1997 were not causing injury or threat of injury on June 1997? This could only have happened if the APCDS had updated its dumping analysis to take into account petitioner's new information, which the APCDS did not.

168. The different periods examined by the DCD and the CNCE in determining whether there was sufficient evidence of dumping and injury, indicates that the dumping and injury evidence was not considered simultaneously in the decision whether or not to initiate the investigation.

169. Second, Argentina failed to comply with Article 5.7 of the Anti-Dumping Agreement by not considering the evidence of both dumping and injury simultaneously *in the same decision* to initiate the investigation.

170. According to the facts, the APCDS determined in its report of 7 January 1998 that there was sufficient evidence of dumping in the export transactions of poultry from Brazil into Argentina. On 22 September 1998, the CNCE determined in Acta No. 464 that there was sufficient evidence of *threat* of injury to justify the initiation of the investigation. On 20 January 1999, the MEOSP issued Resolution No. 11, a public notice announcing the initiation of an anti-dumping investigation on imports of poultry from Brazil.

171. As shown in the paragraph above, the evidence of dumping and injury were considered at different times. Sufficient evidence of dumping was determined on 7 January 1998 and sufficient evidence of threat of injury was determined on 22 September 1998, more than eight months after the dumping consideration. To this regard, Article 5.7 of the Anti-Dumping Agreement sets forth that:

> "The evidence of both dumping and injury shall be considered simultaneously (a) in the decision whether or not to initiate an investigation (...)"

172. Article 5.7 of the Anti-Dumping Agreement mandates that *in the decision to initiate an investigation*, the investigating authority consider the evidence of dumping and injury simultaneously. According to plain language interpretation, the term "simultaneous" is defined as "occurring or operating at the same time".[71]

173. In the present case, the authorities considered the evidence of injury more than eight months after the dumping evidence was considered, which cannot be interpreted as being considered at the same time.

174. Based on the arguments above, Argentina has violated Article 5.7 of the Anti-Dumping Agreement by not considering the evidence of dumping and injury simultaneously in the decision to initiate the investigation.

---

[71] *The Concise Oxford Dictionary - Ninth Edition,* Oxford University Press, 1995, p. 1294.

(x) Claim 31: Inconsistency with Article 5.8 of the Anti-Dumping Agreement

Text of Article 5.8

175. The relevant part of Article 5.8 of the Anti-Dumping Agreement sets forth that:

> "An application under paragraph 1 shall be rejected and an investigation shall be terminated promptly as soon as the authorities concerned are satisfied that there is not sufficient evidence of either dumping or of injury to justify proceeding with the case (...)"

Legal Argument Relative to Claim 31

176. Article 5.8 requires the investigating authorities to reject the application as soon as the investigating authorities are satisfied that there is not sufficient evidence of dumping or injury.

177. According to the plain text meaning of the term "satisfied" and the interpretation of Article 5.8, authorities shall reject an application when the evidence provided therein does not "adequately meet, fulfill or comply with conditions"[72] that indicate that dumping or injury exist.

178. When the CNCE issued Acta No. 405, it had no doubt from the evidence presented in the application that the there was no injury or threat of injury to justify the initiation. Acta No. 405 provided an examination and the reasoning why the conditions to meet the necessary injury standard were not met.

179. Brazil affirms that the CNCE's negative injury determination in Acta No. 405 was the moment which the CNCE was "satisfied" that there was not sufficient evidence of injury to justify proceeding with the case and, therefore, the CNCE should have promptly rejected the application.

180. More specifically, we do not believe that Acta No. 405 was merely an opportunity given by the Argentinean authority for petitioner to provide more information and amend the application. If the CNCE wanted petitioner to provide more information, the CNCE should have sent a letter, requesting petitioner to do so, similarly to what it had previously done.[73] Instead, the CNCE issued a determination based on the evidence presented in the application that the imports of poultry were not injuring or threatening to injure the domestic industry.

181. From the moment the CNCE determined that there was insufficient evidence to justify the initiation of the investigation, the CNCE should have rejected the application and waited for the domestic industry to submit a *new* application with revised and updated information for both injury and dumping.

182. Furthermore, Article 5.8 requires that the investigating authority reject the application "promptly as soon as" it is satisfied that there is not sufficient evidence to justify proceeding with the case. In that respect, Article 5.8 requires that the rejection of the application be carried out or performed without delay. However, instead of rejecting the application, as required by Article 5.8, the CNCE was requested to examine the new information submitted by CEPA more than 30 days after the

---

[72] *The Concise Oxford Dictionary - Ninth Edition,* Oxford University Press, 1995, p. 1226.
[73] *See,* Exhibit BRA-18.

negative injury determination was issued. As provided in the facts related to this claim, Acta No. 405 was issued on 7 January 1998 and petitioner presented new and updated information to SICM on 17 February 1998, more than a month after the CNCE issued the negative injury determination to initiate the investigation.

183. To this regard, we point out language found in the Argentinean Anti-Dumping Regulation (Decree No.2121/94) that provides timeframes for the rejection of an application by the investigating authorities:

> "Art. 38 - The competent authority shall notify the petitioner of any error or omission in the application within 30 business days of presentation of the application. The petitioner shall have 15 business days from the date of the notification to provide the corrections. If the petitioner does not provide the requested corrections within this period, the application shall be rejected without any further proceedings." [74]

184. The Argentinean Anti-Dumping Regulation in effect during the investigation established that if petitioner did not provide the requested corrections within the period of notification, the application must be rejected without any further proceedings.

185. According to the facts related to these claims, the CNCE requested on 24 July 1998 that CEPA update the information presented on 17 February 1998. CEPA presented the requested information on 2 September 1998, a period in excess of the 15-day requirement set out in Article 38 of the Decree No. 2121/94.

186. Brazil does not contend that Acta No. 405 was a notification or opportunity given to petitioner to provide corrections to the application. Acta No. 405 was the moment that the CNCE arrived at a decision or conclusion that the evidence in the application indicated that there was no injury or threat of injury to the domestic industry. Once the CNCE was satisfied that there was not sufficient evidence of injury to justify the initiation of the investigation, it should have rejected the application without delay as required in Article 5.8 of the Anti-Dumping Agreement.

187. If Argentina understands that Acta No. 405 was a notification or opportunity given to petitioner to amend an error or omission in the application, then the Argentinean authorities did not comply with the timeframe required in its own anti-dumping regulations to reject the application.

C. Conduct of the Anti-Dumping Investigation - Evidentiary and Public Notice Requirements

1. Article 12.1

188. **Claim 10:** Argentina failed to notify seven Brazilian exporters when it was satisfied that there was sufficient evidence to justify the initiation of an anti-dumping investigation. By not notifying these exporters when the investigation was initiated, Argentina acted inconsistently with Article 12.1 of the Anti-Dumping Agreement.

---

[74] *See*, Exhibit BRA-21.

(a) Facts

189. On 20 January 1999, the MEOSP issued Resolution No. 11/1999 announcing the initiation of the anti-dumping investigation on imports of poultry from Brazil.[75] On 10 February 1999, the CNCE sent letters to five Brazilian exporters Sadia, Avipal, Nicolini, Seara, and Frangosul communicating of the initiation of the investigation and requesting that they provide responses to the questionnaires sent by the CNCE.[76] On 16 February 1999, the SSCE sent letters to the same five Brazilian exporters inviting them to participate in a hearing on 25 February 1999 for consultations regarding the initiation of the dumping investigation and for receipt of the questionnaires.[77]

190. On 15 September 1999, the DCD sent letters to other Brazilian exporters CCLP, Catarinense, Chapecó, Minuano, Perdigão, Comaves, and Pena Branca notifying of the investigation and requesting that they provide responses to the questionnaire.[78] The CNCE never notified nor provided its questionnaire to these exporters.

(i) Claim 10: Inconsistency with Article 12.1 of the Anti-Dumping Agreement

Text of Article 12.1

191. Article 12.1 provides as follows:

"When the authorities are satisfied that there is sufficient evidence to justify the initiation of an anti-dumping investigation pursuant to Article 5, the Member or Members the products of which are subject to such investigation and other interested parties known to the investigating authorities to have an interest therein shall be notified and a public notice shall be given."

Legal Argument Relative to Claim 10

192. Article 12.1 is a general provision that requires public notice and notification to interested parties known to the investigating authorities.

193. The first part of Article 12.1 establishes a time reference for when the authorities should give public notice and notify the Member and interested parties. This time reference is set for the moment when the authorities are satisfied that there is sufficient evidence to justify the initiation of the investigation.

194. Brazil understands that a public notice was given when Resolution No. 11/99 was issued announcing the initiation of the investigation. However, Article 12.1 requires that in addition to a public notice, a *notification* be given when the authorities are satisfied that there is sufficient evidence to justify the initiation of an investigation. Notification of the initiation of the investigation to the Member the products of which are subject to such investigation was given on 10 February 1999,

---

[75] *See*, Exhibit BRA-7.
[76] *See*, Exhibit BRA-8.
[77] *See*, Exhibit BRA-9.
[78] *See*, Exhibit BRA-13. From the documents of the investigation to which Brazil has access to, Brazil was not able to find the DCD's notification to the Brazilian exporter Pena Branca.

when the CNCE sent the letter to the five Brazilian exporters and on 16 February 1999, when the SSCE sent letters to the five Brazilian exporters.

195. However, the other seven exporters, that were also participating in the investigation, were notified of the initiation and of the need to submit responses to the questionnaire eight months after the investigation had been initiated. Notification occurred on 15 September 1999, when the DCD sent letters to the Brazilian exporters CCLP, Catarinense, Chapecó, Minuano, Perdigão, Comaves and Pena Branca requesting their responses to the questionnaire.

196. In light of this delay, Brazil believes that the notification to the seven exporters did not comply with Article 12.1 because it was not made once the investigation was initiated.

197. The second part of Article 12.1 establishes who has to be notified: the Members of the product of which are subject to the investigation *and* other interested parties known to the investigating authorities to have an interest therein. According to Article 6.11 of the Anti-Dumping Agreement, "interested parties" include:

> "(i) *an exporter or foreign producer* or the importer of a product subject to investigation, or a trade or business association a majority of the members of which are producers, exporters or importers of such product;
>
> (ii) the government of the exporting Member; and
>
> (iii) a producer of the like product in the importing Member or a trade and business association a majority of the members of which produce the like product in the territory of the importing member" (emphasis added)

198. Thus, the exporters or foreign producers of a product subject to investigation must be notified of the initiation.

199. More specifically, the second part of Article 12.1 requires that the investigating authority notify other *known parties* to have an interest in the initiation. Out of the seven exporters notified by the DCD on 15 September 1999, at least five (Comaves, Catarinense, Minuano, Chapecó and Perdigão) were known to the investigating authority at the time the investigation was initiated. Brazil knows this to be a fact because on 7 January 1998, the APCDS concluded, in its report regarding the viability of the initiation of the investigation, that there was dumping into the Argentinean market of poultry exports from Brazil. This report listed ten Brazilian exporters, among them Comaves, Catarinense, Minuano, Chapecó, and Perdigão, five of the seven Brazilian exporters that were notified eight months after the investigation had initiated.[79]

200. Furthermore, Argentinean authorities and Argentinean importers of poultry from Brazil, who were also participating in the investigation, knew who the Brazilian exporters of poultry were for the dumping period of investigation.

201. In view of the fact that the seven Brazilian exporters were notified of the investigation eight months after it had been initiated and that these exporters were interested parties *known* to the investigating authorities, Argentina has incurred in a *prima facie* violation of Article 12.1 of the Anti-Dumping Agreement.

---

[79] *See*, Page 5 of Exhibit BRA-2.

2. Articles 6.1.1, 6.1.2, 6.1.3 and 6.2

202. The following four claims arise from the facts described below:

Claim 11: Argentina failed to give the seven Brazilian exporters at least 30 days to reply to the dumping questionnaires provided by the DCD in a *prima facie* violation of Article 6.1.1. Moreover, the CNCE never notified these seven exporters and never provided them with injury questionnaires.

Claim 12: Argentina also failed to promptly make available to the seven Brazilian exporters evidence presented in writing by the other interested parties involved in the investigation, in violation of Article 6.1.2.

Claim 13: By failing to give the seven exporters the required time to respond to the questionnaires and not promptly making available to these exporters the evidence presented in writing by the other interested parties involved in the investigation, Argentina did not give these exporters full opportunity for the defense of their interests as required by Article 6.2.

Claim 14: Argentina acted inconsistently with Article 6.1.3 by not providing the text of the written application to the Brazilian exporters and to the Government of Brazil as soon as the investigation was initiated.

(a) Facts

203. On 20 January 1999, the MEOSP issued Resolution No. 11/1999 announcing the initiation of the anti-dumping investigation on imports of poultry from Brazil.[80] On 10 February 1999, the CNCE sent letters to the Brazilian exporters Sadia, Avipal, Nicolini, Seara, and Frangosul communicating the initiation of the investigation and requesting that they provide responses to the questionnaires sent by the CNCE.[81] On 16 February 1999, the SSCE sent letters to the five Brazilian exporters inviting them to participate in a hearing on 25 February 1999 for consultations regarding the initiation of the dumping investigation and for receipt of the questionnaires.[82] The DCD and the CNCE never provided the text of the written application to the five Brazilian exporters and to the Government of Brazil as soon as the investigation was initiated.

204. On 28 June 1999, the CNCE issued in Acta No. 531 an affirmative preliminary injury determination.[83] On 6 August 1999, the DCD issued an affirmative preliminary dumping determination.[84] On 20 August 1999, the SSCE issued an affirmative preliminary determination of causal link between dumping and the injury to the domestic industry.[85]

205. On 15 September 1999, eight months after the investigation was initiated, the DCD sent letters to seven other Brazilian exporters: CCLP, Catarinense, Chapecó, Minuano, Perdigão, Comaves, and Pena Branca, notifying of the investigation and requesting that they provide responses to the questionnaire.[86] The letter sent by the DCD to the seven Brazilian exporters required that they provide responses to the questionnaire for the period of January 1998 through January 1999 within 20 days

---

[80] *See*, Exhibit BRA-7.
[81] *See*, Exhibit BRA-8.
[82] *See*, Exhibit BRA-9.
[83] *See*, Exhibit BRA-10.
[84] *See*, Exhibit BRA-11.
[85] *See*, Exhibit BRA-12.
[86] *See*, Exhibit BRA-13.

Report of the Panel

from receipt of the notification.[87] The CNCE never notified or provided injury questionnaires to these seven exporters. Moreover, the DCD and the CNCE never provided the text of the written application to these exporters.

(i) Claim 11: Inconsistency with Article 6.1.1 of the Anti-Dumping Agreement

Text of Article 6.1.1

206. Article 6.1.1 provides that:

"Exporters or foreign producers receiving questionnaires used in an anti-dumping investigation shall be given at least 30 days for reply. Due consideration, should be given to any request for an extension of the 30-day period and, upon cause shown, such an extension should be granted whenever applicable."

Legal Argument Relative to Claim 11

207. Article 6.1.1 of the Anti-Dumping Agreement is the only evidentiary provision in the Agreement that establishes a specific timeframe for the accomplishment of an obligation. The first part of Article 6.1.1 requires that the investigating authority give at least 30 days for exporters or foreign producers to respond to the questionnaires.

208. As explained before in this submission, two agencies share the responsibility for administering the anti-dumping law and investigation procedures in Argentina: the DCD is in charge of the dumping investigation and the CNCE is in charge of the injury investigation.

209. The anti-dumping investigation was initiated on 20 January 1999, when the MEOSP issued Resolution No. 11/1999. The anti-dumping investigation was on imports of poultry from Brazil and, therefore, directed to *all* Brazilian producers and exporters of the subject merchandise. However, only five Brazilian producers/exporters of the subject merchandise were notified of the initiation of the investigation and the need to provide responses to questionnaires. These notifications to the five Brazilian exporters were sent by the CNCE on 10 February 1999 and by the DCD on 16 February 1999.

210. On 15 September 1999, eight months after the investigation had been initiated, the DCD sent notifications of the investigation and the need to respond to questionnaires to CCLP, Catarinense, Chapecó, Minuano, Perdigão, Comaves, and Pena Branca, Brazilian producers/exporters of the subject merchandise that were already included in the investigation without knowledge of the investigation.

211. The DCD's notification to these seven Brazilian exporters requested that they provide responses to the questionnaire within 20 days from receipt of the notification. The timeframe required by the DCD in the notification was on its face contrary to the 30-day period required for responses to questionnaires, provided in the first part of Article 6.1.1 of the Anti-Dumping Agreement.

---

[87] *Ibid.*

212. The CNCE never notified these seven exporters of the investigation and the need to provide responses to the questionnaire. In fact, these seven exporters never received the injury questionnaire.

213. By not giving these seven Brazilian exporters at least 30 days to reply to the dumping questionnaire and by not providing the injury questionnaire to these exporters to respond to, Argentina failed to comply with Article 6.1.1 of the Anti-Dumping Agreement.

(ii) Claim 12: Inconsistency with Article 6.1.2 of the Anti-Dumping Agreement

Text of Article 6.1.2

214. The text of Article 6.1.2 provides that:

"Subject to the requirement to protect confidential information, evidence presented in writing by one interested party shall be made available promptly to other interested parties participating in the investigation."

Legal Argument Relative to Claim 12

215. Article 6.1.2 of the Anti-Dumping Agreement provides that evidence presented by one interested party shall be "made available promptly" to other interested parties.

216. Without knowing, CCLP, Catarinense, Chapecó, Minuano, Perdigão, Comaves, and PenaBranca, participated in the investigation for eight months before they were notified of the investigation and the need to provide responses to the questionnaire.

217. Because the DCD and the CNCE did not inform them of the investigation and of the need to submit responses, these seven exporters did not have evidence that was presented in writing by other interested party made promptly available to them.

218. With regards to the term "made available promptly", we agree with the Panel's interpretation in *Guatemala - Cement II* that on its face, Article 6.1.2 does not necessarily require that one have access to the file to comply with this provision.[88] The Panel in that case provided examples of how evidence can be made available in an investigation without parties having access to the files. For example, an investigating authority can require each interested party to serve its submissions on all other interested parties; or, an investigating authority can undertake to provide copies of each interested party's submission to other interested parties.

219. However, because the seven exporters had not been notified of the initiation of the investigation or given the questionnaires to respond, but were in any event included in the investigation because they exported the subject merchandise to Argentina in the period of investigation, they did not even know that evidence had been presented by the other interested parties in the investigation, much less that they should, or could, have had access to that evidence.

220. Furthermore, Article 6.1.2 mandates the investigating authorities to make the evidence available "promptly". According to textual interpretation, the term

---

[88] *Guatemala - Cement II*, at para. 8.133.

"promptly" means "to make or do readily or at once".[89] Brazil considers that evidence could not be made readily or immediately available to these exporters if they were notified to participate eight months after the investigation had already initiated and a preliminary determination of dumping, injury and causal link had already been made.

(iii) Claim 13: Inconsistency with Article 6.2 of the Anti-Dumping Agreement

Text of Article 6.2

221. Relevant portion of Article 6.2 sets forth that:

"Throughout the anti-dumping investigation all interested parties shall have a full opportunity for the defense of their interests (...)"

Legal Argument Relative to Claim 13

222. Article 6.2 imposes a general duty on investigating authorities to ensure that interested parties have a full opportunity throughout an anti-dumping investigation for the defense of their interests. Even though Article 6.2 does not provide specific guidance as to what steps investigating authorities must take in practice, Brazil considers that notification of the investigation and the request to submit responses to the injury questionnaire eight months after the investigation has initiated is a violation of Article 6.2.

223. First, the seven exporters were given a 20-day deadline to submit their responses to the dumping questionnaire, contrary to the required 30-day deadline provided in Article 6.1.1.

224. Furthermore, the CNCE did not notify any of the seven exporters of the investigation and did not provide them with injury questionnaires. Therefore, these exporters did not have any opportunity for the defense of their interests.

225. Second, because the seven Brazilian exporters were only notified of the investigation and the need to present responses to the dumping questionnaires eight months after the investigation had been initiated, the seven exporters did not have evidence presented by the other interested parties promptly available to them.

226. These facts indicate that the seven Brazilian exporters did not have full opportunity to defend their interests in a clear violation of Article 6.2 of the Anti-Dumping Agreement.

(iv) Claim 14: Inconsistency with Article 6.1.3 of the Anti-Dumping Agreement.

Text of Article 6.1.3

227. Article 6 of the Anti-Dumping Agreement provides for the evidentiary requirements in an anti-dumping investigation. Specifically, Article 6.1.3 sets forth that:

"As soon as an investigation has been initiated, the authorities shall provide the full text of the written application received under

---

[89] *The Concise Oxford Dictionary - Ninth Edition,* Oxford University Press, 1995, p. 1096.

paragraph 1 of Article 5 to the known exporters and to the authorities of the exporting Member and shall make it available, upon request, to other interested parties involved. Due regard shall be paid to the requirement for the protection of confidential information, as provided for in paragraph 5."

Legal Argument Relative to Claim 14

228. The language of Article 6.1.3 sets out a timeframe for authorities to provide the full text of the written application to the known exporters and to the authorities of the exporting Member. Argentina failed to meet this timeframe requirement by never providing the text of the application to the exporters or to the Government of Brazil.

229. With respect to our understanding of Article 6.1.3, Brazil makes reference to the case *Guatemala - Cement II*, where the Panel provided explanation of the purpose and function of Article 6.1.3, by considering that:

> "(...) Timely access to the application is important for the exporters to enable preparation of the arguments in defense of their interests before the investigating authorities."[90] (emphasis added)

That Panel further clarified that:

> "(...) Since deadlines in the timetable of an investigation are counted from the date of initiation it is critical that the investigating authority provide the text of the application "as soon as an investigation has been initiated", for the exporter to be able to devise a strategy to defend the allegations it is being confronted with."[91] (emphasis added)

230. Regarding the instant claim, the Argentinean authorities never provided the text of the written application to the Government of Brazil and the exporters, making it impossible for the exporters to prepare arguments in the defense of their interests and to devise a strategy to defend the allegations made by petitioner in the application.

231. During consultations, Brazil in its communication of 5 December 2001 to Argentina presented questions regarding the investigation. In particular, the following question regarding Article 6.1.3 was presented:

Question 25:

Please explain why Authorities did not provide the full text of the written application to the known exporters and the Brazilian authorities as soon as the investigation was initiated.

Argentina responded on 11 January 2002 by stating that:

> "By means of note ex-SSCE No. 121 of 1 February 1999, notification of the initiation of the investigation was made to the Head of the Brazilian Business in Argentina, Ministro Conselheiro Pedro Motta, requesting cooperation in identifying the interested producers/exporters in the investigation and delivery of the respective questionnaires sent with that intent by the technical area ("área técnica").

---

[90] *Guatemala - Cement II*, at para. 8.102.
[91] *Ibid.*

Report of the Panel

Notification of the initiation of the investigation was also sent to the Subsecretary of American Economic Integration, Ambassador Alfredo Morelli by means of note ex-SSCE No. 122/99 and the ex-Subsecretary of International Economic Negotiations, Ambassador Eduardo Sadous, both notifications were sent on 1 February 1999.

Once the investigation was initiated, Argentina *made available* to the interested parties, among them the exporters, the importers and the authorities of the country in question, the proceedings that generated the investigation in question. *At all times, the interested parties had the opportunity to see the administrative file and to obtain a copy of it, not only of the application but also of all the proceedings that make up the investigation."* (emphasis added)

232. Based on the response provided by Argentina during consultations, the application was "made available" to the interested parties once the investigation was initiated. Brazil understands that Argentina's response that it "made the application available" does not meet the requirement set forth in Article 6.1.3, which requires the investigating authority "to provide" the application.

233. Article 6.1.3 mandates authorities "to provide" the full text of the written application. In this context, the verb "to provide" is a synonym of the verb "to supply".[92] It is our understanding that Argentina was obligated to supply the Government of Brazil and the exporters with the full text of the written application. Argentina's position that the verb "to provide" could be understood to mean that authorities were only required "to make available" the full text of the written application once the investigation was initiated is incorrect. Article 6.1.3 carefully differentiates the obligation that the investigating authorities have with the exporters and the exporting Member from the obligation the investigating authorities have with other interested parties. In the first case, the investigating authority must actively "provide" the full text of the written application to the exporting Member and to the exporters involved in the investigation. In the second case, the investigating authorities must "make available", upon request, the full text of the written application to other interested parties. Brazil believes that if the requirement imposed on the investigating authority was to be understood as being the same for the exporters/exporting Member as that for the other interested parties, there would be no need for the use of different language in Article 6.1.3

234. Furthermore and still based on Argentina's response during consultations, even if the term "to provide" could be understood by the Panel as a synonym of "to make available", which in this case it cannot, Argentina's response that it notified Brazilian Authorities on 1 February 1999 of the initiation of an investigation does not mean that Argentina made the full text of the written application "available" at that time.

235. Even under the assumption that the notification to initiate contained language that the full text of the written application was "available" for all interested parties, the notification of the initiation still occurred on 1 February 1999, 12 days after the investigation was initiated, and not "as soon" as the investigation was initiated, as required by Article 6.1.3 of the Anti-Dumping Agreement.

---

[92] *The Concise Oxford Dictionary - Ninth Edition,* Oxford University Press, 1995, p. 1102.

236. Our understanding of the timeframe provided by the term "as soon as" in Article 6.1.3 comes from the conclusion by the Panel in *Guatemala - Cement II*. In that case, the Panel concluded that:

> "(...) Having determined that Guatemala sent the full text of the application at the earliest 8 days after initiation of the investigation. We are of the view that given the nature of the obligation in Article 6.1.3 sending the application even *8 days after the initiation of investigation is not adequate to fulfill the requirement that it be done "as soon as an investigation has been initiated.""* [93] (emphasis added)

237. Brazil understands that if the Panel in Guatemala - Cement II concluded that 8 days after the initiation was not adequate to fulfill the requirement in Article 6.1.3; in this case, a period of 12 days after the initiation should also be considered not adequate to fulfill the requirement in Article 6.1.3 of the Anti-Dumping Agreement.

3. Articles 6.8, 6.10, 12.2.2 and Annex II

238. Seven claims arise from the facts described below and from the legal requirements of the Anti-Dumping Agreement:

Claim 15: Argentina disregarded the responses submitted by Brazilian exporters with respect to the description of the product sold to Argentina and in Brazil, and applied the normal value adjustment provided by petitioner in the application. Argentina's application of adverse facts available was inconsistent with Article 6.8 and paragraphs 3, 6 and 7 of Annex II.

Claim 16: Argentina acted inconsistently with Article 12.2.2 by failing to adequately explain in the final determination its decision to disregard the information provided by the exporters regarding the product description and to use, instead, the normal value adjustment proposed by petitioner.

Claim 17: Argentina disregarded all export price data provided by Brazilian exporters, and resorted to the export price data provided by the Argentinean agency *Ganaderia*. Argentina's application of adverse facts available was inconsistent with Article 6.8 and paragraphs 3 and 5 of Annex II.

Claim 18: Argentina acted inconsistently with Article 12.2.2 by failing to adequately explain in the final determination its decision to disregard the export price data provided by the Brazilian exporters, and to resort to the export price information provided by the Argentinean agency *Ganaderia*.

Claim 19: Argentina disregarded all normal value information submitted by Frangosul and Catarinense, and resorted to the information provided by petitioner. Argentina's application of adverse facts available was inconsistent with Article 6.8 and paragraphs 3, 5 and 7 of Annex II.

Claim 20: Argentina acted inconsistently with Article 12.2.2 by failing to adequately explain in the final determination its decision to disregard all normal value information submitted by Frangosul and Catarinense, and resort to the information provided by petitioner.

Claim 22: Argentina failed to establish individual margins of dumping for Frangosul and Catarinense, as required by Article 6.10.

---

[93] *Guatemala - Cement II*, at para. 8.104.

(a) Facts

Brazilian Exporters' Response to the Questionnaire

239. On 7 January 1998, the DCD issued a determination to initiate the dumping investigation on poultry from Brazil.[94] In that determination, the DCD established normal value according to the information provided in the application and made an adjustment to normal value, proposed by petitioner, to account for differences in the physical characteristics of the product sold in Brazil and to Argentina.[95]

240. Petitioner alleged that an adjustment to normal value was warranted because in Brazil eviscerated poultry is sold with giblets (heart, stomach, neck and liver), with head and feet, and in Argentina eviscerated poultry is sold without head and feet.[96]

241. Petitioner further alleged that to fairly compare the prices of poultry sold in Brazil (normal value) to the prices of poultry sold in Argentina (export price), the DCD would have to add 9.09 per cent to the price of poultry sold in Brazil to compensate for the fact that poultry in Argentina is sold without head and feet and poultry in Brazil is sold with head and feet. Petitioner's normal value adjustment was based on the prices published by the Brazilian company JOX on 30 June 1997, for chilled poultry, with head and feet, for the São Paulo wholesale market.[97]

242. Annex II of Section A of the dumping questionnaire for the producer/exporter, requested that the exporters provide a complete product description with technical specifications for each model/type/code for the merchandise sold in the internal market and for the merchandise exported to Argentina.[98] Question 2 of Section B (sales to Argentina) of the questionnaire requested that the producer/exporter identify by model/type/code if the merchandise exported to Argentina was identical or similar to the merchandise sold in the internal market. Question 2 further requested that, in the event the merchandise was not identical, the producer/exporter identify the technical differences and how these differences influence the export price.

Sadia

243. On 20 April 1999, Sadia submitted the questionnaire response, providing sales information for the home market and for Argentina for the period 1996 through 1998 and January and February of 1999.[99] In Annex II of Section A of the questionnaire, Sadia described the product as whole, frozen, eviscerated poultry with giblets.[100] More specifically, Sadia reported the product for the internal market as whole, frozen, eviscerated poultry, with giblets, box of 18kg - individual weight of 1.750 to 2.750 kg; and the product for Argentina as whole, frozen, eviscerated poultry, with giblets box of 18kg - individual weight of 1.700 to 2.700 kg.[101]

---

[94] *See*, Exhibit BRA-2.
[95] *See*, Pages 8, 9, 12 and 13 of Exhibit BRA-2.
[96] *See*, Pages 7 and 8 of Exhibit BRA-2.
[97] *See*, Pages 8 and 9 of Exhibit BRA-2.
[98] *See*, Exhibits BRA-22, 23, 24 and 25.
[99] *See*, Exhibit BRA-22.
[100] *Ibid.*
[101] *Ibid.*

According to Sadia's response there were no differences in the physical characteristics for the products sold to Argentina and in Brazil.

244. On 28 April 1999, Sadia submitted a supplemental response to the questionnaire.[102] In this response, Sadia indicated in the supplemental information relative to Annex V of Section A, that whole, frozen, eviscerated poultry, without giblets, was sold to the internal market but not to Argentina during the period of January 1996 through February 1999.[103] The DCD never requested additional, specific information regarding the description of the product sold to Argentina and in Brazil.

Avipal

245. On 21 April 1999, Avipal submitted a diskette with the questionnaire response, providing sales information for the home market and for Argentina for the period 1996 through 1998 and January and February of 1999.[104]

246. On 7 May 1999, Avipal submitted a hard copy of the non-confidential information in the questionnaire response.[105] In Annex II of Section A of that questionnaire response, Avipal described the product as whole, frozen, eviscerated poultry. Avipal further divided the product into two types: (i) broiler (with giblets) containing a plastic package with neck *without head*, gizzard and liver; and, (ii) griler (without giblets).[106] In Annex V of that response, Avipal reported that both broiler and griler type poultry were sold to Argentina and Brazil.[107] According to Avipal's response, there were no differences in the physical characteristics for the product sold to Argentina and in Brazil. The DCD never requested additional, specific information regarding the description of the product sold to Argentina and in Brazil.

Frangosul

247. On 27 April 1999, Frangosul submitted the questionnaire response, providing sales information for the home market and Argentina for the period 1996 through 1998 and January through March of 1999.[108] In Annex II of Section A of the questionnaire, Frangosul described the product as whole, frozen, eviscerated poultry, with giblets (broiler type), and whole, frozen, eviscerated poultry, without giblets (griler type).[109] Both broiler and griler type poultry were sold to Argentina and in Brazil.

248. On 19 August 1999, Frangosul also attached a product brochure to its response (in English and Spanish), describing the types of products produced and sold.[110] According to the description in the brochure, griler type poultry is fresh, frozen poultry, white or yellow skin, fully eviscerated, *headless and feetless*, without giblets; and, broiler type poultry is fresh, frozen poultry, white skin, fully eviscerated,

---

[102] *Ibid.*
[103] *Ibid.*
[104] *See*, Exhibit BRA-23.
[105] *Ibid.*
[106] *Ibid.*
[107] *Ibid.*
[108] *See*, Exhibit BRA-24.
[109] *Ibid.*
[110] *See*, Exhibit BRA-26.

Report of the Panel

headless and feetless, with giblets.[111] Based on Frangosul's response, the exporter did not sell poultry with head and feet and there were no differences in the physical characteristics for the product sold to Argentina and in Brazil. The DCD never requested additional, specific information regarding the description of the product sold to Argentina and in Brazil.

Catarinense

249. On 15 September 1999, the DCD sent a letter to Catarinense notifying of the investigation and requesting that it provide responses to the questionnaire for the producer/exporter.[112]

250. On 20 October 1999, Catarinense requested an extension of the deadline to submit the questionnaire response.[113] On 3 November 1999, Catarinense provided the questionnaire responses.[114] In Annex II of Section A of the questionnaire, Catarinense described the product as whole, frozen poultry with (broiler) and without giblets (griler).[115] For the export market, the broiler type poultry (with giblets) contains liver, gizzard and neck. For the internal market, the broiler type poultry (with giblets) contains liver, gizzard, paws,[116] head and neck. The griler type poultry sold to Argentina and in Brazil do not contain giblets.[117] Catarinense reported that it sold broiler and griler type poultry in the home market and that the broiler type poultry sold in the home market contained *head but not feet*.[118] The DCD never requested additional, specific information regarding the description of the product sold to Argentina and in Brazil.

Final Dumping Determination

251. On 23 June 2000, the DCD issued the final affirmative dumping determination.[119]

Normal Value

252. In the final dumping determination, the DCD established the following non-adjusted normal values for the Brazilian exporters: for Sadia, US$ 0,852; for Avipal, U$S 0,9988; and, for Frangosul and Catarinense the same as that applied to all other exporters, U$S 0,9519.[120] To these values found in the final dumping determination, the DCD made an adjustment of 9.09 per cent in order to find the adjusted normal value to compensate for the alleged difference that poultry in Brazil is sold with head and feet and poultry to Argentina is sold without head and feet.[121] The DCD followed

---

[111] *Ibid.*
[112] *See*, Exhibit BRA-13.
[113] *See*, Page 38 of Exhibit BRA-28.
[114] *See*, Exhibit BRA-25.
[115] *Ibid.*
[116] The term "paw" is not the same as the term "feet". In Spanish, "paw" is "garra" and the term "feet" is "pata". "Paws" are the lower extremity of poultry's "feet", not the "feet" themselves. *See*, Exhibit BRA-34.
[117] *See*, Exhibit BRA-25.
[118] *Ibid.*
[119] *See*, Exhibit BRA-15.
[120] *See*, Pages 55, 63, and 65 of Exhibit BRA-15.
[121] *See*, Pages 55, 63, 65, 67 and 69 of Exhibit BRA-15.

petitioner's adjustment calculation as proposed in the application, which was unsubstantiated by relevant evidence, and disregarded the responses of the exporters.

Export Price

253. The DCD established export price based on the import information from the Argentinean agency *Ganaderia* and disregarded all export price data submitted by the Brazilian exporters.[122]

        (i)   Claim 15: Inconsistency with Article 6.8 and Annex II of the Anti-Dumping Agreement

Text of Article 6.8 and Annex II

254. Article 6.8 of the Anti-Dumping Agreement governs the use of "facts available" by an investigating authority in an anti-dumping investigation. It allows investigating authorities to resort to the use of "facts available" under specific circumstances. Article 6.8 provides:

> "In cases in which any interested party refuses access to, or otherwise does not provide, necessary information within a reasonable period or significantly impedes the investigation, preliminary and final determinations, affirmative or negative, may be made on the basis of the facts available. The provisions of Annex II shall be observed in the application of this paragraph."

Annex II sets out additional conditions and considerations relevant to the application of facts available in a particular case.

The relevant portion of Paragraph 3 of Annex II provides that:

> "All information which is verifiable, which is appropriately submitted so that it can be used in the investigation without undue difficulties, which is supplied in a timely fashion, and, where applicable, which is supplied in a medium or computer language requested by the authorities, should be taken into account when determinations are made. (...)"

Paragraph 6 of Annex II requires that the investigating authority immediately inform the supplying party of the reasons for not accepting evidence or information. Paragraph 6 requires that:

> "If evidence or information is not accepted, the supplying party should be informed forthwith of the reasons therefor, and should have an opportunity to provide further explanations within a reasonable period due account being taken of the time-limits of the investigation. If the explanations are considered by the authorities as not being satisfactory, the reasons for the rejection of such evidence or information should be given in any published determinations."

Paragraph 7 of Annex II establishes that:

> "If authorities have to base their findings, including those with respect to normal value, on information from a secondary source, including

---

[122] *See*, Pages 76, 77 and 104 of Exhibit BRA-15.

the information supplied in the application for the initiation of the investigation, they should do so with special circumspection. In such cases, the authorities should, where practicable, check the information from other independent sources at their disposal, such as published price lists, official import statistics and customs returns, and from the information obtained from other interested parties during the investigation. It is clear, however, that if an interested party does not cooperate and thus relevant information is being withheld from the authorities, this situation could lead to a result which is less favorable to the party than if the party did cooperate."

Legal Argument Relative to Claim 15

255. The conditions for applying "facts available" under Article 6.8 are straightforward. If an interested party: (i) "refuses access to" necessary information within a reasonable period; (ii) "otherwise does not provide" necessary information within a reasonable period; or (iii) "significantly impedes the investigation", the investigating authority *may* make determinations on the basis of the facts available.

256. As shown in the facts related to these claims, the exporters Sadia, Avipal and Frangosul reported that the poultry sold to Argentina was identical to the poultry sold in Brazil. The Brazilian exporter Catarinense reported that from the two types of poultry sold (broiler and griler), there was a difference in the broiler type poultry sold to Argentina and in Brazil. The broiler type poultry sold to Argentina did not contain head and feet, while the broiler type poultry sold in Brazil contained head *but not feet*.

257. Sadia, Avipal, Frangosul and Catarinense did not refuse access or failed to make available this information within a reasonable period, nor did these exporters significantly impede the investigation. These responses were provided as responses to the DCD's dumping questionnaire, submitted within reasonable time for evaluation by the investigating authority.

258. The DCD failed to take into account these responses and applied the normal value adjustment calculation even though, according to the exporters' responses, this adjustment was not warranted.

259. In particular, Paragraph 3 of Annex II provides that all information which is subject to verification, appropriately provided and done so in a timely fashion should be taken into account when determinations are made.

260. In the present case, the product description information appropriately submitted by the exporters, and in a timely fashion, was not taken into account in the final determination.

261. With respect to the application of facts available and Paragraph 3 of Annex II, Brazil agrees with the reasoning set forth by the Panel in *United States - Hot Rolled Steel Products*, that:

> "(...)The AD Agreement establishes that facts available may be used if necessary information is not provided within a reasonable period. *What is a "reasonable period" will not, in all instances be commensurate with pre-established deadlines set out in general regulations.* We recognize that in the interest of orderly administration investigating authorities do, and indeed must establish such deadlines.

Argentina - Poultry Anti-Dumping Duties

However, *a rigid adherence to such deadlines does not in all cases suffice as the basis for a conclusion that information was not submitted within a reasonable period and consequently that facts available may be applied.*

In this regard, we note that paragraph 3 of Annex II, which provides, in pertinent part "All information which is verifiable, which is appropriately submitted so that it can be used in the investigation without undue difficulties, which is supplied in a timely fashion, (...) should be taken into account when determinations are made." *Particularly where information is actually submitted in time to be verified, and actually could be verified, we consider that it should generally be accepted, unless to do so would impede the ability of the investigating authority to complete the investigation within the time limits established by the Agreement. Such might be the case, for instance, if an entire questionnaire response were submitted only just before the time scheduled for verification. However, in this case, it seems clear that the information could have been verified and used, but was instead rejected as untimely.* One of the principle elements governing anti-dumping investigations that emerges from the whole of the AD Agreement is the goal of ensuring objective decision-making based on facts. Article 6.8 and Annex II advance that goal by ensuring that even where the investigating authority is unable to obtain the "first-best" information as the basis of its decision, it will nonetheless base its decision on facts, albeit perhaps "second-best" facts. *This does not however, justify refusing to consider information simply because it submitted outside a pre-determined time-period, if it is submitted within a period that is reasonable under the circumstances - that is, a period that allows the information to be verified and used in the determination, due account being taken of the time limits in the AD Agreement for completing the investigation and the time needed for the investigating authority to do so.* We consider it significant, in this case, that the information submitted past the deadline, but before verification, was not new information concerning such matters as prices, costs, or adjustments that had never previously been provided, and which would require extensive verification (...)"[123] (emphasis added)

262. In the instant case, Sadia, Avipal and Frangosul reported that there were no differences in the physical characteristics of the poultry sold to Argentina and in Brazil. More specifically, these responses were submitted in April of 1999, more than one year before the DCD issued its final affirmative dumping determination, on 23 June 2000. The information provided by the exporters could have been verified and

---

[123] *United States - Anti-Dumping Measures on Certain Hot-Rolled Steel Products from Japan*, 28 February 2001, WT/DS184/R, DSR 2001:X, 4769, at paras. 7.54 and 7.55 ("*United States - Hot Rolled Steel Products*"). The Appellate Body upheld the Panel's findings with respect to the United States inconsistency with Article 6.8 and Annex II of the Anti-Dumping Agreement in its application of facts available. *United States - Anti-Dumping Measures on Certain Hot-Rolled Steel Products from Japan*, 24 July 2001, WT/DS184/AB/R, DSR 2001:X, 4697, at para. 240 (adopted on 23 August 2001) ("*AB - United States - Hot Rolled Steel Products*").

Report of the Panel

used, since it was submitted within a reasonable period for the investigating authority to do so.

263. Catarinense reported the difference in the broiler type poultry sold to Argentina and to Brazil on 3 November 1999, approximately seven months prior to the final affirmative dumping determination. Brazil recalls that Catarinense was only notified of the investigation on 15 September 1999, eight months after the investigation had been initiated.

264. With respect to Catarinense's response, Brazil points out that the exporter reported that it sold both griler (without giblets) and broiler (with giblets) type poultry to Argentina and in Brazil. However, the DCD chose to apply the normal value adjustment to all of the poultry sales in Brazil even though some of these sales did not warrant an adjustment because they were sales of griler type poultry, that is, poultry sold without head and feet.

265. Furthermore, the DCD's normal value adjustment took into account a yield rate of eviscerated poultry based on the allegation that poultry in Brazil was sold with head and feet. According to the information provided by Catarinense, the broiler type poultry sold in Brazil contained head *but did not contain feet*. Thus, the yield rate proposed in the adjustment calculation presented by petitioner for poultry sold in Brazil was inconsistent with the yield rate of poultry sold by Catarinense in Brazil. In Catarinense's case, the DCD should have considered these facts in establishing an adjustment to normal value for the purpose of making a fair comparison.

266. The DCD did not request further specific information from the exporters on the alleged differences in the physical characteristics of the poultry sold to Argentina and in Brazil. The DCD simply rejected exporters' information and used the adjustment proposed by petitioner in the application.

267. In this respect, Brazil turns to the Panel's consideration in *Guatemala - Cement II* on the interpretation of Article 6.8 of the Anti-Dumping Agreement:

> "(...) We do not consider that a failure to cooperate necessarily constitutes significant impediment of an investigation, since in our view the AD Agreement does not require cooperation by interested parties at any cost. Although there are certain consequences (under Article 6.8) for interested parties if they fail to cooperate with an investigating authority, in our view such consequences only arise if the investigating authority itself has acted in a reasonable, objective and impartial manner (...)"[124] (emphasis added)

268. Brazil believes that in the present case the DCD did not act in a reasonable, objective and impartial manner. The DCD had access to the information provided by exporters regarding the product description long before the final determination was issued. Had the DCD questions regarding the exporters' reported information it should have asked them during the investigation, but it did not. The exporters did not refuse or did not fail to provide the necessary information for the DCD to consider whether an adjustment to normal value was warranted. The DCD simply ignored and disregarded the information reported by the exporters.

269. As provided in Paragraph 6 of Annex II, if evidence or information is not accepted the investigating authority must inform the reasons why it has not been

---

[124] *Guatemala - Cement II*, at para. 8.251.

accepted and should give an opportunity for the party to provide further explanations within a reasonable period. If the explanations are considered by the authorities as not being satisfactory, the reasons for the rejection of the evidence or information provided should be given in any published determination.

270. That was not the case for Sadia, Avipal, Frangosul and Catarinense. The DCD never requested specific information on the product description of the poultry sold in Brazil and to Argentina. Had the DCD any questions or doubts regarding the information reported by these exporters that would justify the rejection of this information, the DCD should have requested clarifications on the issue and given the opportunity for exporters to provide explanations during the investigation. The DCD did not do so.

271. Because Sadia, Avipal, Frangosul and Catarinense provided the necessary information for the DCD to conclude that there was *no* need to adjust the normal value for these exporters, the DCD did *not have to* base its finding of normal value on facts available, which in this case was the information provided by petitioner in the application.

272. Even if the DCD *had to* base its finding with respect to normal value on information from a secondary source, which is not the case, Paragraph 7 of Annex II instructs the investigating authority to do so with special circumspection.

273. Brazil affirms that the DCD did not base its finding that normal value warranted adjustment on special circumspection or careful consideration of the information supplied in the application. Had it done so, the DCD would have requested additional information and clarification regarding the type and physical characteristics of the product sold to Argentina and in Brazil and would have checked the information provided in the application with information from other independent sources. The DCD never raised the issue during the investigation.

> (ii) Claim 16: Inconsistency with Article 12.2.2 of the Anti-Dumping Agreement

Text of Article 12.2.2

274. Article 12 governs the contents of public notices issued in the course of an anti-dumping investigation. It provides, in pertinent part:

> "12.2 Public notice shall be given of any preliminary or final determination, whether affirmative or negative, of any decision to accept an undertaking pursuant to Article 8, of the termination of such an undertaking, and of the termination of a definitive anti-dumping duty. Each such notice shall set forth, or otherwise make available through a separate report, in sufficient detail the findings and conclusions reached on all issues of fact and law considered material by the investigating authorities. All such notices and reports shall be forwarded to the Member or the Members the product of which are subject to such determination or undertaking and to other interested parties known to have an interest therein.
>
> 12.2.1 A public notice of the imposition of provisional measures shall set forth, or otherwise make available through a separate report, sufficiently detailed explanations for the preliminary determinations

on dumping and injury and shall refer to the matters of fact and law which have led to arguments being accepted or rejected. Such notice or report shall, due regard being paid to the requirement for the protection of confidential information, contain in particular:

(i) The names of the suppliers, or when this is impracticable, the supplying countries involved;

(ii) A description of the product which is sufficient for customs purposes;

(iii) The margins of dumping established and a full explanation of the reasons for the methodology used in the establishment and comparison of the export price and the normal value under Article 2.

(iv) Considerations relevant to the injury determination as set out in Article 3;

(v) The main reasons leading to the determination.

12.2.2 A public notice of conclusion or suspension of an investigation in the case of an affirmative determination providing for the imposition of a definitive duty or the acceptance of a price undertaking shall contain, or otherwise make available through a separate report, all relevant information on matters of fact and law and reasons which have led to the imposition of final measures or the acceptance of a price undertaking, due regard being paid to the requirement for the protection of confidential information. In particular, the notice or report shall contain the information described in subparagraph 2.1, as well as the reasons for the acceptance or rejection of relevant arguments or claims made by the exporters and importers, and the basis for any decision made under subparagraph 10.2 of Article 6."

Legal Argument Relative to Claim 16

275. The question presented to the Panel is whether any reasoning has been provided in the final determination, sufficient to satisfy the requirements of Article 12.2.2 of the Anti-Dumping Agreement, explaining why the DCD did not use Sadia, Avipal, Frangosul and Catarinense's information on the description of the products sold to Argentina and in Brazil.

276. The questionnaire responses submitted by Sadia, Avipal and Frangosul indicated no difference between the poultry sold to Argentina and in Brazil. The Brazilian exporter Catarinense reported that from the two types of poultry sold (broiler and griler), there was a difference in the broiler type poultry sold to Argentina and in Brazil. The broiler type poultry sold to Argentina did not contain head and feet, while the broiler type poultry sold in Brazil contained head *but not feet*.

277. During the investigation, the DCD did not request further specific information as to the physical characteristics of the product sold to Argentina and in Brazil, and whether such differences affected price comparability between the poultry sold in those markets.

278. In the final determination, the DCD applied the adjustment calculation to normal value provided by petitioner in the application, without providing explanation as to why the information presented by the exporters on the description of the product sold to Argentina and in Brazil were not accepted and, thus, disregarded.

279. In the case of an affirmative determination providing for the imposition of a definitive duty, Article 12.2.2. mandates that a public notice of conclusion of the investigation contain, or otherwise make available through a separate report, *all relevant information on matters of fact and law and reasons which have led to the imposition of final measures*. Included as relevant information are the established margins of dumping and a full explanation of the reasons for the methodology used in the establishment and comparison of the export price and the normal value under Article 2.

280. According to the final dumping determination, the DCD adjusted normal value, to account for alleged physical characteristic differences between the products sold to Argentina and in Brazil, in order to make a fair comparison between the export price and normal value. The DCD provided no explanation on why it did not consider exporters' information on the product description that indicated that no adjustment to normal value was needed to make a fair comparison between the export price and the normal value. The DCD simply applied the normal value adjustment calculation as proposed by petitioner in the application.

281. By not providing this information, Argentina has incurred in a *prima facie* violation of Article 12.2.2 of the Anti-Dumping Agreement.

          (iii)   Claim 17: Inconsistency with Article 6.8 and Annex II of the Anti-Dumping Agreement

Text of Article 6.8

282. Article 6.8 provides that:

"In cases in which any interested party refuses access to, or otherwise does not provide, necessary information within a reasonable period or significantly impedes the investigation, preliminary and final determinations, affirmative or negative, may be made on the basis of the facts available. The provisions of Annex II shall be observed in the application of this paragraph."

The relevant provisions in Annex II are transcribed below.

Paragraph 3 of Annex II provides in part that:

"All information which is verifiable, which is appropriately submitted so that it can be used in the investigation without undue difficulties, which is supplied in a timely fashion, and, where applicable, which is supplied in a medium or computer language requested by the authorities, should be taken into account when determinations are made. (...)"

Paragraph 5 of Annex II sets forth that:

"Even though the information provided may not be ideal in all respects, this should not justify the authorities from disregarding it, provided the interested party has acted to the best of its ability."

Legal Argument Relative to Claim 17

283. In the final determination, the DCD established export price for all Brazilian exporters based on the import information from the Argentinean agency Ganaderia.

284. Sadia provided export price information of poultry sold to Argentina for the period 1996 through February 1999.[125] Avipal provided export price information of poultry sold to Argentina for the period 1996 through March 1999.[126] Frangosul provided export price information for individual export transactions of poultry sold to Argentina from January 1996 through March 1999, with respective invoices.[127] Catarinense provided export price information for individual transactions of poultry sold to Argentina from January 1998 through January 1999, with respective invoices.[128]

285. As stated above, Article 6.8 limits the use of facts available to the following circumstances: (i) cases in which any interested party refuses access to, or otherwise does not provide, necessary information within a reasonable period, or (ii) cases in which any interested party significantly impedes the investigation.

286. In this case, the exporters neither refused nor failed to provide the information on export price within a reasonable period. Frangosul and Catarinense even provided the export price information for individual export transactions to Argentina with the respective invoices.

287. Paragraph 3 of Annex II directs the authorities to consider, when determinations are made, all information, which is verifiable and appropriately submitted. More importantly, Paragraph 5 of Annex II explicitly provides that even though the information provided may not be ideal in all respects, this should not justify the authorities from disregarding it, provided the interested party has acted to the best of its ability.

288. In this respect, Sadia, Avipal, Frangosul and Catarinense have provided information to the best of their abilities and have never refused to cooperate with the DCD. Moreover, the Panel should take into account that the DCD only determined the period of investigation nine months after the investigation had been initiated. During those nine months, Sadia, Avipal and Frangosul provided information on normal value and export price in excess of the period of investigation,[129] which was later defined as from January 1998 through January 1999.[130] The DCD originally did not establish the period of investigation for dumping purposes and exporters had to present export price and normal value information for 1996, 1997, 1998 and the months where data was available for 1999.[131]

289. The exporters never refused to provide such information even though the burden was excessive. With that in mind, the responses may not have been submitted in exactly the form or with the content expected, or desired, by the DCD, but they were nevertheless submitted. To that regard, Brazil recalls that Paragraph 5 of Annex

---

[125] *See*, Exhibit BRA-22 and Pages 18 and 43 of Exhibit BRA-15.
[126] *See*, Exhibit BRA-23 and Pages 22 and 45 of Exhibit BRA-15.
[127] *See*, Exhibit BRA-24 and Pages 29 and 49 of Exhibit BRA-15.
[128] *See*, Exhibit BRA-25 and Pages 38 and 39 of Exhibit BRA-15.
[129] *See*, Exhibits BRA-22, 23 and 24.
[130] *See*, Exhibits BRA-13 and 26.
[131] *See*, Pages 18, 22 and 29 of Exhibit BRA-15.

II provides that the mere fact that the information provided may not be ideal in all respects, does not justify the authorities from disregarding it.

290. By completely disregarding all the export price information provided by the exporters and applying, instead, the information from *Ganaderia*, Argentina has acted inconsistently with Article 6.8 and Paragraphs 3 and 5 of Annex II of the Anti-Dumping Agreement.

> (iv) Claim 18: Inconsistency with Article 12.2.2 of the Anti-Dumping Agreement

Text of Article 12.2.2

291. Article 12.2.2 provides for what information must be included in the public notice of conclusion in the case of an affirmative determination providing for the imposition of a definitive duty. It provides, in pertinent part:

> "12.2.2 A public notice of conclusion or suspension of an investigation in the case of an affirmative determination providing for the imposition of a definitive duty or the acceptance of a price undertaking shall contain, or otherwise make available through a separate report, all relevant information on matters of fact and law and reasons which have led to the imposition of final measures or the acceptance of a price undertaking, due regard being paid to the requirement for the protection of confidential information. In particular, the notice or report shall contain the information described in subparagraph 2.1, as well as the reasons for the acceptance or rejection of relevant arguments or claims made by the exporters and importers, and the basis for any decision made under subparagraph 10.2 of Article 6."

Legal Argument Relative to Claim 18

292. The question presented to the Panel is whether any reasoning has been provided in the final determination, sufficient to satisfy the requirements of Article 12.2.2 of the Anti-Dumping Agreement, regarding why the DCD did not use Sadia, Avipal, Frangosul and Catarinense's export price information.

293. In the final determination, the DCD established export price for all Brazilian exporters based on the import information from the Argentinean agency *Ganaderia* and disregarded the export price reported by Sadia, Avipal, Frangosul and Catarinense.

294. The DCD limited its explanation of the use of the export price information by stating that:

> "For this stage of the proceeding and observant of the most complete and detailed source of information, the DCD considers appropriate to use the FOB export value derived from the Dirección de Ganaderia, Secretaria de Agricultura, Ganaderia, Pesca y Alimentación, listed for each company (...)"[132]

---

[132] *See*, Pages 76 of Exhibit BRA-15.

Report of the Panel

295. No further explanation was given as to why the export price information reported by the exporters was not accepted.

296. Article 12.2.2 specifically requires that the notice or report contain the information described in subparagraph 2.1, as well as the reasons for the acceptance or rejection of relevant arguments or claims made by the exporters and importers. Among the relevant information described in Article 12.2.1 are the established margins of dumping and a full explanation of the reasons for the methodology used in the establishment and comparison of the export price and the normal value.

297. Contrary to Article 12.2.2 of the Anti-Dumping Agreement, no explanation was given as to why the DCD did not establish the export price based on the information provided by exporters.

> (v) Claim 19: Inconsistency with Article 6.8 and Annex II of the Anti-Dumping Agreement

Text of Article 6.8

298. Article 6.8 provides that:

> "In cases in which any interested party refuses access to, or otherwise does not provide, necessary information within a reasonable period or significantly impedes the investigation, preliminary and final determinations, affirmative or negative, may be made on the basis of the facts available. The provisions of Annex II shall be observed in the application of this paragraph."

Paragraph 3 of Annex II provides that:

> "All information which is verifiable, which is appropriately submitted so that it can be used in the investigation without undue difficulties, which is supplied in a timely fashion, and, where applicable, which is supplied in a medium or computer language requested by the authorities, should be taken into account when determinations are made. (...)"

Paragraph 5 of Annex II sets forth that:

> "Even though the information provided may not be ideal in all respects, this should not justify the authorities from disregarding it, provided the interested party has acted to the best of its ability."

Paragraph 7 of Annex II:

> "If authorities have to base their findings, including those with respect to normal value, on information from a secondary source, including the information supplied in the application for the initiation of the investigation, they should do so with special circumspection. In such cases, the authorities should, where practicable, check the information from other independent sources at their disposal, such as published price lists, official import statistics and customs returns, and from the information obtained from other interested parties during the investigation. It is clear, however, that if an interested party does not cooperate and thus relevant information is being withheld from the authorities, this situation could lead to a result which is less favorable to the party than if the party did cooperate."

Legal Argument Relative to Claim 19

299. Pursuant to the facts related to these claims, Frangosul submitted the questionnaire responses, including normal value data on 27 April 1999. On 19 August 1999, Frangosul provided explanation that the great volume of sales in the home market did not make it possible for it to provide copies of invoices for each transaction. Frangosul in this response invited the DCD to verify in loco or to choose a sample of the transactions, so that it could provide invoice copies of the selected transactions.[133] On 12 October 1999, the DCD sent a letter to Frangosul requesting a new list of invoices for the period covering January 1998 through January 1999, so that the DCD could pick out sample transactions it wanted documentation from.[134] On 30 December 1999, Frangosul presented the list of invoices in diskette.[135] On 5 January 2000, the DCD sent a letter to Frangosul informing of the end of the stage to produce evidence.[136] The DCD never selected the transactions for which it wanted Frangosul to provide invoice copies.

300. With respect to the responses provided by Catarinense, Brazil recalls that the DCD notified the exporter of the investigation on 15 September 1999, eight months after the investigation initiated. On 20 October 1999, Catarinense requested an extension of the deadline to submit the questionnaire response. On 3 November 1999, Catarinense provided the questionnaire response with a list of the transactions in the internal market for the period January 1998 through January 1999. On 8 November 1999, the DCD sent a letter to Catarinense granting the extension of the deadline until 8 November 1999.[137] Brazil observes that the DCD sent the letter granting Catarinense the extension on the same day of the end of the deadline granted. After this date, the DCD did not request further information from Catarinense.

301. On 23 June 2000, the DCD issued the final dumping determination without taking into account the normal value information provided by Frangosul and Catarinense in the investigation and, thus, did not establish normal value for these two exporters. Instead, the DCD applied to Frangosul and Catarinense the normal value assigned for all other exporters based on the information provided by petitioner on 26 July 1999.[138] Petitioner presented a spreadsheet with an updated normal value calculation for 1998 through 1999 based on prices published by JOX. Petitioner's calculation used prices from three reference dates for each month of the period January 1998 through January 1999. The prices were for *chilled* poultry, with head and feet, sold in the São Paulo wholesale market.

302. Article 6.8 of the Anti-Dumping Agreement limits the cases in which facts available may be used. These cases occur when any interested party refuses access to or otherwise does not provide necessary information within a reasonable period or significantly impedes the investigation. Throughout the entire investigation Frangosul and Catarinense cooperated with the DCD in providing the information requested.

---

[133] *See*, Exhibit BRA-26.
[134] *Ibid.*
[135] *Ibid.*
[136] *Ibid.*
[137] *See*, Exhibit BRA-27.
[138] *See*, Pages 55 and 104 of Exhibit BRA-15.

303. If the DCD considered that the normal value information was not submitted within the deadlines established by the authority and, thus, was not submitted within a reasonable period, Brazil recalls that a "reasonable period" will not, in all instances, be commensurate with the pre-established deadlines set out in general regulations, particularly if the investigating authority has not acted in a reasonable, objective, and impartial manner.

304. To that regard, Brazil recalls that Frangosul was subject to an excessive burden in presenting dumping data from 1996 through 1999, a period outside the investigating period of January 1998 through January 1999. With respect to Catarinense's response, the exporter submitted the information requested by the DCD even though it was notified of the investigation eight months after the investigation had been initiated. All of these actions by the investigating authority indicate that the DCD did not act in a reasonable, objective and impartial manner.

305. Furthermore, in the case of Frangosul, the exporter invited the DCD to verify the information provided in its response.

306. Paragraph 3 of Annex II provides that all information which is verifiable, which is appropriately submitted so that it can be used in the investigation without undue difficulties, and which is supplied in a timely fashion, should be taken into account when determinations are made. The fact that Frangosul submitted normal value information in time to be verified, and actually could be verified, indicates that the DCD should have considered and accepted the normal value information.

307. Paragraph 5 of Annex II also instructs authorities that information provided may not always be ideal in all respects and that this should not be the reason for disregarding the information if the interested party has acted to the best of its ability.

308. As a final note, the DCD did not have to base its finding with respect to normal value for Frangosul and Catarinense on information provided by petitioner, since it had available information submitted by Frangosul and Catarinense. Petitioner's normal value for all other exporters was established based on prices published by JOX for *chilled* poultry, *with head and feet*, sold in the São Paulo wholesale market. According to Frangosul and Catarinense's responses, the normal value reported was for *frozen* poultry, *without head and feet*.[139] No doubt the normal value provided by the two exporters was more accurate than the normal value provided by petitioner.

309. In that sense, Paragraph 7 of Annex II instructs the investigating authority to use information from a secondary source, including information with respect to normal value, with special circumspection.

310. Even though Frangosul and Catarinense had appropriately provided normal value information, the DCD decided to use petitioner's normal value information, which was based on the price of poultry with different characteristics than that reported by the two exporters. To that effect, Brazil believes that the DCD failed to use special circumspection when it decided to apply the normal value from a secondary source.

---

[139] *See*, Exhibits BRA-24 and 25. We observe that the Brazilian exporter Catarinense reported that the broiler type poultry sold in the home market (Brazil) contained head but *not* feet.

(vi) Claim 20: Inconsistency with Article 12.2.2 of the Anti-Dumping Agreement

Text of Article 12.2.2

311. Article 12.2.2 provides that:

"12.2.2 A public notice of conclusion or suspension of an investigation in the case of an affirmative determination providing for the imposition of a definitive duty or the acceptance of a price undertaking shall contain, or otherwise make available through a separate report, all relevant information on matters of fact and law and reasons which have led to the imposition of final measures or the acceptance of a price undertaking, due regard being paid to the requirement for the protection of confidential information. In particular, the notice or report shall contain the information described in subparagraph 2.1, as well as the reasons for the acceptance or rejection of relevant arguments or claims made by the exporters and importers, and the basis for any decision made under subparagraph 10.2 of Article 6."

Legal Argument Relative to Claim 20

312. The question presented to the Panel is whether any reasoning has been provided in the final determination, sufficient to satisfy the requirements of Article 12.2.2 of the Anti-Dumping Agreement, regarding why the DCD did not use Frangosul and Catarinense's normal value information.

313. In the final determination, the DCD did not establish normal value for Frangosul and Catarinense. In fact, the DCD did not establish an individual margin of dumping for these two exporters, even though they provided information on normal value and export price.

314. The only explanation given by the DCD for not using the information provided by Frangosul and Catarinense was that the authority did not count on additional information or sufficient supporting documentation that would make it possible for it to proceed with a final determination of an individual dumping margin.[140]

315. No further explanation was given to why the normal value information reported by the exporters was not accepted.

316. Article 12.2.2 specifically requires that the notice or report contain the information described in subparagraph 2.1, as well as the reasons for the acceptance or rejection of relevant arguments or claims made by the exporters and importers. Among the relevant information described in Article 12.2.1 are the established margins of dumping and a full explanation of the reasons for the methodology used in the establishment and comparison of the export price and the normal value.

317. Contrary to Article 12.2.2 of the Anti-Dumping Agreement, no explanation was given for the reasons why none of the normal value information provided Frangosul and Catarinense were used in the establishment of the normal value.

---

[140] *See*, Page 76 of Exhibit BRA-15.

(vii) Claim 22: Inconsistency with Article 6.10 of the Anti-Dumping Agreement

Text of Article 6.10

318. Article 6.10 provides as follows:

"The authorities shall, as a rule, determine an individual margin of dumping for each known exporter or producer concerned of the product under investigation. In cases where the number of exporters, producers, importers or types of products involved is so large as to make such determination impracticable, the authorities may limit their examination either to a reasonable number of interested parties or products by using samples which are statistically valid on the basis of information available to the authorities at the time of the selection, or to the largest percentage of the volume of the exports from the country in questions which can reasonably be investigated."

Legal Argument Relative to Claim 22

319. As demonstrated in the facts related to these claims, Frangosul and Catarinense were known producers/exporters of the subject merchandise under investigation. Both Frangosul and Catarinense submitted the requested information on normal value and export price, which was disregarded by the DCD without explanation. Instead, the DCD decided to apply facts available and used the information for normal value submitted by petitioner and the information for export price provided by the Argentinean agency SENASA,[141] in order to establish the dumping margin for all other exporters. The dumping margin applied to all other exporters was applied to Frangosul and Catarinense, even though these exporters appropriately submitted normal value and export price data requested by the DCD within a reasonable period. Pursuant to these facts, the DCD was required to determine an individual margin of dumping for Frangosul and Catarinense.

320. The first sentence of Article 6.10 sets forth a general rule that authorities must determine an individual margin of dumping for each known exporter or producer of the product under investigation.

321. The second sentence of Article 6.10 of the Anti-Dumping Agreement permits an investigating authority to deviate from the general rule, in cases where the number of exporters, producers, importers or types of products involved is so large as to make such determination impracticable, by allowing the investigating authorities to "limit their examination either to a reasonable number of interested parties or products by using samples (...) or to the largest percentage of the volume of the exports from the country in question which can reasonably be investigated".

322. Brazil indicates that the second sentence of Article 6.10 of the Anti-Dumping Agreement, which is the exception to the rule set on the first part of that Article, is only applicable when the number of exporters, producers, importers or types of products involved in an investigation is so large as to make an individual margin determination impracticable.

---

[141] *See*, Page 104 of Exhibit BRA-15.

323. Brazil affirms that this was not the case at issue. The argument that the number of known Brazilian producers and exporters of poultry involved in the investigation was so large as to make an individual margin of dumping determination impracticable was never raised by the DCD during the investigation. In that regard, subparagraph 1 of Article 6.10 provides that such selection "shall preferably be chosen in consultations with and with the consent of the exporters, producers or importers concerned". The DCD did not at any time during the investigation indicate, consult with, or request the consent of the Brazilian producers/exporters concerned that it would make a selection of exporters in accordance with Article 6.10. In fact, the DCD sent dumping questionnaires for Frangosul and Catarinense to respond to, in a clear indication that the investigating authority had the intention of examining the information provided by these two exporters.

324. In addition, the DCD provided no explanation, either in the final determination or in any other document on the record of the investigation, as to why, in this case, it was not possible to determine an individual margin for Frangosul and Catarinense. The DCD failed to provide any evaluation of the facts on the record that could have formed the basis for such a conclusion, indicating that the DCD failed to perform an objective and an unbiased evaluation of the facts which, under the applicable dumping standard of review, the Panel is requested to review.

325. By failing to determine an individual margin of dumping for Frangosul and Catarinense and by applying, instead, the rate established for all other exporters, Argentina has acted inconsistently with the general rule set forth in Article 6.10 of the Anti-Dumping Agreement.

4. Article 6.9

326. **Claim 21:** Argentina failed to inform the Brazilian exporters of the essential facts under consideration which formed the basis for the decision whether to apply definitive measures, thereby preventing the Brazilian exporters from adequately defending their interests, contrary to the requirement in Article 6.9 of the Anti-Dumping Agreement.

(a) Facts

327. On January 4, 2000, the DCD issued the memorandum *Relevamiento de lo Actuado con Anterioridad al Cierre de la Etapa Probatoria*, the report prior to the end of the evidence-producing stage of the dumping investigation.[142] In item VIII of such report, the DCD provided a technical analysis of the information in the dumping investigation, including the elements for the determination of normal value and elements for the definition of the export price.[143] All of which were facts under consideration that would be used to form the basis for the decision whether to apply definitive measures.

Normal Value

---

[142] *See*, Exhibit BRA-28.
[143] *See*, Page 50 of Exhibit BRA-28.

Sadia

328. In the report prior to the final determination, the DCD stated that Sadia provided on 26 August 1999 lists of invoices issued from 1996 through February 1999 and a copy of one invoice with the corresponding translation.[144] Due to the extensive volume of invoices to be examined and for which supporting documentation would have to be provided, the DCD made a statistic sample for the period starting January 1998 through January 1999.[145] According to the DCD, the sample was done randomly and considered 372 transactions.[146] The DCD then requested supporting documentation for the sample it had made. According to the report, Sadia had not presented the referred documentation up to that moment.[147]

329. On 23 June 2000, the DCD issued the final affirmative dumping determination.[148] In the determination, the DCD stated that on 13 January 2000, Sadia presented part of the supporting documentation requested by the DCD (268 invoices).[149] The DCD calculated normal value for Sadia based on the sample it chose, and for which Sadia presented supporting documentation.[150]

Avipal

330. The report prior to the final determination provided that on 12 August 1999, Avipal explained that due to the great number of invoices (around 545 invoices a day and 196,200 invoices per year) it would not be feasible to send copy of all invoices.[151] On 1 September 1999, Avipal submitted copies of the translation of invoice forms.[152] On 21 December 1999, Avipal submitted diskette with the list of the invoices and attached spreadsheets with deductions to be made to the referred list.[153] The DCD noted that the mentioned information had not yet been examined up to that moment.[154]

331. On 23 June 2000, the DCD issued the final affirmative dumping determination.[155] In the determination, the DCD explained that from the information submitted by Avipal on 12 August 1999, the DCD made a calculation based on the transactions, for which Avipal submitted invoice copies (25 invoices).[156] The DCD further stated that the information submitted on 21 December 1999 was not accompanied by supporting documentation and that the DCD only made discounts for which it was able to corroborate.[157] The DCD calculated normal value for Avipal based only on the information of transactions, for which Avipal submitted invoice copies.[158]

---

[144] *See*, Pages 60 and 61 of Exhibit BRA-28.
[145] *See*, Page 61 of Exhibit BRA-28.
[146] *Ibid.*
[147] *See*, Page 61 of Exhibit BRA-28.
[148] *See*, Exhibit BRA-15.
[149] *See*, Page 62 of Exhibit BRA-15.
[150] *See*, Page 63 of Exhibit BRA-15.
[151] *See*, Page 62 of Exhibit BRA-28.
[152] *Ibid.*
[153] *Ibid.*
[154] *Ibid.*
[155] *See*, Exhibit BRA-15.
[156] *See*, Page 64 of Exhibit BRA-15.
[157] *See*, Pages 64 and 65 of Exhibit BRA-15.
[158] *See*, Page 65 of Exhibit BRA-15.

Frangosul

332. Oddly, the report issued by the DCD prior to the final determination made no reference to the normal value information provided by Frangosul throughout the investigation.[159] In this regard, it is important to note that Frangosul invited the DCD to verify *in loco* or to select a sample of the transactions so that it could provide the corresponding invoices.[160] On 30 December 1999, Frangosul presented a list of invoices for transactions in the home market for January 1998 through January 1999 in a diskette.[161] The DCD never selected the transactions for which Frangosul was supposed to provide invoice copies.

333. On 23 June 2000, the DCD issued the final affirmative dumping determination.[162] The DCD applied to Frangosul the normal value found for all other exporters, which was based on information presented by the petitioner on 26 August 1999.[163]

Catarinense

334. In the report prior to the final determination, the DCD stated that Catarinense submitted the response to the dumping questionnaire on 3 November 1999.[164] It is important to note that Catarinense was notified of the investigation and was requested to provide responses to the questionnaire only on 15 September 1999.[165] The DCD report prior to the final determination presented the following table based on the data submitted by Catarinense.

NORMAL VALUE REPORTED BY CATARINENSE

Year	Total Kg.	Total US$	Price Per Kg	Normal Value (+9,09%)
1998	52,528,211	47,068,340.55	0.8961	0.9775
1999*	43,475,875	24,424,618.28	0.5618	0.6129
Weighted Average	96,004,086	71,492,958.83	0.7447	0.8124

Source: Page 66 of Exhibit BRA-28.

335. The DCD indicated that the values in the table came from the aggregate data presented in Annexes V and VI of the exporter's questionnaire and corresponded to a period greater than the period under investigation.[166]

336. On 23 June 2000, the DCD issued the final affirmative dumping determination.[167] In the final determination, the DCD provided that Catarinense did not present supporting documentation for the listed home market sales and applied

---

[159] *See*, Exhibit BRA-28.
[160] *See*, Exhibit BRA-26.
[161] *Ibid.*
[162] *See*, Exhibit BRA-15.
[163] *See*, Pages 54, 55, 103 and 104 of Exhibit BRA-15.
[164] *See*, Page 66 of Exhibit BRA-28.
[165] *See*, Exhibit BRA-13.
[166] *See*, Page 66 of Exhibit BRA-28.
[167] *See*, Exhibit BRA-15.

Report of the Panel

the normal value found for all other exporters, which was based on information presented by the petitioner on 26 August 1999.[168]

Export Price

337. In the report prior to the final determination, the DCD provided that on 13 September 1999, the Subdirector General de Operaciones Aduaneras del Interior submitted lists of import transactions,[169] and that CEPA had also provided on 17 November and 16 December 1999 information regarding imports for the month of October and November 1999.[170] The exporters also submitted lists of invoices for the sales transactions to Argentina throughout the investigation. The report, however, did not mention the export price information submitted by the Brazilian exporters. The information that was considered by the DCD as the most complete and detailed source of information to establish the FOB export price was that provided by the agency *Ganaderia*.[171]

338. On 23 June 2000, the DCD issued the final affirmative dumping determination.[172] In the final determination, the DCD established export price based on the import information from *Ganaderia*.[173] For the export price established for all other exporters, the DCD used the information provided by SENASA.[174]

(i) Claim 21: Inconsistency with Article 6.9 of the Anti-Dumping Agreement

Text of Article 6.9

339. Article 6.9 provides as follows:

"The authorities shall, before a final determination is made, inform all interested parties of the essential facts under consideration which form the basis for the decision whether to apply definitive measures. Such disclosure should take place in sufficient time for the parties to defend their interests."

Legal Argument Relative to Claim 21

340. Article 6.9 of the Anti-Dumping Agreement mandates authorities to inform all interested parties of the essential facts under consideration that will form the basis for the decision whether to apply definitive measures. Article 6.9 further provides that such disclosure of the essential facts take place in sufficient time for the parties to defend their interests.

341. Information regarding normal value and export price, which are used to establish dumping margins, are considered essential facts to be considered in the final determination. By not indicating in the report prior to the final determination that the normal value and export price reported by the exporters was not going to be used and by not giving the reasons why that information would be disregarded, the DCD has

---

[168] *See*, Pages 103 and 104 of Exhibit BRA-15.
[169] *See*, Page 72 of Exhibit BRA-28.
[170] *See*, Pages 72 and 73 of Exhibit BRA-28.
[171] *See*, Page 72 of Exhibit BRA-28.
[172] *See*, Exhibit BRA-15.
[173] *See*, Pages 76 and 77 of Exhibit BRA-15.
[174] *See*, Page 104 of Exhibit BRA-15.

not informed of the essential facts under consideration considered in the decision whether to apply definitive measures and has not given the exporters the opportunity to defend their interests.

342. In particular, the DCD report prior to the final determination did not indicate: (i) that the information in the lists of invoices provided by Sadia that covered the extensive period of 1996 through February 1999 would not be used to establish normal value; (ii) that the only information considered to establish normal value for Sadia in the final determination would correspond to the information for the transactions chosen through the sample made by the DCD, for which supporting documentation was actually provided to the DCD; and, (iii) the reason why the DCD would not consider the information provided by Sadia for all sales in the home market.

343. In addition, the report did not indicate that the only information that would be considered to establish normal value for Avipal would be the information for the transactions, for which supporting documentation was submitted to the DCD (25 invoices).

344. With respect to Frangosul and Catarinense, the DCD simply disregarded the information submitted by the two exporters and applied the normal value found for all other exporters, based on the information provided by petitioner.

345. Likewise, the report did not indicate why the information submitted by the exporters was not considered for purposes of determining the FOB export price, nor did the DCD explain why it considered the information provided by the agency *Ganaderia* more complete and, thus, denied the exporters the right to defend their interests.

346. Our understanding of Article 6.9 comes from the Panel's reasoning on *Argentina - Ceramic Floor Tiles:*

> "(...) the DCD relied primarily upon evidence submitted by petitioners and derived from secondary sources, rather than upon information provided by the exporters, as the factual basis for a determination of the existence of dumping. Thus, petitioner and secondary source information, rather than exporters' information, represented (with respect to the existence of dumping) the essential facts which formed the basis for the decision whether to apply definitive measures. *We therefore examined the record in order to determine whether exporters were informed by the Argentine authority, through access to the file, that it was on these facts that the authority would primarily rely in its determination regarding the existence of dumping.*"[175]
> (emphasis added)

347. Furthermore, Brazil agrees with that Panel's conclusion that exporters cannot be aware simply by reviewing the record of the investigation that evidence submitted by petitioners and derived from secondary sources, rather than facts submitted by the exporters, would form the primary basis for the determination of the existence and extent of dumping.[176] Brazil agrees with that Panel's conclusion that:

---

[175] *Argentina - Definitive Measures on Imports of Ceramic Floor Tiles from Italy*, 28 September 2001, WT/DS189/R, at para. 6.127 (adopted on 5 November 2001) (*"Argentina - Ceramic Floor Tiles"*).

[176] *Argentina - Ceramic Floor Tiles*, DSR 2001:XII, 6241, at para. 6.129.

"(...) The DCD thus failed to put the exporters on notice of an essential fact under consideration. As a result, the exporters were unable to defend their interests within the meaning of Article 6.9, for example, by giving reasons why their responses should not be rejected and by suggesting alternative sources for facts available if their responses were nonetheless disregarded. Under these circumstances, we find that the DCD did not, by referring the exporters to the complete file of the investigation, fulfil its obligation under Article 6.9 to inform the exporters of the "essential facts under consideration which form the basis for the decision whether to apply definitive measures."[177](emphasis added)

348. Brazil believes that the analysis and conclusions of the Panel in *Argentina - Ceramic Floor Tiles* apply to the present claim. The DCD failed to provide the exporters the essential facts, which would form the basis for the application of the definitive measures, and that the information submitted by exporters was not to be used.

349. By not explaining the reasons why such information was rejected, the DCD denied the exporters the opportunity to defend their interests within the meaning of Article 6.9. This constitutes a *prima facie* violation of Article 6.9 of the Anti-Dumping Agreement.

350. Also, to the extent that Argentina, in order to justify its activities in the investigation, may bring forth information or documents not disclosed to the exporters during the investigation (particularly in regard to Claim 39), Brazil submits that such non-disclosure of essential facts should also be considered a violation of Article 6.9.

D. Conduct of the Anti-Dumping Investigation and Final Affirmative Determination

1. Article 2.4 and 2.4.2

351. Five claims follow from the facts described below and the legal text of the Anti-Dumping Agreement:

Claim 23: Argentina acted inconsistently with Article 2.4 by not making due allowance for differences in freight in the normal value established for Sadia and Avipal.

Claim 24: Argentina acted inconsistently with Article 2.4 by not making due allowance for differences in taxation, freight and financial cost in the normal value established for all other exporters.

Claim 25: Argentina acted inconsistently with Article 2.4 by incorrectly making due allowances to normal value based on alleged physical characteristic differences between the product sold in Brazil and to Argentina.

Claim 26: Argentina acted inconsistently with Article 2.4 by imposing an unreasonable burden of proof on Sadia, Avipal and Frangosul by not determining the period of investigation and by allowing the exporters to submit dumping information

---

[177] *Argentina - Ceramic Floor Tiles,* at para. 6.129.

for the years 1996 through 1999, when the dumping period of investigation was later determined as from January 1998 through January 1999.

Claim 27: Argentina acted inconsistently with Article 2.4.2 by incorrectly making a comparison between the export price and the normal value for Sadia and Avipal based only on internal market transactions for which invoices were presented, instead of determining normal value based on all the transactions in the internal market for the period, listed and submitted to the DCD. The DCD established the margins of dumping for Sadia and Avipal on the basis of a comparison of a weighted average *statistical sample* of normal value with a weighted average of prices of all comparable export transactions.

(a) Facts

352. On 23 June 2000, the DCD issued the final affirmative dumping determination.[178] The export price, normal value and the dumping margin calculation in the final determination were established as follows.

Export Price

353. In the final dumping determination, the DCD established export price based on the import information from *Ganaderia*.[179] The DCD used a weighted average FOB export price for the period January 1998 through January 1999 for each exporter. The table used by the DCD to establish export price is the following:

Total By Producer	US$ FOB	Net Kgs	US$/Kgs
Sadia S.A.	16216345	20049051	0.80883
Comaves	3015738	3380321	0.89215
Da Granja Agroi	1652300	1820106	0.90780
Sadia Concordia	1398960	1519560	0.92063
Minuano Alimentos	3139461	3390151	0.92605
Avipal	3554693	3767350	0.94355
Acaua Industria	39824	41920	0.95000
Felipe Avícola	306650	322000	0.95233
Nicolini - SIF	5172876	5397254	0.95843
Catarinense Ltd.	1163894	1158307	1.00482
Perdigão Agroin	1564110	1551753	1.00796
Seara Alimentos	11147872	11038851	1.00988
Ceval Alimentos	947993	917261	1.03350
Frangosul	2663240	2558914	1.04077
Veneto	67252	64050	1.04999
Chapecó CI	1445063	1363221	1.06004
Litoral Aliment	523440	482000	1.08598
TOTAL	**54019711**	**58822070**	**0.91836**

Source: Pages 76 and 77 of Exhibit BRA-15.

---

[178] *See*, Exhibit BRA-15.
[179] *See*, Pages 76, 77, 103 and 104 of Exhibit BRA-15.

Export Price for All Other Exporters

354. In the final determination, the DCD calculated export price for all other exporters based on the information provided by SENASA.[180] The following is the table used by the DCD to establish that export price:

FOB EXPORT PRICE 1998 - January 1999

Producer	US$/Kg	Net Kg	US$ FOB
Comaves	0.89215	3.380.321,00	3.015.738,00
Da Granja Agroi	0.90780	1.820.106,00	1.652.300,00
Sadia Concordia	0.92063	1.820.106,00	1.652.300,00
Minuano Alimentos	0.92605	3.390.151,00	3.139.461,00
Acaua Industria	0.95000	41.920,00	39.824,00
Felipe Avicola	0.95233	322.000,00	306.650,00
Catarinense Ltd	1.00482	1.158.307,00	1.163.894,00
Perdigão Agroin	1.00796	1.551.753,00	1.564.110,00
Frangosul	1.04077	2.558.914,00	2.663.240,00
Veneto	1.04999	64.050,00	67.252,00
Chapecó CI	1.06004	1.363.221,00	1.445.063,00
Litoral Aliment	1.08598	482.000,00	523.440,00
TOTAL	**0.95992**	**17.952.849,00**	**17.233.272,00**

Source: Annex "Precio FOB de exportación de las firmas brasileñas con escasa o sin participación en la investigación" in Exhibit BRA-15.

Normal Value

Sadia

355. On 20 April 1999, Sadia submitted the questionnaire response, providing sales information for the home market and for Argentina for the period 1996 through 1998 and January and February of 1999.[181] On 26 August 1999, Sadia sent a letter to the DCD providing a list of the sales transactions in the home market for 1996 through 1999 and explaining that the great volume of sales in the home market made it impossible to provide an invoice copy for each transaction. In this letter, Sadia invited the DCD to verify *in loco* the transactions listed or to select a sample of transactions so it could provide the corresponding invoices.[182] On 3 December 1999, the DCD sent a letter to Sadia requesting invoice copies of 372 selected sales transactions in the home market, establishing a 5-day deadline to submit the invoice copies.[183] On January 4, 2000, the DCD issued the memorandum *Relevamiento de lo Actuado con Anterioridad al Cierre de la Etapa Probatoria*, the report prior to the end of the evidence-producing stage of the dumping investigation.[184] On 13 January

---

[180] *See*, Page 104 of Exhibit BRA-15.
[181] *See*, Pages 18 and 19 of Exhibit BRA-15 and Exhibit BRA-22.
[182] *See*, Exhibit BRA-29.
[183] *See*, Exhibit BRA-30.
[184] *See*, Exhibit BRA-28.

2000, Sadia submitted copies of the invoices requested by the DCD.[185] On 23 June 2000, the DCD issued the final affirmative dumping determination.[186]

356. In its determination, the DCD explained how it established normal value for Sadia. From the information submitted by Sadia on 26 August 1999, the DCD stated that due to the great volume of information to be analyzed and for which supporting documentation was required, the DCD chose a statistical sample for the period of January 1998 through 1999.[187] The DCD did not explain how this sample was made. The only explanation given was that the DCD determined that the size of the sample would be of 166, considering a tolerable error of 2 per cent and a trusted gap ("*intervalo de confianza*") of 95 per cent.[188] Without further explanation, the DCD stated that it decided to choose a greater sample size for Sadia of 372 transactions.[189]

357. Based on that sample, the DCD requested Sadia to provide supporting documentation (copies of invoices) for that sample. The DCD stated that Sadia requested an extension of the deadline, which was granted, and that on 13 January 2000, Sadia presented part of the supporting documentation requested (268 invoices).[190] The DCD further indicated that according to the memorandum prior to the final determination of 4 January 2000, for purposes of the final determination, the investigating authority would consider the information submitted until that date.[191] The DCD calculated normal value for Sadia based on the information provided by Sadia for the sample chosen by the DCD and for which Sadia had presented supporting documentation. The normal calculation for Sadia was as follows:

STATISTICAL SAMPLE
SADIA S.A.

Period	Gross Simple Average Price R$	Net Simple Average Price R$	Gross Simple Average Price US$	Net Simple Average Price US$	Normal Value + 9,09%	Gross Weight Average Price US$	Net Weight Average Price US$	Normal Value + 9,09%
Jan 98- Jan 99	1,2409	1,1465	1,0527	0,9726	1,061	0,9222	0,852	0,9294

Source: Page 63 of Exhibit BRA-15.

Avipal

358. On 21 April 1999, Avipal submitted its questionnaire response.[192] On 7 May 1999, Avipal submitted a hard copy of the response with the non-confidential information.[193] On 12 August 1999, Avipal submitted a list of sales transactions in the home market for 1996 through 1999, with a sample invoice for each month in 1997 and 1998, and explanation that the great volume of sales in the home market made it impossible to provide an invoice copy for each transaction. In its letter dated

---

[185] *See*, Page 62 of Exhibit BRA-15.
[186] *See*, Exhibit BRA-15.
[187] *See*, Page 62 of Exhibit BRA-15.
[188] *Ibid.*
[189] *Ibid.*
[190] *Ibid.*
[191] *See*, Page 63 of Exhibit BRA-15.
[192] *See*, Exhibit BRA-23.
[193] *Ibid.*

Report of the Panel

12 August 1999, Avipal invited the DCD to verify *in loco* the transactions listed or to select a sample of transactions so it could provide the corresponding invoices.[194] On 1 September 1999, Avipal provided translation of a standard invoice from Portuguese into Spanish.[195] On 21 December 1999, Avipal submitted a diskette with a list of invoices for sales of poultry in the home market for the period January 1998 through January 1999, including deductions and taxes.[196] The DCD never selected the transactions for which Avipal offered to provide invoice copies. On January 4, 2000, the DCD issued the memorandum *Relevamiento de lo Actuado con Anterioridad al Cierre de la Etapa Probatoria*, the report prior to the end of the evidence-producing stage of the dumping investigation.[197] On 23 June 2000, the DCD issued the final affirmative dumping determination.[198]

359. In the final dumping determination, the DCD explained how it established normal value for Avipal. From the information submitted by Avipal on 12 August 1999, the DCD made a calculation based on the transactions, for which Avipal sent invoice copies (25 invoices).[199]

INVOICES HOME MARKET
AVIPAL SA

Year	# of Inv. Presented	Total Kgs	Gross Simple Average Price US$	Net simple Average Price US$	Normal Value +9,09%	Net Weight Average Price R$	Gross Weight Average Price US$	Net Weight Average Price US$	Normal Value +9,09%
1998	25	174.030,9	1,102	1,007	1,0985	1,2220	1,0806	1,0437	1,1385

Source: Page 64 of Exhibit BRA-15.

360. The DCD further stated that on 1 September 1999, Avipal sent a translation of a standard invoice. The DCD indicated that on 21 December 1999, Avipal sent a diskette with the list of invoices and that spreadsheets were attached to the response with deductions to be made to the listed figures.[200] From the analysis of the submitted information, the DCD created the following table:

---

[194] *See*, Exhibit BRA-31.
[195] *See*, Page 64 of Exhibit BRA-15.
[196] *Ibid*.
[197] *See*, Exhibit BRA-28.
[198] *See*, Exhibit BRA-15.
[199] *See*, Page 64 of Exhibit BRA-15.
[200] *Ibid*.

Argentina - Poultry Anti-Dumping Duties

AVIPAL SA
List of sales in the Home Market

Period	Total Kgs	Gross Simple Average Price R$	Net Simple Average Price R$	Gross Weight Average Price US$	Net Weight Average Price US$	Normal Value +9,09%
Jan 98 - Jan 99	126,828,110.36	1,2183	1,1358	1,011	0,9421	1,028

Source: Pages 64 and 65 of Exhibit BRA-15.

361. The DCD indicated that the information submitted on the 21 December 1999 did not present supporting documentation and that the DCD only made discounts for which it was able to corroborate.[201]

362. The DCD calculated normal value for Avipal based on the information of the transactions that accompanied invoice copies. The normal value calculation for Avipal was as follows:

INVOICES HOME MARKET
AVIPAL SA

Year	# of Inv. Presented	Total Kgs	Gross Simple Average Price US$	Net Simple Average Price US$	Normal Value +9,09%	Net Weight Average Price R$	Gross Weight Average Price US$	Net Weight Average Price US$	Normal Value +9,09%
1998	25	174.030,9	1,102	0,986	1,0756	1,1695	1,0806	0,9988	1,0896

Source: Page 65 of Exhibit BRA-15.

Frangosul

363. On 27 April 1999, Frangosul submitted its questionnaire response.[202] On 19 August 1999, Frangosul provided translation of four invoices of sales to Argentina, translation of product brochure, and explanation that the great volume of sales in the home market made it impossible to provide invoice copies for each transaction. Frangosul in this response invited the DCD to verify *in loco* or to select a sample of the transactions so that it could provide the corresponding invoices.[203] On 30 December 1999, Frangosul presented a list of invoices for transactions in the internal market for January 1998 through January 1999 in a diskette.[204] The DCD never selected the transactions for which Frangosul offered to provide invoice copies. On 4 January 2000, the DCD issued the memorandum *Relevamiento de lo Actuado con Anterioridad al Cierre de la Etapa Probatoria*, the report prior to the end of the evidence-producing stage of the dumping investigation.[205] On 23 June 2000, the DCD issued the final affirmative dumping determination.[206]

---

[201] *See*, Page 65 of Exhibit BRA-15.
[202] *See*, Exhibit BRA-24.
[203] *See*, Exhibit BRA-26.
[204] *Ibid*.
[205] *See*, Exhibit BRA-28.
[206] *See*, Exhibit BRA-15.

Report of the Panel

364. In the final determination, the DCD did not consider Frangosul's response nor did it provide an explanation for why the information provided was not used.[207]

Catarinense

365. On 15 September 1999, the DCD sent a letter to Catarinense notifying it of the investigation and requesting it provide responses to the questionnaire. In this letter the DCD established, for the first time, the period of investigation for data collection from January 1998 until January 1999.[208] On 13 October 1999, Catarinense requested an extension of 20 days to submit the responses. On 3 November 1999, Catarinense provided its questionnaire responses. For sales to Argentina, Catarinense provided a list of invoices and copy of the invoices for 1998 and 1999. For sales in the home market, Catarinense provided a list of sales transactions.[209] On 8 November 1999, in reference to Catarinense's request of 13 October 1999, the DCD sent a letter to Catarinense granting the extension of the deadline until 8 November 1999.[210] After this date, the DCD did not request further information from Catarinense. On 23 June 2000, the DCD issued the final affirmative dumping determination, without taking into account the responses submitted by Catarinense in the investigation.[211]

366. In the final determination, the DCD presented the following table from the information submitted by Catarinense on 3 November 1999:

NORMAL VALUE REPORTED BY CATARINENSE

Year	Total Kg.	Total US$	Price Per Kg	Normal Value (+9,09%)
1998	52,528,211	47,068,340.55	0.8961	0.9775
1999*	43,475,875	24,424,618.28	0.5618	0.6129
Weighted Average	96,004,086	71,492,958.83	0.7447	0.8124

Source: Pages 69 and 70 of Exhibit BRA-15.

367. In the final determination, the DCD indicated that the values in the table came from the aggregate data presented in Annexes V and VI of Section A of Catarinense's questionnaire response and corresponded to a period greater than the period under investigation, and that the information provided by Catarinense did not present supporting documentation.[212]

Normal Value for All Other Exporters

368. In the final determination, the DCD calculated the normal value for all other exporters based on the information provided by petitioner on 26 July 1999.[213] Petitioner presented a spreadsheet with the normal value calculation in the home

---

[207] *See*, Pages 103 and 104 of Exhibit BRA-15.
[208] *See*, Exhibit BRA-13.
[209] *See*, Pages 38 and 39 of Exhibit BRA-15 and Exhibit BRA-25.
[210] *See*, Exhibit BRA-27.
[211] *See*, Pages 103 and 104 of Exhibit BRA-15.
[212] *See*, Page 70 of Exhibit BRA-15.
[213] *See*, Page 54 of Exhibit BRA-15.

market for the period 1998 through 1999 based on prices published by JOX.[214] Petitioner's calculation used prices from three reference dates, for each month of the period January 1998 - January 1999.[215] These prices were for *chilled* poultry, with head and feet, sold in the São Paulo wholesale market. Petitioner's calculation is as follows:

NORMAL VALUE
SÃO PAULO - CHILLED POULTRY

Date	Average R$	Exchange Rate	Average US$	Adjustment 9,09%
5/01/98	1.175	1.1161	1.0528	1.1485
14/01/98	1.065	1.1195	0.9513	1.0378
30/01/98	1.167	1.123	1.0392	1.1336
January				1.107
10/02/98	1.217	1.1261	1.0807	1.1790
16/02/98	1.235	1.1281	1.0948	1.1943
27/02/98	1.215	1.1301	1.0751	1.1729
February				1.182
4/03/98	1.240	1.1311	1.0963	1.1959
17/03/98	1.203	1.1341	1.0608	1.1572
27/03/98	1.190	1.1361	1.0474	1.1427
March				1.165
8/04/98	1.212	1.1319	1.0708	1.1681
17/04/98	1.183	1.1409	1.0369	1.1312
30/04/98	1.187	1.144	1.0376	1.1319
April				1.144
6/05/98	1.187	1.1445	1.0371	1.1314
11/05/98	1.187	1.145	1.0367	1.1309
18/05/98	1.132	1.1465	0.9874	1.0771
May				1.113
4/06/98	1.017	1.1514	0.8833	0.9636
16/06/98	1.120	1.1538	0.9707	1.0589
24/06/98	1.032	1.1547	0.8937	0.9750
June				0.999
3/07/98	1.005	1.1566	0.8689	0.9479
14/07/98	1.078	1.1645	0.9257	1.0099
30/07/98	0.990	1.162	0.8520	0.9294
July				0.962
7/08/98	1.090	1.17	0.9316	1.0163
13/08/98	1.088	1.17	0.9299	1.0144
31/08/98	0.998	1.18	0.8458	0.9226
August				0.984
4/09/98	1.07	1.18	0.9068	0.9892
16/09/98	1.052	1.18	0.8915	0.9726
29/09/98	0.987	1.19	0.8294	0.9048

---

[214] *See*, Exhibit BRA-19.
[215] *Ibid.*

Report of the Panel

Date	Average R$	Exchange Rate	Average US$	Adjustment 9,09%
September				0.956
5/10/98	0.97	1.19	0.8151	0.8892
14/10/98	1.092	1.19	0.9176	1.0011
29/10/98	1.007	1.19	0.8462	0.9231
October				0.938
4/11/98	1.048	1.19	0.8807	0.9607
16/11/98	1.020	1.19	0.8571	0.9351
30/11/98	1.015	1.2	0.8458	0.9227
November				0.940
4/12/98	1.053	1.2	0.8775	0.9573
16/12/98	1.170	1.21	0.9669	1.0548
29/12/98	1.252	1.21	1.0347	1.1288
December			34.476	1.0470
Average 1998 NV			0.9577	1.0447
4/01/99	1.232	1.21	1.0182	1.1107
15/01/99	0.972	1.43	0.6797	0.7415
January			0.8490	0.9261
Total 98 and 99			36.174	39.4620
Average 98/99 NV			0.9519	1.0385

Source: Pages 54 and 55 of Exhibit BRA-15 and Exhibit BRA-19.

Dumping Margin

369.   In the final determination, the DCD calculated the dumping margin based on the export price and normal value explained above. The following tables indicate how the dumping margins were calculated:

SADIA SA

Normal value US$/Kg A	FOB Price Average US$/Kg B	Dumping Margin % (A-B)/B
0,9294	0,80883	14,91

Source: Page 102 of Exhibit BRA-15.

AVIPAL SA

Normal value US$/Kg A	FOB Price Average US$/Kg B	Dumping Margin % (A-B)/B
1,0896	0,94355	15,48

Source: Page 103 of Exhibit BRA-15.

ALL OTHER EXPORTERS

Normal value US$/Kg A	FOB Price Average US$/Kg B	Dumping Margin % (A-B)/B
1,0385	0,95992	8,19

Source: Page 104 of Exhibit BRA-15.

370. The DCD further indicated that for the companies Catarinense, Frangosul, Comaves, Da Granja Agroi, Sadia Concordia, Minuano, Acaua, Felipe, Perdigão, Veneto, Chapecó and Litoral Aliment, the investigating authority did not have sufficient additional information or supporting documentation that would enable the final determination of an individual dumping margin.[216]

    (i)   Claim 23: Inconsistency with Article 2.4 of the Anti-Dumping Agreement

Text of Article 2.4

371. Article 2.4 of the Anti-Dumping Agreement provides how a fair comparison between the export price and normal shall be made:

> "A fair comparison shall be made between the export price and the normal value. This comparison shall be made at the same level of trade, normally at ex-factory level, in respect of sales made at as nearly as possible the same time. Due allowance shall be made in each case, on its merits, for differences which affect price comparability, including differences in conditions and terms of sale, taxation, levels of trade, quantities, physical characteristics, and any other differences which are also demonstrated to affect price comparability. In the cases referred to in paragraph 3, allowances for costs, including duties and taxes, incurred between the importation and resale, and for profits accruing, should also be made. If in these case price comparability has been affected, the authorities shall establish the normal value at a level f trade equivalent to the level of trade of the constructed export price, or shall make due allowance as warranted under this paragraph. The authorities shall indicate to the parties in question what information is necessary to ensure a fair, comparison and shall not impose an unreasonable burden of proof on those parties."

Legal Argument Relative to Claim 23

372. On 20 April 1999, Sadia submitted the questionnaire response, providing sales information for the home market and Argentina for the period 1996 through 1998 and January and February of 1999. In Annex VIII, Section C of its questionnaire response, Sadia reported internal freight costs for sales in the internal market for the years 1996, 1997, 1998 and for January and February 1999.

373. On 21 April 1999, Avipal submitted the questionnaire response. On 12 October 1999 the DCD requested a list of invoices for all the sales of poultry in the

---

[216] *See*, Pages 103 and 104 of Exhibit BRA-15.

Report of the Panel

home market for the period January 1998 through January 1999. The DCD did not provide a deadline for Avipal to submit this information. On 21 December 1999, Avipal submitted a diskette with a list of invoices for sales of poultry in the home market for the period January 1998 through January 1999, including a spreadsheet with taxes (ICMS/PIS/COFINS), commission, freight and financial costs included in the normal value that should be deducted for an *ex-factory* comparison with the export price.

374. In its final dumping determination, the DCD calculated normal value for Sadia based on the information provided by Sadia, which was accompanied by supporting documentation, for the sample chosen by the DCD. In its normal value calculation, the DCD failed to make the freight deductions as reported in Sadia's 20 April 1999 response to the questionnaire.

375. Also in the final dumping determination, the DCD calculated normal value for Avipal based on the transactions in the internal market for which Avipal provided copies of invoices. The DCD failed to make the freight deductions as reported by Avipal on 21 December 1999.

376. Article 2.4 of the Anti-Dumping Agreement requires due allowance to be made for differences which affect price comparability, including differences in conditions and terms of sale, taxation, levels of trade, quantities, physical characteristics, *and any other differences which are also demonstrated to affect price comparability.*

377. The requirement to make due allowance for such differences means, at a minimum, that the authority has to evaluate identified differences to see whether an adjustment is required to maintain price comparability and to ensure a fair comparison between normal value and export price, pursuant to Article 2.4. From the evaluation of the identified differences, the authorities must make adjustments where necessary.

378. From the facts of this investigation, the DCD violated Article 2.4 by not making due allowance for freight, as demonstrated by Sadia and Avipal in their responses submitted during the investigation.

(ii) Claim 24: Inconsistency with Article 2.4 of the Anti-Dumping Agreement

Text of Article 2.4

379. Article 2.4 provides in part that:

"(...) Due allowance shall be made in each case, on its merits, for differences which affect price comparability, including differences in conditions and terms of sale, taxation, levels of trade, quantities, physical characteristics, and any other differences which are also demonstrated to affect price comparability.(...)"

Legal Argument Relative to Claim 24

380. On 25 June 1999, the DCD requested JOX to clarify the taxes included in the prices published and used to determine normal value in the preliminary

determination.[217] On 27 July 1999, the DCD sent once again the request for clarification to JOX.[218] On 3 August 1999, JOX sent a letter to the DCD explaining that the prices published by JOX include the following taxes: 12 per cent ICMS (Value Added Tax) and 2.65 per cent PIS/COFINS (Social Contribution on Revenue). JOX further explained that the prices published include: financial costs, depending on the sales term; sales commission of 0.5 per cent to 1 per cent over the value of the sale; and, a variable freight for delivery, depending on the geographic location of the seller and the buyer.[219] JOX provided these responses in Portuguese.

381. According to the facts related to these claims, the DCD established normal value for all other exporters based on the information provided by petitioner on 26 July 1999. This information included a spreadsheet with the calculated normal value. Petitioner's calculation used prices published by JOX for three reference dates, for each month of the period January 1998 - January 1999. The published prices were for *chilled* poultry, with head and feet, sold in the São Paulo wholesale market.

382. Even though the DCD decided to use JOX published prices of poultry to establish the normal value for all other exporters, it did not make due allowance to account for taxes, financial costs, sales commission and freight included in the published prices, as explained by JOX. The DCD simply disregarded the information it had requested JOX and decided not to make any adjustment to the normal value, which was demonstrated to affect price comparability.

383. In the final determination, the DCD simply stated that the information JOX provided was in Portuguese.[220]

384. Article 2.4 of the Anti-Dumping Agreement requires due allowance to be made for differences which affect price comparability, including differences in conditions and terms of sale, *taxation*, levels of trade, quantities, physical characteristics, and *any other differences which are also demonstrated to affect price comparability*. The DCD violated Article 2.4 by not making due allowance for taxes and other differences that affect comparability (financial cost, sales commission, and freight), as demonstrated by JOX in the letter sent to the DCD on 3 August 1999.

385. During the consultation stage of this dispute, Brazil presented on 5 December 2001 questions to Argentina regarding the investigation. Specifically, Brazil requested the following explanations.

Question 39:

Please provide explanation why Authorities disregarded the information they requested of JOX clarifying that the reference price published by them include taxes (ICMS and PIS/COFINS), freight and financial cost.

Argentina responded on 11 January 2002 by stating that:

> "With respect to the JOX publication, the authority requested through notification DCD No. 273-000788/99 that JOX provide clarification regarding the taxes included in the prices published, as well as the general conditions to which these prices are subject. The request was repeated subsequently through another notification.

---

[217] *See*, Exhibit BRA-32.
[218] *Ibid.*
[219] *Ibid.*
[220] *See*, Page 56 of Exhibit BRA-15.

Report of the Panel

Finally, on 28 July 1999 and on 3 August 1999, JOX presented information in Portuguese, which did not allow the authority to use the information once it did not comply with the formal requirements required by the laws and rules regarding the administrative proceedings regime"

Question 40:

If authorities disregarded JOX's explanation due to lack of translation, please provide whether Authorities requested such translation and why Authorities, themselves, did not provide the translation since they were the ones requesting the information.

Argentina responded on 11 January 2002 by stating that:

"We refer to the response provided in question 39. (...) It should be observed that the proceedings of unfair trade practices are governed by the Law of Administrative Proceedings that require that documentation presented be translated, a fact known to the parties intervening in the proceedings"

386. Brazil recalls that the clarification provided by JOX was not requested by the Brazilian exporters or CEPA, but by the authorities themselves. In fact, the JOX publication of *chilled* poultry sold in São Paulo was not a source of information used by the Brazilian exporters. However, Brazil believes that if the DCD decided to use JOX information to establish normal value for all other exporters, it should also have taken into account JOX's explanation on taxes, financial cost, sales commission and freight for the published prices.

387. Brazil also recalls that JOX was not an interested party in this proceeding. To that regard, "interested parties" are defined in Article 6.11 of the Anti-Dumping Agreement as:

"(i) *an exporter or foreign producer* or the importer of a product subject to investigation, or a trade or business association a majority of the members of which are producers, exporters or importers of such product;

(ii) the government of the exporting Member; and

(iii) a producer of the like product in the importing Member or a trade and business association a majority of the members of which produce the like product in the territory of the importing member" (emphasis added)

388. JOX is not included in the definition of "interested parties" as provided in the Agreement and, thus, did not have to comply with the Law of Administrative Proceedings as indicated by Argentina.

389. Furthermore and as stated in footnote 25 of this submission, JOX is a private entity, not related to the Brazilian government or any of the Brazilian exporters subject to the investigation, and was, therefore, under no obligation to respond to the Argentinean authorities much less to provide a translation of its response in Spanish. By responding to the DCD's request, JOX was doing the Argentinean authorities a favor.

390. Brazil understands that when Argentina requested JOX clarification regarding what was included in the published prices, it was checking the data received from

petitioner with the source of that information. Thus, it was up to the DCD to have JOX's explanation translated.

391.   Furthermore, the DCD never requested a translation of the explanation from JOX, which further indicates that the investigating authority was not unbiased and objective in evaluating the normal value information provided in the investigation.

392.   In addition, Sadia, Avipal, Frangosul, Nicolini and Seara presented on 26 August 1999 arguments with respect to the comparison between export price and normal value.[221] Among the arguments presented was that out of the normal value price provided by CEPA, taxes, freight and financial cost should be deducted.[222] The exporters presented the following table to demonstrate what should be the normal value price comparable to the *ex-factory* export price:

JOX PRICE

Jox Price		US$ 0,920
Deductions		
ICMS 12%	0,110	
PIS/COFINS 2,65% /US$ 0,92	0,024	
National Freight	0,055	
Financial Cost	0,016	
Total		**0,715**

Source: Exhibit BRA-33.

393.   Even with the information provided by JOX and exporters requesting that due allowance be made to account for these differences which affect the normal value price, the DCD did not comply with the requirements set forth in Article 2.4 of the Anti-Dumping Agreement.

(iii)   Claim 25: Inconsistency with Article 2.4 of the Anti-Dumping Agreement

Text of Article 2.4

394.   Article 2.4 provides in part that:

"(...) Due allowance shall be made in each case, on its merits, for differences which affect price comparability, including differences in conditions and terms of sale, taxation, levels of trade, quantities, physical characteristics, and any other differences which are also demonstrated to affect price comparability.(...)"

Legal Argument Relative to Claim 25

395.   On 7 January 1998, the DCD issued a notice to initiate the dumping investigation against imports of poultry from Brazil. In that notice, the DCD decided to initiate the investigation based on the normal value information provided by petitioner in the application, which took into account prices published by the

---
[221] *See*, Exhibit BRA-33.
[222] *Ibid*.

Brazilian company JOX on 30 June 1997, for *chilled* poultry, with head and feet, for the São Paulo wholesale market. Based on the JOX published price, the DCD made an adjustment to normal value, proposed by petitioner, to account for physical characteristic differences in the poultry sold in Brazil and to Argentina.

396. According to the suggested adjustment, the average weight of the live poultry raised in Brazil is 2.250 kgs. Petitioner alleged, without submitting any evidence, that the yield of the product in Brazil is 88 per cent and, therefore, out of 1 kg of live poultry 880 gm of eviscerated poultry is obtained, with giblets (heart, stomach, neck and liver), and with head and feet. Petitioner also alleged that the yield of the product sold in Argentina differs from the yield obtained in Brazil. In Argentina, the yield of the product is 80 per cent, considering that head and feet are discarded. Petitioner's conclusion was that out of a live poultry weighing 2.250 kgs, for every 1kg, 800 gm of eviscerated poultry is obtained that can actually be sold in the Argentinean market.

397. Still according to petitioner, the yield rate difference occurs because poultry is sold to Argentina without head and feet while poultry is sold in Brazil with head and feet. The DCD added 9.09 per cent to the price of poultry sold in Brazil to compensate for the allegation that poultry to Argentina is sold without head and feet. No evidence was presented to support petitioner's allegation of physical characteristic differences.

398. Throughout the investigation, the exporters Sadia, Avipal and Frangosul reported that the poultry sold to Argentina was identical to the poultry sold in Brazil. The Brazilian exporter Catarinense reported that from the two types of poultry it sells (broiler and griler), there is a difference in the broiler type poultry sold to Argentina and in Brazil. The broiler type poultry sold to Argentina did not contain head and feet, while the broiler type poultry sold to Brazil contained head *but not feet*.

399. On 23 June 2000, the DCD issued the final affirmative dumping determination. In the fair comparison made between the export price and the normal value, the DCD decided to make allowance for the alleged difference in the physical characteristics of the poultry sold to Argentina and in Brazil. The DCD made a 9.09 per cent adjustment to the normal value, even though the exporters had reported in their responses that there were no differences in the physical characteristics of the products sold to both markets.

400. Article 2.4 mandates that a fair comparison be made between the export price and the normal value. In order to obtain a fair comparison between export price and normal value, Article 2.4 further requires that due allowances be made in each case, on its merits, for differences which affect price comparability. Article 2.4 lists, but does not limit, these differences. They include differences in conditions and terms of sale, taxation, levels of trade, quantities, physical characteristics, and any other differences which are also demonstrated to affect price comparability.

401. In view of the fact that the Brazilian exporters submitted information providing that there were no differences in physical characteristics between the poultry sold in Brazil and the poultry sold to Argentina, there was no due allowance to be made by the DCD for differences related to physical characteristics.

402. It is important to note that Article 2.4 requires due allowance to be made for differences, which *affect* price comparability. The DCD adjusted normal value based on petitioner's unsubstantiated allegation that there were differences in physical characteristics between the poultry sold to Argentina and in Brazil. Exporters submitted responses, and evidence, demonstrating that no such differences existed.

Furthermore, due allowance is only warranted for differences which affect price comparability. Petitioner did not provide evidence nor demonstrate that the alleged differences affected price comparability.

403. Based on exporters response to the questionnaire and the lack of evidence presented by petitioner to prove the existence of differences in physical characteristics in the poultry sold to Argentina and in Brazil, and that such differences affected price comparability, Brazil claims that Argentina acted inconsistently with Article 2.4 of the Anti-Dumping Agreement by incorrectly making allowances to normal value.

(iv) Claim 26: Inconsistency with Article 2.4 of the Anti-Dumping Agreement

Text of Article 2.4

404. Relevant part of Article 2.4 provides that:

"(...) The authorities shall indicate to the parties in question what information is necessary to ensure a fair comparison and shall not impose an unreasonable burden of proof on those parties."

Legal Argument Relative to Claim 26

405. On 20 January 1999, the MEOSP issued a public notice announcing the initiation of the anti-dumping investigation on imports of poultry from Brazil. In the public notice of initiation, Argentina did not establish the period of data collection for the dumping investigation. On 16 February 1999, the SSCE sent letters to Sadia, Avipal, Frangosul, Nicolini and Seara inviting them to participate in a hearing on 25 February 1999 for consultations regarding the initiation of the dumping investigation and to receive the dumping questionnaires.

406. The dumping questionnaires did not establish the period of data collection for the dumping investigation. The five exporters presented normal value and export price information for the years 1996, 1997, 1998, and the available months in 1999. The DCD requested further information without limiting the scope of the dumping period of investigation.

407. On 15 September 1999, the DCD sent letters to CCLP, Catarinense, Chapeco, Minuano, Perdigão, Comaves and Pena Branca notifying of the investigation and inviting these exporters to provide responses to the dumping questionnaire. In this letter, the DCD established *for the first time* in the investigation that the period of data collection for dumping was from January 1998 through January 1999.

408. On 12 October 1999, the DCD sent letters to Frangosul and Avipal requesting they provide list of transaction and invoices for sales in the internal market from January 1998 through January 1999. On 18 October 1999, the DCD sent letters to Sadia, Nicolini and Seara requesting they provide list of transaction and invoices for sales in the internal market from January 1998 through January 1999. Nine months after the investigation was initiated and after a preliminary determination had been issued, the DCD chose to establish the data collection period for the dumping investigation.

409. Article 2.4 of the Anti-Dumping Agreement requires that the authorities indicate to the parties in question what information is necessary to ensure a fair

Report of the Panel

comparison and further requires that investigating authorities not impose an unreasonable burden of proof on those parties.

410. Export price and normal value data constitute necessary information needed in making a fair comparison. However, a request that such information be provided for an undetermined period of time is not in accordance with the requirement of Article 2.4. This provision establishes that authorities must indicate what information is necessary to ensure a fair comparison. Information for one particular period may differ from the information for another period, therefore, defining the period of investigation is essential for the exporter, who must know what information must be provided to ensure a fair comparison.

411. The request by authorities that the exporters provide normal value and export price data for a period exceeding that of the period of investigation is an unreasonable burden of proof imposed by the authority on the exporters. By not clearly indicating to the five exporters the scope of the period of data collection, the Brazilian exporters were imposed an excessive and unreasonable burden of proof in presenting data for a period outside the data collection period of dumping. This unreasonable burden of proof, which prevailed for nine months of the investigation, made it impossible for exporters to provide complete, accurate and timely responses.

412. Brazil considers that the establishment of the data collection period *nine* months after the initiation of the investigation and after a preliminary determination had been made does not comply with Article 2.4.

413. Brazil also considers that the last part of Article 2.4 has been violated by the fact that Argentina only established normal value (in the case of Sadia and Avipal) based on transactions in the internal market for which exporters presented invoices.

414. As demonstrated throughout the investigation, the great volume of sales of poultry in Brazil made it impossible for exporters to attach all invoices corresponding to those transactions. Exporters invited the DCD to verify *in loco* the responses provided, so as to ascertain that the responses were accurate and complete. The DCD chose not to verify these exporters, which does not mean that the information provided by them was not verifiable.

415. Considering the great volume of sales transactions of poultry in Brazil and the fact that only the sales transactions for which exporters presented invoices were considered in the establishment of normal value, exporters were imposed with an unreasonable and impossible burden of proof, contrary to the requirement in Article 2.4.

(v) Claim 27: Inconsistency with Article 2.4.2 of the Anti-Dumping Agreement

Text of Article 2.4.2

416. Pertinent language of Article 2.4.2 of the Anti-Dumping Agreement provides as follows:

"Subject to the provisions governing fair comparison in paragraph 4, the existence of margins of dumping during the investigation phase shall normally be established on the basis of a comparison of a weighted average normal value with a weighted average of prices of all comparable export transactions or by a comparison of normal value and export prices on a transaction-to-transaction basis (...)"

Legal Argument Relative to Claim 27

417. Article 2.4.2 of the Anti-Dumping Agreement provides for how margins of dumping must be established. The first part of this provision sets out the general rule that a comparison be made on the basis of: (1) weighted average normal value with a weighted average of prices of all comparable export transactions; or, (2) individual transactions of normal value and export prices.

418. In the final determination, the DCD established the margins of dumping for the exporters Sadia and Avipal based on the normal value information for which invoices were presented, and not based on all the sales transactions in the internal market reported for the period. The fact that the DCD did not take into account all of the transactions in the internal market to establish the normal value violated how Article 2.4.2. requires a comparison to be made for purposes of establishing the existence of dumping margins.

419. In the final determination, the DCD established the margins of dumping for Sadia and Avipal on the basis of a comparison of a weighted average *statistical sample* of normal value with a weighted average of prices of all comparable export transactions.

420. Brazil understands that if the investigating authority had access to information regarding all transactions in the internal market, even if invoices did not accompany these transactions, it could not select through a sample, even if randomly, and use a limited portion of these transactions for purposes of establishing normal value and for purposes of making the comparison for establishment of the dumping margin. A weighted average of a statistical sample of normal value is not the same as a weighted average of normal value of *all* transactions reported by the exporters.

421. As shown in the facts above, Sadia and Avipal reported that the sales transactions in the internal market were too voluminous for the exporters to present an invoice for each sale transaction. Sadia and Avipal presented a list of all the transactions in the internal market for the period. Invoices were presented for only some transactions in order for the DCD to verify the accuracy of the data submitted in the responses as a whole and not just those for which invoices were provided. Brazil understands that the magnitude of the information submitted may mean that not all data will actually be examined, however this *does not exclude the validity of the data provided*, particularly, if that data could be verified.

422. Not only did Sadia and Avipal report their transactions for the period of investigation (January 1998 - January 1999) but they also provided information on the sales transactions outside the period of investigation (1996, 1997, 1998 and available data for 1999), which they also reported. To have that burden imposed on exporters, and then for the investigating authority to use only some of the transactions during 1998 and January 1999 is contrary to how a margin should be established pursuant to Article 2.4.2 of the Anti-Dumping Agreement.

2. *Articles 3.1, 3.4, 3.5 and 12.2.2*

423. The following two claims arise from the facts described below:

Claim 32: By using different periods to evaluate the relevant economic factors and indices listed in Article 3.4, Argentina failed to make an injury determination based on positive evidence and involving an objective examination as provided for in Article 3.1, 3.4 and 3.5.

Claim 33: Argentina acted inconsistently with Article 12.2.2 by failing to explain in the final determination why the CNCE examined the relevant economic factors and indices listed in Article 3.4 based on different periods.

(a) Facts

424. On 23 December 1999, the CNCE issued the final affirmative injury determination.[223] In the determination, the CNCE stated that the period of injury analysis was from January 1996 until December 1998, taking into account data for the year 1995 as a reference year.[224] The CNCE further explained that for some factors such as: output, prices, imports, exports, and apparent consumption, the period of analysis was from January 1996 until June 1999; and that for the remaining factors the period of analysis was from January 1996 until December 1998.[225]

(i) Claim 32: Inconsistency with Articles 3.1, 3.4 and 3.5 of the Anti-Dumping Agreement

Text of Article 3.1

425. Article 3.1 of the Anti-Dumping Agreement sets forth the general requirements for a determination of injury.

> "A determination of injury for purposes of Article VI of GATT 1994 shall be based on positive evidence and involve an objective examination of both (a) the volume of the dumped imports and the effect of the dumped imports on prices in the domestic market for like products, and (b) the consequent impact of these imports on domestic producers of such products."

Legal Argument Relative to Claim 32

426. According to Article 3.1 of the Anti-Dumping Agreement, an injury determination must involve an *objective examination* of the volume of the dumped imports, the effect of the dumped imports on prices in the domestic market, and the impact of the dumped imports on domestic producers.

427. Based on textual interpretation, the term "objective" means that which is "not subjective".[226] The term "subjective" refers to something that is "imaginary", "partial" or "distorted".[227] Thus, in order for an objective examination to occur, the factors subject to examination must be evaluated within the same parameters and not subject to different or distorted parameters. That said, Article 3.4 of the Anti-Dumping Agreement provides what economic factors must be evaluated in the examination of the impact of the dumped imports on the domestic industry. For an objective

---

[223] *See,* Exhibit BRA-14.
[224] *See,* Page 9 of Exhibit BRA-14.
[225] *Ibid.*
[226] *The Concise Oxford Dictionary - Ninth Edition,* Oxford University Press, 1995, p. 938.
[227] *Ibid.,* p. 1387.

examination to occur, the economic factors and indices listed in Article 3.4 must be examined based on the same parameters.

428. The fact that the CNCE evaluated data for output, prices, imports, exports, and apparent consumption for the period January 1996 through June 1999; and, data for the remaining factors and indices listed in Article 3.4 based on data for the period January 1996 through December 1998, indicates that different parameters of evaluation were used. Thus, the examination of the impact of the dumped imports on domestic producers was not objective and, therefore, contrary to Article 3.1 of the Anti-Dumping Agreement.

429. The examination of the impact of the dumped imports on the domestic industry concerned must be objective, since Article 3.1 of the Anti-Dumping Agreement imposes this obligation on all the factors to be examined in an injury determination. Once the Panel establishes that the injury determination was not based on an objective examination, the Panel must also establish that Argentina violated Articles 3.4 and 3.5 of the Anti-Dumping Agreement.

430. With respect to Article 3.5, some of the factors in the injury analysis were examined in a period that went until June 1999. Since dumping was only ascertained for a period that went until January 1999, there is no basis on which the authorities could attribute the June 1999 injury to the January 1999 dumping. At the very least, some very convincing explanation on how this link existed would be needed in the final determination on causal link.

(ii) Claim 33: Inconsistency with Article 12.2.2 of the Anti-Dumping Agreement

Text of Article 12.2.2

431. Article 12.2.2 provides in part that:

"A public notice of conclusion or suspension of an investigation in the case of an affirmative determination providing for the imposition of a definitive duty or the acceptance of a price undertaking shall contain, or otherwise make available through a separate report, all relevant information on matters of fact and law and reasons which have led to the imposition of final measures or the acceptance of a price undertaking, due regard being paid to the requirement for the protection of confidential information. In particular, the notice or report shall contain the information described in subparagraph 2.1, as well as the reasons for the acceptance or rejection of relevant arguments or claims made by the exporters and importers, and the basis for any decision made under subparagraph 10.2 of Article 6."

Legal Argument Relative to Claim 33

432. The question presented to the Panel is whether any reasoning has been provided in the final determination, sufficient to satisfy the requirements of Article 12.2.2 of the Anti-Dumping Agreement, regarding why the DCD used different periods to evaluate the relevant economic factors and indices listed in Article 3.4 of the Anti-Dumping Agreement.

433. In the case of an affirmative determination providing for the imposition of a definitive duty, Article 12.2.2. mandates that a public notice of conclusion of the investigation contain, or otherwise make available through a separate report, all relevant information on matters of fact and law and reasons which have led to the imposition of final measures. In particular, the public notice of conclusion must contain information described in subparagraph 2.1 of Article 12. Among the information required in subparagraph 2.1 of Article 12 are considerations relevant to the injury determination as set out in Article 3 of the Anti-Dumping Agreement.

434. As shown in the Claim above, the examination by the CNCE of the economic factors and indices listed in Article 3.4 was not objective because it used different parameters to evaluate the factors. Some factors were evaluated taking into account the period from January 1996 through June 1999 and other factors were evaluated taking into account the period from January 1996 through December 1998.

435. In the final injury determination, the CNCE simply stated that the period under analysis corresponded to January 1996 through December 1998. The CNCE further stated that for some variables, such as national production, prices, imports, national exports and apparent consumption, data for the first semester of 1999 was included.

436. No explanation or consideration was offered in the final determination as to why the CNCE evaluated data for output, prices, imports, exports, and apparent consumption for the period January 1996 through June 1999, which was outside the injury period of investigation.

437. By not providing in the final determination considerations relevant to the injury determination as set out in Article 3, Argentina violated Article 12.2.2 of the Anti-Dumping Agreement.

3. *Articles 3.1, 3.2, 3.4 and 3.5*

438. The following four claims arise from the facts transcribed below:

Claim 34: The injury analysis in the final determination did not exclude Nicolini and Seara's imports even though the DCD considered that these were not "dumped imports". By not excluding the imports from Nicolini and Seara from the volume of the "dumped imports", the CNCE did not properly consider whether there had been a significant increase in "dumped imports", thereby violating Article 3.2.

Claim 35: The flawed evaluation of the "dumped imports" indicates that the final injury determination was not based on positive evidence and did not involve an objective examination as required by Article 3.1.

Claim 36: By not excluding the imports from Nicolini and Seara from the volume of the "dumped imports", the CNCE failed to properly examine the impact of the "dumped imports" on the domestic industry, as required by Article 3.4.

Claim 37: By not excluding the imports from Nicolini and Seara from the volume of the "dumped imports", the CNCE did not properly consider injury as prescribed in Article 3.1, and, consequently, did not properly demonstrate the causal link between the dumped imports and the injury to the domestic industry, as required in Article 3.5.

(a) Facts

439. On 23 December 1999, the CNCE issued the final affirmative injury determination.[228] On 23 June 2000, the DCD issued the final affirmative dumping determination.[229] In the dumping determination, the DCD determined that the Brazilian exporters Nicolini and Seara were not exporting the subject merchandise at dumped prices and that poultry from Sadia, Avipal, and all other exporters were being exported at dumped prices.[230]

440. On 17 July 2000, the SSCE issued the final affirmative determination on causal link between the allegedly dumped imports and the injury to the domestic industry.[231]

(i) Claim 34: Inconsistency with Article 3.2 of the Anti-Dumping Agreement

Text of Article 3.2

441. Article 3.2 of the Anti-Dumping Agreement provides factors to be considered with regards to the increase in the volume of "dumped imports", which Article 3.1 requires to be examined. The relevant portion of Article 3.2 sets forth that:

> "With regard to the volume of the dumped imports, the investigating authorities shall consider whether there has been a significant increase in dumped imports, either in absolute terms or relative to production or consumption in the importing Member. (...)"

Legal Argument Relative to Claim 34

442. The language set out throughout Article 3 of the Anti-Dumping Agreement is consistent, the injury to the domestic industry must have been caused by "dumped imports". Article 2.1 of the Anti-Dumping Agreement provides definition of what constitutes a product that is being dumped. In this regard, Article 2.1 provides the definition as follows:

> "For the purposes of this Agreement, a product is to be considered as being dumped, i.e. introduced into the commerce of another country at less than its normal value, if the export price of the product exported from one country to another is less than the comparable price, in the ordinary course of trade, for the like product when destined for consumption in the exporting country"

443. From the language of Article 2.1, "imports are dumped" when a product is introduced into the commerce of another country at a price that is less than the price of the like product in the exporting country.

444. Brazil understands that the definition of the term "dumped imports", as provided in Article 2.1, is applicable to all articles under the Anti-Dumping Agreement.

---

[228] *See*, Exhibit BRA-14
[229] *See*, Exhibit BRA-15.
[230] *See*, Pages 102, 103 and 104 of Exhibit BRA-15.
[231] *See*, Exhibit BRA-16.

445. In the final dumping determination, the DCD determined that the Brazilian exporters Nicolini and Seara were not exporting the subject merchandise at dumped prices.

446. As stated previously in this submission, the DCD established export price in the final dumping determination based on the import information from *Ganaderia*. The DCD listed the net volume of poultry imports in kilograms, the total FOB value of poultry imports in US dollars, and the per unit FOB US dollar per kilogram price of the exports of each Brazilian exporter for the period January 1998 through January 1999.[232]

447. According to that list, for the period of January 1998 through January 1999, Nicolini exported 5,397,254 kilograms to Argentina of the product under investigation, Seara exported 11,038,851 kilograms to Argentina of the product under investigation, and the total volume of the product exported by all Brazilian exporters was 58,822,070 kilograms.

448. Out of the total volume exported by the Brazilian exporters for the period of investigation, Nicolini exported 9.18 per cent and Seara 18.77 per cent of the total volume.

Product	Net Kgs	Participation in Total %
Nicolini	5.397.254	9.18%
Seara	11.038.851	18.77%
Total	58.822.070	100%

Source: Pages 76 and 77 of Exhibit BRA-15.

449. Together, Nicolini and Seara exported 27.95 per cent of total exports from Brazil of the product under investigation, almost one third of total exports of poultry from Brazil for the period. Brazil understands this to be a *significant* volume and a relevant factor in the injury analysis.

450. The injury analysis in the final injury determination, did not exclude the imports from Nicolini and Seara from the "dumped imports" analyzed in the injury examination.

451. Brazil knows this to be fact, since the final injury determination, which was issued on 23 December 1999, preceded the final dumping determination, issued on 23 June 2000, by six months.

452. Article 3.2 of the Anti-Dumping Agreement requires the investigating authority to consider whether there has been a significant increase in "dumped imports", either in absolute terms or relative to the production or consumption in the importing Member. Brazil affirms that the consideration by the investigating authorities of whether there was a significant increase in the "dumped imports" never occurred, since the significant volume of imports from Nicolini and Seara were not excluded from the volume of the "dumped imports".

453. By not excluding the imports from Nicolini and Seara from the total volume of "dumped imports", Argentina has failed to adequately consider whether there had been a significant increase in the "dumped imports", in violation of Article 3.2 of the Anti-Dumping Agreement.

---

[232] *See*, Page 76 of Exhibit BRA-15.

(ii) Claim 35: Inconsistency with Article 3.1 of the Anti-Dumping Agreement

Text of Article 3.1

454. Article 3.1 of the Anti-Dumping Agreement sets forth the general requirements for a determination of injury.

> "A determination of injury for purposes of Article VI of GATT 1994 shall be based on positive evidence and involve an objective examination of both (a) the volume of the dumped imports and the effect of the dumped imports on prices in the domestic market for like products, and (b) the consequent impact of these imports on domestic producers of such products."

Legal Argument Relative to Claim 35

455. Article 3.1 mandates that a determination of injury by the investigating authority be based upon positive evidence and involve an objective examination of three factors: (1) the volume of the "dumped imports"; (2) the effect of the "dumped imports" on prices in the domestic market for like products; and, (3) the consequent impact of the "dumped imports" on domestic producers of such products.

456. According to the facts above, Argentina has failed to base its final injury determination upon positive evidence and make an objective examination of the factors set out in Article 3.1, by incorrectly establishing "dumped imports".

457. As demonstrated in the previous claim, Article 2.1 of the Anti-Dumping Agreement considers a product as being dumped, when it is introduced into the commerce of another country at less than its normal value.

458. Thus, "dumped imports" are those imports that are introduced into the commerce of another country at a price lower than the normal value price. In the final dumping determination, the DCD found that Nicolini and Seara's imports of poultry into Argentina were not being dumped.

459. However, the final injury determination included the imports from Nicolini and Seara as part of the "dumped imports" examined pursuant to Article 3.1.

460. Because the CNCE did not exclude the imports of poultry from Nicoli and Seara from the total of the "dumped imports", the injury examination, as set out in Article 3.1, cannot be considered objective.

(iii) Claim 36: Inconsistency with Article 3.4 of the Anti-Dumping Agreement

Text of Article 3.4

461. Article 3.4 of the Anti-Dumping Agreement provides for the examination of the impact of the "dumped imports" on the domestic industry. Article 3.4 sets forth that:

> "The examination of the impact of the dumped imports on the domestic industry concerned shall include an evaluation of all relevant economic factors and indices having a bearing on the state of the industry, including actual and potential decline in sales, profits,

output, market share, productivity, return on investments, or utilization of capacity; factors affecting domestic prices; the magnitude of the margin of dumping; actual and potential negative effects on cash flow, inventories, employment, wages, growth, ability to raise capital or investments. This list is not exhaustive, nor can one or several of these factors necessarily give decisive guidance."

Legal Argument Relative to Claim 36

462. Article 3.4 of the Anti-Dumping Agreement requires that the examination of the impact of the "dumped imports" on the domestic industry include an evaluation of all relevant economic factors and indices having a bearing on the state of the domestic industry. In particular, the examination to be made is of the impact of the "dumped imports" on the domestic industry.

463. A textual interpretation of the first sentence of Article 3.4 indicates that the investigating authority must examine the impact in the domestic industry of the imports that are being dumped, and not of all imports from a certain destination.

464. In the final dumping determination, a significant part (almost 30 per cent) of the imports of poultry from Brazil were considered not to be "dumped imports". However, for purposes of the injury determination, these imports that were not considered as "dumped imports" were not excluded from the injury analysis of "dumped imports". By not excluding these imports from the total imports of poultry, the CNCE made an incorrect examination of the impact of the "dumped imports" on the domestic industry.

465. A previous GATT Panel raised a similar issue in EC - Cotton Yarn:

"(...) the Panel noted that in responding to a question by the Panel the EC has stated 'Regarding the volume to be considered for injury purposes, the Community took into account all imports, whether dumped or non-dumped, for the reasons mentioned above.' Articles 3.2 and 3.4 of the Agreement required that the investigating authorities examined the volume and effects of the "dumped imports". The Panel noted that the EC stated in its response that it had, for the purposes of its injury analysis, taken into account the effects of all imports from Brazil, whether dumped or non-dumped. As Brazil had not made a Claim that the EC had thereby acted inconsistently with the Agreement, the Panel could not pronounce itself on any such claim"[233] (emphasis added)

466. That Panel indicated that had Brazil made a Claim that the EC had acted inconsistently with the Agreement by taking into account the effects of all imports from Brazil in the injury analysis, and not only the imports that were being dumped, the Panel might have been able to rule on that claim.

467. Unlike the above-mentioned GATT panel proceeding, Brazil does Claim that Argentina's determination is inconsistent with Articles 3.1, 3.2, 3.4 and 3.5 of the Anti-Dumping Agreement.

---

[233] *EC - Imposition of Anti-Dumping Duties on Imports of Cotton Yarn from Brazil*, 4 July 1995, ADP/137, at para. 525 (*"EC - Cotton Yarn"*).

468. With respect to the Claim at issue, by no excluding the imports from Nicolini and Seara from the total of "dumped imports", Argentina has failed to correctly examine the impact of the "dumped imports" on the domestic industry concerned, contrary to the provision in Article 3.4 of the Anti-Dumping Agreement.

(iv) Claim 37: Inconsistency with Article 3.5 of the Anti-Dumping Agreement

Text of Article 3.5

469. Article 3.5 of the Anti-Dumping Agreement establishes the requirements for the analysis of the causal relationship between the dumped imports and the injury to the domestic industry:

> "It must be demonstrated that the dumped imports are, through the effects of dumping, as set forth in paragraphs 2 and 4, causing injury within the meaning of this Agreement. The demonstration of a causal relationship between the dumped imports and the injury to the domestic industry shall be based on an examination of all relevant evidence before the authorities. The authorities shall also examine any known factors other than the dumped imports at which at the same time are injuring the domestic industry, and the injuries caused by these other factors may not be attributed to the dumped imports. (...)"

Legal Argument Relative to Claim 37

470. Article 3.5 of the Anti-Dumping Agreement clarifies how the causal link between dumping and injury to the domestic industry is to be established.

471. First, Article 3.5 requires that the demonstration of a causal relationship be based on the examination of all relevant evidence. Second, Article 3.5 provides that the authorities shall examine any known factors other than the "dumped imports", which are at the same time injuring the domestic industry. Third, the authorities are to make sure that injuries caused by these factors are not attributed to the "dumped imports".

472. The SSCE did not make a causal link analysis. The SSCE simply reproduced the margins of dumping found in the final affirmative dumping determination, some of the factors examined in the final affirmative injury determination, and concluded that there was causal link between the two, without providing the reasons why they believed such link existed. No demonstration of causal link between the two was made in the final affirmative determination of causal relationship.

473. Furthermore, Article 3.5 mandate authorities to determine that "dumped imports" are the cause of injury to the domestic industry. As indicated above, the authorities knew before the causal relationship determination was issued that the imports of Nicolini and Seara were not considered "dumped imports". However, the causal relationship determination failed to evaluate that factor and exclude Nicolini and Seara's imports from the total "dumped imports".

474. Brazil considers that in the absence of a valid injury finding, which was flawed by the inclusion of the imports from Nicolini and Seara in the total "dumped imports", there was no basis for a causal relationship finding.

4. Articles 3.1, 3.4 and 12.2.2

475. The following three claims arise follow from the facts described below and from the legal requirements in the Anti-Dumping Agreement:

Claim 38: Argentina acted inconsistently with Article 3.4 by failing to evaluate all the relevant economic factors and indices listed in Article 3.4.

Claim 39: By failing to evaluate all the relevant economic factors and indices listed in Article 3.4 in its final determination, Argentina's injury determination was not based on positive evidence and did not involve an objective evaluation, as required by Article 3.1.

Claim 40: Argentina acted inconsistently with Article 12.2.2 by failing to adequately explain and provide in its final determination an evaluation of all relevant economic factors and indices listed in Article 3.4.

(a) Facts

476. On 23 December 1999, the CNCE issued its final affirmative injury determination.[234] The examination of the impact of the dumped imports on the domestic industry did not contain an evaluation of all the relevant economic factors and indices having a bearing on the state of the industry. In particular, the CNCE did not evaluate the actual and potential decline in productivity; factors affecting domestic price; the magnitude of the dumping margin; and, the actual and potential negative effects on cash flow, growth and the ability to raise capital or investments.

(i) Claim 38: Inconsistency with Article 3.4 of the Anti-Dumping Agreement

Text of Article 3.4

477. Article 3.4 provides for the examination of the impact of the dumped imports on the domestic industry. The examination must include an evaluation of all relevant economic factors and indices having a bearing on the state of the domestic industry, including:

> "(...) actual and potential decline in sales, profits, output, market share, productivity, return on investments, or utilization of capacity; factors affecting domestic prices; the magnitude of the margin of dumping; actual and potential negative effects on cash flow, inventories, employment, wages, growth, ability to raise capital or investments"

Legal Argument Relative to Claim 38

478. Article 3.4 of the Anti-Dumping Agreement sets specific requirements for examination of factor (b) in Article 3.1. It mandates that in the examination of the impact of the dumped imports on the domestic industry, the authorities evaluate all relevant economic factors and indices having a bearing on the state of the industry. Article 3.4 includes, but does not limit, the factors that must be evaluated by the investigating authority.

---

[234] *See*, Exhibit BRA-14.

479.   In its final injury determination, the CNCE failed to evaluate the actual and potential decline in productivity; factors affecting domestic price; the magnitude of the dumping margin; and, the actual and potential negative effects on cash flow, growth and the ability to raise capital or investments. The CNCE did not refer to actual and potential decline in productivity for the period of analysis nor did it evaluate the productivity of the domestic industry. Similarly, other factors affecting domestic price were neither mentioned nor evaluated by the investigating authority. With respect to the magnitude of the dumping margin, the CNCE did not and could not have evaluated it, since the final dumping determination with the dumping margin was issued on 23 June 2000, six months after the final injury determination was issued. Specific data and analysis of actual and potential negative effects on cash flow, growth and the ability to raise capital or investments were not included in the final injury determination either. All these are factors set out in Article 3.4 and should have been examined.

480.   This understanding that the list of factors set out in Article 3.4 is mandatory, and not illustrative, derives from the language of Article 3.4, as well as from various Panel interpretations of this provision.

481.   The phrase in Article 3.4 that "the examination of the impact of the dumped imports on the domestic industry concerned *shall include* an evaluation of all relevant economic factors", strongly suggests that the evaluation of the listed factors in that provision is mandatory in all cases. Article 3.4 further provides that the evaluation of all relevant economic factors having a bearing on the state of the industry *include* the actual and potential decline in sales, profits, output, market share, productivity, return on investments, or utilization of capacity; factors affecting domestic prices; the magnitude of the margin of dumping; actual and potential negative effects on cash flow, inventories, employment, wages, growth, ability to raise capital or investments. The term "include" as set forth in Article 3.4 simply indicates that there may be other relevant, additional economic factors to be evaluated among *all* the factors that must be evaluated.

482.   Furthermore, various WTO Panels have concluded that the evaluation of the economic factors and indices listed in Article 3.4 is mandatory. For example, the Panel in *Thailand - H-Beams* read the Article 3.4 phrase "shall include and evaluation of all relevant factors and indices having a bearing on the state of the industry, including ..." as:

> "(...) introducing a mandatory list of relevant factors which must be evaluated in every case. We are of the view that the change that occurred in the wording of the relevant provision during the Uruguay Round (from "such as" to "including") was made for a reason and that it supports an interpretation of the current text of Article 3.4 as setting forth a list that is not merely indicative or illustrative, but, rather, mandatory. (...)"[235] (emphasis added)

483.   That Panel further stated that:

> "We are of the view that the language in Article 3.4 makes it clear that all of the listed factors in Article 3.4 must be considered in all cases.

---

[235] *Thailand - Anti-Dumping Duties on Angles, Shapes and Sections of Iron or Non-Alloy Steel and H-Beams from Poland*, 28 September 2000, WT/DS122/R, DSR 2001:VII, 2741, at para. 7.225 (*"Thailand - H-Beams"*).

Report of the Panel

> *The provision is specific and mandatory in this regard.(...)*"[236] (emphasis added)

484. That Panel concluded by stating that:

> "On the basis of a textual analysis of Article 3.4, we are therefore of the view that each of the fifteen individual factors listed in the mandatory list of factors in Article 3.4 must be evaluated by the investigating authorities. (...)"[237] (emphasis added)

485. The Appellate Body upheld that Panel's findings with respect to the Panel's interpretation that Article 3.4 requires a mandatory evaluation of all the factors listed in that provision.[238]

486. Likewise, the Panel on *Mexico - HFCS* dealt with this specific issue by stating that:

> "(...) The text of Article 3.4 is mandatory:
>
> 'The examination of the impact of the dumped imports on the domestic industry concerned **shall include** an evaluation of **all relevant economic factors** and indices having a bearing on the state of the industry, **including** ...'
>
> In our view, this language makes it clear that the listed factors in Article 3.4 must be considered in all cases. There may be other relevant economic factors in the circumstances of a particular case, consideration of which would also be required"[239] (emphasis added by the Panel)

487. That interpretation is also supported by the Panel in EC - Bed Linen, which concluded that:

> "(...) **each** of the fifteen factors listed in Article 3.4 of the AD Agreement must be evaluated by the investigating authorities in each case in examining the impact of the dumped imports on the domestic industry concerned."[240] (emphasis added by the Panel)

488. Furthermore, the nature of the evaluation of the factors listed in Article 3.4 cannot be limited to a mere referral of the factors but must address the data provided, put it into context and analyze it. An evaluation of the factors listed in Article 3.4 requires the investigating authority to determine the significance and value of the information by careful appraisal and study.

489. This can be supported by the understanding of the Panel in *United States - Hot-Rolled Steel Products*, that it would not be sufficient if the investigating

---

[236] *Thailand - H-Beams*, at para. 7.229.
[237] *Thailand - H-Beams*, at para. 7.231.
[238] *Thailand - Anti-Dumping Duties on Angles, Shapes and Sections of Iron or Non-Alloy Steel and H-Beams from Poland*, 12 March 2001, WT/DS122/AB/R, DSR 2001:VII, 2701, at para. 139 (adopted on 05 April 2001) ("*AB - Thailand - H-Beams*").
[239] Mexico - HFCS, DSR 2000:III, 1345, at para. 7.128. The Appellate Body found that the Panel satisfied its duty under Article 12.7 of the DSU to set out a "basic rationale behind [its] findings" with respect to Article 3.4 of the Anti-Dumping Agreement. *Mexico - Anti-Dumping Investigation of High Fructose Corn Syrup (HFCS) from the United States*, 22 October 2001, WT/DS132/AB/RW, DSR 2001:XIII, 6675, at para. 135 (adopted on 21 November 2001) ("*AB - Mexico - HFCS*").
[240] *European Communities - Anti-Dumping Duties on Imports of Cotton-Type Bed Linen from India*, 30 October 2000, WT/DS141/R, DSR 2001:VI, 2077, at para. 6.159 (adopted on 12 March 2001) ("*EC - Bed Linen*"). The Panel's findings on the Claim related to Article 3.4 were not appealed.

authority merely mentioned data for certain factors of Article 3.4 without undertaking an evaluation of that factor. According to that Panel:

> "(...) *An evaluation of a factor implies putting data in context and assessing such data both in their internal evolution and vis-à-vis other factors examined. Only on the basis of the evaluation of data in the determination would a reviewing panel be able to access whether the conclusions drawn from the examination are those of an unbiased and objective authority.*"[241] (emphasis added)

490. More support is found in *Thailand - H-Beams*, where the Panel presented the following view:

> "(...) Therefore, in determining that Article 3.4 contains a mandatory list of fifteen factors to be looked at, *we do not mean to establish a mere "checklist approach"* that would consist of a mechanical exercise of merely ensuring that each listed factor is in some way referred to by the investigating authority. (...) Rather, we are of the view that Article 3.4 requires the authorities properly to establish whether a factual basis exists to support a well-reasoned and meaningful analysis of the state of the industry and a finding of injury. *This analysis does not derive from a mere characterization of the degree of "relevance or irrelevance" of each and every individual factor, but rather must be based on a thorough evaluation of the state of the industry and, in light of the last sentence of Article 3.4, must contain a persuasive explanation as to how the evaluation of relevant factors led to the determination of injury.*"[242] (emphasis added)

491. Likewise, the Panel in *EC - Bed Linen* concluded that:

> "Regarding the nature of the evaluation of each factor that is required, the panel determined that while authorities may determine that some factors are not relevant or do not weigh significantly in the decision, *the authorities may not simply disregard such factors, but must explain their conclusion as to the lack of relevance or significance of such factors.*"[243] (emphasis added)

492. From the considerations above and from the final injury determination, the Panel will verify not only that all the factors listed in Article 3.4 were not considered by the investigating authority, but also that not all factors were properly evaluated, which constitutes a *prima facie* violation of Article 3.4 of the Anti-Dumping Agreement.

(ii) Claim 39: Inconsistency with Article 3.1 of the Anti-Dumping Agreement

Text of Article 3.1

493. Article 3.1 of the Anti-Dumping Agreement sets forth the overall structure of an authority's injury analysis:

---

[241] *United States - Hot-Rolled Steel Products*, DSR 2001:X, 4769, at para. 7.232.
[242] *Thailand - H-Beams*, at para. 7.236.
[243] *EC - Bed Linen*, DSR 2001:VI, 2077, at para. 6.159.

"A determination of injury for purposes of Article VI of GATT 1994 shall be based on positive evidence and involve an objective examination of both (a) the volume of the dumped imports and the effect of the dumped imports on prices in the domestic market for like products, and (b) the consequent impact of these imports on domestic producers of such products."

Legal Argument Relative to Claim 39

494. Article 3.1 sets out the general requirements for a determination of injury based on consideration of the volume, price and consequent impact of the "dumped imports" on the domestic industry. The succeeding sections of Article 3 provide for more specific guidance for such determinations. Article 3.4 sets forth factors to be considered in examining the impact of the dumped imports on the domestic industry, as required by Article 3.1. This examination requires an evaluation of all relevant economic factors and indices, listed in Article 3.4, which have a bearing on the domestic industry.

495. To that regard, the requirement under Article 3.4 of an "evaluation of all relevant factors" must be read in conjunction with the overreaching requirements imposed by Article 3.1 of "positive evidence" and "objective examination" in determining the existence of injury.

496. In the final injury determination, the CNCE failed to evaluate the actual and potential decline in productivity; factors affecting domestic price; the magnitude of the dumping margin; and, the actual and potential negative effects on cash flow, growth and the ability to raise capital or investments. In order for the injury finding by the CNCE to have been based on positive evidence and on an objective examination, the investigating authorities would have had to explicitly state and evaluate in the injury determination *all* the relevant economic factors listed in Article 3.4. This was not the case.

497. The CNCE did not refer to actual and potential decline in productivity for the period of analysis nor did it evaluate the productivity of the domestic industry. Similarly, other factors affecting domestic price were neither mentioned nor evaluated by the investigating authority. With respect to the magnitude of the dumping margin, the CNCE did not and could not have evaluated it, since the final dumping determination with the dumping margin was issued on 23 June 2000, six months after the final injury determination was issued. Specific data and analysis of actual and potential negative effects on cash flow, growth and the ability to raise capital or investments were not included in the final injury determination either.

498. These factors are part of the mandatory list of factors that have to be evaluated in the examination of the impact of the imports on the domestic industry. An objective examination based on positive evidence of the impact of the dumped imports on domestic producers requires that all of the listed factors in Article 3.4 be evaluated.

499. By failing to evaluate all of these factors, Argentina acted inconsistently with Article 3.1 of the Anti-Dumping Agreement.

(iii) Claim 40: Inconsistency with Article 12.2.2 of the Anti-Dumping Agreement

Text of Article 12.2.2

500. Article 12.2.2 provides in part that:

"A public notice of conclusion or suspension of an investigation in the case of an affirmative determination providing for the imposition of a definitive duty or the acceptance of a price undertaking shall contain, or otherwise make available through a separate report, all relevant information on matters of fact and law and reasons which have led to the imposition of final measures or the acceptance of a price undertaking, due regard being paid to the requirement for the protection of confidential information. In particular, the notice or report shall contain the information described in subparagraph 2.1, as well as the reasons for the acceptance or rejection of relevant arguments or claims made by the exporters and importers, and the basis for any decision made under subparagraph 10.2 of Article 6."

Legal Argument Relative to Claim 40

501. The question before the Panel is whether the final determination listed and sufficiently considered all the economic factors and indices in Article 3.4, to satisfy the requirements of Article 12.2.2 of the Anti-Dumping Agreement.

502. In the case of an affirmative determination providing for the imposition of a definitive duty, Article 12.2.2. mandates that a public notice of conclusion of the investigation contain, or otherwise make available through a separate report, all relevant information on matters of fact and law and reasons which have led to the imposition of final measures. In particular, the public notice of conclusion must contain information described in subparagraph 2.1 of Article 12. Among the information required in subparagraph 2.1 of Article 12 are considerations relevant to the injury determination as set out in Article 3 of the Anti-Dumping Agreement.

503. Pursuant to claims 28 and 29, not all relevant economic factors listed in Article 3.4, which must be included in the examination of the impact of the dumped imports on the domestic industry, were referred to or evaluated in the final injury determination.

504. In particular, the CNCE did not refer or evaluate the actual and potential decline in productivity for the period; other factors affecting domestic price were neither mentioned nor evaluated by the investigating authority; and, specific data and analysis of actual and potential negative effects on cash flow, growth and the ability to raise capital or investments were also not included in the final injury determination. With respect to the magnitude of the dumping margin, the CNCE did not, and could not, evaluate the magnitude of the margin of dumping because the final dumping determination, establishing the dumping margin, was issued only on 23 June 2000, six months after the final injury determination was issued.

505. With respect to what has to be considered in the written final determination, Brazil refers to the understanding of the Panel in *Mexico - HFCS*. That Panel confirmed that Article 3.4 requires that:

Report of the Panel

"(...) the consideration of each of the Article 3.4 factors *must be apparent in the final determination of the investigating authority.*".[244] (emphasis added)

506. Similarly, the Panel in *EC - Bed Linen* concluded that:

"(...) The nature of the consideration of each factor listed in Article 3.4, including whether the investigating authority considered the factor relevant in its analysis of the impact of dumped imports on the domestic industry, *must be apparent in the final determination.*"[245] (emphasis added)

507. Because productivity; factors affecting domestic price; the magnitude of the dumping margin; cash flow, growth and the ability to raise capital or investments were not referred to or considered in the final determination, Brazil understands that Argentina incurred in a *prima facie* violation of Article 12.2.2.

5. Article 4.1

508. **Claim 41:** Argentina acted inconsistently with Article 4.1 of the Anti-Dumping Agreement by considering that 46 per cent constituted the major proportion of the total domestic production and, thus, qualified as the domestic industry.

(a) Facts

509. On 23 December 1999, the CNCE issued the final injury determination.[246] In that determination, the CNCE stated that the Argentinean companies San Sebastian, Rasic Hnos, Granja Tres Arroyos, Avicola Roque Perrez, Domvil, F.E.P.A.S.A, Frigorifico de Aves Soychu, Miralejos, Las Camelias, Frigorifico Cumini, Industrial Avicola Cordobesa, Nestor Eggs, and Super had formally adhered to the application presented by CEPA.[247] Out of the thirteen companies listed above, ten responded to the injury questionnaires submitted by the CNCE to the national producer.[248] Out of the ten domestic producers that responded to CNCE's injury questionnaire, responses of only six domestic producers were verified.[249]

510. Examination of the impact of the dumped imports on the domestic industry was based on data provided by the ten companies that responded to the questionnaires. These companies composed 45 per cent of the total domestic production of the like products during the period under analysis (January 1996 through December 1998), and 46 per cent of the total production in 1998.[250]

---

[244] *Mexico - HFCS*, at para. 7.128.
[245] *EC - Bed Linen*, at para. 6.162.
[246] *See*, Exhibit BRA-14.
[247] *See*, Page 61 of the "Informe Técnico Previo a La Determinación Final" in Exhibit BRA-14.
[248] The national producers that responded to the CNCE's questionnaire were: San Sebastian, Rasic Hnos, Granja Tres Arroyos, Avicola Roque Perez, Domvil, F.E.P.A.S.A., Frigorifico de Aves Soychu, Miralejos, Las Camelias, and Super. *See*, Page 61 of the "Informe Técnico Previo a La Determinación Final" in Exhibit BRA-14.
[249] The CNCE verified the responses to the injury questionnaires of: San Sebastian, Rasic, Granja Tres Arroyos, Avicola Roque Perez, Frigorifico de Aves Soychu, and Las Camelias. *See*, Page 61 of the "Informe Técnico Previo a La Determinación Final" in Exhibit BRA-14.
[250] *See*, Page 62 of the "Informe Técnico Previo a La Determinación Final" in Exhibit BRA-14.

(i) Claim 41: Inconsistency with Article 4.1 of the Anti-Dumping Agreement

Text of Article 4.1

511. Relevant part of Article 4.1 states that:

"For the purposes of this Agreement, the term "domestic industry" shall be interpreted as referring to the domestic producers as a whole of the like products or to those of them whose collective output of the products constitutes a major proportion of the total domestic production of those products"

Legal Argument Relative to Claim 41

512. The issue before the Panel is whether 46 per cent of the total domestic production of poultry in Argentina constitutes a major proportion of the total domestic production.

513. The definition of "domestic industry" in Article 4.1 requires authorities to consider the domestic industry taken as a whole or whose collective output constitutes a *major proportion* of the total domestic production, and not a segment of that industry. In order to examine the issue, the Panel must interpret the meaning of the term "major proportion" in Article 4.1 of the Anti-Dumping Agreement.

514. According to ordinary meaning interpretation, the term "major part"[251] is defined as "the majority".[252] "Majority" is understood to mean "the greater number or part".[253] From these definitions, the phrase "major proportion" can be understood as the greater part in relation to the whole. If the whole in question is 100 per cent of the total domestic production of the like product, 46 per cent cannot be considered as the greater part in relation to the whole.

515. As stated, Article 4.1 defines the "domestic industry" as the domestic producers representing the whole of the like products or to those of them whose collective output of the products constitutes *a major proportion* of the total domestic production of those products.

516. Brazil understands Article 4.1 to provide that the domestic industry can either be represented by 100 per cent of the producers of the like product or by those whose production, jointly considered, constitutes more than half of the total domestic production. If the domestic producer's output, jointly considered, is less than 50 per cent of the total production, the domestic producers do not comply with the definition of Article 4.1 of the Anti-Dumping Agreement.

517. The establishment of the domestic industry is important, particularly with respect to the injury analysis. Because the injury examination takes into account the impact of the dumped imports on the domestic industry, if the domestic industry is not properly constituted, the impact examination in the injury analysis may be flawed.

---

[251] The terms "proportion" and "part" are viewed and used as synonyms. *Concise Oxford Dictionary - Ninth Edition,* Oxford University Press, 1995, pages 995 and 1098.
[252] *Concise Oxford Dictionary - Ninth Edition,* Oxford University Press, 1995, p. 822.
[253] *Concise Oxford Dictionary - Ninth Edition,* Oxford University Press, 1995, p. 822.

Report of the Panel

518. Thus, the requirement to make a determination of injury to the domestic industry read in light of the definition of the domestic industry of Article 4.1 implies that the injury must be analyzed with regard to domestic producers as a whole of the like product or to those whose collective output constitutes a major proportion, or the majority, of the total domestic production of those products. Injury cannot be evaluated in respect to a segment or a part of the domestic industry.

519. The CNCE's determination that 46 per cent of the total domestic production of the like product constituted the major proportion of the collective output of the domestic producers is on its face inconsistent with Article 4.1 of the Anti-Dumping Agreement.

E. Imposition and Collection of Anti-Dumping Duties as a Result of the Anti-Dumping Investigation

1. Articles 9.2, 9.3 and 12.2.2

520. The following three claims arise from the facts transcribed below and from the legal requirements in the Anti-Dumping Agreement:

Claim 28: Argentina has acted inconsistently with Article 9.2 by imposing a variable anti-dumping duty that can be collected in an inappropriate amount.

Claim 29: Argentina has acted inconsistently with Article 9.3 by imposing a variable anti-dumping duty that can exceed the margin of dumping established in the final determination.

Claim 30: Argentina acted inconsistently with Article 12.2.2 by failing to provide how the "minimum export price" was established in the determination to impose definitive anti-dumping duties.

(a) Facts

521. On 23 June 2000, the DCD issued its final affirmative dumping determination.[254] In its determination, the DCD calculated and determined margins of dumping of 14,91 per cent for exports of the subject merchandise from Sadia,[255] of 15,48 per cent for exports of the subject merchandise from Avipal,[256] and of 8,19 per cent for exports of the subject merchandise from all other exporters.[257] The DCD determined that the Brazilian exporters Nicolini and Seara were not exporting the subject merchandise at dumped prices.[258] The dumping margins were calculated as follows:

SADIA S.A.

Normal value US$/Kg	FOB Price Average US$/Kg	Dumping Margin %
A	B	(A-B)/B
0,9294	0,80883	14,91

Source: Page 102 of Exhibit BRA-15.

---

[254] *See*, Exhibit BRA-15.
[255] *See*, Page 102 of Exhibit BRA-15.
[256] *See*, Page 103 of Exhibit BRA-15.
[257] *See*, Page 104 of Exhibit BRA-15.
[258] *See*, Page 103 of Exhibit BRA-15.

AVIPAL S.A.

Normal value US$/Kg	FOB Price Average US$/Kg	Dumping Margin %
A	B	(A-B)/B
1,0896	0,94355	15,48

Source: Page 103 of Exhibit BRA-15.

FRIGORÍFICO NICOLINI LTDA.

Normal value US$/Kg	FOB Price Average US$/Kg	Dumping Margin %
A	B	(A-B)/B
0,8027	0,95843	----

Source: Page 103 of Exhibit BRA-15.

SEARA ALIMENTOS S.A.

Normal value US$/Kg	FOB Price Average US$/Kg	Dumping Margin %
A	B	(A-B)/B
0,9104	1,00988	----

Source: Page 103 of Exhibit BRA-15.

ALL OTHER EXPORTERS

Normal value US$/Kg	FOB Price Average US$/Kg	Dumping Margin %
A	B	(A-B)/B
1,0385	0,95992	8,19

Source: Page 104 of Exhibit BRA-15.

522. On 21 July 2000, based upon the final dumping, injury and causal link determinations, the MEOSP issued Resolution No. 574/2000, imposing definitive dumping measures on imports of poultry from Brazil for a period of three years.[259]

523. Such measures took the form of specific anti-dumping duties to be collected as the absolute difference between the FOB price invoiced in any one shipment and a designated "minimum export price" also fixed in FOB terms, to be applied whenever the former price is lower than the latter. The "minimum export price" established for each exporter was US$ 0,92 per kilogram for Sadia, US$ 0,98 per kilogram for Avipal, and US$ 0,98 per kilogram for all other exporters.[260] The public notice of the decision to impose the anti-dumping duties did not explain how the "minimum export prices" were determined. The Brazilian exporters Nicolini and Seara did not have dumping measures since they were found not to be exporting poultry at dumped prices.[261] The public notice also set forth the dumping margins found for Sadia (14.91 per cent), Avipal (15.48 per cent) and all other exporters (8.19 per cent).[262]

---

[259] *See*, Exhibit BRA-17.
[260] *Ibid*.
[261] *Ibid*.
[262] *Ibid*.

(i) Claim 28: Inconsistency with Article 9.2 of the Anti-Dumping Agreement

Text of Article 9.2

524. The relevant portion of Article 9.2 of the Anti-Dumping Agreement provides that:

> "When an anti-dumping duty is imposed in respect of any product, such an anti-dumping duty shall be collected in the appropriate amounts in each case, on a non-discriminatory basis on imports of such product from all sources found to be dumped and causing injury (...)"

Legal Argument Relative to Claim 28

525. Brazil asserts that the variable anti-dumping duties imposed on imports of poultry from Brazil, that is, the absolute difference between the FOB price invoiced in any one shipment and a designated "minimum export price" also fixed in FOB terms, to be applied whenever the FOB export price is lower than the designated "minimum export price", can exceed the margin of dumping established in the final determination, and thus can be collected in inappropriate amounts.

526. A hypothetical example of this circumstance is presented in the exercise below:

TABLE 1

Exporter	"Minimum Export Price" in Resolution No. 574	Ad Valorem Duty in Final Determination
Sadia	0.92 US$/Kg	14.91%
Avipal	0.98 US$/Kg	15.48%
All Others	0.98 US$/Kg	8.19%

TABLE 2

Exporter	"Minimum Export Price"	Example of FOB Export Price	Ad Valorem Dumping Margin per cent
	(A)	(B)	(A) - (B)/(B) x100%
Sadia	0.92 US$/Kg	0.75 US$/Kg	22.66%
Avipal	0.98 US$/Kg	0.75 US$/Kg	30.66%
All Others	0.98 US$/Kg	0.75 US$/Kg	30.66%

TABLE 3

Exporter	Ad Valorem Duty in Final Determination	Ad Valorem Duty in Exercise	Difference
	(A)	(B)	(B) - (A)
Sadia	14.91%	22.66%	7.75%
Avipal	15.48%	30.66%	15.18%
All Others	8.19%	30.66%	22.47%

527. In the above exercise, Brazil has simulated a dumping margin calculation, assuming that the FOB price invoiced in a shipment is US$ 0.75 per kilogram and that the "minimum export price" is the one determined in Resolution No. 574 for each company (Table 2 above).

528. In this hypothetical exercise, specific anti-dumping duties to be collected as the absolute difference between the FOB price invoiced in that shipment and the designated "minimum export price" also fixed in FOB terms, result in the *ad valorem* duty of 22.66 per cent for Sadia, 30.66 per cent for Avipal and 30.66 per cent for all other exporters (Table 2 above).

529. If we compare the margins of dumping found in the DCD's final affirmative dumping determination with the margins found in the exercise above, the Panel will verify that the dumping duty to be applied in the hypothetical case would greatly exceed the margin of dumping established in the final determination (Table 3 above).

530. According to the exercise above, if the Brazilian exporters choose to export poultry into Argentina at a determined lower price, they will be imposed anti-dumping duties to be collected at inappropriate amounts, that is, in excess to the dumping margin found in the investigation and provided in the final determination.

531. This situation would violate the requirement in Article 9.2 of the Anti-Dumping Agreement that an anti-dumping duty must be collected in the appropriate amounts in each case.

(ii) Claim 29: Inconsistency with Article 9.3 of the Anti-Dumping Agreement

Text of Article 9.3

532. Relevant portion of Article 9.3 sets forth that:
"The amount of the anti-dumping duty shall not exceed the margin of dumping as established under Article 2."

Legal Argument Relative to Claim 29

533. After Argentina imposed variable anti-dumping duties on imports of poultry from Brazil, Brazilian exporters have not exported poultry into Argentina at less than the "minimum export price" in order not to pay an amount of anti-dumping duty in excess of the margin established under Article 2.

534. Article 9.3 of the Anti-Dumping Agreement specifically requires that the amount of the antidumping duty must *not* exceed the margin of dumping as established under Article 2. To that effect, Article 2.4.2 of the Anti-Dumping

Agreement provides that the "existence of margins of dumping *during the investigation phase* shall normally be established on the basis of a comparison of a weighted average normal value with a weighted average of all comparable export transactions or by a comparison of normal value and export prices on a transaction-to-transaction basis".

535. In this case, the dumping margin as established under Article 2 of the Anti-Dumping Agreement is that established during the investigation phase, based on the normal value and export price data collected from January 1998 through January 1999. The "minimum export price" determined in Resolution No. 574 does not qualify as a dumping margin established under Article 2, since it does not reflect the normal value and export price as provided by the exporters and examined by the investigating authority.

536. Also, as provided in the hypothetical exercise presented in Claim 28 above, if the Brazilian exporters choose to export poultry into Argentina at a determined lower price, they will be imposed anti-dumping duties to be collected in *excess* of the dumping margin found in the final determination.

537. By establishing a variable anti-dumping measure on imports of poultry from Brazil, which can exceed the margin of dumping established under Article 2, Argentina has acted inconsistently with Article 9.3 of the Anti-Dumping Agreement.

(iii) Claim 30: Inconsistency with Article 12.2.2 of the Anti-Dumping Agreement

Text of Article 12.2.2

538. Article 12.2.2 provides in part that:

"A public notice of conclusion or suspension of an investigation in the case of an affirmative determination providing for the imposition of a definitive duty or the acceptance of a price undertaking shall contain, or otherwise make available through a separate report, all relevant information on matters of fact and law and reasons which have led to the imposition of final measures or the acceptance of a price undertaking, due regard being paid to the requirement for the protection of confidential information. In particular, the notice or report shall contain the information described in subparagraph 2.1, as well as the reasons for the acceptance or rejection of relevant arguments or claims made by the exporters and importers, and the basis for any decision made under subparagraph 10.2 of Article 6."

Legal Argument Relative to Claim 30

539. The question presented to the Panel is whether information has been provided in the final determination, sufficient to satisfy the requirements of Article 12.2.2 of the Anti-Dumping Agreement, as to how the Argentinean authority calculated the "minimum export price" established in Resolution No. 574/2000.

540. Resolution No. 574/2000 was the public notice of conclusion that provided for the imposition of a definitive duty. Resolution No. 574/2000 imposed dumping measures in the form of specific anti-dumping duties to be collected as the absolute difference between the FOB price invoiced in any one shipment and a designated

"minimum export price" also fixed in FOB terms, to be applied whenever the former price is lower than the latter. No explanation was provided in Resolution No. 574/2000 as to how Argentina calculated the "minimum export price".

541. Article 12.2.2 requires that a public notice providing for the imposition of a definitive duty contain, or otherwise make available through a separate report, all relevant information on the matters of fact and law *and reasons which have lead to the imposition of final measures.*

542. Argentina did not provide relevant information as to why the margin established in the final determination was not applied and how the "minimum export price" was calculated.

543. Brazil considers the application of the dumping measures to be relevant information that must be included in the public notice providing for the imposition of a definitive duty. An exporter is entitled to know how the information and arguments presented during the investigation were considered by the investigating authority and how that information was used in arriving at a dumping measure.

544. By not providing relevant information in the public notice as to how and why the investigating authority established a "minimum export price", Argentina has failed to comply with Article 12.2.2 of the Anti-Dumping Agreement.

V. CONCLUSION AND REQUESTS

A. Conclusion

545. The claims set forth in Part III of this submission provide the facts and legal basis on which Brazil believes that Argentina has acted inconsistently with GATT 1994 and the various provisions in the Anti-Dumping Agreement. Brazil believes that the anti-dumping proceeding that lead to the application of definitive anti-dumping measures on imports of poultry from Brazil should never have been initiated (Part III.B of this submission - Initiation of the Anti-Dumping Investigation). Not only did the application not provide relevant evidence to be considered sufficient to meet the requirements of the necessary evidence in an application, but also the Argentinean authorities failed to examine the accuracy and adequacy of that evidence in order to justify the initiation of the investigation. By failing to do this, the Argentinean authorities failed to reject the application based on insufficient evidence of dumping and injury.

546. After Argentina incorrectly initiated the investigation, the Argentinean authorities acted inconsistently with the rules on notification, public notice, evidence and overall procedure set forth in the Anti-Dumping Agreement (Part III.C of this submission - Conduct of the Anti-Dumping Investigation - Evidentiary and Public Notice Requirements). The failure to comply with these provisions of the Agreement has impaired the rights of the exporters for a 'full opportunity' to defend their interests in the investigation at issue. Furthermore, the final determinations of dumping and injury presented material errors regarding the establishment of normal value, adjustments to the normal value, export price, fair comparison; the examination of injury, and its elements, and the establishment of the domestic industry (Part III.D of this submission - Conduct of the Anti-Dumping Investigation and Final Affirmative Determination).

547. When Argentina imposed definitive measures, it further tarnished the proceeding by imposing duties that can exceed the margin of dumping found in the final determination and that, thus, can be collected in inappropriate amounts (Part III.E of this submission - Imposition and Collection of Anti-Dumping Duties as a Result of the Anti-Dumping Investigation).

548. As a final note, Brazil observes that under Article 3.8 of the DSU, in cases where there is infringement of the obligations assumed under a covered agreement, the action is considered *prima facie* to constitute a case of nullification or impairment of the benefits under that Agreement. Accordingly and pursuant to the claims in this submission, to the extent that Argentina has acted inconsistently with the provisions of the Anti-Dumping Agreement, Argentina has nullified or impaired benefits accruing to Brazil under the Agreement.

B. Requests

549. For the reasons shown above, Brazil respectfully requests the Panel to find that Argentina has acted inconsistently with the Anti-Dumping Agreement as per the claims above, which are summarized as follows:

- The initiation of the anti-dumping proceedings against poultry from Brazil by Argentina is inconsistent with Articles 5.2, 5.3, 5.7 and 5.8 of the Anti-Dumping Agreement;
- The initiation and conduct of the anti-dumping investigation against poultry from Brazil by Argentina was inconsistent with Article 12.1 of the Anti-Dumping Agreement;
- The conduct of the anti-dumping investigation against poultry from Brazil by Argentina was inconsistent with Articles 6.1.1, 6.1.2, 6.1.3, 6.2, 6.8, paragraphs 3, 5, 6 and 7 of Annex II, Articles 6.9 and 6.10 of the Anti-Dumping Agreement;
- The final dumping determination by Argentina on poultry from Brazil is inconsistent with Articles 2.4, 2.4.2 and 12.2.2 of the Anti-Dumping Agreement;
- The final injury determination by Argentina on poultry from Brazil is inconsistent with Articles 3.1, 3.2, 3.4, 3.5 and 12.2.2 of the Anti-Dumping Agreement;
- The final injury determination and the imposition of the definitive anti-dumping measures by Argentina on poultry from Brazil is inconsistent with Article 4.1 of the Anti-Dumping Agreement; and,
- The imposition of the definitive anti-dumping measures by Argentina on poultry from Brazil is inconsistent with Articles 9.2, 9.3 and 12.2.2 of the Anti-Dumping Agreement.

550. Accordingly, Brazil respectfully requests that the Panel:

- Recommend that the DSB request Argentina to bring these actions into conformity with GATT 1994 and the Anti-Dumping Agreement;
- Use its right to make suggestions on ways which Argentina could implement the Panel's recommendations, as provided in Article 19.1 of the DSU; and,
- Suggest that, in light of the numerous outcome-decisive violations of the Anti-Dumping Agreement that Argentina immediately repeal Resolution No. 574/2000 imposing definitive anti-dumping duties.

ANNEX A-2

FIRST ORAL STATEMENT OF BRAZIL
(25 September 2002)

INTRODUCTION

1. Brazil appreciates the opportunity to appear before the Panel to explain its position in this dispute. We would like to note our appreciation for the time and effort devoted by the Panel and the secretariat to this matter.

2. In this statement, Brazil will not repeat the arguments already stated in its first submission (BFS) and will simply address some of the central issues before the Panel in light of the arguments raised by Argentina in its first submission (AFS).

3. However, before turning to the specific arguments, we would first like to address an issues raised in AFS. It relates to Argentina's claim that the dispute before this Panel has already been "debated and resolved" in a previous Mercosul Ad Hoc Arbitral Tribunal. Argentina suggests that, for this reason, the Panel should dismiss Brazil's complaint.

THE MERCOSUL AD HOC TRIBUNAL - *Res Judicata*

4. Although Argentina does not clearly state this in its first submission, it appears that Argentina claims that the ruling by the Mercosul Tribunal on the dispute has the effect of *res judicata*.[1] Under the principle of *res judicata* a final judgement rendered by a court or competent jurisdiction on the merits of a case is conclusive as to the rights of the parties and their privies, and as to these parties, constitutes an absolute bar to a subsequent action involving the same claim, demand, or cause of action. In other words, the principle of *res judicata* is only applied if the subsequent action involves the same parties, the same measures and the same claims as the previous action.

5. Having said that, we underscore that although we have the same parties (Brazil and Argentina) and the measure (Resolution No. 574/2000) before this Panel, the claims of the present dispute are not the same.

6. Since Argentina has gone at length with this argument, we would like to explain that the matter before the Mercosul Tribunal had to be decided according to Mercosul anti-dumping rules for trade within the region. The Mercosul Tribunal, however, found that Mercosul anti-dumping rules for trade within the region were not properly in force. Within that context, the Tribunal found that Mercosul Member States were allowed to apply their domestic anti-dumping legislation with respect to regional trade. The Tribunal also concluded that it did not have to decide on any of the substantive issues concerning the investigation, such as the existence of dumping, injury to the domestic industry, and causal link.

7. Brazil notes that the Mercosul arbitrators dealt with the dispute under the umbrella of the Brasilia Protocol, the dispute settlement mechanism that applies

---

[1] AFS, para. 17.

strictly to the Mercosul legal texts, that is, the Treaty of Asuncion and all other agreements and decisions that make up Mercosul's legal framework.

8. Brazil's claims before this Panel are not related to the interpretation, application or non-compliance with the provisions of any of the Mercosul texts. Brazil's claims before this Panel relate to the consistency of the Argentinean anti-dumping investigation and measure with the provisions of the Anti-Dumping Agreement and Article VI of GATT 1994, issues that were never addressed by the Mercosul arbitrators.

9. We make special note that Paraguay also argues, in its third party submission that the ruling by the Mercosul Ad Hoc Arbitral Tribunal has the effect of *res judicata*.[2] In developing its arguments, Paraguay considers relevant to mention the Olivos Protocol. At this point, Brazil will simply recall that the Olivos Protocol is not even in force yet.

10. At any rate, what Paraguay and Argentina bring before this Panel is a situation where Mercosul Members potentially have divergent views on what their rights and obligations under the Mercosul legal texts may be. Yet, Article 1 of the DSU confines the jurisdiction of this Panel to disputes brought pursuant to the "covered agreements" (those listed in Appendix 1 of the DSU), the "WTO Agreement", and the DSU, taken in isolation or in combination with each other. The Brasilia Protocol and the Olivos Protocol are not listed in Article 1 of the DSU.

11. In bringing this *res judicata* claim to the Panel, Argentina cites no provision of the WTO legal texts to support its contention. It simply makes a reference to Article 3.2 of the DSU without clearly indicating how that provision would support the *res judicata* argument. This is not surprising, for Article 3.2 of the DSU deals exclusively with the clarification of the existing provisions of the WTO Agreement and bears no relation whatsoever to the relationship between previous rulings by an international tribunal and the rights and obligations of WTO Members under the "covered agreements", the "WTO Agreement" and the DSU.

12. What Article 3.2 of the DSU provides is that the WTO dispute settlement system "serves to preserve the rights and obligations of Members *under the covered agreements*, and to clarify the existing provisions *of those agreements* in accordance with customary rules of interpretation of public international law." In fact, Article 3.2 affirms the right of Brazil to have the Panel hear its claims that the Argentinean anti-dumping measure impairs Brazil's WTO rights.

INITIATION OF THE DUMPING INVESTIGATION

(a) *Article 5.2 - Evidence in the Application*

13. Regarding the claims of violation of Article 5.2 of the ADA, Argentina claims that an applicant is not obligated to prove without doubt the existence of dumping, but acknowledges that simple assertion of the existence of dumping, injury, and causal link is not sufficient if that assertion is not substantiated by relevant evidence. According to Argentina, an application substantiated by relevant evidence is conditioned on what information is "reasonably available" to the applicant.[3]

---

[2] Paraguay's submission, para. 5.
[3] AFS, para. 34.

14. Argentina states that there are two levels of requirements regarding the quality and quantity of evidence that should be submitted. The first level is the evidence presented in an application for initiation, which according to the Agreement is that which is "reasonably available" to the applicant. The second level is the evidence that should be submitted once the investigation has initiated. To that regard, Argentina cites previous WTO Panel Reports that support the idea that the quantum and quality of evidence required prior to initiation has to be necessarily less than that required for a final determination.[4]

15. Brazil agrees. What Argentina fails to state, however, is that previous WTO Panels have also found that the evidence required at the time of initiation *nonetheless* had to be *relevant* in establishing the elements in the Agreement, and that the *type* of evidence needed to justify initiation *is the same as* that needed to make a preliminary or final determination of dumping, although the quality and quantity is less.

16. The existence, in the application, of *relevant* evidence of the *type* necessary to conduct an investigation is particularly important when it is obvious on the face of the application that adjustments will unavoidably be made to normal value and export price data.

17. That said, Argentina has neither presented arguments nor indicated the evidence in the application to support that: 1) poultry sold in Brazil was physically different from the poultry sold to Argentina; 2) that the alleged differences in physical characteristics actually affect price comparability; and, 3) that the yield rate difference alleged by petitioner was correct.

18. In Brazil's submission, we have shown that the petitioner, in suggesting the calculation adjustment to compensate the alleged difference between the poultry sold in Brazil and to Argentina, provided no "evidence" - that is, no information drawn from a document tending to prove a fact or a proposition - that would justify such an adjustment. Likewise, no evidence was presented showing that price comparability would be affected or that the yield rate proposed by the petitioner was justified.

19. Brazil has also shown that the normal value submitted in the application was for only one day in 1997 (30 June 30), while export data covered a period of six months in 1997 (January through May 1997 and August 1997). According to the Anti-Dumping Agreement, a fair comparison must be made in respect of sales made at as nearly as possible the same time. From the data provided in the application, such a comparison would not be possible.

20. Argentina repeatedly makes the argument that an application substantiated by relevant evidence is conditioned on what information is "reasonably available" to the applicant.[5] We have indicated that normal value information for all of 1996 and 1997 was reasonably available to the petitioner, even though the petitioner only presented normal value information for one day in 1997.[6] The petitioner could have attached prices on poultry published by JOX for all months of 1997. Nonetheless, it chose to provide it for one single day in that year.

---

[4] *Ibid.*, para. 37.
[5] *Ibid.*, paras. 31, 32 and 39.
[6] BFS, para. 124.

(b)   Article 5.3 - Accuracy and Adequacy of the Evidence in the Application

21.   Regarding the claims of violation of Article 5.3 of the ADA, Argentina again argues that the level of evidence sufficient to justify the initiation of an investigation is considerably inferior to that required in a determination to apply a preliminary or definitive measure. Argentina cites selected passages of previous WTO Panel Reports.

22.   We repeat that we do not contest such standard. What Argentina again fails to state that those same reports conclude that "when from the face of an application it is obvious that there are substantial questions of comparability between the export price and home market prices being compared, the investigating authority will *at least* acknowledge that differences in the prices generate questions with regards to their comparability, and either give some consideration as to the impact of those differences on the sufficiency of the evidence of dumping or seek further evidence as might be necessary."

23.   In the present case, the investigating authority neither gave consideration to the impact of the possible differences on the sufficiency of the evidence submitted in the application, nor did it seek further evidence, which was clearly necessary.

24.   Still under Article 5.3, Brazil showed in its first submission that Argentina established export prices - and consequently the dumping margins - based only on export transactions below normal value. We simply refer to Exhibit BRA-2. There, the Panel will verify that the investigating authority considered, from the import data presented in the application, only the portion of the imports of the product that entered Argentina at prices inferior to those for the product sold in Brazil.[7]

25.   By selecting certain export transactions, namely those below normal value, from the total export transactions in the application, Argentina not only failed to examine the accuracy and adequacy of *all* the evidence that was presented in the application but also inflated the dumping margin. It is obvious that the adoption of this methodology would always result in a dumping margin.

26.   In explaining the methodology used to establish the export price, Argentina provided in its first submission a different explanation from that found in the decision to initiate the investigation. In its first submission, Argentina states that the investigating authority examined the import transactions "in an attempt to determine which of them corresponded closest to the product under investigation, and it did so for the sole purpose of calculating the most appropriate and comparable export price possible at this pre-initiation stage."[8] Members of the Panel, this is a convoluted way of trying to explain what in effect is the "zeroing" methodology. We could not agree with the statement that a more adjusted and comparable export price is that which is inferior to those prices for the product sold in the domestic market.

27.   Furthermore, had the investigating authority properly examined the accuracy and adequacy of the evidence provided in the application, it would have realized that the normal value data in the application was for one single day in 1997 and that the export price data was for a period of six months in 1997. Because prices vary over a period of time, a fair comparison must be made in respect of sales made at as nearly as possible the same time, even for purposes of initiation of an investigation.

---

[7] Pages 10 and 11 of BRA-2.
[8] AFS, paras. 78 and 79.

Report of the Panel

Obviously, it is insufficient or inadequate to compare normal value of a single day to export prices covering six non-consecutive months.

CONDUCT OF THE ANTI-DUMPING INVESTIGATION - EVIDENTIARY AND PUBLIC NOTICE REQUIREMENTS

(a)   Article 12.1 - Notification and Public Notice of the Initiation

28.   Regarding the claim of violation of Article 12.1 of the Agreement, Argentina argues that it was impossible to notify the seven exporters, since the interest of these parties was unknown at the time the investigating authority was satisfied that there was sufficient evidence to justify the initiation of the investigation.[9]

29.   First, it is of the utmost importance to reaffirm that Article 12.1 mandates that the investigating authorities notify "the Member ... the products of which are subject to the investigation *and* other interested parties known to the investigating authorities." This obligation falls exclusively upon the investigating authority. Argentina tries to share this obligation with Brazil when it states that it notified Brazil of the initiation of the investigation and requested that it cooperate in identifying the producers and exporters interested in the investigation.[10]

30.   Second, it is simply not true that Argentina did not notify these seven exporters because it did not know that these were parties with an interest in the investigation. As stated and proven in paragraph 199 and Exhibit BRA-2 of Brazil's first submission, out of the seven Brazilian exporters that were not notified of the initiation, *at least* five of these exporters (Comaves, Catarinense, Minuano, Chapecó and Perdigão) were listed as Brazilian exporters in the determination to initiate.[11]

31.   Even though Argentina knew these seven exporters to be interested parties in the investigation it only notified them eight months after the investigation had initiated.

(b)   Article 6.1.1 - Deadlines for Responses

32.   On the claim of violation of Article 6.1.1 of the Agreement, Argentina states that it provided a period of more than 30 days for exporters to reply to the questionnaire.

33.   This is not true. Brazil has provided as Exhibit BRA-13 the letters from the DCD to the seven Brazilian exporters inviting them to provide questionnaire responses within a period no longer than 20 days from receipt of the mentioned letter. It is evident that the timeframe required by the DCD in these letters was on its face contrary to the 30-day period required under Article 6.1.1 of the Agreement.

34.   In paragraph 133 of its first submission, Argentina confirms that it sent the questionnaires to the Brazilian exporters Catarinense, Chapecó, Minuano, Perdigão, Comaves and Pena Branca on 15 September 1999. However, Argentina fails to inform the Panel that in that communication of 15 September, DCD allows a period "not longer than 20 days from the receipt of the [communication]".[12]

---

[9]   *Ibid.*, para. 110.
[10]   *Ibid.*, paras. 112 to 116.
[11]   Exhibit BRA-2, page 5.
[12]   Exhibit BRA-13.

35. We also reaffirm that these seven exporters were never notified by the CNCE of the investigation and of the need to provide responses to the injury questionnaire. In fact, these exporters never even received such questionnaires. Argentina confirms that the CNCE only sent the injury questionnaires to eight exporters - in fact only five exporters received them.[13] By not sending the injury questionnaires to all exporters participating in the investigation, Argentina impaired their rights for defence, again violating Article 6.1.1.

> (c) *Article 6.1.2 - Evidence Submitted ... Shall be Made Available Promptly*

36. With respect to the claim of violation of Article 6.1.2 of the Agreement, Brazil has already established that Argentina knew these exporters to be interested parties in the investigation at the time of initiation. We have also presented evidence to the effect that these exporters were notified of the investigation and the need to participate eight months after the investigation had already been initiated. Such evidence is in Exhibit BRA-13 of Brazil's submission.

37. In that sense, how could evidence presented by the other interested parties in the investigation be made "promptly" available, as required under Article 6.1.2, if these seven exporters were notified to participate in the investigation eight months after the investigation had already initiated and a preliminary determination of dumping, injury and causal link had already been issued?

> (d) *Article 6.1.3 - ... Shall Provide the Full Text of the Written Application*

38. On the claim of violation of Article 6.1.3 of the Agreement, Argentina first argues that in the Spanish version of the Agreement the term "provide" is set forth as "facilitar". Thus, based on the Spanish version of the Agreement, Argentina claims that the investigating authorities have complied with the requirement in Article 6.1.3 when they made the written application available to the interested parties once the investigation was initiated.

39. In fact, any reasonable interpretation of Article 6.1.3 would conclude that Argentina was obligated to supply the Government of Brazil and the exporters with the full text of the written application. Argentina's position that the verb "to provide" could be understood to mean that authorities were only required to "make available" the full text of the written application is incorrect.

40. The first sentence of Article 6.1.3 of the Agreement states that "as soon as an investigation has been initiated, the authorities *shall provide* the full text of the written application received under paragraph 1 of Article 5 to the known exporters and to the authorities of the exporting Member and *shall make it available*, upon request, to other interested parties involved."

41. Article 6.1.3 of the Agreement carefully differentiates the obligation that the investigating authorities have with the exporters and the exporting Member from the obligation the investigating authorities have with other interested parties. In the first case, the investigating authority must actively "provide" the full text of the written

---

[13] AFS, para.135.

application to the exporting Member and to the exporters involved in the investigation. In the second case, the investigating authorities must "make available", upon request, the full text of the written application to other interested parties. Brazil believes that if the requirement imposed on the investigation authority was to be understood as being the same for the exporters and exporting Member as that for the other interested parties, there would be no need for the use of different language in Article 6.1.3 of the Agreement.

42. The same reasoning applies to the text in Spanish. The requirement imposed on the investigating authorities to provide, or "facilitar", the full text of the written application to exporters and the exporting Member is different from the requirement imposed on the authorities to "make available", or "pondrán a disposición", the full text of the written application to other interested parties. Finally, the dictionary of the *Real Academia Española* defines the word "facilitar" as "proporcionar o entregar", a definition entirely compatible with the word "provide", used in the English version.

(e) Article 6.8 - Facts Available

43. On the claims of incorrect use of facts available by Argentina, we note that the authority disregarded the responses provided by the Brazilian exporters with respect to the description of the product sold to Argentina and in Brazil. Instead, the authority applied the normal value adjustment suggested in the application. Argentina claims that it was impossible to take into account the allegations made by the exporters without supporting documentation that could be verified.

44. We have shown in Exhibits BRA-22, BRA-23, BRA-24 and BRA-26 that the exporters Sadia, Avipal and Frangosul reported that the poultry sold to Argentina was identical to the poultry sold in Brazil. We have also shown in Exhibit BRA-25 that the Brazilian exporter Catarinense reported that from the two types of poultry sold (broiler and griler), there was a difference in the broiler type poultry sold to Argentina and in Brazil. The broiler type poultry sold by Catarinense to Argentina did not contain head and feet, while the broiler type poultry sold in Brazil contained head but not feet.

45. Even though the exporters reported this important information within a reasonable period and the authority did not question the exporters on such information - or require further clarifications - the DCD still chose to apply the arbitrary normal value adjustment proposed by the petitioner in the application.

46. Argentina claims that the information reported in the questionnaires was not accompanied by supporting documentation that could be verified.

47. The Panel will note that not only did the questionnaire not specify that this information required supporting documentation but also that the authority never, throughout the investigation, requested any supporting documentation in order to verify the product description reported by these exporters. The investigating authorities also never informed the exporters that their evidence and information was not accepted, pursuant to paragraph 6 of Annex II.

48. Furthermore, the investigating authority decided that the information provided by the petitioner in the application, without any supporting documentation, was more "accurate" and "verifiable" than the precise information provided by the exporters with regard to their own product. We recall that the information used by the petitioner in the application, to indicate that an adjustment to normal value was

necessary, was based on JOX information for chilled poultry, with head and feet, for the São Paulo wholesale market. JOX information was for chilled poultry with head and feet, a product that was different from the product under investigation, frozen poultry without head and feet.

49. We recall that these exporters invited the investigating authority to verify their responses *in loco,* but the authorities decided not to carry out this verification visit. Brazil understands that, in this case, even the information submitted without supporting documentation was still information that could be verified. Argentina seems to confuse the meaning of "verifiable" information, that is, information "that *can* be verified", with information "that has not yet been verified".

50. Moreover, paragraph 7 of Annex II instructs the investigating authority to use "special circumspection" if the authority has to base its findings, including with respect to normal value, on information from a secondary source, including the information supplied in the application by the petitioner. Argentina did not use "special circumspection" when it unjustifiably ignored the responses provided by these exporters and decided to apply the arbitrary adjustment to normal value suggested by the petitioner in the application.

CONDUCT OF THE ANTI-DUMPING INVESTIGATION - FINAL AFFIRMATIVE DETERMINATION

(a) Article 2.4 - Fair Comparison

51. On the claim that Argentina failed to make due allowance for freight in the normal value of two exporters, Argentina claims that the investigating authority could not have made the freight adjustment, even though Sadia reported that such adjustments were warranted, because these deductions were not properly documented.

52. Even though Argentina considers this adjustment has "a decisive and significant impact on price comparability"[14], it still considered that the investigating authority would have acted incorrectly if it had made this specific discount. According to Argentina, no documented evidence was provided and the freight information provided by the exporter was too general to be used.

53. Even though Argentina knows that this adjustment is warranted and that it is "decisive and significant" for the price comparison it simply decided not to make it, instead of using a secondary source of information to estimate such deduction, as it did with the normal value adjustment to compensate the alleged characteristic differences between poultry sold to Argentina and in Brazil.

54. Regarding Argentina's failure to make due allowance for differences in taxation, freight and financial cost in the normal value established for all other exporters, it is important that the Panel not be confused by Argentina's hazy arguments.

55. During the investigation, the DCD requested that JOX clarify the taxes included in the prices published and used to determine normal value in the preliminary determination.[15] In the final determination, the DCD simply stated that

---

[14] *Ibid.*, para. 211.
[15] Exhibit BRA-32.

the information provided by JOX was in Portuguese.[16] We underline the fact that no further explanation by the authorities was provided in the final determination except that the JOX information was in Portuguese.

56. During the consultation stage of this dispute, Brazil requested an explanation on why the investigating authorities disregarded the information provided by JOX. Argentina responded that JOX presented information in Portuguese, which did not comply with the formal requirements of the Argentinean laws and regulations for administrative proceedings.

57. Now, in its first submission, Argentina provides an entirely different response. Argentina argues that for the comparison to be fair it has to be made in the same level of trade, and that is why it did not take into account the deductions informed by JOX, since that would be a comparison between an ex-factory price for normal value and an FOB price for export price.

58. It is noteworthy that for all other purposes, including the normal value adjustment, Argentina has used JOX information. With respect to the alleged differences in characteristics, the DCD did use JOX information even though the exporters submitted information indicating and proving that there were no such differences. With respect to normal value for all other exporters, the DCD also used all other information provided by JOX in establishing the normal value.

59. An ex-factory price is the price with no charges included since this represents the price at the factory. An FOB price includes inland freight to the port of exportation, inland insurance, handling and loading charges. The FOB price does not include taxes and financial costs. That said and with the information provided by JOX, the investigating authority should still have made deductions from the normal value with respect to the taxes and financial costs included in the JOX published prices. These deductions would have permitted a fair comparison on the same level of trade.

60. With respect to the claim that Argentina incorrectly made allowances to normal value based on alleged differences in physical characteristics, the authorities again refused all information submitted by the exporters alleging that no supporting documentation existed. The authorities never asked for such documentation nor did they take the initiative to verify the information provided.

61. Still in its claims of violation of Article 2.4, Brazil asserts that Argentina has imposed an unreasonable burden of proof on exporters Sadia, Avipal and Frangosul by allowing exporters to submit normal value and export price information for the years 1996 - 1999, when the dumping period of investigation was later fixed for January 1998 to January 1999.

62. Argentina admits that it did not define the dumping period of data collection on purpose.[17] Argentina tries to justify its action by stating that the Agreement does not define the period of data collection. Argentina further affirms that the authority has the discretion to request the documentation that it considers necessary in determining dumping and may request more information if needed to ensure due process.

63. Brazil agrees that the Anti-Dumping Agreement does not define or establish what the period of data collection must be. However, the Agreement does provide in

---

[16] Exhibit BRA-15.
[17] AFS, para. 243.

Article 2.4 that the investigating authorities have the obligation of indicating to the parties what information is necessary to ensure a fair comparison and cannot impose an unreasonable burden of proof on the parties.

64. The DCD only established that the dumping data collection period would be from January 1998 through January 1999, on October of 1999, that is, nine months after the investigation was initiated, after a preliminary determination had been issued, and after Sadia, Avipal, and Frangosul had presented their questionnaire responses with normal value and export price information for the years 1996 through 1999. The time and resource spent by these exporters in collecting normal value and export price for the years 1996 through 1999 is an unreasonable burden of proof imposed on these exporters.

65. Furthermore, an excessive burden of proof was also imposed on exporters Sadia, Avipal, and Frangosul when the investigating authority required that these exporters provide an invoice copy for all of the sales transactions in the home market in order to establish normal value and, consequently, make a "fair comparison".

66. These same exporters provided letters to the DCD stating that the great volume of sales of poultry in Brazil made it impossible for exporters to attach all invoices corresponding to those transactions. These exporters attached invoices for a few transactions as sample. The exporters also invited the investigating authority to verify *in loco* the responses provided, so as to ascertain that they were accurate and complete.[18] The DCD chose not to verify these exporters.

(b) Article 3 - Injury Determination

67. Brazil's claims of violation of Articles 3.1, 3.4, 3.5 and 12.2.2 of the Agreement, relate to the use of different periods to evaluate the relevant economic factors and indices listed in Article 3.4, and the lack of explanation in the final determination on why the investigating authority decided to examine the relevant economic factors and indices based on different periods.

68. Once again, Argentina tries to confuse the Panel by making the argument that in threat of injury cases, international law and practice allows for the possibility of analysis of a period longer than the period of investigation so as to verify whether or not there is a trend of increasing imports.[19]

69. We stress that this is not the issue before the Panel. We are not challenging whether in a threat of injury case the investigating authority may or may not analyse data for a period longer than that of the investigation. What we are challenging is that in the investigation at issue, the authority considered a certain period of injury analysis for some factors and another period for other factors.

70. In the final determination, the CNCE stated that the period under analysis corresponded to January 1996 through December 1998. However, only for some variables, such as national production, prices, imports, exports, and apparent consumption did the authority include data corresponding to the first semester of 1999.

71. To that regard, the US disagrees with Brazil's contention that an analysis of differing time periods cannot be objective and thus violates Article 3.1 of the

---

[18] Exhibits BRA-26, BRA-29 and BRA-31.
[19] AFS, paras. 252 to 254.

Agreement. To support its view, the US cites the Panel report in *United States - Hot Rolled Steel*. In that investigation, the US gathered information on all factors over the entire three-year period of investigation, and it evaluated the various factors, at various instances, over the three-year period.

72. We will not go further into the analysis of that Panel report because we believe that the facts of that investigation and the claim of violation presented here by Brazil are very different from that case. First, in the instant case, the investigating authority did not gather information on all factors over the same period, that it is, from January 1996 through December 1998. For the factors national production, prices, imports, exports, and apparent consumption the period of injury analysis was from January 1996 through June 1999. Second, the Argentinean investigating authority did not evaluate all the factors listed in Article 3.4 over the same period of injury analysis.

73. We believe that the US argument is that over one determined period of injury analysis, the investigating authority can compare data for certain years without explicitly discussing data for other years. However, all factors are analyzed under a certain, defined period of injury analysis. Here, unlike the case cited by the US, the Argentinean authorities decided that for certain factors the injury analysis period would be from January 1996 through December 1998 and for other factors the injury analysis period would be from January 1996 through June 1999. What the investigating authorities cannot do, and thus our claim of violation of Articles 3.1 and 3.4 of the Agreement, is establish a certain period of injury analysis for some factors and another period of injury analysis for other factors.

74. Regarding the claim that the CNCE's injury analysis in the final determination was flawed because it did not exclude the imports of the Brazilian exporters Nicolini and Seara from the "dumped imports" under analysis, Argentina argues that in the final causal link determination the authority took into account the dumping determination that the imports from the Brazilian exporters Nicolini and Seara were not being dumped.[20] This is not true.

75. First, the injury analysis in the final injury determination never mentioned the exclusion of the imports from these two Brazilian exporters from the total "dumped imports" under analysis. The Panel can verify this in Exhibit BRA-14. As stated in BFS paragraph 450, we know this to be a fact because the final injury determination was issued on 23 December 1999, and preceded the final dumping determination, issued on 23 June 2000, by six months. It was in the final dumping determination that the investigating authority reached the conclusion that the exporters Nicolini and Seara were not exporting the subject merchandise at dumped prices.

76. In its first submission, Argentina effectively admits that it did not exclude imports from Nicolini and Seara from the injury examination. This, in itself, is a blatant violation of Articles 3.1, 3.2, and 3.4. It is, after all, in the injury determination, that the authorities must examine the volume, the effect, and the impact of the dumped imports.

77. Argentina tries to remedy this situation claiming that it was in establishing the causal link that it took into account the fact that those imports were not dumped.[21] However, the causal link determination contains no indication whatsoever that

---

[20] *Ibid.*, para. 266.
[21] *Ibid.*

Nicolini and Seara's imports were excluded from the total "dumped imports". The final causal link determination simply restated what was already provided in the final dumping determination.

78. On the claim of violation that Argentina failed to evaluate all the relevant economic factors and indices listed in Article 3.4, Argentina tries to convince the Panel that these factors were evaluated by citing various pages in the final injury determination where it claims such information was provided. We will demonstrate that the investigating authority has not evaluated these factors.

79. With respect to the actual and potential decline in productivity, Argentina cites pages 12 through 14 and 20 in the final determination and pages 26 through 30 and 95 of the Technical Report in an attempt to demonstrate that this factor was evaluated. We ask the Panel to check those pages and verify that the factors evaluated in them refer to production, capacity, capacity utilization, employment and wages, that is, other factors listed in Article 3.4 of the Agreement other than actual and potential decline in productivity. Argentina also cites to Annexes 1, 11, 12, 13 and 14 of the Technical Report of the final determination. The Panel must be aware that these Annexes refer to production, employment, wages, and cost structure but do not relate to the factor productivity.

80. Concerning factors affecting domestic prices, Argentina claims that it has analysed the evolution of the price indices of substitute products, basically red meat, as well as the general level of activity and price indices of the most important sectors.[22] We have not identified such evaluation. Argentina further cites Table 16 of the Technical Report, which presents the average sales revenue by kilogram of fresh or chilled poultry. Brazil fails to see how that relates to factors affecting the domestic price.

81. With respect to the magnitude of the dumping margin, instead of citing the final determination to demonstrate that the factor was evaluated, Argentina tries to evaluate this factor in its submission. To this regard, we restate that the investigating authority did not and could not have evaluated the magnitude of the dumping margin because the final dumping determination, with the dumping margin, was issued on 23 June 2000, six months after the final injury determination was issued.

82. With respect to remaining factors, regarding actual and potential negative effects on cash flow, growth, and the ability to raise capital or investments, Argentina admits that it made no cash flow evaluation and claims that such an evaluation would be impossible given some peculiarities of the Argentinean market.[23] Brazil notes that no explanation of the kind offered in AFS is present in the final determination, where this issue is not even mentioned. With respect to the other factors (growth, and the ability to raise capital or investments), Argentina does not indicate, in its first submission, if and where these factors were evaluated in the injury analysis contained in the final injury determination.

83. We find it appropriate at this moment to address the US comment on these claims. First, the US agrees that the Agreement requires an investigating authority to evaluate each of the Article 3.4 factors. Second, the US disagrees that the failure to refer to a particular factor in the published determination necessarily breaches Article 12.2.2. In arguing this position, the US states that Article 12.2.2 requires only that the

---

[22] *Ibid.*, para. 292.
[23] *Ibid.*, paras. 297 to 299.

authorities set forth "in sufficient detail the findings and conclusions reached on all issues of fact and law considered material by the investigating authorities". The US argues that while all enumerated factors must be evaluated, not all are necessarily material in any particular case.

84. We have demonstrated in our submission that Argentina has not even enumerated in the final determination all the factors in Article 3.4, let alone evaluated them. Furthermore, it is not discernible from the published determination that authorities have evaluated all of Article 3.4 factors. More importantly, Brazil recalls that the evaluation of all Article 3.4 injury factors is mandatory and, as such, an inherently material issue of fact and law. Even if a particular factor does not have a material effect in the injury determination, its evaluation *cannot* be considered immaterial by the authorities. The final determination, therefore, must necessarily indicate if and how all factors were evaluated in the underlying investigation and, at a minimum, explain why a particular factor was considered immaterial.

(c) Article 4.1 - Major Proportion

85. Regarding the claim of violation of Article 4.1 of the Agreement, we agree with Argentina that the Agreement does not stipulate an exact percentage of what constitutes a "major proportion" of the total domestic production. That is exactly the issue before the Panel, whether 46 per cent of the total domestic production of poultry in Argentina constitutes a major proportion of the total domestic production.

86. At this point in time, Brazil will simply reiterate the terms of its first submission. Brazil however takes note of the arguments advanced by some of the Third Parties and submits that should the Panel find that a "major proportion" could mean less than 50 per cent of national production, the following considerations should apply.

87. First, contrary to what the EC suggests, nothing in Article 5.4 equates "producers expressly supporting the application" to the "domestic industry". Secondly, if the Agreement provides no specific benchmark for what would constitute a major proportion of total domestic production, then the investigating authorities are under the obligation to expressly elucidate how it found that a percentage lower than 50 per cent could be considered a major proportion.

IMPOSITION AND COLLECTION OF ANTI-DUMPING DUTIES AS A RESULT OF THE ANTI-DUMPING INVESTIGATION

88. Members of the Panel, regarding the claims of violation of Articles 9.2 and 9.3 of the Agreement, due to the imposition of anti-dumping duties pegged to minimum export prices, Brazil takes note of the arguments raised by Argentina and some Third Parties. At this point in time, Brazil would refrain from advancing any further arguments other than those set out in its first submission. Brazil is still evaluating the new elements brought into this discussion and will provide a more substantive and robust analysis of this issue in our second submission. Nonetheless, if necessary, Brazil would endeavour to offer preliminary answers to any questions raised by the Panel in this meeting.

89. Mr. Chairman, members of the Panel, this oral statement merely touches on some of the issues raised in Brazil's first submission. We tried to offer the Panel a

fresh view on some of the core issues and arguments of this case, bearing in mind some of the points raised by Argentina and the Third Parties in their submissions. We did not intend to exhaust the arguments that could and will be raised by Brazil in the following stages of these proceedings. Any omissions should not be construed as lack of interest on the points not addressed, or that Brazil has given up any of the claims raised in its first submission.

90.   Let me thank you again for your time and attention.

Report of the Panel

ANNEX A-3

SECOND WRITTEN SUBMISSION OF BRAZIL
(17 October 2002)

TABLE OF CONTENTS

	Page
INTRODUCTION	A-1979
I. ARTICLE 18.2 OF THE DSU	A-1979
II. ANTI-DUMPING STANDARD OF REVIEW	A-1980
III. RULING BY THE MERCOSUL AD HOC ARBITRAL TRIBUNAL	A-1981
IV. CLAIMS RELATED TO THE INITIATION OF THE ANTI-DUMPING INVESTIGATION	A-1986
Article 5.3	A-1986
Claim 4 - Export Price Below Normal Value	A-1986
V. CLAIMS RELATED TO THE CONDUCT OF THE ANTI-DUMPING INVESTIGATION - EVIDENTIARY AND PUBLIC NOTICE REQUIREMENTS	A-1987
Articles 12.1, 6.1.1, 6.8, 6.9 and Annex II	A-1987
Claim 10 - Failure to Notify Seven Brazilian Exporters	A-1987
Claim 11 - Failure to Give 30-Day Deadline to Respond to Questionnaire	A-1988
Claim 15 - Disregard of Exporters' Product Description	A-1989
Claim 17 - Disregard of Exporters' Export Price Information	A-1992
Claim 21 - Failure to Inform the Essential Facts Under Consideration	A-1993
VI. CLAIMS RELATED TO THE CONDUCT OF THE ANTI-DUMPING INVESTIGATION AND FINAL AFFIRMATIVE DETERMINATION	A-1994
Articles 2.4, 3.1, 3.4, 3.5 and 12.2.2	A-1994
Claim 26 - Unreasonable Burden on Exporters	A-1994
Claim 32 - Failure to Use the Same Period to Evaluate Article 3.4 Factors	A-1996
Claim 38 - Failure to Evaluate All Article 3.4 Factors	A-1998
Claim 40 - Failure to Provide Adequate Final Notice	A-1999
VII. CLAIMS RELATED TO THE IMPOSITION AND COLLECTION OF ANTI-DUMPING DUTIES AS A RESULT OF THE ANTI-DUMPING INVESTIGATION	A-2000
Articles 9.2, 9.3 and 12.2.2	A-2000

		Page
	Claims 28 and 29 - Duty in Excess of the Dumping Margin......	A-2000
	Claim 30 - Failure to Provide How "Minimum Export Prices" Were Established...................................	A-2005
VIII.	CONCLUSION AND REQUESTS	A-2006
	A. Conclusion	A-2006
	B. Requests	A-2006

INTRODUCTION

1. Brazil thanks the Panel for its continued attention and welcomes this opportunity to rebut the arguments presented by Argentina in its first written submission and in its oral statements. Jointly with the second submission, Brazil is also providing the written responses to the list of questions of the Panel, provided on the first substantive meeting of 25 September 2002. In essence, the present submission serves to further point out factual inconsistencies and mistaken interpretations of provisions in the Agreement on the Implementation of Article VI of GATT 1994 ("Anti-Dumping Agreement"), that have not been dealt with in Brazil's first submission and in the written response to the Panel's questions.

2. In order to facilitate, Brazil has divided this rebuttal into 8 parts:

I. Article 18.2 of the Dispute Settlement Understanding ("DSU");

II. Anti-Dumping Standard of Review;

III. Ruling by the Mercosul Ad Hoc Tribunal;

IV. Claims Related to the Initiation of the Anti-Dumping Investigation;

V. Claims Related to the Conduct of the Anti-Dumping Investigation - Evidentiary and Public Notice Requirements;

VI. Claims Related to the Conduct of the Anti-Dumping Investigation and Final Affirmative Determination;

VII. Claims Related to the Imposition and Collection of Anti-Dumping Duties as a Result of the Anti-Dumping Investigation; and,

VIII. Conclusion and Requests.

3. Before making considerations relative to the specific claims, Brazil would like to address three issues raised by Argentina. The first issue relates to Argentina's allegation that Brazil has acted inconsistently with Article 18.2 of the DSU. The second relates to the standard of review in anti-dumping cases as set out in Article 17.6 of the Anti-Dumping Agreement. The third issue deals with Argentina's claim that the dispute before this Panel has already been "discussed and settled" in a previous ruling by a Mercosul Ad Hoc Arbitral Tribunal ("Mercosul Tribunal").

I. ARTICLE 18.2 OF THE DSU

4. Brazil has characterized its first written submission as not having any confidential information, with the exceptions of Exhibits. To that effect, Brazil has offered Argentina, as a courtesy, the opportunity to identify any portion of Brazil's

first submission that Argentina might view as confidential. Argentina has not identified any specific portion of that document as confidential.

5. Argentina has claimed, however, that by classifying its whole first submission as non-confidential, Brazil has acted contrary to Article 18.2 of the DSU and has "impaired" Argentina's rights under the DSU.[1]

6. In Argentina's view, the first sentence of Article 18.2 requires written submissions to always be treated as confidential, regardless of the fact that written submissions may sometimes *not* include confidential information. Argentina understands that the second sentence of Article 18.2 allows only the public disclosure of a party's "statements" of positions. Brazil understands that the DSU does not limit the scope, form, length or content of a party's "statements" and that, in this instance, Brazil's first submission, without the Exhibits, is identical to the "statements" provided in the second sentence of Article 18.2.

7. This is in accordance with Rule 3 of the Working Procedures for this Panel, that provides the following:

> "(...) *Where a party to a dispute submits a confidential version of its written submissions to the Panel, it shall also, upon request of a Member, provide a non-confidential summary of the information contained in its submissions that could be disclosed to the public.*" (emphasis added)

8. In this case, there was no confidential version of Brazil's written submission and, therefore, Brazil was not required to provide a non-confidential summary of the information contained in its first submission.

9. We recall that the purpose of Article 18.2 is to safeguard the protection of confidential information. If no confidential information is included in the first submission there is nothing to be safeguarded and the submission may be disclosed to the public without restrictions.

10. As a final comment, we note that Argentina has failed to demonstrate how the disclosure of any information contained in Brazil's first submission "impairs" Argentina's rights under the DSU.

II. ANTI-DUMPING STANDARD OF REVIEW

11. Regarding the anti-dumping standard of review, Argentina alleges that Brazil has put forward a generic argument without identifying the instances in Argentina's investigation in which it considers that Argentina did not act in good faith.[2] According to Argentina, "accusations of a generic nature are out of place in a WTO proceeding in which, ultimately, the law must be applied to the identified facts of the case".[3]

12. The Panel should note that Argentina's allegation is not correct. In its first submission, Brazil has developed arguments that properly identify the various aspects in the Argentinean investigation that were conducted contrary to the Anti-Dumping Agreement. Specifically, in paragraphs 3 and 4 of the first submission,

---

[1] Argentina's letter to the Panel, n° 220/02, dated 15 August 2002.
[2] Argentina's first submission, para. 11.
[3] *Ibid.*

Brazil has provided a summary of the 41 claims, identifying the specific actions taken by the Argentinean authorities in the investigation. In paragraphs 11 through 544, Brazil has also provided the specific claims, facts and legal arguments relative to each of the 41 claims. The identification of these claims, the related facts and legal arguments are *not* general in nature and are *not* without relevance in this WTO proceeding.

13. In addition, Argentina alleges that Brazil has not substantiated the arguments in any of the paragraphs under the heading "Anti-Dumping Agreement Standard of Review", and has merely set forth allegations which it fails to develop.[4]

14. Brazil has indicated that the violation of each claim is demonstrated in detail throughout the first submission.[5] Accordingly, we have substantiated all our claims of violation and understand that the Panel will carefully examine them in order to assess whether the Argentinean investigating authorities properly established the facts and whether the evaluation of those facts was unbiased and objective.

15. Contrary to what Argentina has provided, Brazil has *never* affirmed, nor implied, that the language in Article 17.6(i) of the Agreement is addressed to the parties, rather than to the Panel.[6] Consequently, we have also *never* claimed in this dispute that Argentina has violated Article 17.6(i) of the Agreement.

III. RULING BY THE MERCOSUL AD HOC ARBITRAL TRIBUNAL

16. In Section II.2 of Argentina's first submission, Argentina claims that Brazil has not acted in good faith by omitting reference to the ruling by the Mercosul Tribunal on the same dispute before the Common Market of the South ("Mercosul").[7] Argentina further provides that this case has already been "discussed and settled" within Mercosul's framework, and that by omitting such reference Brazil has incurred in an abusive exercise of its rights under the WTO covered Agreements.[8]

17. Furthermore, Argentina seems to conclude, that with the purpose of clarifying the scope of the obligations at issue, the Panel should take into account in the instant case Mercosul's legal framework and the consequences of the application of the Brasília Protocol.[9] Alternatively, Argentina concludes that the principle of *estoppel* should be applied to this dispute, since, according to Argentina, there has been a "consistent and unequivocal" behavior on behalf of Brazil that has created a conviction in Argentina with respect to matters involving trade dispute settlement between both Members within Mercosul's framework and with respect to the scope of rulings by a Tribunal.[10]

18. Even though Argentina has stated that it has *not* argued the application of *res judicata*[11], from the arguments presented in its first submission (case has already been "discussed and settled"), it appears, in fact, that Argentina is suggesting that the ruling by the Mercosul Tribunal has the effect of *res judicata*. In the event that

---

[4] Argentina's first submission, para. 12.
[5] Brazil's first submission, para. 6.
[6] Argentina's oral statement, para. 3.
[7] Argentina's first submission, para. 16.
[8] *Ibid.*, para. 17.
[9] *Ibid.*, para. 22.
[10] *Ibid.*
[11] Argentina's oral statement, para. 7.

Argentina *is* alleging the application of *res judicata,* we would like the Panel to take into account the following considerations.

19. *Res judicata* is a "rule that a final judgment rendered by a court of competent jurisdiction on the merits is conclusive as to the rights of the parties and their privies, and, as to them, constitutes an absolute bar to a subsequent action involving the same claim, demand or cause of action".[12] Thus, in order for a ruling or a decision to have the effect of *res judicata* the claims brought in a new action have to be *the same* as those in the previous action, where a final judgement has been rendered.

20. Regarding the applicability of *res judicata* in WTO dispute settlement, we refer to the Panel's reasoning in *India-Autos*. In that case, the Panel found it appropriate to first consider whether the factual circumstances for the application of *res judicata* could be met in the circumstances of that case before ruling on its applicability as a doctrine.[13] In conducting this analysis, that Panel identified a benchmark by which disputes might be seen as distinct or similar for the purposes of rejecting or applying *res judicata.*[14] The Panel established that benchmark as follows:

> "*In the context of WTO dispute settlement, the notion of "matter", as referred to in Article 7.1 of the DSU, determines the scope of what is submitted, and what can be ruled upon, by a panel. As confirmed by the Appellate Body in the Guatemala - Cement case, the matter referred to the DSB consists of two elements: the specific measures at issue and the legal basis of the complaint (or the claims). This appears to the Panel to be the most appropriate minimal benchmark by which to assess whether the conditions of res judicata could conceivably be met, if such notion was of relevance.*
>
> *The Panel therefore considers that for res judicata to have any possible role in WTO dispute settlement, there should, at the very least, be in essence identity between the matter previously ruled on and that submitted to the subsequent panel. This requires identity between both the measures and the claims pertaining to them. There is also, for the purposes of res judicata, a requirement of identity of parties (...)* "[15] (emphasis added)

21. Brazil agrees with that benchmark and believes that in this instance the Panel should also apply this standard. To that regard, we re-state our position that although the parties and the measure currently before this Panel are identical to the parties and measure before the Mercosul Tribunal, the claims of the dispute before this Panel are *not* the same as the claims that were before the Mercosul Tribunal.

22. In order for the Panel to verify this, we find it appropriate to provide background information on the scope of application of the Mercosul dispute settlement system.

23. On 17 December 1991, the Member States of Mercosul approved the Brasília Protocol, establishing Mercosul's dispute settlement mechanism. The Protocol set

---

[12] Black's Law Dictionary, Sixth Edition by the Publisher's Editorial Staff, St. Paul, Minn., West Publishing Co. 1990, at page 1305.
[13] India - Measures Affecting the Automotive Sector, 21 December 2001, WT/DS146/R and WT/DS175/R, at para. 7.60 (adopted on 05 April 2002) ("*India - Autos*"). The Panel's findings related to the principle of *res judicata* were not appealed.
[14] *India - Autos*, at para. 7.61.
[15] *Ibid.*, at paras. 7.65 and 7.66.

forth the scope of the dispute mechanism by providing that "disputes between Mercosul Member States regarding the interpretation, application or non-compliance with provisions of the Treaty of Asunción and the agreements and decisions integrated in its framework must be submitted to the dispute settlement procedure established in the Protocol".[16] According to the Protocol, the scope of application of the dispute settlement mechanism relates to the interpretation, application or non-compliance with provisions of the Treaty of Asunción and the agreements and decisions integrated in its framework.[17]

24. It is important to note that the claims raised in Brazil's request for the establishment of a WTO panel are not related to the interpretation, application or non-compliance with the provisions of the Treaty of Asunción and all other agreements and decisions that make up Mercosul's legal framework. The object of Brazil's challenge in the WTO relates to Argentina's non-compliance of its obligations in the WTO, and in particular to the Anti-Dumping Agreement and GATT 1994.[18]

25. The Mercosul Tribunal dealt with the dispute based on the scope of application set forth in the Protocol, that is, whether provisions that make up Mercosul's framework were correctly interpreted, applied or complied with in the anti-dumping investigation conducted by Argentina on imports of poultry from Brazil. It was ***not*** before the Tribunal the examination and decision of whether Argentina complied with its WTO obligations in the conduct and imposition of anti-dumping measures on poultry from Brazil. Brazil believes that this Panel has the appropriate jurisdiction to examine such claims.

26. In that regard, Article 23 of the DSU mandates exclusive jurisdiction in favour of the DSU for WTO violations. Relevant part of Article 23 provides that:

"1. When Members seek the redress of a violation of obligations or other nullification or impairment of benefits under the covered agreements or impediment to the attainment of any objective of the covered agreements, they shall have recourse to, and abide by, the rules and procedures of this Understanding.

2. In such cases, Members shall:

(a) not make a determination to the effect that a violation has occurred, that benefits have been nullified or impaired or that the attainment of any objective of the covered agreements has been impeded, except through the recourse to dispute settlement in accordance with rules and procedures of this Understanding, and shall make any such determination consistent with the findings contained in the panel or Appellate Body report adopted by the DSB or an arbitration award rendered under the Understanding.(...)"
(emphasis added).

27. Thus, the claims presented to the Panel on Argentina's violation of its WTO obligations entitles Brazil to trigger and use the WTO dispute settlement mechanism,

---

[16] *See*, Article 1 of the Brasília Protocol.
[17] *Ibid.*
[18] *See, Argentina - Definitive Anti-Dumping Duties on Poultry from Brazil: Request for the Establishment of a Panel by Brazil*, WT/DS241/3 (26 Feb. 2002).

excluding thereby the competence of any other mechanism to examine WTO law violation claims.

28. Argentina also makes the argument that the principle of *estoppel* should be applied to this dispute, since there is a conviction on the part of Argentina, based on previous rulings of the Mercosul Tribunal, that Brazil would relinquish its right to use WTO dispute settlement whenever a case is decided by a Mercosul Tribunal. To that regard, Brazil once again affirms that the dispute before the Mercosul Tribunal was grounded on **a different legal basis** from the dispute before this Panel.

29. Nevertheless, if the Panel considers the examination of this argument relevant, Brazil notes that it is to interpret the principle of *estoppel* and whether it is applicable in WTO dispute settlement.

30. *Estoppel* means that "a party is prevented by his own acts from claiming a right to detriment of other party who was entitled to rely on such conduct and has acted accordingly."[19] As noted by the European Communities ("EC") in its third part submission,[20] the Panel in *EC - Bananas I*, correctly concluded that "*estoppel* could only result from the express, or in exceptional cases implied, consent of such parties or of the CONTRACTING PARTIES".[21] That Panel further considered that:

> "(...) The decision of a contracting party not to invoke a right vis-à-vis another contracting party at a particular point in time can therefore, by itself, not reasonably be assumed to be a decision to release that other contracting party from its obligations under the General Agreement. The Panel noted in this context that previous panels had based their findings on measures which had remained unchallenged for long periods of time. The Panel therefore found that the mere fact that the complaining parties had not invoked their rights under the General Agreement in the past had not modified these rights and did not prevent them from invoking these rights now."[22] (emphasis added)

31. The same applies in the instant case. The simple fact that Brazil has brought a similar dispute to the Mercosul Tribunal does not represent that Brazil has consented not to bring the current dispute before the WTO. Specially when the dispute before this Panel is based on **a different legal basis** than the dispute brought before the Mercosul Tribunal.

32. We also call to the Panel's attention that the Mercosul Protocol of Olivos on Dispute Settlement, signed on 18 February 2002, cannot be raised here as an implicit or express consent by Brazil to refrain from bringing the present case to the WTO dispute settlement.

33. To that regard, we are aware that the Protocol of Olivos provides that "disputes within the scope of application of the Protocol, that may also be submitted to the WTO dispute settlement system, may be submitted to either one or the other forum, according to the choice made by the complainant".[23] The Protocol further

---

[19] Black's Law Dictionary, Sixth Edition by the Publisher's Editorial Staff, St. Paul, Minn., West Publishing Co. 1990, at page 551.
[20] EC's third party submission, at. Para. 16.
[21] EEC - Member States' Import Regimes for Bananas 3 June 1993, WT/DS32/R, at para. 361 (unadopted) (*EC - Bananas I*). The Panel's conclusion related to the principle of *estoppel* was not appealed.
[22] *EC - Bananas I*, at para. 362.
[23] *See,* Article 1.2 of the Protocol of Olivos.

states that "once a dispute settlement has been initiated, neither one of the parties may have recourse to other dispute settlement mechanisms in other forums with respect to the same *object* as defined in Article 14 of the Protocol".[24]

34. We note, and repeat, that the object before the Mercosul Tribunal is ***different*** from the object before this Panel. Furthermore, the Protocol of Olivos has not yet entered into force, and even if it had and the object of the dispute was the same, the Protocol of Olivos provides that "disputes underway initiated in accordance with the Protocol of Brasília will continue to be exclusively governed by that Protocol until the dispute has been concluded".[25] Furthermore, the Protocol also states that "while the disputes initiated under the regime of the Protocol of Brasília are not completely concluded and until the proceedings under Article 49 are completed, the Protocol of Brasília will continue to be applied".[26] Therefore, the Protocol of Olivos does not apply to disputes that have already been concluded under the Brasília Protocol.

35. Argentina also errs in its understanding that the existence of Mercosul's legal framework and adjudications of its dispute settlement mechanism must be taken into account by the Panel in fulfilling its responsibilities in accordance with the DSU.[27] Argentina states that this in accordance with Article 3.2 of the DSU, in respect to the clarification of the obligations of the Agreements in accordance with customary rules of interpretation of public international law.[28]

36. We recall that Article 3.2 deals exclusively with the clarification of the existing provisions of the WTO Agreement and does ***not*** provide that a previous ruling by an international tribunal constrains a WTO Panel's interpretation of a WTO Agreement.

37. What Article 3.2, in fact, provides is that:

> *"The dispute settlement system of the WTO is a central element in providing security and predictability to the multilateral trading system. It serves to preserve the rights and obligations of Members under the covered agreements, and to clarify the existing provisions of WTO Agreements in accordance with customary rules of interpretation of public international law."* (emphasis added)

38. Based on this provision, Brazil understands that the Panel must consider a claim brought by a Member with respect to a violation of a covered agreement in order to preserve that Member's rights under that agreement.

39. As a final comment on this issue, Brazil notes that contrary to Argentina's allegations, Brazil has not incurred in an abusive exercise of its rights under the WTO Agreements,[29] nor has its conduct been contrary to good faith by not mentioning in the first submission the ruling by the Mercosul Tribunal.[30] Brazil has not made reference to that ruling simply because it believes that it has no relevance to this case, since the claims currently before the Panel ***are not the same*** as the claims that were before the Mercosul Tribunal.

---

[24] *Ibid.*
[25] *See,* Article 50 of the Protocol of Olivos.
[26] *See,* Paragraph 2 of Article 55 of the Protocol of Olivos.
[27] Argentina's first submission, at para. 18.
[28] *Ibid.*
[29] Argentina's first submission, at para. 23.
[30] *Ibid.*, at para. 16.

Report of the Panel

IV. CLAIMS RELATED TO THE INITIATION OF THE ANTI-DUMPING INVESTIGATION

Article 5.3

Claim 4 - Export Price Below Normal Value

40. Argentina has affirmed that Brazil's statement that, for the purpose of establishing the export price, the selection of data was inappropriate and biased is untrue.[31] To prove that Brazil's statement is untrue, Argentina explained that "the implementing authority analyzed the import transactions in an attempt to determine which of them corresponded closest to the product under investigation, and it did so for the sole purpose of calculating the *most appropriate* and *comparable export price* possible at the pre-initiation stage".[32] Argentina further provided that "it worked out an average of the appropriate transactions, *without in fact making any selection which might distort the difference between the export value and the normal value*".[33]

41. Brazil cannot accept this response as an account of how the export price was established in the initiation stage of the investigation. We have demonstrated in the first submission that the DCD *did* make a selection of export transactions, namely those with prices below normal value, and this selection *did* distort the difference between the export price and the normal value.

42. Brazil will once again show this to the Panel. The Table in Page 10 of Exhibit BRA-2 provides the total export price information submitted by petitioner in the application. The average export price found from that information was **US$1,014/ton**. From that information provided in the application, the investigating authority considered that a significant portion of the product was being imported into Argentina at dumping condition, that is, at prices inferior to those sold in the domestic market of Brazil.[34] The DCD, then, considered only the prices of those export transactions that were below the normal value.

43. The Table in Page 11 of Exhibit BRA-2 shows the volume and value of the export transactions below normal value for the period January through May of 1997. Specifically, the DCD provided that the same selection was made for the month of August 1997 (exports transactions with prices below the normal value).[35] Next, the authority added the export transactions below normal value for August 1997 to the export transactions below normal value for the period January through June 1997.[36] This resulted in an amount of US$4,390,836.38 and a volume of 4,854.24 tons for the exports of poultry from Brazil with prices inferior to the normal value for the period January through August 1997.[37] This resulted in the average f.o.b. export price of **US$0.904536/kg** used to initiate the investigation, which appears on Page 12 of Exhibit BRA-2.

44. Obviously, this method adopted by the DCD distorted (and decreased) the export price and, consequently, distorted the dumping margin. Argentina has not only

---

[31] *Ibid.*, at para. 78.
[32] *Ibid.*
[33] *Ibid.*
[34] *See,* Page 10 of Exhibit BRA-2.
[35] *See,* First paragraph of Page 11 of Exhibit BRA-2.
[36] *Ibid.*
[37] *Ibid.*

failed to examine the accuracy and adequacy of *all* the evidence that was presented in the application but has also inflated the dumping margin.

V. CLAIMS RELATED TO THE CONDUCT OF THE ANTI-DUMPING INVESTIGATION - EVIDENTIARY AND PUBLIC NOTICE REQUIREMENTS

Articles 12.1, 6.1.1, 6.8, 6.9 and Annex II

Claim 10 - Failure to Notify Seven Brazilian Exporters

45.   Regarding the claim of violation of Article 12.1 of the Agreement, Brazil has provided documentation that supports the fact that the investigating authorities had recognized and identified the Brazilian exporters Comaves, Minuano, Chapecó, Catarinense and Perdigão prior to the initiation of the investigation.[38]

46.   The authorities first became aware of the existence of these producers/exporters on 17 February 1998, when petitioner submitted additional information that included lists of imports of poultry from Brazil broken down by producer and exporter.[39] The name of these Brazilian exporters appeared in all lists submitted by petitioner. In fact, the information on these lists came from two Argentinean agencies: *SENASA - Dirección Nacional de Fiscalización Agroalimentaria* ("*SENASA*") and the *Secretaria de Agricultura, Ganaderia, Pesca y Alimentacion Dirección de Ganaderia* ("*Ganaderia*"). How, then, can Argentina allege that these exporters were unknown to them at the time of initiation, when the identification of these Brazilian producers/exporters actually came from two Argentinean agencies?

47.   On 7 January 19998, at a second moment but still prior to initiation, the DCD issued the report regarding the viability of the initiation of the dumping investigation, identifying once again these same exporters.[40] This time, the identification of these exporters was made by the authorities *themselves*.

48.   Brazil has also demonstrated that these five exporters were notified of the investigation and the need to provide responses to the dumping questionnaire only on 15 September 1999,[41] almost eight months after initiation and after a preliminary injury, dumping and causal link determination had been issued.[42]

49.   The timing of this notification to these exporters proves that the authorities did not comply with the requirement in Article 12.1 of the Agreement.

50.   It is interesting that Argentina tries to share the obligation under Article 12.1 with Brazil, when it states that it requested Brazil's cooperation in identifying the producers/exporters.[43] Even though Argentina states this, Argentina never requested Brazil's cooperation in providing the address or contact information of these specific exporters, which it had already identified.

---

[38] *See,* Annexes 1 and 2 of Exhibit BRA-4 and Pages 4 and 5 of Exhibit BRA-2.
[39] *See,* Exhibit BRA-4.
[40] *See,* Pages 4 and 5 of Exhibit BRA-2.
[41] *See,* Exhibit BRA-13.
[42] *See,* Exhibits BRA-10, BRA-11 and BRA-12.
[43] Argentina's first submission, paras. 112 - 116.

Report of the Panel

51. It is also curious how Argentina implicitly tries to equate the obligation of notification with the obligation of publication. In particular, Argentina states that "the initiation of an investigation is a general administrative procedure and published as such in the Official Journal, which constitutes sufficient *notification* of a general scope".[44]

52. We cannot agree with such statement, specially in light of the express distinction of obligations set forth in Article 12.1. Relevant part of that Article provides:

> "When the authorities are satisfied that there is sufficient evidence to justify the initiation of an anti-dumping investigation pursuant to Article 5, the Member or Members the products of which are subject to such investigation and other interested parties known to the investigating authorities to have an interest therein shall be notified *and* a public notice shall be given" (emphasis added)

53. It is clear that Article 12.1 requires that *in addition* to a public notice, a *notification* be given when the authorities are satisfied that there is sufficient evidence to justify the initiation of an investigation. Thus, the requirement of notification is not fulfilled simply by the issuance of the public notice.

Claim 11 - Failure to Give 30-Day Deadline to Respond to Questionnaire

54. In its first submission, Argentina categorically states that it granted the seven Brazilian exporters a *period of more than 30 days* to reply to the DCD's questionnaire and also dully acceded to their requests for extension.[45]

55. Brazil reaffirms that this is simply *not* true. The DCD's notification of the investigation and the need to provide responses to the questionnaires sent to the Brazilian exporters CCLP, Catarinense, Chapecó, Minuano, Perdigão, Comaves and PenaBranca *expressly* indicated that these exporters had *no more than 20* days to respond to the questionnaire.[46] It is evident that the timeframe required by the DCD in these letters was on its face contrary to the 30-day period required under Article 6.1.1 to respond to questionnaires.

56. The requirement in Article 6.1.1 is of such importance that it is the only provision under Article 6 that establishes a specific timeframe for the accomplishment of an obligation. It is simple, if authorities do not provide at least 30 days for exporters or foreign producers to respond to the questionnaires, authorities are in violation of Article 6.1.1 of the Agreement.

57. Under Article 6.1.1, it is *not* permissible for authorities to simply provide a lesser period for response from the outset, just as long as the total period allowed for response (including extension) is at least 30 days. That interpretation would render meaningless the obligation in Article 6.1.1 of the Agreement:

> "Exporters and foreign producers receiving the questionnaires used in an anti-dumping investigation shall be given at least 30 days for reply. Due consideration should be given to any request for an extension of

---

[44] *Ibid.*, at para. 167.
[45] *Ibid.*, at para. 126.
[46] *See,* Exhibit BRA-13.

the 30-day period, and upon cause shown, such an extension should be granted whenever practicable." (emphasis added)

58.   Article 6.1.1 is divided into two sentences. The first sentence specifically relates to the original deadline that authorities must give for exporters/producers to respond to the questionnaire. The second sentence relates to extensions that authorities may give to such responses. The first sentence is an ***obligation*** imposed on the authorities and must be read separately from the second sentence, which is ***not an obligation***. If authorities could simply give any period of time, inferior to 30 days, for exporters/producers to respond to the questionnaire and afterwards provide extensions for a period that, in total, would make up the 30 days, there would be no need for the second sentence in Article 6.1.1. We do not believe that to be the intention in Article 6.1.1 of the Agreement.

59.   Furthermore, when exporters and producers receive a questionnaire they rely on that 30-day period to plan and allocate the necessary resources in order to respond. The great volume of information required in a questionnaire demands time and available personnel to collect and report such information. If from the outset these exporters/producers receive a questionnaire with a deadline for response inferior to 30 days, they will either not even try to respond to the questionnaire or provide incomplete/insufficient responses. In a way, the opportunity to defend their interests is impaired.

60.   This is even more so, if the Panel considers that in this case these seven Brazilian exporters were notified of the investigation almost eight months after initiation and after a preliminary injury, dumping and causal link determination had been issued. These exporters had already had their right of defense impaired. In addition, they were faced with having to respond the dumping questionnaire in ***only*** 20 days.

61.   As a final remark, the Panel should also note that Article 6.1.1 refers to responses to the questionnaires. In this case, ***none*** of the seven exporters received the injury questionnaire and, thus, were not even afforded the opportunity to respond.

Claim 15 - Disregard of Exporters' Product Description

62.   Brazil has demonstrated in Exhibits BRA-22, BRA-23, BRA-24 and BRA-26 that Sadia, Avipal and Frangosul reported in their questionnaire responses that there were no physical characteristic differences between poultry sold to Argentina and in Brazil. Even so, the investigating authority disregarded that information and used the normal value adjustment proposed by petitioner in the application.

63.   Brazil has also demonstrated in Exhibit BRA-25 that Catarinense sold both griler (without giblets) and broiler (with giblets) type poultry to Argentina and in Brazil. However, the investigating authority chose to apply the normal value adjustment to all of the poultry sales in Brazil even though some of these sales did not warrant an adjustment because they were sales of griler type poultry, that is, poultry sold without head and feet.

64.   In the first submission, Argentina seems to justify not using the product description information reported by the Brazilian exporters in their questionnaire

Report of the Panel

responses simply on the basis of lack of supporting documentation.[47] We understand that in this case the DCD was not entitled to resort to facts available.

65. Under Article 6.8, an investigating authority is only authorized to resort to facts available where a party refuses access to, or otherwise does not provide, **necessary information**, or where a party significantly impedes the investigation. In the evidence-producing stage of an investigation, it is a basic obligation of the investigating authority to indicate the information that is required for the investigation. In that respect, Article 6.1 of the Agreement sets forth that:

> "All interested parties in an anti-dumping investigation shall be given notice of the information which the authorities require and ample opportunity to present in writing all evidence which they consider relevant in respect of the investigation in question." (emphasis added)

66. Article 6.1 requires that authorities give notice of the information that is required. So, if an investigating authority does not clearly specify what information is required, the investigating authority cannot punish the interested party (use of facts available) for not submitting such information.

67. Furthermore, Paragraph 1 of Annex II of the Agreement reaffirms the obligation under Article 6.1, by stating that:

> "As soon as possible after the initiation of the investigation, the investigating authorities should specify in detail the information required from any interested party, and the manner in which that information should be structured by the interested party in its response. The authorities should also ensure that the party is aware that if information is not supplied within a reasonable time, the authorities will be free to make determinations on the basis of the facts available, including those contained in the application for the initiation of the investigation by the domestic industry" (emphasis added)

68. Paragraph 1 of Annex II requires investigating authorities to specify **in detail** the required information. If that information is not provided within a reasonable period, the investigating authorities must inform the interested party that a determination may be made on the basis of facts available. Accordingly, investigating authorities **are not** entitled to resort to facts available if the interested party did not provide certain information because the investigating authority failed to specifically indicate that it was required.

69. We find further support in Article 6.6 of the Agreement to our understanding that the DCD was not entitled to resort to facts available in view of the lack of supporting documentation. Article 6.6 states the following:

> "Except in circumstances provided for in paragraph 8, the authorities shall during the course of the investigation satisfy themselves as to the accuracy of the information supplied by the interested parties upon which their findings are based." (emphasis added)

70. From the language in Article 6.6, unless the authorities specifically indicate, exporters are not required to submit supporting documentation for all information submitted, in order to demonstrate the accuracy of such information.

---

[47] Argentina's first submission, at paras. 176 - 185.

71. That was also the conclusion of the Panel in *Argentina - Ceramic Tiles*:

> "(...) we conclude that an investigating authority may not disregard information and resort to facts available under Article 6.8 on the grounds that a party has failed to provide sufficient supporting documentation in respect of information provided **unless** the investigating authority has clearly requested that the party provide such supporting documentation."[48] (emphasis added)

72. To that regard, after Sadia, Avipal, Frangosul and Catarinense provided their product description responses to the dumping questionnaire, the investigating authority did not, at any moment during the course of the investigation, request specific information/clarification or supporting documentation on the product description submitted by these exporters.

73. In fact, not even the dumping questionnaire specifically required that the exporters submit supporting documentation for the product description.[49] In the section "Instructions for Completing the Producer/Exporter Questionnaire", under "Objective & Scope", the questionnaire provides that the producer/exporter shall respond to the questionnaire as precisely as possible, attaching supporting documentation for its responses, or in case this is not possible, indicating the source of information.[50] Likewise, the "General Instructions for Completing the Questionnaire" section provides that the producer/exporter is required to mention on each of the pages it presents, the case number, detailed response to each question, information on the sources used, and attachment of corresponding documentation, as a necessary condition to uphold the veracity of the source.[51]

74. From the general instructions in the questionnaire regarding the need for supporting documentation, we do not believe that the authority provided sufficient information on the precise supporting documentation that was expected from the exporters.

75. We cannot reasonably assume that the questionnaire requested supporting documentation for **all** the information provided by exporters in their responses. At a minimum, this would impose an unreasonable burden on the exporters in responding to the questionnaire. Not to mention the fact that it would be ***impossible*** for exporters to comply with the 30-day deadline to respond to questionnaires, as provided in Article 6.1.1 of the Agreement.

76. The fact that the DCD never requested clarifications or supporting documentation for the information reported by the exporters indicated that the information that had been submitted would be accepted. In that sense, Paragraph 6 of Annex II provides that:

> "*If evidence or information is not accepted, the supplying party should be informed forthwith of the reasons therefor, and should have an opportunity to provide further explanations within a reasonable period, due account being taken of the time-limits of the investigation.*

---

[48] Argentina- Definitive Anti-Dumping Measures on Imports of Ceramic Floor Tiles from Italy, 28 September 2001, WT/DS189/R, DSR 2001:XII, 6241, at para. 6.58 (adopted on 5 November 2001) ("*Argentina - Ceramic Floor Tiles*")
[49] *See,* Pages 19 and 21 of Exhibit BRA-22.
[50] *See,* Page 19 of Exhibit BRA-22.
[51] *See,* Page 21 of Exhibit BRA-22.

If the explanations are considered by the authorities as not being satisfactory, the reasons for the rejection of such evidence or information should be given in any published determinations."
(emphasis added)

77. As previously stated, the investigating authority ***never*** informed the exporters that the product description information reported by them was insufficient or unacceptable. By doing so, the authority acted inconsistently with Paragraph 6 of Annex II of the Agreement.

78. Furthermore, Argentina confirms that the adjustment was based on the method of calculation provided by petitioner in the application and that the validity of such method was confirmed by the absence of any objection by exporters.[52] To that regard, the following considerations should be taken into account.

79. First, by submitting the precise product description information, exporters were already indicating that the need for the adjustment proposed by petitioner was not warranted. In addition, the Brazilian Embassy in Buenos Aires sent a letter prior to the final determination with its considerations regarding the adjustment proposed by petitioner and that would be used by the authorities in the final determination.[53] In that letter, the Brazilian Embassy provided that the investigating authority, in making a fair comparison, should observe for ***each exporter*** the characteristics of the product sold to Argentina and in Brazil.[54] The Brazilian Embassy further stated that the 9.09 per cent adjustment corresponding to head and feet was absurd, since there were exporters that sold in the internal market ***the same*** poultry that was sold to Argentina.[55] Other considerations regarding the methodology used in the adjustment calculation were also put forth by the Embassy, but were not taken into account by the authority in the final determination.[56]

80. Second, petitioner did not submit, for purposes of initiation and during the investigation, any supporting documentation that there existed physical characteristic differences between the poultry sold to Argentina and in Brazil, that such alleged differences affect price comparability, and that the yield rate difference presented was correct. Furthermore, the adjustment information used by petitioner in the application was based on JOX information for chilled poultry, with head and feet, a product different from the product under investigation, frozen poultry without head and feet. Even so, the investigating authority considered JOX information as acceptable evidence that an adjustment was warranted.[57]

81. By considering petitioner's information rather than exporters, the investigating authority failed to use "special circumspection" in their normal value finding and, thus, also violated Paragraph 7 of Annex II of the Agreement.

Claim 17 - Disregard of Exporters' Export Price Information

82. With respect to the claim that Argentina disregarded the export price data provided by the Brazilian exporters and resorted, instead, to the export price

---

[52] Argentina's first submission, at para. 179.
[53] *See,* Exhibit BRA-39.
[54] *See,* Page 5 of Exhibit BRA-39.
[55] *Ibid.*
[56] *See,* Page 6 of Exhibit BRA-39.
[57] *See,* Argentina's first submission, at para. 50.

information provided by the Argentinean agency the *Ganaderia,* we have shown that Sadia, Avipal, Frangosul and Catarinense submitted such information during the investigation.

83.   On 23 April 1999, Sadia provided export price information of poultry sold to Argentina for the period 1996 through February 1999.[58] On 7 May 1999, Avipal provided export price information of poultry sold to Argentina for the period 1996 through March 1999.[59]

84.   On 27 April 1999, Frangosul provided export price information for individual export transactions of poultry sold to Argentina from January 1996 through March 1999, with supporting documentation.[60] Even though Frangosul presented export price data for each sale transaction to Argentina for the period 1996 through March 1999, with corresponding supporting documentation, the investigating authority did not accept that information alleging that these invoices had not been translated.[61] We have provided in Exhibit BRA-26 that Frangosul submitted a few translated invoices of sales to Argentina as sample of all invoices submitted. Furthermore, most of the information in the invoices to Argentina were already in Spanish.

85.   On 3 November 1999, Catarinense provided export price information for individual transactions of poultry sold to Argentina from January 1998 through January 1999, with supporting documentation.[62] The DCD never requested translation of the supporting documentation provided for the export price data. In addition, most of the information in the invoices to Argentina was already in Spanish.

86.   Here, not only did the authority require information in excess of the dumping period of data collection (January 1998 through January 1999), but the authority also decided that the specific information with supporting documentation submitted by exporters was not as complete and detailed as the information from the Argentina agency the *Ganaderia.*[63] We fail to see how the authority could have reached such conclusion. We also fail to see the grounds for the authority to have used best information available as provided under Article 6.8 of the Agreement.

Claim 21 - Failure to Inform the Essential Facts Under Consideration

87.   Brazil has provide in Exhibit BRA-28 the report prior to the end of the evidence-producing stage of the dumping investigation ("*Relevamiento de lo Actuado com Anterioridad al Cierre de la Etapa Probatoria*"). In particular, Brazil has provide that this report did not indicate that:

(1)   The normal value information in the list of invoices provided by Sadia, covering the period January 1996 through February 1999, would not be used in establishing Sadia's normal value;

(2)   That the only information considered to establish normal value for Sadia in the final determination would correspond to the information

---

[58] *See,* Exhibit BRA-22 and Pages 18 and 43 of Exhibit BRA-15.
[59] *See,* Exhibit BRA-23 and Pages 22 and 45 of Exhibit BRA-15.
[60] *See,* Exhibit BRA-24 and Pages 29 and 49 of Exhibit BRA-15.
[61] *See,* Page 75 of Exhibit BRA-15.
[62] *See,* Exhibit BRA-25 and Pages 38 and 39 of Exhibit BRA-15.
[63] *See,* Page 75 of Exhibit BRA-15.

Report of the Panel

(3) The reason why the DCD would not consider the information provided by Sadia for all reported sales in the home market;

(4) That the only information that would be considered to establish normal value for Avipal would be the information for the transactions for which supporting documentation was submitted;

(5) The reason why the DCD would not consider the information provided by Avipal for all reported sales in the home market;

(6) That none of the normal value information submitted by Frangosul and Catarinense would be considered in establishing the normal value and an individual margin of dumping for these two exporters;

(7) The reason why the DCD would not consider the normal value information provided by Frangosul and Catarinense;

(8) Why the information submitted by all Brazilian exporters would not be considered for purposes of determining the f.o.b. export price; and,

(9) Why the product description provided by exporters in the investigation would not considered in evaluating whether the normal value adjustment to account for differences in physical characteristics was warranted.

88. Brazil reaffirms its position that exporters cannot be aware simply by reviewing the record of the investigation that evidence submitted by petitioner and derived from secondary sources, rather than facts submitted by the exporters, would be used as the primary basis for the determination of the existence and the extent of dumping. By not explaining the reasons why such information was rejected, the investigating authority denied the exporters the opportunity to defend their interests within the meaning of Article 6.9 of the Agreement.

89. As stated in the first submission, in the event Argentina provides information or documents not disclosed to exporters during the investigation as means of justification of its actions during the investigation, Brazil submits that such non-disclosure of essential facts should also be considered a violation of Article 6.9 of the Agreement.[64]

VI. CLAIMS RELATED TO THE CONDUCT OF THE ANTI-DUMPING INVESTIGATION AND FINAL AFFIRMATIVE DETERMINATION

Articles 2.4, 3.1, 3.4, 3.5 and 12.2.2

Claim 26 - Unreasonable Burden on Exporters

90. The DCD has imposed an unreasonable burden on the Brazilian exporters Sadia, Avipal and Frangosul by allowing exporters to submit normal value and export price information for the years 1996 through 1999, when the dumping period of investigation was later defined as January 1998 through January 1999. The investigating authority also imposed an excessive burden on Brazilian exporters by requiring that they provide an invoice copy for all of the sales transactions in the

---

[64] Brazil's first submission, at para. 350.

home market in order to consider all reported sales in the establishment of the normal value and, consequently, make a "fair comparison".

91.   Argentina admits that it did not define the dumping period of data collection on purpose.[65] As justification, Argentina states that the Agreement does not define the period for collecting information or for the investigation itself, having the authority *discretion to request documentation it deems necessary in order to determine dumping*, and may require *further information when this is necessary to guarantee due process to the interested parties.*[66]

92.   Brazil fails to see how normal value and export price information for January 1996 through December 1997 was necessary to determine dumping for the period January 1998 through January 1999. Likewise, Brazil fails to see how the normal value and export price information for January 1996 through December 1997 was necessary to guarantee due process of any interested party in the investigation.

93.   Argentina tries to make the argument that Brazil's claim is contradictory because at times it alleges that the investigating authority did not request more information.[67] Argentina further states that 'whenever the implementing authority has sought further information for a particular purpose, Brazil complains that the information requested represents an 'unreasonable burden on exporters' ".[68]

94.   There is an obvious difference between the relevant type of information that the investigating authority must require in an investigation and information that is not relevant to the investigation.

95.   For example, product description is the type of information that was relevant in this investigation. The authorities were required under Article 2.4 of the Agreement to make adjustments in the fair comparison between the export price and the normal value. If authorities were unsure whether such adjustments should have been made, since there were exporters that reported no differences between the product sold in Brazil and to Argentina, the investigating authority was required to request more information. But they did not. The application of the head/feet adjustment had a direct impact on the normal value and on the final dumping margin. This was the type of information that was relevant in this investigation and which the authority was required to request.

96.   However, information on normal value and export price for a period outside of the period of investigation, which therefore was not even used in establishing the margin of dumping, was *not* the type of information that was relevant to the investigation. Thus, requiring the submission of this information, with supporting documentation, was an unreasonable burden on exporters.

97.   Regarding this claim, the EC argues that Article 2.4 of the Agreement does not address the issue raised by Brazil.[69] In doing so, the EC recalls the Panel report in *Egypt - Steel Rebar*, that provides that Article 2.4 is concerned exclusively with the comparison between normal value and the export price and that, therefore, it does not apply to the determination of normal value and export price.[70]

---

[65]   Argentina's first submission, at para. 243.
[66]   *Ibid.*
[67]   Argentina's first submission, at para. 244.
[68]   *Ibid.*
[69]   EC third party submission, at para. 27.
[70]   *Ibid.*

Report of the Panel

98. Brazil considers that the interpretation of the term "unreasonable burden" in Article 2.4 made in that report is incorrect in so far as that Panel found that the burden requirement applies only to comparison of export price and normal value, through various adjustments as appropriate, and not to the establishment of normal value.

99. Brazil understands Article 2.4 to provide for how a fair comparison is to be made between the export price and the normal value. More specifically, the last sentence of Article 2.4 states that "the authorities shall indicate to the parties in question what information is necessary to ensure a fair comparison and shall not impose an unreasonable burden of proof on those parties." That being so, normal value information *is* included in the information necessary to ensure a fair comparison. If authorities do not indicate exactly what information is needed to establish normal value how can a fair comparison be made?

100. In this particular case, normal value and export price information for the period January 1996 through December 1997 was *not* information that was necessary for a fair comparison to be made. Thus, by requesting that information the investigating authority imposed an unreasonable burden on exporters.

Claim 32 - Failure to Use the Same Period to Evaluate Article 3.4 Factors

101. Brazil has presented as Exhibit BRA-14 the final affirmative injury determination by the CNCE. In that determination, the CNCE stated that the period of injury under analysis corresponded to the period from January 1996 through December 1998.[71] However, only for some variables, such as national production, prices, imports, exports, and apparent consumption, did the CNCE include data in its analysis corresponding to the first semester of 1999.[72]

102. The fact that some of the factors under Article 3.4 were evaluated for a certain period while other factors were evaluated for a different period, indicates that different parameters of evaluation were used. This demonstrates that the examination of the impact of the dumped imports on domestic producers was not objective and was, thus, inconsistent with the requirement in Article 3.1 of the Agreement.

103. Argentina has argued that in threat of injury cases, such as this one, "international rules and relevant practice" provide that it is possible to undertake an analysis *beyond the period of investigation* in order to find out whether or not there is a growing trend in imports and, thus, give the investigation a more substantial factual basis.[73]

104. This is not the issue presented before the Panel. Brazil is not challenging whether in a threat of injury case the investigating authority may or may not analyze data for a period beyond the period of investigation. What we are challenging is that in this investigation the CNCE considered a certain period of injury analysis for some factors and considered another period of injury analysis for other factors. Had the CNCE decided to analyze data for *all* factors under Article 3.4 for a period *beyond* the period of investigation, the examination of the impact of the dumped imports on

---

[71] *See,* Page 9 of Exhibit BRA-14.
[72] *Ibid.*
[73] Argentina's first submission, at para. 252.

domestic producers would have been, at least, objective within the meaning of Article 3.1 of the Agreement. That was not the case.

105. The injury analysis considered the data for the factors production, prices, imports, exports and apparent consumption for the period 1996 through June of 1999. The Panel can verify this by looking at the following pages of the injury analysis in the final determination : **production** (Page 9 and Table 1 of Exhibit BRA-14); **prices of product in the domestic market** (Page 14 and Tables 15b - 16 of Exhibit BRA-14): **volume and value of imports** (Pages 15 - 16 and Tables 22 - 29 of Exhibit BRA-14); **exports** (Page 10 and Table 5 of Exhibit BRA-14); and, **apparent consumption** (Page 25 and Tables 30 and 31 of Exhibit BRA-14).

106. For all other factors under Article 3.4 of the Agreement, the CNCE considered data in its analysis for the period January 1996 through December 1998.

107. In its third party submission, the United States ("US") seems to disagree with Brazil's contention that an analysis of differing periods cannot be objective, and thus per se breaches Article 3.1 of the Agreement.[74]

108. To supports it view, the US cites the Panel report in *United States - Hot Rolled Steel Products*. In that investigation, Japan had alleged that the USITC focused on two years of the three-year period of investigation.[75] We understand that in that investigation the US collected information on *all relevant economic factors having a bearing on the state of the domestic industry over the entire three-year period of investigation*, and analyzed all those factors on the basis of data covering that period. Also in that case, Japan *acknowledged* that the USITC gathered data for the entire three-year period and that those data were mentioned in the USITC report in various tables and annexes.[76]

109. The case mentioned by the US bears no relation to the case at issue. We believe that the facts of that investigation and the facts and claim of violation presented here by Brazil are very different. First, there was no discussion in that investigation on the period of investigation. Apparently, data was collected and analyzed for the entire three-year period of investigation. In this instance, the investigating authority did *not* gather information on all factors over the same period, that is, from January 1996 through December 1998. As stated above, for the factors national production, prices, imports, exports, and apparent consumption the period of injury analysis was from January 1996 through June 1999. Second, in that investigation the USITC analyzed *all* the relevant economic factors for the entire three-year period of investigation. Here, the Argentinean investigating authority did *not* evaluate *all* the factors listed in Article 3.4 over the same injury analysis period.

110. It seems that the US argues that over one determined period of injury analysis, the investigating authority can compare data for certain years without *explicitly* discussing data for other years. However, all factors are analyzed under a certain, determined period of injury analysis. Here, unlike the case cited by the US, the Argentinean authorities decided that for certain factors the injury analysis period

---

[74] US third party submission, at para. 12.
[75] United States - Anti-Dumping Measures on Certain Hot-Rolled Steel Products from Japan, 28 February 2001, WT/DS184/R, at para. 7.226 ("*US - Hot Rolled Steel Products*"). This issue was not appealed. United States - Anti-Dumping Measures on Certain Hot-Rolled Steel Products from Japan, 24 July 2001, WT/DS184/AB/R, DSR 2001:X, 4697, at para. 240 (adopted on 23 August 2001) ("*AB - United States - Hot Rolled Steel Products*").
[76] *Ibid.*

would be from January 1996 through December 1998 and for other factors the injury analysis period would be from January 1996 through June 1999.

111. If an investigating authority establishes a certain period of injury analysis for some factors and another period of injury analysis for other factors, that authority has not made an objective examination of the impact of dumped imports on domestic producers within the meaning of Article 3.1 of the Agreement.

Claim 38 - Failure to Evaluate All Article 3.4 Factors

112. In examining the impact of the dumped imports on the state of the domestic industry, investigating authorities are obligated to evaluated **all** relevant economic factors and indices listed in Article 3.4 of the Agreement. In the final injury determination, the CNCE failed to evaluate the following relevant economic factors under Article 3.4: actual and potential decline in productivity; factors affecting domestic price; the magnitude of the dumping margin; and, the actual and potential negative effects on cash flow, growth and the ability to raise capital or investments.

113. Argentina alleges that applicants submitted information on the "productivity situation" in the sector during the course of the investigation.[77] Argentina claims that this information is reflected in the final injury determination in Pages 12, 13, 14, 20 and in the Technical Report in Pages 26, 28, 29, 30 and 95. We ask the Panel to verify this information. Brazil has found that these pages present an analysis of the following factors: production capacity; utilization of capacity; employment; wages; cost structure; and, sales in the internal market, but do not present any data information for the period under analysis or any evaluation for that period for the factor productivity.

114. For factors affecting the domestic price, Argentina also affirms that the CNCE has properly considered all the factors which, in addition to imports, might have had an impact on the price of the domestic product.[78] To support this statement, Argentina refers the Panel to Table 16 in the Technical Report.[79] Table 16 presents the average sales revenue by kilogram of fresh or chilled poultry. Brazil does not see the connection between the information contained in Table 16 and factors affecting the domestic price.

115. With respect to the magnitude of the dumping margin, Argentina proposes to make the evaluation that was intended in the final injury determination in its first submission.[80] Accordingly, Argentina fails to cite where in its final injury determination the authority evaluated the magnitude of the dumping margin. Once again, we state that the authority did not and could not have evaluated the magnitude of the dumping margin because the final dumping determination, with the dumping margin, was issued on 23 June 2000, that is, six months after the final injury determination was issued. Still, Argentina argues in the first submission that margins of 8 - 14 per cent are significant and were evaluated by the authority because of their potential impact on Argentine production.[81] First, no such evaluation was made in the final injury determination. Second, even if the CNCE had considered, which it did

---

[77] Argentina's first submission, at para. 275.
[78] Ibid., at para. 292.
[79] Ibid.
[80] Argentina's first submission, at para. 294.
[81] Ibid., at para. 295.

not, margins of 8 - 14 per cent in the final injury determination, these margins referred to the margins used to initiate the investigation[82] and did not account for the normal value or export price information presented during the investigation.

116. For the factor cash flow, Argentina states, for the first time, that the cash-flow analysis requirement was not relevant and could not be met due to particular characteristics of the Argentinean market.[83] Brazil notes that no explanation of the kind was offered in the final injury determination, where this factor is not even mentioned. For the factors growth and the ability to raise capital or investments, Argentina makes no indication in its first submission where, and if, these factors were evaluated in the injury analysis in the final determination.

Claim 40 - Failure to Provide Adequate Final Notice

117. The US seems to agree with Brazil that the Anti-Dumping Agreement requires an investigating authority to evaluate **all** of the factors listed in Article 3.4 of the Agreement.[84] However, the US has affirmed that the failure to refer to a particular factor in the published determination does not necessarily breach Article 12.2.2 of the Agreement.[85]

118. The US understands that Article 12.2 requires only that the authorities set forth "in sufficient detail the findings and conclusions reached on all issues of fact and law *considered material by the investigating authorities*".[86] The US argues that while all enumerated factors must be evaluated, not all factors are necessarily material in any particular case.[87]

119. Brazil has demonstrated that in the final injury determination Argentina has not even enumerated all of Article 3.4 factors, let alone evaluated them. Brazil understands that if the Panel finds that Argentina has failed to evaluate all the economic factors set forth in Article 3.4 of the Agreement (Claim 38), then the Panel need not address Brazil's claim with respect to the failure by Argentina to give adequate explanation of the evaluation of those factors in the final notice (Claim 40). We understand that a notice may adequately explain in the determination that was made, but if the determination was substantively inconsistent with the requirements under the Agreement, the adequacy of the notice is meaningless. Nevertheless, if the Panel does not find that Argentina has failed to evaluate all Article 3.4 factors, the Panel must address Brazil's claim with respect to the failure of adequate notice (Claim 40).

120. The US has also provided that it should, nonetheless, be discernible from the published determination that the authorities have evaluated all of the factors in Article 3.4.[88] To that regard, Brazil notes that the evaluation of **all** Article 3.4 injury factors is **mandatory** and, as such, this evaluation is an inherently material issue of fact and law. Even if a particular factor does not have a material effect in the injury determination, its evaluation **cannot** be considered immaterial by the authorities and

---

[82] *See,* Page 12 of Exhibit BRA-2.
[83] Argentina's first submission, at para. 299.
[84] US third party submission, at para. 14.
[85] *Ibid.*, at para. 15.
[86] *Ibid.*
[87] *Ibid.*
[88] US third party submission, at para. 16.

Report of the Panel

must be provided for in the final notice. Therefore, the final determination must necessarily indicate if and how all factors were evaluated in the underlying investigation and, at a minimum, explain why a particular factor was considered immaterial.

VII. CLAIMS RELATED TO THE IMPOSITION AND COLLECTION OF ANTI-DUMPING DUTIES AS A RESULT OF THE ANTI-DUMPING INVESTIGATION

Articles 9.2, 9.3 and 12.2.2

Claims 28 and 29 - Duty in Excess of the Dumping Margin

121. Regarding the claims of violation of Articles 9.2, 9.3 and 12.2.2 of the Agreement, relative to the specific anti-dumping duties to be collected as the absolute difference between the f.o.b. price invoiced in any one shipment and a designated "minimum export price", we have taken into consideration the arguments raised by Argentina[89] and by the EC and Canada, in their third party submissions,[90] in preparing the following analysis of the issue.

122. We begin by examining the language in Article 9 of the Agreement, which provides for how anti-dumping duties are to be imposed and collected. Specifically, relevant part of Article 9.2 of the Agreement establishes that:

> "When an anti-dumping duty is imposed in respect of any product, such anti-dumping duty shall be collected in the appropriate amounts in each case, on a non-discriminatory basis on imports of such product from all sources found to be dumped and causing injury,(...)" (emphasis added)

123. Article 9.3. of the Agreement further provides:

> "The amount of the anti-dumping duty shall not exceed the margin of dumping as established under Article 2." (emphasis added)

124. From the language of these two provisions, we understand the requirement under Article 9.2 (collection of anti-dumping duties in appropriate amounts) to be closely related to the requirement under Article 9.3 of the Agreement (duties shall not exceed the margin of dumping as established under Article 2). In other words, if the amount of an anti-dumping duty exceeds the margin as established under Article 2, than the anti-dumping duty will consequently be collected in inappropriate amounts. That being so, a violation of Article 9.2 is entirely dependent on a violation of Article 9.3 of the Agreement.

125. Thus, we turn to a closer examination of Article 9.3 of the Agreement.

126. Article 9.3 of the Agreement imposes a limit on the amount of the anti-dumping duty. That limit is the margin of dumping found in the investigation, as established under Article 2 of the Agreement. Article 2 of the Agreement provides for the determination of dumping. We find that, under Article 2, the ***only*** provision that defines how margins of dumping are to be established is paragraph 4.2 of that Article. Relevant portion of Article 2.4.2 provides that:

---

[89] Argentina's first submission, at paras. 305 - 321.
[90] EC's third party submission, at paras. 29 - 37; Canada's third party submission, at paras. 1 - 18.

> *"Subject to the provisions governing fair comparison in paragraph 4, the existence of margins of dumping during the investigation phase shall normally be established on the basis of a comparison of a weighted average normal value with a weighted average of all comparable export transactions or by a comparison of normal value and export prices on a transaction-to-transaction basis(...)"* (emphasis added)

127. In the instant case, the dumping margin as established under Article 2 of the Agreement was that established during the investigation phase. That is, the dumping margin based on the normal value and export price data submitted by the exporters during the investigation, for the period January 1998 through January 1999, and used by the authority in the final determination.[91] From the moment the anti-dumping duty is imposed until a review of the imposition of that duty is made, the only margin of dumping available, calculated pursuant to Article 2, is the margin assessed in the investigation, found in the final determination, and informed to all interested parties through a public notice, as provided in Article 12.2 of the Agreement. In that regard, Article 12.2.2 requires that the public notice of a conclusion of an investigation contain the following information:

> *"(...) (iii) the margins of dumping established and a full explanation of the reasons for the methodology used in the establishment and comparison of the export price and the normal value under Article 2;(...)"* (emphasis added)

128. The "minimum export price" determined in Resolution No. 574/2000 does not qualify as a dumping margin established under Article 2, since it does not reflect the normal value and export price as provided by the exporters and examined by the investigating authority in the investigation.

129. In that regard, Canada has stated in its third party submission that Article 2.4.2 of the Agreement does not appear immediately relevant to this case,[92] since in determining the "margin of dumping" for purposes of Article 9.3, Article 2 should be examined in its entirety.[93] In doing so, Canada argues that the ***margin of dumping*** is simply the difference between the export price and "the comparable prices ... in the exporting country", as set out in Article 2.1.[94]

130. We remind the Panel that Article 2.1 does not define, or even refer to, how a margin of dumping is to be established. Article 2.1 simply defines what dumping is. In fact, the only provision in the Agreement that specifically explains how the dumping margin is to be established is Article 2.4.2.

131. Both, Argentina and Canada, appear to have the same understanding that the margin of dumping found in the course of the original investigation does not limit the amount of anti-dumping duties that may be imposed when future imports take place.[95] Canada further provides that when such future imports are dumped at a

---

[91] *See*, Pages 102 - 104 of Exhibit BRA-15.
[92] Canada's third party submission, at para. 11.
[93] Canada's third party submission, at para. 10.
[94] *Ibid.*
[95] Argentina's oral statement, at para. 60; Canada's third party submission, at para. 17.

higher margin than that determined to exist at the time of the final determination, the importing Member may impose anti-dumping measures equal to that margin.[96]

132. In making this statement, Canada does not take into account the fact that this alleged "higher margin of dumping" caused by future imports, would only take into account the export prices of the subject merchandise without considering any possible changes in the prices in the internal market. It is not unlikely, that changes in market conditions or exporter's improvement in productivity create a situation where the price of the product, in the internal market and the export market, is reduced. Apparently, Canada does not consider the possibility that such a situation could occur, since in proposes that anti-dumping duties can change based only on future imports.

133. Furthermore, if we were to assume, based on Canada's argument, that the "margin of dumping" to be imposed and collected simply refers to the difference between the export price and the comparable price in the exporting country *for any given period*, what would be the purpose of the "margin of dumping" found in a final determination? Obviously, the dumping margin found in the final determination of an investigation is that which is established on the basis of the normal value and the export price provided during the investigation. In that sense, the dumping margin is that found in the period of investigation.

134. Contrary to Canada's position, we find that that Article 2.4.2 of the Agreement is *extremely* relevant in interpreting the language of Article 9.3 of the Agreement.

135. The same reasoning applies to the EC's arguments related to the interpretation of Article 9.3. In particular, the EC states that "(...) from the fact that Article 2.4.2 applies to the investigation phase, it does not follow that the application of all other provisions of Article 2 is also restricted to the investigation phase".[97]

136. We call the Panel's attention to the fact that Brazil has *never* affirmed, or implied, that all other provisions of Article 2 are restricted to the investigation phase. What we have argued is that the margin of dumping is established based on the information collected and examined during the investigation and, in that sense, dumping margins are restricted to the investigation period, as set out in Article 2.4.2 of the Agreement.

137. Regarding this issue, a clarification is in order. Article 2.4 establishes how a fair comparison between export price and normal value has to be made (same level of trade, sales made at as nearly as possible the same time, possibility of allowances, etc). This provision is valid in making a fair comparison under any proceeding, since Article 2.1 defines what dumping is for purposes of the Agreement, that is, in investigations and reviews. Likewise, the provisions under Article 2 regarding normal value and export price are also applicable to any proceeding (investigations and reviews). However, the methodology for the establishment of a dumping margin is provided under Article 2.4.2 and *is* limited to investigations.

138. The EC further provides that Brazil's interpretation is contradicted by the immediate context of Article 9.3.[98] In making its argument, the EC states that "Article 9.3.1 envisages the possibility to collect duties on a retrospective basis,

---

[96] Canada's third party submission, at para. 17.
[97] EC's third party submission, at para. 32.
[98] EC's third party submission, at para. 33.

which, by definition, presupposes the possibility to calculate the dumping margins on the basis of data for individual shipments or for time-periods outside the investigation period".[99] The EC also cites to Article 9.3.2 of the Agreement that provides that in cases "where duties are assessed prospectively, the authorities shall *refund* the duties 'paid in excess of the dumping margin'".[100] According to the EC, that "dumping margin" is *not* the margin established for the investigation period, but rather the margin established for individual shipments or time-periods *after* the imposition of the duties.[101] That also seems to be the understanding of Argentina in its first submission.[102]

139. We cannot agree with this understanding.

140. Article 9.3.1 provides for duties assessed on a retrospective basis. In such cases, a positive dumping margin, as a result of an investigation, not only allows the collection of duties but also serves as basis for the establishment of the deposit made by importers, until that duty is effectively collected. For purposes of collection, whenever requested, an administrative review is made to determine the margin of dumping corresponding to a new period. For example, during the first year that the dumping measure is in place, the importers deposit an amount equivalent to the dumping margin assessed in the investigation for each transaction made (liability). In the end of that year, if requested, an administrative review is initiated and will determine a normal value and export price corresponding to that year. The comparison between this new normal value and export price will result in a dumping margin that will serve as the basis for the duty to be effectively collected and for the new liability to be established for the following year.

141. Article 9.3.2 provides for the assessment of duties on a prospective basis. In such cases, the duty to be collected is established and may not exceed the margin of dumping found. This duty will be the basis for collection until a new margin of dumping (through a review) is determined. Since the duty is fixed, there is the possibility of collection in excess of the margin found for specific transactions. For that reason, Article 9.3 provides for refunds. A refund, however, only occurs if an *importer* requests it and does not imply modification of the duty. In order for the duty to be changed, a new margin of dumping would have to be determined, which would take into account data provided by the exporters (normal value and export price) for a different period than that considered in the investigation.

142. Thus, in the prospective system, when the duty is imposed the only margin of dumping available to be considered for the assessment of the duty to be collected is the margin of dumping determined in the investigation, as established under Article 2.

143. Regarding refunds for duties paid in excess of the margin of dumping, the Panel should note that such refunds do not imply that a Member has the discretion (or the right) to collect duties in any given amount. It is also important to note that the importer has the burden of requesting such a refund. The objective of the refund is to guarantee that the importer will not pay in excess of the margin found in the investigation in cases where the dumping margin related to an importer's specific

---

[99] *Ibid.*
[100] *Ibid.*
[101] *Ibid.*
[102] Argentina's first submission, at paras. 309 - 316.

transaction is inferior to the dumping margin found in the investigation. We note that the refund proceeding is not immediate since it requires a new calculation of the margin and the deadlines to make such calculations are equivalent to the deadlines in an investigation.

144. Specifically with respect to the "minimum export prices" imposed by Argentina, there is no limit in the amount of the duties to be collected and, thus, in essence, it is not in compliance with the Agreement. As stated previously, we cannot agree that the reference to the dumping margin in Article 9.3.2 of the Agreement does not relate to the dumping margin established for the investigation period.

145. Furthermore, Article 9.3.2 does not provide for how the dumping margin is established but rather for refund situations as explained above. We cannot presume that Article 9.3.2 allows for a permanent review of the anti-dumping duty, where only the export price is reviewed and the normal value remains unchanged (that is, the normal value found in the investigation). At a minimum, that new margin of dumping would not be in accordance with Article 2.4 of the Agreement, in that the comparison between the export price and the normal value would not be made in respect of sales made at as nearly as possible the same time. A comparison between a current export price for a specific transaction and an average normal value based on data for one year ago is not in conformity with Articles 2.1 and 2.4 (prices must be *comparable*).

146. If Article 9.3.2 was to be understood that way, that would also mean that the exporters, interested parties in the investigation that provided the export price and normal value data, would have absolutely *no* right of defense with respect to this "review" in Article 9.3.2, since it is up to the importer, and not the exporter, to request refunds under Article 9.3.2. We repeat, *Article 9.3.2 of the Agreement does not provide for a review of the margin of dumping found in the investigation*. If a review is warranted the Agreement provides for such a situation under Article 11. There, all interested parties participate, including the exporter, and are able to submit new export price and normal value information and to defend their interests.

147. Furthermore, when the EC affirms that Article 9.4 of the Agreement *expressly* contemplates for "the collection of variable duties equal to the difference between *the normal value established for the investigation period and the export prices of the shipments made after the imposition of the duties*",[103] we can under *no* circumstance agree with that position.

148. In examining the EC's argument, we turn to the relevant language in Article 9.4:

> "When the authorities have limited their examination in accordance with the second sentence of paragraph 10 of Article 6, any anti-dumping duty applied to imports from exporters or producers not included in the examination shall not exceed:
>
> > (i) the weighted average margin of dumping established with respect to the selected exporters or producer or,
> >
> > (ii) where the liability for payment of anti-dumping duties is calculated on the basis of a prospective normal value, the difference between the weighted average normal value of the

---

[103] EC's third party submission, at para. 35.

selected exporters or producers and the export prices of exporters or producers not individually examined , (...)" (emphasis added)

149. Article 9.4 of the Agreement identifies a ceiling which investigating authorities shall not exceed in establishing an "all others" rate. We understand that Article 9.4(i) refers to cases where the anti-dumping duty is assessed on a prospective basis (Article 9.3.2), and Article 9.4(ii) refers to cases where duties are assessed on a retrospective basis (Article 9.3.1). We know this to be true, since the language in Article 9.4(i) *expressly* refers to the "margin of dumping", that is, the "margin of dumping" found in the investigation.

150. This interpretation is supported by the Appellate Body's understanding in *United States - Hot Rolled Steel Products*:

> *"Before focusing on the qualifying language in Article 9.4 of the Anti-Dumping Agreement, we recall that the word "margins", which appears in Article 2.4.2 of that Agreement, has been interpreted in European Communities - Bed Linen. The Panel found, in that dispute, and we agreed, that "margins" means the individual margin of dumping determined for each of the **investigated** exporters and producers of the product **under investigation**, for that particular product. This margin reflects a comparison that is based upon examination of all of the relevant **home market** and **export market transactions**. We see no reason, in Article 9.4, to interpret the word "margins" differently from the meaning it has in Article 2.4.2,(...)"*[104] (emphasis added)

151. Because Article 9.4(ii) refers to the "liability for payment of anti-dumping duties", we understand that provision to refer to duties assessed on a retrospective basis, and not on a prospective basis.

152. That said, Brazil has demonstrated in the first submission that Argentina has imposed a variable anti-dumping duty that can exceed the margin of dumping found in the final determination[105] and, thus, can be collected in inappropriate amounts.

Claim 30 - Failure to Provide How "Minimum Export Prices" Were Established

153. As a final note, the EC has stated in its submission that the precise method followed by the Argentinean authorities in order to calculate the "minimum export prices" is unclear.[106] According to the EC, it is unclear whether, and if so how, the "minimum export prices" relate to the normal values established during the investigation.[107]

154. It is also unclear for Brazil how the investigating authority established the "minimum export prices". That is precisely our claim of violation of Article 12.2.2 of the Agreement. In the final determination and in Resolution No. 574/2000, no

---

[104] United States - Anti-Dumping Measures on Certain Hot Rolled Steel Products from Japan, 24 July 2001, WT/DS184/AB/R, DSR 2001:X, 4697, DSR 2000:XI, 5295, para. 118 (adopted on 23 August 2001) ("*AB - United States - Hot Rolled Steel Products*").
[105] Brazil's first submission, at paras. 520 - 531.
[106] EC's third party submission, at para. 37.
[107] *Ibid.*

explanation was provided as to how Argentina calculated the "minimum export prices". We have alleged in our first submission that Argentina did not provide relevant information as to why the margin established in the final determination was not applied and how the "minimum export price" was calculated.[108] We consider the application of the dumping measures to be relevant information that must be included in the public notice providing for the imposition of a definitive duty. An exporter is entitled to know how the information and arguments presented during the investigation were considered by the investigating authority and how that information was used in arriving at a dumping measure.

155. To that regard, even if the "minimum export price" are equivalent to or lower than the relevant normal values established during the investigation, Argentina still failed to provide in the final dumping determination, or in Resolution No. 574/2000, why the margin established in the final determination was not applied and how the "minimum export prices" were calculated, as required under Article 12.2.2 of the Agreement.

VIII. CONCLUSION AND REQUESTS

A. Conclusion

156. Brazil has raised 41 claims in this dispute. These claims have been presented in detail in Brazil's first submission, which also included 34 Exhibits that support Brazil's various allegations. Further evidence and arguments related to the 41 claims were raised and presented by Brazil in its first oral statement, as well as in the present submission. Thus, any claims that have not been addressed in the present submission should not be construed as claims which Brazil has renounced to.

157. Brazil believes to have covered all the points raised by the Panel, Argentina and Third Parties in this dispute and understands that additional issues or considerations regarding the arguments here presented may be forthcoming. In such instance, Brazil welcomes the opportunity to present its views and arguments at that moment.

B. Requests

158. For the reasons presented throughout this dispute, Brazil respectfully reiterates its request in the first submission that the Panel find that Argentina has acted inconsistently with the Anti-Dumping Agreement with respect to Articles 5.2, 5.3, 5.7, 5.8, 12.1, 6.1.1, 6.1.2, 6.1.3, 6.2, 6.8, paragraphs 3, 5, 6 and 7 of Annex II, 6.9, 6.10, 2.4, 2.4.2, 12.2.2, 3.1, 3.2, 3.4, 3.5, 4.1, 9.2 and 9.3.

159. Accordingly, Brazil also reiterates its request that the Panel recommend that the DSB request Argentina to bring these actions into conformity with GATT 1994 and the Anti-Dumping Agreement and, in doing so, use its right to make suggestions on ways which Argentina could implement the Panel's recommendations, as provided in Article 19.1 of the DSU.

---

[108] Brazil's first submission, at para. 542.

160. In light of the numerous outcome-decisive violations of the Anti-Dumping Agreement, we request that the Panel suggest that Argentina immediately repeal Resolution No. 574/2000 imposing definitive anti-dumping duties.

ANNEX A-4

REPLIES OF BRAZIL TO QUESTIONS OF THE PANEL - FIRST MEETING

(25 September 2002)

Claim 1

To both parties

2. In the view of the parties, which are the obligations under Article 5.2? In addition, would the parties agree that Article 5.2 imposes obligations on the applicant and not on the investigating authority as stated in *Guatemala - Cement II*? Please explain. In the event of agreement with the conclusions in *Guatemala - Cement II*, what recommendation should a panel reach in case that a breach of Article 5.2 ADA is found? In particular, would a recommendation that a Member bring the measure into conformity be appropriate?

Response

Article 5.2 of the Anti-Dumping Agreement requires an application to include evidence of dumping, injury and causal link. Specifically, the application must contain information required in items (i) through (iv) of Article 5.2. We cannot presume from the language in Article 5.2 that these obligations are imposed on the applicant. Relevant part of Article 5.2 provides that:

"(...) Simple assertion, unsubstantiated by relevant evidence, cannot be considered sufficient to meet the requirements of this paragraph.(...)".(emphasis added)

The **consideration** of sufficient evidence to meet the requirements of the paragraph in Article 5.2 is made by the investigating authority and not by the applicant. After all, the applicant is not the one to consider whether the evidence it submitted in the application is sufficient to meet the requirements of Article 5.2.

Furthermore, the WTO and its Agreements provide for obligations and rights of **Members** of the WTO. Consequently, the Anti-Dumping Agreement also imposes obligations on **Members** of the WTO and not on specific interested parties in an investigation. We cannot, therefore, infer that the obligations under Article 5.2 are obligations of the applicant and not the investigating authority.

Under Article 5.2 of the Agreement, the investigating authority must check the application to see whether the information required by that Article is present in the application. In order for an investigating authority to accept an application it must **consider** whether information and evidence in the application is sufficient to meet the requirements set forth in items (i) through (iv) of Article 5.2. At a subsequent stage, and once the application has be considered and accepted by the authority as meeting the requirements in Article 5.2, Article 5.3 of the Agreement imposes another obligation on the investigating authority. This obligation is the examination of the accuracy and adequacy of the evidence provided in the application to determine whether it is sufficient to justify the initiation of the investigation.

To Brazil

3. Does Article 5.2 ADA require that the application contain reasonably available relevant evidence on any adjustment to be made if such adjustment is required for applicant to allege "dumping". In this regard, should such evidence identify:

    (a)   that an adjustment is required;

    (b)   the nature and extent of the adjustment;

    (c)   the basis/methodology for making such adjustment?

Please explain.

Response

Article 5.2 of the Anti-Dumping Agreement requires that the application include evidence of ***dumping***. Pursuant to Article 2.1 of the Agreement, "dumping" is the introduction of a product into the commerce of another country at an export price lower then the normal value (comparable price in the exporting country's market). To prove whether dumping exists, or whether there is an indication of dumping, a comparison between the export price and the normal value must be made. In making this comparison, adjustments are made for differences which affect price comparability. Thus, if an applicant alleges that an adjustment is required in order for a fair comparison to be made, and for there to be an indication of dumping, relevant evidence of such adjustment ***must*** be included in the application.

In view of the above, we understand that Article 5.2 of the Agreement requires that the application contain reasonably available relevant evidence on adjustments to be made, specially if that adjustment is so important that without it the applicant could not have alleged the existence of dumping. Obviously, not all adjustments have such an impact in determining whether dumping exists. However, that is not the case here.

In the instant case, had the investigating authority not accepted the adjustment to normal value (9.09 per cent) as proposed by petitioner and considered the export price for all transactions, and not only those with prices inferior to normal value, there would be no indication of the existence of dumping and the investigation would not have been initiated.

To demonstrate this, we have simulated an exercise to show that there would be no indication of dumping had the authorities considered:

1.   The average f.o.b. price for all export transactions, and not only those at prices lower than the normal value in the establishment of the export price; and,

2.   That an adjustment to normal value was not warranted because petitioner did not present relevant evidence to support such an adjustment.

For the normal value, we have used the JOX price published on 30 June 1997, as provided in the application, without the 9.09 per cent adjustment to normal value. In this scenario, the normal value would have been **0.957** US$/kg.[1]

For the export price, we have considered all the data offered by petitioner for the period January through June and August of 1997, instead of considering only the

---

[1]   *See,* Page 9 of Exhibit BRA-2.

export transactions at prices below the price of eviscerated poultry in Brazil. Using this methodology, the export price for that period would have been **1.014** US$/Kg.[2]

Still with respect to the export price, we have also considered all the export data provided by the Argentinean agency Delegación II - Unidade de Informatica ("DUI") for the period August through October of 1996, instead of considering only the export transactions at prices below the price of eviscerated poultry in Brazil. The export price for that period would have been **1.091** US$/Kg.[3]

In comparing the above export prices (**1.014** US$/Kg or **1.091** US$/Kg) with the unadjusted normal value (**0.957** US$/kg), the Panel will be able to verify that the normal value was lower than the export prices and, therefore, there was *no* indication that poultry from Brazil was entering the Argentinean market at dumped prices.

This exercise serves to show the Panel how important it was for the investigating authority to have considered and required that the relevant evidence in the application identify and indicate that:

1. An adjustment was required;
2. The nature and extent of that adjustment; and,
3. The basis/methodology for making such adjustment.

Brazil considers that evidence of the relevant *type* is required in a case where it is obvious from the face of the application that normal value and export price alleged in the application will require significant adjustments in order to effectuate a fair comparison. At a minimum, the investigating authorities in examining the application should have required relevant evidence to support the allegation that an adjustment, with such an impact, was warranted. Relevant evidence, that is, information drawn from a document tending to prove a fact or a proposition, must support the need for an adjustment (specially whether the alleged physical characteristic differences that lead to the adjustment affect price comparability) and the methodology adopted for making such an adjustment.

4. Was information on the adjustments referred to in paras. 70 and 71 of Brazil's First Written Submission ("FWS") 'reasonably available' to the applicant at the time of filing the application? Please explain.

Response

Yes, we believe that information regarding poultry sold in Brazil (including physical characteristics) was reasonably available to the applicant at the time the application was filed.

We do not propose here to indicate how and where the applicant should search for such information in order to provide the evidence required in an application. Nevertheless, we have found that there are several (national and regional) poultry associations and publications in Brazil, where the applicant could have gathered the necessary evidence. In that regard, we cite to the Brazilian publication presented by the importer Interamericana Comercial S.R.L. ("Interamericana"), the Folha de Londrina/Folha do Paraná.[4] More specifically, the

---

[2] *See,* Page 10 of Exhibit BRA-2 and Annex to Exhibit BRA-2 with export data for the period January through June and August 1997.
[3] *See,* Last Page of Exhibit BRA-2 with export data for the period August through October 1996.
[4] *See,* Page 13 of Exhibit BRA-15.

Brazilian exporters also presented during the investigation price publication from the Associação Nacional dos Abatedouros Avícolas ("ANAB") regarding frozen poultry sold in the internal market for all of 1997 and the first seven months of 1998.[5]

Claim 2

To Brazil

14. Is Brazil's claim under Article 5.3 regarding frozen / chilled adjustment dependent on a finding by the Panel that Argentina was correct to make the head / feet adjustment at the time of initiation? In other words, is Brazil arguing that if the need for a head / feet adjustment was obvious from the face of the application, then so was the need for a frozen / chilled adjustment?

Response

Claim 2 in Brazil's submission, relative to the violation of Article 5.3 of the Agreement, is not whether the investigating authority should have made the frozen/chilled adjustment. The argument presented in Claim 2 is that if the authorities considered from the information provided in the application that an adjustment to compensate for the head/feet differences was required, then, at a minimum, the investigating authorities should have also made an adjustment to compensate for the differences between frozen/chilled poultry.

We recall that petitioner's application is provided in Exhibit BRA-1. From that Exhibit, the Panel will be able to verify that the export price data submitted by petitioner, and used by the authority, referred to *frozen* poultry (Mercosul Common Nomenclature NCM 0207.12.00)[6], a product different from that corresponding to the JOX price publication used to establish the normal value, which was for chilled poultry (NCM 0207.11.00).[7] If Argentina found there to be sufficient evidence to make the head and feet adjustment, Argentina should have also found, from the information submitted in the application, that a frozen and chilled adjustment was also required.

That said, Brazil's Claim 2 is that there was ***not*** sufficient evidence from the information provided in the application for the Argentinean authorities to have accepted that an adjustment to normal value was needed to compensate for the alleged physical characteristic differences (head/feet) between the poultry sold to Argentina and in Brazil.

The normal value information provided in the application by petitioner was information provided by JOX exclusively with regards to prices of *chilled* poultry, sold in São Paulo, with head, feet and giblets for one day in 1997. The information in the JOX price publication did not provide or affirm that all poultry sold in Brazil contained head, feet and giblets. The information presented did not correspond to prices at which the product in question was sold when destined for consumption in Brazil.

We understand that petitioner tried to make the JOX price published for chilled poultry with head and feet into evidence that all poultry sold in Brazil is

---

[5] *See,* Pages 16, 20 and 24 of Exhibit BRA-15.
[6] *See,* Page 6 of Exhibit BRA-1.
[7] *See,* Page 2 of Exhibit BRA-1.

chilled and includes head and feet. That is not true. However, the investigating authority incorrectly accepted the JOX information as evidence that all poultry sold in Brazil is chilled and contains head and feet.

Petitioner further alleged that it was necessary to compensate for these physical characteristic differences and assumed that such differences affect price comparability. Again, no evidence was presented in the application to support the allegation that these differences affect price comparability.

Petitioner, then, presented a calculation of compensation where the yield rate of eviscerate poultry sold in Brazil is 88 per cent of the live poultry and that the yield rate of eviscerated poultry sold in Argentina is 80 per cent of the live poultry. Nowhere in the application or in the determination to initiate is there indication of a document supporting the allegation that the yield rate of poultry sold in Brazil is 88 per cent and that in Argentina it is 80 per cent. This calculation and the yield rates proposed were accepted by the investigating authority even though no supporting evidence was presented in the application to sustain such allegations.

Claim 6

To Brazil

21. **Para. 136 of Brazil's FWS reads in relevant part:**
    'if authorities had examined the accuracy and adequacy of the evidence provided in the application they would have required that petitioner provide prices of poultry for the entire period under analysis in order to correctly make a fair comparison with export prices for the same period.'
    In the view of Brazil, which is the 'entire period under analysis'?

Response

Brazil's response to this question does not address whether we find the period under analysis established by Argentina, prior to initiation, to be appropriate. Brazil will limit its response to what it considers to be the entire period under analysis based on the normal value and export price data used by the authority in the initiation.

In assessing whether there is sufficient evidence of dumping in the application to justify the initiation, the investigating authority may not ignore the provisions of Article 2 of the Anti-Dumping Agreement, which defines what dumping is. In particular, Article 2.4 of the Agreement requires a fair comparison be made between the export price and the normal value *in respect of sales made at as nearly as possible the same time.*

Taking into account that for purposes of initiation the data considered by the DCD in the establishment of the export price was from August through October of 1996 and January through June and August of 1997[8], we consider that for a fair comparison to have occurred the authority should have, *at least*, considered normal value data for the same period, that is, from August through October of 1996 and January through June and August of 1997. That was not the case.

---

[8] *See,* Page 12 of Exhibit BRA-2.

Petitioner and the investigating authority considered normal value for purposes of initiation based on only one day in 1997 (30 June). In that regard, we know from the information provided by petitioner prior to initiation and during the investigation that normal value information for all of 1996 and 1997 was reasonably available.

On 17 February 1998, prior to initiation, petitioner submitted to the authority additional information that included, among other information, JOX price publication for chilled poultry with head and feet in the Brazilian market for July and December of 1997 and January and February of 1998.[9] Even with this information, the authority chose to initiate the investigation based only on normal value information for one day in 1997.

In addition, on 26 July 1999, during the investigation, petitioner once again submitted updated information on normal value for three days in each of the twelve months of 1998 and two days in January 1999.[10]

From the facts above, we have shown that the JOX price publication was (and is) reasonably available to petitioner for any desired period, and could have been submitted in the application. Likewise, we have shown that the authorities did not examine the accuracy and adequacy of the evidence provided in the application (or the additional information provided by petitioner) to determine whether it was sufficient to justify the initiation of the investigation.

Claim 9

To both parties

22. In the present case, by virtue of which legal instrument was the investigation initiated?

Response

Brazil understands that the investigation was initiated when the Ministerio de Economia y Obras y Serviços Publicos ("MEOSP") issued Resolution No. 11/1999, announcing the initiation of the anti-dumping investigation on imports of poultry from Brazil.[11]

That said, the Panel should take account of the fact that the ***consideration*** of the dumping and injury evidence, that lead to the decision to initiate the investigation, was not done simultaneously. For the sake of clarification, we will present the sequence of facts related to this claim in order for the Panel to verify what we have argued.

1. *On 7 January 1998*, the DCD issued a report regarding the viability of the initiation of the dumping investigation, determining that there was sufficient evidence of dumping in the export transactions of poultry from Brazil into Argentina.[12]

---

[9] *See,* Exhibit BRA-4.
[10] *See,* Exhibit BRA-19.
[11] *See,* Exhibit BRA-7.
[12] *See,* Exhibit BRA-2.

Report of the Panel

2. *On 7 January 1998*, the CNCE issued Acta No. 405, determining *insufficient* evidence of injury to justify the initiation of the investigation.[13]

3. *On 17 February 1998*, after having access to Acta No. 405, petitioner submitted additional information to the authority.[14]

4. *On 22 September 1998*, the CNCE issued Acta No. 464, determining sufficient evidence of threat of injury to justify the initiation of the investigation.[15]

5. *On 29 December 1999*, the authority in charge of the causal link analysis issued the report on causal link. In it, the authority stated that the DCD based its report on the elements that were included in the original application that took into account the period January through June of 1997.[16] The causal link determination also pointed out that petitioner submitted additional updated information for all of 1997 and the first semester of 1998.[17] However, the DCD did not make or issue a new dumping analysis, taking into account petitioner's additional information.

6. *On 20 January 1999*, the MEOSP issued Resolution No. 11/1999, announcing the initiation of the anti-dumping investigation on imports of poultry from Brazil.[18] This Resolution was published in the Argentinean Official Journal on 25 January 1999.

From the sequence of the facts related above, we can conclude that the evidence of dumping and injury was considered at different times. The dumping evidence was considered on 7 January 1998, and the injury evidence on 22 September 1998, *more than eight months after the evidence of dumping was considered*. If the term "simultaneously" is defined as "occurring or operating at the same time"[19] and the Panel understands that Article 5.7 require authorities to examine evidence simultaneously rather than sequentially, how could the authority have simultaneously considered the dumping and injury evidence if there was an eight-month gap between the two considerations?

For Argentina to have met the requirement in Article 5.7, a new dumping consideration taking into account the updated information presented by petitioner should have occurred on 22 September 1998, but that did not happen. In this case, the timing of the consideration of the dumping and injury evidence was not simultaneous.

Therefore, even though we understand the MEOSP to be the authority that issued the decision to initiate the investigation, that decision was based on the evidence of dumping considered by the DCD on 7 January 1998 and on the evidence of injury considered by the CNCE on 22 September 1998.

23. What interpretation is given by the parties to the following excerpt from the panel report in *Guatemala - Cement II*: we are of the view that Article 5.7

---

[13] *See*, Exhibit BRA-3.
[14] *See*, Exhibit BRA-4.
[15] *See*, Exhibit BRA-6.
[16] *See*, Page 2 of Exhibit BRA-20.
[17] *See*, Page 4 of Exhibit BRA-20.
[18] *See*, Exhibit BRA-7.
[19] *The Concise Oxford Dictionary - Ninth Edition*, Oxford University Press, 1995, p. 1294.

requires the investigating authority to examine the evidence before it on dumping and injury simultaneously, rather than sequentially?

Response

First, we would like to indicate that we do not find it possible for an authority to *consider* evidence of dumping and injury simultaneously if the evidence considered by the authorities indisputably refers to non-related periods for dumping and injury.

The Panel will verify that the causal link analysis, prior to initiation, was issued on 29 December 1999, and in it the authority stated that the DCD made a dumping analysis based on the elements that were included in the *original* application, which took into account the period January through June of 1997.[20] The causal link determination also pointed out that petitioner submitted additional updated information for all of 1997 and the first semester of 1998.[21] However, the DCD did not *consider* petitioner's updated information and did not issue a new dumping analysis.

On the other hand, the first injury analysis, Acta No. 405, *considered* there to be insufficient evidence of injury to justify the initiation of the investigation. The data collected for that injury analysis went from January 1994 through June 1997.[22] Eight months after the dumping and the first injury analysis had been made, the CNCE issued a second injury analysis, Acta No. 464, considering there to be sufficient evidence of threat of injury to justify the initiation of the investigation. The second injury analysis was based on the data collected for the period January 1994 through June 1998.[23]

If the first injury analysis considered that the dumping found on June 1997 was not causing injury or threat of injury on June 1997, how could Argentina have found threat of injury on June 1998 if the dumped imports on June 1997 were not causing injury on June 1997?

Second, even if the language in Article 5.7 of the Agreement could be interpreted in accordance with the understanding of the Panel in *Guatemala - Cement II* (simultaneous, rather than sequential, examination of the dumping and injury evidence), in this case that also did not occur.

Our response to question 22 above presents the sequence of events that clearly indicate that the evidence of injury was considered eight months after the evidence of dumping was considered. An eight-month gap between these two considerations is not in accordance with the understanding of the Panel in *Guatemala - Cement II* of the requirement in Article 5.7 of the Agreement.

Claim 10

To both parties

24.   What are 'interested parties known to the investigating authorities to have an interest' within the meaning of Article 12.1 ADA?

---

[20] *See,* Page 2 of Exhibit BRA-20.
[21] *See,* Page 4 of Exhibit BRA-20.
[22] *See,* Exhibit BRA-3.
[23] *See,* Page 8 of the "*Informe Técnico Prévio a la Apertura*" in Exhibit BRA-6.

Report of the Panel

Response

The definition of "interested parties", for the purposes of the Anti-Dumping Agreement, is provided in Article 6.11 of the Agreement. It includes the exporter, the foreign producer and the importer of a product subject to investigation; the government of the exporting Member; and, the producer of the like product in the importing Member.

From that definition, we understand the phrase "interested parties known to the investigating authorities to have an interest" to mean the interested parties, as defined by Article 6.11, recognized or identified by the investigating authorities to have an interest in the investigation.

In that regard, we remind the Panel that prior to initiation, petitioner submitted on 17 February 1998 additional information, including lists of imports of poultry from Brazil, *broken down by producer and exporter*.[24] These lists identified by name fifteen Brazilian producers of poultry and twenty Brazilian exporters of poultry. These lists provided by petitioner were, in fact, a document from two Argentinean agencies: *SENASA - Dirección Nacional de Fiscalización Agroalimentaria* ("*SENASA*") and the *Secretaria de Agricultura, Ganaderia, Pesca y Alimentación Dirección de Ganaderia* ("*Ganaderia*").[25] Identified in these two lists were five Brazilian producers/exporters (Comaves, Minuano, Chapecó, Catarinense and Perdigão) of the seven producers/exporters that were notified of the investigation almost eight months after it had been initiated.[26] We understand that at that moment, prior to initiation, petitioner had identified and provided the names of the Brazilian producers/exporters of poultry to the investigating authority.

In addition, in the report regarding the viability of the initiation of the dumping investigation, of 7 January 1998, the investigating authority identified ten Brazilian exporters of the subject merchandise.[27] The identification of these Brazilian exporters was made by the investigating authorities, ***themselves***, prior to the initiation of the investigation. These ten exporters were "interested parties known to the investigating authority" within the meaning of Article 12.1 of the Agreement. Among these ten exporters identified were five (Comaves, Minuano, Chapecó, Catarinense and Perdigão) of the seven exporters that were notified of the investigation almost eight months after it had been initiated, and after a preliminary injury, dumping and causal link determination had been issued.

As a final comment, we find it quite evident that an exporter, that exports the product subject to an investigation, will undoubtedly have an interest in the investigation. After all, the exports of these companies might be subject, at the end of the investigation, to the imposition of anti-dumping duties.

Thus, from the facts above, we have shown that these exporters were "interested parties known to the investigating authorities" and should have been notified of the investigation as soon as it was initiated.

25. When were each of the following parties notified of the initiation of the investigation:

---

[24] *See*, Exhibit BRA-4.
[25] *See*, Annexes 1 and 2 of Exhibit BRA-4.
[26] *See*, Brazil's first submission, at paras. 192 - 201.
[27] *See*, Pages 4 and 5 of Exhibit BRA-2.

Government of Brazil, Avipal, Seara, Frigorifico Nicolini, Sadia, Frangosul, Chapecó, Minuano, Perdigão, Catarinense, CCLP, PenaBranca, and Comaves?

Response

The Government of Brazil was notified of the initiation of the investigation on 1 February 1999.[28]

The Brazilian exporters Avipal, Seara, Nicolini, Sadia and Frangosul were notified by the DCD of the initiation and the need to provide responses to the dumping questionnaire on 10 February 1999.[29] These same exporters were notified by the CNCE of the initiation and the need to provide responses to the injury questionnaire on 16 February 1999.[30]

The Brazilian exporters Chapecó, Minuano, Perdigão, Catarinense, CCLP, PenaBranca and Comaves were notified by the DCD of the initiation of the investigation and the need to provide responses to the dumping questionnaire on 15 September 1999[31], almost eight months after the investigation had been initiated. These exporters were never notified nor did they receive an injury questionnaire from the CNCE.

In this regard, we refer to Argentina's explanation that the injury questionnaire was only sent to 8 exporters (when, in fact, was sent to only 5 exporters) because the injury analysis basically considers the injury to the domestic industry and, therefore, there is no need for *all* exporters to receive and respond to the injury questionnaire.

We call the attention of the Panel to the fact that an injury analysis takes into account not only the impact of the dumped imports on the domestic industry (Article 3.4 of the Agreement) but also the volume of the alleged dumped imports (Article 3.2 of the Agreement) and the effect of the dumped imports on prices in the domestic market (Article 3.2 of the Agreement). Therefore, the information on volume and price of imports provided by exporters is important and required in an injury analysis.

Furthermore, it was important and, in fact, a right of all exporters to receive the injury questionnaire and have the opportunity to respond to the questions made by the CNCE. If other exporters, and interested parties, had the opportunity to defend their interests by responding to the injury questionnaire, these seven exporters should also have had that opportunity. Whether or not these exporters would have responded to the injury questionnaire was a decision to be made by them and not by the investigating authority.

---

[28] *See*, Exhibit ARG-III.
[29] *See*, Exhibit BRA-8.
[30] *See*, Exhibit BRA-9.
[31] *See*, Exhibit BRA-13.

Claim 11

To both parties

27. What is the meaning of the word 'questionnaires' in Article 6.1.1 ADA? In the view of the parties, is the word 'questionnaires' confined to the questionnaires provided at the initial stage of the investigation only?

Response

Brazil understands that the term "questionnaires" in Article 6.1.1 of the Anti-Dumping Agreement refers to the questionnaires provided at the initial stage of the investigation. Subsequently, if the investigating authorities require additional, supplemental information or clarification of the information provided (by exporters, importers or the domestic industry) in the response to the questionnaires, the investigating authority will request such information.

In particular, the term "questionnaires" in Article 6.1.1, used in an anti-dumping investigation, refers to the dumping questionnaire as well as the injury questionnaire. We understand that some Members adopt a system where two agencies share the responsibility for administering the anti-dumping law and investigation procedures. One agency being responsible for determining the existence of dumping and calculating the dumping margin and the other for determining whether the domestic industry has been injured by the allegedly dumped imports. We understand that Argentina adopts such a system.

Consequently, Argentina also failed to comply with Article 6.1.1 of the Agreement when it did not send the injury questionnaire to the Brazilian exporters CCLP, Comaves, Minuano, Chapecó, Catarinense, Perdigão and PenaBranca.

Claim 12

To both parties

32. What is the meaning of the word 'participating' in Article 6.1.2 ADA? Would the parties consider that companies that are aware of an ongoing investigation but that do not show an interest in it qualify as 'parties participating in the investigation'?

Response

To participate means to be a part or "an essential member or constituent of anything".[32] A producer or exporter of a product under investigation is an essential member or constituent of an investigation.

Companies that *are aware*, that is, that have knowledge of an ongoing investigation, qualify as "interested parties participating in the investigation", even if they do not show an interest in the investigation. The lack of interest of an interested party in an investigation does not exclude or diminish the obligation of the investigating authorities of "promptly" making available to them evidence presented in writing by other interested parties. Interested parties that do not show an interest in

---

[32] *The Concise Oxford Dictionary - Ninth Edition,* Oxford University Press, 1995, p. 995.

the investigation may still want to defend their rights in an investigation based on certain allegations or evidence presented by other parties.

That said, Brazil reaffirms that the Brazilian exporters CCLP, Catarinense, Chapecó, Minuano, Perdigão, Comaves and PenaBranca were *not aware* of the ongoing investigation until they were notified by the authorities, eight months after it had been initiated.

33.   What is the meaning of the word 'promptly' in Article 6.1.2 ADA?

Response

According to textual interpretation, the term "promptly" means "to make or do readily or at once".[33] Brazil considers that evidence presented in writing by one interested party could not be made readily or immediately available to the Brazilian exporters CCLP, Catarinense, Chapecó, Minuano, Perdigão, Comaves and PenaBranca, if these exporters were notified of the investigation almost eight months after it had been initiated.

We stress that these seven exporters had not been notified of the initiation or given the questionnaires to respond during eight months of the investigation but were, in any event, included in the investigation because they exported the subject merchandise to Argentina in the period of investigation.

Any evidence that was presented during these eight months could not be understood as being "promptly" available to these exporters if they were *not aware* of the existence of this investigation and their need to participate.

Claim 14

To both parties

34.   What are 'known exporters' within the meaning of Article 6.1.3 ADA? In particular, would producers in the exporting country that have been identified as exporters of the product concerned by the applicant in the application qualify as 'known exporters'?

Response

Brazil would first like to clarify that Argentina *never* provided the full text of the written application to the Government of Brazil (authorities of the exporting Member) nor to any exporter (known or allegedly unknown) of the product under investigation.

That said, we understand the phrase "known exporters" in Article 6.1.3 of the Agreement to mean exporters that were recognized or identified by the investigating authorities. Information submitted in Brazil's Exhibits demonstrate that the investigating authorities knew, prior to the initiation, of the existence of the Brazilian exporters CCLP, Catarinense, Chapecó, Minuano, Perdigão, Comaves and PenaBranca.

Prior to initiation, petitioner submitted on 17 February 1998 additional information, including lists of imports of poultry from Brazil, *broken down by*

---

[33] *Ibid.*, p. 1096.

Report of the Panel

producer and exporter.[34] These lists identified by name fifteen Brazilian producers of poultry and twenty Brazilian exporters of poultry. These lists provided by petitioner were, in fact, a document from two Argentinean agencies: *SENASA - Dirección Nacional de Fiscalización Agroalimentaria* ("*SENASA*") and the *Secretaria de Agricultura, Ganaderia, Pesca y Alimentación Dirección de Ganaderia* ("*Ganaderia*").[35] Identified in these two lists were five Brazilian producers/exporters (Comaves, Minuano, Chapecó, Catarinense and Perdigão) of the seven producers/exporters that were notified of the investigation almost eight months after it had been initiated.[36] We understand that at that moment, prior to initiation, petitioner had identified and provided the names of the Brazilian producers/exporters of poultry to the investigating authority.

Still prior to initiation and in the report regarding the viability of the initiation of the dumping investigation, of 7 January 1998, the investigating authority identified ten Brazilian exporters of the subject merchandise.[37] We point out that here the identification of these Brazilian exporters was made by the investigating authorities **themselves**. Among these ten exporters identified were five (Comaves, Minuano, Chapecó, Catarinense and Perdigão) of the seven exporters that were notified of the investigation almost eight months after it had been initiated, and after a preliminary injury, dumping and causal link determination had been issued. These ten exporters were "known exporters" within the meaning of Article 6.1.3 of the Agreement.

35. Would the parties agree with the finding of the panel *Guatemala - Cement II* that 'the term "as soon as" conveys a sense of substantial urgency' and that "as soon as" and "immediately" can be considered interchangeable terms? Please explain.

Response

Brazil notes that the issue here is not so much related to the timing in Article 6.1.3 but to the fact that the Argentinean authorities *never* provided the written application to the Government of Brazil and the exporters.

That being so, Brazil agrees with the finding of the Panel in *Guatemala - Cement II* that the term "as soon as" conveys a sense of substantial urgency. In particular, we find the following conclusion of that Panel to be relevant and applicable to this case:

> "We note that Article 6.1.3 does not specify the number of days within which the text of the application shall be provided. What it does specify is that the text of the application be provided "as soon as" the investigation has been initiated. In this regard, the term "as soon as" conveys a sense of substantial urgency. In fact, the terms "immediately" and "as soon as" are considered to be interchangeable. We do not consider that providing the text of the application 24 or 18 days after the date of initiation fulfils the requirement of Article 6.1.3

---

[34] *See,* Exhibit BRA-4.
[35] *See,* Annexes 1 and 2 of Exhibit BRA-4.
[36] *See,* Brazil's first submission, at paras. 192 - 201.
[37] *See,* Pages 4 and 5 of Exhibit BRA-2.

that the text be provided "as soon as an investigation has been initiated"[38] (emphasis added)

Immediate access to the application is important for exporters to prepare their arguments in defence of their interests and to devise a strategy to defend the allegations made by petitioner in the application.

To Brazil

36. What is the meaning of the words 'as soon as an investigation has been initiated' in Article 6.1.3 ADA? In the particular case at stake, when was the investigation initiated?

Response

Brazil once more makes note of the fact that the Argentinean authorities **never** provided the text of the written application to the Government of Brazil and the exporters, as required under Article 6.1.3 of the Anti-Dumping Agreement. We repeat, the Argentinean authorities **never** provided the text of the application.

We understand that Argentina argues that in the Spanish version of the Agreement the term "provide" is set forth as "facilitar" and that based on that meaning the Argentinean authorities complied with the requirement in Article 6.1.3 of the Agreement when they made the written application **available** to the interested parties once the investigation was initiated.[39] Argentina's position that the verb "to provide" could be understood to mean that authorities were only required to "make available" the full text of the written application is incorrect.

We restate that Article 6.1.3 carefully differentiates the obligation that the investigating authorities have with the exporters and the exporting Member from the obligation the investigating authorities have with other interested parties. In the first case, the investigating authority must actively "provide" the full text of the written application to the exporting Member and to the exporters involved in the investigation. In the second case, the investigating authority must "make available", upon request, the full text of the written application to other interested parties. Brazil believes that if the requirement imposed on the investigating authority was to be understood as being the same for the exporters and the exporting Member as that for the other interested parties, there would be no need for the use of different language in Article 6.1.3 of the Agreement.

The same reasoning applies to the text in Spanish. The requirement imposed on the investigating authorities to provide, or "facilitar", the full text of the written application to exporters and the exporting Member is different from the requirement imposed on the authorities to "make available", or "podrán a disposición", the full text of the written application to other interested parties.

Furthermore, the verb "facilitar" is understood to mean "proporcionar o entregar", a definition entirely compatible with the verb "provide" used in the English version.[40]

---

[38] Guatemala - Definitive Anti-Dumping Measures on Grey Portland Cement from Mexico, 24 October 2000, WT/DS156/R, DSR 2000:XI, 5295, at para. 8.101 (adopted on 17 November 2000) ("*Guatemala - Cement II*").
[39] *See,* Argentina's first submission, at para. 164.
[40] *Real Academia Española,* Editorial Espasa Calpe, S.A, 2001.

Report of the Panel

That said, we return to the Panel's question. The phrase "as soon as an investigation has been initiated" in Article 6.1.3 of the Agreement means that the authority must actively provide the text of the application *immediately* after the investigation is initiated. We note the urgency required in Article 6.1.3. Brazil notes that the investigation was initiated when the MEOSP published, on 25 January 1999, Resolution No. 11/1999, of 20 January 1999. Argentina notified (*but did not provide the application*) the Government of Brazil of the initiation of the investigation on 1 February 1999[41], that is, seven days after the initiation had been published.

Claim 15

To Brazil

38. With regard to Exhibits BRA-22, 23, 24 and 26, please indicate precisely where exporters reported that the poultry sold to Argentina was identical to the poultry sold in Brazil.

Response

Sadia

Exhibit BRA-22 includes Section A of Sadia's questionnaire response submitted on 20 April 1999, and Section A of Sadia's supplemental response submitted on 28 April 1999. In Annex II (*"Identificación del Produto Denunciado"*) of Section A, the questionnaire requests a complete product description with technical specifications for each model/type/code for the merchandise sold in the internal market and exported to Argentina.[42]

In its response of 20 April 1999, Sadia described the product as whole, frozen, eviscerated poultry with giblets. More specifically, for the internal market, Sadia reported the product as whole, frozen, eviscerated poultry, with giblets, box of 18kg - individual weight of 1.750 to 2.750 kg. For the Argentinean market, Sadia reported the product as whole, frozen, eviscerated poultry, with giblets, box of 18kg - individual weight of 1.700 to 2.700 kg.[43] In addition, Sadia submitted a detailed description of the poultry produced by the company. In this description, Sadia reports that a bag of giblets containing heart, liver, gizzard and neck, previously cleaned and chilled, is put into the abdominal cavity of the animal.[44] No mention is made to the head and feet of the poultry. According to Sadia's response there were no differences in the physical characteristics for the products sold to Argentina and in Brazil.

In its supplemental response of 28 April 1999, Sadia indicated in Annex V of Section A, that whole, frozen, eviscerated poultry, *without* giblets, was sold to the internal market but not to Argentina during the period January 1996 through February 1999.[45] Thus, poultry without head and feet was, in fact, sold in Brazil.

The DCD never requested additional information or clarification regarding the description of the product sold to Argentina and in Brazil.

---

[41] *See,* Exhibit ARG-III.
[42] *See,* Page 4 of Exhibit BRA-22.
[43] *Ibid.*
[44] *See,* Page 12 of Exhibit BRA-22.
[45] *See,* Last page of Exhibit BRA-22.

Avipal

Exhibit BRA-23 includes a letter from Avipal submitting the questionnaire in a diskette on 21 April 1999, and the non-confidential part of Section A of Avipal's questionnaire response on 7 May April 1999. In Annex II (*"Identificación del Produto Denunciado"*) of Section A, the questionnaire requests a complete product description with technical specifications for each model/type/code for the merchandise sold in the internal market and exported to Argentina.[46]

In its response, Avipal described the product as whole, frozen, eviscerated poultry. More specifically, Avipal divided the product into two types: (i) **broiler** - whole, frozen eviscerated, containing a plastic bag with neck ***without head***, gizzard and liver; and, (ii) **griler** - whole, frozen eviscerated without giblets.[47] In Annex V of that response, Avipal reported that both broiler and griler type poultry were sold to Argentina and Brazil.[48] According to Avipal's response, there were no differences in the physical characteristics of the product sold to Argentina and in Brazil.

We also recall that throughout the investigation the DCD never requested additional information or clarification regarding the description of the product.

Frangosul

Exhibit BRA-24 includes Section A of Frangosul's questionnaire response submitted on 27 April 1999. Exhibit BRA-26 includes Frangosul's response to the DCD with the translation of the product brochure in Spanish submitted on 19 August 1999. In Annex II (*"Identificación del Produto Denunciado"*) of Section A, the questionnaire requests a complete product description with technical specifications for each model/type/code for the merchandise sold in the internal market and exported to Argentina.[49]

In its response of 27 April 1999, Frangosul described the product as whole, frozen, eviscerated poultry with giblets (**broiler type**) and whole, frozen, eviscerated poultry without giblets (**griler type**).[50] Both broiler and griler type poultry were sold to Argentina and in Brazil.

In its response of 19 August 1999, Frangosul attached a product brochure (in English and Spanish), describing the types of products sold. According to the description on the product brochure, griler type poultry is fresh, frozen poultry, white or yellow skin, fully eviscerated, ***headless and footless***, without giblets; and broiler type poultry is fresh, frozen poultry, white skin, fully eviscerated, ***headless and footless***, with giblets.[51]

Once again, throughout the investigation the DCD never requested additional information or clarification regarding the description of the product sold to Argentina and in Brazil.

---

[46] *See,* Page 7 of Exhibit BRA-23.
[47] *Ibid.*
[48] *See,* Page 11 of Exhibit BRA-23.
[49] *See,* Page 5 of Exhibit BRA-24.
[50] *See,* Pages 5 and 6 of Exhibit BRA-24.
[51] *See,* Page 8 of Exhibit BRA-26.

Catarinense

Exhibit BRA-25 includes Section A of Catarinense's questionnaire response submitted on 3 November 1999. In Annex II (*"Identificación del Produto Denunciado"*) of Section A, the questionnaire requests a complete product description with technical specifications for each model/type/code for the merchandise sold in the internal market and exported to Argentina.[52]

In its response, Catarinense described the product as whole, frozen poultry with giblets (**broiler type**) and whole frozen poultry without giblets (**griler type**).[53] For the export market, the broiler type poultry (with giblets) contains liver, gizzard and neck.[54] The griler type poultry sold to Argentina and in Brazil do not contain giblets.[55] Catarinense reported that it sold both broiler and griler type poultry in the home market.

The DCD never requested additional information or clarification regarding the description of the product sold to Argentina and in Brazil.

Claim 19

To Brazil

41. Argentina asserts that Frangosul's normal value data was submitted out-of-time. Please comment.

Response

In order to respond to this question, we find it necessary to provide and explain the chronology of the responses submitted by Frangosul and the requests for extension to submit such responses, as well as the requests by the DCD for information.

1. On 16 February 1999, the DCD notified Frangosul of the initiation of the investigation and fixed a deadline of 29 March 1999 for Frangosul to respond to the dumping questionnaire.[56]
2. On 15 March 1999, Frangosul requested an extension of the deadline to submit the response to the questionnaire by 20 April 1999.[57]
3. On 26 March 1999, the DCD granted the extension until 20 April 1999.[58]
4. On 27 April 1999, Frangosul submitted the response to the dumping questionnaire.[59] In particular, Frangosul responded to Section C of the questionnaire regarding sales to the domestic market. This information included sales of poultry made in Brazil (internal market) corresponding to the years 1996, 1997, 1998 and the first three months of 1999, separated by month.[60] We make special note that, subsequently, the authority requested

---

[52] *See,* Page 8 of Exhibit BRA-25.
[53] *Ibid.*
[54] *See,* Page 9 of Exhibit BRA-25.
[55] *See,* Pages 10 and 36 of Exhibit BRA-25.
[56] *See,* Exhibit BRA-9.
[57] *See,* Page 28 of Exhibit BRA-15.
[58] *Ibid.*
[59] *See,* Page 29 of Exhibit BRA-15.
[60] *Ibid.*

supporting documentation for all of the sales transactions in the internal market covering that period.[61] Even though Frangosul submitted this information seven days after the deadline of 20 April 1999, Frangosul still provided this information within a reasonable period for the authority to consider that information, specially taking into account the volume of data submitted for a period in excess of what was needed.

5. On 12 July 1999, the DCD requested that Frangosul provide additional information. This information included translation of all supporting documentation corresponding to the export transactions of the product under investigation (even though most of the information provided in these invoices were already in Spanish); information on export transactions to the five largest export markets (aside from Argentina) where the product was sold; translation of the product brochure (even though the product brochure had already been provided in Spanish); and, supporting documentation for all the sales transactions in the domestic market for the period.[62] The DCD fixed a deadline of ten days for Frangosul to submit this information.

6. On 28 July 1999, Frangosul requested an extension of the deadline to submit the information requested by the DCD.[63]

7. On 9 August 1999, the DCD granted the extension for Frangosul to submit the requested information within fifteen days.[64]

8. On 19 August 1999, Frangosul provided a translation of invoices for a few export transactions, as sample of all export transactions, which it had reported; information on the export transactions to the five largest export markets for the period 1996 through 1999; translation of the product brochure with the description of the product; and, an explanation that the great volume of sales in the internal market did not make it possible for it to provide copies of invoices for each transaction.[65] To support its explanation, Frangosul indicated that more than 320,000 invoices are issued in one given year for sales transactions in the internal market and that on 27 April 1999 it had submitted a list of invoices for the sales transactions in the internal market. Frangosul further stated that the invoices were available to the investigating authorities for a verification *in loco* or for a selection of such documents for specific transactions to be used as sample.[66]

9. On 12 October 1999, the DCD requested a new list of invoices with the total transactions in the internal market for the period January 1998 through January 1999, so that the DCD could select a statistic sample and subsequently request the supporting documentation for that sample.[67] In this request, the DCD also informed, for the first time in the investigation, that the list of invoices sent on 27 April 1999, did not include specific information necessary for the authority's analysis.[68] We also call to the Panel's attention

---

[61] *See,* Pages 29 and 30of Exhibit BRA-15.
[62] *See,* Page 49 of Exhibit BRA-15.
[63] *Ibid.*
[64] *Ibid.*
[65] *See,* Exhibit BRA-26.
[66] *Ibid.*
[67] *Ibid.*
[68] *Ibid.*

Report of the Panel

the fact that this was the *first time* that the investigating authority informed Frangosul what the dumping period of data collection was.

10. On 18 November 1999, the DCD renewed its request for a list of invoices for the sales transactions in the internal market for the period January 1998 through January 1999 and that Frangosul submit this information in a diskette within 5 days. No mention is made to the supporting documentation.[69]

11. On 30 December 1999, Frangosul presented in a diskette the list of invoices for the sales transactions in the internal market for the period January 1998 through January 1999.[70]

12. On 4 January 2000, the DCD issued the report prior to the final determination (disclosure of essential facts under consideration). This report does not mention the list of invoices submitted by Frangosul.[71]

13. On 5 January 2000, the DCD notified Frangosul of the end of the evidence-producing stage of the investigation.[72]

With respect to the sequence of events above, Brazil would like to make the following considerations.

First, the Panel must not forget under what circumstances Article 6.8 of the Agreement allows an investigating authority to resort to the use of facts available. According to Article 6.8 of the Agreement, where interested parties do not "significantly impede" the investigation, recourse may be had to facts available **only** if an interested party fails to submit *necessary information* "within a reasonable period". If information is, in fact, supplied "within a reasonable period", the investigating authority cannot use facts available and must use the information submitted by the interested party. In the case at issue, Frangosul did not incur in any of the circumstances set forth in Article 6.8 of the Agreement for the application of facts available.

Even though Frangosul responded to the questionnaire seven days after the deadline, Frangosul still submitted responses "within a reasonable period". To that regard, Brazil recalls that "a reasonable period" will not necessarily be equivalent to the established deadlines set out by investigating authorities. Our understanding of a "reasonable period" is aligned with the understanding of the Panel in *United States - Hot Rolled Steel Products*:

> *"(...) The AD Agreement establishes that facts available may be used if necessary information is not provided within a reasonable period. What is a "reasonable period" will not, in all instances be commensurate with pre-established deadlines set out in general regulations. We recognize that in the interest of orderly administration investigating authorities do, and indeed must establish deadlines. However, a rigid adherence to such deadlines does not in all cases suffice as the basis for a conclusion that information was not*

---

[69] *See,* Exhibit ARG-XXVIII.
[70] *See,* Exhibit BRA-26.
[71] *See,* Exhibit BRA-28.
[72] *See,* Exhibit BRA-26.

submitted within a reasonable period and consequently that facts available may be applied."[73] (emphasis added)

We do not propose to affirm or imply that Article 6.8 and Annex II of the Agreement is a license for interested parties to simply disregard the time-limits set out by investigating authorities. However, we understand that the word "reasonable" in Article 6.8 suggests a degree of flexibility by authorities that involves consideration of *all* of the circumstances of a particular case.

Second, Brazil understands that the application of Article 6.8 of the Agreement is also dependent upon the actions of the investigating authority in an investigation. If an investigating authority does not act in a proper manner during the investigation, it cannot claim that the interested party did not comply with the requirements of Article 6.8 and, thus, resort to the application of facts available.

In this respect, Brazil turns to the Panel's consideration in *Guatemala - Cement II* on the interpretation of the application of Article 6.8 of the Agreement:

*"(...) We do not consider that a failure to cooperate necessarily constitutes significant impediment of an investigation, since in our view the AD Agreement does not require cooperation by interested parties at any cost. Although there are certain consequences (under Article 6.8) for interested parties if they fail to cooperate with an investigating authority, in our view such consequences **only** arise if the investigating authority itself has acted in a reasonable, objective and impartial manner(...)"*[74] (emphasis added)

The sequence of facts presented above demonstrate that the investigating authority in this case did not acted in a reasonable, objective and impartial manner. The fact that Frangosul was originally required to submit normal value and export price information for an excessively long period (January 1996 through March 1999) and that more than eight months after the initiation the authority fixed a much smaller dumping period of data collection (January 1998 through January 1999) indicates how unreasonable, non-objective and partial the authority was in this investigation. Specially, if you consider that the authority, at a subsequent stage, requested supporting documentation for all sales transactions in the internal market for the period January 1996 through March 1999. In this regard, the Panel should understand that Frangosul spent a considerable amount of time and resource collecting and reporting normal value and export price information for a period in excess of three years. In particular, we recall that in Frangosul's case there were over 320,000 transactions in the internal market for just one given year.

Third, it was not until 12 October 1999, that the DCD informed Frangosul that the information submitted on 27 April 1999 was not sufficient to make a dumping analysis. It was also at that moment that the DCD established the dumping data collection period. Thus, in accordance with the authority's instructions (more

---

[73] United States - Anti-Dumping Measures on Certain Hot-Rolled Steel Products from Japan, 28 February 2001, WT/DS184/R, DSR 2001:X, 4769, at para. 7.54 ("*United States - Hot Rolled Steel Products*"). The Appellate Body upheld the Panel's findings with respect to the United States inconsistency with Article 6.8 and Annex II of the Anti-Dumping Agreement in its application of facts available. United States - Anti-Dumping Measures on Certain Hot-Rolled Steel Products from Japan, 24 July 2001, WT/DS184/AB/R, DSR 2001:X, 4697, at para. 240 (adopted on 23 August 2001) ("*AB - United States - Hot Rolled Steel Products*").

[74] *Guatemala - Cement II*, DSR 2000:XI, 5295, at para. 8.251.

than eight months after initiation), Frangosul had to submit a new and more specific set of normal value data for a new period. This meant that Frangosul had to go back and collect specific information for the period January 1998 through January 1999, which sometimes meant manually having to search the many invoices (over 320.000) to find the information requested by the authority. Even though such information was submitted outside the deadline established by the DCD, it was still provided prior to the disclosure of the essential facts under consideration and the final determination.

Brazil considers that in light of the nature and quantity of the information submitted, the unreasonable burden imposed by the authority throughout the investigation, and the fact that Frangosul invited the authority to verify in its premises all documents of sales transactions (in the internal market and to Argentina), the authority should have considered that the information was submitted within a "reasonable period" and should have used it in the final determination.

Claim 19

To Brazil

46(a). Please provide a copy of Catarinense's questionnaire response of 3 November 1999.

Response

We have provided as Exhibit BRA-25 Catarinense's response to Section A of the dumping questionnaire. Catarinense's complete dumping questionnaire response, with list of invoices for all sales transactions to Argentina (Section B) with copies of invoices, list of invoices for all sales transactions in the internal market (Section C), and cost breakdown (Section D), comprises over 1.500 pages. We believe that such volume of information would not only be burdensome to collect and copy but would also serve very little purpose, since we understand that the Panel's objective is not whether the authority wrongfully calculated the normal value and export price for Catarinense but that it did *not* even consider any of the information submitted by the exporter.

We are, however, providing as Exhibit BRA-37 Catarinense's response to Section B of the questionnaire with a sample of the list of invoices of sales to Argentina for each month in 1998 and January 1999, as well as a sample of invoices reported for sales in each month of 1998 and January 1999; the response to Section C of the questionnaire with a sample of the list of invoices of sales in the internal market for each month in 1998 and January 1999; and, the response to Section D of the questionnaire.

If the Panel considers this information to be insufficient to examine the claims put forth by Brazil, we will gladly provide the complete set of Catarinense's response to the questionnaire.

46(b). Argentina asserts that Frangosul's normal value data was submitted out-of-time. Please comment.

Response

Please see the response to question 41 above.

Claim 23

To Brazil

49. When did Avipal first request a normal value adjustment for freight charges? Did Avipal provide supporting documentation with its request? If so, please provide a copy of that supporting documentation.

Response

Article 2.4 of the Anti-Dumping Agreement imposes an obligation on the investigating authority to make a fair comparison between the export price and the normal value. In making this fair comparison, due allowances must be made for differences, which affect price comparability. We understand freight charges to be included in such adjustments.

We note that the obligation in Article 2.4 of the Agreement is imposed on the investigating authority and that the exporter does not have to request that such an adjustment be made. Accordingly, in the course of the investigation, the DCD never requested supporting documentation from Avipal for such freight charges.

That being so, we point out that on 20 April 1999, Avipal and other exporters submitted a letter to the DCD that stated, among other things, that in order to compare the normal value proposed by petitioner (JOX publication) to the *ex factory* export price certain adjustments had to be made. Avipal provided a list with the value of such adjustments, including tax, ***national freight charges*** and financial cost.[75]

On 12 October 1999, the DCD established and informed Avipal, for the first time in the investigation, that the dumping period of data collection was from January 1998 through January 1999.[76] In this communication, the DCD also requested that Avipal present a list of invoices for all sales of poultry in the internal market for that period. The DCD did not provide a deadline for Avipal to submit this information.

On 21 December 1999, Avipal submitted a diskette with a list of invoices for sales of poultry in the home market for the period January 1998 through January 1999, including a spreadsheet with taxes (ICMS/PIS/COFINS), commission, ***freight*** and financial costs included in the normal value that should be deducted from an *ex factory* comparison with the export price.[77]

We understand that Argentina considers freight adjustment to have "a decisive and significant impact on price comparability".[78] It is interesting, however, that even though Argentina knows this adjustment is warranted and that it is "decisive and significant" for the price comparison, it simply decided not to make it. Even if no supporting documentation was provided (when, in fact, it was not even requested), Argentina still could have used a secondary source of information to estimate such deduction, as it did with the normal value adjustment to compensate the alleged characteristic differences between poultry sold to Argentina and in Brazil.

---

[75] *See*, Exhibit BRA-35.
[76] *See*, Page 44 of Exhibit BRA-15.
[77] *See*, Exhibit BRA-36.
[78] *See*, Argentina's first submission, at para. 211.

In that sense, we remind the Panel that JOX provided a response to the investigating authority's request for clarification of what taxes and charges were included in the prices published and used to determine normal value.[79] JOX letter to the DCD, of 3 August 1999, explained that the prices published by JOX included taxes (12 per cent - ICMS; 2.65 per cent - PIS/COFINS); financial costs; sales commission of 0.5 per cent to 1 per cent over the value of the sale; and, *a variable freight for delivery*, depending on the geographic location of the seller and the buyer.[80]

Even with this explanation provided by JOX, the investigating authority still chose not to make the freight adjustments to Avipal's normal value, required in a fair comparison.

50.   Is Brazil's argument regarding the investigating authority's failure to use information submitted by exporters limited to adjustments for the purpose of Article 2.4, or also to other factors / claims?

Response

Brazil's arguments regarding the investigating authority's failure to use information submitted by exporters is ***not*** limited to adjustments for purpose of Article 2.4 of the Agreement. Brazil has also argued failure of the investigating authority to use information submitted by exporters in the following claims:

Claim 17 - Argentina disregarded the export price provided by the Brazilian exporters and resorted, instead, to the export price information provided by the Argentinean agency *Ganaderia*;[81]

Claim 19 - Argentina disregarded all normal value information submitted by the Brazilian exporters Frangosul and Catarinense and resorted, instead, to information provided by petitioner[82], and,

Claim 27 - Argentina disregarded all listed and reported transactions in the internal market for the Brazilian exporters Sadia and Avipal in establishing normal value and in making the fair comparison and used, instead, only the internal market transactions for which invoices were submitted.[83]

Claims 23 - 27

To Brazil

51.   Please explain precisely what evidence was in the record that you consider the investigating authorities failed to use.

Response

We refer to the response to question 50 above.

Regarding **Claim 17**, Sadia provided export price information of poultry sold to Argentina for the period 1996 through February 1999.[84] Avipal provided export

---

[79] *See*, Exhibit BRA-32.
[80] *Ibid*.
[81] *See*, Brazil's first submission, at paras. 282 - 290.
[82] *See*, Brazil's first submission, at paras. 298 - 310.
[83] *See*, Brazil's first submission, at paras. 416 - 422.
[84] *See*, Exhibit BRA-22 and Pages 18 and 43 of Exhibit BRA-15.

price information of poultry sold to Argentina for the period 1996 through March 1999.[85] Frangosul provided export price information for individual export transactions of poultry sold to Argentina from January 1996 through March 1999, with respective supporting documentation.[86] Catarinesne provided export price information for individual transactions of poultry sold to Argentina from January 1998 through January 1999, with respective supporting documentation.[87]

In the final determination, the DCD established export price for all Brazilian exporters based on the import information from the Argentinean agency *Ganaderia* and disregarded (without justification) all export price data submitted by the Brazilian exporters.[88]

Regarding **Claim 19**, please refer to the responses to question 41 (Frangosul) and question 46(a) (Catarinense) above. Specifically, all normal value information submitted by these two exporters was disregarded in the final determination and the DCD used, instead, the normal value calculated for all other exporters. We note the fact that in the final determination the normal value used by the authority for all other exporters was that submitted by petitioner based on JOX published prices for chilled poultry with head and feet.

Regarding **Claim 27**, the following took place:

On 26 August 1999, Sadia sent a letter to the DCD with a list of invoices issued for the sales transactions in the home market for 1996 through 1998, and January and February 1999.[89] In this letter, Sadia explained that the great volume of sales in the home market made it impossible to provide an invoice copy for each transaction and invited the DCD to verify in *loco* the transactions listed or to select a sample of transactions so it could provide the corresponding invoices.[90] On 3 December 1999, the DCD sent a letter to Sadia requesting invoice copies of 372 selected sales transactions in the home market, establishing a 5-day deadline to submit the invoice copies.[91] On 13 January 2000, Sadia submitted copies of the invoices requested by the DCD.[92]

In the final determination, the DCD established normal value for Sadia based only on information for which supporting documentation was provided and not for all reported internal market transactions.[93]

On 12 August 1999, Avipal submitted a list of sales transactions in the home market for 1996 through 1999, with a sample invoice for each month in 1997 and 1998, and explanation that the great volume of sales in the home market made it impossible to provide an invoice copy for each transaction. In this letter, Avipal invited the DCD to verify *in loco* the transactions listed or to select a sample of transactions so it could provide the corresponding invoices.[94] On 1 September 1999,

---

[85] *See,* Exhibit BRA-23 and Pages 22 and 45 of Exhibit BRA-15.
[86] *See,* Exhibit BRA-24 and Pages 29 and 49 of Exhibit BRA-15.
[87] *See,* Exhibit BRA-25 and Pages 38 and 39 of Exhibit BRA-15.
[88] *See,* Pages 76, 77 and 104 of Exhibit BRA-15.
[89] *See,* Exhibit BRA-29.
[90] *Ibid.*
[91] *See,* Exhibit BRA-30.
[92] *See,* Page 62 of Exhibit BRA-15.
[93] *See,* Pages 62 and 63 of Exhibit BRA-15.
[94] *See,* Exhibit BRA-31.

Report of the Panel

Avipal provided translation of a standard invoice from Portuguese into Spanish.[95] On 21 December 1999, Avipal submitted a diskette with a list of invoices for sales of poultry in the home market for the period January 1998 through January 1999, including deductions and taxes.[96] The DCD never selected the transactions for which Avipal offered to provide invoice copies.

In the final determination, the DCD established normal value for Avipal based only on the transactions for which Avipal had provided invoice copies and not on all reported transactions in the internal market.[97]

As shown, Sadia and Avipal presented a list of all transactions in the internal market for the period. Invoices were presented for only some transactions in order for the DCD to verify the accuracy of the data submitted in the responses as a whole and not just those for which invoices were provided. Brazil understands that the magnitude of the information submitted may mean that not all data will accurately be examined, however, this does not exclude the validity of the data provided, particularly if that data could be verified.

It is important to note that not only did Sadia and Avipal report transactions for the period of investigation (January 1998 through January 1999) but they also provided information on the sales transactions outside the period of investigation (1996, 1997, 1998 and available data in 1999). To have that burden imposed on exporters and, then, for the investigating authority to use only some of the transactions during 1998 and January 1999 is contrary to how a margin should be established pursuant to Article 2.4 of the Agreement.

Claim 25

To Brazil

54. Please provide all of the exporters' replies to Sections B.2 and C.1.1 of the DCD's questionnaire (as set forth on "folios" 8 and 9 in Exhibit BRA-22).

Response

From the documents of the investigation to which Brazil had access to, Brazil was not able to identify the responses to Sections B.2 and C.1.1 of the dumping questionnaire for the Brazil exporters Sadia, Avipal and Frangosul.

If the Panel considers that the information on product description reported by the exporters in the investigation and, thus far, presented by Brazil in this dispute is not sufficient to examine this claim, we ask that the Panel request that Argentina provide the responses of these companies to Sections B.2 and C.1.1 of the dumping questionnaire. We understand that the Argentinean investigating authority has all of the confidential and non-confidential responses of the exporters submitted in the investigation and will be able to provide the requested information to the Panel.

We are providing, however, as Exhibit BRA-38 the injury questionnaire responses of the Brazilian exporters Sadia, Avipal and Frangosul, that also contains information on the product description. Also in Exhibit BRA-38, the Panel will find

---

[95] *See*, Page 64 of Exhibit BRA-15.
[96] *Ibid.*
[97] *Ibid.*

Catarinense's response to Section B.2 and Section C.1.1 of the dumping questionnaire.

Claim 34

To Brazil

61. If non-dumped imports are to be excluded for the purpose of an Article 3 injury analysis, doesn't this suggest that the determination of dumping must precede the determination of injury? If so, how is a Member to ensure that evidence of dumping and injury will be considered simultaneously in conformity with Article 5.7?

Response

Article 3.1 of the Agreement requires a determination of injury to be based upon positive evidence and involve an objective examination of the volume, the effect, and the impact of *"dumped imports"* on domestic producers. We understand that the injury analysis, as provided in Article 3 of the Agreement, must exclude imports that are *found not to be dumped* from the total imports subject to the investigation. To this regard, we find several indications in the provisions related to anti-dumping investigations that support our understanding.

First, Article VI:1 of the General Agreement on Tariffs and Trade of 1994 ("GATT") provides that dumping occurs when the *products* of one country are introduced into the commerce of another country at less than the normal value of the product. Thus, if certain products by one country are not being entered into the commerce of another country at prices below normal value, dumping does not occur. Consequently, those *products* from that country cannot be considered *"dumped imports"*.

Likewise, Article 2.1 of the Anti-Dumping Agreement provides that a *product* is to be considered as *being dumped* if the export price of the product exported from one country to another is less than the comparable price. The same reasoning applies, if the export price of a product exported from one country is not inferior to the comparable price in the exporting country, then those products cannot be considered as *being dumped*.

From the language of these provisions, it is clear that the definition of dumping is not related to all exports of a certain country that enter the commerce of another but to the exports of the *products* from a certain country, which enter the commerce of another at prices below the normal value.

Second, all of Article 3, with the exception of Article 3.3, refers to *"dumped imports"* as those imports that are *found to be dumped*. We find this to be true, since Articles 3.1, 3.2, 3.4, 3.5, 3.6, 3.7 and 3.8 explicitly refer to *"dumped imports"*, and not to imports subject to an investigation.

Since the definition of *"dumped imports"*, in Article 2.1, is used for purposes of the Agreement, and not only for purposes of that Article, we understand that the term in Article 3 conveys the same meaning.

Specifically, Article 3.5 of the Agreement is where this is most evident. Article 3.5 requires the demonstration that *"dumped imports"* are, through the effects of *dumping*, causing injury to the domestic industry. Thus, the causal link

Report of the Panel

analysis requires a demonstration that the imports with *"dumping effects"* be the cause of injury to the domestic industry, and not all imports, which also includes those imports found not to be dumped. Article 3.5 further requires that the demonstration of causal link, between the *"dumped imports"* and the injury to the domestic industry, be based on examination of all relevant evidence before the authorities. We find that evidence that imports from certain producers/exporters are not found to be dumped to be relevant evidence before the authorities. More importantly, Article 3.5 requires the investigating authority to examine *any known factors other than the dumped imports* which at the same time are injuring the domestic industry. Imports of the product found not to be dumped qualify as known factors other than the *"dumped imports"*. Article 3.5 even exemplifies such factors which may be relevant in this respect, such as the volume and prices of ***imports not sold at dumping prices***. In this sense, the volume and value of the imports from Nicolini and Seara was an important factor that should have been examined by the investigating authority in the causal link analysis.

As mentioned above, Article 3.3 is an exception to Article 3 of the Agreement. Article 3.3 refers to cumulation cases, where the authority may cumulatively assess the effects of *imports* where *imports* of more than one country are simultaneously subject to an anti-dumping investigation. It is important to mention that not only is this not the case here, since only the imports of one country were subject to the investigation, but also that Article 3.3 expressly refers to *"imports of a product"* rather than to *"dumped imports"*, being understood that for reasons of cumulation *all imports* are considered and not only the ones that are *being dumped*.

Third, further clarification is found when we look at the language in Article 9.2 of the Agreement:

> "When an anti-dumping duty is imposed in respect of any product, such anti-dumping duty shall be collected in the appropriate amounts in each case, or in a non-discriminatory basis on imports of such product from all sources found to be dumped and causing injury.(...)"
> (emphasis added)

The language in this provision supports the idea that only imports of a product, *which where found to be dumped*, from a certain producer/exporter may be considered as dumped imports. Again, not all imports of the product are subject to anti-dumping duties, only those products from producers/exporters that were *found* to be dumped.

This understanding is in agreement with the Panel's understanding in *EC - Bed Linen*:

> "(...) we consider that dumping is a determination made with reference to a **product** from a **particular producer/exporter**, and not with reference to individual transactions. That is, the determination of dumping is made on the basis of consideration of transactions involving a particular product from **particular producers/exporters**. If the result of that consideration is a conclusion that the product in question from **particular producers/exporters is dumped**, we are of the view that the conclusion applies to all imports of the product *from*

such source(s), at least over the period for which dumping was considered. (...)"[98] (emphasis added)

That Panel also found that:

*"(...) It is possible that a calculation conducted consistently with the AD Agreement would lead to the conclusion that one or another Indian producer should be attributed a zero or de minimis margin of dumping. In such a case, it is our view that the **imports attributable to such a producer/exporter may not be considered as "dumped" for purposes of the injury analysis. (...)"*[99] (emphasis added)

Likewise, in the present investigation, we believe that the Panel should come to the same conclusion, that is, that **only the total imports from any producer/exporter that was actually found to be dumping be considered as "dumped imports"**. Accordingly, The imports from Nicolini and Seara should not be included in the **"dumped imports"** evaluated under Article 3 of the Agreement.

That being said, we understand that the dumping analysis in an investigation should always precede the injury analysis. It has to be this way in order for the provisions in the Agreement to make sense.

For example, in Article 3.4 of the Agreement, one of the mandatory relevant economic factors to be evaluated in the examination of the impact of the dumped imports on the domestic industry is the magnitude of the *dumping margin*. If an injury analysis precedes the dumping analysis how can the injury analysis evaluate the magnitude of the dumping margin?

Also, if the injury analysis precedes the dumping analysis, the **"dumped imports"** in the injury analysis will always include the totality of the imports and not only those imports that the dumping analysis found to be dumped. For the reasons indicated above, we do not believe that the Agreement meant for imports found **not to be dumped** to be included in the term **"dumped imports"** for purposes of the injury and causal link analysis.

The injury analysis depends upon the findings in the dumping analysis and cannot, therefore, be subsequent to it.

In the response to question 23 above, we have provided our understanding of Article 5.7 of the Agreement. There, we have stated that we do not find it possible for an authority to consider evidence of dumping and injury simultaneously if the evidence considered by the authorities indisputably refers to non-related periods for dumping and injury. The *different periods* examined by the DCD and the CNCE in determining whether there was sufficient evidence of dumping and injury, indicates that the dumping and injury evidence was *not* considered simultaneously in the decision whether or not to initiate the investigation. We understand that the dumping determination need not consider trends over time, whereas the injury determination will normally require information covering more than one year in order to evaluate

---

[98] European Communities - Anti-Dumping Duties on Imports of Cotton-Type Bed Linen from India, 30 October 2000, WT/DS141/R, at DSR 2001:VI, 2077, para. 6.136 ("*EC - Bed Linen*"). The EC did not appeal the Panel's understanding of "dumped imports" in Articles 3.1, 3.4 and 3.5 of the Anti-Dumping Agreement. European Communities - Anti-Dumping Duties on Imports of Cotton-Type Bed Linen from India, 1 March 2001, WT/DS141/AB/R (adopted on 12 March 2001) ("*AB - EC- Bed Linen*"), DSR 2001:V, 2049.

[99] *EC - Bed Linen*, at para. 6.138.

volume and price changes. However, in order for an authority to consider dumping and injury evidence simultaneously, the evidence of dumping and injury should, at a minimum, relate to the same period, in order for that evidence to justify the initiation of an investigation. We repeat, evidence of dumping and injury cannot be considered simultaneously if such evidence relates to *different periods*.

To that regard, we turn to the considerations of the United States ("US") regarding this claim. The US affirms that the obligation in Article 5.7 of the Agreement is to consider the evidence of dumping and injury simultaneously.[100] According to the US, the term "simultaneously" is linked to the term "considered" and not to the term "evidence".[101] The US provides as an example of simultaneous consideration, consideration of dumping and injury evidence in "concurrent investigations".[102]

Brazil does not understand "simultaneous consideration" to mean consideration of dumping and evidence in concurrent investigations. Obviously, in all investigations evidence of dumping and injury have to be considered in concurrent investigations, otherwise the requirements in Article 5.2 and 5.3 of the Agreement are not met. If evidence of injury is considered in a different investigation than the investigation where evidence of dumping is considered, how could the requirement in Article 5.2, that the application include evidence of dumping, injury and causal link, be met? Likewise, how could the authorities examine the accuracy and adequacy of evidence provided in the application if dumping evidence is considered in a separate investigation from the injury evidence? We do not consider that the term "simultaneously" in Article 5.7 of the Agreement refers to consideration of dumping and injury evidence in concurrent investigations.

In addition, Brazil understands that the US Department of Commerce ("DOC"), responsible for dumping investigations, and the US International Trade Commission ("USITC"), responsible for injury investigations, do not issue their dumping and injury determination at the same time. In that sense and according to the interpretation of the term "simultaneously" given by the Panel in *Guatemala - Cement II*, the DOC and the ITC's consideration of dumping and injury evidence is not made simultaneously.

Even if Article 5.7 of the Agreement is to be understood as simultaneous consideration of evidence of dumping and injury, rather than sequential consideration, that also did not occur in this investigation. The Panel will be able to verify that the final affirmative injury determination was issued on 23 December 1999[103] and the final dumping determination was issued on 23 June 2000[104], exactly six months after the dumping evidence was considered. How could authorities have simultaneously considered the dumping and injury evidence if there was a six-month gap between the two considerations?

---

[100] *See*, US third party submission, at para. 3.
[101] *Ibid.*
[102] *Ibid.*
[103] *See*, Exhibit BRA-14.
[104] *See*, Exhibit BRA-15.

Claim 41

To Brazil

65. Regarding para. 87 of its first oral statement, is Brazil alleging that Argentina's failure to explain why it considered a percentage lower than 50 per cent "a major proportion" constitutes a violation of Article 4.1, or of some other provision of the AD Agreement? If so, please explain how this claim falls within the Panel's terms of reference.

Response

Brazil does not believe that CNCE's determination that 46 per cent of the total domestic production of the like product constituted the "major proportion" of the collective output of the domestic producers is consistent with Article 4.1 of the Agreement. We remind the Panel that the issue is exactly whether 46 per cent of the total domestic production of poultry in Argentina constitutes a "major proportion" of the total domestic production.

We have provided our understanding of the term "major proportion" in our first submission and, according to that interpretation, we understand Article 4.1 of the Agreement to provide that the domestic industry can either be represented by 100 per cent of the producers of the like product or by those whose production, jointly considered, constitutes *more than half* of the total domestic production. We understand this to be an objective benchmark that leaves very little room for confusion or abuse. There is no question that 51 per cent, 60 per cent, or 70 per cent of the total domestic production constitutes a "major proportion" of the total (100 per cent) domestic production.

Here, we find it appropriate to consider the arguments presented by Third Parties in respect to this claim.

First, Guatemala recognizes that the term "major" in the English version of the Agreement could imply a higher level of requirement than the term "importante" in the Spanish version.[105] However, Guatemala incorrectly considers that the term "importante" could not, *in any case*, be meant to constitute more than half of a whole, as provided by Brazil.[106] We do not agree that the term "importante" could not be understood *in any case* as more than half of the total production. If we follow Guatemala's reasoning, we could not consider the domestic industry as a "proporción importante" in a case where the domestic industry represents 70 per cent of the total domestic production, which is clearly the majority of the total production.

Second, the US provides as an initial matter that Article 4.1 of the Agreement is just a definition and, as such, does not impose an independent obligation on WTO Members.[107] We respectfully disagree with that position. Article 4.1 of the Agreement requires that the term "domestic industry" be interpreted as referring to the domestic producers as a whole or to those of them whose collective output of the products constitutes a major proportion of the total domestic industry. The term "domestic industry" cannot be interpreted any other way than that provided in Article

---

[105] *See*, Guatemala third party submission, at para. 21.
[106] *Ibid*.
[107] *See*, US third party submission, at para. 8.

4.1 of the Agreement. If a Member's investigating authority does so, it is not in compliance with what is required in Article 4.1 of the Agreement.

Furthermore, the US is mistaken when it states that the meaning of the term "major" cannot connote to mean "the majority".[108] We have provided in our fist submission that the term can have that connotation.[109]

The US also argues that Brazil's understanding that the term "major proportion" means "majority" "directly conflicts with the fact that the drafters were quite explicit, elsewhere in the Agreement, when they intended to impose a majority requirement for a particular obligation".[110] According to the US, Article 5.4 clearly imposes a "majority" requirement, whereas Article 4.1 establishes a "major proportion" requirement, which is a different standard.[111]

We agree with the US that the standard under Article 5.4 is different from that under Article 4.1 of the Agreement. In Article 5.4 of the Agreement, the requirement in order for an application to be considered as made by or on behalf of the domestic industry, is that the application be supported by those domestic producers whose collective output constitutes more than 50 per cent of the total production by that portion of the domestic industry expressing either support for or opposition to the application, as long as those producers that express support for the application constitute at least 25 per cent of the total domestic production. Article 5.4 refers to the standing of the producers supporting the application, while Article 4.1 refers to the definition of "domestic industry", with implications regarding the injury analysis. In fact, the threshold in Article 5.4 is lower than in Article 4.1 of the Agreement, since they refer to different standards.

Third, unlike the US, the European Communities ("EC") supports the position that the term "domestic industry" has the same meaning throughout the Anti-Dumping Agreement.[112] Here, the EC seems to imply that "major proportion" is defined by reference to the standing requirements of Article 5.4 of the Agreement, that is, producers accounting for at least 25 per cent of the total domestic production. We cannot agree that the term "major proportion" in Article 4.1, which is used as an alternative to domestic producers as a whole (100 per cent), could mean 25 per cent of the total domestic production. Nothing in the Anti-Dumping Agreement provides, or implies, that "producers expressly supporting the application" is equivalent to the "domestic industry" in an investigation.

Our view is that the term "major proportion" in Article 4.1 allows for determinations to be made in situations where the information for the industry as a whole is not available, so long as that information relates to producers that constitute more than 50 per cent of the total domestic production.

However, if the Panel understands that the Anti-Dumping Agreement does not provide a specific benchmark for what constitutes a "major proportion" of the total domestic production, then we believe that the investigating authority must elucidate how it found a percentage lower than 50 per cent to be a "major proportion". Otherwise, investigating authorities will have such wide discretion as to

---

[108] *See*, US third party submission, at para. 9.
[109] *See*, Brazil's first submission, at para. 514.
[110] *See*, US third party submission, at para. 10.
[111] *Ibid*.
[112] *See*, EC third party submission, at para. 51.

consider 46 per cent, 25 per cent or 10 per cent of the total domestic production as sufficient to constitute a "major proportion" of the total domestic industry. We cannot believe that this is the intention of the Agreement.

It is in the Panel's terms of reference to decide whether 46 per cent of the total domestic production of poultry in Argentina constitutes a "major proportion" of the total domestic production. In doing so, the Panel must consider the meaning of the term "major proportion". Such consideration must set forth what the investigating authority's reasoning is (or should be) in determining "major proportion" as a percentage lower than 50 per cent of total domestic production.

We recall that in Argentina's first submission, the only argument set forth was that Brazil's understanding of the term "major proportion" is subjective.[113] On the contrary, we understand that a finding by an investigating authority that a percentage lower than 50 per cent constitutes the "major proportion" of the total domestic production to be subjective. Accordingly, we believe that investigating authorities must elucidate how, in such instances, that proportion of the domestic industry can be understood as constituting a "major proportion".

---

[113] *See,* Argentina's first submission, at para. 302.

ANNEX A-5

SECOND ORAL STATEMENT OF BRAZIL
(26 November 2002)

INTRODUCTION

1. Brazil welcomes the opportunity to once again appear before the Panel and to present its positions on the dispute regarding Argentina's imposition of definitive anti-dumping duties on poultry from Brazil. We would like to reiterate our appreciation for the time and effort devoted by the Panel and the secretariat to this matter.

2. Similarly to what we have done in the first oral statement, Brazil will endeavour not to repeat the arguments that have already been offered many times in this proceeding. Brazil will simply address some of the main issues before the Panel in light of the arguments and responses provided by Argentina in its second submission (ASS) and in its response to the Panel's questions in the first substantive meeting (AR).

3. Before turning to our specific arguments, we will briefly comment on Argentina's position regarding the ruling by the Mercosul Ad Hoc Arbitral Tribunal and the applicability of the principle of good faith and *estoppel* to this case.

RULING BY THE MERCOSUL AD HOC TRIBUNAL

4. Argentina argues that Brazil's conduct in bringing the present dispute to the WTO is contrary to the principle of good faith because a similar dispute has already been brought, discussed and settled within Mercosul. According to Argentina, the present dispute before the Panel represents an exercise of Brazil's right that is contrary to the principle of good faith and, thus, the Panel should prevent Brazil from invoking its rights under the WTO by applying the principle of *estoppel*.[1]

5. Brazil strongly opposes Argentina's allegation and affirms that the exercise of its rights under the WTO is ***not*** contrary to the principle of good faith.

6. In that regard, we recall that the claims of the dispute before this Panel are ***not*** the same as the claims that were before the Mercosul Tribunal. The Mercosul Tribunal dealt with the dispute based on whether provisions that make up Mercosul's framework were correctly interpreted, applied or complied with in the anti-dumping investigation carried out by the Argentinean authorities.[2] The claims raised in Brazil's request for the establishment of a WTO Panel relate to Argentina's non-compliance of its obligations in the WTO, in particular under the Anti-Dumping Agreement.[3]

7. Argentina's allegation that Brazil has not acted in accordance with the principle of good faith by first resorting to the Mercosul dispute settlement

---

[1] Argentina Second Submission ("ASS"), para. 6.
[2] *See*, Article 1 of the Brasília Protocol.
[3] *Argentina - Definitive Anti-Dumping Duties on Poultry from Brazil: Request for the Establishment of a Panel by Brazil*, WT/DS241/3 (26 Feb. 2002).

mechanism and then resorting to the WTO dispute settlement system with respect to the same dispute[4] is not correct. We have shown that the disputes are not the same.

8. Furthermore, the Mercosul Tribunal itself found that it did not have the appropriate jurisdiction to examine claims of WTO violations. We recall that the Mercosul Tribunal found that Mercosul anti-dumping rules for trade within the region were not properly in force[5] and that Mercosul Member States were allowed to apply their domestic anti-dumping legislation with respect to regional trade.[6]

9. The Tribunal further established that the discrepancies related to the existence of requirements for the application of anti-dumping duties, that is, whether there was dumping, injury and causal link, were not aspects that were up to the Tribunal to clarify.[7] Thus, the Tribunal itself recognized that its jurisdiction was limited.

10. Moreover, we understand that Article 23 of the DSU mandates exclusive jurisdiction in favor of the DSU for WTO violations.

11. Article 3.2 of the DSU provides that the WTO dispute settlement system "serves to preserve the rights and obligations of Members under the covered agreements". Accordingly, it is Brazil's right to have the Panel hear and decide its claims brought before it. To interpret otherwise would diminish Brazil's rights under the WTO covered agreements.

12. Regarding Argentina's allegation that the principle of *estoppel* should be invoked in this WTO dispute, we restate that simply because Brazil has brought a related - but different - dispute to the Mercosul Tribunal does not mean that Brazil has accepted to relinquish its right to bring the current dispute before the Panel. We accentuate the fact that the dispute before this Panel is based on a different legal basis than the dispute brought before the Mercosul Tribunal.

13. Even by Argentina's standard of what constitutes estoppel - a statement of fact which is clear, unambiguous, voluntary, unconditional and authorized, which is relied upon in good faith[8] - the Panel will verify that no such statement was made on behalf of Brazil renouncing its right to bring a dispute, based on different claims, to the WTO.

14. Alternatively, Argentina appears to argue that, in considering the claims brought forth by Brazil in this dispute, the Panel cannot ignore the ruling by the Mercosul Tribunal in keeping with the rules of international law applicable in the relations between the parties, pursuant to Article 31.3(c) of the Vienna Convention on the Law of Treaties ("Vienna Convention"), and as provided in Article 3.2 of the DSU.[9] Concerning this allegation, the following considerations are in order.

15. First, Argentina requests that the Panel consider the Mercosul rules used by the Mercosul Tribunal in interpreting the current dispute before the Panel.[10] We cannot reasonably presume that a ruling by the Mercosul Tribunal, which does not even address the Anti-Dumping Agreement, is to be used in the interpretation of

---

[4] ASS, para. 10.
[5] Award of the Fourth Mercosul *Ad Hoc* Arbitral Tribunal, 21 May 2001, at paragraph 131.
[6] *Ibid.*, para. 153.
[7] *Ibid.*, para. 214.
[8] ASS, para. 13.
[9] *Ibid.*, para. 7.
[10] *Ibid.*, para. 29.

provisions of that Agreement, which binds over 140 WTO Members that are not Members of Mercosul.

16. Second, Brazil reaffirms that Article 3.2 of the DSU deals exclusively with the clarification of the existing provisions of the WTO Agreement. It is clear from the language in Article 3.2 that the dispute settlement system "serves to preserve the rights and obligations of Members under the "covered agreements" and to clarify the existing provisions of *those agreements*".

17. Contrary to Argentina's understanding,[11] Article 3.2 of the DSU is, in fact, limited to the rules of interpretation used to clarify the existing provisions of the WTO Agreement and bears no association to the relationship between previous rulings by an international tribunal and the rights and obligations of WTO Members under the "covered agreements".

INITIATION OF THE DUMPING INVESTIGATION

(a) Article 5.2 - Lack of Evidence in the Application

18. According to Argentina, the JOX publication of 30 June 1997, presented in the application, contained information on "whole poultry". Specifically, that publication provides the price of chilled poultry with head, feet and giblets sold in São Paulo, Brazil.[12] Argentina has *affirmed* that this "physical characteristic" difference affects prices and that the difference holds a value equivalent to the demand in view of markets' characteristics.[13]

19. Even though Argentina alleges that these differences affect prices, Argentina failed to show where in the application or in the determination to initiate the investigation evidence was presented to support this allegation. In fact, Argentina *assumes* that the alleged differences have such effects *solely* based on the product description of the JOX publication.

20. Argentina has also stated that the evidence presented by petitioner to the authority contained sufficient data, within the meaning of Article 5.2 of the Agreement, that: (1) there were physical characteristic differences in the product used as basis to calculate normal value; (2) that in so far as these differences affected the commercial yield of the products object of comparison, there *unquestionably* was an impact in the price comparability; and, (3) that such differences merited an adjustment that would allow, prior to initiation, a fair comparison, for which an adjustment methodology was presented.[14]

21. Apparently, Argentina *assumes* that from the data provided in the JOX price publication an investigating authority could *infer* that all poultry sold in Brazil contains head and feet; that such differences affect price comparability; that an adjustment was, thus, warranted and that the methodology presented by petitioner was justified. However, once again, Argentina does not indicate the *evidence* presented in the application that would support the investigating authority's conclusions that petitioner's adjustment, as proposed, was necessary for purposes of making a fair comparison between export price and normal value.

---

[11] *Ibid.*, para. 23.
[12] Argentina Response to the Panel's Questions in the First Substantive Meeting ("AR"), question 5.
[13] *Ibid.*
[14] ASS, para. 36.

22. Even though Argentina appears to agree with Brazil's definition of "evidence"[15], Argentina still fails to indicate what "information drawn from a document tending to prove a fact or proposition"[16] was used to support the allegation that these differences affect price comparability and justify the methodology used for the normal value adjustment.

23. In responding to the Panel's question as to whether Argentina considered that the JOX price publication for only one day (30 June) was all the information "reasonably available to the applicant" on normal value, Argentina replied that although petitioner submitted the value for one day, this value indicated the *trend* of prices in the market as well as the causes of the existence of its variations.[17]

24. Here, Brazil cannot agree that the JOX price published for only one day in 1997 could reasonably indicate *a trend* of prices in the market for a six-month period.

25. In that regard, Argentina affirms that the "evidence provided [in the application] is a representative value taken from a specialized publication for a given period."[18] When asked what the term "given period" meant, Argentina categorically stated that even though the JOX publication provides for the price in effect on 30 June 1997, one can see in the right margin of that publication that the "production of the parallel market of São Paulo's inland is clearly inferior, which has maintained the price in solid ground".[19] According to Argentina, this information reflects that the price published by JOX did not vary considerably and has maintained its stability.[20] We understand this to be Argentina's reasoning for not providing JOX price publication for other months in 1997, in the establishment of the normal value.

26. Here, we call the attention of the Panel to the fact that the information quoted by Argentina in the JOX publication refers to the **live** poultry market and ***not*** to the frozen or chilled poultry market (slaughtered poultry), a market, whose description by the same publication, does not contain the reference cited by Argentina. Thus, Argentina tries to use the explanation in the JOX publication for a different product, **live poultry**, to justify not requesting, or using, prices for more than one day in 1997 for chilled poultry, a product that is completely different from live poultry. Brazil does not accept this as a reasonable explanation for the establishment of normal value based on only one day in 1997.

27. Furthermore, the JOX price publication used by petitioner in the application is a daily publication. Accordingly, Brazil has provided Exhibit BRA-19, which demonstrates that normal value information for all of 1996 and 1997 was "reasonably available" to petitioner. This Exhibit shows that petitioner could have attached information on prices of poultry published by JOX for all months of 1997 but, instead, chose to provide it for one single day in that year.

28. According to Argentina's own definition, the phrase "reasonably available evidence to the applicant" in Article 5.2 is defined as evidence that may be obtained

---

[15] AR, question 6.
[16] Brazil First Submission ("BFS"), para. 63.
[17] AR, question 7.
[18] Argentina First Submission ("AFS"), para. 50.
[19] AR, question 12.
[20] *Ibid.*

by an applicant without an excessive burden of proof that would make the presentation of the application impossible.[21]

29. Brazil understands that the JOX price publication for all months of 1997 was information that could have been obtained by the applicant without an excessive burden of proof and would have made the presentation of the application possible.

30. Argentina also affirms that the JOX price publication for 30 June 1997 was considered normal value evidence submitted in the application and that the investigating authority did not require additional information on it.[22] Argentina understands that the authority did not find it necessary to request additional information with respect to the physical characteristic differences mentioned in the application and the adjustment provided by the applicant, taking into account the standard of information to be considered in that stage of the investigation (that is, prior to initiation).[23]

31. We find that this statement actually proves that the authority failed to examine the accuracy and adequacy of the information provided in the application. This adjustment to normal value was so important that without it the applicant could not have alleged the existence of dumping and, thus, the investigation could not have been initiated. It was obvious from the information provided in the application that the investigating authority, fully aware of the impact of the adjustment, should have required, and used, additional information.

32. Accordingly, Brazil understands that Argentina neither gave consideration to the impact of the possible differences on the sufficiency of the evidence submitted in the application, nor did it seek further evidence, as confirmed by Argentina.

(b) *Article 5.3 - Accuracy and Adequacy of the Evidence Provided in the Application*

33. Brazil reaffirms its position that the method adopted by Argentina to establish the export price, and consequently the dumping margin, was based only on export prices below the normal value, which in turn would always result in a dumping margin.[24] Brazil has also affirmed that the methodology adopted by the Argentinean authority is, in fact, the "zeroing" methodology.[25]

34. Argentina has confirmed our understanding that in establishing the dumping margin for purposes of initiation, the investigating authority has taken all export transactions with prices below normal value, excluding those transactions that would result in a negative dumping margin.[26] Therefore, there is no doubt that the Argentinean methodology inflated the dumping margin and made sure that one existed.

---

[21] AR, question 8.
[22] AR, question 9.
[23] AR, question 11.
[24] Brazil First Oral Statement ("BFO"), paras. 24 and 25.
[25] BFO, para. 26.
[26] AR, question 11.b.

CONDUCT OF THE ANTI-DUMPING INVESTIGATION - EVIDENTIARY AND PUBLIC NOTICE REQUIREMENTS

(a)   Article 12.1 - Notification and Public Notice of the Initiation

35.   Regarding the claim of violation of Article 12.1 of the Agreement, Brazil has already demonstrated that the investigating authority **knew**, prior to initiation, of the existence and interest of at least five of the seven exporters that were not notified of the investigation almost eight months after it had been initiated.[27]

36.   Argentina seems to imply that the authority must notify only those parties that consider themselves interested in the investigation, within the meaning of Article 6.1.1 of the Agreement.[28] Argentina's reasoning is untenable; how can a party present itself as an interested party if it does not even know that an investigation has been initiated? That is exactly why Article 12.1 requires the authority to notify interested parties known to them.

37.   In explaining how it reconciles the fact that five exporters were listed (and identified) in the report initiating the investigation, but notified only eight months after initiation, Argentina confirms that it "knew" these exporters but that this alone did not constitute an "identification" that would have made it possible for the authority to send the corresponding questionnaires.[29] Presumably, Argentina is claiming that it did not have the addresses of those companies.

38.   Once again, Argentina tries to share the notification obligation imposed on the investigating authority with Brazil, by stating that the authority requested the co-operation of the Brazilian government in this identification.[30] This is simply not true; Brazil never received any communication from the Argentinean authorities requesting such information concerning those five **specific** exporters identified in the report.

(b)   Article 6.1.1 - Deadlines for Responses

39.   In response to the panel's question on the Article 6.1.1 issue, Argentina has explicitly stated that it does **not** apply a system where a lesser period is provided at the outset, as long as the total period, including extensions, is at least 30 days.[31] Argentina, in fact, confirms that the 30-day deadline from the outset is applicable in all situations. Nonetheless, in Argentina's Exhibits ARG-XLVI through ARG-LIII, we verify that the deadline set forth by the authority for the questionnaire responses was for a period **no longer than 20 days** from receipt of the mentioned notification.

40.   Taking into account the statement made by Argentina together with the fact that the deadline provided by the DCD was for a period no longer than 20 days and that the CNCE never sent the injury questionnaire to the seven exporters, it is clear that the investigating authorities were in violation of Article 6.1.1 of the Agreement.

---

[27] Brazil Second Submission ("BSS"), paras. 45 through 53.
[28] AR, question 24.
[29] AR, question 26.
[30] *Ibid.*
[31] AR, question 31.

(c) *Article 6.1.2 - Evidence Shall Be Made Available Promptly*

41. Brazil has asserted that Argentina did not make promptly available the evidence presented by the other interested parties in the investigation to the seven Brazilian exporters that were notified of the investigation almost eight months after it had been initiated.[32]

42. Once again, Argentina confuses the requirement under Article 6.1.2 by explaining that interested parties in the investigation are the parties that have qualified themselves in the investigation as interested parties and have manifested an interest to participate in the investigation.[33]

43. We do not agree with Argentina's understanding of Article 6.1.2. First, a party cannot qualify itself as an interested party in an investigation if it is not aware of the investigation. Second, a party need not qualify itself in an investigation in order to be a part of it. Third, the lack of interest of a party in an investigation does not exclude or diminish the obligation of the investigating authorities of promptly making available to them evidence presented in writing by other interested parties.

44. Argentina seems to think that an interested party is only included in an investigation once it has requested to participate in that investigation.[34] This reasoning simply does not make sense. There is nothing in the Anti-Dumping Agreement that requires parties to request participation in an investigation in order to be included in that investigation. In order for a party to be included in an investigation, the party must simply be a producer/exporter of the product subject to the investigation.

(d) *Article 6.8 and Article 12.2.2 - Inappropriate Use of Facts Available*

45. With respect to the authority's disregard of the responses provided by the Brazilian exporters on the description of the product sold to Argentina and in Brazil, Argentina has firmed its position that only information provided by the exporters that was accompanied by supporting documentation was used by the authority in establishing the normal value.[35]

46. In its second submission, Brazil has demonstrated that Argentina's lack of supporting documentation argument did not entitle the authority to resort to facts available.[36] The Panel will note that Sadia, Avipal, Frangosul and Catarinense provided responses in the questionnaire regarding the description of the product sold to Argentina and in Brazil.[37] The Panel will also note that the questionnaires did not **specify** that the product description information required supporting documentation. Furthermore, the investigating authority did not, at any moment during the course of the investigation, request specific information, clarification or supporting documentation on the product description responses submitted by these exporters.

47. In addition, the investigating authorities never informed these exporters that their information would not be accepted and, thus, never provided the exporters an

---

[32] BFS, paras. 215 through 220.
[33] AR, question 32.
[34] ASS, para. 50 (last sentence).
[35] *Ibid.*, para. 54.
[36] BSS, paras. 62 through 81.
[37] Exhibits BRA-22, BRA-23, BRA-24, BRA-25 and BRA-26.

opportunity to provide explanations or supplemental documentation, pursuant to Paragraph 6 of Annex II of the Agreement.

48. Brazil understands that Article 6.1 of the Agreement requires authorities to give notice to all interested parties of the information that is required. Consequently, if an investigating authority does not clearly specify what information is required, the investigating authority cannot resort to facts available and punish the interested party for not submitting such information. Likewise, Paragraph 1 of Annex II of the Agreement also requires authorities to specify in detail the information required from any interested party.

49. Furthermore, the Brazilian Government specifically objected the authority's adjustment calculation. Nonetheless, the Argentinean authority still made the adjustment to normal value based on the adjustment proposed in the application, even though petitioner did not provide supporting documentation for its proposed adjustment.

50. In this regard, we understand that the authority failed to use "special circumspection", within the meaning of Paragraph 7 of Annex II, in applying the arbitrary adjustment to normal value as suggested by petitioner in the application.

51. Still with respect to Article 6.8 of the Agreement, the authority also disregarded the export price provided by all Brazilian exporters and, instead, established the export price based on the import information from the Argentinean agency *Ganaderia*.

52. In particular, Argentina explains, for the first time, that the information provided by Frangosul and Catarinense was not used simply because in Frangosul's case the information submitted was insufficient and outside the deadline, and in the case of Catarinense because the information was considered insufficient.[38]

53. This explanation seems to contradict Argentina's own response that Frangosul provided supporting documentation for the export prices reported in the investigation.[39] It is noteworthy that Argentina does not respond to the Panel's question on whether the DCD had sufficient export price data for Frangosul and Catarinense.[40] The answer to that question would be that not only did Frangosul and Catarinense provide all the export price data requested by the authority within a reasonable period but they also provided the corresponding supporting documentation.[41]

54. The Panel should also note that the Brazilian exporters Sadia, Avipal, Frangosul and Catarinense provided export price information on poultry sold to Argentina for the period 1996 through 1999, as required by the authority.[42]

(e) *Article 6.10 - Individual Margin of Dumping*

55. On the claim of violation of Article 6.10, Argentina apparently seems to justify not calculating individual margins for Frangosul and Catarinense based on the

---

[38] ASS, para. 56.
[39] AR, question 45.
[40] *Ibid.*
[41] Pages 29, 38, 39 and 49 of Exhibit BRA-15.
[42] Pages 18, 22, 29, 38, 39, 43, 45 and 49 of Exhibit BRA-15.

argument that the normal value information provided by these companies was not accompanied by supporting documentation.[43]

56. We have already presented our views as to Argentina's inappropriate use of facts available based on lack of supporting documentation. In the case of Frangosul, the authority changed the scope of the dumping period of data collection more than eight months after the investigation had initiated and requested supporting documentation for all sales transactions in the internal market. By doing so, the investigating authority did not act in a reasonable, objective and impartial manner and could not have resorted to facts available.[44] In the case of Catarinense, the investigating authority never requested supporting documentation for the sales transactions in the home market reported by the company.[45]

57. Furthermore, we have demonstrated that both Frangosul and Catarinense provided the required export price data with supporting documentation but the authority nonetheless disregarded that information.

58. In that regard, we refer to Argentina's explanation that it was evident that the investigating authority did not count on the necessary elements to calculate the individual margins of dumping.[46] According to Argentina, this margin appears from the relationship between both values, the export price and the normal value; no supporting documentation was provided for the latter.[47]

59. We point out to the Panel that even though the investigating authority also disregarded the export price information submitted by the exporters Sadia and Avipal, the investigating authority still calculated the individual margins of dumping for those two companies. Brazil fails to see the reason why the authority decided to proceed differently with respect to the information provided by Frangosul and Catarinense.

CONDUCT OF THE ANTI-DUMPING INVESTIGATION - FINAL AFFIRMATIVE DETEMINATION

(a) Article 2.4 - Fair Comparison

60. On the claim that Argentina failed to make due allowance for freight in the normal value of the exporters Sadia and Avipal, Argentina admits that Sadia presented in Annex VIII the internal freight costs for sales in the internal market.[48] Argentina further explains that this adjustment should have been made had Sadia presented supporting documentation.[49]

61. What Argentina fails to state is that after Sadia submitted the internal freight cost data in Annex VIII of its questionnaire response, the investigating authority never requested additional information, clarification or supporting documentation regarding internal freight costs.[50]

---

[43] AR, questions 44 and 45.
[44] Brazil's Response to the Panel's Questions in the First Substantive Meeting ("BR"), question 41.
[45] BFS, para. 250.
[46] AR, question 45.
[47] Ibid.
[48] ASS, para. 71.
[49] Ibid.
[50] AR, question 47, Exhibit ARG-XLIV.

62. Even though Argentina agrees that this adjustment has "a decisive and significant impact on price comparability",[51] it still maintains that the investigating authority would have acted incorrectly if it had made this specific discount.

63. We have already demonstrated that the authority could have used a secondary source of information to estimate such deduction, as it did with the normal value adjustment to compensate the alleged characteristic differences between poultry sold to Argentina and in Brazil, but it chose not to.[52]

64. Furthermore, Exhibit ARG-LVI presents a letter from Sadia and Avipal's attorney to the investigating authority *explicitly* stating that the normal value established for Sadia and Avipal incorrectly included internal freight costs.[53] Even so, the investigating authority still did not make the required freight adjustment to the normal value of these two companies.

65. On the claim relative to Argentina's failure to make due allowance for differences in taxation, freight and financial cost in the normal value established for all other exporters, if the authority found that the JOX information was so reliable as to make adjustments concerning physical characteristics that were not warranted, why did the authorities not consider the JOX information on taxation, freight and financial cost adjustments reliable?

66. We underline that the JOX information on taxation, freight and financial cost adjustments was provided as a result of a request made by the investigating authority and not by any interested party in the investigation. If the JOX response was provided in Portuguese, the authorities themselves should have either translated the information or requested that JOX provide a translation. Instead, the investigating authority chose not to consider that information and not to make the required adjustments.

67. Argentina argues that the JOX information was not taken into account because it would result in an improper comparison between an *ex factory* price for the normal value and an FOB export price. According to Argentina, there was no identical information on the deductions to be made from the export values of the goods.[54]

68. Brazil recalls that an FOB price includes inland freight to the port of exportation, inland insurance, handling and loading charges. An FOB price, however, does not include taxes and financial cost. Thus, there were no adjustments to be made to the FOB export price with respect to taxes and financial cost. Because the FOB price does not include taxes and financial cost the authority should have, at least, made an adjustment in the normal value to exclude taxes and financial cost (included in JOX prices), in making a fair comparison. In doing so, the authority would still be left with a normal value price that was not exactly *ex factory* - for it would still include internal freight charges - but the comparison would be on a more similar level of trade. These deductions would have permitted a fair comparison.

69. On the claim that the investigating authority imposed an "unreasonable burden" on exporters, Brazil would merely like to clarify that Argentina's statement

---

[51] AFS, para. 211.
[52] BFO, para. 53.
[53] Exhibit ARG-LVI.
[54] AFS, para. 229.

Report of the Panel

that the investigating authority did not request or require during the investigation that all invoices be presented is not true.[55]

70. The investigating authority did, in fact, request supporting documentation for all of the sales transactions in Brazil and to Argentina. The Panel will confirm this by looking at pages 18, 19, 22, 23, 27, 29 and 30 of Exhibit BRA-15. We recall that exporters Sadia, Avipal and Frangosul complained that this requirement was excessive and impossible to meet due to the great volume of sales in the home market.[56]

(b)   Article 3 - Injury Determination

71. Regarding the claims of violation on the use of different periods to evaluate the relevant economic factors and indices listed in Article 3.4, Argentina maintains that an authority is not obligated to examine any of the factors outside the period of investigation.[57]

72. We agree with Argentina that an authority is not obligated to examine any Article 3.4 factor outside the period of investigation. However, this is not the case at issue. In this investigation, the Argentinean authority considered a certain period of injury analysis for the factors production, prices, imports, exports and apparent consumption and considered another period of injury analysis for the remaining Article 3.4 factors.

73. In explaining its position, Argentina provides that the authority considered some factors with the purpose of ratifying the trend observed during the period of investigation.[58] In that sense, the investigating authority evaluates certain relevant factors for a given period outside the period of investigation by way of reference.[59]

74. The Panel can verify that, in this investigation, that is not how the Argentinean authority proceeded. Brazil believes that if the investigating authority had examined the factors production, prices, imports, exports and apparent consumption for the first semester of 1999 by way of reference, the authority would have stated so in the final injury determination just as it did with respect to the data for the year 1995.[60]

75. In the final injury determination, the authority explicitly stated that it took into account data for the year 1995 as a reference year. Because the data collected for 1995 was used just as a reference and was not included in the authority's examination, the investigating authority didn't even mention the year 1995 in its narrative evaluation of Article 3.4 factors. The Panel will note that for all factors that were evaluated in the injury determination, the authority begins its evaluation with the year 1996. Likewise, in the Tables attached to the final injury determination, the data for 1995 even appears in a different shade from the rest of the data with an indication at the bottom of each Table that the year 1995 is used as a reference period.

---

[55] AR, question 52.
[56] Exhibits BRA-29, BRA-31 and BRA-26.
[57] AR, question 59.
[58] Ibid.
[59] Ibid.
[60] Page 9 of Exhibit BRA-14.

76. Unlike the data for 1995, the investigating authority made a narrative evaluation for the factors production, prices, imports, exports and apparent consumption, taking into account the first semester of 1999.[61] In the same manner, the data for the first semester of 1999 in the Tables relating to the factors production, prices, imports, exports and apparent consumption appear in the same shade as the data for the period January 1996 through December 1998,[62] and there is *no* indication that the data for the first semester of 1999 is used only by way of reference.[63]

77. Regarding the authority's failure to exclude the imports of the Brazilian exporters Nicolini and Seara from the "dumped imports" in the injury analysis, we must point out that instead of citing the final determination to ensure that non-dumped imports were excluded for the purposes of the injury analysis, Argentina tries in its first submission to explain that because "the average FOB prices for the other imports investigated were lower than the prices of companies that did not practice dumping, it follows that their sale on the domestic market would inevitably yield international prices even lower than the prices determined by the CNCE in its final determination".[64]

78. We fail to see how this explanation proves that the imports from Nicolini and Seara were *effectively* taken out of the total "dumped imports" in the injury analysis.

79. On the other hand, Brazil has shown that the injury analysis in the final determination never mentioned the exclusion of the imports from these two Brazilian exporters.[65] Brazil has found additional support on the fact that the final injury determination was issued on 23 December 1999, and preceded by six months the final dumping determination, which was issued on 23 June 2000.

80. Furthermore, Argentina states that the investigating authority took into account the determination that there was no dumping by Nicolini and Seara, when analysing the causal link relationship.[66] This alone is a clear indication that in the injury analysis the authority did not exclude the non-dumped imports. After all, it is in the injury determination that authorities must examine the volume, the effect, and the impact of the "dumped imports".

81. Even if we look at the causal link determination, we find no indication that Nicolini and Seara's imports were excluded from the total "dumped imports".[67] We repeat, the final causal link determination simply restated what was already provided in the final dumping determination.

82. Let's now turn to Argentina's allegation that the factor actual and potential decline in productivity was specifically analysed in the final injury determination.[68]

83. Brazil has not found in the final determination a specific analysis of the factor productivity over the injury period of investigation. There is also no specific data in the final determination or in the Tables attached to the determination that present an explicit analysis of that factor. What Argentina has presented is the evaluation by the authority of the factors production capacity, utilization of capacity, employment,

---

[61] Pages 9, 10, 14, 15, 16 and 25 of Exhibit BRA-14.
[62] Tables 1, 5, 15b- 16, 22-29 and 30-31 of Exhibit BRA-14.
[63] *Ibid.*
[64] AFS, para. 269.
[65] Exhibit BRA-14.
[66] AFS, para. 266.
[67] Exhibit BRA-16.
[68] AR, question 59.

wages, cost structure and sales in the internal market, but *not* the evaluation for the factor productivity.

84.   To that effect, Argentina mentions that the determination provided that "in general terms, the relative stability of the number of employees in relation to the increase observed in the production, would be indicating a greater physical productivity of labour, probably due to the incorporation of the aforementioned technology".[69] We fail to see how that qualifies as a specific analysis of the factor productivity for the injury period of investigation and where the data regarding productivity for that period is indicated.

85.   Furthermore, Argentina indicates that the investigating authority relied on a letter presented by petitioner on 2 December 1999 to evaluate the factor productivity.[70] On this issue, Brazil makes the following considerations.

86.   First, the letter presented by petitioner contained no data, or supporting documentation, regarding its allegation.[71] Second, Argentina cites a passage in the final determination that refers to the arguments by the parties and not to the authority's evaluation of factors in the impact examination.[72] The authority simply restated in the final determination part of the letter presented by petitioner and failed to evaluate and consider data for the factor productivity for the injury period of investigation.[73]

87.   Brazil also stresses the fact that Argentina has not indicated where in the final determination the factor magnitude of the dumping margin was evaluated. In this respect, Argentina has not responded to the Panel's question to comment on paragraph 81 of Brazil's first oral statement.[74] This omission is not surprising. Brazil has already established that the investigating authority did not and could not have evaluated this factor because the final dumping determination, with the dumping margin, was issued six months after the final injury determination was issued.

88.   In addition, Argentina has also failed to indicate where in the final determination there is a *specific* evaluation of data for the factors cash flow, growth and ability to raise capital and investments for the injury period of investigation.

89.   In examining claims 38 through 40, the Panel should keep in mind that even though some factors may not have been relevant or weighed significantly in the decision of the investigating authority, the authority was still obligated to explain its conclusion as to the lack of relevance or significance of such factors and could not have simply disregarded them.

CONCLUSION

90.   Members of the Panel, the purpose of this statement is merely to address some of the main or new arguments raised by Argentina in its second written submission and in its response to the Panel's questions. We have tried not to repeat the arguments already set forth in previous stages of this proceeding and to offer

---

[69] Page 13 of Exhibit BRA-14.
[70] AFS, para. 279.
[71] Exhibit ARG-LX.
[72] Page 95 of Exhibit BRA-14.
[73] *Ibid.*
[74] AR, question 59.

additional clarification on the fundamental issues of this dispute. In this statement, we did not mention claims where Argentina's second submission and answers to the Panel's questions did not introduce any new or significant arguments.

91. In conclusion, we request that the Panel find that Argentina has acted inconsistently with the provisions of the Anti-Dumping Agreement as provided in the 41 claims presented in Brazil's first submission. We thank you for your time and attention and will be pleased to answer any questions you may have.

ANNEX A-6

REPLIES OF BRAZIL TO QUESTIONS OF THE PANEL - SECOND MEETING

(28 November 2002)

Questions to Brazil

Claim 22

90. It is stated in para. 319 of Brazil's First Written Submission that 'Frangosul and Catarinense submitted the requested information on normal value and export price, which was disregarded by the DCD without explanation.' Would Brazil agree that, if the data submitted by Frangosul and Catarinense had been disregarded in accordance with relevant provisions of the ADA, the investigating authority would not have been required to calculate an individual dumping margin for Frangosul and Catarinense? Please explain.

Response

Brazil would first like to clarify that Frangosul and Catarinense did, in fact, submit the requested normal value and export price information and that, therefore, the investigating authority could not have disregarded that information based on the relevant provisions of the Anti-Dumping Agreement. Consequently, the Argentinean authority was, in fact, required to calculate an individual dumping margin for Frangosul and Catarinense.

We understand that Argentina has alleged that the investigating authority could not calculate an individual margin of dumping for these two companies because the normal value information presented by them was not accompanied by supporting documentation.[1] In that regard, we present, once again, the chronology of the normal value and export price information presented by these two companies and the reasons why the DCD could have, and should have, calculated an individual margin of dumping for them.

Frangosul's Normal Value

Regarding the normal value data submitted by Frangosul, the Panel can verify that on **27 April 1999**, Frangosul responded to Section C of the questionnaire regarding sales to the domestic market. This information included sales of poultry in Brazil corresponding to the years 1996, 1997, 1998 and the first three months of 1999, separated by month.[2] The Panel will also note that, subsequently, the Argentinean authority requested supporting documentation for all of the sales transactions in the internal market covering that period.[3]

On 19 August 1999, Frangosul sent a letter to the DCD explaining that the great volume of sales in the internal market did not make it possible for the company

---

[1] Argentina Response to the Panel's Questions in the First Substantive Meeting ("AR"), questions 44 and 45.
[2] Page 29 of Exhibit BRA-15.
[3] Pages 29 and 30 of Exhibit BRA-15.

to provide copies of invoices for each transaction.⁴ In this letter, Frangosul indicated that over 320,000 invoices are issued in one given year for sales transactions in the internal market and that the invoices were available to the investigating authority for a verification *in loco* or for a selection of such documents for specific transactions to be used as sample.⁵

On **12 October 1999**, the DCD requested a new list of invoices with the total transactions in the internal market for the period January 1998 through January 1999, so that the DCD could select a sample and subsequently request the supporting documentation for that sample.⁶ This was the *first time* that the investigating authority informed Frangosul what the dumping period of data collection was.

On **30 December 1999**, Frangosul presented a diskette with the list of invoices for the sales transactions in the internal market for the period January 1998 through January 1999.⁷ The investigating authority never selected the specific transactions for which Frangosul was supposed to present the supporting documentation.

On **5 January 2000**, the DCD notified Frangosul of the end of the evidence-producing stage of the investigation.⁸

Brazil understands that the application of Article 6.8 of the Agreement is also dependent upon the actions of the authority in an investigation. If an investigating authority does not act in a proper manner during the investigation, it cannot claim that the interested party did not comply with the requirements of Article 6.8 and, thus, resort to the application of facts available. To support this understanding, we have turned to the Panel's consideration in *Guatemala - Cement II* on the interpretation of the application of Article 6.8 of the Agreement:

> "(...) We do not consider that a failure to cooperate necessarily constitutes significant impediment of an investigation, since in our view the AD Agreement does not require cooperation by interested parties at any cost. Although there are certain consequences (under Article 6.8) for interested parties if they fail to cooperate with an investigating authority, in our view such consequences **only** arise if the investigating authority itself has acted in a reasonable, objective and impartial manner (...)"⁹ (emphasis added)

Because the Argentinean authority changed the scope of the dumping period of data collection more than eight months after the investigation had initiated and, in the beginning of the investigation, requested supporting documentation for all sales transactions in the internal market for a period over 3 years, we understand that the authority did not act in a reasonable, objective and impartial manner and could not have resorted to the use of facts available.

---

⁴ Exhibit BRA-26.
⁵ *Ibid.*
⁶ *Ibid.*
⁷ *Ibid.*
⁸ *Ibid.*
⁹ Guatemala - Definitive Anti-Dumping Measures on Grey Portland Cement from Mexico, 24 October 2000, WT/DS156/R, DSR 2000:XI, 5295, at para. 8.251 (adopted on 17 November 2000) (*"Guatemala - Cement II"*).

Catarinense's Normal Value

With respect to the normal value data submitted by Catarinense, we observe that Catarinense was notified of the investigation and the need to respond to the dumping questionnaire on **15 September 1999**, almost eight months after the investigation had initiated.[10] In this notification, the DCD established that the normal value and export price information to be provided was for the period January 1998 through January 1999.

On 3 November 1999, Catarinense provided the questionnaire response with information on sales transactions to Argentina, disaggregated by transaction, with supporting documentation, as well as the information on sales transactions in Brazil, disaggregated by transaction, without supporting documentation.[11] The Argentinean authority never requested the supporting documentation for Catarinense's sales transactions in the internal market, nor did it select specific transactions in the internal market for Catarinense to provide the corresponding supporting documentation.

Even though the authority notified Catarinense almost eight months after the investigation had initiated and after a preliminary dumping, injury and causal link determination had been issued, Catarinense still submitted the requested information. Nonetheless, the DCD disregarded the normal value information submitted by the exporter.

Frangosul and Catarinense's Export Price

Regarding the export price submitted by Frangosul and Catarinense, the Panel will note that both exporters reported the information, disaggregated by transaction, with the supporting documentation.[12] Apparently, even Argentina concurs with this fact.[13]

Even though Frangosul and Catarinense submitted the requested export price information with supporting documentation, the Argentinean authority still disregarded the export price data provided by them and resorted to facts available.

Here, it is important to note that even though the Argentinean authority also disregarded the export price data submitted by Sadia and Avipal, the authority still calculated the individual dumping margins for those two companies. We do not agree with Argentina's disregard of Sadia and Avipal's export price information, but we find it correct that the investigating authority still proceeded to calculate an individual dumping margin for those companies. We do not understand why, and cannot agree that, the investigating authority proceeded differently with respect to the information provided by Frangosul and Catarinense. There simply was no reason under Article 6.8 of the Agreement for the Argentinean authority to have disregarded the normal value and the export price (with supporting documentation) provided by these two exporters.

With that in mind, we respond the Panel's question by stating that there simply was no basis in the Agreement for the Argentinean authority to disregard the information provided by the exporters Frangosul and Catarinense.

---

[10] Exhibit BRA-13.
[11] Page 39 of Exhibit BRA-15.
[12] Pages 29 and 39 of Exhibit BRA-15.
[13] AR, question 45.

We point out that even if the two exporters had not submitted the appropriate information and the authority had correctly disregarded it in accordance with the relevant provisions of the Agreement, the investigating authority was still required to calculate an individual dumping margin for the two exporters, as provided under Article 6.10 of the Agreement. The fact that an exporter has not submitted the relevant and appropriate information to establish normal value and export price does not exclude the authority's obligation under Article 6.10 to calculate an individual margin of dumping for that exporter. The Panel will find a more detailed response regarding the difference between the obligation under Article 6.10 and the use of facts available under Article 6.8 in our response to questions 97 and 98.

91. It is stated in para. 324 of Brazil's First Written Submission that 'the DCD provided no explanation, either in the final determination or in any other document on the record of the investigation, as to why, in this case, it was not possible to determine an individual margin for Frangosul and Catarinense.' Would Brazil agree that, if the investigating authority had disregarded the data submitted by Frangosul and Catarinense in accordance with relevant provisions of the ADA, it would not have been required to explain in the final determination or in any other document on the record of the investigation why an individual dumping of margin for those exporters had not been calculated?

Response

We have provided in the response to question 90, that the investigating authority did not have legal basis under the Agreement to disregard the normal value and the export price data submitted by Frangosul and Catarinense and that, therefore, the authority was required to calculate an individual dumping margin for the two exporters.

However, even if the Argentinean authority could have disregarded the data submitted by Frangosul and Catarinense in accordance with the provisions of the Agreement, that is Article 6.8, the authority was still required to explain before the final determination and in the final determination why an individual dumping margin for those exporters had not been calculated.

In that sense, Article 6.9 of the Agreement provides that:

> "The authorities shall, before the final determination is made, inform all interested parties of the **essential facts** under consideration which form the basis for the decision whether or not to apply definitive measure. Such disclosure should take place in sufficient time for the parties to defend their interests" (emphasis added)

The calculation of the dumping margin is an essential fact under consideration as provided in Article 6.9 of the Agreement. Accordingly, if an authority decides to calculate the dumping margin for certain exporters based on information other than that provided by the exporters during the investigation, that too is an essential fact that should be informed prior to the final determination so that the parties can defend their interests. Even if the authority only provides that the information was disregarded in accordance with the relevant provisions of the Agreement but does not explain why the information was disregarded and why an individual margin of dumping was not calculated, how can the exporters defend their interests, as provided in Article 6.9?

Likewise, Article 12.2.2 requires that a public notice of conclusion with the imposition of a definitive duty contain "**all relevant information** on the matters of **fact and law and reasons** which have led to the imposition of final measures". In particular, Article 12.2.2. provides that such notice must contain:

"(...) (iii) the margins of dumping established and a full explanation of the reasons for the methodology used in the establishment and comparison of the export price and the normal value under Article 2(...)" (emphasis added)

Brazil understands that included in the *full explanation* of the reasons for the methodology used in the establishment of the export price and the normal value is the reason why the authority disregarded the export price and normal value provided by the exporters and why an individual margin of dumping for those exporters was not calculated.

Claim 23

92. Please comment on para. 210 of Argentina's first written submission.

Response

Argentina agrees that the investigating authority did not make the required freight reductions to Sadia's normal value. To justify the authority's error, Argentina argues that the authority could not have made the adjustment because it had not been properly documented. Argentina further argues that in Annex VIII of Sadia's questionnaire response, the exporter provided a general estimate of freight deductions. According to Argentina, the information used to calculate the normal value was based on an analysis of all invoices provided by Sadia in accordance with the sample used by the authority and that these invoices were not accompanied by any details concerning freight charges to be deducted.

Concerning these allegations, the Panel should note the following considerations.

It is a fact that Sadia presented, in Annex VIII of its questionnaire response of 20 April 1999, the costs of freight in the internal market.[14] If Argentina considers that the freight adjustment should have been made if supporting documentation had been submitted,[15] why didn't the Argentinean authority specifically request that Sadia provide additional or supplemental information, clarification or supporting documentation on the internal freight costs? Article 6.1 of the Agreement requires authorities to give notice of the information, which interested parties are required to present. Likewise, Paragraph 1 of Annex II of the Agreement **expressly** states that "investigating authorities should specify in **detail** the information required from interested parties". The Argentinean authority should have specified that supporting documentation for freight deductions was the type of information that Sadia was required to present. By not specifically indicating this to Sadia, there was no way that the exporter could have known that the information reported in Annex VIII was not going to be used.

Brazil is convinced that Argentina was fully aware of the need to make freight adjustments to Sadia's normal value. First, Sadia reported the freight cost in

---

[14] Argentina Second Submission ("ASS"), para. 71.
[15] *Ibid.*

the internal market in Annex VIII of its questionnaire response. Second, Exhibit BRA-32 provides a letter from JOX to the authority stating that the quoted prices in its publication include taxation, **freight** and financial costs. Third, Exhibit ARG-LVI presents a letter from Sadia and Avipal's attorney to the investigating authority explicitly stating that the normal value established for Sadia and Avipal incorrectly included internal freight costs. Even though the Argentinean authority was aware that the adjustment was warranted, it still did not request that Sadia provide such information.

We understand that if the freight costs reported by Sadia were not considered reliable, the authority could have also used a secondary source of information to estimate such deduction, as it did with the normal value to compensate for the alleged characteristic differences between the poultry sold to Argentina and in Brazil.

As a final observation, it is important that the Panel note that even though the authority knew, and Argentina admits, that the freight adjustment has a *"decisive and significant impact on price comparability"*,[16] Argentina still considers that the investigating authority would have acted incorrectly if it had made this specific discount. Here, we remind the Panel that Article 2.4 of the Agreement requires authorities to make due allowance for any *difference that affects price comparability*. In our view, the failure to make the freight adjustment to Sadia's normal value was contrary to the requirement under Article 2.4 of the Agreement.

Claim 24

93.   Please comment on paras 77 - 79 of ASS.

Response

Exhibit BRA-32 provides the JOX letter to the investigating authority explaining that the prices quoted in its publication, used by the authority to establish the normal value for all other exporters, includes Value Added Tax (ICMS) of 12per cent; Social Contribution on Revenue (PIS/COFINS) of 2.65per cent; financial cost, depending on the sales term; sales commission of 0.5 to 1per cent over the value of the sale; and, a variable freight for delivery, depending on the geographic location of the seller and the buyer.

Article 2.4 of the Agreement provides that a fair comparison shall be made at the same level of trade, normally at the ex-factory level. We have established, and Argentina apparently does not dispute this, that an ex-factory price is the price with no charges included, since this represents the price at the factory. In other words, the buyer bears all costs and risks involved in taking the goods from the seller's premises. We also believe that it is fair to state that the JOX price is not an ex-factory price, since it includes taxes, freight and financial cost.

Argentina appears to agree with Brazil that an F.O.B. price includes inland freight to the port of exportation, inland insurance, handling and loading charges.[17] Its is also safe to say that an f.o.b. price does not include taxes and financial cost. Thus, there are no adjustments to be made to the f.o.b. export price with respect to taxes and financial cost.

---

[16]   Argentina First Submission ("AFR"), para. 211.
[17]   ASS, para. 77.

What we have argued is that because the f.o.b. export price does not include taxes and financial cost, the authority should have, at a minimum, made an adjustment in the JOX price (normal value), excluding the taxes and financial cost, when making a fair comparison. In doing so, the authority would still be left with a normal value that was not ex-factory because it would still include internal freight charges. We recall that Article 2.4 of the Agreement requires that the comparison be made at the same level of trade, which is normally at ex-factory. However, if a comparison on an ex-factory level is not possible, the comparison still has to be on the same level of trade. The deductions of taxes and financial cost from the JOX price would have permitted a fair comparison on the same, or at least a more similar, level of trade.

The Panel should note that the investigating authority, when calculating the normal value for the exporters Sadia, Avipal, Nicolini and Seara, adjusted the normal value of these exporters by excluding the Value Added Tax (ICMS) of 12per cent and the Social Contribution on Revenue (PIS/COFINS) of 2.65per cent.[18] For Sadia and Avipal the investigating authority also adjusted the normal value by excluding the financial cost.[19] This adjusted normal value, without taxes and financial cost, was used by the authority in making the fair comparison with the f.o.b. export price.[20] We see no reason why the authority could not have made the same adjustment to the normal value established for all other exporters. This adjustment would have allowed a fair comparison with the f.o.b. export price.

Claim 27

94. Does Brazil consider that the investigating authority would have violated Article 2.4.2 if the exporters had agreed that the investigating authority could calculate normal value on the basis of those domestic transactions for which invoices had been requested?

Response

Brazil considers that the investigating authority would still have violated Article 2.4.2 even if the exporters had agreed that the investigating authority could calculate normal value on the basis of those domestic transactions for which invoices had been requested.

We remind the Panel that when the investigation was initiated and the authority sent the dumping questionnaire to the exporters Sadia, Avipal, Frangosul, Nicolini and Seara, the authority had required normal value and export price information for the years 1996, 1997, 1998 and the months where data was available in 1999.[21] Subsequently, the investigating authority required supporting documentation for all sales transactions in Brazil and to Argentina for that same period.[22] Because of the enormous volume of sales transactions in the internal market, the exporters were forced to send a letter to the authority explaining that it was impossible to provide an invoice for each sale transaction in the internal

---

[18] Annex to Exhibit BRA-15.
[19] Ibid.
[20] Pages 63, 65, 67, 69, 102 and 103 of Exhibit BRA-15.
[21] Pages 18, 22, 23, 26, 27 and 29 of Exhibit BRA-15.
[22] Pages 18, 19, 22, 23, 27, 29 and 30 of Exhibit BRA-15.

market.²³ In this letter, the exporters recommended that the authority either verify the transaction *in loco* or select a sample of transactions so that supporting documentation could be presented.²⁴

The idea behind the exporters' suggestion was to give the authority, through a sample, the ability to verify the accuracy and veracity of the universe of normal value information reported in the questionnaire response. The Panel must not forget that the exporters had already gone through the burdensome task of collecting and reporting normal value and export price data for several years, which was not used by the authority in the final determination. Brazil understands that the magnitude of the information provided may mean that not all data will actually be examined, however, this *does not exclude the validity of all the data provided*, particularly if that data could be verified.

Furthermore, we understand that the establishment of the period of data collection, for dumping purposes, is intrinsically related to the dumping margin methodology under Article 2.4.2 of the Agreement. Article 2.4.2 provides that the existence of margins of dumping "shall normally be established on the basis of a comparison of a weighted average normal value with a weighted average of prices of all comparable export transactions (...)". Normally, the weighted average normal value is compared to the weighted average export price for a comparable product sold during the period of investigation. It is important to note that the weighted average prices are usually calculated for the entire period of investigation. This comparison of prices for products sold during a certain period ensures a more accurate picture of the price patterns to export and domestic markets. We understand that this is one of the reasons why the Committee on Anti-Dumping Practices has recommended that the period of data collection for dumping investigations normally be 12 months and, in any case, no less than 6 months.²⁵ A limited period of data collection also means limited transactions for comparison and cannot substitute a comparison analysis based on all sales transactions for the entire period.

Likewise, if an authority limits the transactions that are to be used in the comparison, be it those transactions selected by the authority and for which invoices were presented, there is a risk that the prices provided will not reflect the actual price patterns for the entire period.

Questions To Both Parties

Claim 21

95.   What are 'essential facts under consideration which form the basis for the decisions whether to apply definitive measures' within the meaning of Article 6.9 ADA? In particular, would 'essential facts' cover only facts or also reasoning supporting a certain conclusion?

---

²³   Exhibit BRA-26, Exhibit BRA-29 and Exhibit BRA-31.
²⁴   *Ibid.*
²⁵   Committee on Anti-Dumping Practices - Recommendation Concerning the Periods of Data Collection for Anti-Dumping Investigations, adopted by the Committee on 5 May 2000 - G/ADP/6 - 16 May 2000.

Report of the Panel

Response

The term "essential" means "absolutely necessary; indispensable".[26] "Fact" is "a thing that is known to have occurred, to exist, or to be true".[27] Thus, "essential facts", within the meaning of Article 6.9 of the Agreement, are assertions of something existing or done, which are indispensable for the authority's consideration in forming the basis for the decision whether or not to apply definitive measures. Information regarding the establishment of the normal value and the export price, used to calculate the dumping margin, are essential facts to be considered in the final determination.

It is important to note that the term "facts" is also present in Article 17.6(i) of the Agreement. According to Article 17.6(i), "in its assessment of the *facts* of the matter, the panel shall determine whether the authorities' establishment of the *facts* was proper and whether their evaluation of those *facts* was unbiased and objective (...)". Under that Article, "facts" is not merely the data established and evaluated by the authority but also the reasoning supporting a certain conclusion in establishing a fact.

Accordingly, we understand that in Article 6.9 the phrase "essential facts" covers the data collected *and* the reasoning supporting a certain conclusion made by an authority in establishing the facts. The conclusion made by an authority relates to the authority's establishment of the facts. For example, it is not sufficient for an authority to simply state that it has disregarded the normal value submitted by a certain exporter based on Article 6.8 of the Agreement. The authority must inform the reasons why certain information was disregarded pursuant to Article 6.8.

This is our understanding of the phrase "essential facts" in Article 6.9 of the Agreement. We note that the first sentence of Article 6.9 should be read and construed together with the second sentence of Article 6.9, that is, that the disclosure of the "essential facts" should take place in sufficient time for the parties to **defend their interests**. Within the meaning of Article 6.9, a party needs to know the reasoning supporting a certain conclusion made by an authority in order to provide arguments and reasons in its defense. If the phrase "essential facts" is interpreted otherwise, the second sentence of Article 6.9 would be rendered meaningless.

96. At para. 8.229 of its report, the panel in *Guatemala - Cement II* found that:

> 'An interested party will not know whether a particular fact is "important" or not unless the investigating authority has explicitly identified it as one of the "essential facts" which form the basis of the authority's decision whether to impose definitive measures.'

Would you agree with the above finding? Please explain.

Response

Brazil agrees with the Panel's findings in *Guatemala - Cement II* that an interested party will only know whether a particular fact is important if the authority explicitly identifies it as an "essential fact" to be considered in forming the basis of

---

[26] *The Concise Oxford Dictionary - Ninth Edition,* Oxford University Press, 1995, p. 461.
[27] *Ibid.,* p. 482.

the authority's decision whether or not to impose definitive measures. We emphasize that the obligation of the authority under Article 6.9 is not to inform all interested parties of just any "fact", but to inform interested parties of the "essential facts". In fact, the requirement under Article 6.9 is even more specific. Authorities are not only required to inform the "essential facts", but the "essential facts" that will form the basis for the decision whether or not to apply definitive measures.

If an authority simply summarizes the vast amount of information that was submitted to the files of the investigation without specifically indicating what information is important in forming the basis of the authority's decision, how can an exporter know what "essential fact" will be used in the authority's decision whether or not to impose definitive measures? Likewise, how can an exporter defend its interest?

For example, in the instant case, Frangosul and Catarinense submitted export price information with supporting documentation. Even though the authority acknowledged this in the report prior to the end of the evidence-producing stage of the dumping investigation,[28] the authority still disregarded that export price information in the final determination. In the disclosure report prior to the final determination, the authority neither indicated nor did it provide why that information would be disregarded. The exporters had no reason to suspect that that information would not be considered by the authority and, thus, were not able to defend their interests.

In that sense, we find it useful to also cite to another passage of the Panel's findings in the *Guatemala - Cement II* report:

> *"(...) The difficulty for an interested party with access to the file, however, is that it will not know whether particular information in the file forms the basis of the authority's final determination. One purpose of Article 6.9 is to resolve this difficulty for interested parties. This has been acknowledged by Guatemala, which has itself asserted that "[t]he object and purpose of Article 6.9 is to allow exporters a fair opportunity to comment on the important issue in an investigation after the record is closed to new facts". An interested party will not know whether a particular fact is "important" or not unless the investigating authority has explicitly identified it as one of the "essential facts" which form the basis of the authority's decision whether to impose definitive measures.*[29] (emphasis added)

The purpose of Article 6.9 is exactly that, to provide interested parties the opportunity to present arguments and to comment on the important issues in an investigation after the evidence-producing stage is finished but prior to the final determination.

Claim 22

97. What do parties understand by the words "for each known exporter or producer concerned of the product under investigation" contained in the first sentence of Article 6.10? In the view of the parties, would the cited portion of the first sentence of Article 6.10 require the calculation of an individual margin of

---

[28] Pages 29 and 38 of Exhibit BRA-28.
[29] *Guatemala - Cement II*, DSR 2000:XI, 5295 para. 8.229.

dumping for each exporter known to the investigating authority? Would that also be the case when a known exporter does not provide relevant information requested by the investigating authority? Please explain.

Response

The first sentence of Article 6.10 of the Agreement requires authorities to determine an individual margin of dumping for each known exporter or producer concerned of the product under investigation. Thus, if an exporter is known to the authority, the authority is required, and Article 6.10 expressly states this as a rule, to calculate an individual dumping margin for that exporter.

If the known exporter provides the relevant information necessary to calculate the individual margin of dumping, there is no question, the authority must do so. That was the case for Frangosul and Catarinense. If the known exporter does not provide the relevant information necessary to calculate the normal value and the export price, but the authority still has access to individual information for that exporter, the investigating authority is still required to calculate the individual margin of dumping.

It is important to note the difference between applying facts available, in accordance with Article 6.8 of the Agreement, to a specific exporter and not calculating the individual margin of dumping for that exporter. In cases where the authority does not have the relevant normal value or export price information and the authority is entitled to resort to facts available, the facts available applicable to a specific exporter may not be the same as the facts available applicable to another exporter. Accordingly, the calculation of the individual dumping margins for those two exporters will not be the same.

For instance, in the final determination the Argentinean authority disregarded the export price submitted by the exporters Sadia, Avipal, Nicolini and Seara and applied the individual weighted average export price for these exporters as provided by the Argentinean agency *Ganaderia*.[30] However, for Frangosul and Catarinense, the authority also disregarded the export price submitted by these exporters but failed to use the individual weighted average export price as provided by the *Ganaderia*.[31] Because the authority did not calculate an individual margin of dumping for Frangosul and Catarinense, the authority used as the export price for these two exporters a weighted average f.o.b. export price of US$0,95992, that took into account the weighted average export price of all other exporters with little or no participation in the investigation.[32] This export price of US$0,95992 was lower than the individual weighted average export price provided by the *Ganaderia* for Frangosul (US$1,0407) and Catarinense (US$1,0048).[33] Had the authority used this individual weighted average export price instead of the weighted average export price for all other exporters, there would have been no dumping margin for Frangosul and a dumping margin of 3.35per cent for Catarinense.

We point out, however, that specifically in this case, Frangosul and Catarinense **did** provide the required export price information with supporting

---

[30] Pages 76 and 77 of Exhibit BRA-15.
[31] *Ibid.*
[32] Page 103 and the last page of Exhibit BRA-15.
[33] Pages 76 and 77 of Exhibit BRA-15.

documentation and the authority should have used that information to calculate the individual dumping margin for the two exporters.

Thus, in the instant case, the authority not only incorrectly disregarded the information submitted by Frangosul and Catarinense during the investigation, and thus erred in not calculating the individual dumping margin, but the authority also had access to individual weighted average export price for those two exporters as provided by the *Ganaderia* but decided to apply the weighted average f.o.b. export price for all other exporters. Consequently, the authority incorrectly applied the dumping margin for all others exporters to Frangosul and Catarinense.

98. **In the view of the parties, would the findings in paras. 6.86 to 6.101 (both included) of the panel *Argentina - Ceramic tiles* be applicable to the facts in this dispute? In particular, would the following finding of the panel be relevant to the current dispute: 'The basis of the normal value determination has no bearing on the ability to calculate an individual dumping margin for the producer whose normal value is in question.'? Would the lack of information on normal value, export price or cost of production, automatically allow the non-calculation of an individual dumping of margin in accordance with Article 6.10? Please explain, identifying and providing relevant factual support to the Panel.**

Response

Even though the facts of the case *Argentina- Ceramic Tiles* are somewhat different from the facts in the instant case, the reasoning provided by that Panel regarding the interpretation of Article 6.10 is still valid.

First, we agree with the Panel's views in *Argentina - Ceramic Tiles* that Article 6.10 requires that an individual margin of dumping has to be determined for each exporter with regard to the product subject to investigation. Relevant part of that report provides that:

> *"While the second sentence of Article 6.10 allows an investigating authority to limit its examination to certain exporters and producers, it does not provide for a deviation from the general rule that individual margins be determined for those exporters or producers that are examined. To the contrary, Article 9.4 provides that, where the authorities limit their examination under Article 6.10, the anti-dumping duty for exporters or producers that are not examined shall not exceed a level determined on the basis of he results of the examination of those exporters or producers that were examined. That Article 9.4 does not provide any methodology for determining the level of duties applicable to exporters or producers that are examined in our view confirms that the general rule requiring individual margins remains applicable to those exporters or producers. We find further confirmation in Article 6.10.2, which requires that, in general, an individual margin of dumping must be calculated even for the producers/exporters not initially included in the sample, if they provide the necessary information and if to do so is not unduly burdensome. If even producers not included in the original sample are entitled to an individual margin calculation, then it follows that producers that were included in the original sample are entitled as well. Indeed, the parties appear to agree that Article 6.10 of the AD*

Agreement requires that as a rule an individual margin of dumping has to be determined for each exporter with regard to the product subject to investigation."[34] (emphasis added)

We point out the fact that in the instant case the authority did not limit their examination pursuant to the second sentence of Article 6.10 of the Agreement and the authority was, thus, required to determine an individual margin of dumping for each known exporter or producer concerned.

Second, we have presented in the response to question 90 above that Frangosul and Catarinense **did** submit the required normal value and export price information during the investigation. In particular, these two exporters also submitted supporting documentation with the export price information. Brazil fails to see the reason why the Argentinean authority did not use that information to calculate the individual margin of dumping for Frangosul and Catarinense.

Third, we agree with the Panel's finding in *Argentina - Ceramic Tiles* that *"(...) the basis of the normal value determination has no bearing on the ability to calculate an individual dumping margin for the producer whose normal value is in question"*.[35] We have provided in the response to question 97 above, that there is a difference between applying facts available, based on Article 6.8 of the Agreement, in order to establish normal value and export price for a specific exporter and not calculating the individual margin of dumping for that exporter. In establishing the normal value or the export price, the authority may be entitled to resort to facts available under specific circumstances. However, that does not mean that the authority is not required to calculate an individual margin of dumping.

For example, the facts available applied by an authority to determine an exporter's normal value may be different from the facts available applied by an authority to determine another exporter's normal value. Another example occurs when an authority applies facts available to determine an exporter's normal value but uses the export price reported by the exporter, while for another exporter the authority applies facts available to determine the export price and uses the exporter's reported normal value. In such situations, the authority will still calculate an individual margin of dumping for each known exporter or producer concerned of the product under investigation.

Thus, we do not agree that the lack of information on normal value, export price or cost of production **automatically** allows the non-calculation of an individual dumping margin. To accept that as true would violate the requirement in the first sentence in Article 6.10 of the Agreement.

---

[34] Argentina - Definitive Measures on Imports of Ceramic Floor Tiles from Italy, 28 September 2001, WT/DS189/R, at para. 6.90 (adopted on 5 November 2001) ("*Argentina - Ceramic Tiles*").

[35] *Argentina - Ceramic Tiles*, DSR 2001:XII, 6241, para. 6.96.

ANNEX A-7

COMMENTS OF BRAZIL ON THE RESPONSES OF ARGENTINA TO THE PANEL'S AND TO BRAZIL'S QUESTIONS - SECOND MEETING

(28 November 2002)

Questions to Argentina

Preliminary issues

66. Regarding para. 13 of Argentina's second submission ("ASS"), what was the "statement of fact" (point I) allegedly made by Brazil? Please explain how Argentina relied in good faith upon that alleged statement (point III).

Response from Argentina

Firstly, Argentina considers that Brazil's conduct in successively filing its case and activating dispute settlement proceedings in different fora, first in MERCOSUR and then in the WTO - particularly in view of the precedents described in Argentina's first written submission[1], i.e. recourse to the dispute settlement mechanism under the Protocol of Brasilia to settle conflicts with other MERCOSUR States parties and compliance with the content and scope of the arbitral awards in all of the disputes - provides statements of fact which meet the requirement of being clear, unambiguous, voluntary, unconditional and authorized, the essential elements of estoppel under the definition provided in paragraph 13 of Argentina's submission.

In paragraph 20 of its rebuttal submission[2], Argentina sets out the elements which are present in the current dispute brought by Brazil before the WTO. Among these elements, the last sentence of subparagraph (iii) of paragraph 20 states that: "Consequently Brazil's previous conduct with respect to the acceptance of awards, confirmed by the signature of the Protocol of Olivos, invalidates the complaint against Argentina that Brazil is now trying to substantiate on the basis of the DSU."

Moreover, the fact that Brazil signed the Protocol of Olivos on 18 February 2002 - by which it expressly accepted the choice of forum clause - and then, seven days later, on 25 February 2002, requested the establishment of a Panel in the current dispute, displays a clear contradiction in its conduct, in which Argentina had had full confidence, both countries being member states of MERCOSUR; and Argentina is now suffering the negative impact of this change of position.[3] This fact was also raised in the submissions of the EC[4] and Paraguay[5] as third parties.

---

[1] First written submission of Argentina, 29 August 2002, paras. 18-22 and corresponding footnotes.
[2] Rebuttal submission of Argentina, 17 October 2002, para. 20.
[3] In fact, Argentina has already approved the Protocol of Olivos. On 9 October 2002, the National Congress adopted the Protocol of Olivos by Law 25.663, promulgated by the Executive through Decree 2091/02 of 18 October 2002 and published in Official Bulletin of the Republic of Argentina No. 30008 of 21 October 2002.
[4] Third party submission of the European Communities, 9 September 2002, para. 17 and footnote 17.
[5] Third party submission of Paraguay, 9 September 2002, para. 8.

Brazil's Comments

Brazil understands that the phrase "statement of fact" means "the act or an instance of stating or being stated; expression in words"[6] of "a thing that is known to have occurred, to exist, or to be true".[7] Within that meaning, Brazil reiterates that it has never declared that it would renounce its right to bring a dispute, based on different claims, to the WTO because a similar dispute had been brought to the Mercosul Tribunal.

We recall that the Mercosul Protocol of Olivos on Dispute Settlement cannot be raised here as an implicit or express consent by Brazil to refrain from bringing the present case to the WTO dispute settlement. First, we note that the object before the Mercosul Tribunal was different from the object before this Panel. Second, The Protocol of Olivos has not yet entered into force, and even if it had and the object of the dispute were the same, the Protocol of Olivos provides that "disputes underway initiated in accordance with the Protocol of Brasília will continue to be exclusively governed by that Protocol until the dispute has been concluded".[8] The Protocol also states that "while the disputes initiated under the regime of the Protocol of Brasília are not completely concluded and until the proceedings under Article 49 are completed, the Protocol of Brasília will continue to be applied".[9] Based on those provisions, it is fair to state that the Protocol of Olivos does not apply to disputes that have already been concluded under the Brasília Protocol. Third, what Argentina brings before this Panel is a situation where Mercosul Members potentially have divergent views on what their rights and obligations are under Mercosul legal framework. We remind the Panel that Article 1 of the DSU confines the jurisdiction of this Panel to disputes brought pursuant to the "covered agreements", the "WTO Agreement", and the DSU, taken in isolation or in combination with each other. The provisions of the Brasília Protocol and the Protocol of Olivos are not listed in Article 1 of the DSU. Thus, the rules and procedures of the DSU do not apply to consultations and the settlement of disputes concerning the rights and obligations of Mercosul Members under the Mercosul legal framework.

67. **At para. 13 of ASS, Argentina asserts that the principle of estoppel is a general principle of international law. Is the principle of estoppel a "customary rule[] of interpretation of public international law" within the meaning of Article 3.2 of the DSU? Please explain. Is a general principle of international law the same as a rule of interpretation of international law? Please explain.**

Response from Argentina

The rules of interpretation of public international law to which Article 3.2 of the DSU refers concern Article 31 of the Vienna Convention on the Law of Treaties.

Article 31 of the Vienna Convention sets forth the rules to be followed with respect to interpretation; and the rules of interpretation are applied by the adjudicating body taking account, in all cases, of the sources of law.

---

[6] *The Concise Oxford Dictionary - Ninth Edition,* Oxford University Press, 1995, p. 1361.
[7] *Ibid.*, 1995, p. 482.
[8] Article 50 of the Protocol of Olivos.
[9] Paragraph 2 of Article 55 of the Protocol of Olivos.

The sources that may be applied to interpretation are set forth in Article 38 of the Statute of the International Court of Justice, which lists, as a principal source, treaties, international custom, and the general principles of international law.

Consequently, Argentina understands the principle of estoppel, as a general principle of international law, to constitute a legitimate source to which any international tribunal called upon to settle a dispute may have recourse.

In the current dispute, it is in this light that Argentina considers that the principle of estoppel argument should be taken into account by the Panel in carrying out its functions under the DSU. This is in keeping with the obligation laid down in Article 3.2 of the DSU to clarify the existing provisions of the agreements in accordance with customary rules of interpretation of public international law.

Moreover, Argentina repeats what it stated in its second written submission[10], namely that other panels have already examined the principle of estoppel in past disputes: "*European Communities - Asbestos*"[11] and "*Guatemala - Cement*"[12].

Brazil's Comments

No comments.

Claim 1

68. In reply to question 6, Argentina refers to the *Aves & Ovos* review. If the applicant submitted more extracts from that review than are contained in Exhibit BRA-1, please provide a copy of such additional extracts. Please explain precisely how information from the *Aves & Ovos* review, as supplied by the applicant, supported the need for a 9.09 per cent adjustment to normal value. Furthermore, on what basis did the investigating authority assign the same value to the head and feet as to other parts of the chicken?

Response from Argentina

We stress that the review Aves & Ovos does not provide any information with respect to the 9.09 per cent adjustment carried out. The mention of the said review in Argentina's reply to question 6 of the Panel following the first meeting was made in connection with the listing of evidence provided by the applicant in its application. As regards the question concerning the basis on which the investigating authority assigned the same value to the head and feet as to the other parts of the chicken, we note once again that the head and feet were not considered to have the same value as the other parts of the animal for the purposes of assessing the adjustment. On the contrary the 9.09 per cent adjustment is the result of an evaluation of the specific recovery of heads and feet.

Brazil's Comments

We point out that Argentina confirms that the investigating authority did **not** consider whether the value of the head and feet was the same as the value of the other

---

[10] Second written submission of Argentina, 17 October 2002, paras. 17, 18 and 19.
[11] WT/DS135/R, *European Communities - Measures Affecting Asbestos and Asbestos-Containing Products*, Report adopted on 5 April 2001, para. 8.60.
[12] WT/DS156/R, *Guatemala - Definitive Anti-Dumping Measure on Grey Portland Cement from Mexico*, Report adopted on 17 November 2000, DSR 2000:XI, 5295, para. 8.23.

parts of the chicken for the purpose of evaluating the necessary adjustments.[13] Based on Exhibit BRA-1, the Panel can verify that the application contained no evidence or indication that there were physical characteristic differences in the product sold in Brazil and to Argentina, that such alleged differences affect price comparability, that the yield rate as proposed by the applicant was appropriate, and that, therefore, the adjustment methodology presented was justified.

Claim 2

69. Regarding Argentina's reply to question 12, the Panel notes that the extract from the JOX document quoted by Argentina is included under the heading "Frango Vivo"? Is there a similar statement for eviscerated poultry? What does it mean to say that "the price remains on very firm ground"?

Response from Argentina

No, the JOX publication specifically refers to live poultry. Nevertheless, the reference to the words "production on the parallel market within São Paulo is sharply lower, so that the price remains on very firm ground" relates to the fact that live poultry is the fundamental and principle input for the product under investigation. Thus, it is perfectly reasonable, at this stage prior to the opening of the investigation, to deduce that if the price of the input remains essentially unaltered, the price of the end-product - i.e. the product under investigation - will not vary substantially.

In other words, the phrase "so that the price remains on very firm ground" means that the price would remain essentially unaltered, thus constituting an acceptable element at this stage prior to the investigation.

Brazil's Comments

Argentina confirms that the quoted extract from the JOX document refers to **live** poultry and that there is no similar statement in the JOX publication for **eviscerated** poultry.[14]

We disagree with Argentina that the reference in the JOX publication for **live** poultry is sufficient to establish the trend of normal value prices for **eviscerated** poultry (a different product), because **live** poultry is the raw material of the product under investigation.[15] The Panel should note that the extract from the JOX publication under heading "Frango Vivo" (**live** poultry) monitors daily changes in the market and cannot possibly be used to indicate price trends over a longer period of time. Furthermore, the Panel should note that there is another heading in the JOX publication titled "Frango Abatido" (slaughtered poultry). This heading provides that "the sales of slaughtered and cuts of poultry at the end of the week have not demonstrated any recovery in volume. The cold storage plants (freezers) continue trying to re-pass higher prices, without success, in view of the existing surplus in offer. Even though the beginning of the month is near, it will be difficult to re-pass the adjustments while the offer is still inadequate".[16] Even though "frango abatido" (slaughtered poultry) is also a product made from **live** poultry, the extract in the JOX

---

[13] Argentina Response to the Panel's Questions in the Second Substantive Meeting ("ARS"), question 68.
[14] ARS, question 69.
[15] Ibid.
[16] Exhibit BRA-1

publication for slaughtered poultry indicates the inability to raise prices because of the excess volume of poultry offered in the Brazilian market.

It is also interesting that Argentina considers valid, in the initiation stage of the investigation, that the authority consider as sufficient evidence to establish normal value the price of poultry for only one day in 1997, when the export price was established based on a six-month period. We have demonstrated that the JOX report used to establish the normal value is a daily publication, which was reasonably available to the applicant. Accordingly, the applicant could, and should, have presented the prices in the JOX publication for a period of at least six months in 1997, but chose not to.

Claim 3

70. When did the Secretary receive Act No. 405 from the CNCE (dated 7 January 1998)? When did the Secretary receive the report from the APCDS (also dated 7 January 1998)?

Response from Argentina

The Secretary of Industry, Trade and Mining received Record No. 405 on 9 January 1998, and the DCD Report on Dumping on 27 January 1998.

Brazil's Comments

No comments.

71. Regarding the first sentence of the third paragraph of Argentina's reply to question 16, what is meant by the phrase "in keeping with the requirements of the application on 17 February 1998"? What precisely are the "requirements of the application"?

Response from Argentina

The requirements of the application are those contained in form 349 provided in Annex ARG-XXXIX. The meaning of the phrase is that on 17 February 1998, the applicants provided updated information on the basis of what was requested in the mentioned form 349. This information, on the basis of a legal finding by the relevant ministerial department and in conformity with Law No. 19549 on Administrative Procedures, was transmitted to the CNCE with the instruction that it be analysed. The analysis resulted in the issue by the CNCE of Record No. 464 and the corresponding Technical Report.

Brazil's Comments

No comments.

Claim 10

72. How and when did the Authority obtain the addresses of the Brazilian exporters which were contacted in February 1999? If those addresses were obtained from a document on the record of the investigation, please provide a copy of this document.

Response from Argentina

The addresses of the producers/exporters notified in February 1999 were provided by telephone through the importers interested in the investigation. Having learned of the initiation of the investigation through the Official Bulletin, they contacted the investigating authority and provided the said addresses.

Brazil's Comments

According to Argentina, the investigating authority obtained the addresses of the Brazilian exporters, contacted on February 1999, through interested importers in the investigation.[17] Once the initiation of the investigation was published, these importers contacted the investigating authority and provided such information.[18]

Brazil recalls that the investigating authority knew, prior to initiation, of the existence and interest of at least five of the seven Brazilian exporters that were only notified of the investigation on 15 September 1999.[19] If the investigating authority knew of the existence of these exporters prior to initiation but did not have their contact information, why didn't the authority inquire in February 1999 with the interested importers on the addresses of these Brazilian exporters? In particular, if the investigating authority was only able to contact the seven Brazilian exporters after the importer Interamericana Comercial ("Interamericana") provided their addresses[20], why didn't the authority inquire in February 1999 with the importer Interamericana about the addresses of these seven exporters? Likewise, the authority could have also requested that the Brazilian government provide the contact information of those *specific* exporters identified in the report regarding the viability of the investigation.

Still on Argentina's response, Brazil wonders whether it is normal procedure for an Argentinean authority to wait for importers to contact them with addresses of exporters so that the authority can then notify the interested exporters known to them. If that is the normal procedure, what happens when interested importers do not contact the authority, providing the addresses of the known exporters? In such cases, does it mean that the interested exporters known to the authorities are not notified?

73. Please comment on para. 36 of Brazil's Second Oral Statement.

Response from Argentina

With respect to paragraph 36 of Brazil's Statement, we refer to what Argentina has already stated in connection with Article 6.1.1, namely that the parties interested in the investigation were given ample opportunity to participate, with due regard for the requests for extensions that were submitted.

Brazil's Comments

No comments.

---

[17] ARS, question 72.
[18] *Ibid.*
[19] Pages 4 and 5 of Exhibit BRA-2.
[20] Argentina Response to the Panel's Questions in the First Substantive Meeting ("AR"), questions 26 and 28.

Claim 11

74. **Following on from Argentina's reply to question 29, was all of the information contained in the application sent to both the DCD and the CNCE, or did they only receive those parts of the application dealing with dumping and injury respectively?**

Response from Argentina

Both entities received the same application, with the same information. Upon submitting an application for the initiation of an investigation, the applicant had to complete the form approved by Resolution No. 349 of the former Secretariat for Industry and Trade before the former Under-Secretariat for Foreign Trade (SSCE). In keeping with Articles 36 to 40 of Decree No. 2121/94, the application was filed with the former SSCE, which transmitted a complete copy thereof to the CNCE so that the latter could make an injury determination.

The CNCE received, on 9 September 1997, a copy of the application for the initiation of the investigation filed by CEPA with the SSCE on 2 September 1997. The two submissions are identical, and the submission transmitted to the CNCE can be found in Section I of file CNCE No. 43/1997 (folios 2 to 284). Thus, both entities had at their disposal complete copies of the application for measures submitted by CEPA.

Brazil's Comments

No comments.

Claim 15

75. **Regarding the second sentence of Argentina's reply to question 39, what precisely is the "procedure" (for supporting documentation) followed by the investigating authority? How was an interested party to know what supporting documentation it was required to provide? Where exactly has the "procedure" been specified? Where exactly is the request for supporting documentation set forth? Please provide copies of the relevant sources.**

Response from Argentina

Regarding the procedure followed by the investigating authority to obtain supporting documentation, attached to the questionnaire are instructions explaining how it should be completed and stating that it should be accompanied by supporting documentation. At the same time, the instructions state that where it is not possible to provide supporting documentation, the source of the information should be indicated. By supporting documentation, the authority means documentation that backs the statements or arguments of the interested parties. For example, if the implementing authority is expected to make an adjustment for freight, it would be helpful for the interested party to attach the contract with the shipping company or any other documentation at its disposal which records the value or percentage that should be discounted for freight.

These instructions can be found in the first part of the questionnaire to be completed by the exporter.

A blank copy of the questionnaire for exporters is provided as Annex ARG-LXIII.

Report of the Panel

Brazil's Comments

Article 6.1 and Paragraph 1 of Annex II of the Agreement require authorities to give notice and specify in detail the information required from interested parties. We note that the dumping questionnaire did not specifically require that the exporters submit supporting documentation for the product description. The Panel should look at Pages 19 and 21 of Exhibit BRA-22, where the instructions for completing the producer/exporter questionnaire are provided.[21] From these general instructions, one can see that there was not sufficient information on the precise supporting documentation that was expected from the exporters. Furthermore, the fact that the authority never requested clarifications or supporting documentation for the information reported by the exporters indicated that the information that had been submitted would be accepted. In that sense, the authority never informed the exporters that the product description information reported by them was insufficient or unacceptable. By doing so, the authority acted inconsistently with Paragraph 6 of Annex II of the Agreement.

Claim 20

76. Regarding question 43, please indicate precisely what normal value data Catarinense was asked to provide. Please specify the document(s) in which the request was made. Furthermore, for what period of time was Catarinense asked to provide the relevant normal value data?

Response from Argentina

The information that the company Catarinense was asked to supply was the information requested in Note DCD No. 273-001065/99, provided by Brazil in exhibit BRA-13, in which it can be seen that the period for which the information was requested was 1998 - January 1999. We recall in this connection that independently of the documentation requested, in the last note sent by the implementing authority - Note DCD No. 273-001321/99 provided in exhibit BRA-27 - the companies were reminded that they were to comply with the requirements of the National Law on Administrative Procedures, particularly as regards certification of legal status, a basic prerequisite for a party to be considered in an investigation.

Brazil's Comments

No comments.

77. With regard to Catarinense's normal value data, Argentina asserts that those data were submitted in an aggregate form. However, it is apparently stated in Section VII.3.2 of the Final Dumping Determination that Catarinense had submitted information on sales made in the domestic market corresponding to 1998 and January 1999 disaggregated by transaction. Please comment?

Response from Argentina

As stated, in Section VII.3.2 of the Final Report on the Determination of the Margin of Dumping there is a reference to Annex VIII: "Sales in the domestic market for 1998 and January 1999, disaggregated by transaction" at folio 3023. That is, with respect to normal value for the requested period, Catarinense submitted a list of

---

[21] Brazil Second Written Submission, para. 73.

domestic market sales transactions without providing any supporting documentation and without any magnetic media. Finally, we repeat that Catarinense at no time provided any certification of legal status although this had been requested in Note DCD 273-001321/99.

Section VIII.1.3.3.5 of the Report on the Final Determination on the Margin of Dumping, at folios 3053/3054, states that the values reproduced at folio 3054 were obtained from the information from the exporting company in aggregate form in Annexes V and VI of the questionnaire for exporters and that it covered a longer period than that requested by the implementing authority. Thus, the processing of the information in Annexes V and VI yields the detailed values in the table appearing at folio 3054. As indicated in the footnotes to Annexes V and VI, in the case of 1999 the information was accumulated until September. We attach as Annex ARG-LXIV a copy of Annexes V and VI, as submitted by Catarinense.

Brazil's Comments

Argentina confirms that the Brazilian exporter Catarinense provided information on sales made in the domestic market corresponding to 1998 and January 1999, disaggregated by transaction.[22]

We recall that Catarinense was notified of the investigation and the need to respond to the dumping questionnaire only on 15 September 1999.[23] Even though Catarinense was notified of the investigation almost eight months after it had initiated, Catarinense still provided the questionnaire response with complete information on sales transactions to Argentina, disaggregated by transaction, with supporting documentation, as well as complete information on sales transactions in Brazil, disaggregated by transaction, without supporting documentation.[24] To that regard, the Argentinean authority never requested the supporting documentation for Catarinense's sales transactions in the internal market, nor did it request that the information be provided in a diskette. Furthermore, the authority never selected specific transactions in the internal market, as it did with other exporters, for Catarinense to provide the corresponding supporting documentation.

During the investigation, Catarinense provided complete normal value and export price data that should have been used by the authority in determining the exporter's individual margin of dumping.

78. Please comment on the first two sentences of para. 53 of Brazil's Second Oral Statement.

Response from Argentina

With respect to the first two sentences of paragraph 53, there is no contradiction whatsoever as Brazil tries to suggest, since Argentina said that the export price information was indeed provided, but since for the reasons already given the determination of normal value could not be made, the notified export prices could not be considered. In this connection, Argentina had official information on export prices for both companies which is the information that was used in the final determination.

---

[22] ARS, question 77.
[23] Exhibit BRA-13.
[24] Page 39 of Exhibit BRA-15.

Brazil's Comments

Argentina confirms that the export price data submitted by the exporters Frangosul and Catarinense was, in fact, accompanied by supporting documentation.[25] Nevertheless, Argentina alleges that since it was not able to establish normal value for these two exporters, the authority was not able to consider the export price data submitted by them.[26] We disagree with Argentina's position that the normal value information for Frangosul and Catarinense could not be established. However, even if that were true, that does not exclude the fact that the authority could, and should, have used Frangosul and Catarinense's export price data and calculated an individual dumping margin for the two exporters. In that sense, we remind the Panel that even though the Argentinean authority disregarded the export price data submitted by the exporters Sadia and Avipal, the authority still calculated an individual dumping margin for those two companies. We understand that the Argentinean authority should have proceeded accordingly with respect to Frangosul and Catarinense. The fact that the authority does not have normal value or export price information for a certain exporter does not exclude the authority's obligation under Article 6.10 to calculate an individual margin of dumping for that exporter.

It is true that Argentina had official information on the export price for Frangosul and Catarinense.[27] However, it is **not** true that the authority used that information in the final determination. In the final determination, the Argentinean authority disregarded the export price submitted by the exporters Sadia, Avipal, Nicolini and Seara and applied the individual weighted average export price for these exporters as provided by the Argentinean agency *Ganaderia*.[28] However, for Frangosul and Catarinense, the authority also disregarded the export price submitted by these exporters but failed to use the individual weighted average export price as provided by the *Ganaderia*.[29] Because the authority did not calculate an individual margin of dumping for Frangosul and Catarinense, the authority used as the export price for these two exporters a weighted average f.o.b. export price of US$0,95992, that took into account the weighted average export price of all other exporters with little or no participation in the investigation.[30] This export price of US$0,95992 was lower than the individual weighted average export price provided by the *Ganaderia* for Frangosul (US$1,0407) and Catarinense (US$1,0048).[31] Had the authority used this individual weighted average export price instead of the weighted average export price for all other exporters, there would have been a negative dumping margin for Frangosul and a dumping margin of 3.35 per cent for Catarinense.

We emphasize, nevertheless, the fact that Frangosul and Catarinense **did** provide the required export price information with supporting documentation and the authority should have used that information to calculate the individual dumping margin for the two exporters.

---

[25] ARS, question 78.
[26] *Ibid.*
[27] *Ibid.*
[28] Pages 76 and 77 of Exhibit BRA-15.
[29] *Ibid.*
[30] Page 103 and the last page of Exhibit BRA-15.
[31] Pages 76 and 77 of Exhibit BRA-15.

Claim 21

79.   It would seem from para. 185 of Argentina's First Written Submission that parties were informed of the 'essential facts' through the Report on Action Taken of 4 January 2002. Could Argentina confirm that this is the only instrument on the record of the investigation through which the investigating authority informed interested parties of the 'essential facts'?

Response from Argentina

Yes, the Report on Action Taken is the document by which the investigating authority informed the interested parties of the essential facts. In this connection, Argentina reaffirms what it stated in paragraph 185 of its first written submission.

Brazil's Comments

No comments.

80.   The Panel notes Argentina's reply to question 47(a). As a follow-up question, the Panel would appreciate it if Argentina could reply the following questions:

(1)   In the investigation at stake, which were the 'essential facts' informed by the investigating authority to interested parties?

(2)   Where, if at all, the information referred to in paras. 340-350 of Brazil's First Written Submission and para. 87 of Brazil's Second Written Submission can be found?

In replying to these questions, Argentina is requested to point out with precision the paragraph or page number where the information is contained on the record of the investigation, if any, and to provide a copy of the relevant documents.

Response from Argentina

The essential facts are those which appear throughout the Report on Action Taken of January 2000 (folio 2757).

However, to be more precise with respect to the normal value and the export price, we refer by way of example to Section VIII.1 and VIII.1.3.3 of the said report, which explains the methodology used by SADIA for the calculation of normal value. The same is done for AVIPAL SA in Section VIII.1.3.3.2, which contains detailed information and a description of the methodology applied to calculate normal value for that company. Corresponding information is also provided for NICOLINI (folios 2819 and 2820) and for SEARA (folio 2821).

Consequently, what Brazil stated in paragraphs 340-350 of its first written submission does not correspond to reality. Indeed, the interested parties were given ample opportunity to express their views with respect to the essential facts that the authority considered for the calculation of normal value and the export price.

Concerning the copy of the essential facts report, see EXHIBIT BRA-28.

Brazil's Comments

Brazil understands that Argentina has failed to indicate, in its response to question 80(2), precisely where in the report prior to the final determination (Exhibit

Report of the Panel

BRA-28), the information referred to in paras. 340-350 of Brazil's First Written Submission and para. 87 of Brazil's Second Written Submission can be found.

Claim 23

81. At para. 73 of ASS, Argentina suggests that the exporter had ample opportunity to inform the DCD of any adjustments that needed to be made when it submitted the invoices requested by the DCD. Why should Sadia have requested an adjustment for freight costs when submitting its invoices if it had already requested that adjustment in its questionnaire response?

Response from Argentina

Argentina reaffirms what it said in paragraphs 210 and 211 of its first written submission. Indeed, SADIA replied to the questionnaire item concerning internal freight, but never provided any supporting documentation for that item. Nor do the invoices submitted provide any indication of the percentage and/or amount of the adjustment to be made.

In other words, although in Annex X SADIA provided a US$/Ton value to be discounted for freight, and also did so in Annex VIII - Sales in the domestic market - these values were presented in annualized form without any supporting documentation that would have enabled the authority to verify whether they corresponded to the reality and hence carry out the said adjustment.

In this connection, a "*nota fiscal*" (tax receipt) from SADIA has been provided showing clearly that the box corresponding to cost of freight does not contain any figure at all. And the box corresponding to "*frete por conta*" contains the indication "1", which corresponds to "*emitente*".

The kind of supporting documentation to which we refer in this case would be, for example, a contract between SADIA and a shipping company or any other documentation from the company which clearly indicates the amount to be discounted for freight. We insist that the "*notas fiscales*", which did not reveal the indicative amount of the requested adjustment, were the only documentation on hand.

Attached hereto as Annex ARG-LXV is a photocopy of the invoice and a photocopy of Annexes VIII and X of the Questionnaire for Exporters.

Brazil's Comments

No comments.

82. Argentina has asserted that it did not grant Sadia's request for a freight cost adjustment because Sadia failed to support its request with documentary evidence. Please indicate *precisely* (page number, paragraph number, line number) where the investigating authority explained the reason for rejecting Sadia's request in its final determination, or in any other document prepared by the investigating authority at the time of its determination. If the Panel does not already have a copy of the relevant document, please provide a copy thereof.

Response from Argentina

The relevant explanation can be found in Section VIII.1.3.3.1 of the Report on Action Taken. In that report, the DCD identified the information that it would use for the determination of normal value, which did not include any adjustment for freight.

Brazil's Comments

We ask that the Panel examine Section VIII.1.3.3.1 of the report prior to the final determination[32] and Section VIII.1.3.3.1 of the dumping final determination,[33] in order to verify that the investigating authority did ***not*** provide an explanation for rejecting Sadia's freight cost adjustment.

Claim 22

83.   Please comment on para. 59 of Brazil's Second Oral Statement.

Response from Argentina

To begin with, it should be noted with respect to Brazil's question as to why the authority did not proceed in the same manner with CATARINENSE and FRANGOSUL, that CATARINENSE never provided certification of legal status, i.e. it did not comply with an essential requirement that must be met by any interested party wishing to participate in the investigation in accordance with the National Law on Administrative Procedures (Law No. 19.49) which, pursuant to Article 76 of Decree No. 2121/94, applies on a residual basis in investigation proceedings.

This law was duly notified to the WTO Anti-Dumping Committee, which is why the last note sent to CATARINENSE, which appears in EXHIBIT BRA-27, states that it should comply with the requirements of the National Law on Administrative Procedures. Instead, not only did Catarinense persist in not making any submission, but as mentioned, it failed to provide certification of legal status.

In the case of FRANGOSUL, in spite of the successive extensions granted and the numerous requests for information from the implementing authority (see the summary table for the company in question, which was transmitted to the Panel together with Argentina's replies to the questions posed following the first meeting), no information was available in connection with domestic market sales transactions, needed by the authority to determine the individual margin of dumping.

We recall in this connection that, as can be seen in the summary table for FRANGOSUL, by Note DCD No. 272-001181/99 of 12 October 1999 and Note DCD No. 273-001412/99 of 18 November of 1999, the implementing authority asked FRANGOSUL for the last time to provide lists of domestic market sales. In the second of these two notes, it granted a maximum of five days to do so. The purpose of this time-limit was to ensure that the implementing authority would have sufficient time to analyse and process the requested information.

However, FRANGOSUL, once the time-limit for the submission for the information had elapsed, provided, in magnetic form only (diskette), the list of *notas fiscales*. Indeed, FRANGOSUL failed to provide a hard copy of the list as required under the National Law on Administrative Procedures. This Law applies on a residual basis to anti-dumping proceedings pursuant to Article 76 of Decree No. 2121/94.

---

[32]   Pages 58 - 62 of Exhibit BRA-28.
[33]   Pages 59 - 63 of Exhibit BRA-15.

Report of the Panel

For the sake of clarity, we cite below Article 7 and 15 of Decree No. 1759/72 which regulates the mentioned Law.

"*Article 7 - The identification under which a record of proceedings is initiated shall be retained throughout successive proceeding regardless of the bodies participating in them. All of the units are under obligation to provide information from a file on the basis of its initial identification.*

The title page shall indicate the body with primary responsibility for the proceedings and the time-limit for its settlement."

"Article 15 - Documents shall be typed or legibly handwritten in ink, in the national language". The top of the page shall contain a summary of the pleadings. They shall be signed by the interested parties, or their legal representatives or attorneys. Each document, with the sole exception of the document initiating the proceedings, shall be headed by the identification of the file to which it corresponds, and where appropriate, shall contain a precise indication of the representation exercised ...."

Administrative proceedings in Argentina are written.

Once again, Argentina would like to draw the Panel's attention to the numerous requests by the implementing authority to the exporting companies concerning documentation to be submitted, and is ready to provide the Panel with any documents that it may consider relevant in this respect.

Brazil's Comments

Regarding Argentina's response, the following observation is in order. We believe that Argentina has failed to respond to the Panel's question, that is, to comment on para. 59 of Brazil's Second Oral Statement. Paragraph 59 provides that:

> "*We point out to the Panel that even though the investigating authority also disregarded the export price information submitted by the exporters Sadia and Avipal, the investigating authority still calculated the individual margins of dumping for those two companies. Brazil fails to see the reason why the authority decided to proceed differently with respect to the information provided by Frangosul and Catarinense.*"

We have already established, and Argentina confirms, that the export price data submitted by Frangosul and Catarinense was complete and accompanied by supporting documentation. The authority could, and should, have used that information to establish the export price data for the two exporters. We believe that the authority should have also used the normal value information submitted by Frangosul and Catarinense in the investigation. However, even if the authority was entitled to disregard the normal value information of these two exporters, which it wasn't, the authority could have still determined an individual dumping margin for them. That is exactly what the authority did with respect to the exporters Sadia and Avipal. While the authority accepted the normal value information and disregarded the export price data submitted by them, the authority still went on to calculate the individual margins of dumping for Sadia and Avipal. Argentina has ***not*** explained why the authority acted differently with respect to Frangosul and Catarinense.

The Panel should note that this is the first time in this proceeding that Argentina presents the argument that the investigating authority did not accept the information submitted by Catarinense because the company did not accredit representation. We point out that nowhere in the report prior to the final determination[34] or in the final determination[35] does the authority offer that explanation as the reason why the information submitted by Catarinense was disregarded.

Claim 24

84. **In respect of claim 24, please indicate precisely (page number, paragraph number, line number) where the investigating authority gave the reasons for not making the various adjustments to the JOX domestic price data, either in the investigating authority's final determination, or in any other document prepared by the investigating authority at the time of its determination. If the Panel does not already have a copy of the relevant document, please provide a copy thereof.**

Response from Argentina

At folio 3040 of the Report on the Final Determination, Section VIII.1.3, there is an explanation of the circumstances of the request for information by the implementing authority to the President of the JOX publication.

Brazil's Comments

In responding to the Panel's question, Argentina refers to Section VIII.1.3 of the final determination[36], where supposedly the investigating authority gave the reasons for not making the various adjustments to the JOX domestic price data. We note that the passage referred to by Argentina simply provides that the Argentinean authority requested JOX, on 25 June 1999 and on 27 July 1999, to provide an explanation of the taxes included in the published prices, as well as the general conditions to which the prices were subject to. That passage further provides that, on 28 July 1999 and on 3 August 1999, JOX submitted the requested information in Portuguese. The Panel will note that in the final determination the investigating authority did *not* indicate that the various adjustments reported by JOX would not be made to the domestic price data, nor did it provide the reasons for not making such adjustments.

85. **Did the investigating authority ask JOX to provide a Spanish translation of its letter of 3 August 1999 through which JOX had given information in Portuguese? If so, please provide a copy of the document containing that request.**

Response from Argentina

The translation was not requested because it was assumed that the parties to the anti-dumping proceedings, to which the National Law on Administrative Procedures applies on a residual basis, would know what was required under that Law.

---

[34] Exhibit BRA-28.
[35] Exhibit BRA-15.
[36] Page 56 of Exhibit BRA-15.

Brazil's Comments

Argentina confirms that the investigating authority did not ask JOX to provide a Spanish translation of its 3 August 1999 letter.[37] Argentina justifies the authority's failure to request the translation by stating that the parties intervening in a dumping proceeding know the requirements for submitting such information.[38]

Regarding Argentina's justification, we remind the panel the following. First, the information submitted by JOX was a result of a request made by the investigating authority and not by the Brazilian exporters or petitioner. It is important that the Panel note that JOX is a private entity, not related to the Brazilian government or any of the Brazilian exporters subject to the investigation. Thus, according to the definition of "interested parties" in Article 6.11 of the Agreement, JOX did not qualify as an interested party in the investigation proceeding, and was under no obligation to respond to the Argentinean authorities much less to provide a translation of its response in Spanish. Second, even after JOX provided information on the various adjustments to its published domestic prices, the authority still did not request the translation. We point out that the authority could, and should, have requested the translation or translated the information themselves. Brazil believes that if the Argentinean authority decided to use the JOX information to establish the normal value for all other exporters, it should have taken into account JOX's explanation on taxes, financial discount, sales commission and freight for the published prices. Third, under Article 2.4 of the Agreement due allowance in a fair comparison is an obligation of the investigating authority. If the authority knows that there are differences between the export price and the normal value, which affect price comparability, the authority is required to make that adjustment. Once JOX provided that its published domestic prices include taxes, financial cost, sales commission and freight, the authority was obligated to make these adjustments.

86. Please comment on para. 68 of Brazil's second oral statement.

Response from Argentina

We agree with Brazil in theory that to conduct a fair comparison, all of the appropriate adjustments need to be made both to the normal value and the export price.

However, in the case at issue, with respect to the JOX publication the information that would have made it possible to carry out some of the adjustments that Brazil mentions did not comply with the requirements of the National Law on Administrative Procedures (Law No. 19549) in that under Article 28 of Decree No. 1759/72 regulating the said Law, documentation in a foreign language must be translated into Spanish by a registered translator.

Brazil's Comments

Apparently, Argentina agrees with Brazil that in order to make a fair comparison, all necessary adjustments should be made to normal value and export price.[39] Argentina, however, fails to comment on paragraph 68 of Brazil's second oral statement, where we explain why the authority should have, at least, made an

---

[37] ARS, question 85.
[38] *Ibid.*
[39] ARS, question 86.

adjustment in the normal value to exclude taxes and financial cost included in the JOX prices, in order to make a fair comparison. A more detailed explanation on why the authority should have excluded taxes and financial cost from the JOX published domestic prices is provided in our response to the Panel's questions in the second substantive meeting.[40]

Claim 32

87. Please indicate precisely (page number, paragraph number, line number) where the investigating authority explained why it looked at 1999 data for only certain injury factors and not others, either in the investigating authority's final determination, or in any other document prepared by the investigating authority at the time of its determination. If the Panel does not already have a copy of the relevant document, please provide a copy thereof.

Response from Argentina

Lines 1 to 6 in the second paragraph of Section V (State of the Domestic Industry) of Record No. 576 of 23 December 1999, which appears in CNCE File No. 43/1997 (folio 7313), clearly state that:

"The 'period under analysis' corresponds to the period from January 1996 to December 1998. For certain variables, such as domestic production, prices, imports, national exports and apparent consumption, data is included for the first half of 1999. Data for 1995 is provided for reference purposes. Variations for the first half of 1999 are against the same period for the previous year." (Emphasis added)

Nevertheless, Argentina reiterates what it stated in its two previous submissions, and for a better understanding of the overall context, we repeat our reply that:

"First of all, there is no obligation to analyse any indicator outside the period established by the authorities as the investigation period.

In accordance with international practice in certain countries, Argentina considered a number of variables accessible to the public in order to double check the trends observed during the investigation period. If we were to insist on the constant updating of all indicators during the investigation, as Brazil seems to suggest in this case, the investigation would be endless. We repeat that this is not the objective of the AD Agreement, nor is it the practice of those countries which, like Argentina, examine certain relevant indicators of reference data."

It should be noted that the determination of threat of injury was based on the period from January 1996 to December 1998, and the other data, as stated in previous replies and in the Record in question was used for reference purposes.

Brazil's Comments

In responding to the Panel's question, Argentina fails to provide where the investigating authority explained why it looked at 1999 data for only certain injury

---

[40] Brazil Response to the Panel's Questions in the Second Substantive Meeting ("BRS"), question 93.

factors and not others. The passage referred to by Argentina clearly states that the data corresponding to the year 1995 is used by way of reference.[41] However, that same passage does **not** provide that the data corresponding to the first semester of 1999 is used by way of reference. What that passage provides is that the data for the variables national production, prices, imports, national exports and apparent consumption corresponding to the first semester of 1999 were included[42] in the period of injury analysis. Had the authority intended to use the data for the first semester of 1999 merely as reference, the authority would have clearly stated this in the final determination, just as it did with the data for the year 1995. In this investigation, the Argentinean authority considered a certain period of injury analysis for the factors production, prices, imports, exports and apparent consumption and considered another period of injury analysis for the remaining Article 3.4 factors.

Claim 38

88. Please explain precisely how Table 16 of Act No. 576 (para. 292 of Argentina's first written submission) constitutes an evaluation of "factors affecting domestic prices" within the meaning of Article 3.4 of the AD Agreement. Please provide a more detailed explanation than that set forth in paragraph 74 of Argentina's second oral statement.

Response from Argentina

Table No. 16, which belongs to Technical Report GEGE/1TDF No. 03/99 and is an integral part of Record No. 576, provides the average sales revenue for one kilogram of eviscerated poultry, fresh or chilled, and the relative prices of the comparable product, with regard to the price of industrial goods taken as a whole and of bovine meat - represented respectively by the Wholesale Industrial Price Index for Manufactured Goods and the simple average of the consumer price indices for fresh bovine meat, front and hind cuts.

The comparison made with respect to the Wholesale Industrial Price Index for Manufactured Goods was based on the need to assess whether the price of the product in question was following the same trend as the other manufactured goods.

With regard to the second index, Argentina has traditionally been a consumer of red meat, so that it was considered appropriate to use this index to analyse the impact of variations in that product on poultry meat as from a certain degree of substitution between bovine meat and poultry meat.

As can be seen from the table, the two relative prices analysed followed the same trend as average sales revenue for the product in question, although in the case of the price in relation to the simple average for bovine meat the annual variations reflected a stronger decrease in 1998 as a result of the increase in the price of bovine meat recorded that year. Indeed, as indicated in the Market Chapter of Technical Report GEGE/ITDF No. 03/99, Section VI.5 (Recent evolution of the market), folio 7371, paragraph 3: during 1998 there was a further increase in the demand for poultry as a result of the substitution effect following the sharp increases in the price of bovine meat, which reached its peak in the middle of 1998. No decline in the consumption of poultry was recorded following the subsequent fall in the price of

---

[41] ARS, question 87 and Page 9 of Exhibit BRA-14.
[42] *Ibid.*

bovine meat. This is because the market perception is that the price of poultry is so low that it is even pushing the price of bovine meat downwards.

Consequently Article 3.4 was clearly taken into consideration where it provides that "[t]he examination of the impact of the dumped imports on the domestic industry concerned shall include an evaluation of all relevant economic factors and indices having a bearing on the state of the industry, including ... factors affecting domestic prices ...".

Brazil's Comments

No comments.

89. Regarding Argentina's reply to question 59 concerning paragraph 80 of Brazil's first oral statement, please provide exact citations (e.g., page number, paragraph number, line number) for the various extracts from Act No. 576.

Response from Argentina

Concerning the citations referred to in paragraph 80:

- The citation "An econometric exercise was conducted which showed that for the period from January 1995 to June 1999, the price of the product on the domestic market depended on the volume of imports for the previous month, the price of the imported product and the price of bovine meat. The inclusion of the price of maize in the mentioned model did not produce satisfactory results, indicating that the considerable variability of the price of whole eviscerated poultry does not coincide with the price of maize. Nevertheless, both variables showed similar patterns ... " can be found in Section VIII (Conditions of Competition between the Like Product and the Imported Product), § 1, folio 7328, last paragraph, and folio 7329, first paragraph.

- The citation according to which "[t]he economic recession did not particularly affect the consumption of whole eviscerated poultry, which continued to increase (in 1998 it increased by 14 per cent)" can be found in Section VIII (Conditions of Competition between the Like Product and the Imported Product), § 1, folio 7329, second paragraph.

- Finally, the citation "... with regard to the price of industrial goods taken as a whole and of bovine meat - represented respectively by the Wholesale Industrial Price Index for Manufactured Goods and the simple average of the consumer price indices for fresh bovine meat, front and hind cuts - followed the same trend as the sales revenue described above, although in the case of bovine meat, the annual variations reflected a stronger decrease in 1998 as a result of the increase in the price of bovine meat recorded that year" can be found in Section V (State of the Domestic Industry), at folio 7318, last paragraph.

Brazil's Comments

No comments.

Questions to both parties

Claim 21

95. What are 'essential facts under consideration which form the basis for the decisions whether to apply definitive measures' within the meaning of Article 6.9 ADA? In particular, would 'essential facts' cover only facts or also reasoning supporting a certain conclusion?

Response from Argentina

>They are the facts upon which the implementing authority bases its conclusions.

Brazil's Comments

>No comments.

96. At para. 9.229 of its report, the panel in *Guatemala - Cement II* found that:

>'An interested party will not know whether a particular fact is "important" or not unless the investigating authority has explicitly identified it as one of the "essential facts" which form the basis of the authority's decision whether to impose definitive measures.'

Would you agree with the above finding? Please explain.

Response from Argentina

>Argentina agrees with the position of the Panel in *Guatemala - Cement II* - indeed, all that is reported in the Report on Action Taken makes up the facts which will form the basis of the authority's decision, a circumstance of which the implementing authority informs the interested parties.

Brazil's Comments

>Argentina states that all information contained in the report prior to the final determination (Exhibit BRA-28) make up the facts which form the basis of the authority's decision whether to impose definitive measures.[43] We do not agree with Argentina's statement. The Panel should carefully look at Exhibit BRA-28 in order to verify that the authority did **not** explicitly identify what facts were considered "essential facts", which would form the basis of the authority's decision whether to impose definitive measures. In fact, what Exhibit BRA-28 presents is a summary of the information submitted by the various interested parties in the files of the investigation. Without explicitly indicating to the interested parties what the "essential facts" under consideration were, the authority failed to provide the exporters with the opportunity to defend their interests.

Claim 22

97. What do parties understand by the words "for each known exporter or producer concerned of the product under investigation" contained in the first sentence of Article 6.10? In the view of the parties, would the cited portion of the

---

[43] ARS, question 96.

first sentence of Article 6.10 require the calculation of an individual margin of dumping for each exporter known to the investigating authority? Would that also be the case when a known exporter does not provide relevant information requested by the investigating authority? Please explain.

Response from Argentina

A condition for the determination of an individual margin of dumping for each exporter is that the exporter should be known, and should supply the documentation needed to reach such a determination.

Brazil's Comments

According to Argentina, in order for the authority to determine an individual margin of dumping, two conditions are required: (1) that the exporter be known to the authority; and, (2) that the exporter present the necessary documentation to enable the calculation of the individual margin.[44]

We must point out that nothing in Article 6.10 of the Agreement requires that the exporter present the necessary documentation, as a condition for the authority to determine an individual dumping margin. Under Article 6.10, the authority must determine an individual margin of dumping for each known exporter or producer concerned of the product under investigation. In that regard, the exporters Frangosul and Catarinenese were known exporters/producers of the product under investigation. Both companies presented normal value and export price information during the investigation, being that the export price data submitted by these exporters was accompanied by supporting documentation. Accordingly, the authority was obligated to determine an individual dumping margin for the two exporters.

We have, nonetheless, also provided that the fact that an exporter has not submitted the relevant or appropriate information to establish normal value or export price does not exclude the authority's obligation under Article 6.10 to determine an individual margin of dumping for that exporter.[45] If the known exporter does not provide the relevant information necessary to calculate normal value or export price, but the authority still has access to individual information for that exporter, the investigating authority is still required to calculate the individual margin of dumping. We emphasize that there is a difference between applying facts available, as provided in Article 6.8 of the Agreement, to a specific exporter and not calculating the individual dumping margin for that exporter. In cases where the authority does not have the relevant normal value or export price data and the authority is entitled to resort to facts available, the facts available applicable to a specific exporter may be different from the facts available applicable to another exporter. Accordingly, the calculation of the individual margins for those two exporters will also be different.

98. In the view of the parties, would the findings in paras. 6.86 to 6.101 (both included) of the panel *Argentina - Ceramic Tiles* be applicable to the facts in this dispute? In particular, would the following finding of the panel be relevant to the current dispute: 'The basis of the normal value determination has no bearing on the ability to calculate an individual dumping margin for the producer whose normal value is in question.'? Would the lack of information on

---

[44] *Ibid.*, question 97.
[45] BRS, questions 90, 97 and 98.

Report of the Panel

normal value, export price or cost of production, automatically allow the non-calculation of an individual dumping of margin in accordance with Article 6.10? Please explain, identifying and providing relevant factual support to the Panel.

Response from Argentina

It does not apply to the present case, since in the arguments of the *Ceramic Tiles* case, the investigating authority, in calculating the margin of dumping, took account of circumstances relating to "cases where the number of exporters, producers, importers or types of products involved is so large as to make such a determination impracticable ...". In other words, the considerations on which the Panel relied were related to the fact that the Argentine authority had decided to determine the margin of dumping on the basis of "a reasonable number of interested parties ... using samples which are statistically valid on the basis of information available to the authorities at the time of the selection, ...". Thus, the findings are not applicable to this case.

Brazil's Comments

Even though in *Argentina - Ceramic Tiles* the Argentinean authority calculated the dumping margin based on the second sentence of Article 6.10, which limits the examination of the authority to certain producers and exporters, the reasoning provided by that Panel with respect to the interpretation of Article 6.10 is, nonetheless, correct and applicable to this case.

In particular, we cite to the following passage in that report:

"(...) Article 9.4 provides that, where the authorities limit their examination under Article 6.10, the anti-dumping duty for exporters or producers that are not examined shall not exceed a level determined on the basis of the results of the examination of those exporters or producers that were examined. That Article 9.4 does not provide any methodology for determining the level of duties applicable to exporters or producers that are examined in our view confirms that the general rule requiring individual margins remains applicable to those exporters or producers. We find further confirmation in Article 6.10.2, which requires that, in general, an individual margin of dumping must be calculated even for the producers/exporters not initially included in the sample, if they provide the necessary information and if to do so is not unduly burdensome. If even producers not included in the original sample are entitled to an individual margin calculation, then it follows that producers that were included in the original sample are entitled as well. Indeed, the parties appear to agree that Article 6.10 of the AD Agreement requires that as a rule an individual margin of dumping has to be determined for each exporter with regard to the product subject to investigation."[46] (emphasis added)

---

[46] Argentina - *Definitive Measures on Imports of Ceramic Floor Tiles from Italy*, 28 September 2001, WT/DS189/R, DSR 2001:XII, 6241, at para. 6.90 (adopted on 5 November 2001) (*"Argentina - Ceramic Tiles"*).

Thus, if that Panel found that producers included or not in a sample, in situations where a sample was needed, were entitled to an individual margin calculation, then this Panel should also conclude that in the instant case the producers that were examined, in situations where a sample was not needed, were also entitled to an individual margin calculation.

REPLIES BY ARGENTINA TO THE QUESTIONS OF BRAZIL

1 and 2. The Brazilian exporters were informed of the period of data collection at the preliminary determination stage of the investigation.

As can be seen in the annexes to the Report on the Preliminary Determination, the implementing authority had already decided that the investigation period would be January 1998 to January 1999.

All of the exporting companies could clearly see what investigation period was being examined by the authority. In the case of AVIPAL, SADIA and FRANGOSUL, the requests for documentation by the DCD provided indications of what the investigation period to be examined would be.

Likewise, we refer to the Summary Table attached as a supplement to Argentina's replies to the questionnaire provided by the Panel following the First Meeting of the Panel with the Parties.

3. What basis did the investigating authority use to select January 1998 through January 1999 as the period of data collection for dumping purposes, as opposed to the period 1996 through 1998, indicated in the dumping questionnaires sent to Sadia, Avipal and Frangosul?

Brazil's Comments

The Panel should observe that the Argentinean investigating authority did not clearly and specifically establish in the preliminary determination that the dumping period of data collection was from January 1998 through January 1999.[47] It is also important to note that the investigating authority sent a letter to petitioner on 1 June 1999, requesting that petitioner update the information regarding normal value in Brazil for the period January 1998 through January 1999.[48] No similar letter was sent from the authority to the Brazilian exporters prior to the preliminary determination. In fact, the investigating authority did not use any of the normal value and export price information submitted by the Brazilian exporters for the years 1996 through 1999 in the preliminary dumping determination. It was only on 12 October 1999 and on 18 October 1999, that the authority sent a letter to Avipal, Frangosul, Sadia, Nicolini and Seara requesting that they provide a list of transactions and invoices for sales in the internal market from January 1998 through January 1999. Nine months after the investigation was initiated and after a preliminary determination had been issued, the authority chose to establish and inform the Brazilian exporters of the data collection period for the dumping investigation.

It was also only on 15 September 1999, that the authority sent a letter to the Brazilian exporters CCLP, Catarinense, Chapecó, Minuano, Perdigão, Comaves and

---

[47] Exhibit BRA-11
[48] Page 10 of Exhibit BRA-11.

Pena Branca notifying them of the investigation and inviting them to provide questionnaire responses.[49]

On a final note, if the authority determined the period of investigation based on the information corresponding to the period closest to initiation, why did the authority request normal value and export price information for the years 1996 through 1999, and why didn't the authority establish the period of investigation as soon as the investigation was initiated?

---

[49] Exhibit BRA-13.

ANNEX B

Argentina

	Contents	Page
Annex B-1	First Written Submission of Argentina	B-2092
Annex B-2	First Oral Statement of Argentina	B-2160
Annex B-3	Second Written Submission of Argentina	B-2173
Annex B-4	Replies of Argentina to Questions of the Panel - First Meeting	B-2188
Annex B-5	Second Oral Statement of Argentina	B-2215
Annex B-6	Replies of Argentina to Questions of the Panel - Second Meeting	B-2233
Annex B-7	Replies of Argentina to Questions of Brazil - Second Meeting	B-2247
Annex B-8	Comments of Argentina on the Responses of Brazil to the Panel's Questions - Second Meeting	B-2248
Annex B-9	Comments of Argentina on the Second Oral Statement of Brazil	B-2252

ANNEX B-1

FIRST WRITTEN SUBMISSION OF ARGENTINA
(29 August 2002)

TABLE OF CONTENTS

			Page
INTRODUCTION			B-2093
I.	BACKGROUND		B-2093
II.	PRELIMINARY ARGUMENTS: RELEVANT RULES AND PRINCIPLES OF PUBLIC INTERNATIONAL LAW APPLICABLE TO THIS PROCEEDING		B-2094
	II.1	STANDARD OF REVIEW	B-2094
	II.2	OTHER PRINCIPLES AND RULES OF PUBLIC INTERNATIONAL LAW APPLICABLE TO THE CASE	B-2096
	II.3	PLEADINGS PERTAINING TO THIS SECTION	B-2098
III.	SUBSTANTIVE CLAIMS		B-2099
	III.1	INITIATION OF THE INVESTIGATION	B-2099
		III.1.1 CLAIMS 1 AND 5: CONSISTENCY WITH ARTICLE 5.2	B-2099
		III.1.2 CLAIMS 2, 4, 6 AND 8: CONSISTENCY WITH ARTICLE 5.3	B-2104
		III.1.3 CLAIM 9: CONSISTENCY WITH ARTICLE 5.7	B-2109
		III.1.4 CLAIMS 3, 7 AND 31: CONSISTENCY WITH ARTICLE 5.8	B-2110
	III.2	CONDUCT OF AN ANTI-DUMPING INVESTIGATION - EVIDENTIARY AND PUBLIC NOTICE REQUIREMENTS	B-2112
		III.2.1 CLAIM 10: CONSISTENCY WITH ARTICLE 12.1	B-2112
		III.2.2 CLAIMS 11 TO 14: CONSISTENCY WITH ARTICLE 6	B-2114
		III.2.2.1 CLAIM 11: CONSISTENCY WITH ARTICLE 6.1.1	B-2115
		III.2.2.2 CLAIM 12: CONSISTENCY WITH ARTICLE 6.1.2	B-2118
		III.2.2.3 CLAIM 13: CONSISTENCY WITH ARTICLE 6.2	B-2120
		III.2.2.4 CLAIM 14: CONSISTENCY WITH ARTICLE 6.1.3	B-2123
		III.2.3 CLAIMS 15, 16, 17 AND 21: CONSISTENCY WITH ARTICLES 6.8 (ANNEX II), 6.9 AND 12.2.2	B-2124

			Page
	III.2.4	CLAIMS 18, 19, 20 AND 22: CONSISTENCY WITH ARTICLES 12.2.2, 6.8 (ANNEX II) AND 6.10	B-2127
III.3		CONDUCT OF THE INVESTIGATION AND FINAL DETERMINATION	B-2133
	III.3.1	CLAIM 23: CONSISTENCY WITH ARTICLE 2.4	B-2133
	III.3.2	CLAIM 24: CONSISTENCY WITH ARTICLE 2.4	B-2135
	III.3.3	CLAIM 25: CONSISTENCY WITH ARTICLE 2.4	B-2137
	III.3.4	CLAIM 26: CONSISTENCY WITH ARTICLE 2.4	B-2138
	III.3.5	CLAIM 27: CONSISTENCY WITH ARTICLE 2.4.2	B-2140
	III.3.6	CLAIMS 32 AND 33: CONSISTENCY WITH ARTICLES 3.1, 3.4, 3.5 AND 12.2.2	B-2140
	III.3.7	CLAIMS 34, 35, 36 AND 37. CONSISTENCY WITH ARTICLE 3.1, 3.2, 3.4 AND 3.5	B-2143
	III.3.8	CLAIMS 38, 39 AND 40: CONSISTENCY WITH ARTICLES 3.4 AND 3.1, AND ARTICLE 12.2.2	B-2149
	III.3.9	CLAIM 41: CONSISTENCY WITH ARTICLE 4.1	B-2153
III.4		IMPOSITION AND COLLECTION OF ANTI-DUMPING DUTIES AS A RESULT OF THE ANTI-DUMPING INVESTIGATION	B-2154
	III.4.1	CLAIMS 28, 29 AND 30: CONSISTENCY WITH ARTICLES 9.2, 9.3 AND 12.2.2	B-2154
IV.	PLEADINGS		B-2159

INTRODUCTION

In this submission, Argentina rejects the doubts raised by Brazil concerning Resolution 574/2000 of the Ministry of the Economy of the Argentine Republic on the basis of various considerations of fact and law which are presented below in two main sections as follows: Section II, dealing with the standard of review and the rules and principles of public international law applicable to the case, and Section III, which refutes the substantive arguments contained in Brazil's 41 claims.

I. BACKGROUND

1. On 21 July 2000, the Ministry of the Economy of the Argentine Republic issued Resolution No. 574, imposing definitive anti-dumping measures on imports of poultry from Brazil, classified under MERCOSUR tariff headings 0207.11.00 and 0207.12.00 for a period of three years. The Resolution was published in the Official Bulletin of the Argentine Republic of 24 July 2000.

2. On 30 August 2000, in conformity with Article 2 of the Protocol of Brasilia, Brazil requested the initiation of direct negotiations with Argentina on the application of anti-dumping duties on Brazilian poultry exports (Resolution ME 574/00).

Report of the Panel

3. On 24 January 2001, Brazil gave notice of its intention to initiate the arbitral proceedings laid down in Article 7 of the Protocol of Brasilia.

4. On 21 May 2001, the dispute was settled by the award of the MERCOSUR Ad Hoc Arbitral Tribunal set up to rule on the *dispute between the Federative Republic of Brazil and the Argentine Republic on "Imposition of Anti-dumping Duties on Exports of Whole Poultry from Brazil (Res. 574/2000 of the Ministry of the Economy of the Argentine Republic)."* In accordance with Article 22 of the Protocol of Brasilia, following the award, the Arbitral Tribunal issued a clarification thereof on 18 June 2001.

5. On 7 November 2001, Brazil requested consultations with Argentina under Article 4 of the Understanding on Rules and Procedures Governing the Settlement of Disputes (DSU), Article XXII of the General Agreement on Tariffs and Trade 1994 (GATT 1994), Article 17 of the Agreement on Implementation of Article VI of the GATT 1994 (Anti-Dumping Agreement), including Article 17.4 thereof, and Article 19 of the Agreement on Implementation of Article VII of the GATT 1994 (Agreement on Customs Valuation), in respect of Resolution ME 574/00.

6. On 10 December 2001, consultations were held in Geneva between the delegations of the two countries.

7. On 25 February 2002, the Government of Brazil, pursuant to Article XXII of the GATT 1994, Article 6 of the DSU and Article 17 of the Anti-Dumping Agreement, requested the establishment of a panel.

8. On 17 April 2002, the Dispute Settlement Body established the Panel that was to examine the claims of the Government of Brazil. The Panel was constituted on 27 June 2002.

II. PRELIMINARY ARGUMENTS: RELEVANT RULES AND PRINCIPLES OF PUBLIC INTERNATIONAL LAW APPLICABLE TO THIS PROCEEDING

II.1 STANDARD OF REVIEW

9. Argentina agrees that there is a separate standard of review[1] in the case of Article 17.6 of the Anti-Dumping Agreement. However, the recognition of a different standard cannot be understood as an acknowledgement of the existence of the presumption of bad faith in international relations, let alone entitle Brazil to make

---

[1] The peculiarity of the Anti-Dumping Agreement as the only one of the Agreements that contains a specific standard for the review of provisional or definitive anti-dumping measures or price agreements when they are challenged under the DSU was recognized in Panel Report WT/DS24/R of 8 November 1996: "We note that the ATC does not establish a standard of review for panels, contrary, for example, to the WTO Agreement on Implementation of Article VI of the General Agreement on Tariffs and Trade 1994, where Article 17.6 defines the standard of review that panels have to apply when reviewing cases arising under that Agreement. We further note that the DSU does not contain a provision mandating a specific standard of review", (para. 7.8, page 74).

Similarly, the Report of the Appellate Body in *Argentina - Safeguard Measures on Imports of Footwear* (WT/DS121/AB/R) of 14 December 1999 asserts that: "We have stated, on more than one occasion, that, for all but one of the covered agreements, Article 11 of the DSU sets forth the appropriate standard of review for panels. The only exception is the Agreement on Implementation of Article VI of the General Agreement on Tariffs and Trade 1994, in which a specific provision, Article 17.6, sets out a special standard of review for disputes arising under that Agreement".

an accusation against Argentina on the basis of such a presumption. On the contrary, the principle of good faith "informs the provisions of the Anti-Dumping Agreement, as well as the other covered agreements."[2]

10. Contrary to what Brazil has said[3], Argentina did not act in bad faith, but conducts its international relations according to the "pervasive"[4] principle of good faith that underlies all treaties.

11. Brazil puts forward a generic argument without identifying the instances in Argentina's investigation in which it considers that Argentina did not act in good faith, and without substantiating its assertions in this respect. Accusations of a generic nature are out of place in a WTO proceeding in which, ultimately, the law must be applied to the identified facts of the case.

12. Argentina considers that Brazil's arguments should be rejected: indeed, in none of the paragraphs under the heading "Anti-Dumping Agreement Standard of Review" does Brazil substantiate those arguments - it merely sets forth allegations which it fails to develop.

13. Argentina also rejects Brazil's argument[5] that the Argentine Government improperly established the facts and conducted a non-objective and biased evaluation of the facts so as to favour the interests of the domestic industry in a manner inconsistent with the provisions of the Anti-Dumping Agreement. Here once again, Brazil fails to provide evidence substantiating its assertion that the evaluation was "non-objective" or that the investigation was biased.

14. Similarly, Argentina notes that according to Article 17.6 (ii), the Panel "shall interpret the relevant provisions of the Agreement in accordance with customary rules of interpretation of public international law". That is to say, according to the Vienna Convention on the Law of Treaties, the correct way to proceed is to examine the ordinary meaning of the provision in its context and in the light of its object and purpose. Contrary to Brazil's unsubstantiated statement[6], the principle of good faith is at the basis of the rule *pacta sunt servanda*, i.e. treaties must be performed by the parties to them in good faith.

15. Similarly, Argentina also considers that the failure by Brazil to identify the case of bad faith which it attributes to Argentina seriously impairs its ability to defend itself under Article 3.10 of the DSU, according to which, if a dispute arises, the parties must engage in dispute settlement procedures "in good faith in an effort to resolve the dispute". Thus, in *United States - Tax Treatment for "Foreign Sales Corporations"*[7], the Appellate Body maintained that: "By good faith compliance,

---

[2] Report of the Appellate Body in *United States - Anti-Dumping Measures on Certain Hot-Rolled Steel Products from Japan (United States - Hot-Rolled Steel)*, WT/DS184/AB/R adopted on 23 August 2001, DSR 2001:X, 4697, para. 101.
[3] First written submission of Brazil, para. 31.
[4] Report of the Appellate Body in *United States - Tax Treatment for "Foreign Sales Corporations"* (WT/DS108/AB/R) adopted on 20 March 2000, DSR 2000:III, 1619, para. 166: " ... This is another specific manifestation of the principle of good faith which, we have pointed out, is at once a general principle of law and a principle of general international law. This pervasive principle requires both complaining and responding Members to comply with the requirements of the DSU (and related requirements in other covered agreements) in good faith ... ".
[5] First written submission of Brazil, para. 28.
[6] *Ibid.*, para. 31.
[7] Report of the Appellate Body, *United States - Tax Treatment for "Foreign Sales Corporations"* (WT/DS108/AB/R) adopted on 20 March 2000, DSR 2000:III, 1619, para. 166.

complaining Members accord to the responding Members the full measure of protection and opportunity to defend, contemplated by the letter and spirit of the procedural rules. The same principle of good faith requires that responding Members seasonably and promptly bring claimed procedural deficiencies to the attention of the complaining Member, and to the DSB or the Panel, so that corrections, if needed, can be made to resolve disputes."

II.2 OTHER PRINCIPLES AND RULES OF PUBLIC INTERNATIONAL LAW APPLICABLE TO THE CASE

16. Brazil's claim also contradicts general principles of international law and disregards relevant rules of interpretation of WTO obligations. In this connection, Argentina would like to point out that Brazil's conduct in omitting any reference to the arbitral award relating to the same complaint in the framework of MERCOSUR, in which its claims were not upheld, is contrary to the principle of good faith in the fulfilment of agreements and in the actions of States. Brazil is now trying to reverse this negative result, rearguing its case under the WTO Dispute Settlement Understanding.

17. Argentina also wonders whether by omitting any reference to the fact that the case had already previously been *discussed* and *settled* in the framework of MERCOSUR, Brazil may have abused its rights under the WTO Agreements.

18. Argentina and Brazil are not only WTO Members, but also States party to MERCOSUR, and as such, cannot ignore the *legal framework* and the particular relationship resulting from the integration process. The existence of this legal framework and the adjudications of its dispute settlement system must be taken into account by the Panel when acting in accordance with the DSU. This fits in with the obligation contained in Article 3.2 of the DSU to clarify the existing provisions of the agreements in accordance with the customary rules of interpretation of public international law.

19. Both Argentina and Brazil, as States party to MERCOSUR, have assumed a set of commitments based on the Treaty of Asunción for the creation of the Southern Cone Common Market and the Protocol of Brasilia for the Settlement of Disputes (Protocol of Brasilia)[8] intended to resolve conflicts between States parties. These instruments are particularly relevant because Brazil's complaint against Argentina in this case has already been addressed[9] and settled through the procedure regulated by those regional agreements.

20. Brazil's decision to resort to the Protocol of Brasilia mechanism as the appropriate framework for the settlement of the dispute, added to the fact that this was not the first instance of dispute settlement at the regional level - three awards had

---

[8] Treaty for the Creation of a Common Market between the Argentine Republic, the Federative Republic of Brazil, the Republic of Paraguay and the Eastern Republic of Uruguay, signed on 26 March 1991, which entered into force on 29 November 1991 and was notified under the GATT/WTO on 5 March 1992. Protocol of Brasilia for the Settlement of Disputes, signed on 17 December 1991. Available on: http:/www.mercosur.org.uy

[9] Award of the MERCOSUR Ad Hoc Arbitral Tribunal constituted to rule on the dispute between the Federative Republic of Brazil and the Argentine Republic regarding the imposition of anti-dumping measures on exports of whole poultry from Brazil (Res. 574/2000) of the Ministry of the Economy of the Argentine Republic. Date: 21 May 2001.

already been made previously between Argentina and Brazil[10] - implies full acceptance of the MERCOSUR legal framework and acceptance of the dispute settlement procedure *in totum*, including the unappealable and definitive nature of its awards.[11] Brazil has been consistent in repeatedly accepting the MERCOSUR dispute settlement system and its consequences, the arbitral awards. This is not an isolated practice, but a procedure regulated by a Protocol currently in force that has been applied in a total of eight cases since 1999[12], seven of which have involved Brazil

---

[10] I. Award of the MERCOSUR Ad Hoc Arbitral Tribunal constituted to hear the dispute on communications Nos. 37 of 17 December 1997 and 7 of 20 February 1998 from the Department of Foreign Trade Operations (Decex) of the Secretariat for Foreign Trade (Secex): Application of restrictive measures to reciprocal trade. Date: 28 April 1999.

II Award of the MERCOSUR Ad Hoc Arbitral Tribunal constituted to hear the complaint of the Argentine Republic against the Federative Republic of Brazil on subsidies for the production and exportation of pork. Date: 27 September 1999.

III Award of the MERCOSUR Ad Hoc Arbitral Tribunal constituted to rule on the application of safeguard measures to textile products (Res. 861/99) by the Ministry of the Economy and Public Works and Services. Date: 10 March 2000.
Available on: http:/www.mercosur.org.uy

[11] Articles 8 and 21 of the Protocol of Brasilia:
"Article 8: The State Parties declare that they recognize as obligatory, *ipso facto* and without need of a special agreement, the jurisdiction of the Arbitral Tribunal which in each case is established to hear and resolve all controversies which are referred to in the present Protocol."
"Article 21:
1. The decisions of the Arbitral Tribunal cannot be appealed, and are binding on the State Parties to the controversies from the moment the respective notification is received and will be deemed by them to have the effect of res judicata.
2. The decisions should be complied with within a time-limit of fifteen (15) days, unless the Arbitral Tribunal fixes a different time-limit."
(See Annex ARG-XXXII)

[12] I Award of the MERCOSUR Ad Hoc Arbitral Tribunal constituted to hear the dispute on communications Nos. 37 of 17 December 1997 and 7 of 20 February 1998 of the Department of Foreign Trade Operations (Decex) of the Secretariat for Foreign Trade (Secex): Application of restrictive measures to reciprocal trade. Date: 28 April 1999.

II. Award of the MERCOSUR Ad Hoc Arbitral Tribunal constituted to hear the complaint of the Argentine Republic against the Federative Republic of Brazil on subsidies for the production and exportation of pork. Date: 27 September 1999.

III. Award of the MERCOSUR Ad Hoc Arbitral Tribunal constituted to rule on the application of safeguard measures to textile products (Res. 861/99) of the Ministry of the Economy and Public Works and Services. Date: 10 March 2000.

IV. Award of the MERCOSUR Ad Hoc Arbitral Tribunal constituted to rule on the dispute between the Federative Republic of Brazil and the Argentine Republic regarding the imposition of anti-dumping duties on exports of whole poultry from Brazil (Res. 574/2000) of the Ministry of the Economy of the Argentine Republic. Date: 21 May 2001.

V. Award of the MERCOSUR Ad Hoc Arbitral Tribunal constituted to hear the dispute brought by the Eastern Republic of Uruguay against the Argentine Republic concerning restrictions on access to the Argentine market of bicycles of Uruguayan origin. Date: 29 September 2001.

VI. Award of the MERCOSUR Ad Hoc Arbitral Tribunal constituted to hear the dispute brought by the Eastern Republic of Uruguay against the Federative Republic of Brazil concerning the prohibition on imports of remoulded tyres from Uruguay. Date: 9 January 2002.

VII. Award of the MERCOSUR Ad Hoc Arbitral Tribunal constituted to hear the dispute brought by the Argentine Republic against the Federative Republic of Brazil concerning barriers to the importation of Argentine phytosanitary products into the Brazilian market. Failure to incorporate Resolutions GMC Nos. 48/96, 87/96, 149/96, 156/96 and 71/98, preventing their entry into force in MERCOSUR. Date: 19 April 2002.

and five of which have involved disputes between Argentina and Brazil. The Panel cannot ignore this fact and the legal consequences associated with an arbitral award by an international tribunal.

21. Brazil's complaint within the framework of the WTO contradicts: (a) its consistent practice, as a MERCOSUR State party since 1991, of fulfilling the commitments it has assumed and having recourse to the dispute settlement procedure provided for under the Protocol of Brasilia and reaffirmed through the signature of the Protocol of Olivos[13]; (b) its consistent and unequivocal practice of accepting the scope of the arbitral awards, of which there have been eight thus far, seven of them involving Brazil either as complainant or respondent.

22. Argentina concludes that:

- For the purposes of clarifying the scope of the obligations *in casu*, account must be taken of the regulatory framework and the consequences of the fact that the Protocol of Brasilia was applied in the dispute at issue;

- in the alternative, the principle of estoppel and the consequences thereof are applicable to this dispute, since Brazil has consistently and unequivocally behaved in such a way as to lead Argentina to a conviction in respect of trade dispute settlement between the two parties in the framework of MERCOSUR and respect for the scope of the rulings.

II.3   PLEADINGS PERTAINING TO THIS SECTION

23. As Argentina has pointed out, the omission by Brazil of any reference to the dispute previously discussed and settled by another international tribunal clearly reveals that the current submission of the case to the WTO reflects an abusive exercise by Brazil of its rights.

24. Moreover, in the light of the international commitments in force, Brazil's prior and subsequent practice of accepting the framework of MERCOSUR for the discussion and settlement of trade disputes with Argentina as a fellow MERCOSUR State party, and given the terms under which the dispute was brought, Brazil's complaint in the framework of the WTO has given rise to an estoppel situation for which Brazil is liable under the DSU.

25. For the above reasons, and considering in particular that Brazil's complaint involves challenging a measure which is identical in the current dispute to the measure at issue in the dispute within the framework of MERCOSUR, Argentina requests the Panel to refrain from ruling on the 41 claims of alleged inconsistency of the Argentine regulations with the Anti-Dumping Agreement contained in paragraph

---

VIII Award of the MERCOSUR Ad Hoc Arbitral Tribunal constituted to rule on the dispute between the Republic of Paraguay and the Eastern Republic of Uruguay concerning the application of the IMESI (*Impuesto específico interno* - Specific Internal Tax) on the sale of cigarettes. Date: 21 May 2002.
Complete texts of the above-mentioned awards available on: http:/www.mercosur.org.uy

[13] Protocol of Olivos for dispute settlement in MERCOSUR, signed on 18 February 2002 by the four MERCOSUR States parties (not yet in force). Complete text of the Protocol of Olivos available on: http:/www.mercosur.org.uy

549 of Brazil's first written submission, and consequently to reject the requests contained in paragraph 550 of that submission.

26. In case the Panel should reject these pleadings and consider that it must rule on all of Brazil's claims, Argentina has provided substantive justification in respect of each one of those claims in Section III below.

III. SUBSTANTIVE CLAIMS

III.1 INITIATION OF THE INVESTIGATION

III.1.1 CLAIMS 1 AND 5: CONSISTENCY WITH ARTICLE 5.2

27. Brazil claims that the information provided by CEPA in its application for the initiation of an investigation - in respect of the required adjustment of normal value in view of differences in physical characteristics - was not backed by the documentation (Claim 1) and that the normal value and the export price were calculated on the basis of different periods (Claim 5).

Text of Article 5.2

The relevant part of Article 5.2 stipulates as follows:

"An application under paragraph 1 shall include evidence of (a) dumping; (b) injury within the meaning of Article VI of GATT 1994 as interpreted by this Agreement and (c) a causal link between the dumped imports and the alleged injury. Simple assertion, unsubstantiated by relevant evidence, cannot be considered sufficient to meet the requirements of this paragraph. The application shall contain such information as is reasonably available to the applicant on the following: (Emphasis added)

(...)

(iii)   information on prices at which the product in question is sold when destined for consumption in the domestic markets of the country or countries of origin or export (or, where appropriate, information on the prices at which the product is sold from the country or countries of origin or export to a third country or countries, or on the constructed value of the product) and information on export prices or, where appropriate, on the prices at which the product is first resold to an independent buyer in the territory of the importing Member;

(iv)   information on the evolution of the volume of the allegedly dumped imports, the effect of these imports on prices of the like product in the domestic market and the consequent impact of the imports on the domestic industry, as demonstrated by relevant factors and indices having a bearing on the state of the domestic industry, such as those listed in paragraphs 2 and 4 of Article 3."

Argentine claim

28. Contrary to what Brazil contends in its Claims 1 and 5, the applicant provided *all of the necessary evidence* with respect to the normal value and the export value as well as the relevant evidence for the adjustments needed in order to make a fair comparison between the normal value and the export value.

29.   We agree with Brazil, given that Article 5.2 so requires, that the applicant must provide evidence - and not simple allegations or assertions - of dumping injury to the domestic industry and a causal link, as set forth in the various subparagraphs of Article 5.2.

30.   However, Article 5.2 also stipulates that the applicant shall provide, with its applications, such information as is reasonably available to it on: the applicant and the domestic industry where applicable (Article 5.2(i)), the like product (5.2(ii)), prices - normal value and export value (Article 5.2(iii)) and the evolution of the volume of dumped imports, their effects, consequences and influence, both on the injury and on the causal link (Article 5.2(iv)).

31.   In Argentina's view, when Article 5.2 states that: "[t]he application shall contain such information as is reasonably available to the applicant ... ", it is anticipating the difficulties that domestic producers might encounter in their efforts to obtain documentary evidence of the situation at issue in their complaint.

32.   It should be noted that the applicant supplied, with its application, the documentation that was available to it. The implementing authority cannot impose upon domestic producers requirements so stringent that they would effectively block their access to such proceedings. The above-mentioned provision in Article 5.2 provides applicants with access to proceedings of this kind in keeping with the right of parties to defend themselves; to require evidence that was beyond their reach would be to deny them that right.

33.   In Argentina's view, the standards of evidence applied during the stage running from the submission of the application to the declaration of initiation of the investigation are revised upwards at later stages of the proceeding with the possible involvement of the producers-exporters concerned and other interested parties.

34.   In other words, the applicant for the initiation of an investigation is not required to prove beyond all doubt the existence of dumping, injury and causal link, since the final determination of these elements is the responsibility of the investigating authority, which conducts a thorough investigation once the initiation has been decided. As stated in the Agreement, simple assertion of dumping, injury and causal link, unsubstantiated by relevant evidence within the limits of the information reasonably available to the applicant, is not sufficient. The authority examines the accuracy and adequacy of the evidence for the sole purpose of determining whether the initiation of an investigation is justified. Once the investigation has been initiated, the respondent companies as well as the importers have the right to defend themselves at every stage of the proceeding.

35.   One of the reasons why the Anti-Dumping Agreement allows Members as much as 12 to 18 months to conduct an investigation is the complexity and detail involved in analysing, verifying and evaluating objectively the evidence that all of the participants are called upon to submit during the proceedings, in order to determine whether or not the situation justifies the imposition of anti-dumping duties in conformity with the Agreement.

36.   In other words, in the course of the proceedings, the evidence initially supplied by the applicant and the evidence supplied subsequently are compared against the evidence provided by the respondent companies and the other interested parties, verified on site, where necessary, by the implementing authority, in order to carry out an objective evaluation and arrive at reasoned conclusions.

37.   There are clearly two different standards under the Agreement as regards, *inter alia*, the quality and quantity of evidence to be submitted. On the one hand, there is the evidence to be supplied with the application for initiation which, according to the Agreement, is the evidence reasonably available to the applicant; and, on the other hand, there is the evidence to be supplied once the investigation stage has begun. Likewise, as stipulated in the Agreement itself, the standard of examination of the evidence required of the authority in deciding on the initiation of an investigation must clearly be different from the standard of evaluation and analysis required of the same authority in respect of the evidence supplied by all of the interested parties throughout the investigation *vis-à-vis* the substantive requirements for reaching a conclusion of dumping, injury, and causal link during the investigation stage.

38.   We recall, in this respect, the Panel's statement[14] in *Guatemala - Cement I*, in which it cites the case *United States - Measures Affecting Imports of Softwood Lumber from Canada:*[15]

> *"In analysing further what was meant by the term 'sufficient evidence', the Panel noted that the quantum and quality of evidence to be required of an investigating authority prior to initiation of an investigation would necessarily have to be less than that required of that authority at the time of making a final determination ... ."*[16] (Emphasis added)

39.   The Agreement does not require the applicant to provide evidence in the application that is not reasonably available to it; indeed, evidence concerning normal value and export value *par excellence* are ultimately in the hands of the respondent companies and their importers. Nor, consequently, does the Agreement require the authority to evaluate evidence that is not yet in its hands, since that evidence will be supplied during the course of the proceedings.

40.   It should be borne in mind that although Article 5.2 stipulates that the applicant must provide evidence of dumping, injury and causal link, it does not imply that the evidence supplied in itself should determine the existence of dumping, injury and causal link, but rather that the evidence, even if the Article itself does not say so, should be of **alleged** dumping, injury and causal link, **forming minimum grounds justifying the initiation of an investigation**. This interpretation is supported by an analysis of the context of the Article and the object and purpose of the Agreement. Any other interpretation would imply that an investigation was not necessary, since the evidence supplied with the application would be definitive. This would be illogical and would contradict the Agreement itself.

41.   Article 1 of the Anti-Dumping Agreement establishes, as a principle that informs the Agreement, that: "[a]n anti-dumping measure shall be applied only under circumstances provided for in Article VI of the GATT 1994 and pursuant to investigations initiated and conducted in accordance with the provisions of this Agreement ... ".

42.   The requirements for "initiated" must obviously be different from the requirements for the application of a definitive measure. This is why an investigation

---

[14] *Guatemala - Anti-dumping Investigation Regarding Portland Cement from Mexico* (WT/DS60/R), Report of the Panel, DSR 1998:IX, 3797, paras. 7.55 and 7.56.
[15] SCM/162.
[16] *Ibid.*, para. 332.

can be initiated, provisional duties applied, and a decision possibly taken not to impose a definitive measure.

43. It should also be pointed out that the Argentine implementing authority places at the disposal of applicants for the initiation of an investigation of alleged dumping a **"model form"** listing all of the evidence that these must provide under Article 5.2 of the Anti-Dumping Agreement. The Anti-Dumping Agreement has been incorporated in the Argentine legal system in its totality. Thus, the model forms meet the requirements established by Article 5.2 and its subparagraphs. The applicant filled in the form and provided annexes containing the required evidence.

44. Argentina would like to recall in this respect a statement by the Panel in *Mexico - Anti-Dumping Investigation of High Fructose Corn Syrup (HFCS) from the United States*:

> " ... *Article 5.2 does not require an application to contain analysis, but rather to contain information, in the sense of evidence, in support of allegations. While we recognize that some analysis linking the information and the allegations would be helpful in assessing the merits of an application, we cannot read the text of Article 5.2 as requiring such an analysis in the application itself.*"[17] (Emphasis added)

45. Consequently, Argentina repeats that contrary to what Brazil contends in its Claims 1 and 5, the applicant provided all of the necessary evidence with respect to normal value and export value as well as the relevant evidence to make the necessary adjustments for a fair comparison between the two values.

46. With respect to normal value, the evidence was supplied by the CENTRO DE EMPRESAS PROCESADORAS AVICOLAS (CEPA) based on a publication (JOX) containing values for the product on the Brazilian domestic market. These values were adjusted by CEPA to bring the product sold on the Brazilian domestic market into line with the product sold in Argentina, from which the head and feet are removed.

47. To adjust for differences affecting price comparability, due account was taken of the information provided by the applicant, as explained in the relevant technical report.

48. In Section I, folios 27 to 34, 37, 38, 43 and 44[18], the applicant provides information on the price of poultry (with feet, head and giblets) in São Paulo and the respective weight/meat ratio (recorded in the Directorate's report of the initiation of the investigation).

49. In accordance with Article 5.2, the authority made all of the necessary adjustments on the basis of the information and documentation "reasonably available to the applicant" supplied with the application.

50. In other words, the applicant provided the information reasonably available to it with respect to normal value, adding a publication by JOX *Asesoría Agropecuaria* (Agricultural Consultants*)*. The evidence provided is a representative value taken from a specialized publication for a given period. It is perfectly acceptable to provide a specialized publication as evidence, given that CEPA could hardly be expected to provide the sales invoices of Brazilian exporters for the Brazilian domestic market under the exact conditions of comparison that the Agreement itself requires. The

---

[17] WT/DS132/R, Report of the Panel, para. 7.76.
[18] Annex ARG-I.

majority of Argentine importers are distributors, wholesalers or major wholesale operators. This is why CEPA supplied, as evidence of normal value, the data contained in what is recognized as a serious specialized publication which reflected - within an acceptable margin of approximation in this instance - the same levels of commercial sales.[19]

51. Having provided evidence in the application within an appropriate margin of approximation in the form of a comparable price for a like product destined for consumption in the country of origin, it was unnecessary to make any market-related adjustments in order to carry out a fair comparison, since the price data making up the evidence offered as normal value and the export prices supplied by the applicant corresponded to the same level of trade. Both prices refer to the starting-point in the marketing chain, so that with respect to that point, the comparability of the two was not affected. Thus, the requirements of the Agreement for the determination of dumping during the stage prior to the initiation of the investigation were met.

52. The applicant provided a report from JOX *Asesoría Agropecuaria* which states that " ... the prices for poultry as recorded in our information bulletin refer to chilled poultry with feet, head and giblets."[20]

53. Accordingly, given that poultry is exported to Argentina without feet and head, CEPA provided an annex to Note 220/97 containing the calculation required to make a fair adjustment between poultry with feet and head sold on the Brazilian domestic market and the poultry exported to Argentina.

54. We stress that none of the subparagraphs of Article 5.2 state that the applicant must provide all of the evidence required under Articles 2 and 3 with its application for the initiation of an investigation.

55. In this connection, we cite the Panel Report in *Guatemala - Cement II*:

> *" ... We do not of course mean to suggest that an investigating authority must have before it at the time it initiates an investigation evidence of dumping within the meaning of Article 2 of the quantity and quality that would be necessary to support a preliminary or final determination. An anti-dumping investigation is a process where certainty on the existence of all the elements necessary in order to adopt a measure is reached gradually as the investigation moves forward ...*
>
> *Consistent with our discussion above, we consider that, although these provisions of Article 2 do not 'apply' as such to initiation determinations, they are certainly relevant to an investigating authorities' consideration as to whether sufficient evidence of dumping exists to justify the initiation of an investigation."*[21] (Emphasis added)

56. Article 5.2 does not require the applicant to provide evidence of normal value in respect of the entire period for which evidence of export value was provided, since it is obvious that the information on imports published by the official bodies in the country of the applicant (export price) would be reasonably available to any applicant. In other words, it is clear and reasonable that **the quantity and quality of information available to the applicant on normal sales value in the domestic**

---

[19] See folio 170 of the File.
[20] See folio 180 of the File.
[21] *Guatemala - Definitive Anti-dumping Measures on Grey Portland Cement from Mexico* (WT/DS156/R), Report of the Panel, DSR 2000:XI, 5295, paras. 8.35 and 8.36.

market of the country of origin of the anti-dumping investigation should not be the same as for the export price.

57. For the above reasons, Argentina submits that, in accordance with GATT/WTO precedent, for the purposes of the initiation the applicant provided the necessary evidence of dumping, injury and causal link in compliance with Article 5.2 of the Anti-Dumping Agreement, and that consequently, Claims 1 and 5 of Brazil are without foundation.

III.1.2 CLAIMS 2, 4, 6 AND 8: CONSISTENCY WITH ARTICLE 5.3

58. Brazil claims that by accepting the applicant's calculation to adjust normal value (Claim 2), by establishing export prices based only on export transactions with prices below normal value (Claim 4), by calculating dumping margins between the normal value and the export price based on sales that were not made at as nearly as possible the same time (Claim 6) and given that the data on dumping and injury cover different periods (Claim 8), Argentina acted inconsistently with Article 5.3 of the Anti-Dumping Agreement.

Text of Article 5.3

"The authorities shall examine the accuracy and adequacy of the evidence provided in the application to determine whether there is sufficient evidence to justify the initiation of an investigation."

Argentine argument

59. Contrary to Brazil's contentions with respect to Claims 2, 4, 6 and 8, Argentina submits that the implementing authority examined the accuracy and adequacy of the evidence provided by the applicant and concluded that it was sufficient to justify the initiation of the investigation.

60. Article 5.3 simply requires the investigating authority to examine the accuracy and adequacy of the evidence submitted by the applicant. In other words, the investigating authority must verify whether the evidence comes from a source that is backed by supporting documentation and whether it serves to prove that the requirements laid down in Article 5.2 of the Anti-Dumping Agreement have been met in such a way as to enable the implementing authority to determine the existence of **sufficient evidence to justify the initiation of an investigation.**

61. Thus, Article 5.3 of the Anti-Dumping Agreement does not impose any obligation on the authority to conduct, at that stage, a thorough investigation to establish the existence of dumping, injury and causal link, but rather, the obligation to examine the evidence provided in terms of its accuracy and adequacy.

62. Once the investigation has been initiated in accordance with the Agreement, the authorities have 12 months or a maximum of 18 months to compare the evidence submitted by the applicant against the evidence submitted by all of the interested parties, and to satisfy themselves as to its truth.

63. It must be borne in mind that the procedure leading from the application for initiation of the investigation to the decision as to whether the investigation is warranted is an *inaudita parte* procedure in which the respondents have not yet taken

part or been able to provide evidence to counter the evidence provided by the applicant.

64. Similarly, the standard of "sufficient" evidence to justify the initiation of an investigation is considerably lower than the standard required for the decision to apply a preliminary or definitive measure.

65. As stated by the Chairman of the Panel in *United States - Measures Affecting Imports of Softwood Lumber from Canada*, cited by the Panel in *Guatemala - Cement I*:

> " ... A number of questions arose regarding particular aspects of the evidence addressed by the US Department of Commerce ... However, the Panel had to take into account that it was not reviewing a determination of the existence of subsidy, injury and causality, but a finding that sufficient evidence of these elements existed to warrant an investigation ... [T]he threshold required by Article 2.1 of the Agreement for initiation of a countervailing duty investigation was such that the Panel could not properly find that the United States initiation in this case was inconsistent with that Article, having regard to the standard of review."[22] (Emphasis added)

66. Again, in *Guatemala - Cement I*, the Panel cited the *United States - Softwood Lumber* as follows:

> "In analysing further what was meant by the term 'sufficient evidence', the Panel noted that the quantum and quality of evidence to be required of an investigating authority prior to initiation of an investigation would necessarily have to be less than that required of that authority at the time of making a final determination ... "[23]

- **Concerning Brazil's claim that the implementing authority acted inconsistently with Article 5.3 by accepting the applicant's calculation to adjust normal value (Claim 2), we wish to make the following remarks:**

67. Resolution ex-SCI No. 349/91 concerning the form for the submission of an application for the initiation of an anti-dumping investigation grants the information provided by the applicant therein the status of affidavit. It should be pointed out in this connection that the implementing authority analysed the information on file when deciding to initiate the investigation. This is demonstrated by its effort to gather additional evidence on the basis of the official registers of import transactions, and to take account of that data and reflect its analysis thereof in its technical report.

68. It should be recalled, moreover, that Article 5.2 of the Agreement stipulates that "the application shall contain such information as is reasonably available to the applicant ... ". Bearing this in mind, Argentina proceeded in conformity with Articles 2 and 5.3 of the Anti-Dumping Agreement. Due account was taken, in establishing price comparability, of the adjustments for which there was enough evidence to warrant their consideration, and adjustments were made at this stage of the proceedings on the basis of the evidence on file.

---

[22] Letter from the Chairman of the Panel to the Chairman of the GATT Committee on Subsidies and Countervailing Measures (SCM/163) of 19 February 1993.
[23] WT/DS60/R, Report of the Panel, para. 7.55.

Report of the Panel

69. Once the application had been declared acceptable, during the stage prior to the initiation of the investigation, the technical bodies conducted an analysis of all of the documentation submitted.

70. Now, as regards the evidence of normal value taken for the initiation of the investigation, what was used was a publication by the consulting firm JOX of 30 June 1997 (Section I, folio 27)[24] referring to poultry with feet, heads and giblets; i.e. the reference is to sales prices on the domestic market of the product under investigation, since the said publication falls within the period under analysis at that stage.

71. As regards the statement in paragraph 77 of Brazil's submission that the information provided by JOX referred exclusively to prices of chilled poultry sold in Sao Paolo, with head, feet and giblets, for one day in 1997, we note that the implementing authority, upon examining the accuracy and adequacy of that evidence, began by taking account of the fact that JOX is a specialized publication providing an average representative value reflecting the state of the São Paulo market. That market is one of Brazil's most representative markets which, like Buenos Aires, is a large urban centre which reflects domestic consumption patterns.

72. The Agreement stipulates that identical or like products should be used for the purposes of comparison. If like products are used, adjustments may have to be made where appropriate. However, the ultimate appropriateness of such adjustments is part of the investigation process. Indeed, the final part of Article 2.4 states that the implementing authority shall indicate to the parties in question what information is necessary to ensure a fair comparison.

73. It is in this light that we must consider the mentioned physical differences between the poultry sold on the São Paulo market, for which there was sufficient evidence of value to warrant the initiation of the investigation, and the comparable value for the determination of probable dumping justifying, together with the existence of injury and a causal link, the initiation of an investigation.

74. Likewise, data from a specialized publication on a like product in a representative market of origin (poultry with head and feet on the São Paulo market) is sufficient and adequate as evidence for the purposes of considering the initiation of the requested investigation. This evidence is not meant (and should not be meant) to prove that the totality of the product in the market of origin is identical to the product at issue, but rather, in accordance with the Agreement, to provide adequate and comparable information for the purposes of proving the existence of elements justifying, from the point of view of the dumping, the initiation of the investigation.

75. The physical differences between the product in the market of origin and the product exported to Argentina warranted, in the opinion of the implementing authority, an adjustment to eliminate possible differences affecting price comparability as stipulated in Article 2.4 of the Agreement. This is why the implementing authority decided that it was necessary to make a fair adjustment to allow for the difference between poultry sold in São Paulo with feet and head, and poultry exported by Brazil to Argentina, without feet or head.

76. It is also the responsibility of the implementing authority, as established in Article 5.3 of the Agreement, to determine whether the evidence provided is sufficient to justify the initiation of an investigation. Here, the implementing

---

[24] See the folios cited in Annex ARG-I.

authority, bearing in mind the provisions of the Agreement relating to price comparability and adjustments, considered that since Article 5.3 of the Anti-Dumping Agreement did not define "sufficient evidence", the determination that the evidence supplied for that stage of the proceeding constituted "sufficient evidence" depended on its satisfying the implementing authority, on the understanding that the said evidence was subject to the condition precedent of a positive outcome of the overall review conducted.

- **Concerning Brazil's claim that the implementing authority acted inconsistently with Article 5.3 by establishing export prices based only on export transactions with prices below normal value (Claim 4), we would like to make the following remarks:**

77. Article 5.3 of the Agreement lays down the obligation to examine the accuracy and adequacy of the evidence provided in the application to determine whether it is sufficient to justify the initiation of the investigation. As explained previously, the implementing authority acted consistently with Article 5.3.

78. Brazil's statement that the selection of data by Argentina was inappropriate and biased for the purposes of establishing export prices and subsequently comparing them with the normal value in order to establish alleged dumping which, together with injury and a causal link, would justify the initiation of the investigation, is untrue. The implementing authority analysed the import transactions in an attempt to determine which of them corresponded closest to the product under investigation, and it did so for the sole purpose of calculating the most appropriate and comparable export price possible at this pre-initiation stage. Moreover, it worked out an average of the appropriate transactions, without in fact making any selection which might distort the difference between the export value and the normal value.

79. The technical department concerned examined the import transactions identified in the source in question with a view to determining which ones corresponded closest to the product under investigation so that the calculation of the export price could be as precise as possible.

80. The Report on the Initiation of the Investigation (Section IV, folios 471-518)[25] contains the margins of dumping established on the basis of the average for export transactions to Argentina involving the product under investigation. Consideration was given in this connection to average exports for the period January-August 1997. The alleged margins of dumping calculated in points 3, 4 and 7 of the Report were established for the purpose of conducting an additional analysis of the case at issue.

81. That analysis did not alter the conclusions on alleged dumping reached by the technical department. The methodology set forth in the Anti-Dumping Agreement having been applied, it was in fact unaffected by the additional analysis that Brazil calls into question.

- **Concerning Brazil's claim that the implementing authority acted inconsistently with Article 5.3 by calculating a dumping margin by making a comparison between export price and normal value, in respect of sales that were not made at as nearly as possible the same time (Claim**

---

[25] See Exhibit BRA-2.

6) and that the data on dumping and injury covers different periods (Claim 8), we would like to make the following remarks:

82. Article 5.3 requires the implementing authority to examine the accuracy and adequacy of the evidence provided in the application to determine whether it is sufficient to justify the initiation of an investigation. There is no indication of any time requirements in respect of the export prices and the normal value.

83. The Argentine implementing authority acted consistently with the fair comparison requirement in Article 2.4 of the Agreement with respect to the determination, in keeping with the standard applicable to the initiation of an investigation, of the possible existence of dumping that would warrant, pending fulfilment of the requirement of sufficient evidence of injury and causal link, the initiation of the investigation.

84. The basis for comparison was established in the light of the evidence reasonably available to the applicant, bearing in mind that this evidence was appropriate for proceeding with the initiation. Once the investigation was open, and with the help of the evidence from the other interested parties, the implementing authority was able to have access to elements in keeping with the requirements of the Agreement for the purposes of making its provisional and definitive determinations.

85. As regards the time lapse between the data on dumping and the data on injury, Brazil's interpretation is biased and tendentious to say the least.

86. The Authority, acting in accordance with Article 5.2, examined the evidence submitted by the applicant, i.e. the evidence available to the applicant. Argentina interprets Article 5.3 as requiring an examination of the documentation submitted and a determination of whether it is sufficient, in accordance with the standards required at that stage. The authority should not be expected to meet a standard in respect of that examination similar to the standard required once the investigation has been initiated.

87. At that stage, the implementing authority is entitled to resort to on-site verifications of the information submitted by the exporters. This procedure is not provided for during the stage prior to initiation of the investigation. Moreover, the authority is limited by Article 5.5 of the Anti-Dumping Agreement which, unless the government of the respondent country has been notified of the existence of an application, does not permit any publicizing thereof before the investigation has been declared open. Thus, the authority's power to investigate is restricted by the risk of violating Article 5.5 of the Anti-Dumping Agreement.

88. Finally, reverting to the evidence required by the Anti-Dumping Agreement in order to act on a request for the initiation of an investigation, the existence of dumping was established by the evidence recorded in Section IV, folio 471 of the DCD's Report on the Feasibility of Initiating an Investigation[26] of 7 January 1998; thus, evidence of the three elements having been produced, i.e. injury, dumping and causal link, the corresponding Administrative Act was issued in the form of Resolution SICyM No. 11 of 20 January 1999[27], published in the Official Bulletin on 25 January 1999, declaring the initiation of the investigation.

---

[26] *Ibid.*
[27] See Exhibit BRA-7.

III.1.3 CLAIM 9: CONSISTENCY WITH ARTICLE 5.7

89. Brazil claims that Argentina acted inconsistently with Article 5.7 by not considering, in the decision whether or not to initiate the investigation, the data collected for dumping simultaneously with the data collected for injury.

Text of Article 5.7

The relevant part of Article 5.7 stipulates that:

> *"The evidence of both dumping and injury shall be considered simultaneously: (a) in the decision whether or not to initiate an investigation ... ".*

Argentine argument

90. The determination of injury caused by dumped imports must be based on objective evidence and must involve an objective examination of "the consequent impact of these imports on domestic producers of such products". Brazil over-emphasizes the element of simultaneousness that may emerge from the provisions of the Agreement. The time lapse between the entry of the dumped imports and the impact that can be assessed as injury or threat thereof (in the indicated sequence) depends on the elements that cause the enterprises producing the like product to the imported product to react in the face of dumped imports, elements which may involve a time-lag which, far from precluding the possibility of action for unfair competition, supports that possibility.

91. In this case, Argentina was dealing with an initiation for threat of injury in which the existence of a dumped import price resulted in parameters that pointed to the existence of the conditions required for an affirmative determination of threat of injury during the phase prior to the initiation of the investigation.

92. As explained in the technical report prior to initiation, the business cycle of the industry at issue - the poultry industry - is approximately six months (including the incubation of chicks), so that price and quantity signals from the first half of 1997 would have an impact on indicators in the industry during the months following that period.

93. Thus, while *prices in the domestic industry* up to the first half of 1997 (i.e. during the period for which dumping was demonstrated) did not show signs of being significantly affected, prices for the sample domestic enterprises showed a steady decline after June 1997 in the absence of any factors other than the *price gap* between the price of imports on the domestic market and the price of the like domestic product, and the *steady fall in average f.o.b. import prices from Brazil starting in 1997.*

94. Moreover, Record (*Acta*) No. 464 of the CNCE Board[28] prior to the initiation of the investigation points out that "[t]he prices of the sample of domestic enterprises showed a decline in 1997 that will have to be analysed, should an investigation be initiated, in an ongoing context of declining prices of inputs and fluctuations in substitute products, such as bovine meat".

95. The Record adds: " ... which could explain why up to 1997, domestic sales increased in spite of the dumping in that year, but by the first half of 1998 the rate of

---

[28] See Exhibit BRA-6, point V, page 4.

growth in domestic sales had already declined"[29] *in the context of a growth trend in the market share of Brazilian imports.*

III.1.4 CLAIMS 3, 7 AND 31: CONSISTENCY WITH ARTICLE 5.8

96. Brazil claims that Argentina violated Article 5.8 by failing to reject the application which, according to Brazil, was not based on evidence of dumping, pursuant to claims 1 and 2 (Claim 3) and pursuant to claims 5 and 6 (Claim 7), and by failing to reject the initiation of the investigation as soon as the CNCE determined that there was no injury in Record No. 405 (Claim 31).

Text of Article 5.8

The relevant passage of Article 5.8 stipulates that:

> "5.8 An application under paragraph 1 shall be rejected and an investigation shall be terminated promptly as soon as the authorities concerned are satisfied that there is not sufficient evidence of either dumping or of injury to justify proceeding with the case ... "

Argentine argument

97. Bearing in mind what was stated above with respect to Claims 1, 2, 5 and 6, Brazil's arguments with respect to Claims 3 and 7 are without foundation; indeed, since the applicant had provided all of the documentation available to it, which was examined for accuracy and adequacy, there was no reason for the implementing authority to reject it.

98. What was provided was relevant evidence, and not merely allegation or conjecture as Brazil tries to demonstrate. The competent authority took account of the documentation submitted, which was duly analysed by the competent technical bodies. Moreover, it should be recalled that Article 5.2 of the Agreement stipulates that "[t]he application shall contain such information as is reasonably available to the applicant ... ".

99. Thus, it can rightly be said that, as already mentioned, the implementing authority considered the information and documentation available in the file when deciding on the initiation of these proceedings.

100. As regards Brazil's claim that Argentina should have rejected the application for initiation of the investigation, we note that Article 38 of Decree 2121/94 entitles the investigating authority to grant the applicant a period of time to amend or complete the application should it contain any errors or omissions. This is linked, then, to the fact that an application may lack a particular item of information that is required or contain a clerical error. If so, the implementing authority informs the applicant accordingly so that within a set period of time, the errors or omissions can be corrected or remedied.

101. In this particular case, Brazil states that Argentina, faced with the determination made by the CNCE in Record No. 405 should, pursuant to the above-mentioned Article, have filed the case. In the light of the clarification of the actual meaning of Article 38 invoked by Brazil and the considerations of fact and law set

---

[29] *Ibid.*

forth below, there is no way that Argentina, acting in conformity with the law, could have filed the case.

102. The applicant, as emerges from the file, submitted updated information in keeping with the requirements of the application of 17 February 1998. As a result, the Legal Department of the Ministry of the Economy and Public Works and Services determined that " ... in view of the fact that the information submitted by the *Centro de Empresas Procesadoras Avícolas* (CEPA) in file No. 061-001196/98 was not evaluated by the National Foreign Trade Commission when ruling on injury to the domestic industry in Record No. 405/98, this Directorate-General considers that before proceeding any further, the said National Commission should be asked to intervene once again in order to rule on the items submitted ... " (folio 2302 of File CNCE No. 43/97).[30]

103. The examination of the new information submitted, far from conflicting with Argentine law, is expressly provided for in Article 60 of the Regulations to the National Law on Administrative Procedures (RLNPA), which stipulates that the competent body (in this case, which involves injury, the CNCE) shall intervene once again in the proceedings if any new developments occur or come to its knowledge. In the case at issue, the additional submission by the applicant introduced new items of evidence which called for a further intervention by the CNCE at the request of the competent bodies and in strict conformity with the law.

104. It should also be stressed that during the stage prior to the initiation of the investigation, third party rights are not affected, the only relationship being between the applicant and the implementing authority. Thus, Brazil, which as interested party in the investigation had access to all of the folios making up the file, will have noted that during the period of time between the applicant's submission and the decision to initiate, a number of proceedings took place. In light of the above considerations, the suggested filing of the case would have been contrary to administrative law and would have adversely affected individual rights of the applicant with all of the administrative consequences that such an act would entail.

105. In this connection, Article 5.5 of the Anti-Dumping Agreement is also applicable: "The authorities shall avoid, unless a decision has been made to initiate an investigation, any publicizing of the application for the initiation of an investigation ... ".

106. Thus, paragraph 38 cited above is applicable where the implementing authority, having detected errors or omissions, has asked the applicant to correct or remedy them. Indeed, if the applicant does not do so within the time-period indicated by the authority, the case must be filed.

107. In the case at issue, however, within a specific period of time, the applicant provided updated information that warranted analysis and led to the determination set forth in Record No. 469.

108. Consequently, and in the light of the above-mentioned provisions, until the competent authority has expressly ruled on the initiation of the investigation on the basis of an overall analysis of each and every one of the elements on file, the case should not be filed.

---

[30] See Annex ARG-II.

III.2 CONDUCT OF AN ANTI-DUMPING INVESTIGATION - EVIDENTIARY AND PUBLIC NOTICE REQUIREMENTS

III.2.1 CLAIM 10: CONSISTENCY WITH ARTICLE 12.1

109. In paragraph 188 of its submission, Brazil claims that Argentina failed to notify seven Brazilian exporters when it was satisfied that there was sufficient evidence to justify the initiation of an anti-dumping investigation. Brazil claims that, by not notifying these exporters when the investigation was initiated, Argentina acted inconsistently with Article 12.1 of the Anti-Dumping Agreement.

Text of Article 12.1

When the authorities are satisfied that there is sufficient evidence to justify the initiation of an anti-dumping investigation pursuant to Article 5, the Member or Members the products of which are subject to such investigation and other interested parties known to the investigating authorities to have an interest therein shall be notified and a public notice shall be given. (Emphasis added)

According to Article 6.11, "interested parties" include:

(i) an exporter or foreign producer or the importer of a product subject to investigation, or a trade or business association a majority of the members of which are producers, exporters or importers of such product;

(ii) the government of the exporting Member; and

(iii) a producer of the like product in the importing Member or a trade and business association a majority of the members of which produce the like product in the territory of the importing Member.

Argentina's argument

110. Argentina submits that the investigating authorities have satisfied the Article 12.1 requirement of public notice and notification to interested parties (exporter or foreign producer) "known […] to have an interest", such as the government of the exporting Member, namely Brazil. Indeed, it would have been impossible to notify parties whose interest in the investigation was not known.

111. By Resolution SICyM No. 11/99 of 20 January 1999, published in the Official Journal of 25 January 1999, the Secretary for Industry, Trade and Mining announced the **initiation of the investigation** (Section VI, folios 712 to 715).[31]

112. By Note SSCE No. 121 of 1 February 1999[32], notification of the initiation of the investigation was made to the Chargé d'Affaires of the Federative Republic of Brazil in the Argentine Republic, *requesting his cooperation "in identifying the interested producers/exporters in this investigation and providing them with the attached requests for information, in order that they should supply the Argentine Government with the details requested on the product under investigation"* (Section VI, folios 729 to 731).

113. The Note also specifies that "*a hearing will be held on 25 February 1999 for consultations regarding the scope of the ongoing investigation and to deliver*

---

[31] See Exhibit BRA-7.
[32] See Annex ARG-III.

questionnaires to the participants ... . The Government of the Argentine Republic urges this diplomatic representation to take full cognizance of the aforementioned proceedings". Lastly, the Note expresses readiness to remain at the Brazilian Government's disposal for any additional information that might be required.

114. By Notes SSCE Nos. 122/99 and 123/99[33] of 1 February 1999, notification of the initiation of the investigation was also sent by the Under-Secretariat for Foreign Trade to the Under-Secretary for American Economic Integration and the Under-Secretary for International Economic Negotiations, with a view to informing Argentina's diplomatic representation in the Federative Republic of Brazil and the Permanent Mission of the Argentine Republic to the International Organizations in Geneva, Switzerland, and to ensuring that the aforementioned Resolution was communicated to the relevant Committee (Section VI, folios 736 to 747).

115. In addition, on 16 February 1999, by Notes DCD Nos. 273-000139/99, 273-000138/99, 273-000144/799, 273-000137/99, 273-000140/99 and 273-000141/99[34], the producers/exporters **Avipal S.A. Avicultura e Agropecuaria**, **Frigorífico Nicolini Ltda.**, **Seara Alimentos S.A.** and **Frangosul S.A., Agro Avícola Industrial** were invited to present all the evidence they considered relevant for the proper conduct of the investigation (Section VI, folios 759 and 760; Section VI, folios 757, 758, 769 and 770; Section VI, folios 755 and 756; and Section VI, folios 761 to 764, respectively).

116. Finally, on 25 February 1999, a **hearing** was held for the parties potentially interested in participating in the proceedings, at which DCD officials responded to questions from those who attended.

117. It should be emphasized that, the above notwithstanding, no representative of the Government of the Federative Republic of Brazil attended the hearing, as stated in the record of 25 February 1999 (Section VI, folio 828).[35]

118. It must be underlined, moreover, that Argentina recently learned of the interest of the other seven exporters cited in paragraph 190 of Brazil's submission (Cooperativa Central de Laticinios do Parana (CCLP), Catarinense, Chapecó, Minuano, Perdigão, Comaves and Penabranca), via a questionnaire answered by INTERAMERICANA COMERCIAL S.R.L., in which the company asks that information be sought from those enterprises as well.[36]

119. This is why, deeming the matter to be relevant to the investigation, Argentina acceded to the request made by the importer INTERAMERICANA COMERCIAL S.R.L. By Notes DCD Nos. 273-001062/99, 273-001063/99, 273-001064/99, 273-001065/99, 273-001066/99 and 273-001067/99 of 15 September 1999[37], the DCD asked the Brazilian producers Chapecó, Minuano, Perdigão, Catarinense, CCLP and Comaves to specify the price per kg. of poultry actually paid in the Brazilian market by wholesalers over the period January 1998-January 1999. For the purposes of orderly data presentation, a *questionnaire for exporters/producers was sent to those producers, together with instructions on how to fill in the document*, contrary to

---

[33] See Annex ARG-IV.
[34] See Annex ARG-V.
[35] SeeAnnex ARG-VI.
[36] See Annex ARG-VII.
[37] Annex ARG-VIII attached.

Brazil's statement in Claim 11, paragraph 202, which is addressed separately (Section LIII, folios 2369 and 2370; Section LII, folios 2367 and 2368; Section LII, folios 2361 and 2362; and Section LII, folios 2363 and 2364).

120. Hence, Brazil's claim that Argentina failed to meet its obligation to notify the exporters is without foundation and utterly tendentious.

III.2.2 CLAIMS 11 TO 14: CONSISTENCY WITH ARTICLE 6

121. By way of introduction and regarding the question of violation of Article 6 of the Agreement, it should be pointed out that, in order to help to guide interested firms and parties, the implementing authority rapidly provides them with questionnaires and forms. These specify any information and documentation relevant to the purposes of an investigation.

122. Therefore, even though the Brazilian Government had not singled out specific exporters, the implementing authority, to ensure the full participation of the producers/exporters and having determined the adequacy of the request made by the importer INTERAMERICANA COMERCIAL S.R.L., asked *inter alia* that specific Brazilian companies and institutions, including Comaves, Catarinense, Minuano, Chapecó and Perdigão, be requested to submit reports on actual sales, prices per kg. of poultry actually paid, and so forth (File No. 061-003264 of 21 April 1999, Section X, folio 1007).[38] By Note DCD No. 273-000832/99, the DCD accordingly asked INTERAMERICANA COMERCIAL S.R.L. to provide a list of addresses for the aforementioned firms (Section XXIV, folio 2000).[39]

123. The above-mentioned enterprise duly presented a list giving the particulars and domicile of the firms in question (File No. 061-007231/99 of 12 August 1999, Section XXVII, folio 2296).[40]

124. Reports were thus requested from the following exporters (Section LII, folios 2361, 2363, 2365, 2367, 2369 and 2371):[41]

- COOPERATIVA CENTRAL DE LATICINIOS DO PARANA, by Note DCD No. 273-001066/99
- COOPERATIVA CENTRAL OESTE CATARINENSE LTDA., by Note DCD No. 273-001065/99
- CHAPECO CIA INDUSTRIAL, by Note DCD No. 273-001062/99
- CIA MINUANO DE ALIMENTOS, by Note DCD No. 273-001063/99
- PERDIGÃO INDUSTRIAL, by Note DCD No. 273-001064/99
- COMAVES INDUSTRIA E COMERCIO DE ALIMENTOS LTDA, by Note DCD No. 273-001067/99

As can be seen from the above, the implementing authority sought to offer the widest possible opportunity for participation; moreover, it granted a series of additional deadlines upon good cause shown by those requesting extensions and took

---

[38] See Annex ARG-VII.
[39] See Annex ARG-IX.
[40] See Annex ARG-X.
[41] See Annex ARG-VIII.

account of various participants' difficulties in gathering and actually producing evidence.

III.2.2.1 CLAIM 11: CONSISTENCY WITH ARTICLE 6.1.1

125. Brazil claims that Argentina acted inconsistently with Article 6.1.1. by failing to give seven Brazilian exporters at least 30 days to reply to the dumping questionnaires supplied by the DCD. Brazil also claims that the CNCE never notified these seven exporters and never provided them with the injury questionnaires.

Text of Article 6.1.1

> *Exporters or foreign producers receiving questionnaires used in an anti-dumping investigation shall be given at least 30 days for reply. Due consideration should be given to any request for an extension of the 30-day period and, upon cause shown, such an extension should be granted whenever practicable.*

Argentina's argument

126. Argentina submits that it has not violated Article 6.1.1, because it not only granted the Brazilian exporters a **period of more than 30 days** to reply to the DCD's questionnaires but also duly acceded to their requests for extension by granting them whenever practicable.

127. As regards the seven exporters referred to in Brazil's submission, it should be reiterated that, contrary to Brazil's claim, the investigating authorities *provided them with the questionnaire for exporters/producers, together with instructions on how to fill in the document.*

128. On 25 February 1999, a **hearing** was held for the parties potentially interested in participating in the proceedings, at which DCD officials responded to questions from those who attended.

129. The date of 29 March 1999 was set for the presentation of the relevant forms and questionnaires and the submission of evidence by the firms involved to the DCD.

130. The successive applications for extension of the deadline for the submission of evidence are listed by way of example:[42]

- Application by SADIA S.A. for an extension of the deadline for submission of its questionnaire; granted by the DCD (File No. 061-002094/99 of 15 March 1999, folio 930).
- Application by FRANGUSOL S.A. for an extension of the deadline for submission of its questionnaire; granted by the DCD (File No. 061-002101/99 of 15 March 1999, folio 931).
- Application by FRIGORIFICO NICOLINI LTDA. for an extension of the deadline for submission of its questionnaire; granted by the DCD (File No. 061-002102/99 of 15 March 1999, folio 934).

---

[42] See Annex ARG-XI.

Report of the Panel

- Application by AVIPAL S.A. for an extension of the deadline for submission of its questionnaire; granted by the DCD (File No. 061-002140/99 of 16 March 1999, folio 935).

131. The above examples bear witness to the authorities' determination, throughout the proceedings, to offer interested parties the broadest possible opportunity not only to participate but also to gather the information needed to ensure an accurate final determination.

132. Upon expiry of the new deadline for the presentation of the DCD's questionnaires and the provision of evidence regarded as relevant, the firms involved in the investigation submitted the documentation, which was incorporated in the report on evidence adduced prior to the production of evidence stage (Section XXII, folios 1771 to 1806).

133. The following replies were also received from the seven Brazilian producers (CCLP, Catarinense, Chapecó, Minuano, Perdigão, Comaves and Penabranca) to whom the questionnaires had been delivered by Notes DCD Nos. 273-001062/99, 273-001063/99, 273-001064/99, 273-001065/99, 273-001066/99 and 273-001067/99 of 15 September 1999, in response to a request from INTERAMERICANA COMERCIAL S.R.L.:[43]

> Responding to the DCD's request, Cooperativa Central De Laticinios Do Parana LTDA. stated on 18 October 1999 that it had made **no** exports to Argentina of the product at issue during the period January 1998-January 1999 (File No. 061-009759/99, Section LIII, folio 2387).[44]
>
> COOPERATIVA OESTE CATARINENSE LTDA. requested an extension of the deadline for the submission of additional information and provided the following documentation (File No. 061-010463/99, Sections LIII to LIX, folio 2405):[45]
>
> Annex I - Identification of the producer/exporter. Confirmation of conformity for the purposes of verification.
>
> Annex II - Identification of the product at issue. Technical specifications and copies of labels attached.
>
> Annex III - List of importers in Argentina and third countries of the goods under investigation.
>
> Annex IV - Information on the producer/exporter market. Unit of measure: tonne.
>
> Annex V - Summary of producer/exporter sales. Whole, frozen, eviscerated poultry. Unit of measure: tonne.
>
> Annex VI - Summary of producer/exporter sales. Whole, frozen, eviscerated poultry. Unit of measure: US$ mil.
>
> Additional information: History of the *Cooperativa*, profile, business name, lists of addresses of parent company and branches, main input suppliers, organizational and managerial aspects, functional chart of the management, distribution channels in the domestic, foreign and Argentine markets, list of

---

[43] See Annex ARG-VIII.
[44] See Annex ARG-XXVI.
[45] See Annex ARG-XII.

the company's products, technical specifications of the products at issue, and statements of assets for the financial periods 1997 and 1998.

Annex VII - Actual exports to Argentina by transaction (including documentary evidence).

Annex VIII - Sales in the domestic market for 1998 and January 1999, disaggregated by transaction.

Annex IX - Exports to third countries.

Annex X - Cost structure of imported goods.

Annex XI - Cost structure of exported goods.

The *Cooperativa* supplied both confidential and non-confidential data, along with a non-confidential summary.

It also provided a description of the manufacturing process of the product at issue, and a fluxogram.

The *Cooperativa's* request for extension was granted (Section LIX, folios 2416 and 2417).[46]

On 28 October 1999, CHAPECO COMPANHIA INDUSTRIAL DE ALIMENTOS (Cascavel plant) informed the DCD that it had made **no** sales to Argentina during the period under investigation (File No. 061-010656/99, Section LIX, folio 2418).[47]

On 9 November 1999, MINUANO DE ALIMENTOS requested an extension of the deadline for the submission of information (File No. 061-010773/99, Section LIX, folio 2419).[48] On 18 November 1999, the DCD extended the requested deadline until 22 November 1999 (Note DCD No. 273-001409/99, Section LIX, folios 2429 and 2430).[49] **The Brazilian firm had submitted no information by the time the deadline expired.**

On 18 November 1999, COMAVES INDUSTRIA E COMERCIO DE ALIMENTOS LTDA requested an extension of the deadline for the submission of information (File No. 061-011200/99, Section LIX, folio 2446).[50] On 7 December 1999, the DCD extended the deadline until 13 December 1999 (Note DCD No. 273-001487/99, Section LIX, folios 2487 and 2488).[51] **The Brazilian firm had submitted no information by the time the deadline expired.**

On 11 November 1999, the Brazilian exporter PENABRANCA requested an extension of the deadline for the submission of information on the price per kg. of poultry actually paid in the Brazilian market (File No. 061-010864/99, Section LIX, folio 2421).[52] On 18 November 1999, the DCD extended the deadline until 29 November 1999 (Note DCD No. 273-001406/99, Section

---

[46] See Annex ARG-XIII.
[47] See Annex ARG-XIV.
[48] See Annex ARG-XV.
[49] See Annex ARG-XVI.
[50] See Annex ARG-XVII.
[51] See Annex ARG-XVIII.
[52] See Annex ARG-XIX.

LIX, folios 2423 and 2424).[53] **The Brazilian firm had submitted no information by the time the deadline expired.**

The Brazilian firm PERDIGÃO AGROINDUSTRIAL never responded, not even to request an extension of the deadline.

By Notes DCD Nos. 273-001309/99, 273-001317/99 and 273-001318/99 dated 4 November 1999, and Nos. 273-001319/99 and 273-001321/99 dated 8 November 1999[54], the Brazilian firms COOPERATIVA CENTRAL OESTE CATARINENSE LTDA, CHAPECO CIA INDUSTRIAL, CIA MINUANO DE ALIMENTOS, PERDIGÃO AGROINDUSTRIAL and COMAVES INDUSTRIA E COMERCIO DE ALIMENTOS were informed of the provisions of Law No. 19.549 on Administrative Procedures and Regulatory Decrees Nos. 1759/72 and 1883/91, regarding submissions to the National Public Administration.

134. In view of the foregoing, and contrary to Brazil's claim in paragraph 211 of its submission, Argentina submits that the investigating authorities granted the Brazilian exporters a deadline longer than that specified in the Agreement to reply to the DCD's questionnaires, having due regard for the exporters' requests for extensions, which were granted whenever practicable, pursuant to Article 6.1.1.

135. With respect to paragraph 212 of Brazil's submission, claiming that seven exporters never received the CNCE's injury questionnaire, it should be pointed out that the CNCE delivered the questionnaire to only eight exporters in full conformity with the provisions of Article 6.1, the scope of which appears to be exaggerated by Brazil. Indeed, in the words of the relevant section of Record No. 576:[55] *"Moreover, the exports to Argentina notified by the Brazilian enterprises that replied to the CNCE's 'Questionnaire for Exporters' accounted for more than half of all imports of whole, eviscerated poultry from Brazil ... ."*

136. Argentina therefore considers that the implementing authority satisfied the Article 6.1.1 requirement. Moreover, Brazil never challenged the circumstance now being complained of in its various statements in the course of the investigation.

III.2.2.2 CLAIM 12: CONSISTENCY WITH ARTICLE 6.1.2

137. Brazil claims that Argentina acted inconsistently with Article 6.1.2 by failing promptly to make available to the other interested parties participating in the investigation evidence presented in writing by the interested parties.

Text of Article 6.1.2

Subject to the requirement to protect confidential information, evidence presented in writing by one interested party shall be made available promptly to other interested parties participating in the investigation.

---

[53] See Annex ARG-XX.
[54] See Annex ARG-XXI.
[55] See Exhibit BRA-14.

Argentina's argument

138. Contrary to Brazil's claim, the Argentine authorities fulfilled the obligation in Article 6.1.2 in that they promptly made available to the interested parties participating in the investigation evidence presented in writing by the other interested parties. This is demonstrated by the fact that, once the investigation had started, the Argentine authorities made available to the interested parties - *inter alia* the exporters, importers and the authorities of the country concerned - the documentation relating to the proceedings at issue. Thus, authorized interested parties could at all times consult the file and obtain a copy thereof, that is, not only of the application itself but also of all the other records on file.

139. Brazil therefore incorrectly asserts, in paragraph 216 of its submission, that seven Brazilian exporters participated in the investigation for eight months, unbeknown to themselves, before they were notified thereof. As Argentina points out in connection with the question of consistency with Article 12.1 (Claim 10), the investigating authorities recently learned of the interest of the other seven exporters cited by Brazil in paragraph 216 of its submission (Cooperativa Central de Laticinios do Parana (CCLP), Catarinense, Chapecó, Minuano, Perdigão, Comaves and Penabranca), via the questionnaire answered by INTERAMERICANA COMERCIAL S.R.L, in which the company asks that information be sought from those enterprises as well.

140. The Argentine authorities could hardly have made available to the seven Brazilian exporters evidence presented in writing by the other interested parties participating in the investigation if those exporters were not part of the investigation. Argentina's only obligation was promptly to make available to the other interested parties *participating in the investigation* evidence presented in writing by one interested party - and so Argentina did.

141. Argentina deplores the fact that the Brazilian Government, which was indeed informed prior to the initiation of the investigation and was a party with an interest therein from the outset, did not advise the Argentine authorities of the interest of those firms or suggest that it would be advisable for the latter to participate in the proceedings.

142. Even so, immediately after being apprised of the above, Argentina, in the interest of due process and seeking to obtain relevant information in order to ensure full consistency of its decisions with the legal provisions in force, asked the Brazilian producers CCLP, Catarinense, Chapecó, Minuano, Perdigão and Comaves to specify the price per kg. of poultry actually paid in the Brazilian market by wholesalers over the period January 1998-January 1999 and *sent them the questionnaire for exporters/producers together with instructions on how to fill in the document*, for the purposes of orderly data presentation (Section LIII, folios 2369 to 2372; Section LII, folios 2365 to 2368; folios 2361 and 2362; folios 2363 and 2364).[56]

143. In addition, and contrary to Brazil's claim[57], it should be emphasized that the replies received from those exporters clearly show that two of the seven enterprises (CCLP and CHAPECO) made no exports to Argentina during the period under

---

[56] See Annex ARG-VIII.
[57] Submission of Brazil, para. 219: " ... they exported the subject merchandise to Argentina in the period of investigation ... ".

investigation, while the other four (Minuano, Comaves, Penabranca and Perdigão) stated that they had no interest in the investigation.

144. Indeed, in response to the DCD's request, Cooperativa Central de Laticinios do Parana LTDA. (CCLP) and CHAPECO COMPANHIA INDUSTRIAL DE ALIMENTOS (Cascavel plant) informed the DCD on 18 October 1999 and 28 October 1999, respectively, by means of Files Nos. 061-009759/99 and 061-010656/99, that they had made **no** exports to Argentina of the product at issue over the period January 1998-January 1999 (Section LIII, folio 2387[58] and Section LIX, folio 2418).[59]

145. By Files Nos. 061-010773/99, 061-011200/99 and 061-010864/99 of 9 November 1999, 18 November 1999 and 11 November 1999[60], respectively, MINUANO DE ALIMENTOS, COMAVES INDUSTRIA E COMERCIO DE ALIMENTOS LTDA. and PENABRANCA requested an extension of their deadlines for submitting information. By Notes DCD Nos. 273-001409/99 of 18 November 1999, 273-001487/99 of 7 December 1999 and 273-001406/99 of 18 November 1999, the DCD granted the extensions requested to 22 November 1999 in the first case, 13 December 1999 in the second, and 29 November 1999 in the third.[61] **By the time the deadlines expired, however, none of those enterprises had submitted any information.** The Brazilian firm PERDIGÃO AGROINDUSTRIAL never responded, not even to request an extension.

146. Argentina deems that it has thus given all the interested parties the opportunity to present in writing all the evidence they regard as relevant. However, if the parties with a supposed interest in the investigation did not participate, it was they - and not the implementing authority - that failed to defend their own interests.

147. This is why Argentina maintains that it would have been difficult for the investigating authorities to make the evidence presented by the interested parties promptly available to the enterprises in question, given that the latter did not even join as interested parties. Argentina therefore submits that it acted consistently with Article 6.1.2.

III.2.2.3 CLAIM 13: CONSISTENCY WITH ARTICLE 6.2

148. Brazil claims that Argentina acted inconsistently with Article 6.2 by failing to give the interested parties full opportunity to defend their interests.

Text of Article 6.2

The relevant section of Article 6.2 provides that:

Throughout the anti-dumping investigation all interested parties shall have a full opportunity for the defence of their interests.

---

[58] See Annex ARG-XXVI.
[59] See Annex ARG-XIV.
[60] See Annexes ARG-XVII and XIX.
[61] See Annexes ARG-XVIII and XX.

Argentina's argument

149. Contrary to Brazil's claim, all the interested parties had full opportunity to defend their interests throughout the investigation and, by giving them that opportunity, the investigating authorities satisfied the obligation laid down in Article 6.2.

150. Argentina agrees with paragraph 222 of Brazil's submission that Article 6.2 does not provide specific guidance as to what steps investigating authorities should take in practice. In the light of the facts set forth below, Argentina deems that it has met the Article 6.2 requirement.

151. As already mentioned in relation to the question of consistency with Article 6.1.3 (Claim 14), once the investigation had started Argentina made available to the interested parties - *inter alia* the exporters, importers and the authorities of the country concerned - the documentation relating to the proceedings at issue. Authorized interested parties could thus consult the file and obtain a copy thereof at all times, that is, not only of the application itself but also of all the other records on file, and any other party that considered itself as having an interest therein could present itself at the investigation with such a request. In the specific case of the exporters, the practice is for their governments and the latter's importer-clients to advise ex officio that anti-dumping proceedings have been initiated in the country of origin of the product under investigation.

152. Hence the way in which the Argentine authorities provided access to the proceedings for interested parties clearly did not in any way impair the right of access to the records and even less the right of defence. Argentina consequently deems irrelevant the arguments put forward by Brazil in support of its Article 6.2 claim concerning "impairment of the right of defence".

153. In addition to the above, the authorities' determination, throughout the proceedings, to offer interested parties the broadest possible opportunity not only to participate but also to gather the information needed to ensure an accurate final determination is evidenced by the record of submissions made by the participating firms and the conclusions reached on the basis of those submissions. Thus, the information supplied by the exporters SADIA S.A., AVIPAL S.A., FRIGORIFICO NICOLINI LTDA. and SEARA ALIMENTOS S.A. led to a determination of their respective individual margins of dumping.

154. The work done by the Technical Department in requesting and putting together all this documentation can be seen from the following notifications:[62]

- Note DCD No. 273-001460/99 of 3 December 1999 - SEARA ALIMENTOS S.A.
- Note DCD No. 273-001461/99 of 3 December 1999 - FRIGORIFICO NICOLINI LTDA.
- Note DCD No. 273-001462/99 of 3 December 1999 - SADIA S.A.

155. In the other cases, the implementing authority had to gather the information from other sources.

156. As regards the other firms examined by the implementing authority (DA GRANJA AGROI, SADIA CONCORDIA, ACAUA INDUSTRIA, FELIPE

---

[62] See Annex ARG-XXII.

AVICOLA, VENETO and LITORAL ALIMENT), Argentina reiterates that there was no additional information or sufficient supporting documentation, despite the numerous requests made by the implementing authority. The following are cited as examples:[63]

- Note DCD No. 273-001319/99 - PERDIGÃO AGROINDUSTRIAL
- Note DCD No. 273-001406/99 - PENABRANCA AVICULTURA S.A.
- Note DCD No. 273-001409/99 - COMPANHIA MINUANO DE ALIMENTOS
- Note DCD No. 273-001487/99 - COMAVES IND. E COM. DE ALIMENTOS LTDA.
- File No. 061-008834/99 from the COOPERATIVA CENTRAL OESTE CATARINENSE requesting an extension of the deadline.

157. In broad terms, it should be emphasized that while detailed analysis of the questionnaires provides an approximate picture of companies' trade operations, the supporting documentation is the key source for determining prices, tax adjustments and levels of trade. It is also the basis on which the implementing authority is empowered to verify information on the spot.

158. In a further unsubstantiated statement in paragraph 222 of its submission, Brazil claims that Argentina acted inconsistently with Article 6.2 by notifying the investigation and requesting a response to the injury questionnaires eight months after the initiation of the investigation. That statement is incorrect. Brazil's assertion in paragraph 222 obviously refers once again to the seven exporters which Brazil contends had an interest in the investigation.

159. It should be pointed out in this connection that the obligation to give public notice and to notify the interested parties (exporter or foreign producer) applies only to parties known to have an interest in the investigation (Argentina reiterates its statement in respect of Article 12.1; Claim 10). Indeed, it would have been impossible to notify parties whose interest therein was not known. Argentina also reiterates that it was Brazil itself that had the most obvious opportunity of informing all Brazilian producers of the existence of this investigation and/or of advising the Argentine Government of the existence of such producers. An investigation is opened on the basis of knowledge of each known exporter or foreign producer as notified by the applicant and, once the opening of the investigation has become public, the responsibility of ensuring that all potential actors participate in that investigation does not lie solely with the implementing authority.

160. In a dumping case in which the matter at issue is the competitive behaviour of foreign producers and/or exporters, the direct consequence of delivering the notification to initiate to the Government of the interested exporting Member is that knowledge pertaining to the sphere in which foreign producers operate may be protected. That notion is embodied, *inter alia*, in Article 6.1.3.

161. Such was not the case of the interests of the seven exporters, as amply noted and documented by Argentina in its discussion of the question of consistency with Article 6.1.2 (Claim 12). In the light of the foregoing, Argentina deems that the investigating authorities have fulfilled the Article 6.2 requirement.

---

[63] See Annexes ARG-XXI, XX, XVI, XVIII and XIII.

III.2.2.4 CLAIM 14: CONSISTENCY WITH ARTICLE 6.1.3

162. Brazil claims that Argentina acted inconsistently with Article 6.1.3 by not providing the text of the written application to the Brazilian exporters and the Government of Brazil as soon as the investigation was initiated.

Text of Article 6.1.3

> *As soon as an investigation has been initiated, the authorities shall provide the full text of the written application received under paragraph 1 of Article 5 to the known exporters* and to the authorities of the exporting Member and shall make it available, upon request, to other interested parties involved. Due regard shall be paid to the requirement for the protection of confidential information, as provided for in paragraph 5. (Emphasis added)*

*The footnote reads as follows:

> It being understood that, where the number of exporters involved is particularly high, the full text of the written application should instead be provided only to the authorities of the exporting Member or to the relevant trade association.

Argentina's argument

163. Contrary to Brazil's claim, the Argentine authorities satisfied the requirements of Article 6.1.3 by providing the Brazilian exporters and the Brazilian Government with the full text of the written application as soon as the investigation was initiated.

164. Brazil claims that the Argentine authorities acted inconsistently with Article 6.1.3 in that they failed to transmit the application to the known exporters and to the authorities of the exporting country. In this connection, it should be emphasized that, in its Spanish version, the Article lays down the obligation to "*facilitar*" ("provide"). The Argentine authorities satisfied that obligation by making the records of the proceedings available to authorized interested parties. Argentina fails to understand why Brazil concludes that the term "facilitar" means "to send", and considers Brazil's interpretation to be erroneous.

165. Once the investigation had started, Argentina made available to the interested parties - *inter alia* the exporters, importers and the authorities of the country concerned - the documentation relating to the proceedings at issue. Authorized interested parties could thus consult the file and obtain a copy thereof at all times, that is, not only of the application itself but also of all the other records on file.

166. Argentina consequently considers the claim concerning "curtailment of the right of defence" in paragraph 230 of Brazil's submission to be inadmissible, since Brazil's diplomatic representation in Argentina had available to it, at all times, the full records covering the initiation and entire duration of the investigation, pursuant to Article 6.1.3.

167. Moreover, the initiation of an investigation is a general administrative procedure and published as such in the Official Journal, which constitutes sufficient notification of general scope. From the moment notification appeared in the Official Bulletin, interested parties *with accredited status were able to gain immediate access to the records of the proceedings.*

168. Therefore, the way in which the written application and access for interested parties was provided by the Argentine authorities clearly does not impair the parties' right of access to the records and even less their right of defence.

169. Moreover, once the Argentine authorities had initiated the investigation, notification was given, by Note SSCE No. 121 of 1 February 1999[64], to the Brazilian Chargé d'Affaires in Argentina, pursuant to Article 6 of the Anti-Dumping Agreement. The Note clearly shows that Argentina expects the Brazilian Government to cooperate "*in identifying the interested producers/exporters in this investigation and providing them with the attached requests for information, in order that they could supply the Argentine Government with the details requested on the product under investigation*".

170. The Note further states that "*a hearing will be held on 25 February 1999 for consultations regarding the scope of the ongoing investigation and to deliver questionnaires to the participants ... . The Government of the Argentine Republic urges this diplomatic representation to take full cognizance of the aforementioned proceedings*". Lastly, the Note expresses readiness to remain at the Brazilian Government's disposal for any additional information that might be required.

171. The above notwithstanding, no representative of the Brazilian Government attended the hearing, as stated in the record of 25 February 1999 (Section VI, folio 828)[65], nor is there any record of the presence of any interested party at the hearing. Brazil can hardly claim today that its right of defence was impaired.

172. Furthermore, Argentina fails to understand how the Brazilian Government calculates the deadline for notifying initiation of the investigation, since Resolution SICyM No. 11/99 of 20 January 1999 was published in the Official Bulletin of 25 January 1999, namely the date on which the countdown was to begin.

173. Considering that the Brazilian authorities were notified on 1 February 1999, it can be established that five working days had elapsed and not 12, as Brazil erroneously maintains in paragraph 237 of its submission.

174. Once again, Argentina is surprised to see how Brazil repeatedly seeks to mislead the Panel by misinterpreting not only the Agreement but also the practical steps taken by Argentina's implementing authority.

III.2.3 CLAIMS 15, 16, 17 AND 21: CONSISTENCY WITH ARTICLES 6.8 (ANNEX II), 6.9 AND 12.2.2

175. Brazil claims that Argentina acted inconsistently with Article 6.8 and Annex II by disregarding the responses submitted by Brazilian exporters with respect to the description of the product sold to Argentina and in Brazil, and resorting to the normal value adjustment calculation provided by the applicant (Claim 15). Brazil likewise claims that Argentina acted inconsistently with Article 12.2.2 by failing to adequately explain in the final determination its decision to disregard the information provided by the exporters regarding the product description and to use instead the normal value adjustment proposed by the applicant (Claim 16). Brazil further claims that Argentina acted inconsistently with Article 6.8 and Annex II by disregarding the

---

[64] See Annex ARG-III.
[65] See Annex ARG-VI.

export price data provided by the Brazilian exporters, and resorting to the export price information provided by the Secretariat for Agriculture, Fisheries and Food (Claim 17). Lastly, Brazil claims that Argentina acted inconsistently with Article 6.9 by failing to inform the Brazilian exporters of the essential facts (Claim 21).

Text of Article 6.8

In cases in which any interested party refuses access to, or otherwise does not provide, necessary information within a reasonable period or significantly impedes the investigation, preliminary and final determinations, affirmative or negative, may be made on the basis of the facts available. The provisions of Annex II shall be observed in the application of this paragraph.

Text of Annex II, paragraphs 3, 6 and 7

The relevant section of paragraph 3 provides that:

3. All information which is verifiable, which is appropriately submitted so that it can be used in the investigation without undue difficulties, which is supplied in a timely fashion, and, where applicable, which is supplied in a medium or computer language requested by the authorities, should be taken into account when determinations are made....

6. If evidence or information is not accepted, the supplying party should be informed forthwith of the reasons therefor, and should have an opportunity to provide further explanations within a reasonable period, due account being taken of the time-limits of the investigation. If the explanations are considered by the authorities as not being satisfactory, the reasons for the rejection of such evidence or information should be given in any published determinations.

7. If authorities have to base their findings, including those with respect to normal value, on information from a secondary source, including the information supplied in the application for the initiation of the investigation, they should do so with special circumspection. In such cases, the authorities should, where practicable, check the information from other independent sources at their disposal, such as published price lists, official import statistics and customs returns, and from the information obtained from other interested parties during the investigation. It is clear, however, that if an interested party does not cooperate and thus relevant information is being withheld from the authorities, this situation could lead to a result which is less favourable to the party than if the party did cooperate.

Text of Article 6.9

The authorities shall, before a final determination is made, inform all interested parties of the essential facts under consideration which form the basis for the decision whether to apply definitive measures. Such disclosure should take place in sufficient time for the parties to defend their interests.

Text of Article 12.2.2

A public notice of conclusion or suspension of an investigation in the case of an affirmative determination providing for the imposition of a definitive duty or the acceptance of a price undertaking shall contain, or otherwise make available through a separate report, all relevant information on the matters of fact and law and reasons which have led to the imposition of final measures or the acceptance of a price undertaking, due regard being paid to the requirement for the protection of confidential information. In particular, the notice or report shall contain the information described in subparagraph 2.1, as well as the reasons for the acceptance or rejection of relevant arguments or claims made by the exporters and importers, and the basis for any decision made under subparagraph 10.2 of Article 6.

Argentina's argument

176. Contrary to Brazil's claim, the DCD based its conclusions on " ... [a]ll information which is verifiable, which is appropriately submitted ... ", pursuant to Annex II, paragraph 3, of the Anti-Dumping Agreement.

177. In order to examine the information, the Argentine authorities send questionnaires containing all the elements needed to conduct an accurate analysis with a view to determining the existence or absence of dumping, and specify the need for supporting documentation to substantiate the questionnaire information and to allow those replying to add all further elements they deem to be of interest. The parties enjoy similar rights throughout the investigation procedure.

178. The implementing authority obviously cannot examine claims put forward by the parties without supporting documentation that can be verified. Since "verifiable" means "that can be checked", this can only be done on the basis of supporting documentation for which it is possible to do so.

179. Brazil specifically challenges the adjustment made to the normal value of 9.09 per cent used by the authority in its final determination. The adjustment is indeed based on the method of calculation provided by the applicant, but the validity thereof was confirmed by the absence of any objection supported by verifiable evidence - not by mere allegations. The additional documents provided by various Brazilian firms on 20 April 1999 (File No. 061-003243/99, Section IX, folio 999)[66] and by the diplomatic representation of the Federative Republic of Brazil are mere arguments unsubstantiated by technical data. The appropriateness of the adjustment is further demonstrated by the fact that these documents do not question the need for such adjustment.

180. Likewise, there was no supporting documentation whatsoever regarding the incidence of freezing and/or chilling at the time of determining the normal value of the product at issue, despite the points made in the submission by the ABEF (Brazilian Chicken Producers and Exporters Association) (File No. 061-012582/99, Section LXVI, folio 2507)[67], which, once again, are simple statements regarding the issues under consideration.

181. In view of the foregoing, Argentina considers that the Panel should reject the claims put forward by Brazil, which appears to have a biased view of the investigation. Proof that the action taken by the Argentine authority was both appropriate and consistent with the Agreements resides in the determination that led to the exclusion of the exporting firms Frigorifico Nicolini and Seara from the anti-

---

[66] See Annex ARG-XXIII.
[67] See Annex ARG-XXIV.

dumping measure, precisely because those firms not only claimed that they did not engage in dumping but also - and this is the important point - because they supplied all the information required, along with the corresponding supporting documentation.

182. Likewise, as regards the producers/exporters Sadia and Avipal, it was possible to determine an individual margin of dumping consistent with the data that they themselves had provided and substantiated.

183. Hence the implementing authority did not discriminate in any way between the firms. On the contrary, its primary objective was to act in conformity with the letter of the Anti-Dumping Agreement.

184. Argentina therefore fails to understand Brazil's claim of inconsistency with Article 12.2.2, which stipulates that " ... *shall contain, or otherwise make available through a separate report, all relevant information on the matters of fact and law and reasons which have led to the imposition of final measures ...* ", since both the Report on Action Taken and the Report on the Final Determination of the Margin of Dumping, throughout the text and under different headings, dealt in detail with each of the submissions by the producing-exporting enterprises in order to reach a reasoned conclusion as to the implementing authority's motives for excluding submissions that lacked sufficient supporting documentation or were made after the deadline had expired.

185. Regarding Article 12.2.2, it should be pointed out that, in the Report on Action Taken prior to the closure of the period for obtaining evidence, dated 4 January 2002 (Section LXIII, folio 2757), the DCD made available to the parties all the essential facts on which it intended to base its final decision. This is evidenced by the DCD's notes of 5 January 2000 (Section LXII, folios 2860 to 2880)[68] informing all the parties of the end of the stage for producing evidence and inviting them to consult the records of the proceedings and to submit pleadings if they so wished, all of which demonstrates compliance with the requirements of the Agreement.

III.2.4 CLAIMS 18, 19, 20 AND 22: CONSISTENCY WITH ARTICLES 12.2.2, 6.8 (ANNEX II) AND 6.10

186. Brazil claims that Argentina acted inconsistently with Article 12.2.2 by failing to adequately explain in the final determination its decision to disregard the export price data provided by the exporters, and to resort to the export price data provided by the Secretariat for Agriculture, Fisheries and Food (Claim 18). Brazil also claims that Argentina acted inconsistently with Article 6.8 and Annex II, paragraphs 3, 5 and 7, by disregarding all normal value information submitted by Frangosul and Catarinense and resorting to the information provided by the applicant (Claim 19). Brazil further claims that Argentina acted inconsistently with Article 12.2.2 by failing to adequately explain in the final determination its decision to disregard all normal value information submitted by Frangosul and Catarinense, and to resort to the information provided by the applicant (Claim 20). Lastly, Brazil claims that Argentina acted inconsistently with Article 6.10 by failing to establish individual margins of dumping for Frangosul and Catarinense (Claim 22).

---

[68] See Annex ARG-XXV.

Text of Article 6.8

In cases in which any interested party refuses access to, or otherwise does not provide, necessary information within a reasonable period or significantly impedes the investigation, preliminary and final determinations, affirmative or negative, may be made on the basis of the facts available. The provisions of Annex II shall be observed in the application of this paragraph.

Text of Annex II, paragraphs 3, 5 and 7

The relevant section of paragraph 3 provides that:

3. *All information which is verifiable, which is appropriately submitted so that it can be used in the investigation without undue difficulties, which is supplied in a timely fashion, and, where applicable, which is supplied in a medium or computer language requested by the authorities, should be taken into account when determinations are made ...*

5. *Even though the information provided may not be ideal in all respects, this should not justify the authorities from disregarding it, provided the interested party has acted to the best of its ability.*

7. *If authorities have to base their findings, including those with respect to normal value, on information from a secondary source, including the information supplied in the application for the initiation of the investigation, they should do so with special circumspection. In such cases, the authorities should, where practicable, check the information from other independent sources at their disposal, such as published price lists, official import statistics and customs returns, and from the information obtained from other interested parties during the investigation. It is clear, however, that if an interested party does not cooperate and thus relevant information is being withheld from the authorities, this situation could lead to a result which is less favourable to the party than if the party did cooperate.*

Text of Article 12.2.2

A public notice of conclusion or suspension of an investigation in the case of an affirmative determination providing for the imposition of a definitive duty or the acceptance of a price undertaking shall contain, or otherwise make available through a separate report, all relevant information on the matters of fact and law and reasons which have led to the imposition of final measures or the acceptance of a price undertaking, due regard being paid to the requirement for the protection of confidential information. In particular, the notice or report shall contain the information described in subparagraph 2.1, as well as the reasons for the acceptance or rejection of relevant arguments or claims made by the exporters and importers, and the basis for any decision made under subparagraph 10.2 of Article 6.

Text of Article 6.10

The authorities shall, as a rule, determine an individual margin of dumping for each known exporter or producer concerned of the product under investigation. In cases where the number of exporters, producers, importers or types of products involved is so large as to make such a determination impracticable, the authorities may limit their examination either to a

Argentina - Poultry Anti-Dumping Duties

reasonable number of interested parties or products by using samples which are statistically valid on the basis of information available to the authorities at the time of the selection, or to the largest percentage of the volume of the exports from the country in question which can reasonably be investigated.

Argentina's argument

187. For the purposes of the final determination of the margin of dumping, the implementing authority analysed and examined all the information before it that was consistent with the principles enshrined in the Agreement, i.e. information that was properly provided within the required time-frame and was accompanied by proper evidence.

188. This is in line with the above statement regarding the record of submissions made by the participating firms and the conclusions reached on the basis of those submissions. Thus, the information supplied by the exporters was the source used for determining the respective margins of dumping for SADIA S.A., AVIPAL S.A., FRIGORIFICO NICOLINI LTDA. and SEARA ALIMENTOS S.A.

189. As was duly pointed out in the Final Report, the data received from the producer/exporter COOPERATIVA CENTRAL OESTE CATARINENSE LTDA. was presented on an aggregate basis, without any supporting documentation.

190. In the case of the exporter Frangosul - the relevant details in the following paragraphs notwithstanding - several notifications (Notes DCD Nos. 273-001181/99 of 12 October 1999 and 273-001182/99 of 12 October 1999)[69] were sent to the company with a request to provide the lists of *Notas fiscales* (tax receipts), in order to establish a statistical sample of the formalities required under the Law on Administrative Procedures. A reminder was sent on 18 November 1999 (Notes DCD Nos. 273-001412/99 and 273-001413/99).[70] Two diskettes, without supporting documentation, arrived after the deadline had expired.

191. As regards the other firms examined by the implementing authority (Comaves, Da Granja Agroi, Sadia Concordia, Minuano de Alimentos, Acaua Industria, Felipe AVICOLA, PERDIGÃO AGROIN, VENETO, CHAPECO CL and LITORAL ALIMENT), Argentina reiterates that there was no additional information or sufficient supporting documentation, despite numerous requests by the implementing authority.

192. In broad terms, it should be mentioned that while detailed analysis of the questionnaires provides an approximate picture of companies' trade operations, the supporting documentation is the key source for determining prices, tax adjustments and levels of trade.

193. Special mention should be made of the incorporation of the Report on Action Taken prior to the closure of the period for obtaining evidence, which contains details on the status of information on file in the proceedings.

194. Lastly, as regards the question concerning the period considered for determining the margin of dumping, it should be emphasized that the implementing authority is entitled to request all information deemed relevant for clarifying the facts

---

[69] See Annex ARG-XXVII.
[70] See Annex ARG-XXVIII.

Report of the Panel

under investigation, it being understood that the authority analyses all data on file in the proceedings.

195. Argentina acted consistently with the requirements of Annex II of Agreement, and particularly paragraph 7 thereof, to the extent that it proceeded with " ... *with special circumspection* ... ", basing its conclusions on a " ... *check [of] the information from other independent sources at their disposal, such as* ... *official import statistics* ... ".

196. Finally, as a reminder and renewed proof of the authority's determination to gather additional information from the exporting firms, the submissions by Frangosul and Catarinense and the DCD notes requesting information and/or clarification from them are listed below:[71]

- On 27 April 1999, Frangosul presented, by means of File No. 061-003502/99 (power of attorney) drafted in Portuguese, the questionnaire **minus Annex VIII (sales in the Brazilian domestic market)**, the profile of the company, the production process and balance sheets. It also presented a monthly list of domestic sales by company branch, indicating initial and final invoices but without specifying dates, amounts per unit, total amounts, kgs, types of goods, etc. (Section 11, folio 1022).

- The company chose to present only **invoices for exports to the Argentine market**, omitting to include those requested by the DCD (Sections 11, 12, 13, 14 and 15).

- On 10 May 1999, FRANGOSUL provided a translation of the aforementioned power of attorney (File No. 061-003924/99, Section 21, folio 1618).

- On 11 May 1999, it presented the company's balance sheet (File No. 061-003952/99, Section 21, folio 1620).

- Note DCD No. 273-000837/99 of 12 July 1999 requests FRANGOSUL to supply the following information (Section 25, folios 2076 and 2077):

    1. Translation of the exhibit concerning exports to Argentina (Annex VII).
    2. Supporting documentation for domestic sales (Annex VIII).
    3. Exports to third countries.
    4. Translation of FRANGOSUL'S leaflets.

- On 28 July 1999, FRANGOSUL requested an extension of the deadline (File No. 061-006626/99, Section 26, folio 2107), which was granted for a maximum period of 15 days (Note DCD No. 273-000912/99, Section 27, folio 2274).

- On 19 August 1999, FRANGOSUL presented the following information (File No. 061-007466/99, Section 28, folio 2304):

    1. Translation of the commercial invoices (exhibit) for actual exports to Argentina (Annex VII).

---

[71] See Annex ARG-XXIX. See also Annex ARG-XXVII.

2. Exports to third countries (Annex IX) representing the five most important markets for the goods in question.
3. Translation of the new leaflets for Frangosul products.
4. Regarding invoices for sales in the Brazilian domestic market, Frangosul explains: *"Supporting documentation for sales in the domestic market (Annex VIII). In view of the daily number of invoices drawn up by our sales branches (estimated at over 140 invoices a day and more than 320,000 a year), it is not feasible to send copies of all invoices for domestic sales. This is why on 27 April 1999 we presented File No. 061-003502 containing a list of invoices for our domestic sales. The invoices are at the disposal of the Argentine authorities should they wish to verify them or request specific documents for spot checks."*

- On 1 September 1999, Frangosul presented the invoices of sales to the Argentine market (File No. 061-007964/99, Section 52, folio 2326).
- By Notes DCD Nos. 273-001181/99 and 273-001182/99 of 12 October 1999, the DCD requested a list of invoices, as the one presented by Frangosul was incomplete (no dates, quantities, prices, etc.) (Section 53, folios 2382 to 2385). The DCD explains:

"The aforementioned lists give only the numbers of Notas fiscales for the period under investigation. They specify the month and the branch but not details such as dates, quantities, prices, discounts, tax, freight, etc., which are highly useful for the conduct of the current proceedings".

"Owing to the difficulty in documenting and substantiating all the transactions made during the period under investigation because of the large number of transactions per day, we would ask you to provide the lists of Notas fiscales showing all the transactions made over the period January 1998-end January 1999. This will be used for statistical sampling and we will subsequently ask you to supply the corresponding supporting documentation".

197. Although the aforementioned Note DCD No. 273-001181/99 did not specify a deadline for presenting the requested documentation, in such cases Law No. 19.549 on Administrative Procedures applies on a residual basis, pursuant to the following provision of Article 76 of Decree No. 2121/94: *"The procedure for the imposition of anti-dumping and countervailing duties by the implementing authorities specified in this regulation shall be governed, on a residual basis, by the Law on Administrative Procedures and its regulations"*. In this respect, Article 1(e)(4) of Law No. 19.549 stipulates the following: *"Where no special time period has been set for the conduct of proceedings, notifications and summons, the serving of orders and subpoenas and replies to communications, hearings and reports, the said period shall be ten days"*.

- By Notes DCD Nos. 273-001412/99 and 273-001413/99, the DCD reiterated the request it had made in Note DCD No. 273-001181/99 (Section 59, folios 2435 to 2438).

Report of the Panel

> • Finally, on 30 December 1999 Frangosul presented a diskette containing - according to the company - the list of *Notas fiscales* (File No. 061-012882/99, Section 63, folio 2756).[72]

198. All the above shows that FRANGOSUL did not submit any documentation regarding sales prices in the Brazilian domestic market. Its questionnaire was accompanied by a list of invoice numbers pertaining to certain branches of the company, but the list was incomplete because it did not include the information needed to analyse sales in the Brazilian domestic market. Frangosul therefore did not provide any of the items required in Annex VIII of the exporters' questionnaire. The DCD accordingly requested it to supply that information. FRANGOSUL responded as follows: *"In view of the daily number of invoices drawn up by our sales branches (estimated at over 140 invoices a day and more than 320,000 a year), it is not feasible to send copies of all invoices for domestic sales. This is why on 27 April 1999 we presented File No. 061-003502 containing a list of our invoices for our domestic sales. The invoices are at the disposal of the Argentine authorities should they wish to verify them or request specific documents for spot checks."*

199. As an example, part of the information sent by FRANGOSUL along with its questionnaire, in response to the Annex VIII requirement (sales in the Brazilian domestic market), is detailed below.
DECEMBER 1998

Invoices	Branch 01	Branch 02	Branch 04	Branch 13	Branch 42	Branch 43	Branch 59	Branch 67	Branch 69	Branch 71	Branch 72	Branch 73
Initial	32239/S	38204/S	5425/S	35090/S	19552/S	22439/S	19657/S	37618/S		1762/s	908/M1	801/M1
Final	35373/S	42179/S	5501/S	38332/S	21838/S	24337/S	21940/S	43064/S		1963/s	1192/M1	1017/M1

200. FRANGOSUL contradicts itself in stating that it was impossible to submit invoices for sales in the Brazilian domestic market because of the number of invoices issued daily by all of its branches. In this connection, it should be noted that ALTHOUGH THE COMPANY DID NOT PRESENT A SINGLE INVOICE FOR SALES IN THE BRAZILIAN DOMESTIC MARKET, IT WAS INDEED ABLE TO PROVIDE SOME 600 INVOICES FOR EXPORTS TO ARGENTINA.

201. The foregoing shows that FRANGOSOL never presented any supporting documentation for domestic sales and that its final submission arrived beyond the deadline for analysing the information - the Report on Action Taken being dated 4 January 2002.

202. Concerning the submission made by CATARINENSE on 3 November 1999 (File No. 061-010463/99, Sections LIII to LIX, folio 2405, sheets 1 to 1198)[73], it should be pointed out that the company did not have authorized legal status in conformity with Law No. 19.549 on Administrative Procedures. In that submission, Catarinense requested a 20-day extension of the deadline for presenting information (Section LIII, folio 2405, sheet 3). The extension was granted by Note DCD No. 273-

---

[72] See Annex ARG-XXX.
[73] See Annex ARG-XII.

001321/99 (Section LII, folios 2416 and 2417)[74] and the company made no subsequent requests for further extension.

203.   Lastly, as regards CATARINENSE'S submission, the company failed to provide the Annex VIII information (sales in the Brazilian domestic market). The only supporting documentation was a list of invoices and invoices for exports to Argentina. This was the only submission made, no subsequent submissions having been received. As regards the delay in delivering the questionnaire to Catarinense, reference is made to Argentina's arguments regarding Claims 10 to 14.

204.   The above details show that not once in the course of the proceedings did the Brazilian producer/exporter firms present any formal claims - not to mention any supporting documentation pointing to disagreement with the DCD - thus seemingly endorsing the DCD's description.

205.   As a final comment on Brazil's claims, Argentina points out that on-the-spot verification is a procedure that is left to the discretion of the investigating authority. Indeed, the Anti-Dumping Agreement does not impose such a procedure but imposes the obligation to seek means of verifying the accuracy of the information and documentation submitted, thus triggering the investigation procedure. Moreover, since on-the-spot verification is not the only means of checking information adduced in an investigation, the authority has discretionary power to conduct such verifications as it deems necessary and relevant in the case at issue.

206.   Lastly, and in this connection, it proved equally impossible in the case of FRANGOSUL to carry out a verification on the spot, either because the documentation presented did not warrant such a procedure, or - as in the case of the data on sales in the Brazilian domestic market - because no documentation was presented, making it impracticable to perform on-the-spot verifications."

III.3   CONDUCT OF THE INVESTIGATION AND FINAL DETERMINATION

III.3.1 CLAIM 23: CONSISTENCY WITH ARTICLE 2.4

207.   Brazil claims that Argentina acted inconsistently with Article 2.4 by not making due allowance for freight when determining the normal value in the case of SADIA and AVIPAL.

Text of Article 2.4

The relevant section of Article 2.4 provides the following:

" ... *Due allowance shall be made in each case, on its merits, for differences which affect price comparability, including differences in conditions and terms of sale, taxation, levels of trade, quantities, physical characteristics, and any other differences which are also demonstrated to affect price comparability.*"

Argentina's argument

208.   With regard to the comparison made for the enterprise SADIA S.A., the following comments should be made:

---

[74]   See Annex ARG-XIII.

209. In paragraphs 372 to 374 of its submission, Brazil contends that Argentina did not take into account the information provided on 20 April 1999 in Annex VIII to the reply to the questionnaire when the questionnaire sent to the exporter was returned. In paragraph 374, in particular, Brazil claims that "In its normal value calculation, the DCD failed to make the freight reductions as reported in Sadia's 20 April 1999 response to the questionnaire".

210. It is true that the DCD did not make the freight reductions mentioned by the party. But in this case, the implementing authority did not make any error or omission. The adjustment for freight could not be made because it had not been properly documented. In Annex VIII to the reply to the questionnaire sent to the exporter, SADIA provided a purely illustrative general estimate of freight deductions. The information used to calculate the normal value, however, was based on an analysis of all the invoices provided by the enterprise in accordance with the sample used by the implementing authority, which were not accompanied by any details concerning freight charges to be deducted, neither as an attachment to the invoices nor as part thereof.

211. Thus, it would have been improper for the DCD to make any specific deduction - with a decisive and significant impact on price comparability - that:

   (a) Was not contained in the documentary evidence provided;

   (b) had been submitted in a general way - even though in the form of an amount deductible from the unit value of the goods - and in fact represented an average for an extended period of time, the minimum being one year, as can be seen in Annex VIII accompanying the reply to the Questionnaire by the exporter SADIA, rather than a definite value to be charged to or deducted from the goods and for which there was supporting documentation in due form.

212. As regards the comparison in the case of the enterprise AVIPAL S.A., the following comments should be made:

213. In the case of this enterprise, the DCD used the best available information in order to compare the two prices, inasmuch as it used the information provided by the enterprise itself in its submission dated 12 August 1999 (Section 27, folio 2297)[75] to determine the normal value. After receiving this submission, on 12 October 1999, the Implementing Authority, in Note No. 273-001180/99[76] (Section 53, folio 2380) requested the firm AVIPAL S.A. to provide data on its transactions and supporting documentation.

214. The information requested by the implementing authority was not only submitted belatedly on 21 December 1999 - i.e. two months later - but was not complete (Section 60, folio 2505)[77]. In its aforementioned submission, the company provided the list of transactions requested on a magnetic medium (*notas fiscales* (tax receipts), January 1998-January 1999), together with a spreadsheet showing the amounts that should be deducted from prices. The information was not only transmitted without the proper translation required by the provisions of the Law on Administrative procedure (Law No. 19.549, Article 28), but also without the

---

[75] See Annex ARG-XXXIII.
[76] See Annex ARG-XXXI.
[77] See Annex ARG-XXXIV.

supporting documentation that would have enabled the DSD to verify the accuracy of what had been stated.

215. Furthermore, the party's delay in sending the list made it impossible for the DCD to ask for the invoices that may have been necessary based on a sample, as was done in the case of SADIA.

216. As a result, the authority used the information for which there was documentary evidence, namely, the invoices provided by the firm in the submission in File No. 061-007241/99 of 12 August 1999 - Section 27, folio 2297.[78]

217. It is important to note that the information used was therefore that provided by the enterprise, which could have decided not only to transmit the information required in due time but could also have attached the relevant supporting documentation, as it had previously done.

218. Based on the foregoing, Argentina considers that there is no justification for Brazil's claim that the implementing authority did not make due allowance for the adjustments it should have made, and neither is there any justification for the statement that the companies SADIA and AVIPAL convincingly demonstrated the need to do this.

219. The DCD not only acted in accordance with the requirement clearly spelt out in Article 2.4, but throughout the investigation the criteria used were made perfectly clear.

220. According to Article 2.4: *"Due allowance shall be made in each case, **on its merits**, for differences which affect price comparability ... "* This clearly shows that the obligation of a party conducting an investigation to make due allowance for differences that might affect price comparability is not an absolute obligation. It depends on whether the various factors and circumstances claimed by the parties with a view to affecting the price comparison made by the investigating authority *have sufficient merit* to be taken into account, leaving the authority to determine whether or not the factors put before it are relevant.

III.3.2 CLAIM 24: CONSISTENCY WITH ARTICLE 2.4

221. Brazil claims that Argentina acted inconsistently with Article 2.4 by not making due allowance for differences in taxes, freight charges and financial costs in the normal value established for all the other exporters.

Text of Article 2.4

The relevant section of Article 2.4 states the following:

"Due allowance shall be made in each case, on its merits, for differences which affect price comparability, including differences in conditions and terms of sale, taxation, levels of trade, quantities, physical characteristics, and any other differences which are also demonstrated to affect price comparability."

Argentina's argument

222. Brazil claims that the DCD sent two notes to the firm JOX *Assesoría Agropecuaria* requesting clarification of the taxes in the publication used for the

---

[78] See Annex ARG-XXXIII.

Report of the Panel

preliminary determination and that, despite the persistence shown in requesting this information, it later decided not to use it to make the price deductions which, according to Brazil, should have been made from the normal value.

223. Before replying to Brazil's claim, Argentina wishes to clarify that, although the DCD did indeed send the two notes mentioned by Brazil to JOX requesting clarification of the taxes and other commercial clauses contained in the publication included in the file, the two notes were not in the same terms, as Brazil contends.

224. The first note referred to by Brazil, of 25 June 1999 - Section 22, folio 1808, Note No. 273-000788/99 - is the original note requesting clarification, whereas the second, sent one month later, on 27 July 1999, DCD Note No. 273 - 000883/99 - Section 25, folio 2091[79], is a note in response to another note from JOX dated 2 July 1999 in which the latter requests the DCD to transmit a copy of the note requiring clarification.

225. Argentina considers it necessary to reaffirm the criterion used to interpret the obligation to make due allowance for differences that might affect price comparability in a procedure, as laid down in Article 2.4.

226. As stated when responding to Claim 23, Argentina considers that Article 2.4 determines the criteria to be used in order to ensure that comparisons between the export price and the normal value are made in a fair and equitable manner.

227. The first obligation on the parties is to be found in the first sentence of the Article and although Argentina considers that there is no order of precedence among the various sentences, there are different levels of detail which, following a line that runs from the general to the more specific, qualify the criteria to be taken into account in the comparison.

228. For example, the first sentence of Article 2.4 states that the comparison must be fair. The second sentence is more specific and lays down a minimum criterion for the comparison in order to meet this requirement: the values to be compared must represent the same level of trade, normally the ex-factory level. Subsequently, the Article prescribes that, based on an evaluation of each particular case, due allowance must be made for differences which affect price comparability and it describes some of the factors to be taken into account, without seeking to provide an exhaustive list, and which meet the requirement that it must be demonstrated that these differences have to be taken into account because they affect price comparability.

229. It is precisely because the comparison must be fair, which requires that it should be at the same level of trade, that the deductions communicated by JOX were not taken into account. If this had been done, the comparison would have been - improperly - between an ex-factory price for the normal value and an f.o.b. export price, because there was no identical information on the deductions to be made from the export value of the goods.

230. Regarding Brazil's claim in paragraph 392 of its submission, it should be noted that in this case the information submitted by five exporters on 26 August 1999 was disregarded by the DCD because it was inaccurate. The table presented by the exporters is in fact incorrect. This can clearly be seen simply by trying to reconstruct the final price on the basis of the price obtained after making the suggested deductions.

---

[79] See Annex ARG - XXXV.

231. For the foregoing reasons, we consider that the Panel should reject Brazil's claim that Argentina acted inconsistently with Article 2.4 by not making due allowance for differences in taxation, freight charges and financial costs in the normal value established for all other exporters, as Argentina not only acted within the limits imposed by the legislation in force but also took into account and weighed up all the information provided by the parties in each case and, as prescribed in Article 2.4, it evaluated the adequacy of each item of information according to its merits, with special emphasis on the existence of evidence that would allow it to verify each item.

III.3.3 CLAIM 25: CONSISTENCY WITH ARTICLE 2.4

232. Brazil claims that Argentina acted inconsistently with Article 2.4 by improperly taking into account the alleged physical differences between the product sold in Brazil and that exported to Argentina in order to establish the normal value.

Text of Article 2.4

The relevant section of Article 2.4 states the following:

> "Due allowance shall be made in each case, on its merits, for differences which affect price comparability, including differences in conditions in terms of sale, taxation, levels of trade, quantities, physical characteristics, and any other differences which are also demonstrated to affect price comparability."

Argentina's argument

233. Brazil bases this claim on the fact that the DCD took into account the statement by CEPA (the applicant), in its request for the opening of an investigation that the poultry sold in both countries was not the same as that exported to Argentina, which did not have feet or heads, whereas the poultry for the domestic market had both heads and feet, without verifying the accuracy of the information submitted to it.

234. Brazil therefore contends that, by making an adjustment when it was not necessary, the DCD went beyond its obligation to take due account of the information submitted by the parties and failed to examine its accuracy or adequacy.

235. Argentina once again argues that Brazil's claim regarding application of Article 2.4 is based on arguments that were only partly substantiated during the conduct of the investigation, which was accessible without restrictions to the Government of Brazil itself, the exporters and other interested parties, throughout its duration. Consequently, Brazilian exporting enterprises could not have been unaware of the fact that part of the applicant's submission was the Annex to Note 220/97, which explained the differences between the products sold in both countries, as well as a proposal on the type of adjustment that should be made in order to be able to compare the prices on an equal footing.

236. If Brazilian producers/exporters considered that the alleged differences were not correct, therefore, they had ample opportunity throughout the administrative procedure that was the basis for the investigation to draw attention to the error unequivocally, but they did not do so.

237. Moreover, JOX *Ascesoria Agropecuaria* clarified that the chilled poultry is usually sold in the São Paulo region with feet and heads, as stated in the Note dated 1 August 1997, contained in the file on Folio 177 and forming part of Exhibit BRA-1.

In the second point of the second paragraph of a Note of 23 June 1999[80], the company Jox also informed the implementing authority that:

> "The chilled poultry sold in the State of São Paulo includes heads and feet, unless indicated otherwise, in which case the prices should be around 10 per cent higher"

238. Argentina therefore considers that inasmuch as:

(a) The authority that conducted the investigation was given proof of a physical difference that clearly affected the price comparability to be carried out as part of the procedure;

(b) this proof was also accompanied by an appropriate method for making the necessary adjustment in order to compare prices, and, still more importantly;

(c) during the investigation the Brazilian exporters did not expressly deny that there was a physical difference between the products or reject the proposed method for making the adjustment, which was criticized by exporters although they did not at any time give reasons for the criticism or make any alternative proposals for the comparison;

the implementing authority complied with Article 2.4 of the Anti-Dumping Agreement, which provides that due allowance must be made for all the differences that might affect a fair comparison, when it made the adjustment based on the method proposed.

239. On the basis of the foregoing, Argentina considers that it had to make an adjustment in order to be able to compare the prices. As already stated, this view is backed up by the letters and clarifications from JOX, which have always been part of the evidence contained in the file and, if they had considered it appropriate, the Brazilian exporters could have proposed rectifications; however, they did not do so.

240. Consequently, the Panel is requested to find that Brazil's claim that Argentina acted inconsistently with Article 2.4 because there was no difference that might affect comparability is inadmissible and that, as shown, it was necessary to make an adjustment so that a fair comparison of prices could be made; that despite having manifold opportunities to do so, the interested parties never questioned the need to make the adjustment for physical differences in the product - indeed they only questioned the methodology, without proposing any alternative methodology, and not the actual need to make the adjustment.

III.3.4 CLAIM 26: CONSISTENCY WITH ARTICLE 2.4

241. Brazil claims that Argentina acted inconsistently with Article 2.4, imposing an unreasonable burden of proof on SADIA, AVIPAL and FRANGOSUL by not defining the period of the investigation and allowing exporters to submit information on dumping for the years 1996 to 1999, when the investigation period was subsequently established as January 1998 to January 1999.

---

[80] Exhibit BRA-32.

Text of Article 2.4

The relevant section of Article 2.4 states the following:

"The authorities shall indicate to the parties in question what information is necessary to ensure a fair comparison and shall not impose an unreasonable burden of proof on those parties ... ".

Argentina's argument

242. Argentina does not share the views expressed by Brazil in this claim and totally rejects the idea of an alleged imposition by Argentina of an unreasonable burden of proof on Brazilian exporters, a claim which Brazil tries to substantiate by stating that:

(a) The investigation period was not automatically defined at the time the investigation was initiated;

(b) the normal value was only based on invoices presented by the parties and, considering the large volume of sales on the domestic market, this had the effect of imposing an excessive burden of proof on Brazilian exporters.

243. The Anti-Dumping Agreement does not define the period for collecting information or for the investigation itself. The implementing authority therefore has discretion to request the documentation it deems necessary in order to determine dumping, and may require further information when this is necessary to guarantee due process to the interested parties. It should be noted that this attention to the interests of the parties is used as an argument on the grounds that it represents an "unreasonable burden", with implicit reference to an intention to prejudice exporters.

244. Brazil's argument contradicts what has been said throughout this submission, in that the complaint in some cases has been that the implementing authority did not request more information. Whenever the implementing authority has sought further information for a particular purpose, Brazil complains that the information requested represents an "unreasonable burden on exporters".

245. As an example of the special attention paid by the implementing authority to this aspect, it should be emphasized that, precisely because of the comments made by the parties to the effect that, the large volume of operations by enterprises on the local market made it difficult for them to provide written evidence of all the transactions, the authority only requested the submission of evidence for those operations chosen on the basis of a statistical sample drawn up for the purpose of not imposing an unreasonable burden on exporters.

246. In any event, throughout the procedure, Brazil's producers/exporters did not complain of the burden of information requested by the DCD in relation to the provisions of Article 6.1.3 of the Anti-Dumping Agreement.

247. The difficult balance which Brazil tries to impose on Argentina in defining the volume and type of information to be requested does not appear to be in line with an article such as Article 6, paragraphs 1 and 2, and other related articles in which the Agreement seeks to give the parties the right of legitimate defence which Argentina was careful to give them during this procedure.

III.3.5 CLAIM 27: CONSISTENCY WITH ARTICLE 2.4.2

248. Brazil claims that Argentina acted inconsistently with Article 2.4.2 by incorrectly establishing the normal value for SADIA, AVIPAL and FRANGOSUL solely on the basis of transactions in the domestic market for which invoices were submitted rather than all the transactions contained in the list sent to the DCD. Brazil also claims that the DCD established the margin of dumping for SADIA and AVIPAL by comparing the weighted average of a statistical sample with the weighted average of prices of all export transactions.

Text of Article 2.4.2

> The relevant section of Article 2.4.2 states the following:
>
> *"Subject to the provisions governing fair comparison in paragraph 4, the existence of margins of dumping during the investigation phase shall normally be established on the basis of a comparison of a weighted average normal value with a weighted average of prices of all comparable export transactions or by a comparison of normal value and export prices on a transaction-to-transaction basis."*

Argentina's argument

249. Although the authority established a measure for AVIPAL and SADIA based on a sample, it has been shown that this sample, inasmuch as it was calculated on the basis of a statistically correct methodology/formula, was indicative of the overall sales in the domestic market. The sample was accompanied by the relevant supporting documentation.

250. Consequently, it is difficult to understand the injury claimed by Brazil in that the documentation submitted by the enterprises was used for the sample.

III.3.6 CLAIMS 32 AND 33: CONSISTENCY WITH ARTICLES 3.1, 3.4, 3.5 AND 12.2.2

251. Brazil claims that Argentina acted inconsistently with Article 3.1, 3.4 and 3.5 by using different periods to evaluate the relevant economic factors and indices listed in Article 3.4 and, according to Brazil, this nullifies the final determination of injury based on positive evidence and an objective evaluation (Claim 32). Brazil also argues that Argentina acted inconsistently with Article 12.2.2 by failing to explain in the final determination why the relevant economic factors and indices listed in Article 3.4 were based on different periods (Claim 33).

Text of Article 3.1, 3.4 and 3.5 and Article 12.2.2

> "3.1   A determination of injury for purposes of Article VI of GATT 1994 shall be based on positive evidence and involve an objective examination of both (a) the volume of the dumped imports and the effect of the dumped imports on prices in the domestic market for like products, and (b) the consequent impact of these imports on domestic producers of such products.
>
> 3.4   The examination of the impact of the dumped imports on the domestic industry concerned shall include an evaluation of all relevant economic factors and indices having a bearing on the state of the

> *industry, including actual and potential decline in sales, profits, output, market share, productivity, return on investments, or utilization of capacity; factors affecting domestic prices; the magnitude of the margin of dumping; actual and potential negative effects on cash flow, inventories, employment, wages, growth, ability to raise capital or investments. This list is not exhaustive, nor can one or several of these factors necessarily give decisive guidance.*
>
> *3.5 It must be demonstrated that the dumped imports are, through the effects of dumping, as set forth in paragraphs 2 and 4, causing injury within the meaning of this Agreement. The demonstration of a causal relationship between the dumped imports and the injury to the domestic industry shall be based on an examination of all relevant evidence before the authorities. The authorities shall also examine any known factors other than the dumped imports which at the same time are injuring the domestic industry, and the injuries caused by these other factors must not be attributed to the dumped imports. Factors which may be relevant in this respect include,* inter alia, *the volume and prices of imports not sold at dumping prices, contraction in demand or changes in the patterns of consumption, trade-restrictive practices of and competition between the foreign and domestic producers, developments in technology and the export performance and productivity of the domestic industry.*
>
> *12.2.2 A public notice of conclusion or suspension of an investigation in the case of an affirmative determination providing for the imposition of a definitive duty or the acceptance of a price undertaking shall contain, or otherwise make available through a separate report, all relevant information on the matters of fact and law and reasons which have led to the imposition of final measures or the acceptance of a price undertaking, due regard being paid to the requirement for the protection of confidential information. In particular, the notice or report shall contain the information described in subparagraph 2.1, as well as the reasons for the acceptance or rejection of relevant arguments or claims made by the exporters and importers, and the basis for any decision made under subparagraph 10.2 of Article 6."*

Argentina's argument

252. The initiation of the investigation was prompted by the appraisal of threat of injury. The CNCE therefore considered, as is customary, the possibility of analysing the trend in imports for the first half of 1999. In this connection, it should be emphasized that both international rules and relevant practices in this area provide that, in cases of threat of injury, it is possible to undertake an analysis beyond the period of the investigation in order to find out whether or not there is a growing trend in imports and, as a result, give the investigation a more substantial factual basis. (For example, Mexican legislation specifically allows the period of the investigation to be extended after it has been initiated).

253. In respect of the period under investigation, the National Foreign Trade Commission therefore used information for the three full years and the remaining months prior to the initiation of the investigation for the determination of injury and,

when analysing whether or not there was a threat of injury, it requested information for the months following the decision to initiate the investigation so as to note trends in this particular case import trends, and their effect on market shares and prices.

254. Moreover, the existence of a voluntary agreement between the parties between October 1998 and March 1999 meant that it was necessary to analyse imports without the effects produced by that agreement, so the analysis was extended until June 1999, both for imports and for all apparent consumption variables.

255. As legal evidence of the above and to anticipate Brazil's objection, we refer to Record No. 576 itself, in which the Commission duly stated: " ... *it should be noted that, if there had been no agreement on volumes and prices between Brazilian exporters and Argentine producers, in 1998 imports would have increased even more and, subsequent to the investigation period, in the first half of 1999, the upward trend would have continued ...* ".

256. In paragraph 427 of its submission, Brazil asserts that Argentina failed to respect Article 3.1 of the Agreement and that the determination of injury was not based on an *objective* examination of the factors listed in that Article. It then puts forward a number of linguistic considerations through which - on the basis of the English text of the Article - it seeks to refute the analysis made by the CNCE, indicating that it was subjective.

257. This calls for the following comments:

(a) Also in regard to the meaning of the words used, "*objective*" is something "belonging or relating to the object itself and not to our way of thinking or feeling"[81] whereas *subjective* is something "relating to our way of thinking or feeling and not to the object itself"[82]. It would therefore appear that Argentina agrees with this terminological distinction.

(b) However, there is no way that the Commission's determination can be seen as "imaginary", "partial", "distorted" or discretional. Nor, as the various instruments resulting from the investigation procedure show, were different parameters used to analyse the indicators.

258. With regard to Brazil's statement in paragraphs 432 and 433, Argentina strictly complied with the provision in Article 12.2.2 by means of the public notice provided through the publication in the Official Journal of the MEYOSP Resolution.

259. In addition to the administrative act called a Resolution, by which the public is informed of the decision adopted, any report by the competent technical authorities and determinations adopted as a result are available to all parties interested by the investigation that have come forward and are accredited in the file.

260. As an illustration, in this particular case, Record No. 576 has 30 folios which, added to the 122 in the corresponding technical report (GEGE/ITDF No. 03/99) bring the total to 152 folios. This is why Argentina, in conformity with the provisions in Article 12.2.2, published in the Official Journal the Resolutions which contain, in the recitals, the conclusions of the various authorities involved in the investigation.

---

[81] See "*Diccionario de la Lengua Española de la Real Academia Española*", twenty-first edition, Madrid, 1992, page 1459.
[82] *Ibid.*, page 1911.

261. Argentina's methodology was made public on several occasions at the WTO (particularly in the Ad Hoc Group on Implementation) and was supported by several Members because it is impossible to publish in an official medium all the instruments and reports by technical bodies that are used as a basis for the adoption of final decisions by the higher authorities.

262. One relevant precedent adopted by the Panel was in the *Guatemala - Cement* dispute, where it is stated that:

> "Mexico claims that Guatemala's notice of initiation did not meet the standard of 'adequate information' because it did not contain adequate information on the basis on which dumping was alleged in the application nor adequate information summarising the factors on which the allegation of injury, in this case threat of material injury, was based, as required by Article 12.1.1.
>
> Guatemala responds that the public notice as supplemented by the report of the Directorate of Economic Integration of 17 November 1995 is adequate to fulfil the requirements of Article 12.1.1. Since the file was open to the public Guatemala considered that the report from the Economic Integration Directorate was available to Mexico and contained the relevant information to comply with Article 12.1.1."[83]

III.3.7 CLAIMS 34, 35, 36 AND 37. CONSISTENCY WITH ARTICLE 3.1, 3.2, 3.4 AND 3.5

263. Brazil claims that, by failing to exclude the imports from two Brazilian exporters from the injury analysis, Argentina did not properly consider the volume, the effect on prices and the impact of the dumped imports on the domestic industry, so Argentina acted inconsistently with Article 3.2 (Claim 34) and with Article 3.4 (Claim 36). Likewise, Brazil contends that the evaluation of the dumped imports indicates that the final injury determination was not based on positive evidence and an objective examination, as required by Article 3.1 (Claim 35). Brazil then argues that, by not excluding imports from these two Brazilian exporters from the dumped imports, Argentina had acted inconsistently with Article 3.5 in not properly considering injury in accordance with Article 3.1 and, consequently, did not properly demonstrate the causal relationship between the dumped imports and the injury to domestic industry, as required by Article 3.5 (Claim 37).

Text of the Articles

> *3.1* "A determination of injury for purposes of Article VI of GATT 1994 shall be based on positive evidence and involve an objective examination of both (a) the volume of the dumped imports and the effect of the dumped imports on prices in the domestic market for like products, and (b) the consequent impact of these imports on domestic producers of such products.
>
> *3.2* With regard to the volume of the dumped imports, the investigating authorities shall consider whether there has been a significant increase in dumped imports, either in absolute terms or relative to production or

---

[83] *Guatemala - Definitive Anti-Dumping Measures on Grey Portland Cement from Mexico* (WT/DS156/R) report of the Panel, paras. 8.90 and 8.91.

consumption in the importing Member. With regard to the effect of the dumped imports on prices, the investigating authorities shall consider whether there has been a significant price undercutting by the dumped imports as compared with the price of a like product of the importing Member, or whether the effect of such imports is otherwise to depress prices to a significant degree or prevent price increases, which otherwise would have occurred, to a significant degree. No one or several of these factors can necessarily give decisive guidance.

3.4 The examination of the impact of the dumped imports on the domestic industry concerned shall include an evaluation of all relevant economic factors and indices having a bearing on the state of the industry, including actual and potential decline in sales, profits, output, market share, productivity, return on investments, or utilization of capacity; factors affecting domestic prices; the magnitude of the margin of dumping; actual and potential negative effects on cash flow, inventories, employment, wages, growth, ability to raise capital or investments. This list is not exhaustive, nor can one or several of these factors necessarily give decisive guidance.

3.5 It must be demonstrated that the dumped imports are, through the effects of dumping, as set forth in paragraphs 2 and 4, causing injury within the meaning of this Agreement. The demonstration of a causal relationship between the dumped imports and the injury to the domestic industry shall be based on an examination of all relevant evidence before the authorities. The authorities shall also examine any known factors other than the dumped imports which at the same time are injuring the domestic industry, and the injuries caused by these other factors must not be attributed to the dumped imports. Factors which may be relevant in this respect include, inter alia, the volume and prices of imports not sold at dumping prices, contraction in demand or changes in the patterns of consumption, trade-restrictive practices of and competition between the foreign and domestic producers, developments in technology and the export performance and productivity of the domestic industry."

Argentina's argument

264. Regarding the share of total exports by Brazil attributable to Brazilian exporters for which there is no significant margin of dumping, it should be noted that the major link between the volume of imports and injury is reflected both in the market share and in the import/production ratio. The relevance and sensitivity of these indicators when determining injury is explained below.

265. The CNCE analysed the total volume of imports investigated and concluded *"that the domestic industry producing whole eviscerated poultry suffered material injury caused by allegedly dumped imports from the Federative Republic of Brazil."*

266. In this connection, Brazil makes a wrong assumption in presuming that the implementing authority did not carry out the corresponding analyses. When analysing the causal relationship, contrary to Brazil's statement, the competent authority did take into account the determination that there was no dumping of exports to the Argentine Republic by the Brazilian enterprises NICOLINI and SEARA.

267. As can be seen from folios 4564 and 3469 of file CNCE No. 43/97 and in ITDF No. 03/99[84], the firms NICOLINI and SEARA provided information in response to the CNCE's questionnaires for exporters. According to this information, the average f.o.b. prices of these enterprises were substantially higher than the prices for the other exports from the origin investigated, for which the competent authority determined the existence of an unfair practice. It can also be seen that the volume of exports by the aforementioned enterprises came nowhere close to the levels reached for the majority of exports from Brazil throughout the period analysed by the CNCE.

268. Record No. 576 of the CNCE concluded with regard to prices that "*the imports investigated were present on the market at prices that caused injury to the prices of like domestic products. The price of whole eviscerated poultry on the domestic market fell throughout the period and the imports investigated had an impact on this decrease. The evidence obtained during the investigation indicates that price is the decisive factor on the market and its decrease throughout the period was associated with the presence of the imports investigated and their price.*"

269. Consequently, as the average f.o.b. prices for the other imports investigated were lower than the prices of enterprises that did not practise dumping, it follows that their sale on the domestic market would inevitably yield international prices even lower than the prices determined by the CNCE in its final determination of injury.

270. In order to illustrate the above, a table and the corresponding chart have been added to this section III.3.7 which show that in 1997 and 1998 the average f.o.b. prices of imports without dumping (NICOLINI and SEARA) were 13 per cent higher than the other imports investigated. As the chart shows, this situation recurred month after month, and it can also be seen that for every month, the average monthly f.o.b. prices of imports from these firms remained, except in the case of NICOLINI in October 1997, above the average f.o.b. prices for transactions for which dumping had been determined.

271. Lastly, the fact that exports by NICOLINI and SEARA did not have the major share in any year during the period investigated by the CNCE implied that no radical changes could be expected in the volume and share of the other imports investigated. In the apparent consumption tables, which are also to be found at the end of this section III.3.7, it can be seen that dumped imports clearly represented the majority, rising in 1998 to almost 40,000 tonnes compared with 56,000 tonnes for total imports from Brazil, and that they grew at a similar rate to that for total imports from Brazil and even more rapidly in 1998 (45 per cent in the case of dumped imports and 40 per cent for all imports from Brazil).

272. Consequently, the share of dumped imports in apparent consumption rose, displacing domestic sales of the like domestic product.

273. In conclusion, Argentina points out that the above facts are apparent from the information in the files, to which both the Government of Brazil and the producing/exporting enterprises in Brazil had full access as interested parties. Consequently, there is no justification for the claims made.

---

[84] See exhibit BRA-14.

AVERAGE f.o.b. PRICES FOR IMPORTS OF WHOLE EVISCERATED poultry; FRESH, CHILLED OR FROZEN
In US dollars/kg.

PERIOD	BRAZIL			OTHER ORIGIN	TOTAL ORIGIN
	Total	Subtotal without DUMPING (NICOLINI + SEARA)	Subtotal with DUMPING		
Jan -95	1.12	1.29	1.09	1.13	1.12
Feb-95	1.09	1.26	1.04	1.17	1.09
Mar-95	1.05	1.19	1.01	1.21	1.05
Apr-95	0.98	1.11	0.94		0.98
May-95	0.92	1.03	0.88		0.92
Jun-95	0.89	1.03	0.83		0.89
Jul-95	0.88	1.01	0.86		0.88
Aug-95	0.89	0.97	0.86		0.89
Sep-95	0.95	0.99	0.94	1.14	0.96
Oct-95	1.03	1.05	1.03	1.14	1.04
Nov-95	1.04	1.09	1.03	1.14	1.05
Dec-95	1.04	1.11	1.02	1.14	1.05
Jan-96	1.06	1.11	1.04	0.99	1.05
Feb-96	1.02	1.07	1.00	1.10	1.03
Mar-96	1.01	1.06	1.00	1.15	1.02
Apr-96	1.01	1.11	0.98	1.12	1.01
May-96	1.02	1.06	1.00		1.02
Jun-96	1.02	1.01	1.03	1.07	1.02
Jul-96	1.01	1.02	1.01	1.07	1.02
Aug-96	1.05	1.06	1.05	1.07	1.06
Sep-96	1.09	1.14	1.07	1.07	1.09
Oct-96	1.12	1.18	1.09	2.00	1.12
Nov-96	1.13	1.21	1.10		1.13
Dec-96	1.12	1.20	1.09	1.03	1.12
Jan -97	1.07	1.18	1.02		1.07
Feb-97	1.04	1.18	0.97		1.04
Mar-97	1.05	1.16	1.00		1.05
Apr-97	0.98	1.04	0.95		0.98
May-97	0.93	1.01	0.89		0.93
Jun-97	0.88	0.99	0.85		0.88
Jul-97	0.91	0.98	0.88		0.91
Aug-97	0.91	0.98	0.89		0.91
Sep-97	0.90	1.03	0.87		0.90
Oct-97	0.98	0.99	0.97		0.98
Nov-97	0.95	1.04	0.91	1.00	0.95

Argentina - Poultry Anti-Dumping Duties

	BRAZIL				
Dec-97	0.98	1.08	0.93	0.93	0.98
Jan -98	0.87	1.10	0.80	1.00	0.88
Feb-98	0.90	0.99	0.82	1.00	0.90
Mar-98	0.91	0.98	0.86	1.00	0.91
Apr-98	0.90	0.98	0.84		0.90
May-98	0.91	0.98	0.85		0.91
Jun-98	0.86	0.99	0.82		0.86
Jul-98	0.89	0.99	0.86		0.89
Aug-98	0.89	0.97	0.86	0.94	0.89
Sep-98	0.91	0.97	0.89	1.01	0.91
Oct-98	0.93	0.97	0.92	0.91	0.93
Nov-98	0.95	0.97	0.92	0.91	0.95
Dec-98	0.97	1.01	0.95	0.91	0.97
1995	1.01	1.10	0.99	1.14	1.02
1996	1.06	1.12	1.04	1.07	1.06
1997	0.96	1.05	0.92	0.94	0.96
1998	0.91	0.99	0.88	0.96	0.91
Var. % 96/95	5	2	5	-6	4
Var. % 97/96	-9	-6	-11	-12	-9
Var. % 98/97	-5	-5	-5	2	-5

▢ Reference period

Source: CNCE, based on information from INDEC

Report of the Panel

Average f.o.b. price of imports by exporter

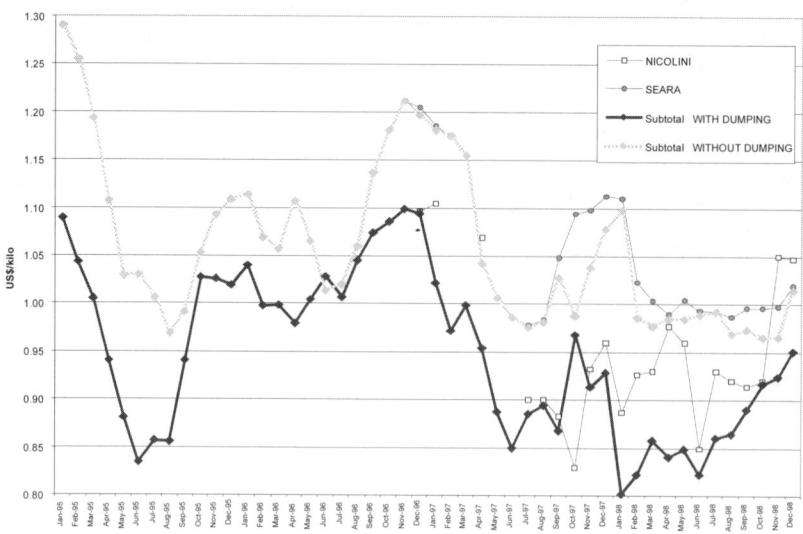

APPARENT CONSUMPTION OF WHOLE EVISCERATED POULTRY

tonnes

Period	Sales of domestic production on the domestic market	Import (1)					Apparent consumption
		Brazil			Other origin	Total	
		Total BRAZIL	Brazil without dumping	Brazil with dumping			
1995	688.725	15.317	3.660	11.657	522	15.939	704.664
1996	667.402	22.544	6.517	16.027	1.843	24.386	691.788
1997	693.641	40.128	12.845	27.283	320	40.448	734.089
1998	782.850	56.291	16.803	39.487	316	56.606	839.457

Var. % 96/95	-3	47	78	37	196	53	-2
Var. % 97/96 (2)	4	78	97	70	-83	66	6
Var. % 98/97	13	40	31	45	-1	40	14

Reference period
(1) Net variation in stocks according to information from importers.
(2) Only as of the last quarter of 1994, imports from NICOLINI exceeded 100 tonnes/month.

STRUCTURE OF APPARENT CONSUMPTION OF WHOLE EVISCERATED POULTRY

Percentage

Period	Sales of domestic production on the domestic market	Import					Apparent consumption
		Brazil			Other origin	Total	
		Total BRAZIL	Brazil without dumping	Brazil with dumping			
1996	96.5	3.3	0.9	2.3	0.3	3.5	100
1997	94.5	5.5	1.7	3.7	0.0	5.5	100
1998	93.3	6.7	2.0	4.7	0.0	6.7	100

Note: The sum of the components may not correspond to the total due to differences in rounding the figures.
Source: CNCE, based on information by INDEC and contained in the reference file.

III.3.8 CLAIMS 38, 39 AND 40: CONSISTENCY WITH ARTICLES 3.4 AND 3.1, AND ARTICLE 12.2.2

274. Brazil contends that Argentina acted inconsistently with Article 3.4 by not evaluating all the relevant economic factors and indices listed in the paragraph in this Article (Claim 38) and, consequently, taking into account the foregoing alleged inconsistency, it also acted inconsistently with Article 3.1, according to Brazil, by not basing the determination of injury on positive evidence and objective evaluation (Claim 39). Brazil also argues that Argentina acted inconsistently with Article 12.2.2 by not taking into account in its final determination the evaluation of all the relevant economic factors and indices listed in Article 3.4 (Claim 40).

Text of Article 3.4 and 3.1

> *"3.4 The examination of the impact of the dumped imports on the domestic industry concerned shall include an evaluation of all relevant economic factors and indices having a bearing on the state of the industry, including actual and potential decline in sales, profits, output, market share, productivity, return on investments, or utilization of capacity; factors affecting domestic prices; the magnitude of the margin of dumping; actual and potential negative effects on cash flow, inventories, employment, wages, growth, ability to raise capital or investments. This list is not exhaustive, nor can one or several of these factors necessarily give decisive guidance.*
>
> *3.1 A determination of injury for purposes of Article VI of GATT 1994 shall be based on positive evidence and involve an objective examination of both (a) the volume of the dumped imports and the effect of the dumped imports on prices in the domestic market for like products, and (b) the consequent impact of these imports on domestic producers of such products."*

Text of Article 12.2.2

> *"12.2.2 A public notice of conclusion or suspension of an investigation in the case of an affirmative determination providing for the imposition of a definitive duty or the acceptance of a price undertaking shall contain, or otherwise make available through a separate report, all relevant information on the matters of fact and law and reasons which have led to the imposition of final measures or the acceptance of a price undertaking, due regard being paid to the requirement for the protection of confidential information. In particular, the notice or report shall contain the information described in subparagraph 2.1, as well as the reasons for the acceptance or rejection of relevant arguments or claims made by the exporters and importers, and the basis for any decision made under subparagraph 10.2 of Article 6."*

Argentina's argument

275. Argentina acted consistently with the provisions in the Anti-Dumping Agreement by evaluating, in respect of injury, all the factors listed in Article 3.4 and their impact on prices of the like domestic product as well as their impact on the domestic industry concerned.

276. There are no grounds for Brazil's claims regarding the absence of any analysis or evaluation of factors such as productivity, variables affecting domestic prices, the magnitude of the margin of dumping, actual and potential effects on the cash flow of the applicant firms, growth, and ability to raise capital.

277. Firstly, during the conduct of the investigation, the applicants submitted information on the productivity situation in the sector which, based on the relevant indicators for such industries, showed that, at the initiation of the investigation by the Argentine authorities, the Argentine poultry industry was on an equal footing with the Brazilian industry and also with the major producers at the global level.

278. This is reflected in Record No. 576, folios 12, 13, 14, 20 and in the Technical Report in folios 26, 28, 29, 30 and 95. These sections basically explain that the growth in productivity that resulted from the production restructuring process in the sector since the early 1990s was a response to the changes taking place in market conditions following Argentina's unilateral opening up of its economy during the period concerned, as well as the integration process taking place between Argentina and Brazil.

279. This is corroborated by the fact that CEPA's contentions in respect of the aforementioned paragraphs were not questioned during the conduct of the investigation, either by Brazilian exporting firms or by importers in the Argentine market. CEPA confirmed that the leading productivity indicators such as the number of eggs per hen to be incubated per cycle, the number of chicks born, the daily weight gain of the chickens being raised, the amount of balanced feed needed to produce 1 kilo of meat, cited in a non-exhaustive list, are similar to those in the Brazilian industry and in some cases, for example, the daily weight gain of the chickens being raised, are higher.

280. Furthermore, some of the indicators contained in the Annex are directly related to productivity, for example, the size of the labour force employed and some headings on average unit costs versus sustained increase in production (see tables 1, 11, 12, 13 and 14 of Annex I to the Technical Report).[85]

281. The Argentine industry's costs are currently comparable to those of the most competitive producers at the international level. This was achieved through a large-scale programme to restructure the industry and adapt production, in accordance with a timetable for investment amounting to over US$270 million between 1994 and 1998.[86] The major part of the investment was used to renovate, extend and equip refrigeration plants and to equip and build farms (essentially for reproduction), and to increase the capacity of the silos, incorporate new technology in plants manufacturing balanced feed, purchase incubators and automate equipment to make by-products and treat effluent, train personnel, purchase vehicles, etc.

282. Much of the investment was affected by the uncertainty caused in the local market by the importation of Brazilian products, which utilized the Argentine market as an alternative market in order to resolve problems of local or foreign demand, thereby negatively affecting price recovery inasmuch as demand remains steady in Argentina.

---

[85] *Ibid.*
[86] See Annex ARG-XXXVI.

- **Characteristics of the Argentine poultry market:**

283. The Argentine poultry sector has traditionally been characterized by local supplies and a low export figure. Consumption of poultry meat has traditionally been seasonal in November and December, due in particular to the end-of-year festivities. The profile of demand for poultry meat, in addition to the price of the product *per se*, is closely tied to the market for red meat or beef, the main substitute given the characteristics of the Argentine market, and the trend in prices compared to the latter product is one of the key variables when analysing the trend in consumption in the poultry sector.

284. Other things being equal, as there are no significant differences in terms of quality compared with Brazilian poultry, competition is essentially based on market prices which, due to the factors set out below, are highly sensitive to minor variations in supply and have to be taken into account when evaluating both threat of injury and injury itself.

285. This is essentially due to the following:

(a) There is relatively stable demand in the market, which showed a strong upward trend in consumption as of the 1990s;

(b) the extent of Brazil's production capacity and the generation of exportable surpluses mean that Brazil can easily redirect its efforts to third markets when there are domestic or external imbalances, despite the large size of its own domestic market[87];

(c) the marginality, in relative terms, of Argentina's poultry market compared with the Brazilian market means that there is a high potential for price discrimination, providing cross subsidies according to the domestic market and third markets (in this connection, see the table on page 21 of Record No. 576)[88];

(d) the proximity of the Brazilian market, which means an effective lead-time of 72 hours in terms of the major consumer market, namely, the Federal Capital and the surrounding area;

(e) the absence of significant access barriers for this product because of the MERCOSUR agreement, and the foreign exchange stability throughout the 1990s resulting from the application of an exchange rate that made one Argentine peso equal to one United States dollar;

(f) the impact of Brazilian imports as price fixers on the Argentine market, even when the volume is relatively low, because of the vast potential for increasing shipments within a very short time;

(g) the technical and financial restrictions that make it difficult to keep stocks for any length of time (pages 92/94 of the Technical Report).

286. In the light of the foregoing and bearing in mind that the marketing characteristics of the product mean that fixing domestic prices is strongly affected by the price in import markets, the imbalances due to surplus supplies in the market of origin and dumped imports necessarily led to price adjustments in the domestic sector.

---

[87] See section VI.2 "MERCOSUR" in the Technical Report (exhibit BRA-14).
[88] See Exhibit BRA-14.

287. For Argentina's poultry industry, this process meant losses in actual and potential terms because the immediate arrival of dumped imports of the Brazilian product in response to the favourable situation in the domestic market had a marked effect on prices, causing them to fall and thereby affecting the recovery of an industry that had invested substantially in improving productivity.

288. The domestic price depression at a time of sustained growth in apparent consumption because of changes in consumer habits can only be explained by the existence of imports under conditions of unfair competition.

289. Brazil clearly has a vast capacity to dump exportable surpluses on the Argentine market under conditions of unfair competition because Argentina is geographically close and has the most easily accessible market.[89] For example, during the period August-September 1997, during the crisis in South East Asia, the volume exported to Argentina increased by 115 per cent, i.e. over a three-month period it rose from 2,349 tonnes to 5,082 tonnes, a figure which is approximately equal to 10 per cent of domestic production for one month or the total production over one month of firms such as San Sebastián or Rasic SA.

290. As Argentina has always contended, this increase occurred because surpluses that could not be channelled into Brazil's traditional markets were directed to alternative markets such as Argentina, which at that time was showing a marked price recovery; however, this recovery could not be sustained in the long term because of the downward pressure exerted by dumped imports from Brazil.

291. Meanwhile Brazil, whose poultry industry recorded losses of 20-25 per cent, increased its sales to Argentina by an annual percentage variation of **70.52 per cent in 1997 and 13.35 per cent in 1998**.

- **Other factors affecting the price of the domestic product:**

292. The CNCE properly considered all the factors which, in addition to imports, might have had an impact on the price of the domestic product. For this purpose, it analysed the trend in the price index for substitute products, mainly red meat, as well as the general level of activity and price indexes in the most important relevant sectors (see Table No. 16 in the Technical Report).[90] In general terms, the arguments put forward by the producer-exporters and Brazil cannot be substantiated because, despite the recession in Argentina, apparent consumption of poultry meat increased steadily, so that this variable could hardly explain the downward pressure on prices. Competition from ready-prepared poultry could not be used as justification either, because not only is it a different product, but it also happens to be produced by the same firms that sell chilled or fresh poultry.

293. Nor could the trend be due to considerations related to changes in the demand profile requiring the introduction of aggressive price policies in order to retain market share, since the aforementioned increase in apparent consumption is in fact the result of a trend that began in the mid-1980s towards growing consumption of lean meat because of its better dietary and health properties in comparison with red meat.

---

[89] See Annex ARG XXXVII.
[90] See Exhibit BRA-14.

- **Remarks concerning the effects caused by the margin of dumping:**

294. In a situation where, in addition to the factors already explained regarding the characteristics of the Argentine market, there is a fixed exchange rate and a recession, the impact of unfair practices such as dumping can be felt all the more strongly, even with relatively small margins. This is particularly true when commodities are the reference product and the price variable is the essential factor in competition.

295. Consequently, bearing in mind the above explanations concerning Brazil's potential to generate surpluses under conditions of unfair competition, margins of 8-14 per cent are significant and were evaluated thus by the investigating authority because of their potential impact on Argentine production.

- **Remarks concerning the failure to analyse cash flow and the ability to raise capital:**

296. A few words, to begin with, on the terms of financing for companies in Argentina, where the capital market has never been an important source, apart from occasional exceptions such as occurred in the 1990s, a fact which is to a large extent reflected in the accounting legislation.

297. At the legislative level, pursuant to Article 299 of Law No. 19550, companies are obliged to submit a "Statement of the Origin and Utilization of Funds" which, unlike the cash flow statement within the strict meaning of financial accounting, is not a detailed breakdown of the cash flow situation but simply a synthetic description of the elements that have led to increases or decreases in funds. These headings, therefore, in no way allow any conclusions to be drawn regarding cash flow trends.

298. Taking account of the above, the indicators which make it possible to undertake such an analysis in terms of the reference variable would be liquidity and the breakeven point, which were analysed in a consistent manner in the Technical Report attached to Record No. 576.

299. Lastly, in relation to paragraph 296 above and the financing mechanisms in this sector, none of the applicants is quoted on the stock exchange or has utilized the capital market, so that irrespective of the rules in force, the cash-flow analysis requirement is not relevant and cannot be met.

300. In view of the considerations of fact and of law set out above in relation to Claims 38, 39 and 40, Argentina considers that it has complied with the requirements laid down in Articles 3.1, 3.4 and 12.2.2, in other words, in its final determination it made due allowance for the evaluation of all the relevant economic factors and indices listed in Article 3.4.

III.3.9 CLAIM 41: CONSISTENCY WITH ARTICLE 4.1

301. Brazil contends that Argentina acted inconsistently with Article 4.1 by considering that 46 per cent constituted the major proportion of total domestic production of poultry in Argentina.

Text of Article 4.1

The relevant section of Article 4.1 states the following:

> *"For the purposes of this Agreement, the term 'domestic industry' shall be interpreted as referring to the domestic producers as a whole of the like*

products or to those of them whose collective output of the products constitutes a major proportion of the total domestic production of those products ... ".

Argentina's argument

302. The definition of domestic industry was consistent with the WTO rules because Argentina considers that 46 per cent of total production is "a major proportion". Brazil's contention that "a major proportion" can only represent at least 50 per cent of the domestic industry is a subjective opinion and is not based on Article 4 of the Anti-Dumping Agreement.

303. According to Record No. 576, the firms concerned represented 46.2 per cent of the domestic industry in 1998, so the CNCE considered that it had complied with the requirement in Article 4.1 of the Anti-Dumping Agreement.

304. For the Argentine Republic, as for other WTO Members (in accordance with previous, consistent decisions in this respect), 46.2 per cent represents a major proportion because it is not simply by chance that the Anti-Dumping Agreement did not establish a fixed percentage in order to show what is meant by "major proportion".

III.4 IMPOSITION AND COLLECTION OF ANTI-DUMPING DUTIES AS A RESULT OF THE ANTI-DUMPING INVESTIGATION

III.4.1 CLAIMS 28, 29 AND 30: CONSISTENCY WITH ARTICLES 9.2, 9.3 AND 12.2.2

305. Brazil claims that Argentina acted inconsistently with Article 9.2 by imposing variable anti-dumping duties that could lead to the collection of an inappropriate amount (Claim 28). For the same reason, Brazil contends that the anti-dumping duty imposed could exceed the margin of dumping established in the final determination (Claim 29). Lastly, Brazil claims that Argentina acted inconsistently with Article 12.2.2 by not explaining how the minimum export price was determined (Claim 30).

Text of Article 9.2

> 9.2. *"When an anti-dumping duty is imposed in respect of any product, such anti-dumping duty shall be collected in the appropriate amounts in each case, on a non-discriminatory basis on imports of such product from all sources found to be dumped and causing injury, except as to imports from those sources from which price undertakings under the terms of this Agreement have been accepted. The authorities shall name the supplier or suppliers of the product concerned. If, however, several suppliers from the same country are involved, and it is impracticable to name all these suppliers, the authorities may name the supplying country concerned. If several suppliers from more than one country are involved, the authorities may name either all the suppliers involved, or, if this is impracticable, all the supplying countries involved.."*

Text of Article 9.3

9.3 *"The amount of the anti-dumping duty shall not exceed the margin of dumping as established under Article 2."*

Text of Article 12.2.2

12.2.2 *"A public notice of conclusion or suspension of an investigation in the case of an affirmative determination providing for the imposition of a definitive duty or the acceptance of a price undertaking shall contain, or otherwise make available through a separate report, all relevant information of the matters of fact and law and reasons which have led to the imposition of final measures or the acceptance of a price undertaking, due regard being paid to the requirement for the protection of confidential information. In particular, the notice or report shall contain the information described in subparagraph 2.1, as well as the reasons for the acceptance or rejection of relevant arguments or claims made by the exporters and importers, and the basis for any decision made under subparagraph 10.2 of Article 6."*

Argentina's argument

306. Argentina acted consistently with Articles 9.2, 9.3 and 12.2.2 of the Anti-Dumping Agreement and the regulations of Law No. 24425, Decree No. 2121/94.

307. After analysing and taking into account all the information collected during the procedure, contrary to the Brazilian Government's position that Argentina did not comply with Article 9.2 and 9.3 of the Agreement, the implementing authority determined for whom it would in due time and form provide the relevant evidence containing all the necessary elements. Thus, it excluded the Brazilian producing/exporting firms NICOLINI and SEARA from the anti-dumping measure and fixed an individual dumping margin for the exporting firms AVIPAL and SADIA.

308. Although Article 9 of the Agreement does not address the methods to be used to collect the anti-dumping duties, i.e. it does not fix any methodology or give indications similar to those fixed by the Agreement in other cases, in practice, Members of the WTO apply anti-dumping duties in three ways: (a) Fixed duties in relation to an *ad valorem* tax; (b) fixed in relation to a specific amount; (c) variable.

309. Article 9.3 provides that "*[t]he amount of the anti-dumping duty shall not exceed the margin of dumping as established under Article 2*". This principle is set out in detail in Article 9.3.1 and 9.3.2. Article 9.3.2, in particular, provides that "[w]*hen the amount of the anti-dumping duty is assessed on a prospective basis, provision shall be made for a prompt refund, upon request, of any duty paid in excess of the margin of dumping*" (Emphasis added). In this particular case, the aforementioned Article was fully respected because Argentina used the prospective system and there was no request from the exporting firms that warranted a revision with a review to refunding the alleged duty paid in excess.

310. The refund of any duty paid in excess has been authorized since the Tokyo Round in Article 8.3 of the Anti-Dumping Code, as well as in Article 8(c) of the Anti-Dumping Code of the Kennedy Round, which are the provisions preceding Article 9.3 of the current Agreement. Article 9.3 of the current Anti-Dumping Agreement lays down the requirement that there must be a **prior request** and that "a

Report of the Panel

request for a refund, *duly supported by evidence*, must be made by an importer of the product subject to the anti-dumping duty" (emphasis added).

311. Argentina repeats once more that there was no such request, nor did Brazil - in the claims being examined - provide proof of its contentions regarding the collection of excess anti-dumping duties.

312. Without prejudice to the foregoing which, in itself, is conclusive, Argentina deems it relevant to clarify certain issues. The system of collecting anti-dumping duties in variable amounts used by Argentina (the difference between the normal value and the declared f.o.b. value of the shipment in question), in the view of the implementing authority, is precisely designed to ensure that the anti-dumping duty effectively paid does not exceed the margin of dumping determined. For example, if the margin of dumping disappears in the course of applying the duties because the export price is aligned on the normal value, under this system the duty to be paid would be zero. As can be seen, this is perfectly consistent with the principles set out in Article 9.3.

313. If, as a result of this application, a situation arises in which the duty paid is higher than the margin of dumping determined in the investigation, the exporter is fully entitled to request a prompt refund, subject to a duly substantiated request, and the implementing authority will carry out the relevant review. Thus, it can be seen that the Agreement itself, in Articles 9.3.1 and 9.3.2, provides the "remedy" for any excess payment by allowing for a review that may lead to the payment of a refund of the amount paid in excess; so that the Agreement accepts that an amount in excess of the anti-dumping duty may be paid.

314. If Brazil's position is that a single system for payment of a fixed *ad valorem* rate should be adopted - a situation that is not provided for in the Agreement - such a system would have similar disadvantages, for example, the following: applying a fixed *ad valorem* rate on a prospective basis would mean that, even if the margin of dumping disappeared because the export price was aligned on the normal value, the anti-dumping duty would still have to be paid in the expectation that the payment in excess would be refunded once there had been a review. Moreover, combining the price aligned on the normal value with the payment of an *ad valorem* duty at a higher rate (the export price aligned on the normal value) could incite exporters to stay out of the market and, in such a situation, there would be no new imports, nor would it be possible to undertake a review that would result in a refund either. On the contrary, in such a situation, the system of paying a variable amount of anti-dumping duties would not lead to excess payment and so would be much fairer for the exporter.

315. As already explained, in practice WTO Members apply the following anti-dumping duties: (a) fixed in relation to an *ad valorem* rate; (b) fixed in relation to a specific amount; and (c) variable amounts. Canada also applies variable amounts of anti-dumping duties. Consequently, the methodology adopted by Argentina is consistent with the Anti-Dumping Agreement.

316. In accordance with Article 9.3, a minimum f.o.b. export price was fixed as an anti-dumping measure that was equivalent, and in some cases was lower than the normal value determined so "[t]he amount of the anti-dumping duty shall not exceed the margin of dumping as established ... ". This is shown in the table below:

Exporter	Normal value US$/kg.	Average f.o.b. price US$/kg.	Margin of dumping %	Anti-dumping measure minimum f.o.b. US$/kg.
	A	B	(A-B)/B	
Sadia	0.9294	0.80883	14.91	0.92
Avipal	1.0896	0.94355	15.48	0.98
Other	1.0385	0.95992	8.19	0.98

317. Lastly, the simple exercise below (Tables 1, 2 and 3) shows that the calculation of the anti-dumping duty to be collected may also be above (or below) the margin of dumping determined when this is calculated as a fraction of the f.o.b. price invoiced, in other words, when a measure is fixed in "*ad valorem*" form.

- **TABLE 1**

	A	B	C	D	E
Exporter	Normal value [US$/kg.]	Average f.o.b. price [US$/kg.]	Margin of Dumping (A-B)/B [%]	Margin of Dumping (A-B) [US$/kg.]	Anti-dumping duty (A-B) [US$/kg.]
Sadia	0.93	0.81	14.91%	0.12	0.12
Avipal	1.09	0.94	15.48%	0.15	0.15
Other	1.04	0.96	8.19%	0.08	0.08

- **TABLE 2**

	A	B	C
Exporter	*Ad Valorem** (Table 1.C)	f.o.b. Price Example [US$/kg.]	Anti-dumping duty (A*B) [US$/kg.]
Sadia	14.91%	1.20	0.18
Avipal	15.48%	1.20	0.19
Other	8.19%	1.20	0.10

* The "*ad valorem*" is deemed to be equal to the dumping margin expressed as a percentage.

- **TABLE 3**

Exporter	A Anti-Dumping Duty (Table 2.C) [US$ /kg.]	B Anti-Dumping Duty (Table 1.E) [US$ /kg.]	C Variation (A-B) [US$ /kg.]
Sadia	0.18	0.12	0.06
Avipal	0.19	0.15	0.04
Other	0.10	0.08	0.02

This exercise assumes that the Brazilian exporting firms decide to export their products at a higher price (US$1.20/kg.).

As a result of this practice, it can clearly be seen that, when applying an anti-dumping measure in "*ad valorem*" form, the anti-dumping duties to be collected rise from US$0.12/kg. to US$0.18/kg., in the case of Sadia, from US$0.15/kg. to US$0.19/kg. in the case of Avipal, and from US$0.08/kg. to US$0.10/kg. for the other exporters (table 3).

In this way as well, the dumping margin established in the final determination would presumably be exceeded (table 1.D), although the difference in this case is that companies that wish to discontinue unfair competition practices by aligning their export prices on those in the domestic market, as indicated above, would still pay a duty.

318. It is thus clear that these systems, because of their particular features, are liable to generate variations or excess duties. The Agreement acknowledges this and regulates the situation by providing appropriate "remedies". Failure to use these remedies cannot be attributed to the implementing authority, as a cause of injury or violation of the Agreements in effect.

319. With regard to Brazil's contentions regarding Article 12.2.2 of the Anti-Dumping Agreement, Argentina complied with the requirements in this Agreement because both in the Report on Action Taken and the Report on the Final Determination of the Margin of Dumping, throughout the text, under different topics, each of the submissions by the producing/exporting enterprises was looked at in detail in order to reach a reasoned conclusion on the motives for which the implementing authority determined the measures to be applied including exclusion of the enterprises which met the requirements for this decision.

320. In the Report on Action Taken, which preceded the closure of the period for obtaining evidence, dated 4 January 2002 (Section LXIII, folio 2757), the DCD made available to the parties all the essential facts on which it intended to base its final decision and, on the basis of these facts, the implementing authority fixed a minimum value.

321. As Argentina has shown, Brazil has merely made allegations in this complaint and has not proved any failure to comply with the Article in question on the part of Argentina, which made the determinations on the basis of the documentation attached to the records of proceedings in conformity with the provisions of the Agreement.

IV. PLEADINGS

322. On the basis of the arguments set out in the sections above, Argentina respectfully requests the Panel to proceed as follows:

(i) Pursuant to the arguments set out in Section II and as explained in paragraphs 23, 24 and 25 of this Submission, Argentina requests the Panel to refrain from ruling on the 41 claims of inconsistency with various provisions of the Agreement on Implementation of Article VI of the General Agreement on Tariffs and Trade 1994 (Anti-Dumping Agreement) submitted by Brazil.

If the Panel should decide not to accede to Argentina's request as set out in paragraph 26 of this Submission, and in the light of the arguments developed in Section III, Argentina respectfully requests that the Panel:

(ii) Reject Brazil's claims that Resolution 574/2000 of the Ministry of the Economy of the Argentine Republic is inconsistent with:

- Article 5.2, 5.3, 5.7 and 5.8 of the Anti-Dumping Agreement;
- Article 12.1 of the Anti-Dumping Agreement;
- Article 6.1.1, 6.1.2, 6.1.3, 6.2 and 6.8, and paragraphs 5, 6 and 7 of Annex II, and Article 6.9 and 6.10 of the Anti-Dumping Agreement;
- Article 2.4 and 2.4.2 of the Anti-Dumping Agreement;
- Article 3.1, 3.2, 3.4 and 3.5 of the Anti-Dumping Agreement;
- Article 4.1 of the Anti-Dumping Agreement;
- Article 9.2 and 9.3 of the Anti-Dumping Agreement;
- the various claims related to Article 12.2.2.

(iii) Reject the request for the immediate repeal of Resolution 574/2000 imposing definitive anti-dumping duties.

ANNEX B-2

FIRST ORAL STATEMENT OF ARGENTINA
(25 September 2002)

I. INTRODUCTION

1. The Argentine Republic is grateful for the opportunity to present its arguments before the Panel in the light of Brazil's Written Submission of 8 August 2002, and to refute the doubts raised by Brazil concerning Resolution 574/2000 of the Ministry of the Economy of the Argentine Republic on the basis of various considerations of fact and law which are presented below in two main sections as follows: Section II, dealing with the standard of review and the rules and principles of public international law applicable to the case, and Section III, which refutes the substantive arguments contained in Brazil's 41 claims.

II. PRELIMINARY ARGUMENTS: RELEVANT RULES AND PRINCIPLES OF PUBLIC INTERNATIONAL LAW APPLICABLE TO THIS PROCEEDING

II.1 STANDARD OF REVIEW

2. Argentina repeats its agreement that there is a separate standard of review[1] in the case of Article 17.6 of the Anti-Dumping Agreement. However, in view of the allegations made by Brazil in paragraphs 26, 27 and 28 of its first written submission[2], Argentina wishes to question whether in all cases a presumed infringement of Article 17.6(i) may become the subject of an allegation by a party to a dispute.

3. In the view of the Argentine Republic, a literal interpretation of Article 17.6(i) of the Anti-Dumping Agreement (AD) establishes a standard of review that panels must apply in determining whether the investigating authority adequately established the facts and whether its assessment was impartial and objective. The text of the article is not meant for the Parties to the Agreement but for the Panel. There is consequently some doubt as to the possibility of according parties the right to allege infringements thereof, except where a situation of "due process" will arise.

4. In the Report on the case *"Egypt-Steel"*:[3] the Panel made this same point:

"Furthermore, while, given our dismissal of this claim on procedural grounds, we need not rule on whether a violation of Article 17.6(i) can be the subject of a claim by a party in a dispute, we have considerable doubts in this regard. What is clear nevertheless, and in any case, is that Article 17.6(i) lays down the standard which a panel has to apply in examining the matter referred to it in terms of Article 17.5 of the AD Agreement. As such, we are of

---

[1] First written submission by the Argentine Republic, 29 August 2002, para. 9.
[2] First written submission by Brazil, 8 August 2002.
[3] Report of the Panel on "Egypt - Definitive Anti-Dumping Measures on Steel Rebar from Turkey", WT/DS211/R, 8 August 2002, para. 7.142.

course bound by it in our consideration of the claims in this dispute" (emphasis added)

II.2. OTHER PRINCIPLES AND RULES OF PUBLIC INTERNATIONAL LAW APPLICABLE TO THE CASE

II.2.1. Content of Argentina's complaint

5. Argentina considers it timely to refute some of the arguments made in the first written submission of the EC concerning *res iudicata*[4], and to offer some clarifications.

6. First, Argentina considers inaccurate the EC statement that *"this Panel need not reach this issue because it is plain that, in any event, the requirements for the existence of res judicata are not met"* .[5]

7. In addition to reaffirming that the Argentine Republic *has not argued* primarily for the application of the doctrine of "Res judicata", Argentina considers that the EC's affirmation should certainly be based on demonstrating that requirements of that doctrine are not satisfied in this case. In the *"India/Autos"* case [6], the Panel maintained[7], with respect to the application of the doctrine of *res judicata* that it would first examine the applicability of the doctrine in the WTO and secondly, if it were applicable to WTO dispute settlement, whether the facts of the dispute satisfied the requirements of the doctrine.

8. As the EC indeed acknowledges, "The measure before this Panel is the same as the measure in dispute before MERCOSUR Ad Hoc Arbitral Tribunal".[8] Without prejudice to the applicability of the doctrine, Argentina believes it necessary to point out that the requirements *are indeed fulfilled* in this case:

- **The identity of the parties** is beyond doubt on both occasions, with an element of "added value", in that they are States party to a an integration process, namely MERCOSUR. As such, Argentina and Brazil have designed an organisational structure and agreed that their disputes would be adjudicated by means of the procedure contemplated in the Brasilia Protocol, by the same token accepting the arbitral awards in their totality, as argued by Argentina[9] and endorsed by Paraguay, another State party to MERCOSUR; in its First Written Submission.[10]

- **the identity of the measure being challenged**: Resolution 574/2000 of the Ministry of the Economy of the Argentine Republic, as stated by Argentina in its first written submission [11] and also acknowledged by the EC.[12]

---

[4] Third party submission of the EC, 9 September 2002, para. 5.
[5] Third party submission of the EC, para. 6.
[6] WT/DS 146/R, WT/DS175/R, India - Measures affecting the Automotive Sector, 21 December 2001.
[7] WT/DS 146/R, WT/DS 175/R, para. 7.55.
[8] Third party submission of the EC, para. 7.
[9] First written submission of Argentina, paras. 18 and 19.
[10] Third party submission of Paraguay, para. 7.
[11] First written submission of Argentina, para. 16.
[12] Third party submission of the EC, para. 7.

- **the identity of the legal basis of the claim**: in MERCOSUR, Section II of the claim filed by Brazil (entitled FUNDAMENTAÇAO JURIDICA), has two parts: in part A (ASPECTOS PRELIMINARES), Brazil includes a paragraph 4 titled "Evolução das normas do Mercosul sobre antidumping e normas aplicáveis à utilização de medidas antidumping no comercio intrazona" containing Decisión N°11/97 according to which, as Brazil itself recognises: "o texto incorpora, portanto, todas as disciplinas da WTO sobre a matéria (não podería ser diferente)".[13] Brazil then confirms that "[d]esde 1997, a aplicação de medidas antidumping no comércio intrazona, repita-se, deve dar-se em conformidade com o Marco Normativo, o qual reflete o entendimento comum alcancado pelos Estados Parte a respeito das regras e procedimentos estabelecidos pelo Acordo Antidumping da WTO".[14] In other words, Brazil's intention was to base its claim on the alleged inconsistency of the Argentine measure with the WTO Anti-Dumping Agreement, which can be substantiated in subsection II.B "DAS INCONSISTÊNCIAS LEGAIS" and in paragraph 6."O Processo de Investigação e a Aplicação do Direito Antidumping". All throughout subsection II.B of its submission within MERCOSUR, Brazil confirms that the legal basis of its submission was the presumed WTO-inconsistency of the Argentine measure.

9. It is noteworthy that the submission of Paraguay, another State party to MERCOSUR, **is conclusive** as to the significance it attaches to Brazil's current complaint before the WTO when it states that: "Paraguay considers that, in accordance with the general principles of public international law, this case is "res judicata"[15], because it has already been brought under the dispute settlement procedure established within the framework of MERCOSUR, and under the Brasilia Protocol in particular". Paraguay further confirms: "In view of the foregoing, Paraguay considers this case as having been subject to a prior dispute settlement procedure, as recognised by both parties and resolved by a ruling that is binding on and mandatory for those parties. Hence this case should not be addressed by this Panel, for if it were, this would constitute a violation of the principles and rules of public international law and failure to abide by decisions handed down by MERCOSUR institutions, in this instance the award of an Ad Hoc Arbitral Tribunal constituted under the Brasilia Protocol."[16]

10. Argentina wishes to reiterate that Brazil's conduct in omitting any reference to the arbitral award relating to the same complaint in the framework of MERCOSUR, in which its claims were not upheld, is contrary to the **principle of good faith in the observance and application of international agreements** *in two spheres simultaneously*: the treaties and protocols signed, first within MERCOSUR, and second, in the WTO.[17]

---

[13] Submission of Brazil dated 16 March 2001 to the MERCOSUR Ad Hoc Arbitral Tribunal, page 22.
[14] Submission of Brazil dated 16 March 2001 within Mercosur, page 25.
[15] Third party submission of Paraguay, para. 5.
[16] *Ibid.*, para.10.
[17] First written submission of Argentina, paras. 16 and 17.

11. In the WTO framework, the significance of the principle of good faith was elucidated in the case *United States - Shrimps*, in which the Appellate Body stated that: "... This principle, at once a general principle of law and a general principle of international law, controls the exercise of rights by states. One application of this general principle, the application widely known as the doctrine of *abus de droit*, prohibits the abusive exercise of a state's rights and enjoins that whenever the assertion of a right "impinges on the field covered by [a] treaty obligation, it must be exercised bona fide, that is to say, reasonably." An abusive exercise by a Member of its own treaty right thus results in a breach of the treaty rights of the other Members and, as well, a violation of the treaty obligation of the Member so acting ...".[18]

12. Furthermore, Argentina believes that the present dispute initiated by Brazil within the WTO violates not only Article 21 of the Brasilia Protocol, which was pointed out in the submission of Paraguay[19], but also the principle of good faith in the WTO framework. For, "a State cannot be allowed to avail itself of the advantages of a treaty when convenient and to reject that treaty when compliance becomes burdensome. It is of very little consequence whether the said rule is based on what is known in English law as the principle of estoppel or on the requirement of good faith. The first is but one aspect of the second".[20]

13. This estoppel-good faith binomial has also been underlined by Georg Scwarzenberger, who argues that the violation of a treaty implies an infringement of the principle of good faith that prevails in international relations.

14. The Argentine Republic reiterates[21] that Brazil's complaint within the framework of the WTO contradicts: (a) its consistent practice, as a MERCOSUR State party since 1991, of fulfilling the commitments it has assumed and having recourse to the dispute settlement procedure provided for under the Protocol of Brasilia and reaffirmed through the signature of the Protocol of Olivos; (b) its consistent and unequivocal practice of accepting the scope of the arbitral awards, of which there have been eight thus far, seven of them involving Brazil either as complainant or respondent.

15. Brazil's conduct in raising this dispute within the WTO thus displays some common features of "estoppel"- which as stated above, is closely linked to the principle of good faith -

" ... on the one hand, commitment to the responsibility born of appearances created; on the other, and in consequence, the obligation on the party subject to that responsibility to accept the risk of the reactions that its attitude or actions could elicit from another party".[22]

16. The disqualifying effect of **estoppel** therefore **annuls the validity or effectiveness of accusations that contradict one's own acts or statements.**

---

[18] Report of the Appellate Body, United States, Prohibition of imports of certain shrimp and shrimp products ("*United States - Shrimp*"), WT/DS58/AB/R, adopted on 6 November 1998, DSR 1998:VII, 2755, para. 158.
[19] Third party submission of Paraguay, paras. 6 and 10.
[20] Lauterpacht Hersch, cited by Enrique Pecourt Garcia in *El principio del estoppel en Derecho Internacional Público. Revista Española de Derecho Internacional Público*, Madrid, 1962, pp. 107-108.
[21] First written submission of Argentina, para. 21.
[22] Enrique Pecourt Garcia, op.cit., p. 100.

17. The Argentine Republic likewise considers it timely to point out that Brazil's conduct as evidenced within the MERCOSUR framework until the establishment of this Panel underscores the case for estoppel. Indeed, the States party to MERCOSUR - including Brazil of course - completed all the stages leading to the conclusion of a treaty signed on 18 February 2002, namely the Protocol of Olivos the purpose of which is to settle disputes within MERCOSUR. This Protocol includes a choice of forum provision. As the EC points out in its submission[23] and also confirmed by Paraguay,[24] the commitment assumed by Brazil with the signing of the Protocol of Olivos on 18 February 2002 is not consistent with Brazil's request for the establishment of a WTO panel submitted on 25 February 2002.[25]

18. In short, Argentina concludes that Brazil displayed consistent conduct in MERCOSUR as pertained to submitting its trade disputes with other States party to the dispute settlement procedure contemplated in the Protocol of Brasilia. Furthermore, Brazil had accepted the significance of awards under the Protocol of Brasilia itself before and after the Arbitral Award concerning poultry. Thirdly, Brazil gave yet another sign of this conduct by negotiating and signing the Protocol of Olivos in February 2002. Obviously, Brazil's conduct gave rise to rights and expectations, and more than this, a firm conviction amongst the other States Members of MERCOSUR as to Brazil's acceptance of the framework, the prosecution of the process and the scope of the awards under the terms of the legal instruments of MERCOSUR. Fourthly, Argentina emphasises that no subregional instrument provides for any possibility whatsoever of submitting a dispute that has already been resolved to successive forums - judicial or arbitral- within MERCOSUR or elsewhere. Lastly, Argentina reiterates[26] that Brazil's conduct cannot be viewed as isolated or sporadic, as there are a good many awards in which Brazil was involved whether as complainant or respondent, and accepted the award in all cases.

19. In Argentina's view, by virtue of the application of the principle of good faith[27], no interpretation given by the Panel in respect of the dispute raised by Brazil, **can overlook the existence of the arbitral award[28]** that settled the dispute within MERCOSUR and **the special relationship** between Argentina and Brazil as **States party emanating from the regional integration treaties and protocols** existing in the MERCOSUR framework. In keeping with the reasoning concerning the "customary rules of interpretation of public international law" in the cases *"United*

---

[23] Third party submission of the EC, para. 17 and note 18.
[24] Third party submission of Paraguay, para. 8.
[25] Document WT/DS241/3, 26 February 2002.
[26] First written submission of Argentina, para. 20 and note 12.
[27] "Il n'en reste pas moins que les diverses méthodes d'interprétation se rattachent toutes à une règle essentielle: celle de l'interprétation de bonne foi, formulée par l'article 31, para.e 1, de la Convention de Vienne. Ce principe fondamental est à l'origine des divers moyens et règles utilisés pour interpréter les traités et c'est en fonction de cette exigence fondamentale que le choix entre ces différentes méthodes doit être effectué." Dinh Nguyen Quoc, Daillier Patrick and Pellet Alain, Droit International Public, 4th Edition, Librairie générale de droit et de jurisprudence (LGDJ), Paris, 1992, p.252.
[28] Award of the MERCOSUR Ad Hoc Arbitral Tribunal set up to rule on the dispute between the Federative Republic of Brazil and the Argentine Republic on "Imposition of Anti-dumping Duties on Exports of Whole Poultry from Brazil (Res. 574/2000 of the Ministry of the Economy of the Argentine Republic)." Dated 21 May 2001.

States - Standards for Reformulated and Conventional Gasoline"[29] *and "Japan-Alcoholic Beverages"*[30], Argentina maintains that for the purposes of a full examination and depending on the context, the interpretation must take account of all the facts and factors relating to the case, within the meaning of Article 31 of the Vienna Convention on the Law of Treaties.[31]

II.2.2. Pleadings pertaining to this section

20. In the light of the above, the Argentina Republic respectfully repeats the request it made in its First Written Submission, that based on the omission by Brazil of any reference to the dispute previously discussed and settled by another international tribunal, the Panel find that the current submission of the case to the WTO reflects an abusive exercise by Brazil of its rights.

21. Similarly, Argentina reiterates that the Panel's finding cannot overlook the fact that in the light of the international commitments in force, Brazil's prior and subsequent practice of accepting the framework of MERCOSUR for the discussion and settlement of trade disputes with Argentina as a fellow MERCOSUR State party, and given the terms under which the dispute was brought, Brazil's complaint in the framework of the WTO has given rise to an estoppel situation for which Brazil is liable under the DSU.

22. For the above reasons, and considering in particular that Brazil's complaint involves challenging a measure which is identical in the current dispute to the measure at issue in the dispute within the framework of MERCOSUR, Argentina requests the Panel to refrain from ruling on the 41 claims of alleged inconsistency of the Argentine regulations with various provisions of the Agreement on the Application of Article VI of the General Agreement on Tariffs and Trade of 1994 (Anti-Dumping Agreement) contained in paragraph 549 of Brazil's first written submission, and consequently to reject the requests contained in paragraph 550 of that submission.

---

[29] Report of the Appellate Body on the case "United States - Standards for Reformulated and Conventional Gasoline", WT/DS2/AB/R, adopted on 20 May 1996, DSR 1996:I, 3, at 16.

[30] Report of the Panel on the case "Japan - Taxes on Alcoholic Beverages", WT/DS8/R, WT/DS10/R, WT/DS11/R., 11 July 1996, DSR 1996:I, 97.

[31] Vienna Convention on the Law of Treaties
Article 31 - General rule of interpretation
1. A treaty shall be interpreted in good faith in accordance with the ordinary meaning to be given to the terms of the treaty in their context and in the light of its object and purpose.
2. The context for the purpose of the interpretation of a treaty shall comprise, in addition to the text, including its preamble and annexes:
   (a) any agreement relating to the treaty which was made between all the parties in connection with the conclusion of the treaty;
   (b) any instrument which was made by one or more parties in connection with the conclusion of the treaty and accepted by the other parties as an instrument related to the treaty.
3. There shall be taken into account, together with the context:
   (a) any subsequent agreement between the parties regarding the interpretation of the treaty or the application of its provisions;
   (b) any subsequent practice in the application of the treaty which establishes the agreement of the parties regarding its interpretation;
   (c) any relevant rules of international law applicable in the relations between the parties.
4. A special meaning shall be given to a term if it is established that the parties so intended.

Report of the Panel

23. Should the Panel reject these pleadings and consider that it must rule on Brazil's claims, Argentina has set out its reasoning in the following section concerning the WTO-consistency of Resolution 574/00.

III. THE CONDUCT OF THE ANTI-DUMPING INVESTIGATION

III.1 GENERAL

24. Argentina maintains that throughout the investigation it complied with all aspects of the relevant provisions of the Anti-Dumping Agreement, though in particular as regards giving "due consideration" to all the factors that impinge on price comparability, and the provisions establishing the obligation duly to examine *all the information submitted by the parties to the procedure* and to fulfil the obligations of the Agreement regarding *notification of the Parties*.

25. Throughout all the phases of the procedure, Argentina effectively kept Brazilian exporters and the Government of that country abreast of the various actions that were taking place.

III.2 NOTIFICATIONS

26. Argentina therefore disputes the veracity of Brazil's claim of failure to notify seven Brazilian exporters in sufficiently good time to allow them to reply to the questionnaires or that the text of the application was not delivered to the exporters and to the Government of Brazil as soon as the investigation began.

27. Throughout the entire process, the Implementing Authority consistently demonstrated its readiness to provide the scope for the right of defence of the parties concerned, by all the means at its disposal and insofar as it was able.

28. Proof of this is that as the various stages of the procedure unfolded, not only did it accord all the extensions requested by the parties as shown by way of example in paragraph 130 of Argentina's First Written Submission, but it also granted the Brazilian exporters a period longer than the 30 days prescribed in the Agreement for replying to the questionnaires.

29. Argentina wishes to stress that as soon as the Implementing Authority became aware of the seven exporters whose inclusion had been requested by INTERAMERICANA COMERCIAL S.R.L., the request was granted. This is clear evidence of the readiness to open the way for participation by all parties in the procedure and in a manner conducive to the optimum obtention of information so as to arrive at an accurate determination.

30. Argentina refutes Brazil's claim that this action amounts to lack of compliance with the Agreement, as it would have been illogical to expect the Authority to send the relevant questionnaires to those exporters, having been unaware of their existence.

31. In Argentina's opinion, this situation could have been remedied early in the investigation if the Government of Brazil had decided to participate in the investigation as soon as it had been invited and notified, i.e. from the very beginning, even ahead of the notifications in the WTO framework and the consultations under the regional agreement.

32. This is also applicable to the treatment given to the information submitted by the parties during the investigation.

33. Contrary to Brazil's allegation, Argentina duly considered all the information submitted by the parties in the course of the investigation concerning its various aspects. This was done as prescribed in Article 2.4, bearing in mind the relevance to the procedure of the information furnished, and based on the Authority's assessment of its authenticity and verifiability.

34. In keeping with Article 2.4, each party was told expressly what information was required by the Implementing Authority for the investigation in question, and it was made clear that it should be accompanied by documentary evidence that would facilitate its use and confirm it reliability.

35. Argentina wishes to make clear in this connection that whenever possible, the information supplied by the parties to the Implementing Authority was used, provided that it was verifiable.

36. Brazil nonetheless believes that, having failed to meet the Authority's request to furnish the necessary documentary proof, the Authority should have conducted an *in situ* verification, apparently as the only viable way of remedying this omission.

37. Argentina is not denying the possibility of conducting verifications under the Agreement. It wishes to make clear, however, that its interpretation of this possibility differs somewhat from that of Brazil.

38. Argentina believes that as foreseen in the same Agreement, this mechanism allows for a method of verification of the information contributed during an investigation, that must not necessarily be used by the Authority when it needs to ascertain the veracity and/or relevance of any evidence, and all the more so when the private sector has not complied with the Implementing Authority's request to submit information.

39. The possibility to undertake verifications of the kind being proposed by Brazil is foreseen in Article 6.7 of the Agreement, which establishes that:

> *"in order to verify information provided or to obtain further details, the authorities may carry out investigations in the territory of other Members ... "* (Emphasis added)

40. Argentina repeats that according to its interpretation, the Article provides that the decision to carry out verifications in the territory of the Member under investigation is optional for the Authority and not an obligation under the Agreement.

III.3 ESSENTIAL FACTS

41. Argentina does not consider that there has been any infringement of the obligation to inform the interested parties "of the essential facts under consideration which form the basis for the decision whether to apply definitive measures", as stated in Article 6.9 of the Anti-Dumping Agreement. On the contrary, in earlier cases, WTO precedent clearly defined the scope of obligation contained in Article 6.9, AD, and Argentina believes it has fully complied with the stipulations of that Article as was defined in WTO precedent.[32]

---

[32] Report of the Panel on Guatemala - Definitive Anti-Dumping Measures on Grey Portland Cement from Mexico, WT/DS156/R, dated 24 October 2000, DSR 2000:XI, 5295, para. 8.230:
" ... We do not accept an interpretation of Article 6.9 that would effectively reduce its substantive requirements to those of Article 6.4. In our view,

42. Accordingly, it is agreed that merely "giving access" to the records of the investigation to the parties did not satisfy the requirement of Article 6.9, AD, which is intended to enable the interested parties to defend their interests based on due access to the relevant information. Argentina did not contravene that purpose in the present case, for at no point in the investigation was there a cessation of the additional task of processing the records and extracting the relevant information to compose a separate report that was made available to the interested parties.

43. Contrary to Brazil's assertion, Argentina maintains that the relevant information *was duly broken down and made available to the interested parties through the* Report on Action Taken prior to the Closure of the Period for Obtaining Evidence (*Relevamiento de lo Actuado con Anterioridad al Cierre de la Etapa probatoria*), dated 4 January 2002. The obligation in Article 6.9, AD entails the additional task of breaking down sufficient relevant information in good time so that the parties may have access to the data actually used. This assures the due handling of information and the right of defence of the parties.

44. That is the value that Argentina ascribes to the Report on Action Taken prior to the Closure of the Period for Obtaining Evidence, by considering it an additional procedural step, in other words, an "active step" (as the EC describes it in its submission)[33], whereby the Implementing Authority decided that all the information gathered - which would not be further expanded - was to be duly processed, broken down and ordered so as to identify the essential facts. The interested parties would then be informed that the relevant documentation was available to them (DCD Notes of 5 January 2000). In this way the right of the interested parties to defend their interests was duly safeguarded.

---

an investigating authority must do more than simply provide "timely opportunities for interested parties to see all information that is relevant to the presentation of their cases ... and that is used by the authorities ..." in order to "inform all interested parties of the essential facts under consideration which form the basis for the decision whether to apply definitive measures".

Similarly, the Report of the Panel on Argentina - Definitive anti-dumping measures on imports of ceramic floor tiles from Italy ("Argentina - Tiles"), WT/DS189/R, dated 28 September 2001, DSR 2001:XII, 6241, para. 6.125, stated:

" ... the requirement to inform all interested parties of the essential facts under consideration may be complied with in a number of ways. Article 6.9 of the AD Agreement does not prescribe the manner in which the authority is to comply with this disclosure obligation. The requirement to disclose the "essential facts under consideration" may well be met, for example, by disclosing a specially prepared document summarizing the essential facts under consideration by the investigating authority or through the inclusion in the record of documents - such as verification reports, a preliminary determination, or correspondence exchanged between the investigating authorities and individual exporters - which actually disclose to the interested parties the essential facts which, being under consideration, are anticipated by the authorities as being those which will form the basis for the decision whether to apply definitive measures. This view is based on our understanding that Article 6.9 anticipates that a final determination will be made and that the authorities have identified and are considering the essential facts on which that decision is to be made. Under Article 6.9, these facts must be disclosed so that parties can defend their interests, for example by commenting on the completeness of the essential facts under consideration."

[33] Third party submission of the EC, para. 23.

45. Argentina believes that it fully complied with the obligation under Article 6.9, AD, by means of the Report on Action Taken prior to the Closure of the Period for Obtaining Evidence, having duly identified the essential facts, in a separate procedural stage and in due time and form, so that the interested parties could defend their interests.

III.4 MAJOR PROPORTION OF THE INDUSTRY

46. Argentina submits that it does not share Brazil's view that the reference to "una proporción importante de la producción nacional" (*a major proportion of [the total] domestic production*) in Article 4.1, AD means a proportion greater than 50 per cent.

47. We believe that a categorical affirmation that Article 4.1, AD necessarily refers to at least 50 per cent cannot be accepted as valid by the WTO, and that moreover, there can be no claim here of lack of compliance of Article 4.1, AD by Argentina.

48. In the first place, the Spanish version of Article 4.1 speaks of "una proporción importante", and not of "la proporción más importante", or "la mayor proporción", or "la mayoría". We share the EC's view which notes that in the English version Article 4.1 speaks of "a major proportion" and not of "the major proportion".[34]

49. Both the Spanish and English versions of Article 4.1, AD use terms that are more limited than the categorical "mayoría" (*majority*) or "superior al 50%" *(more than 50 per cent)* that Brazil is attempting to introduce. Argentina's view is that the words used in Article 4.1, AD cannot be taken as equivalent, for example, to the stipulations of Article 5.4, AD, (which expressly provides for "más del 50 por ciento" de la producción total) *[more than 50 per cent of the total production ...].*

50. Finally, even though Argentina agrees with Brazil that 46 per cent certainly does not constitute "una mayoría" *[a majority]* - by very little - we would venture to suggest that Brazil could hardly deny, on the other hand, that 46 per cent does indeed constitute a "proporción importante que no es mayoría" *[a major proportion that is not a majority].* Argentina believes that it has fully complied Article 4.1, AD, the purpose of which is to define the expression "domestic industry".

III.5 THE ADJUSTMENT

51. Argentina submits that the adjustment made by the Authority in accordance with the method supplied by the Petitioner must not be considered as anything but additional proof of the degree of compliance of this procedure with the Anti-Dumping Agreement.

52. In this regard, Argentina wishes to make clear its position, which was at any rate already outlined in its written submission to the Panel. As there was proof that the chickens being sold in the city of São Paulo - which formed the basis for starting the investigation - did not have their head and feet removed, unlike those being exported, the Implementing Authority was compelled to make the adjustment, because the heads and feet represent a factor that - undeniably - influences price comparability.

---

[34] *Ibid.*, para. 49.

Report of the Panel

53. At no time did the Brazilian exporters object to the need for the adjustment. But moreover, in response to a request by the Authority for clarification, JOX sent a note[35] confirming the percentage adjustment indicated by the Petitioner. This was used by the Implementing Authority for lack of any other information that was shown to be more suitable and which could have been included in the course of the investigation if the Brazilian exporters believed that the data used was not accurate.

III.6 CALCULATION OF ANTI-DUMPING DUTIES

54. The Argentine Republic insists that the system it used to impose anti-dumping duties is consistent with Article 9 of the Anti-Dumping Agreement and that it is the Agreement itself and the practice of WTO Members that underpin the possibility of applying anti-dumping duties, based on the decision of the Implementing Authority, in the following manner:

(a) Fixed duties in relation to an *ad valorem* tax; (b) fixed in relation to a specific amount; (c) variable.

55. The system of variable amounts used by Argentina to set prospective anti-dumping duties (the difference between normal value and the FOB value declared for the shipment concerned) - Article 9.3.2, AD - is designed precisely to ensure that the anti-dumping duty actually collected does not exceed the margin of dumping determined. Hence, for example, if in the process of imposing the duties the margin of dumping should disappear because the export price has been aligned with normal value, the duty payable would be zero under this system. It is clear that this is perfectly consistent with the principle set out in Article 9.3.

56. Similarly, if the imposition of duties could possibly give rise to a situation in which the duties collected were higher than the margin of dumping determined, Articles 9.3.1 and 9.3.2 of the Agreement prescribe the way in which to correct this situation, and it can by no means be inferred that under the system applied by Argentina, the interested parties so requesting could be denied reimbursement of excess duties paid, by the means and in the manner foreseen under the applicable regulations.

57. We would like to make absolutely clear that without prejudice to the general remarks made about the system used by Argentina, in the present case, the minimum export value set for each of the exporters for whom an individual margin of dumping was determined, as well as that set for the rest of the exporters covered by the general level determined, were less than the Normal value determined for each case during the investigation. As such, while the margins of dumping determined by the Implementing Authority during the investigation were 14.91 per cent for SADIA SA, 15.48 per cent for AVIPAL SA, and 8.19 per cent for the rest, the minimum export values, which stood at USD 0.92, USD 0.98 and USD 0.98 respectively, represent a difference of 13.74 per cent, 10.05 per cent and 5.63 per cent in each specific case, *vis-à-vis* the f.o.b. values determined for each one during the procedure.

58. Article 9.3 provides that "*[t]he amount of the anti-dumping duty shall not exceed the margin of dumping as established under Article 2*". In the light of the preceding paragraph and of the relevant provision of the Agreement, it can be seen that Argentina has acted in a manner consistent therewith.

---

[35] First written submission of Brazil, Exhibit BRA-32.

59. The resort to anti-dumping duties is the remedy open to a Member in particular circumstances for correcting an unfair trade practice which, based on the findings of a prior investigation under the terms of the AD, causes injury to a sector of its domestic industry.

60. The obligation arising from Article 9.3 for any Member that imposes such duties is that the latter must not exceed the amount of the margin established in Article 2, without such margin being necessarily determined under the stipulations of Article 2.4.2, as Brazil would wish. In this regard, Argentina shares the opinion of Canada to the effect that the margin of dumping determined during the investigation imposes no limit on the duty that may be applied to future imports.[36]

61. As can be seen, the alleged inconsistency is false, because:

    (a)   The AD does not prescribe WHAT system must be used to collect -anti-dumping duties;

    (b)   the AD itself envisages the possibility that the duty paid could in some situations diverge from the determined margin, and also includes the remedy for such a situation; and

    (c)   nothing in the present case suggests that any such excess duty could be withheld from Brazilian exporters.

62. Argentina wishes to draw the Panel's attention to a situation that could possibly result from an erroneous interpretation of the provisions of the Anti-Dumping Agreement pertaining to the levying of anti-dumping duties, which is obviously what Brazil is attempting to achieve.

63. If the system of variable duties were deemed to be inconsistent with the Anti-Dumping Agreement merely because in a particular context - foreseen elsewhere in the Anti-Dumping Agreement together with the remedy therefor - the duties collected were in excess of the determined margin, a Member could easily arrange for a measure taken to correct the distortions caused by an unfair trade practice to be challenged as inconsistent, simply by intensifying the unfair practice, i.e. by widening the margin of dumping involved.

64. The purpose of Article VI would be completely thwarted in this way.

IV. CONCLUSION

65. In the light of the arguments put forward in the sections above, the Argentine Republic respectfully requests of the Panel the following:

    (1)   That, in keeping with the reasoning developed in Section II and as already mentioned in paragraphs 20, 21 and 22 of this Submission, the Panel refrain from ruling on the 41 claims of alleged inconsistency with various provisions of the Agreement on the application of Article VI of the General Agreement on Tariffs ad Trade of 1994 (Anti-Dumping Agreement) submitted by Brazil.

66. Should the Panel decide not to accede to the above pleading by the Argentine Republic, as set out in paragraph 23 of this submission and in the light of the arguments submitted in Section II, it is respectfully requested to:

---

[36] Third party submission of Canada, page 4.

Report of the Panel

(2) Reject the Brazil's claims that Resolution 574/00 of the Ministry of the Economy of the Argentine Republic is inconsistent with:
- Articles 5.2, 5.3, 5.7 and 5.8 of the Anti-Dumping Agreement;
- Article 12.1 of the Anti-Dumping Agreement;
- Articles 6.1.1, 6.1.2, 6.1.3, 6.2 and 6.8, as well as paragraphs 5, 6, and 7 of Annex II, and with Articles 6.9, and 6.10 of the Anti-Dumping Agreement;
- Articles 2.4, 2.4.2, of the Anti-Dumping Agreement;
- Articles 3.1, 3.2, 3.4, 3.5 of the Anti-Dumping Agreement;
- Article 4.1 of the Anti-Dumping Agreement;
- Articles 9.2, 9.3 of the Anti-Dumping Agreement;
- As well as the various claims related to Article 12.2.2.

(3) Reject the request for the immediate repeal of Resolution 574/2000 imposing the definitive anti-dumping duties.

ANNEX B-3

SECOND WRITTEN SUBMISSION OF ARGENTINA
(17 October 2002)

The Government of Argentina would like to thank the members of the Panel for this opportunity to submit, for their consideration, its rebuttal to the arguments put forward by the Government of Brazil in the course of these proceedings.

I. INTRODUCTION

1. *"The provisions of the WTO - AD Agreement (**WTO Anti-Dumping Agreement**) were incorporated in community legislation by DEC CMC No. 11/97 (Regulatory Framework, RF). Since by definition of Article 1, the RF is in conformity with the WTO-AD Agreement, failure to comply with the former implies failure to comply with the latter. Furthermore, should the RF disciplines not be applicable for some legal reason that excludes such application, the provisions of the WTO AD Agreement would apply pursuant to Article 19 of the Protocol of Brasilia (PB) as 'applicable principles and rules of international law'. The rules of the WTO Anti-Dumping Agreement are binding for WTO Members, which include the **States parties to MERCOSUR"**. (Emphasis added).*

2. This paragraph from Brazil's submission (paragraph 30 of the Award[1]) before the MERCOSUR Ad Hoc Arbitral Tribunal helps to understand that Brazil's "insistence" on filing a complaint at the regional level using the procedure laid down in the Protocol of Brasilia in the knowledge that there was no MERCOSUR legislation governing intra-zone dumping shows that it chose this course, in spite of the fact that Argentina repeatedly explained that the MERCOSUR should be rejected as a forum for the settlement of the dispute[2], because it wanted the dispute to be settled at the regional level, and it was only following the unfavourable ruling in that forum that it decided to bring the case before the WTO.

3. The actual Ad Hoc Tribunal set up to hear and settle the dispute brought before MERCOSUR ruled that: "In this situation, the WTO Anti-Dumping Agreement stands as an appropriate reference, not as MERCOSUR legislation, which it is not, but by virtue of Article 19 of the Protocol of Brasilia[3] as an applicable

---

[1] "Award on poultry" - Award of the MERCOSUR Ad Hoc Arbitral Tribunal set up to rule on the dispute between the Federative Republic of Brazil and the Argentine Republic on "Imposition of Anti-Dumping Duties on Exports of whole poultry from Brazil (Res. 574/2000 of the Ministry of the Economy of the Argentine Republic)." Date: 21 May 2001.
[2] *Ibid.*, para. 80.
[3] The Protocol of Brasilia was signed by the four MERCOSUR States parties on 17 December 1991. Article 19 thereof reads as follows:
"(1) The Arbitral Tribunal shall settle the dispute by applying: the provisions of the Treaty of Asunción, agreements concluded within the framework thereof, the decisions of the Council of the Common Market, the resolutions of the Common Market Group, and applicable principles and rules of international law.
(2) This provision shall not prejudice the power of the Arbitral Tribunal to decide a Dispute *ex aequo et bono* if the parties agree thereto."

principle of international law (Cfr. Second Arbitral Tribunal, paragraphs 59 et. seq., for a clarification of the concept of subsidies), in this case to shed light on the meaning and purpose of anti-dumping proceedings."[4] (Footnotes added).

4. Argentina respectfully requests the Panel to evaluate, in its analysis of the case, the fact that Brazil successively brought its complaint first before MERCOSUR, and then, in view of the unfavourable outcome, before the WTO.

5. Since Brazil's way of proceeding makes it clear that it intended to reverse the previous unfavourable ruling, Argentina repeats[5] that the Panel should bear in mind, in settling this case, that Argentina and Brazil are not only WTO Member States, but also States parties to MERCOSUR, and as such they must honour the commitments assumed in both fora. Indeed, both fora generate a set of legal relationships which bind the parties under public international law.

6. In short, Argentina considers that Brazil's conduct in bringing the dispute successively before different fora, first MERCOSUR and then the WTO, as well as the legal arguments that Brazil put forward in its submission to the Ad Hoc Arbitral Tribunal at the regional level, based not only on MERCOSUR rules, but also on the provisions of the WTO Anti-Dumping Agreement[6], constitutes a legal approach that is contrary to the principle of good faith and which, in the case at issue, warrants invocation of the principle of estoppel.

7. Should the Panel reject the basis of Argentina's claim as set forth in the paragraph above, Argentina submits, in the alternative, that in view of the relevant rule of international law applicable in the relations between parties pursuant to Article 31.3(c) of the Vienna Convention on the Law of Treaties, in the light of Article 3.2 of the DSU the Panel cannot disregard, in its consideration and substantiation of the present case brought by Brazil, the precedents set by the proceedings in the framework of MERCOSUR.

8. As argued in its first written submission, Argentina rejects the doubts raised by Brazil concerning Resolution 574/2000 of the Ministry of the Economy on the basis of various considerations of fact and law which are presented in the two main sections making up that submission, namely Section II, dealing with the rules and principles of public international law applicable to the case, and Section III, which refutes the substantive arguments contained in Brazil's 41 claims.

II. PRELIMINARY ARGUMENTS: PRINCIPLES AND RULES OF INTERNATIONAL LAW APPLICABLE TO THE CASE

II(a) Good faith - principle of estoppel

9. Brazil and Argentina assumed rights and obligations within the framework of MERCOSUR. In Argentina's view, the Panel in the current case cannot disregard the fact that the dispute was already discussed and resolved previously.

---

[4] "Award on Poultry" para. 159.

[5] First written submission of Argentina, 29 August 2002, para. 18, and third party submission of Paraguay, 9 September 2002, para. 7.

[6] Submission by Brazil in the framework of MERCOSUR (paras. 30, 31, 32, 33, 34, 35, 36, 37, 38, 39 and 40 of the "Award on Poultry."

10. Moreover, in the framework of MERCOSUR it is a standing practice for all parties - obviously including Brazil - to accept the obligations deriving from the legislative framework in force, including the Treaty of Asunción and the Protocol of Brasilia. In Argentina's view, a State party is not acting in good faith if it first has recourse to the mechanism of the integration process to settle its dispute with another State party and then, dissatisfied with the outcome, files the same complaint within a different framework, making matters worse by omitting any reference to the previous procedure and its outcome. This conduct, as corroborated by Brazil's peaceful acceptance of previous awards, not to mention the fact that in some of these cases, the conclusions have revolved around the principle of estoppel, cannot be disregarded by the Panel.

11. Contrary to what the United States has said[7], Argentina does not claim in its first written submission a breach of the Protocol of Brasilia by Brazil for the purposes of having the Panel reject its claims; rather, Argentina points out that the complaint existed, that Brazil has brought the case at issue before the WTO in the full knowledge of that fact and by virtue of the unfavourable outcome of its complaint at the regional level - and that it omits any reference to the matter.

12. Similarly, Argentina disagrees with the United States where it argues that it "also disagrees with Argentina that the Panel may apply what Argentina calls the principle of estoppel. The fact that Argentina cites no textual basis for its request reflects the fact that Members have not consented to provide for the application of any such principle of estoppel in WTO dispute settlement. The term estoppel appears nowhere in the text nor does Argentina cite to any provision which in substance provides Argentina the type of defence it asserts."[8]

13. Argentina repeats[9] that the essential elements of estoppel are "(i) A statement of fact which is clear and unambiguous; (ii) this statement must be voluntary, unconditional, and authorized; (iii) there must be reliance in good faith upon the statement or the advantage of the party making the statement".[10] Similarly, "[a] considerable weight of authority supports the view that estoppel is a general principle of international law, resting on principles of good faith and consistency, and shorn of the technical features to be found in municipal law.(...). Thus before a tribunal the principle may operate to resolve ambiguities and as a principle of equity and justice: here it becomes a part of the evidence and judicial reasoning."[11]

14. Firstly, with respect to the possibility for a panel to apply the principle of estoppel, Argentina can find no provision or rule whatsoever that prohibits a panel from examining, and where it deems appropriate applying, that principle.

15. Similarly, in the case *United States - Standards for Reformulated and Conventional Gasolene*[12], the report made it clear that:

---

[7] Oral Statement of the United States at the Third-Party Session with the Panel, 26 September 2002, para. 4.
[8] *Ibid.*, para. 5.
[9] Intervention by the Argentine Republic at the meeting of the Panel with the Parties, 25 September 2002, paras. 12, 13, 14, 15 and 16.
[10] Brownlie Ian, "Principles of Public International Law", Fourth Edition, Clarendon Press. Oxford, 1990, page 641.
[11] *Ibid.*, page 641.
[12] Report of the Appellate Body in *United States - Standards for Reformulated and Conventional Gasolene*, adopted on 20 May 1996, DSR 1996:I, 3.

"That direction reflects a measure of recognition that the *General Agreement* is not to be read in clinical isolation from public international law." [13]

16. In other words, the GATT and the WTO are subject to the general rules of international law.

The Appellate Body recognized, in *United States - Standards for Reformulated and Conventional Gasolene*, that GATT/WTO legislation forms part of international law, and hence the general principles of international law apply to the work of the panel and the Appellate Body.

17. Among the arguments put forward by the United States is the statement that no panel to date has applied a principle of estoppel.[14] In Argentina's view, this argument is devoid of any legal foundation and can be refuted empirically. It is devoid of legal foundation because the panels are called upon to apply public international law to settle the disputes brought before them. And it can be refuted empirically because the United States itself [15], in its oral submission, mentions two cases[16] in which the scope of estoppel is expressly discussed.

18. In *European Communities - Asbestos*:[17]

"From a legal point of view, the question seems to be whether there is *estoppel* on the part of the EC because they notified the Decree or because of their statements, including those during the consultations. This would be the case if it was determined that Canada had legitimately relied on the notification of the Decree and was now suffering the negative consequences resulting from a change in the EC's position."

19. In the case *"Guatemala - Cement:*[18]

"Guatemala uses both the concepts of 'acquiescence' and 'estoppel' in support of this argument. We note that 'acquiescence' amounts to 'qualified silence', whereby silence in the face of events that call for a reaction of some sort may be interpreted as a presumed consent. The concept of estoppel, also relied on by Guatemala in support of its argument, is akin to that of acquiescence. Estoppel is premised on the view that where one party has been induced to act in reliance on the assurances of another party, in such a way that it would be prejudiced were the other party later to change its position, such a change in position is 'estopped', that is precluded." (Footnotes 789 and 790 omitted)

---

[13] *Ibid.*, page 20.
[14] Oral Statement of the United States at the Third-Party Session with the Panel, 26 September 2002, para. 6.
[15] *Ibid.*, para. 6.
[16] WT/DS135/R, *European Communities - Measures Affecting Asbestos and Asbestos-Containing Products,* report adopted on 5 April 2001, and WT/DS156/R, *Guatemala - Definitive Anti-Dumping Measure on Grey Portland Cement from Mexico,* report adopted on 17 November 2000, DSR 2000:XI, 5295.
[17] WT/DS135/R, *European Communities - Measures Affecting Asbestos and Asbestos-Containing Products,* DSR 2001:VIII, 3305, para. 8.60.
[18] WT/DS156/R, *Guatemala - Definitive Anti-Dumping Measure on Grey Portland Cement from Mexico*, para. 8.23.

20. Argentina respectfully requests the Panel to examine the case in the light of the principle of estoppel because the current dispute brought by **Brazil before the WTO** involves the following elements:

(i) Brazil contradicts itself by filing the complaint against Argentina first within the framework of MERCOSUR, on the understanding that it was a bilateral dispute in the framework of a regional integration scheme in which WTO anti-dumping legislation was applied, and then maintaining that the same dispute exceeded the scope of MERCOSUR;

(ii) taking advantage of its own contradictions after having brought its complaint before MERCOSUR and obtained an adverse ruling, Brazil turned to the WTO in order to reverse the unfavourable ruling contained in the arbitral award, invoking the same legislation, but acting contrary to its previous practice of respecting awards based on the Protocol of Brasilia;

(iii) prior to[19] and following[20] this case Brazil, through its conduct and/or silence, maintained an attitude that was clearly favourable to the acceptance of the scope of the obligations deriving from MERCOSUR, and created favourable expectations among the other States parties with respect to the behaviour that is was reasonable for the three remaining parties to expect from it. *Consequently Brazil's previous conduct with respect to the acceptance of awards, confirmed by the signature of the Protocol of Olivos, invalidates the complaint against Argentina that Brazil is now trying to substantiate on the basis of the DSU.*

21. Finally, Argentina refutes the arguments by Brazil[21] and the EC[22], and repeats[23] that it has not argued primarily for the application of the doctrine of "res judicata".

II(b) Evidence

22. In the interest of transparency and to ensure that it is possible for the Panel to make an objective assessment under Article 11 of the DSU, Argentina would like to state to the Panel that it is prepared to hand over its submissions in the MERCOSUR proceedings and invites Brazil to do likewise, thereby providing the Panel with the full evidence of the procedures that took place within MERCOSUR with respect to the subject of the current dispute.[24]

---

[19] First written submission of Argentina, para. 20 and footnote 12.
[20] Signature of the Protocol of Olivos, expressly including a choice of forum clause.
[21] Oral Statement of Brazil, First Meeting with the Panel, 25 September 2002, para. 4.
[22] Third party submission of the European Communities, 9 September, para. 5.
[23] Intervention by the Argentine Republic at the meeting of the Panel with the parties, 25 September 2002, para. 7.
[24] Annex ARG-LXII - Table comparing the MERCOSUR dispute with the WTO dispute.

II(c) The relevant rule of public international law: Art. 31(c) of the Vienna Convention

23. Firstly, Argentina does not agree with the statement of the United States that "[b]y its plain terms, Article 3.2 is limited to the rules of interpretation used to clarify the existing provisions of the WTO Agreement."[25]

24. Argentina submits that Article 3.2 of the DSU provides a rule of interpretation for the Panel and WTO legal practice has confirmed that rule by referring to Articles 31 and 32 of the Vienna Convention on the Law of Treaties.

25. Article 31.3(c) of the Vienna Convention on the Law of Treaties specifically stipulates that for the purposes of interpretation, account shall be taken of " ... any relevant rules of international law applicable in the relations between the parties."

26. In the words of Jiménez de Arechaga[26] "[t]his provision means that a treaty must be interpreted **within the framework of the rules of international law in force between the parties**".

27. The same author also refers to a 1975 resolution by the International Law Institute[27] in which it is stated that: "The interpretation of a treaty must take account of all relevant rules of international law applicable between the parties at the time of implementation."

28. In Argentina's view, the regulatory framework of MERCOSUR and the legal consequences deriving from the implementation of the Protocol of Brasilia by the Ad Hoc Arbitral Tribunal in the case at issue are relevant rules of public international law within the meaning of Article 31.3(c) of the Vienna Convention on the Law of Treaties.

29. Argentina respectfully requests the Panel to take into consideration, for the purposes of interpretation of the current dispute under the WTO and under the terms set forth in the preceding paragraph, the rules forming part of the regulatory framework of MERCOSUR on which the ruling of the MERCOSUR Ad Hoc Tribunal was based.

II(d) Summary

30. To summarize, Argentina submits that in the case at issue, Brazil's current complaint against it under the WTO is invalid in that Brazil's conduct not only runs counter to the principle of good faith, but warrants estoppel.

31. For the reasons set forth in the preceding paragraph, the case for estoppel which the United States defines as a procedural argument and which has been recognized as such in the WTO, and which is more generally considered by doctrine to be a substantive defence should, in Argentina's view lead the Panel to refrain from ruling in the case at issue. Even if the Panel considers that estoppel in the WTO is only applicable as a procedural defence, it is more than enough to reject Brazil's substantive arguments.

---

[25] Oral Statement of the United States at the Third-Party Session with the Panel, 26 September 2002, para. 7.
[26] Jiménez de Arechaga, Eduardo "El derecho internacional contemporáneo", Editorial Tecnos, Madrid 1980, page 61.
[27] *Ibid.*, page 63.

32.   In the alternative, if the Panel should reject the arguments set forth in the previous paragraphs, Argentina considers that the Panel should in any case refrain from making any findings or conclusions regarding the consistency and compatibility of Resolution 574/2002 with the Anti-Dumping Agreement, since the MERCOSUR regulatory framework, which includes the Protocol of Brasilia and the legal consequences of the arbitral award, are relevant rules of international law that are applicable between the parties in conformity with Article 31.3(c) of the Vienna Convention on the Law of Treaties.

III.   SUBSTANTIVE ASPECTS OF THE INVESTIGATION

III(a)   Article 5.2 of the Anti-Dumping Agreement

33.   Argentina reaffirms what it stated in its first written submission, namely that the evidence that the applicant must provide at the initiation of the investigation must be the evidence reasonably available to it. As regards the implementing authority, the obligation contained in this Article is to determine that the evidence accompanying the application is sufficient to justify the initiation of the investigation.

This condition of sufficiency means that the evidence must contain indications that dumping has occurred, causing damage to the domestic industry. However, the detail concerning the facts put forward will always be less than the detail which emerges at a later stage from the investigation.

34.   Thus, the evidence required must be of a standard that makes it possible to initiate the investigation on the basis thereof. As stated in paragraph 32 of its first written submission, Argentina submits that to require of domestic producers a level of detail and knowledge in the evidence they must submit that is materially beyond their reach would amount simply to denying them any access to the proceedings.

With reference to the different standards of evidence required at the different stages of the proceedings, Argentina recalls the statements by the Panels in *United States - Measures Affecting Imports of Softwood Lumber from Canada*[28], and *Mexico - Anti-Dumping Investigation of High-Fructose Corn Syrup (HFCS) from the United States*[29], referred to in paragraphs 38 and 44 of its first written submission of 29 August 2002.

35.   Brazil, which has said that it agrees with this argument by Argentina[30], nevertheless claims that in this case Argentina violated Article 5.2 because the evidence submitted by the applicant was not sufficient to determine that:

(i)   The product sold in Brazil was physically different from that sold in Argentina;

(ii)   the differences in physical characteristics actually affected price comparability;

(iii)   the yield rate difference alleged by the applicant was correct.[31]

---

[28] WT/DS236, para. 332.
[29] WT/DS132/R, para. 7.76.
[30] Oral statement of Brazil at the first meeting with the Panel, para. 15.
[31] *Ibid.*, para. 17.

36. This is not the case. The evidence submitted by the applicant to the investigating authority contained sufficient data within the meaning of Article 5.2 of the Anti-Dumping Agreement that:

(i) Contrary to what Brazil claims, there were physical differences between the product (whole poultry) taken as a basis for the calculation of normal value;

(ii) since these differences affected the trade performance of the products being compared, they unquestionably affected the price comparability;

(iii) these differences called for an adjustment to enable - prior to the initiation of the investigation - a fair comparison to be conducted, for which purpose an adjustment methodology was also provided.

III(b) Article 5.7 of the AD Agreement

37. As regards Brazil's claim that Argentina failed to comply with Article 5.7 of the AD Agreement by not simultaneously considering the evidence of both dumping and injury in the decision to initiate the investigation, Argentina maintains, as it did in its first written submission, that this claim is unfounded.

38. Article 5.7 stipulates that the evidence of both dumping and injury shall be considered simultaneously **in the decision whether or not to initiate an investigation**.

39. Although in its own first written submission[32] Brazil attempts to demonstrate that Argentina violated the AD Agreement simply because the reports respectively establishing the existence of dumping and the existence of injury bear different dates, this does not in any way mean that the Authority, in its decision to initiate the investigation, did not simultaneously consider the evidence in both reports.

40. In this connection, Argentina draws the Panel's attention to the Third Party Submission of the United States, which states that "Brazil appears to believe that this language (i.e. that of Article 5.7) obligates a Member to ensure that its investigating authorities consider dumping and injury information from simultaneous (i.e. identical) time periods. Viewed in context, however, the term 'simultaneously' is linked to the term 'considered', not the term 'evidence'."[33]

41. Argentina concurs with the United States and reiterates the argument made in its first written submission that Brazil over-emphasizes the element of simultaneousness emerging from the provisions of the AD Agreement, interpreting the obligations in Article 5.7 in a manner that is simply incorrect.

42. Argentina repeats once again that the implementing authority, in deciding to initiate the investigation, simultaneously took account of both the injury and the dumping analysis and the causal link between the two.

III(c) Article 5.8 of the AD Agreement

43. As regards Brazil's claim that Argentina should have rejected the application for initiation of the investigation because the application had failed to demonstrate injury, Argentina reiterates the statement made in its first written submission and reaffirmed at the first meeting of the Panel with the parties. Argentina likewise

---

[32] First written submission of Brazil, para. 171.
[33] Third party submission of the United States, para. 3.

reiterates its reply to question 16 of the Panel that since the applicant provided updated information in keeping with the requirements of the application, the new information had to be examined in order to determine its relevance to the ongoing proceedings.

44. As specified in the aforementioned reply, the examination of new information is expressly provided for in Article 60 of the Regulations of the National Law on Administrative Procedures (RLNPA, approved by Decree No. 1759/72 and harmonized by Decree No. 1883/91), which was duly notified to the relevant WTO Committees and stipulates that the competent body (in this case, which involves injury, the CNCE) shall intervene once again in the proceedings if *any new developments occur or come to its knowledge*. In the case at issue, the additional submission by the applicant introduced new items of evidence which called for a further intervention by the CNCE, at the request of the competent bodies and in strict conformity with the law.

45. Argentina wishes to lay special emphasis on the following points, duly brought to the Panel's attention with respect to the above:

(1) The information presented by the applicant supplemented that submitted at the time the case was opened; it was intended to provide the authority with data that had not been included in the initial submission and enabled the CNCE to make an affirmative determination.

(2) During the stage prior to the initiation of the investigation, third party rights are not affected.

(3) Brazil's suggestion to file the case at that stage of the investigation, with the introduction of additional information, would have adversely affected the individual rights of the applicant, in breach of the law.

III(d) Article 12.1 of the AD Agreement

46. Here Argentina simply refers to its first written submission, emphasizing that it fulfilled the obligation to notify all parties known to the investigating authority. It draws attention to paragraphs 112, 113 and 114 of the text so that the Panel can verify the various documents submitted and the steps taken by Argentina in order to comply with Article 12.1.

47. As regards the claim that the exporters were notified eight months after the initiation of the investigation, it would have been impossible to do so any earlier because the authority did not learn of their existence until the firm INTERAMERICANA COMERCIAL made its submission.

The same is true of Brazil's claim under Article. 6.1.2. The Authority cannot be said to have failed to fulfil its obligations towards enterprises that did not join as interested parties.

III(e) Article 6.1.1 of the AD Agreement

48. As specified in Argentina's first written submission, the investigating authority granted all the periods stipulated in the AD Agreement to all the parties with an interest in the investigation. In addition to the procedural time-frames, however, Argentina showed every good will in allowing all the exporters sufficient time to supply the information required to properly defend their interests. This is

evidenced by the successive extensions granted by the Authority in each case, as recorded in paragraphs 126 to 136 of the submission.

III(f) Article 6.2 of the AD Agreement

49. Here again, Brazil refers - as a basis for its claim that Argentina acted inconsistently with Article 6.2 - to the eight exporters involved in the investigation as a result of the request by the firm INTERAMERICANA COMERCIAL.

50. Argentina refers yet again to its first written submission and specifically paragraphs 148 to 161. It also strongly re-emphasizes that although the Brazilian Government had been notified from the very outset of the investigation, through a request for cooperation "in identifying the interested producers/exporters in this investigation and providing them with the attached requests for information...",[34] Argentina was not informed of the alleged interest[35] of the firms whose right of defence it had allegedly impaired and which were only involved in the investigation on the basis of a request by one of the parties.

III(g) Articles 6.8 and 12.2.2 of the AD Agreement

51. As regards Brazil's various claims in respect of the authority's use of the information supplied by the exporters during the investigation and the lack of proper explanation, in some cases, why certain data had been disregarded, Argentina's first written submission gives a detailed list[36] of the different types of information provided by each firm in the course of the investigation and specifies the way in which the information was used, where such use was warranted in the proceedings and met the formal requirements of Argentine legislation, of which each of the parties was duly aware.

52. In spite of the above, Argentina considers it important to revert to a number of points repeatedly raised by Brazil in connection with the use of the information and the possibility of verifying its accuracy.

53. Brazil claims that the Brazilian exporters supplied all the information requested by the investigating authority and that the latter decided, for no apparent reason, to discard that information and use only the data provided by the applicant.

54. This is not the case. Indeed, Argentina has demonstrated that once the exporters had supplied the supporting evidence needed, at a minimum, to corroborate the information they had provided, that information was used.

55. As regards the export price data, Brazil claims that Argentina used the applicant's data. However, it apparently fails to mention that the information actually used by Argentina in this case was the official data from the register of the General Customs Administration, which is the body in charge of supervising and controlling all foreign trade transactions. The register serves as a database for other State, and private, bodies and contains the most detailed and accurate information available on values and prices for each transaction. Any information presented to Customs by economic agents - i.e. exporters and importers - is recorded in the form of a sworn statement.

---

[34] First written submission of Argentina, para. 112.
[35] Ibid., para. 147.
[36] Ibid., paras. 187-206.

56. In other cases such as those of FRANGOSUL and CATARINENSE, the information was not used simply because, in FRANGOSUL's case, the data provided was insufficient and was submitted after the deadline that would have permitted its use had expired[37] and, in CATARINENSE's case, because the data was insufficient.[38]

57. At the risk of belabouring the point, Argentina reiterates that each time the parties supplied the information in the prescribed timely and appropriate fashion, the information was used. Argentina had to resort to other sources of information in cases where any aspect of those requirements had not been met.

58. Brazil claims, moreover, that the Authority should have conducted on-the-spot verifications of the information supplied by the exporters since they had offered it the possibility of doing so during the proceedings.

59. Argentina has repeatedly emphasized that the conduct of on-the-spot verifications is optional for the investigating authority and is not an obligation under the AD Agreement. It nevertheless considers it important to reaffirm its oral statement at the meeting of the Panel with the parties on 25 September 2002.

60. Argentina is not denying the possibility of conducting verifications under the Agreement. It wishes to make clear, however, that its interpretation of this possibility differs somewhat from that of Brazil.

61. The possibility to undertake verifications of the kind proposed by Brazil is foreseen in Article 6.7 of the Agreement, which establishes that:

> "...*the authorities may carry out investigations in the territory of other Members....*" (Emphasis added)

62. Argentina thus considers that, as foreseen in the Agreement, this mechanism allows a method of verification of the information added to the file during an investigation that does not necessarily have to be used by the authority when it needs to ascertain the truth and/or relevance of any evidence, especially when the private sector fails to comply with the implementing authority's request for information.

63. In Argentina's view, this is the most correct interpretation of Annex I, paragraph 1, which details the procedures applicable to Article 6.7 and establishes that:

> "*Upon initiation of an investigation, the authorities of the exporting Member and the firms known to be concerned should be informed of the intention to carry out on-the-spot investigations.*" (Emphasis added)

64. A joint reading of Article 6.7 and Annex I, paragraph 1, of the AD Agreement clearly reveals the discretionary nature of this mechanism, ruling out any claim as to its binding character. Its optional nature is further confirmed by paragraph 3 of that same Annex, which provides that the explicit agreement of the firms concerned should be obtained as a prerequisite to any on-the-spot investigation.

65. Brazil appears, moreover, to interpret the above possibility as an obligation to be fulfilled in addition to the timely and appropriate submission of information requested by the authority.

66. Argentina therefore refers to the relevant part Annex I, paragraph 8, which reads as follows:

---

[37] *Ibid.*, paras. 187-200.
[38] *Ibid.*, para 203.

> *"As the main purpose of the on-the-spot investigation is to verify information provided or to obtain further details, it should be carried out after the response to the questionnaire has been received...; further, it should be standard practice prior to the visit to advise the firms concerned of the general nature of the information to be verified and of any further information which needs to be provided... ."*

67. As this provision shows, on-the-spot investigations do not release the interested parties from the obligation to supply the information requested by the investigating authority - especially where the authority decides to carry out an investigation visit. In other words, Brazil can hardly claim that Argentina has violated a specific rule of the Agreement when the Brazilian exporters themselves did not satisfy the obligation under the Agreement to facilitate the task that Brazil claims has not been fulfilled.

III(h) Article 2.4 of the AD Agreement

68. Brazil claims that Argentina acted inconsistently with the Article 2.4 requirement to make a fair price comparison, holding that its claim is substantiated by the different actions taken by Argentina in the course of the investigation, as outlined below. Brazil further claims that Argentina has placed an unreasonable burden of proof on the Brazilian exporters by not specifying from the outset the period for which the information was being requested.

69. Argentina reiterates that it complied, throughout the investigation, with the Article 2.4 requirement to make a fair comparison.

70. The above claims have already been extensively addressed in Argentina's first written submission. Argentina therefore repeats that it made all the adjustments it considered appropriate, insofar as it had been demonstrated that:

   (a) those adjustments were necessary; and

   (b) the adjustment values were correct, and not merely figures under a general heading covering a certain period of time.

71. Thus, as regards freight adjustment, which Brazil claims Argentina should have made in the case of SADIA, Argentina agrees with Brazil that adjustment would have been necessary - but only to the extent that the investigating authority had received the relevant supporting documentation in a timely and appropriate fashion. Argentina also concurs with Brazil that SADIA did provide an estimate in Annex VIII of the questionnaire sent to the exporters - but this was a purely general and aggregate estimate covering a period of one year.

72. Argentina based its normal value calculation on prices drawn from a series of invoices selected according to the random sampling method. Those documents, which the exporter was duly requested to supply, gave no indication whatsoever of the amounts to be deducted or of the items to which the deductions should apply.

73. This is why the Authority did not make the deduction requested by Brazil, because if it had applied a discount representing a general average for a given stage of the investigation, this would have distorted the price to be used. In any event, the exporter had ample opportunity, when it sent the requested invoices, to inform the Authority of any items and amounts it considered necessary to deduct or add, according to the characteristics specific to the transactions recorded in the documents.

74. As regards the adjustments which, again, Brazil claims should have been made to the normal value calculated for the "other exporters", Argentina notes Brazil's advice to the Panel not to be confused by Argentina's seemingly "hazy" arguments.[39]

75. Argentina agrees that the Panel should not be misled and therefore believes that a few points should be clarified in order to ensure that the Panel is not confused by Brazil's arguments.

76. The first point is that although Brazil claims throughout its Submission that Argentina should not have used the information supplied by JOX, it appears to contradict itself in its oral statement when it asserts that, for the purposes of the above adjustment, Argentina should also have used the information provided by the consulting firm.

77. The second point refers to Brazil's argument that, had Argentina made the aforementioned deduction on the price used to calculate normal value - even acknowledging that the f.o.b. value includes inland freight and insurance, handling, loading and unloading and warehousing, it would have been comparing prices at the same level of trade.[40]

78. Argentina does not understand the reason for Brazil's assertion. It is indeed true, as Brazil points out, that export prices do not include domestic taxes. However, the mere fact that such taxes are not included, or - if they were - that they could be deducted, does not resolve the matter of the Agreement requiring the comparison to be made preferably at ex-factory level.

79. In other words, Brazil appears to believe that it would have been sufficient, for the purposes of fair comparison within the meaning of Article 2.4, to make an adjustment to normal value and not to the f.o.b. value in order to arrive at two prices representative of the same level of trade. Had Argentina done that, however, it would have been comparing an ex-factory value (sales value of goods deposited with the vendor) with an f.o.b. value (value of goods deposited plus the costs listed in paragraph 44).

80. As regards Brazil's claim that an unreasonable burden of proof was imposed on its exporters, Argentina refers to paragraphs 242 to 247 of its first written submission.

III(i) Article 9.2 and 9.3 of the AD Agreement

81. The anti-dumping duties imposed by Argentina are in keeping with the requirements of Article 9.2 and 9.3 of the AD Agreement, which stipulate that such duties "shall be collected in the appropriate amounts in each case" and "shall not exceed the margin of dumping as established under Article 2".

82. As stated in its first written submission and reiterated in its oral intervention on 25 September 2002, Argentina uses the system of variable amounts to assess prospective anti-dumping duties.

83. Although Article 9 of the AD Agreement does not specify the modalities for applying such duties, the practice of WTO Members recognizes the system used by Argentina as one of the possible methods. Article 9.3 provides for the possibility of

---

[39] Oral statement of Brazil - First Meeting with the Panel, para. 54.
[40] *Ibid.*, para. 59.

assessing duties on a retroactive or prospective basis and also establishes the ways in which any duties paid in excess should be corrected.

84. In this case, Brazil claims that Argentina violated Article 9.2 and 9.3 by imposing variable anti-dumping duties.

85. To uphold its Article 9.2 claim, Brazil proceeds from the assumption that if the Brazilian exporters decided to export their product to Argentina with a margin of dumping in excess of that determined during the investigation, their exports would be subject to a duty higher than that which had been established. This is not the case because, as specified in Article 2.1 of the AD Agreement:

> "...a product is to be considered as being dumped, i.e. introduced into the commerce of another country at less than its normal value, if the export price of the product exported from one country to another is less than the comparable price, in the ordinary course of trade, for the like product when destined for consumption in the exporting country."

86. In line with Canada's reasoning in its third party submission, Argentina wishes to make clear that the above claim is not supported by Article 9.2, which merely provides that duties shall be collected in "the appropriate amounts" - the determination thereof being established in Article 9.3.

87. As mentioned earlier, Article 9.3 establishes that the anti-dumping duty shall not exceed the margin of dumping as established under Article 2 in its entirety - and not, as Brazil erroneously contends, under Article 2.4.2, which deals with the margin of dumping during the investigation only.

88. Argentina has established anti-dumping duties and collects these duties in a manner consistent with the Agreement, i.e. they were assessed on the basis of the margin of dumping established under Article 2 and are collected pursuant to Article 9.2 and 9.3. Argentina does not deny the claim that the margin may be exceeded. The fact that such a possibility exists, however, is not sufficient for claiming that Argentina acted in a manner inconsistent with the Agreement. Indeed, if the margin had been exceeded, the exporters could have invoked Article 9.3 (if they so deemed appropriate) to request the refund of duties paid in excess, but they did not do so.

89. In view of the foregoing, Argentina reiterates its request that the Panel reject Brazil's claim of inconsistency with the above articles.

IV. PLEADINGS

90. In the light of the arguments put forward in the sections above, Argentina respectfully requests the Panel:

(1) In keeping with the reasoning developed in Section II and as stated in paragraphs 30, 31 and 32 of this submission, to refrain from ruling on the 41 claims of inconsistency with various provisions of the Agreement on Implementation of Article VI of the General Agreement on Tariffs and Trade 1994 (Anti-Dumping Agreement) submitted by Brazil.

Should the Panel decide not to accede to the above request by Argentina, as set out in Section II(d) of this submission and in the light of the arguments developed in Section III, it is respectfully requested to:

(2) Reject Brazil's claim that Resolution No. 574/2000 of the Ministry of the Economy of the Argentine Republic is inconsistent with:
- Article 5.2, 5.3, 5.7 and 5.8 of the Anti-Dumping Agreement;
- Article 12.1 of the Anti-Dumping Agreement;
- Article 6.1.1, 6.1.2, 6.1.3, 6.2 and 6.8, paragraphs 5, 6, and 7 of Annex II, and Article 6.9 and 6.10 of the Anti-Dumping Agreement;
- Article 2.4 and 2.4.2 of the Anti-Dumping Agreement;
- Article 3.1, 3.2, 3.4 and 3.5 of the Anti-Dumping Agreement;
- Article 4.1 of the Anti-Dumping Agreement;
- Article 9.2 and 9.3 of the Anti-Dumping Agreement;
- and the various claims relating to Article 12.2.2.

(3) Reject Brazil's request for the immediate repeal of Resolution No. 574/2000 imposing the definitive anti-dumping duties.

ANNEX B-4

REPLIES OF ARGENTINA TO QUESTIONS OF THE PANEL - FIRST METING

(25 September 2002)

DSU Article 18.2

To Argentina

1. Argentina stated at this morning's meeting that it was not opposed, as a matter of principle, to Brazil having made its first written submission available to the public. Instead, Argentina was concerned with the timing of Brazil's action. Does this mean that Argentina accepts that a Member may make its written submissions to a panel available to the public at some point in time without infringing Article 18.2 of the DSU? Would Brazil violate DSU Article 18.2 if it made its written submissions available to the public after the Panel issued its final report?

Reply to the first part of the question

Yes, following the provisions of Article 18.2 of the DSU.

Reply to the second part of the question

No.

Claim 1

To both parties

2. In the view of the parties, which are the obligations under Article 5.2? In addition, would the parties agree that Article 5.2 imposes obligations on the applicant and not on the investigating authority as stated in *Guatemala - Cement II*? Please explain. In the event of agreement with the conclusions in *Guatemala - Cement II*, what recommendations should a panel reach in case that a breach of Article 5.2 ADA is found? In particular, would a recommendation that a Member bring the measure into conformity be appropriate?

Reply

It is Argentina's understanding that the Agreement imposes obligations on Members. In principle, Article 5.2 imposes an obligation on Members with respect to the information that is required to be provided with the application for the initiation of an investigation. In other words, Article 5.2 lays down the requirements governing what the sector wishing to file an application for the initiation of an investigation must provide with its application.

In fact, Article 5.2 must be read in conjunction with Article 5.3 of the Anti-Dumping Agreement, since the latter imposes on the authorities the obligation to examine the accuracy and adequacy of the evidence provided by the applicant.

To Brazil

3. Does Article 5.2 ADA require that the application contain reasonably available relevant evidence on any adjustment to be made if such adjustment is required for applicant to allege "dumping". In this regard, should such evidence identify:

(a) That an adjustment is required;
(b) the nature and extent of the adjustment;
(c) the basis/methodology for making such adjustment?

Please explain.

4. Was information on the adjustments referred to in paras. 70 and 71 of Brazil's First written submission ("FWS") 'reasonably available' to the applicant at the time of filing the application? Please explain.

To Argentina

5. Did the application contain evidence to support that: (1) the poultry sold in Brazil was physically different from the poultry sold to Argentina; (2) that the alleged physical characteristics differences affect price comparability; and (3) the alleged yield rate difference presented by petitioner between the poultry sold in Brazil and to Argentina? If so, please provide the evidence supplied in the application.

Reply

The Jox publication of 30 June 1997 - Annex ARG-I - contains information concerning "whole poultry". Specifically, it states that the prices refer to chilled poultry marketed in the city of São Paulo (Brazil), expressed in Reals, with feet, head and giblets. This "physical" difference has an impact on prices, since the difference has a value that is determined by the demand for the poultry depending on the characteristics of the markets. Similarly, the information contained in the file reveals that the product exported to Argentina is eviscerated poultry.

6. Please comment on the definition of "evidence" set forth in paragraphs 63 and 64 of Brazil's FWS. In particular, the statement by Brazil in paragraph 64 that "information provided in the application without supporting documentation does not qualify as evidence". Please explain the basis of your response with specific reference to this case.

Reply

Regarding the requested evidence, the requirement to submit such evidence is clearly stated in the legislation in force, as well as in Form No. 349 which has been valid since 12 November 1991. It is these requirements that must be met by the complainant in an alleged dumping case.

In this connection, and with specific reference to the case at issue, CEPA submitted:

(a) SYSDEC's report on imports of the product under investigation from January to June 1997, the source for which was the Directorate-General of Customs;

(b) a copy of the report by the consulting firm Jox containing prices for chilled poultry in São Paolo expressed in Reals, with head, feet and giblets, as stated in the publication itself. Since it also explains that there are differences requiring adjustments for the purposes of price comparison, the firm adds a copy of the export price statistics for poultry published by the review *Aves & Ovos* of the *Asociación Paulista de Avicultura* of April and May 1997. It also adds evidence of the legal status of CEPA, and SENASA data concerning the representativeness of CEPA, in the area of domestic poultry production.

At the same time, CEPA provided the necessary translations and authentications for each piece of documentation submitted in a foreign language as required by Law No. 19.549 on Administrative Procedures and the regulatory decree applicable on a supplementary basis to alleged dumping or subsidy procedures. Thus, the requirements laid down by the Implementing Authority in connection with the application for initiation of an investigation were met.

In this connection, Argentina agrees with the definition of "evidence" provided by Brazil in paragraphs 63 and 64 of its first written submission, keeping in mind that the elements supplied by CEPA constitute sufficient documentary evidence for the initiation of an investigation. Specifically, the evidence provided as proof of normal value consists of excerpts from specialized journals and a publication by consultants of public notoriety, both of which constitute sufficient evidence of the exact values at which the product in question is marketed.

Consequently, it is clear that the implementing authority complied with the Article 5.3 obligation and examined the " … accuracy and adequacy of the evidence provided in the application …".

Claim 2

To Argentina

7. Could Argentina please clarify what they consider to be "reasonably available" information for an applicant under Article 5.2? In this case, taking into account that Jox is a consulting company that apparently publishes data on prices of poultry regularly, does Argentina consider that information on domestic prices in Brazil from Jox concerning only one day was all the information "reasonably available to the applicant" on normal value within the meaning of Article 5.2 ADA? Please explain.

Reply

The expression " … reasonably available" in Article 5.2 expresses the notion that the applicant must supply such evidence as is available and within its reach, and by which it can demonstrate what it alleges. Such evidence will be what the applicant can obtain at that particular time by the means available to it. CEPA provided Jox, a publication which enabled it to demonstrate the values at which the product in question was being sold, and which, in addition to providing the isolated value for one day, showed the price trend in the market as well as the cause of any variations.

We also repeat what was stated in paragraph 71 of Argentina's first written submission and in the preceding reply, namely that the implementing authority, in examining the accuracy and adequacy of the evidence provided by CEPA, took account, firstly, of the fact that Jox was a specialized publication providing an average representative value reflecting the state of the São Paolo market. That market is one of Brazil's most representative markets, and, like Buenos Aires, it is a large urban centre which reflects domestic consumption patterns.

8.   Reference is made to the following portion of para. 32 of Argentina's FWS:

> **'The above-mentioned provision in Article 5.2 provides applicants with access to proceedings of this kind in keeping with the right of parties to defend themselves; to require evidence that was beyond their reach would be to deny them that right.'**

What does Argentina understand by the words "beyond their reach"? In the present case, what information was "beyond the reach" of the applicant?

Reply

It is Argentina's understanding that what the Anti-Dumping Agreement requires in connection with the application for the initiation of an investigation, i.e. what is "reasonably available to the applicant", in addition to what was stated above, is such evidence as can be obtained without imposing an excessive burden of proof on the applicant that could make the submission of an application impossible, and without placing the applicant in a situation in which knowledge of its search for information could lead to a disclosure of the investigation it intends to apply for, with the commercial implications that such disclosure could entail. Moreover, in Argentina's view, the term used in the Agreement is intended to show the difficulty involved in obtaining evidence, particularly of normal value, in this instance, a difficulty which could be aggravated depending on the characteristics of the market and the possibilities available to the applicant. Moreover, if the applicant had to resort to hiring a consultant to obtain domestic market prices in the country in question, or resort to some dubious artifice to obtain those prices, the anti-dumping procedure would be deprived of any meaning or practical relevance.

9.   Please explain the process used by Argentina to receive and evaluate an application, with particular reference to any additional information that may be supplemented by the applicant. Please explain with specific reference to this case, whether:

(a)   **The investigating authority asked for (or received) more information, in particular on normal value, to decide on initiation;**

(b)   **at what stage of the investigation was additional information requested/received;**

(c)   **was the additional evidence used to determine normal value for the purpose of evaluation under Article 5.3;**

(d)   **if the answer to (c) above is in the negative, was the additional evidence on normal value used at any later stage for determination of normal value?**

Reply

To submit an application for the opening of an investigation, the applicant had to fill out form No. 349. That form explains exactly what data the applicant must provide in conformity with the requirements of Article 5.2 of the Anti-Dumping Agreement. In addition, the applicant must supply all of the supporting documentation for the information provided in the said form so that the Implementing Authority can examine the accuracy and adequacy of the "*evidence provided*". Thus, as regards normal value, the evidence considered was the Jox publication of 30 June 1997 accompanying the application, there being no additional requests by the implementing authority in that respect.

10. Please provide a copy of the model form referred to in para. 43 of its FWS?

Form 349/91 is attached hereto as Annex ARG-XXXIX.

11. Please comment on the following paragraphs of Brazil's first oral statement:

> **(a) Paragraphs 21 to 23, which refer to a Panel report and allege that the investigating authority in this case did not give consideration to the impact of the possible differences on the sufficiency of the evidence submitted in the application, nor did it seek further evidence, which was clearly necessary.**

Reply to question 11(a)

The adjustment made by the implementing authority for the differences between the poultry sold in Brazil and poultry sold in Argentina was included by the applicant when submitting the application, and applied by the authority as from the initiation of the investigation on the understanding that the said information was what was reasonably available to the applicant, that it was reasonable and that the implementing authority did not have knowledge of any elements to suggest that it should not be considered. Having evaluated the said information, the authority did not consider that it was necessary to request additional information in that respect in view of the standards applicable to the information to be considered at that stage of the investigation.

> **(b) Paragraphs 24 to 25 which allege that the method used by Argentina to establish the export price and consequently the dumping margin was based only on export prices below the normal value, which in turn "would always result in a dumping margin". In this response, please explain the methodology used by Argentina in this case.**

Reply to question 11(b)

The methodology used by Argentina to establish the dumping margin can be explained as follows: all of the export transactions that were below the normal value were considered, excluding those which yielded a negative dumping margin. This methodology has also been used by other WTO Members. Indeed, the stage prior to initiation requires sufficient evidence of dumping. The calculation made does not bring in economic effects on the market. What is required is the knowledge that there have been transactions involving dumping which justify, from that point of view, the initiation of an investigation.

12. Reference is made to the following portion of paragraph 50 of Argentina's FWS:

Argentina - Poultry Anti-Dumping Duties

'The evidence provided is a representative value taken from a specialized publication for a given period.'

What does Argentina mean by the words 'a given period'? Does it relate to a period of one day, or longer? Please provide your response with specific reference to this case.

Reply

What Argentina means by those words is a moment in the analysis period considered by the implementing authority. At the same time, although the Jox publication provides the price for 30 June 1997, the right-hand margin of the text contains CEPA's translation of the following words: " ... production on the parallel market within São Paolo is sharply lower, *so that the price remains on very firm ground*...". In other words, the quotation did not vary much, but rather remained stable. (Emphasis added)

13. Reference is made to the following portion of paragraph 50 of Argentine's FWS:

'This is why CEPA supplied, as evidence of normal value, the data contained in what is recognized as a serious specialized publication which reflected - within an acceptable margin of approximation in this instance - the same levels of commercial sales.'

What does Argentina understand by the words 'within an acceptable margin of approximation'?

Reply

By the words "... within an acceptable margin of approximation in this instance", Argentina intended to show that the values taken for the purposes of the comparison required by the Anti-Dumping Agreement were at the same level of trade, i.e. both the normal value and the export price were at wholesale level. In view of the nature of the stage prior to initiation, a precise approximation of the levels of trade cannot be expected. During the ensuing investigation, if it takes place, it is possible to verify the equivalence of the levels of trade and make the necessary adjustments, on the basis chiefly of the information provided by the parties.

To Brazil

14. **Is Brazil's claim under Article 5.3 regarding frozen/chilled adjustment dependent on a finding by the Panel that Argentina was correct to make the head/feet adjustment at the time of initiation? In other words, is Brazil arguing that if the need for a head/feet adjustment was obvious from the face of the application, then so was the need for a frozen chilled adjustment?**

Claim 3

To Argentina

15. Please explain which authority (authorities) have the authority to:
    (a) Accept/reject an application
    (b) Initiate an investigation

(c) **Conduct the investigation**
(d) **Decide on the application of the duty**

Reply

According to the regulatory Decree in force at the time of the investigation at issue, No. 2121/94:

(a) The ex-UNDER-SECRETARIAT FOR FOREIGN TRADE (now the UNDER-SECRETARIAT FOR TRADE POLICY AND MANAGEMENT) is the competent authority to rule on the admissibility of applications for the initiation of an investigation.

(b) The SECRETARIAT FOR INDUSTRY, TRADE AND MINING is the competent authority to rule on the initiation of an investigation.

(c) The UNDER-SECRETARIAT FOR TRADE POLICY AND MANAGEMENT and the NATIONAL FOREIGN TRADE COMMISSION are responsible for conducting proceedings with respect to injury.

(d) The MINISTRY OF PRODUCITON is the implementing authority for the application of anti-dumping duties. At the time of the investigation at issue, the competent authority was the ex-MINISTRY OF THE ECONOMY AND PUBLIC WORKS AND SERVICES.

16. **Following the CNCE's finding that there was no indication of injury or threat thereof suffered by the domestic industry in Acta No. 405, did the investigation authority reject the application? In other words, was Acta No. 405 effectively closing the file on the application? Please explain.**

Reply

Record No. 405 is not, *per se,* a valid instrument for closing the investigation, nor is the CNCE empowered to file the proceedings.

Similarly, it should be pointed out that the mentioned Acta No. 405 was issued on the basis of information provided by the applicant applicable as of the date of issue.

As already stated in writing, and as emerges from the file, the applicants submitted updated information in keeping with the requirements of the application on 17 February 1998. As a result, the Legal Department of the Ministry of the Economy and Public Works and Services, at the request of the then Under-Secretariat for Foreign Trade, determined that " ... in view of the fact that the information submitted by the *Centro de Empresas Procesadoras Avícolas* (CEPA) in file No. 061-001196/98 was not evaluated by the National Foreign Trade Commission when ruling on injury to the domestic industry in Record No. 405/98, this Directorate-General considers that before proceeding any further, the said National Commission should be asked to intervene once again in order to rule on the items submitted ... " (folio 2302 of File CNCE No. 43/97).

The examination of the new information submitted is expressly provided for in Article 60 of the Regulations to the National Law on Administrative Procedures (RLNPA - approved by Decree No. 1759/72, Regulatory Enactment by Decree No. 1883/91), duly notified to the relevant WTO Committees, which stipulates that the competent body (in this case, which involves injury, the CNCE) shall intervene once again in the proceedings if any new developments occur or *come to its knowledge*. In the case at issue, the additional submission by the applicant introduced new items of evidence which called for a further intervention by the CNCE at the request of the competent bodies and in strict conformity with the law.

It should also be repeated that during the stage prior to the initiation of the investigation, third party rights are not affected, the only relationship being between the applicant and the implementing authority. Thus, Brazil, which as interested party in the investigation had access to all of the folios making up the file, will have noted that during the period of time between the applicant's submission and the decision to initiate, a number of proceedings took place. In light of the above considerations, the suggested filing of the case would have been contrary to administrative law and would have adversely affected individual rights of the applicant with all of the administrative consequences that such an act would entail.

In this connection, Article 5.5 of the Anti-Dumping Agreement is also applicable: "The authorities shall avoid, unless a decision has been made to initiate an investigation, any publicizing of the application for the initiation of an investigation…"

In the case at issue, the applicant provided updated information that warranted analysis and led to the determination set forth in Acta No. 469.

Consequently, and in the light of the above-mentioned provisions, CNCE Acta No. 405 in no way constitutes an act by which the competent authority filed the application submitted, and a further intervention by the said authority was ultimately warranted under Argentine law.

17. What time-frame is envisaged by the word "promptly" in Article 5.8 ADA? Please respond with reference to this case.

Reply

Article 5.8 of the AD Agreement stipulates that: "An application under paragraph 1 shall be rejected and an investigation shall be terminated ***promptly*** as soon as the authorities concerned are satisfied that there is not sufficient evidence of either dumping or of injury to justify proceeding with the case …"

Thus, it should be stressed that Argentina did not violate Article 5.8 of the AD Agreement, since until the implementing authority (then the Secretariat for Industry, Trade and Mining) issues a resolution ruling the initiation of the investigation (which is published in the *Boletín Oficial de la Nación*), the activities of the authorities do not technically fall within the confines of an "investigation". There is no way that the two "Actas" of the CNCE prior to the opening of the investigation could terminate promptly an investigation that did not exist. Thus, the scope which Argentina gives to the term "promptly" in Article 5.8 of the AD Agreement is the scope determined by the relevant domestic legislation which, on the occasion of the various notifications, was never the subject of any objection by WTO Members in this respect.

Consequently, the term "promptly" must be interpreted in the context of an investigation that has been initiated, in respect of which the necessary administrative steps must be taken for termination once the authority is certain that there is no dumping or injury to justify continuing with the procedure.

Report of the Panel

Claim 4

To Argentina

18. In paragraph 80 of its FWS, Argentina asserts that:

"the Report on the Initiation of the Investigation ... contains the margins of dumping established on the basis of the average for export transactions to Argentina involving the product under investigation. Consideration was given in this connection to average exports for the period January-August 1997. The alleged margins of dumping calculated in points 1, 3 and 4 of the Report were established for the purpose of conducting an additional analysis of the case at issue."

With respect to this paragraph, this Panel has the following questions:

- Could Argentina explain the methodology used to calculate the f.o.b. export prices reported in points 1 and 2 of Section 7 (Dumping margin') of the Report relating to the Viability of the Initiation of the Dumping Investigation? With respect to the dumping calculation in point 2 of Section 7, could Argentina confirm that the import transactions that were taken into account to calculate the average export price were those contained in pages 489 to 492 of the Record (both included)?

Reply

In point 1 of Section 7, and in this instance prior to the initiation of the investigation, Argentina took the average f.o.b. export price for the period from August-October 1996. Similarly, applying the same methodology used for point 2, it took all of the transactions that were below 1.04, as of in detail on folios 508 and 509 and the lower table at folio 509.

Regarding point 2 of section 7, for the calculation of the export price Argentina considered those import transactions that were under the normal value, which resulted in an f.o.b. export price of 0.90454.

For the purposes of Table 2 in section 7, Argentina used the details for the export transactions set forth in the Annex at folios 485 to 488. Similarly, the information used to calculate the f.o.b. export price for point 2 can be found in the Annex at folios 489 to 492.

- Does the table included in page 10 of Section 6 of the above Report include all imports of the product subject to investigation originating in Brazil during the period January to May and August 1997? Is the total amount reported in that table (US$1,014.75/MT) the average f.o.b. export price for the product concerned imported in Argentina from Brazil during the period January to May and August 1997? Please explain.

Reply

Yes, the table in section 6 includes all of the imports of the product under investigation, with a price ranging from US$700 to US$1,330 per ton.

- The table in page 10 of Section 6 of the Report (folio 480) apparently includes data on f.o.b. export prices supplied by the petitioner for the period *January to May and August 1997*. In page 12 of Section 7 (page 482 of the Record), point (2) reads 'taking into account the f.o.b. export price data supplied by the petitioner for the period *January to June and August 1997* ...'. In paragraph 80 of its FWS, Argentina asserts that 'consideration was given to average exports for the period *January-August 1997.*' Could Argentina kindly clarify which period has been used to calculate the average f.o.b. export price during 1997?

Reply

The period used to determine the f.o.b. export price in this case was January to June 1997 and August 1997. The month of July was not taken into consideration because the official Argentine source the Monitoring Unit of the Secretariat for Industry, Trade and Mining, does not record any imports. In other words, while the period considered was January to August 1997, no imports were recorded for the month of July 1997.

19. Reference is made to paragraph 79 of Argentina's FWS:

"The technical department concerned examined the import transactions identified in the source in question with a view to determining which ones corresponded closest to the product under investigation so that the calculation of the export price could be as precise as possible."

What does Argentina understand by the transactions that 'corresponded closest to the product under investigation'?

Reply

In its examination, Argentina tried to determine which imports corresponded to the products under investigation, placing emphasis on the physical characteristics of the product investigated.

Claim 5

To Argentina

20. Bearing in mind Brazil's statements in paragraph 124 of its FWS, was information on normal value other than that concerning 30 June 1997 'reasonably available' to the applicant?

Reply

By Note 273-000887/99 of 29 July 1999, Section 26, folio 2103 (see Annex ARG-XL), the implementing authority asked the applicant for further information on normal value on the understanding that, with the investigation under way, it would be able to supply data, as it in fact did. This does not alter the fact that prior to initiation, the authority considered that the evidence of 30 June 1997 was the evidence reasonably available to the applicant.

Claim 6

To Brazil

21. **Paragraph 136 of Brazil's FWS reads in relevant part:**
"If authorities had examined the accuracy and adequacy of the evidence provided in the application they would have required that petitioner provide prices of poultry for the entire period under analysis in order to correctly make a fair comparison with export prices for the same period."
In the view of Brazil, which is the 'entire period under analysis'?

Claim 9

To both parties

22. **In the present case, by virtue of which legal instrument was the investigation initiated?**

Reply

The investigation was initiated by Secretariat for Industry, Trade and Mining Resolution No. 1/99, published in the Official Bulletin of 25 January 1999.

23. **What interpretation is given by the parties to the following excerpt from the panel report in *Guatemala - Cement II*: "we are of the view that Article 5.7 requires the investigating authority to examine the evidence before it on dumping and injury simultaneously, rather than sequentially?"**

Reply

As Argentina has already stated, the simultaneous analysis stipulated in Article 5.7 requires that both analyses take place at the same time and that the elements considered in the two analyses correspond to a period that coincides sufficiently, taking into account of the differences involved in investigating dumping on the one hand and injury on the other.

Claim 10

To both parties

24. **What are 'interested parties known to the investigating authorities to have an interest' within the meaning of Article 12.1 ADA?**

Reply

According to Article 12.1, the implementing authority shall notify "the Member or Members ... and other interested parties known to the investigating authorities to have an interest therein ... and a public notice shall be given."

At the same time Article 5.2(ii), identifying the items of information to be supplied by the applicant for an investigation, includes "the names of the country or countries of origin or export in question, the identity of each *known* exporter or foreign producer *and a list of known persons importing the product in question*".

Thus, it is Argentina's understanding that notification must be given to those parties that are considered interested within the meaning of Article 6.11, that are known and identified in such a way as to make such notification possible and identified it as interested parties. Both the notification to the Member country and the public notice are requirements that seek to supplement the knowledge that the implementing authority has either *per se* or on express and substantiated information from third parties.

25. When were each of the following parties notified of the initiation of the investigation: Government of Brazil, Avipal, Seara, Frigorifico Nicolini, Sadia, Fransgosul, Chapeco, Minuano, Perdigao, Catarinense, CCLP, Pena Branca, and Comaves?

Reply

In response to question 25, Argentina refers to the information contained in the tables attached hereto as Annexes ARG-XLI, ARG-XLII, ARG-XLIII, ARG-XLIV, ARG-XLV, ARG-XLVI, ARG-XLVII, ARG-XLVIII, ARG-XLIX, ARG-L, ARG-LI and ARG-LXI. Annex ARG-LXI lists, in addition, the notifications sent by the DCD to the different parties in two different stages: first, once the investigation was formally opened, and second, following the submission by the company Interamericana Comercial.

To Argentina

26. How does Argentina reconcile the fact that while exporters were listed in the Report of 7 January 1998 regarding the Viability of the Initiation of the Dumping Investigation, they appear not to have been notified?

Reply

While Argentina had received indications from a number of exporters, this did not constitute, in itself, an "identification" which made it possible to send them the relevant questionnaires. For the purposes of notification, it requested the cooperation of the Brazilian Government, which had knowledge of the application prior to the initiation of the investigation (see paragraph 112 of Argentina's first written submission). Unfortunately, the relevant information was not forthcoming, and finally, with the investigation already well advanced, it was possible to notify the exporters in question thanks to the information provided by the importing firm Interamericana Comercial, as explained in Argentina's first written submission (paragraphs 118 and 119).

We also refer to folios 3020 and 3021 of the Report on the Final Determination of the Margin of Dumping of 23 June 2000. Although there is, indeed, an obligation to notify the interested parties, Argentina took the necessary action in this respect by directly notifying those exporters that were appropriately identified for the purposes of notification and asking for the cooperation of the exporting member country. This does not, in any way, imply a shift of the burden to Brazil - it was merely an attempt to obtain, through its cooperation, the participation of Brazilian exporters during the investigation and as from its outset, as provided for in the Agreement itself.

Claim 11

To both parties

27. What is meaning of the word 'questionnaires' in Article 6.1.1. ADA? In the view of the parties, is the word 'questionnaires' confined to the questionnaires provided at the initial stage of the investigation only?

Reply

Article 6.1 sets forth the obligation to give notice of the information required to the parties, and to give them the opportunity to present, in writing, all of the relevant evidence. Article 6.1.1 points to the existence of questionnaires to be sent to foreign exporters or producers - either directly or through the representations of the exporting Member country - and stipulates a minimum of 30 days for reply, stating that preferential consideration should be given to requests for extension.

In this connection, Argentine practice, in conformity with the legislation in force, is to send questionnaires upon initiating the investigation, granting the stipulated time-period; and if, as a result of the proceedings, additional or supplementary information is required, the time-limit for the submission of such information is directly related to the content of the requirement, and consideration is also given to requests for an extension.

To Argentina

28. Which is the nature of the requests addressed to certain Brazilian exporters on 15 September 1999? In particular, are those requests original questionnaires? Are they the same as the questionnaires sent to the other exporters earlier in the investigation? Please explain.

Reply

The implementing authority learned of the elements that enabled it to contact the other Brazilian exporters through the importing company Interamericana Comercial at an advanced stage in the proceedings, as the result of a request to seek evidence. Accordingly, the authority proceeded to ask for the said evidence which consisted, *inter alia*, of sales prices in the domestic market, export prices and costs, and for the sole purpose of responding adequately to the general requirements and enabling exporters to attach any other information that they considered important, it also provided a copy of the questionnaire forms sent out at the beginning of the investigation.

We refer as well to paragraphs 118 and 119 of Argentina's first written submission.

29. Reference is made to paragraph 135 of Argentina's first written submission:

" ... it should be pointed out that the CNCE delivered the questionnaire to only eight exporters in full conformity with the provisions of Article 6.1 ... "

Which are the eight exporters to which the CNCE sent the injury questionnaire? When were these questionnaires sent to those exporters? How

and when did the CNCE obtain the addresses for these eight exporters? Please provide copies of the communications from the CNCE to these exporters.

Furthermore, the DCD's questionnaire was sent to five exporters: why wasn't the DCD's questionnaire sent to the same eight exporters that the CNCE sent its questionnaire to?

Reply

To answer the last question first, the DIRECTORATE OF UNFAIR COMPETITION and the NATIONAL FOREIGN TRADE COMMISSION are different bodies, the former being responsible for the determination of dumping, and the latter for the determination of injury.

Under Argentine legal procedure, the DCD and the CNCE act independently in their respective areas of competence.

On 10 February 1999, the CNCE questionnaire for exporters was transmitted to the Brazilian companies Sadia, Frangosul, Avipal, Frigorífico Nicolini and Seara (copies of the respective notes, the originals of which appear at folios 3092 to 3096 of CNCE file No. 43/97, are attached as Annex ARG-LII). As explained in Record (Acta) No. 576, " ... the exports to Argentina reported by the Brazilian companies that responded to the CNCE questionnaire for exporters represented more than half of the total imports of all eviscerated poultry from Brazil for 1995, 1996, 1997 and 1998 ... ".

The list of companies that replied to the said questionnaires between 22 February and 3 May, with references to the corresponding folios in file CNCE 43/97, is provided below:

QUESTIONNAIRE FOR THE EXPORTER	REPLIED
Seara	YES (folio 3464/82)
Frigorífico Nicolini	YES (folio 4556/68)
Avipal	YES (folio 4868/896)
Sadia	YES (folio 5296/308)
Frangosul	YES (folio 4904/61)

30. **Did the invoices attached to the communication of Interamericana Commercial S.R.L. to the DCD of 21 April 1999 (EXHIBIT ARG-VII) contain the address of Comaves Industrial? Can you please provide copies of those invoices?**

Reply

While the implementing authority had before it an invoice submitted by the importing company containing an alleged address for the company Comaves Industrial (Section 27, folio 2296, sheet 4), it was not clear that the company was a producing-exporting firm and that this was its current domicile. A copy of the said invoice is attached as Annex ARG-LIII.

31. **We refer to your statement in paragraph 134 of your First written submission that the "investigating authorities granted the Brazilian exporters a deadline longer than that specified in the Agreement to reply to the DCD's questionnaires". Should the 30-day period provided for in Article 6.1.1 be**

provided from the outset when the questionnaire is first sent out, or is it sufficient to provide a lesser period at the outset, provided that the total period allowed for response is at least 30 days?

Reply

In response to this question, Argentina refers to the information provided in the tables contained in Annexes XLI to LI, and LXI.

Without prejudice to the above, we note that Argentina grants exporters the 30 days stipulated in the AD Agreement for submitting the forms, as stated in the form itself. Exporters have a right to the 30 days, and the 30 days are granted. The alternative examined by the Panel of initially granting a lesser period and then increasing the number of days to 30 does not reflect the system applied by Argentina. What the Argentine authority stated was that in addition to the 30 days, it granted the requested extensions. It is understood that the time-limits granted for responding to the requests should be in keeping with the nature and complexity of those requests. Thus, the initial 30-day period for replying in full to the basic investigation questionnaire at the outset is appropriate.

Claim 12

To both parties

32. What is the meaning of the word "participating" in Article 6.1.2 ADA? Would the parties consider that companies that are aware of an ongoing investigation but that do not show an interest in it qualify as "parties participating in the investigation"?

Reply

In order to be able to answer this question, Argentina would ask the Panel to elaborate. However, we understand that the interested parties are those that have proven to be interested parties during the investigation itself by expressing their interest in participating.

33. What is the meaning of the word "promptly" in Article 6.1.2. ADA?

Reply

In response to this question, we refer to the last paragraph of our reply to question 35.

Claim 14

To both parties

34. What are "known exporters" within the meaning of Article 6.1.3 ADA? In particular, would producers in the exporting country that have been identified as exporters of the product concerned by the applicant in the application qualify as "known exporters"?

Reply

Argentina understands "known exporters" to be those whose domicile is known together with all of the data needed to identify them and transmit to them the relevant notifications. The authority of the Member country initiating an investigation does not necessarily have to complete information on exporters. Indeed, the AD Agreement provides for the participation of the exporting Member country as the appropriate vehicle for obtaining all of the information needed so that its producers can be informed of the existence of the investigation, including the documentation necessary to participate actively in the investigation.

35.   Would the parties agree with the finding of the panel *Guatemala - cement II* that "the term 'as soon as' conveys a sense of substantial urgency" and that "as soon as" and "immediately" can be considered interchangeable terms? Please explain.

Reply

The Panel in *Guatemala - Cement II* states that "as soon as" conveys a sense of substantial urgency. It adds that the terms "as soon as" and "immediately" are interchangeable. Argentina considers that while the Panel's interpretation must be viewed in the context in which it was made, it is essential that the terms be evaluated in the complete context of the applicable legislation and domestic procedures. In the case of Argentina, the said legislation and procedures were notified to the Member countries and were not challenged.

One thing that makes a difference to the interpretation and conclusion that the terms are interchangeable is the full meaning of the context in which they appear. The context and purpose in the *Guatemala II* case is not the same as the context and purpose we are examining in the case at issue.

Indeed, in the case at issue, the objective of the action is to try to ensure that there are no unjustified obstacles to trade between countries. In other words, to ensure that *measures that are in force or investigations under way* are not maintained *when it is learned that they are not appropriate in the framework of the provisions of the AD Agreement.*

In this case, in which there are rights that are protected by legislations, the term "as soon as" must take account of, and be consistent with the need for greater speed, on the one hand, and the need to comply with the relevant legal provisions on the other.

To Brazil

36.   What is the meaning of the words "as soon as an investigation has been initiated" in Article 6.1.3 ADA? In the particular case at stake, when was the investigation initiated?

To Argentina

37. Please comment on paragraphs 42 and 43 of Brazil's first oral statement.

Reply

Regarding paragraph 42 of Brazil's first oral statement, Argentina understands the term "*facilitar*", on the basis of the accepted meaning in our language, as meaning to permit access to a thing or element that is of interest to the other party. In other words, our interpretation is not substantially different from that of Brazil, nor is it different from the interpretation used by various member states with respect to the specific matter at issue. The difference that is being sought to be introduced here applies to the way in which access to the element is "*facilitado*". The copy of the application is available to the interested parties and the government of the exporting country from the outset of the investigation and interested parties that are duly accredited under Argentine law are provided permanent access to the file to the extent possible.

Regarding paragraph 43, it should be pointed out with respect to the documentation supplied by Sadia and Frangosul (Section X, folio 1012, sheet 4) that, for example, although Sadia explains that the technical specifications for the products marketed in Brazil and Argentina are the same, in Section IX, folio 999 (Annex ARG-XXIII to Argentina's first written submission), the representative of the company Sadia, who is also the representative of Frangosul, Seara and Avipal, in a way challenges the adjustment made but without saying how it should be made.

This is why Argentina considers the simple allegations of the representative to have been insufficient - they should have been documented so that they could be verified.

Claim 15

To Brazil

38. With regard to EXHIBITS BRA-22, 23, 24 and 26, please indicate precisely where exporters reported that the poultry sold to Argentina was identical to the poultry sold in Brazil.

To Argentina

39. Brazil has asserted that the investigating authorities did not request supporting documentation for all information requested from exporters. Please comment.

Reply

Brazil's statements on this issue reflect a confusion which would appear to arise from an interpretation of the procedures determined by the particular way in which that country applies them rather than an orderly and systematic reading of the way in which the Argentine implementing authority proceeds. Firstly, it should be explained that the implementing authority follows a procedure which is notified to the parties through its legal provisions and the instructions accompanying the requests for information. Thus, the authority, as is customary and in keeping with its usual procedure, requested supporting documentation for the arguments put forward insofar as those arguments are based on documentation which is substantially in the hands of that party. This methodology is applied concurrently to all of the parties involved, and does not in fact discriminate against, or conceal anything from exporters.

Argentina did not request copies of all of the invoices, but only the supporting documentation for the arguments put forward. On the basis of the information supplied by the parties throughout the proceedings, the authority evaluates the possibility of requesting further documentation, without prejudice to what has already been requested in the questionnaire for exporters.

Claim 17

To Argentina

40. Where in its final determination, or any other document made available to interested parties, does the DCD explain why it rejected the relevant exporters' export price data?

Reply

The Report on Action Taken (folio 2757, Section 63) - EXHIBIT BRA-28 - identifies in detail what information submitted in the course of the proceedings Argentina would take into consideration in its final determination. Similarly the Report on the Final Determination (EXHIBIT RA-15) also mentions the reasons why individual determinations of margin of dumping were not made.

As stated earlier on, and as the parties are aware, the information supplied must be submitted in conformity with the formal and substantive provisions of Argentine law and with the provisions specifically set forth in the request for information. Failure to comply with these provisions means that the implementing authority cannot use the information correctly and legally for the purposes of its determinations.

Claim 19

To Brazil

41. Argentina asserts that Frangosul's normal value data was submitted out-of-time. Please comment.

Claim 20 (*inter alia*)

To Argentina

42. Regarding paragraph 190 of Argentina's first written submission, please provide copies of the "several notifications" that were sent to Frangosul "with a request to provide the lists of *Notas fiscales*" What was the deadline for Frangosul's submission of normal value data?

Reply

Regarding the copies of the "numerous *notas fiscales*" requested from Frangosul, they were attached to Argentina's first written submission as Annexes 27 and 28. However, we attach hereto Annex ARG-XLV, containing a table listing all of the notifications sent to Frangosul. See also Annex ARG-LIV, attached hereto, containing copies of the requested n*otas*.

The final deadline granted to the company Frangosul was indicated in Note DCD No. 273-001413/99, which provided for "a period of no more than five days following the reception of this note". The Note is attached hereto as Annex ARG-LV. After the granted deadline of 29 November 1999 had elapsed, the company made a submission, on 30 December 1999, containing a diskette. In other words, beyond the period of time granted by the DCD.

43. Precisely what normal value data did the DCD ask Cararinense to provide? Please provide supporting documentation.

Reply

In order to help the Panel understand this issue, we note with respect to Catarinense that the Report on the Final Determination, at folios 3053/3054, states that the information supplied on normal value is reported on an aggregate basis in Annexes V and VI, and for a longer period. It was also reported that the information had not been documented. The fact that it was provided in aggregate form made it impossible for the implementing authority to consider only what corresponded to the investigation period.

44. Please indicate where, in the DCD's Final Determination, the reasons are given for not calculating individual dumping margins for Frangosul and Catarinense?

Reply

Once again we note, with respect to Catarinense, that Report on the Final Determination (EXHIBIT BRA-15) states, at folios 3053/3054, that the information provided on normal values was reported on an aggregate basis in Annexes V and VI, and for a longer period. It was also reported that it had not been documented.

Similarly, at folio 3087, the final Report makes the following statement: "Finally, we stress that in the case of the companies Catarinense Limitada, Frangosul, Comave, Da Granja Agroi, Sadia Concordia, Minuano De Alimentos, Acaua Industria, Felipe Avicola, Agroi, Veneto, Chapeco and Litoral Alimen, the implementing authority did not have sufficient additional information or supporting documentation to enable it to reach an individual final determination of the margin of dumping. That being the case, the implementing authority had to fall back on the relevant legislation in force, considering, to that end, the best information that it had obtained prior to the current stage of the proceedings ... ".

45. Please indicate where, in the DCD's final determination, or in any other document prepared by the DCD at that time, the reasons for not calculating individual dumping margins for Frangosul and Catarinense are provided? Did the DCD have sufficient export price data in respect of these two exporters?

Reply

We stress once again that the DCD Report on the Final Determination (EXHIBIT BRA-15) states, at folio 3087, the following: "Finally, we stress that in the case of the companies Catarinense Limitada, Frangosul, Comave, Da Granja

Agroi, Sadia Concordia, Minuano De Alimentos, Acaua Industria, Felipe Avicola, Agroi, Veneto, Chapeco and Litoral Alimen, the implementing authority did not have sufficient additional information or supporting documentation to enable it to reach an individual final determination of the margin of dumping. That being the case, the implementing authority had to fall back on the relevant legislation in force, considering, to that end, the best information that it had obtained prior to the current stage of the proceedings ... ".

With respect to Frangosul, only documentation on export prices was provided - there was no information concerning sales prices on the domestic market. It seems perfectly clear that the implementing authority did not have the necessary elements for calculating individual dumping margins given, as emerges from the Agreement, that this margin reflects the ratio between the two values and that specifically, information on sales prices in the domestic market is in the hands of the exporter. Regarding Catarinense, we refer to our reply to Question 43.

Claim 19

To Brazil

46(a). Please provide a copy of Catarinense's questionnaire response of 3 November 1999.

46(b). Argentina asserts that Frangosul's normal value data was submitted out-of-time. Please comment.

Claim 21

To Argentina

47(a). In paragraphs 340-350 if its FWS, Brazil asserts that certain information was not provided to the exporters. Please indicate precisely where, if at all, this information can be found in the authority's Report of 4 January 2000.

Reply

The Report on Action Taken (EXHIBIT BRA-28) clearly states what information was provided by each one of the exporters in the course of the proceedings, and of that information, what documentation would or would not be used for the final determination of the margin of dumping. Particularly relevant are Parts VIII, VIII.1 and VIII.3 et seq.

However, in order to help clarify this issue, we refer to the tables attached hereto as Annexes XLI to LI, and LXI.

Claim 23

To Argentina

47(b). Did the DCD Sadia to provide additional information regarding its request for "flete interno" adjustment (i.e. after Sadia provided the data set forth in Annex VIII of its questionnaire response?)

Reply

In response to Question 47(b), Argentina refers to the information contained in the table attached hereto as Annex XLIV.

48. Please provide a copy of Expediente No. 061-000739/2000, as referenced at page 95 of the DCD's final dumping determination (EXHIBIT BRA-15). Please also provide a copy of Expediente No. 061-000663/2000, referenced at page 97 of the same document.

Reply

Copies of File No. 061-000739/2000 and 061-000663/2000 are attached hereto as Annex ARG-LVI and ARG LVII respectively.

To Brazil

49. When did Avipal first request a normal value adjustment for freight charges? Did Avipal provide supporting documentation with its request? If so, please provide a copy of that supporting documentation.

50. Is Brazil's argument regarding the investigation authority's failure to use information submitted by exporters limited to adjustments for the purpose of Article 2.4, or also to other factors/claims?

Claims 23-27

To Brazil

51. Please explain precisely what evidence was in the record that you consider the investigation authorities failed to use.

To Argentina

52. Please comment on paragraphs 61 and 65 of Brazil's first oral statement.

Reply

We must begin by determining what, in the view of Members, is meant by the term "excessive burden". If carried to the extreme, the concept of excessive burden could render the request for information from the parties meaningless. The information requested might have had a different weight in proportion to the trade importance of each exporter, but it is equivalent to the information that is requested of all parties, in all investigations, information that is supplied, as in the case at issue, by a few of the producers-exporters. In any case, the exporters, like any other interested parties, were welcome to contact the implementing authority and explain that they considered the evidence they were to provide to be "excessive" (in quality and quantity), providing sufficient justification for their claim. However, the parties did not make use, during the investigation, of the opportunity granted to them under the actual procedure, an "omission" which is now being presented to the Panel as a failure by the implementing authority to take sufficient action. Argentina would further like to explain to the Panel that it never requested, let alone required, that the exporters provide an invoice copy for "all of the sales transactions". Argentina was unable to find the part of the file that Brazil was referring to in this connection, which is not surprising, given that the request was not made.

Without prejudice to the above, Argentina would like to point out with respect to paragraph 61 that it did not consider the request for information from the producers-exporters to be an excessive burden, since certain exporters provided information that did in fact comply with the DCD's requests. Moreover, if certain exporters did in fact consider the evidence requested to be excessive, they should have informed the authority accordingly and explained that it was impossible to comply. However, at no point was this done.

At the same time, Brazil should indicate, in connection with paragraph 65, where in the file Argentina required that the exporters provide "an invoice copy for all of the sales transactions in the home market". The tables attached as Annexes XLI to LI and LXI, show exactly what requests for information were made by Argentina.

Claim 24

To Argentina

53. Certain data (regarding adjustments) submitted by Jox appears to have been rejected because if was submitted in Portuguese. If that was the case, why was the other Jox data - also submitted in Portuguese - accepted by the DCD (EXHIBITS BRA-19 and 32, regarding normal value data and the adjustment for different characteristics)?

Reply

The Jox information submitted by CEPA in File No. 61-006544/99 (Section 25 - folio 2096) (Exhibit Brazil 19) was translated following a request by the implementing authority made in Note No. 273-000887/99 (folio 2103 - Section 26) (see Annex ARG-LVIII). The translation was provided in File No. 061:006874/99 (folio 2115 - Section 26)(see Annex LIX).

As can be seen, the implementing authority considered evidence of normal value that was translated in conformity with the Law on Administrative Procedures and its regulatory Decree.

Claim 25

To Brazil

54. Please provide all of the exporters' replies to Sections B.2 and C.1.1 of the DCD's questionnaire (as set forth on "folios" 8 and 9 in EXHIBIT BRA-22).

Claim 26

To Argentina

55. Was the additional normal value data submitted by CEPA on 26 July 1999 (EXHIBIT BRA-19) relied on by the DCD for the purpose of making a final determination on dumping?

Reply

Yes, that information was considered in making the final determination, as revealed by the Report on Action Taken prior to the closure of the period for obtaining evidence, dated 4 January 1999 (folios 2809 - 2811), Part VIII.1.2.2 and in the Final Determination of the Margin of Dumping (folios 3038-3040), Part VIII.1.2.2.

56. Please comment on paragraph 59 of Brazil's oral statement.

Reply

The implementing authority carried out the adjustments to the extent that they were documented by evidence as required for that purpose under Argentine law, which was known to the parties. In this connection, the Law on Administrative Procedures and its regulatory Decree No. 1759/72 are applicable to anti-dumping procedures, on a residual basis, as stated in the regulatory Decree to Law 24425. The said Decree No. 1759/72 to the Law on Administrative Procedures stipulates in Article 28 that documents under foreign jurisdiction shall be submitted with a translation into Spanish by a certified translator. Pursuant to the said legislation and given that the documentation supplied by Jox Asesoria following an additional request by the implementing authority was not provided with a translation, and that none of the exporters provided translations, the said adjustments for inland freight and taxes were not considered.

The implementing authority made it clear that since it was aware that there were possible factors requiring adjustment, it would require information substantiated by relevant evidence, and if that evidence complied with the legislation in force, it would be considered for the purposes of its determinations. Any other approach would mean violating Argentine law, the Agreement itself and the legitimate right of all parties involved to defend their interests and be treated with equity. In the case at issue, this is clearly revealed by the fact that Brazilian exporters Sadia, Avipal, Nicolini and Ceara did submit the relevant documentation, and that evidence was considered for the purposes of making an individual determination of the margin of dumping.

Claim 27

To Argentina

57. Please explain exactly why the DCD's sample of domestic transactions (used for calculating normal value) was statistically valid. Is any such explanation contained in the DCD's final documentation, or any other document made available to interested parties? If so, where?

Reply

A sample is statistically valid with an acceptable margin of error. The fact that use was not made of the entire range of information is justified by lack of access thereto, lack of time to process it all and the need to reduce the number of errors associated with the processing of large quantities of data. Thus, the aim is to draw inferences concerning population parameters on the basis of sample statistics. We note that the Agreement on implementation of Article VI of the GATT 1994 provides for the use of statistical methods to determine normal value.

We attach hereto the explanation provided by the DCD in the Report on the Final Determination (EXHIBIT BRA-15), folios 3046/3047.

Claims 28-30

To Argentina

58.   With regard to the statement in parenthesis in the second line of paragraph 55 of Argentina's first oral statement, was the "minimum export price" determined for each exporter (for the purpose of the variable anti-dumping duty) less than, equivalent to, or more than the normal value calculated (during the investigation) for each exporter respectively?

Reply

Argentina sought to follow the suggestion made by the AD Agreement and to use a value less than the margin of dumping in the conditions established by the Agreement to ensure that trade between Members can benefit from competition without prejudice to the domestic industry.

In the case of AVIPAL, the value taken was barely less than the normal value determined during the investigation. In the case of SADIA, it was less: the normal value determined was 0.94 and the value applied was 0.92. For the other companies it was also less, the normal value determined being 1.0385 and the minimum export value applied being 0.98.

Claims 32-40

To Argentina

59.   Please comment on paragraphs 69-70, and 79-82 of Brazil's first oral statement.

Reply

Paragraphs 69-70

First of all, there is no obligation to analyse any indicator outside the period established by the authorities as the investigation period.

In accordance with international practice in certain countries, Argentina considered a number of variables accessible to the public in order to double check the trends observed during the investigation period. If we were to insist on the constant updating of all indicators during the investigation, as Brazil seems to suggest in this case, the investigation would be endless. We repeat that this is not the objective of the AD Agreement, nor is it the practice of those countries which, like Argentina, examine certain relevant indicators of reference data.

Comments on paragraphs 79-82

Paragraph 79

We repeat what we stated in our first written submission, in paragraphs 277 to 282. Argentina would like to make it clear to the Panel that the evolution of the productivity factor was analysed specifically in Record CNCE No. 576, as was the case for all of the factors listed in the AD Agreement. Indeed, the said Record states that " … the relative stability of the number of employees in spite of the increased production would indicate higher physical labour productivity, probably due to the above-mentioned introduction of new technology." Brazil calls the attention of the Panel to the fact that the data submitted - production, employment, wages and cost structure - does not refer specifically to the productivity factor. Argentina wonders why Brazil should wish to call the Panel's attention to this issue, since the mentioned factors are those which made the CNCE's analysis possible.

Paragraph 80

Argentina repeats what it stated in paragraph 292 of its first written submission. Regarding the fact that Brazil fails to find an evaluation of other factors affecting the price of whole eviscerated poultry during the investigation period, we note that this evaluation appears both in CNCE Record No. 576 and in the Technical Report. Indeed, regarding the evolution of the price of a substitute product - red meat - the said Record states the following: "An econometric exercise was conducted which showed that for the period from January 1995 to June 1999, the price of the product on the domestic market depended on the volume of imports for the previous month, the price of the imported product and the price of bovine meat. The inclusion of the price of maize in the mentioned model did not produce satisfactory results, indicating that the considerable variability of the price of whole eviscerated poultry does not coincide with the price of maize. Nevertheless, both variables showed similar patterns ... ". This analysis was based on the elements set forth in the Technical Report at folios 7371/2 and 7491/507. CNCE Record No. 576 also refers to the analysis of the evolution of the general level of activity, stating that "[t]he economic recession did not particularly affect the consumption of whole eviscerated poultry, which continued to increase (in 1998 it increased by 14 per cent)." Finally, with respect to relative prices, CNCE Record No. 576 states that "...with regard to the price of industrial goods taken as a whole and of bovine meat - represented respectively by the Wholesale Industrial Price Index for Manufactured Goods and the simple average of the consumer price indices for fresh bovine meat, front and hind cuts - followed the same trend as the sales revenue described above, although in the case of bovine meat, the annual variations reflected a stronger decrease in 1998 as a result of the increase in the price of bovine meat recorded that year." The above analysis was supported by the information provided in the Technical Report, in particular Table No. 16 at folio 7474 and the description at folio 7410. Regarding Table No. 16 of the Technical Report, Argentina notes that according to Brazil it contains only the average sales revenue for poultry, when in fact it also provides the relative prices mentioned above.

Paragraph 82

Argentina evaluated the specific accounts of the companies and the main economic and financial variables contained in the accounting and financial instruments required in connection with the corporate characteristics of the companies. It is these factors that define, among other elements, the capacity of a company to raise capital, and ultimately, its capacity for growth and investment. Contrary to what Brazil claims in paragraph 82 of its oral submission of 25 September 2002, this explanation appears in the Technical Report GEGE/ITDF 03/99 and in Record No. 576.

60. **Please also comment on Brazil's assertion at paragraph 74 of its first oral statement that is "not true" that the CNCE did not take into account imports from Nicolini and Seara for the purpose of its injury determination.**

Reply

With respect to this assertion, Argentina repeats what it stated in paragraphs 269-273 of its first written submission.

Claim 34

To Brazil

61. **If non-dumped imports are to be excluded for the purpose of an Article 3 injury analysis, doesn't this suggest that the determination of dumping must precede the determination of injury? If so, how is a Member to ensure that evidence of dumping and injury will be considered simultaneously in conformity with Article 5.7?**

Claim 34

To Argentina

62. **Please explain how the investigating authorities ensure that non-dumped imports were excluded for the purpose of the injury determination.**

Reply

In response to this question, Argentina refers to its reply to question 60.

Claim 38

To Argentina

63. **At paragraph 278 of its FWS, Argentina refers to a number of page references. Please indicate precisely which documents these page numbers refer to. Please also indicate corresponding file page numbers (for example, page 1 of Acta No. 576 (EXHIBIT BRA-14) is page 7303 of the file). Furthermore, please indicate precisely which extracts from these pages that Argentina is referring to.**

Reply

The references made by Argentina in paragraphs 278 of its first submission concerning improvements in the sector's productivity are the following:
- (a) Record No. 576: page 12 (paragraph 2), page 13 (paragraph 4), page 14 (paragraph 1), page 20 (paragraphs 3 and 4)
- (b) Technical Report: page 26 (paragraph 5), page 28 (paragraphs 5 and /), page 29-30 (paragraph 2) and page 95 (paragraphs 3 and 4).

64. **Regarding paragraph 279 of Argentina's FWS, please indicate in which document 'CEPA confirmed that the leading productivity indicators ... are similar to those in the Brazilian industry'.**

Reply

The exact words used by the Centro de Empresas Procesadoras Avícolas (CEPA) in its submission at folio 7135 of File CNCE No. 43/97, dated 2 December 1999 (post-hearing submission), a copy of which is attached hereto as Annex ARG-LX, were: " ... for a number of years now, there has been no difference between our productive output and that of Brazilian poultry producers ...".

Claim 41

To Brazil

65.   Regarding paragraph 87 of its first oral statement, is Brazil alleging that Argentina's failure to explain why it considered a percentage lower than 50 per cent "a major proportion" constitutes a violation of Article 4.1, or of some other provision of the AD Agreement? If so, please explain how this claim falls within the Panel's terms of reference.

ANNEX B-5

SECOND ORAL STATEMENT OF ARGENTINA
(26 November 2002)

I. INTRODUCTION

1. Argentina is grateful for the possibility of presenting before the Panel its arguments in the light of the second written submission of Brazil (rebuttal submission) dated 17 October 2002.

2. At this stage of the proceedings, Argentina would like to highlight - in summary form - and respond to certain arguments put forward by Brazil in its latest submission.

II. PRELIMINARY ARGUMENTS

3. Argentina repeats that it considers accusations of bad faith[1] of a generic nature such as the one made by Brazil in its first written submission to be out of place, and consequently, the Panel should reject the arguments contained in the second paragraph of the section "Anti-Dumping Standard of Review" in Brazil's second written submission.

4. It is very difficult for Argentina to understand how the use of the term "generic" can be rejected on the grounds of Brazil's attempted justification[2] whereby the listing of the 41 claims in paragraphs 3 and 4 of its first written submission, not to mention the contents of paragraphs 11 through 544 of that submission provide a greater degree of precision to the accusation of bad faith.

5. A distinction has to be drawn between the claims and the legal justifications thereof in respect of which Brazil states that "*the identification of these claims, the related facts and legal arguments are **not** general in nature and are **not** without relevance in this WTO proceeding*"[3] on the one hand, and the accusation of bad faith on the other. The alleged inconsistencies of Argentina's Resolution 574/2000 with WTO rules bear no relationship with the principle of bad faith.

II.2 THE DOCTRINE OF *RES JUDICATA*

6. Contrary to Brazil's statement[4] that "*it appears, in fact, that Argentina is suggesting that the ruling by the Mercosul Tribunal has the effect of res judicata. In*

---

[1] First written submission of Brazil, para. 28, page 12.
[2] Rebuttal submission of Brazil, Section III - "Ruling by MERCOSUL Ad Hoc Arbitral Tribunal", para. 12, page 4.
[3] *Ibid.*
[4] Rebuttal submission of Brazil, Section III - "Ruling by the MERCOSUL Arbitral Tribunal", para. 18, page 5.

Report of the Panel

the event that Argentina is alleging the application of res judicata ... ", Argentina repeats[5] that it has not argued for the application of the doctrine of *"res judicata".*

7. Nevertheless, Argentina feels that it should refute the arguments put forward by Brazil in this connection in its rebuttal submission and provide a number of clarifications.

8. In the case *India - Autos*[6], the Panel stated that it would have to examine the applicability of the doctrine in the WTO, and secondly, that it would be necessary to determine whether the facts in the dispute were such as to satisfy the requirements of the doctrine.

9. However, the examination of the doctrine of *res judicata* in the case *India - Autos* was based on circumstances different from those that apply to the dispute brought by Brazil.

10. In *India - Autos* the treatment of *res judicata* referred to two successive cases: *India - Quantitative Restrictions*[7] and *India - Autos,* both settled under the WTO. And indeed, footnote 333 of the Panel Report in *India - Autos* dwells on the examination of two disputes brought under the WTO. These disputes considered claims calling for the establishment of successive panels concerning the same issue. The two cases referred to were *India - Patents*[8] and *Australia - Automotive Leather II.*[9] Both cases involved disputes brought before the WTO in which *res judicata* was deemed irrelevant since there was no identity between the parties to the disputes *(India -Patents*[10]), or there was a void in the previous decision of the Panel with respect to the matter at issue *(Australia - Automotive Leather II).*[11]

11. As Argentina has argued, the dispute brought by Brazil against Argentina under the WTO is not comparable with any of the three cases in which past panels have had the opportunity to examine the scope of the theory of *res judicata.*

12. Without prejudice to the fact that it did not invoke the applicability of the doctrine, Argentina feels that it is necessary to point out the substantial differences between the current dispute and the cases cited by the EC and Brazil in their respective submissions.

---

[5] Intervention by the Argentine Republic at the meeting of the Panel with the parties, 25 September 2002, para. 7.

[6] *India - Measures Affecting the Automotive Sector* (WT/DS146/R, WT/DS175/R), 21 December 2001, para. 7.55.

[7] *India - Quantitative Restrictions on Imports of Agricultural, Textile and Industrial Products* (WT/DS90/R). Subsequently, complaints were brought by the United States and the EC in the case *India - Measures Affecting the Automotive Sector* (WT/DS146/R and WT/DS175/R),

[8] *India - Patent Protection for Pharmaceutical and Agricultural Chemical Products* (WT/DS79) complaint brought by the EC,

[9] *Australia - Subsidies Provided to Producers and Exporters of Automotive Leather* (WT/DS126/R), report adopted on 16 June 1999.

[10] WT/DS79. The United States had previously filed a similar complaint: *India - Patent Protection for Pharmaceutical and Agricultural Chemical Products* (WT/DS50), DSR 1998:I, 41.

[11] In the case *Australia - Automotive Leather II* (WT/DS126/R) Australia, according to paragraph 9.14, asked the Panel to read into the DSU an implicit prohibition on multiple panels between the same parties regarding the same matter that does not exist in the text of the DSU. However, the Panel ruled that "[n]or is this a case where a complainant has sought a second panel before a first panel has completed its work with respect to the same matter because it was dissatisfied with developments in the first panel. Although the first panel in this case was established, it was never composed and thus never began its work."

- **They are not successive complaints under the same forum**: In the case at issue, we have an arbitral award issued by a tribunal set up at the request of Brazil in the framework of MERCOSUR, and not a prior ruling within the WTO.

- **The identity of the parties** is beyond doubt if we compare the case brought before MERCOSUR and the current case before the WTO. Moreover, as Argentina has pointed out, there is an element of "added value" in that both States are States party to the same integration process, namely MERCOSUR.[12]

- **There is identity of the measure being challenged**, i.e. Resolution ME 574/2000, as stated by Argentina in its first written submission[13] and also acknowledged by the EC.[14]

- **There is identity of the legal basis of the claim**: In this respect, Argentina has already pointed out[15] the high degree of similarity between the arguments made under MERCOSUR and those made under the WTO. A comparative table was included in Annex ARG-LXII which clearly illustrates the mentioned coincidences in Brazil's successive submissions in the two fora.

13. In short, despite the differences between the current dispute brought by Brazil and the cases already settled within the framework of the WTO in which *res judicata* was invoked, Argentina has decided not to argue the application of this doctrine for two basic reasons: firstly, because Argentina recognizes that in the absence of an applicable MERCOSUR regulatory framework in this area, each State Party to MERCOSUR is governed by the provisions of the Anti-Dumping Agreement[16]; and secondly, in spite of this fact Brazil, fully aware of the situation, resorted to MERCOSUR, and the Ad Hoc Tribunal proceeded to examine the case and settle it taking account, because Brazil itself included them in the regulatory framework, both in the legal grounds and in the description of legal inconsistencies, **of the articles of the Anti-Dumping Agreement which in Brazil's view were infringed by Resolution ME 574/2000.**

14. Thus, in Argentina's view the case brought before MERCOSUR and the arbitral award resulting from the complaint filed by Brazil cannot be overlooked, not because of *res judicata*, but because of the pertinence of Brazil's conduct in filing of the complaint twice successively, and because the MERCOSUR regulatory framework comes within the relevant rules applicable to the case under Article 31.3(c) of the Vienna Convention on the Law of Treaties.

---

[12] Intervention by the Argentine Republic at the first meeting of the Panel with the parties, para. 8.
[13] First written submission of Argentina, para. 16.
[14] Third party submission of the EC, para. 7.
[15] Intervention by the Argentine Republic at the meeting of the Panel with the parties, para. 8.
[16] See rebuttal submission of Argentina, para. 2, and para. 18 of this statement by Argentina at the second meeting of the Panel with the parties.

II.3 OTHER PRINCIPLES AND RULES OF PUBLIC INTERNATIONAL LAW APPLICABLE TO THE CASE

15. Argentina would like to provide a few clarifications in connection with Brazil's arguments in the section "Ruling by the MERCOSUL Ad Hoc Arbitral Tribunal" of its rebuttal submission.

16. Firstly, while it is true, as Brazil maintains[17], that Article 1 of the Protocol of Brazil sets forth the scope of the Protocol, Argentina's arguments are directed towards drawing the attention of the Panel to the fact that the dispute brought by Brazil before the WTO had already been heard at the regional level, a fact which must have legal consequences in these proceedings.

17. Indeed, the Panel has a right to be informed of all precedents to the case, and Argentina stresses in that connection that it was Brazil that opted to resort to MERCOSUR to settle the dispute, that invoked and argued its claims on the basis of WTO rules and regulations in defending its case before MERCOSUR, and that avoided any reference to precedent in the request for consultations, the request for the establishment of the Panel, the request for the constitution of the Panel and its first written submission before the WTO.

18. Among the "Preliminary Arguments" of its first written submission to the MERCOSUR Ad Hoc Arbitral Tribunal[18], Argentina requested that "*if it agrees with the Argentine position that there is no MERCOSUR legislation that gives the Tribunal the power to review proceedings with respect to intra-zone dumping and application of anti-dumping duties fully governed by and applied under the domestic law of a State party, the Tribunal terminate its action.*" In other words, throughout the conduct of the proceedings it kept Brazil informed of its dissenting view that the matter was not being settled in the appropriate forum.

19. Nevertheless Brazil, knowing full well that the MERCOSUR regulatory framework did not include any express provision on this subject, persisted in submitting its dispute in that forum, and rather than accepting the unfavourable result, initiated proceedings before the WTO.

20. Argentina agrees with Brazil that the Ad Hoc Tribunal set up to hear the case brought by Brazil before MERCOSUR had to apply MERCOSUR regulations, but in this case it happens to be Brazil itself that has decided to include in its submission to that forum - both in the legal grounds and in the description of legal inconsistencies - the alleged violations of the WTO Anti-Dumping Agreement arising from Resolution 574/2000. In this connection, Brazil argued that "*[t]he provisions of the WTO - AD Agreement were incorporated in community legislation by DEC CMC No. 11/97 (Regulatory Framework, RF). Since by definition of Article 1, the RF is in conformity with the WTO-AD Agreement, failure to comply with the former implies failure to comply with the latter. Furthermore, should the RF disciplines not be applicable for some legal reason that excludes such application, the provisions of the WTO AD Agreement would apply pursuant to Article 19 of the Protocol of Brasilia (PB) as 'applicable principles and rules of international law'. The rules of the WTO Anti-*

---

[17] Rebuttal of Brazil, Section III, "Ruling by the MERCOSUL Ad Hoc Arbitral Tribunal", para. 23.
[18] Arbitral Award (para. 50).

Dumping Agreement are binding for WTO Members, which include the States parties to MERCOSUR".[19] (Emphasis added).

21. It is particularly important in this case to point out that "[t]he tribunal confirms that it is right to apply the Protocol of Brazil in the case at issue"[20], and that, furthermore, *"[t]he Tribunal shall settle the dispute in the framework of the subject as defined above. To that end, it proposes to address and decide on the following questions in order: (...) (b) if there are no MERCOSUR regulations expressly covering this subject, what is the consequence? What legal system should apply?"*[21] The same Tribunal then goes on to state that it was resorting to the WTO Anti-Dumping Agreement, given that *"[i]n this situation, the WTO Anti-Dumping Agreement stands as an appropriate reference, not as MERCOSUR legislation, which it is not, but by virtue of Article 19 of the Protocol of Brasilia as an applicable principle of international law (Cfr. Second Arbitral Tribunal, paragraphs 59 et. seq., for a clarification of the concept of subsidies), in this case to shed light on the meaning and purpose of anti-dumping proceedings."*[22]

22. In conclusion, Argentina repeats that Brazil's conduct in bringing the same case twice successively in different fora - first in the framework of MERCOSUR, and then, faced with an unfavourable result, before the WTO - claiming violations of the same provisions of the WTO Anti-Dumping Agreement in both cases, is in breach of the principle of good faith which calls for compliance with treaties - both the agreements concluded in the framework of MERCOSUR and the obligations assumed under the WTO; and as a result of Brazil's conduct we have a situation of estoppel.[23]

23. In this connection, Argentina rejects Brazil's arguments concerning the Protocol of Olivos.[24] Argentina repeats[25] that the Protocol of Olivos confirms Brazil's previous conduct with respect to the acceptance of awards and their scope, and from that point of view invalidates the complaint against Argentina that Brazil is now trying to substantiate on the basis of the DSU.

II.4 RELEVANT RULE OF PUBLIC INTERNATIONAL LAW

24. Argentina repeats[26] that the regulatory framework of MERCOSUR and the legal consequences deriving from the application of the Protocol of Brasilia by the Ad Hoc Arbitral Tribunal in the case at issue are relevant rules of public international law within the meaning of Article 31.3(c) of the *Vienna Convention on the Law on Treaties.*

25. Argentina respectfully requests the Panel to take into consideration the actions taken and the **regulations applied within the framework of MERCOSUR**, since the fulfilment of obligations under the agreements covered by the WTO cannot

---

[19] Submission of Brazil before MERCOSUR (reference to paragraph 30 of the Arbitral Award).
[20] Arbitral award (para. 101).
[21] *Ibid.,* para. 109.
[22] *Ibid.,* para. 159.
[23] Rebuttal submission of Argentina, para. 20.
[24] Rebuttal submission of Brazil, section entitled "Ruling by the MERCOSUL Ad Hoc Arbitral Tribunal", paras. 32, 33 and 34.
[25] Rebuttal submission of Argentina, para. 20, footnote 20.
[26] *Ibid.,* paras. 28 and 29.

Report of the Panel

be considered in isolation[27], but rather as one more element in the international regulatory system governing relations between WTO Members, which in this case are also States parties to MERCOSUR.

26. In particular, the "*Conclusions*" and "*Decision*" sections and paragraphs of the Arbitral Award[28] are of special significance in that they involve a ruling on the claims and allegations of Brazil which the Panel should take into account in determining the scope, in the case at issue, of the Argentine obligations with respect to the Anti-Dumping Agreement, refraining from ruling on them.

III. SUBSTANTIVE ASPECTS OF THE INVESTIGATION

III.1 INITIATION OF THE INVESTIGATION

27. Argentina repeats that the information submitted by the applicant to the investigating authority contained sufficient evidence within the meaning of Article 5.2 of the Anti-Dumping Agreement and that it represented what was reasonably available to the applicant.

28. Similarly, Argentina repeats that the applicant for the initiation of an investigation is not required to prove beyond all doubt the existence of dumping, injury and causal link, since the final determination of these elements is the responsibility of the investigating authority, which conducts a thorough investigation once the initiation has been decided.

29. Argentina also repeats that there are different standards of evidence according to the different stages of the proceedings. We recall, in this respect, the statements of the panels in *United States - Measures Affecting Imports of Softwood Lumber from Canada*[29] and *Mexico - Anti-Dumping Investigation of High Fructose Corn Syrup (HFCS) from the United States*[30] reproduced in paragraphs 38 and 44 of our first written submission.

30. Thus, the implementing authority having examined the accuracy and adequacy of the evidence submitted, verifying that it contained indications of dumping that was causing injury to the domestic industry, it concluded that this evidence was sufficient to declare the initiation of the investigation.

31. Argentina repeats in this connection that Article 5.3 does not impose any obligation to conduct, at that stage, a thorough investigation, since the standard of "sufficient" evidence to justify the initiation of an investigation is considerably lower than the standard required for the decision to apply a preliminary or definitive measure.

32. As regards Brazil's claim that Argentina failed to comply with Article 5.7 of the AD Agreement simply because the reports respectively establishing the existence of dumping and the existence of injury bear different dates, we repeat that this difference of dates does not in any way mean that the authority, in its decision to

---

[27] See rebuttal submission of Argentina, para. 15.
[28] Arbitral Award, "III. Conclusions" and "IV. Decision".
[29] WT/DS236, para. 332.
[30] WT/DS132/R, para. 7.76.

initiate the investigation, did not simultaneously consider the evidence in both reports.

33. With respect to Brazil's claim that Argentina failed to comply with Article 5.8 of the AD Agreement in that it should have rejected the application for initiation of the investigation because the application had failed to demonstrate injury, Argentina refers to its statements in this connection in its written submissions, its oral statement and its reply to questions 16 and 17 of the Panel.

34. We repeat in this connection that with respect to the submission of new evidence, under the relevant Argentine legislation the competent authority is required to intervene once again in the proceedings if any new developments occur or come to its knowledge. In this case, the additional submission by the applicant introduced new items of evidence which called for a further intervention by the CNCE at the request of the competent bodies and in strict conformity with the law.

III.2 CONDUCT OF AN APPROPRIATE INVESTIGATION - EVIDENTIARY AND PUBLIC NOTICE REQUIREMENTS

ARTICLE 12.1

35. Argentina reaffirms that the investigating authorities acted in accordance with the requirement laid down in Article 12.1 to give public notice and to notify the interested party *known to the investigating authority to have an interest therein*, as well as the Government of Brazil. Indeed, we repeat that it would have been impossible to notify parties whose interest in the investigation was not known. We refer in this connection to Argentina's replies to questions 25 and 26 of the Panel.

36. Argentina reiterates that throughout the proceedings it provided the Government of Brazil with facts concerning the application through its Chargé d'Affaires in Argentina[31], with a view to obtaining its cooperation in identifying the *producers-exporters interested in the investigation*. Similarly, Argentina has noted that although invited[32], no representative of the Government of Brazil attended the information meeting held on 25 February 1999 to which all parties potentially interested in participating in the proceedings were invited and at which officials from the Directorate of Unfair Competition replied to questions from those who attended, nor is there any record that any interested party attended the meeting.

37. This is why it is difficult to understand how Brazil can try to deny any responsibility in this respect by stating in paragraph 50 of its rebuttal submission that Argentina never requested Brazil's cooperation in providing the address or contact information of the companies whose interest in the investigation was not known. Indeed, the means of exporters were mentioned, but this did not, in itself, constitute an "identification" that made it possible to send the questionnaires. As Argentina stated in its reply to question 26 of the Panel, this does not imply shifting the burden to Brazil, but rather, it represents an attempt to obtain through Brazil the participation of the Brazilian exporters during the investigation and from the outset as provided for in Article 10.

---

[31] Note SSCE No.121 of 1 February 1999, provided as Annex ARG-III.
[32] Record of 25 February 1999, Annex ARG-VI.

Report of the Panel

38. We reaffirm in this connection that only through the request from the company INTERAMERICANA COMERCIAL S.R.L. did Argentina learn of the interest of the seven other exporting enterprises mentioned by Brazil.[33] In fact, having determined the adequacy of the request and to ensure full participation of the producers/exporters, even though the Brazilian Government had not singled out specific exporters, the implementing authority asked certain Brazilian companies and institutions to provide reports (Comaves, Catarinense, Minuano, Chapeco and Perdiagao) concerning actual sales, prices for kilogramme of poultry actually paid, etc.[34], and asked the company INTERAMERICANA COMERCIAL S.R.L. to provide a list of addresses of those firms.[35]

ARTICLE 6.1.1

39. In keeping with the evidence already presented, Argentina reaffirms that it granted the Brazilian exporters a period of thirty days to reply to the questionnaires of the DCD. This is proven by the fact that the said questionnaires were provided during the information meeting held on 25 February 1999, with a deadline for submission to the DCD of 29 March 1999. Similarly, as has been documented, due consideration was given to the requests for extensions, which were granted whenever practicable.[36]

40. Regarding the Brazilian claims in paragraphs 59 and 60 of its rebuttal, Argentina agrees with Brazil that because of the large volume of information requested in the questionnaires, the exporters and producers relied on a minimum period of thirty days to allocate the necessary resources in order to respond.

41. However, Argentina does not understand how Brazil can adduce in this respect that there were seven exporters that did not enjoy their right of defense when, as stated in Article 143 of Argentina's first written submission, the replies to the questionnaires received from those exporters clearly show that two of them (CCLP and CHAPECO)[37] did not export to Argentina during the period under investigation, while the other four (MINUANO, COMAVES, PENABRANCA and PERDIGAO) demonstrated their lack of interest in the investigation by not providing any information whatsoever, not even following the expiry of the deadline and the extension granted.[38]

42. This is why, contrary to Brazil's claim, Argentina reaffirms that the investigating authority granted the Brazilian exporters a deadline longer than that specified in the Agreement to reply to the DCD's questionnaires, having due regard for the exporters' requests for extensions, which were granted whenever practicable, pursuant to Article 6.1.1.

43. It also bears repeating that the CNCE delivered the injury questionnaire to five exporters, in full conformity with the provisions of Article 6.1, since the exports to Argentina notified by the Brazilian companies that replied to the CNCE

---

[33] Annex ARG-VII.
[34] *Ibid.*
[35] Annexes ARG-VIII, IX and X.
[36] First written submission, paras. 130 to 132, and Annex ARG-XI.
[37] See Annexes ARG-XXVI and XIV.
[38] See Annexes ARG-VIII, XV, XVI, XVII, XVIII, XIX and XX, and first written submission, para. 133.

questionnaire for exporters represented more than half of the total imports of whole eviscerated poultry from Brazil - so that the claim made by Brazil in paragraph 35 of its rebuttal submission is absolutely unfounded.

44. Thus, in addition to stressing that Brazil never questioned the circumstances now being complained of in its various statements in the course of the investigation, Argentina reaffirms that the implementing authority acted in full conformity with Article 6.1.1.

ARTICLE 6.1.2

45. Argentina reaffirms that the authorities acted consistently with the obligation laid down in Article 6.1.2 in that they promptly made available to the other interested parties participating in the investigation evidence presented in writing by the interested parties, and the other interested parties could at all times consult the file and obtain a copy thereof.

46. Consequently, Argentina repeats that if the parties with a supposed interest in the investigation did not participate, as stated before it was they, and not the implementing authority, that failed to defend their own interests. Indeed, it would have been impossible for the investigating authorities to place evidence presented by the interested parties at the disposal of the seven mentioned Brazilian companies, since those companies did not even join as interested parties. Thus, Argentina submits that it acted consistently with Article 6.1.2.

ARTICLE 6.2

47. In accordance with the above considerations, Argentina reaffirms that all of the interested parties had full opportunity to defend their interests throughout the investigation: they were given access to the proceedings, and their right of access to the records was in no way impaired, let alone their right of defence. Thus, the investigating authorities met the obligation laid down in Article 6.2. Moreover, the authorities allowed any party that considered itself as having an interest to present itself at the investigation, expressing that interest.

48. This determination on the part of the authorities to offer interested parties the broadest possible opportunity not only to participate in the proceedings, but also to gather the information needed to ensure an accurate final determination, is evidenced by the record of the submissions made by the participating firms and the conclusions reached on the basis of those submissions, and in particular the work of the Technical Department in requesting and putting together the documentation.[39]

49. Argentina therefore considers that the investigating authorities complied with the obligation laid down in Article 6.2.

ARTICLE 6.1.3

50. Argentina reaffirms that the competent authorities satisfied the requirements of Article 6.1.3 by providing Brazilian exporters and the Brazilian Government with the full text of the written application as soon as the investigation was initiated. In this connection, the Argentine authorities satisfied the obligation to provide by

---

[39] See Annex ARG-XXII and Annexes ARG-XXI, XX, XVI, XVIII and XIII.

making the records of the proceedings available to the authorized interested parties. Moreover, from the moment notification of initiation of the investigation appeared in the Official Bulletin, interested parties with accredited status were able to gain immediate access to the records of the proceedings.

51. Moreover, and notwithstanding the above, once the initiation of the investigation had been decided upon, the Argentine authorities notified that fact to the Brazilian Chargé d'Affaires in Argentina[40], pursuant to Article 6 of the Anti-Dumping Agreement.

ARTICLES 6.8 and 12.2.2

52. Regarding the treatment of the information provided by the exporters during the investigation, Argentina has repeatedly stated throughout these proceedings that this information was used to the extent that it complied with the formal requirements laid down by Argentine law, which were known to all of the parties.

53. Argentina once again repeats in this connection that the Brazilian claim that its exporters complied in supplying all of the information requested by the investigating authority, and that the investigating authority decided for no reason to reject that information and use only the information provided by the applicant, is untrue. Argentina has shown that wherever the information supplied by the exporters was accompanied by the documentary evidence needed, at a minimum, to corroborate the information they had provided, that information was used.

54. As regards the information used for export prices, Argentina reaffirms that this was official data from the General Customs Administration, which is the body responsible for supervising and controlling all foreign trade transactions. In cases such as CATERINENESE and FRANGOSUL, we repeat that the information was not used simply because, in the case of the former, what was provided was insufficient[41], while in the case of the latter, not only was the information insufficient, but it was submitted after the expiry of the deadline for its use.[42]

55. Argentina has also repeatedly stated, with respect to the claim that the authorities should have conducted on-the-spot verifications of the information provided by the exporters, that this is something which is left to the discretion of the investigating authority, and is not an obligation under the AD Agreement.

III.3 FAIR COMPARISON, INJURY, CAUSAL LINK AND PUBLIC NOTICE

ARTICLES 2.4, 3.1, 3.4, 3.5 and 12.2.2

Excessive burden of proof on exporters

56. Regarding Brazil's claim that the implementing authority imposed an excessive burden of proof on the exporters, Argentina would like to repeat what it stated in its first written submission.

---

[40] See Annex ARG-III.
[41] First written submission of Argentina, para. 203.
[42] *Ibid.*, paras. 187 to 200.

57. Brazil's argument is contradictory in that the complaint in some cases has been that the implementing authority did not request more information, while in other cases the complaint was that too much information was requested. It should be noted that when the implementing authority requested further information, it was for a particular purpose relating to the determination of normal value and export value.

58. It should also be remembered that the implementing authority took account of the comments of the parties to the effect that the large volume of operations by enterprises on the local market made it difficult for them to provide documentary evidence of all of the transactions, and in order to avoid imposing an excessive burden on exporters, only requested the submission of evidence for those transactions chosen on the basis of a statistical sample for which it was essential to have certain basic information.

59. As regards Brazil's statement in paragraph 94 under claim 26 of its rebuttal submission, it would appear that Brazil attributes more relevance to the information on how to make a fair comparison than the evidence required to make a precise determination of normal value and export value, which needs to be done before a fair comparison can be made. Without evidence of normal value and export value from exporters, it is impossible to make a proper fair comparison considering physical differences that affect price comparability.

60. Similarly, with respect to Brazil's statement in paragraph 95 under claim 26 of its rebuttal to the effect that it did not request the information required to make a fair comparison considering physical differences, Argentina would like to point out that the exporters denied that in Brazil, poultry was sold with head and feet, but never contributed any evidence to the file to invalidate the fair comparison put forward and substantiated by the applicant. Similarly, it should be stressed that in an investigation, the parties can supply all of the information and evidence they consider relevant without its being requested by the implementing authority.

61. Concerning Brazil's claim that an excessive burden was imposed on exporters because they were asked for information for years that were not included in the investigation period, Argentina repeats that the Agreement neither defines nor limits the period for collecting information, nor does it define or limit the actual period under investigation. The implementing authority therefore has discretion to request the documentation it deems necessary for the purposes of determining the existence of dumping, and may require further information when this is necessary to guarantee due process to the interested parties.

62. In conclusion, we note that the requests for information by the authority were supported by the requirements imposed under Article 6.1 and 6.2, i.e. to guarantee the parties' right of legitimate defence. These two paragraphs also enable the interested parties to provide all of the evidence which they consider relevant in the course of the investigation, i.e. this is a right of the interested parties.

63. Regarding Brazil's statement concerning the opinion of the EC in paragraph 97 under claim 26 of its rebuttal, Argentina points out that it agrees fully with the interpretation of the Communities, and consequently we understand Brazil to have erred in claiming inconsistency with Article 2.4 under its claim 26.

64. As regards the adjustment made by the implementing authority, Argentina repeats that this was done correctly and on the basis of the evidence and the methodology provided by the applicant. Based on the evidence provided, the adjustment was clearly necessary - poultry with head and feet sold on the São Paolo

market and poultry exported to Argentina without head and feet. Similarly, as we stated earlier, the Brazilian exporters did not provide any evidence to the contrary. Nor did the Brazilian exporters object to the adjustment methodology at any time during the proceedings. We repeat that at the request of the authority, the company JOX sent a note validating the percentage adjustment made by the applicant.

Use of different periods to analyse the injury factors

65. Turning to Brazil's claim that the implementing authority used different periods to evaluate some of the injury factors, Argentina repeats that the use of a longer period for the analysis of certain factors - *in a threat of injury investigation* - than for other factors does not imply, *per se*, that the implementing authority conducted an evaluation of the evidence that was not objective. Argentina's position coincides with the position presented by the United States in its written submission, backed by the Panel in "*United States - Hot-Rolled Steel*".[43]

66. Contrary to what Brazil claims, Argentina considers that the CNCE acted with particular case. Argentina repeats what it said in its first written submission, mainly that the CNCE decided to analyse the trends in imports for the first half of 1999, taking as a basis both international rules and relevant practices in that area which provide that in cases of threat of injury, it is possible to undertake an analysis beyond the period of the investigation in order to find out whether there is a growing trend in imports and, as a result, give the investigation a more substantial factual basis.

67. We recall that the existence of a voluntary agreement between the parties from October 1998 to March 1999 meant that it was necessary to analyse imports without the effects produced by that agreement, so the analysis was extended until June 1999, both for imports and for all apparent consumption variables.

68. In this connection, we refer to Record No. 576, in which the Commission duly stated that if there had been no such agreement between the exporters and the Argentine producers, " ... *in 1998 imports would have increased even more and, subsequent to the investigation period, in the first half of 1999, the upward trend would have continued ...*".

Evaluation of all of the factors

69. Argentina repeats what it has said throughout these proceedings, namely that the implementing authority acted consistently with the provisions of the Anti-Dumping Agreement by evaluating, in respect of injury, all the factors listed in Article 3.4 and their impact on prices of the like domestic product as well as their impact on the domestic industry concerned.

70. We recall, in this connection, what Argentina stated in paragraph 277 of its first written submission, namely that the applicant submitted information on the productivity situation in the sector which showed that, at the initiation of the investigation, the Argentine poultry industry was on an equal footing with the Brazilian industry and also with the leading producers at the global level[44], a

---

[43] WT/DS184.
[44] Record 576, folios 12, 13, 14, 20, and Technical Report, folios 26, 28, 29, 30 and 95 as well as Tables 1, 11, 12, 13 and 14 of Annex I to the Technical Report (EXHIBIT BRA-14).

statement which was not questioned during the course of the investigation either by the Brazilian exporting companies or by importers in the Argentine market.

71. At the same time, we reiterate that the Argentine industry's costs are comparable to those of the most competitive producers at the international level. This was achieved through a large-scale programme to restructure the industry and adapt production[45], which was affected by the uncertainty caused in the local market by the importation of Brazilian products, particularly since Brazil utilized the Argentine market as an alternative market in order to resolve problems of local or foreign demand. We recall that the extent of Brazil's production capacity and the generation of exportable surpluses mean that Brazil can easily redirect its effort to third markets when there are domestic or external imbalances, despite the large size of its own domestic market.[46]

72. We refer, in connection with the above considerations, to paragraphs 283-285 of Argentina's first written submission, which describe the characteristics of the Argentine poultry sector as regards the export coefficient, consumption, demand, demand profile, comparative price behaviour[47], sensitivity to minor variations in supply, etc., as well as Brazil's status as price fixer in the Argentine market, even with relatively low volumes, owing to the enormous potential for increasing shipments on very short notice, all of which necessarily led to price adjustments for the domestic sector.

73. Argentina therefore repeats that the decline in domestic prices in a context of sustained growth in apparent consumption owing to a change in consumer habits can only be explained by the existence of imports under unfair competition.[48]

74. Regarding Brazil's claim in paragraph 113 of its rebuttal (claim 38), it is difficult to understand how Brazil can fail to see the connection between the information contained in Table 16 of the Technical Report and factors affecting domestic prices, since that Table shows the evolution of price indexes for substitute products, mainly red meat, as well as the general level of activity of price indexes in the most important sectors.[49]

75. Argentina therefore reiterates that the CNCE properly considered all of the factors which, in addition to imports, could have had an effect on the prices of the domestic product. Similarly, given the potential impact on Argentine production, bearing in mind the characteristics of the domestic market and the Brazilian market, the investigating authority correctly evaluated that margins of dumping of 8 and 14 per cent were significant.

Public notice of the final determination

76. Argentina repeats that the public notice of the final determination complied with all of the requirements of the Agreement. Article 12.2 - which introduces Article 12.2.2 of the AD Agreement - stipulates that the findings and conclusions considered material by the investigating authorities shall be published in sufficient detail. In other words, the text of Article 12.2 does not require that all of the findings and

---

[45] See Annex ARG XXXVI.
[46] See Section VI.2 ("MERCOSUR") of the Technical Report (BRA-14).
[47] See the Table on page 21 of Record 576 (EXHIBIT BRA-14).
[48] See Annex ARG-XXXVII.
[49] See EXHIBIT BRA-14.

conclusions be published. Moreover, the authority has the discretion to decide which are the findings and conclusions which it considers relevant for the purposes of publication. Here, Argentina fully agrees with the interpretation by the United States[50] to the effect that not all of the factors listed in Article 3.4 must be published.

III.4 COLLECTION OF ANTI-DUMPING DUTIES

ARTICLE 9.2 and 9.3

77. Argentina reiterates, as it has maintained in the various stages of these proceedings, that the manner in which it applies and collects anti-dumping duties is consistent with the requirements of the Agreement.

78. In light of the claims in Brazil's rebuttal, however, Argentina deems necessary to make a number of comments that will give the Panel all the information it needs to reach a reasoned conclusion on the matter.

79. For clarity's sake, we propose to divide our argument on this issue into two parts, namely:

(a) we shall respond to Brazil's various claims that a violation of Article 9.2 is entirely dependent on a violation of Article 9.3; and

(b) we shall demonstrate that Brazil's claim that Argentina applies anti-dumping duties in a manner inconsistent with the AD Agreement has no basis whatsoever.

80. Starting with point (a), Argentina concurs with Brazil that paragraphs 2 and 3 of Article 9 of the AD Agreement are closely related.[51] On the other hand, Argentina disagrees that a violation of Article 9.2 is entirely dependent on a violation of Article 9.3 of the AD Agreement.

81. The express obligation in Article 9.2 is that duties "*shall be collected in the appropriate amounts*", while Article 9.3 provides that these "*shall not exceed the margin of dumping as established under Article 2*". An anti-dumping duty could therefore hypothetically be collected in an inappropriate amount - i.e. in breach of Article 9.2 therefore - without, however, exceeding the margin of dumping established under Article 2, i.e. without violating Article 9.3.

82. Brazil's analysis, which concludes that any violation of Article 9.2 is dependent on failure to respect the limit specified in Article 9.3, stems from its interpretation that the margin referred to in Article 9.3 is that determined pursuant to Article 2.4.2, which sets out the method to be **used during the investigation phase** to determine the existence of margins of dumping. Brazil hence concludes that the Article 9.2 reference to "appropriate amounts" is the margin of dumping established during that stage in the proceedings.

83. Argentina disagrees with this interpretation, which leads it directly to point (b) of its argument. While Article 2.4.2 is clearly the only provision that explains in detail how a margin of dumping is to be established, what is just as clear is that that same Article limits the application of the provision in question to a specified period, namely "**during the investigation phase**".

---

[50] Written submission by the United States as third party, para. 15.
[51] Second written submission of Brazil, Section VII - "Claims related to the imposition and collection of antidumping duties as a result of the antidumping investigation", para. 40.124, page 22.

84. In focusing exclusively on Articles 9.2 and 9.3 and 2.4.2, Brazil apparently fails to consider other relevant provisions of the anti-dumping regime, which not only should be analysed in order to ascertain the alleged violation but also are those which in fact contain the obligations that Brazil claims Argentina has failed to meet.

85. Contrary to Brazil's claim,[52] there is a difference between the margin of dumping determined during the investigation phase and the anti-dumping duty ultimately established as a result of the investigation. The difference is clear from a full reading and interpretation of the Article in its context, namely not only the AD Agreement in its entirety but also Article VI of the GATT 1994, the implementing provisions of which are set out in detail in the AD Agreement.

86. Article 2.1 of the AD Agreement provides that: *"For the purpose of this Agreement, a product is to be considered as being dumped, i.e. introduced into the commerce of another country at less than its normal value, if the export price of the product exported from one country to another is less than the comparable price, in the ordinary course of trade, for the like product when destined for consumption in the exporting country."*

87. Article VI.1 of the GATT 1994 contains a definition of dumping similar to that in Article 2.1 of the AD Agreement. The relevant part of paragraph VI.2 likewise establishes that:

> *" ... For the purposes of this Article, the margin of dumping is the price difference determined in accordance with the provisions of paragraph 1."*

88. Article 9.1 of the AD Agreement stipulates that: *"The decision whether or not to impose an anti-dumping duty in cases where all requirements for the imposition have been fulfilled, and the decision whether the amount of the anti-dumping duty to be imposed shall be the full margin of dumping or less, are decisions to be made by the authorities of the importing Member. It is desirable that the imposition be permissive in the territory of all Members, and that the duty be less than the margin if such lesser duty would be adequate to remove the injury to the domestic industry."*

89. A reading of the Articles cited above raises a question that is crucial in evaluating Brazil's claim that Article 9.2 is dependent on Article 9.3 of the AD Agreement. The margin of dumping established during the investigation phase does not necessarily have to be equivalent to the anti-dumping duty finally established. In the decision to impose anti-dumping duties, the implementing authority is required to take account not only of irrefutable evidence that the unfair practice has taken place but also of the fact that the duty imposed as a result of the investigation is adequate to remove the injury to the domestic industry attributable to dumping. If definitive anti-dumping duties were established solely on the basis of the margin of dumping established during the investigation, the injury analysis would be irrelevant and hence the provisions of Article VI of the GATT 1994 and Article 9.1 of the AD Agreement would be devoid of all substance.

90. In paragraphs 131 et seq. of its second written submission, Brazil claims, moreover, that both Argentina and Canada erred in their interpretation regarding the absence of restriction on the anti-dumping duty collected. This is not so. Argentina recognizes that the restriction on applying anti-dumping duties is that established in

---

[52] *Ibid.*, para. 127.

Article 9.3, and nothing in Canada's written submission appears to uphold Brazil's interpretation.

91. The point on which both Argentina and Canada agree, and Brazil disagrees, is that nothing in the AD Agreement requires a Member to impose duties limited to the margin of dumping established pursuant to Article 2.4.2, that is, during the investigation phase; and, if it does so, as we said before, the implementing authority should analyse the Article in its entirety, in the light of the objectives contained in Article 9.1 of the AD Agreement and Article VI of the GATT 1994.

92. The hypothesis on which Brazil builds its rejection of Canada's argument that changes in market conditions, or exporters' improved productivity, may create a situation where prices in both markets (the exporter's domestic market and the importer's market) are reduced, is perfectly correct. On the other hand, what is equally correct is that this is but one of many hypothetical situations that could arise and that it provides no answer in respect of the other - also highly likely - situation argued by both Canada and Argentina, under which - if Brazil's claim, i.e. that anti-dumping duties are limited to the margin of dumping found during the investigation phase, were to prevail - an exporter with considerable means to exercise international price discrimination could easily disregard a Member's attempt to halt an unfair practice, while deeming the measure imposed to be inconsistent, by practising even greater dumping. Hence Argentina sees nothing in the AD Agreement to support Brazil's position.

93. The situation illustrated by Brazil could in fact easily be remedied through provisions laid down in the AD Agreement for that purpose. Article 11.2 establishes a procedure for dealing with a change in circumstances such as Brazil's example of a drop in prices in both the export and the import market. And under Article 9.3.2, exporters may request the refund of all duties paid in excess.

94. In paragraph 41 of its Rebuttal, Brazil further contends that the minimum export prices determined in Resolution 574/2000 do not qualify as anti-dumping duties, since they do not reflect the normal value and export prices as provided by the exporters and examined by the investigating authority.

95. Argentina fails to understand Brazil's grounds for such a claim. On the one hand, Brazil itself provided, as an annex to its first written submission[53], the various technical reports that were prepared by the bodies in charge of the investigation and were reportedly used by the implementing authority as a basis for determining the applicable duties.

96. On the other, Argentina has also demonstrated that, in accordance with Article VI.2 of the GATT 1994 and Article 9.1 of the AD Agreement, the minimum prices for each of the exporters subject to individual anti-dumping duties and for the "other" exporters were set in amounts lower than the margin of dumping established as a result of the investigation.[54]

97. Here again, Brazil appears to be seeking to induce the Panel to find that the system of variable amounts used by Argentina to set anti-dumping duties on a prospective basis is inconsistent with the AD Agreement.

---

[53] See mainly EXHIBIT BRA-15.
[54] See first written submission of Argentina, para. 316, and intervention by the Argentine Republic at the first meeting of the Panel with the parties, para. 57.

98.   Argentina is therefore compelled to repeat that the AD Agreement contains no provision as to how the Members should assess their anti-dumping duties and that, in practice, they use any of three systems.[55] Moreover, Article 9, entitled "*Imposition and Collection of Anti-Dumping Duties*", describes the manner in which those duties could be collected (on a prospective or a retrospective basis) but does not specify the system to be used by the Members for that purpose.

99.   What Article 9.1 does specify is that "[i]t is desirable that the imposition be permissive in the territory of all Members, and that the duty be less than the margin if such lesser duty would be adequate to remove the injury to the domestic industry".

100.   To summarize, and on the basis of the foregoing, Argentina wishes clearly to point out that:

(i)   Since Article VI of the GATT 1994 and Article 2 of the AD Agreement define what dumping is, they also define what should be considered a margin of dumping, the latter being nothing more than a manner of expressing the former, except in the case of specific provisions that apply to particular stages such as that indicated in Article 2.4.2 of the AD Agreement;

(ii)   the limit imposed by Article 9.3 of the AD Agreement on the imposition of anti-dumping duties therefore refers to Article 2 in its entirety and not to Article 2.4.2, as Brazil maintains;

(iii)   the anti-dumping duty imposed as a result of an investigation conducted in accordance with the AD Agreement does not necessarily have to be equivalent to the margin of dumping established during the investigation phase;

(iv)   the practice of WTO Members, in the absence of specific provisions in the AD Agreement, has established the use of three systems for applying anti-dumping duties, one of them being the system of variable amounts used by Argentina.

101.   Consequently, Argentina respectfully requests the Panel to find that it has acted consistently with the WTO AD Agreement in assessing and collecting the duties imposed in this case, and to reject Brazil's claim of inconsistency with Article 9.2 and 9.3.

IV.   PLEADINGS

102.   In the light of the arguments put forward in the sections above, Argentina respectfully requests the Panel:

(1)   In keeping with the reasoning developed in Section II and as already mentioned in paragraph 26 of this Submission, to refrain from ruling on the 41 claims of inconsistency with various provisions of the Agreement on the Implementation of Article VI of the General Agreement on Tariffs and Trade 1994 (Anti-Dumping Agreement) submitted by Brazil.

---

[55] See first written submission of Argentina, para. 315, and intervention by the Argentine Republic at the first meeting of the Panel with the parties, para. 54.

Report of the Panel

103. Should the Panel decide not to accede to the above request by the Argentine Republic, as set out in Section II:26 of this Submission and in the light of the arguments developed in Section III, it is respectfully requested to:

    (2) Reject Brazil's claim that Resolution 574/2000 of the Ministry of the Economy of the Argentine Republic is inconsistent with:

- Article 5.2, 5.3, 5.7 and 5.8 of the Anti-Dumping Agreement;
- Article 12.1 of the Anti-Dumping Agreement;
- Article 6.1.1, 6.1.2, 6.1.3, 6.2 and 6.8, and paragraphs 5, 6, and 7 of Annex II, and Article 6.9 and 6.10 of the Anti-Dumping Agreement;
- Article 2.4 and 2.4.2 of the Anti-Dumping Agreement;
- Article 3.1, 3.2, 3.4 and 3.5 of the Anti-Dumping Agreement;
- Article 4.1 of the Anti-Dumping Agreement;
- Article 9.2 and 9.3 of the Anti-Dumping Agreement;

as well as the various claims relating to Article 12.2.2.

104. Reject Brazil's request for the immediate repeal of Resolution 574/2000 imposing the definitive anti-dumping duties.

ANNEX B-6

REPLIES OF ARGENTINA TO QUESTIONS FROM THE PANEL - SECOND MEETING

(28 November 2002)

Note: The Panel has referred to claim numbers for ease of reference only.

Questions to Argentina

Preliminary issues

66. Regarding para. 13 of Argentina's second submission ("ASS"), what was the "statement of fact" (point I) allegedly made by Brazil? Please explain how Argentina relied in good faith upon that alleged statement (point III).

Reply

Firstly, Argentina considers that Brazil's conduct in successively filing its case and activating dispute settlement proceedings in different fora, first in MERCOSUR and then in the WTO - particularly in view of the precedents described in Argentina's first written submission[1], i.e. recourse to the dispute settlement mechanism under the Protocol of Brasilia to settle conflicts with other MERCOSUR States parties and compliance with the content and scope of the arbitral awards in all of the disputes - provides statements of fact which meet the requirement of being clear, unambiguous, voluntary, unconditional and authorized, the essential elements of estoppel under the definition provided in paragraph 13 of Argentina's submission.

In paragraph 20 of its rebuttal submission[2], Argentina sets out the elements which are present in the current dispute brought by Brazil before the WTO. Among these elements, the last sentence of subparagraph (iii) of paragraph 20 states that: "Consequently Brazil's previous conduct with respect to the acceptance of awards, confirmed by the signature of the Protocol of Olivos, invalidates the complaint against Argentina that Brazil is now trying to substantiate on the basis of the DSU."

Moreover, the fact that Brazil signed the Protocol of Olivos on 18 February 2002 - by which it expressly accepted the choice of forum clause - and then, seven days later, on 25 February 2002, requested the establishment of a Panel in the current dispute, displays a clear contradiction in its conduct, in which Argentina had had full confidence, both countries being member States of MERCOSUR; and Argentina is

---

[1] First written submission of Argentina, 29 August 2002, paras. 18-22 and corresponding footnotes.
[2] Rebuttal submission of Argentina, 17 October 2002, para. 20.

now suffering the negative impact of this change of position.[3] This fact was also raised in the submissions of the EC[4] and Paraguay[5] as third parties.

67.   At para. 13 of ASS, Argentina asserts that the principle of estoppel is a general principle of international law. Is the principle of estoppel a "customary rule[] of interpretation of public international law" within the meaning of Article 3.2 of the DSU? Please explain. Is a general principle of international law the same as a rule of interpretation of international law? Please explain.

Reply

The rules of interpretation of public international law to which Article 3.2 of the DSU refers concern Article 31 of the Vienna Convention on the Law of Treaties.

Article 31 of the Vienna Convention sets forth the rules to be followed with respect to interpretation; and the rules of interpretation are applied by the adjudicating body taking account, in all cases, of the sources of law.

The sources that may be applied to interpretation are set forth in Article 38 of the Statute of the International Court of Justice, which lists, as a principal source, treaties, international custom, and the general principles of international law.

Consequently, Argentina understands the principle of estoppel, as a general principle of international law, to constitute a legitimate source to which any international tribunal called upon to settle a dispute may have recourse.

In the current dispute, it is in this light that Argentina considers that the principle of estoppel argument should be taken into account by the Panel in carrying out its functions under the DSU. This is in keeping with the obligation laid down in Article 3.2 of the DSU to clarify the existing provisions of the agreements in accordance with customary rules of interpretation of public international law.

Moreover, Argentina repeats what it stated in its second written submission[6], namely that other panels have already examined the principle of estoppel in past disputes: "*European Communities - Asbestos*"[7] and "*Guatemala - Cement*"[8].

Claim 1

68.   In reply to question 6, Argentina refers to the Aves & Ovos review. If the applicant submitted more extracts from that review than are contained in Exhibit BRA-1, please provide a copy of such additional extracts. Please explain precisely how information from the Aves & Ovos review, as supplied by the applicant, supported the need for a 9.09 per cent adjustment to normal value.

---

[3]   In fact, Argentina has already approved the Protocol of Olivos. On 9 October 2002, the National Congress adopted the Protocol of Olivos by Law 25.663, promulgated by the Executive through Decree 2091/02 of 18 October 2002 and published in Official Bulletin of the Republic of Argentina No. 30008 of 21 October 2002.

[4]   Third party submission of the European Communities, 9 September 2002, para. 17 and footnote 17.

[5]   Third party submission of Paraguay, 9 September 2002, para. 8.

[6]   Second written submission of Argentina, 17 October 2002, paras. 17, 18 and 19.

[7]   WT/DS135/R, *European Communities - Measures Affecting Asbestos and Asbestos-Containing Products*, Report adopted on 5 April 2001, para. 8.60.

[8]   WT/DS156/R, *Guatemala - Definitive Anti-Dumping Measure on Grey Portland Cement from Mexico*, Report adopted on 17 November 2000, DSR 2000:XI, 5295, para. 8.23.

Furthermore, on what basis did the investigating authority assign the same value to the head and feet as to other parts of the chicken?

Reply

We stress that the review Aves & Ovos does not provide any information with respect to the 9.09 per cent adjustment carried out. The mention of the said review in Argentina's reply to question 6 of the Panel following the first meeting was made in connection with the listing of evidence provided by the applicant in its application. As regards the question concerning the basis on which the investigating authority assigned the same value to the head and feet as to the other parts of the chicken, we note once again that the head and feet were not considered to have the same value as the other parts of the animal for the purposes of assessing the adjustment. On the contrary the 9.09 per cent adjustment is the result of an evaluation of the specific recovery of heads and feet.

Claim 2

69. Regarding Argentina's reply to question 12, the Panel notes that the extract from the JOX document quoted by Argentina is included under the heading "Frango Vivo"? Is there a similar statement for eviscerated poultry? What does it meant to say that "the price remains on very firm ground"?

Reply

No, the JOX publication specifically refers to live poultry. Nevertheless, the reference to the words "production on the parallel market within São Paulo is sharply lower, so that the price remains on very firm ground" relates to the fact that live poultry is the fundamental and principle input for the product under investigation. Thus, it is perfectly reasonable, at this stage prior to the opening of the investigation, to deduce that if the price of the input remains essentially unaltered, the price of the end-product - i.e. the product under investigation - will not vary substantially.

In other words, the phrase "so that the price remains on very firm ground" means that the price would remain essentially unaltered, thus constituting an acceptable element at this stage prior to the investigation.

Claim 3

70. When did the Secretary receive Act No. 405 from the CNCE (dated 7 January 1998)? When did the Secretary receive the report from the ADPCDS (also dated 7 January 1998)?

Reply

The Secretary of Industry, Trade and Mining received Record No. 405 on 9 January 1998, and the DCD Report on Dumping on 27 January 1998.

71. Regarding the first sentence of the third paragraph of Argentina's reply to question 16, what is meant by the phrase "in keeping with the requirements of the application on 17 February 1998"? What precisely are the "requirements of the application"?

Reply

The requirements of the application are those contained in form 349 provided in Annex ARG-XXXIX. The meaning of the phrase is that on 17 February 1998, the applicants provided updated information on the basis of what was requested in the mentioned form 349. This information, on the basis of a legal finding by the relevant ministerial department and in conformity with Law No. 19549 on Administrative Procedures, was transmitted to the CNCE with the instruction that it be analysed. The analysis resulted in the issue by the CNCE of Record No. 464 and the corresponding Technical Report.

Claim 10

72. How and when did the Authority obtain the addresses of the Brazilian exporters which were contacted in February 1999? If those addresses were obtained from a document on the record of the investigation, please provide a copy of this document.

Reply

The addresses of the producers/exporters notified in February 1999 were provided by telephone through the importers interested in the investigation. Having learned of the initiation of the investigation through the Official Bulletin, they contacted the investigating authority and provided the said addresses.

73. Please comment on para. 36 of Brazil's Second Oral Statement.

Reply

With respect to paragraph 36 of Brazil's Statement, we refer to what Argentina has already stated in connection with Article 6.1.1, namely that the parties interested in the investigation were given ample opportunity to participate, with due regard for the requests for extensions that were submitted.

Claim 11

74. Following on from Argentina's reply to question 29, was all of the information contained in the application sent to both the DCD and the CNCE, or did they only receive those parts of the application dealing with dumping and injury respectively?

Reply

Both entities received the same application, with the same information. Upon submitting an application for the initiation of an investigation, the applicant had to complete the form approved by Resolution No. 349 of the former Secretariat for Industry and Trade before the former Under-Secretariat for Foreign Trade (SSCE). In keeping with Articles 36 to 40 of Decree No. 2121/94, the application was filed with the former SSCE, which transmitted a complete copy thereof to the CNCE so that the latter could make an injury determination.

The CNCE received, on 9 September 1997, a copy of the application for the initiation of the investigation filed by CEPA with the SSCE on 2 September 1997. The two submissions are identical, and the submission transmitted to the CNCE can be found in Section I of file CNCE No. 43/1997 (folios 2 to 284). Thus, both entities had at their disposal complete copies of the application for measures submitted by CEPA.

Claim 15

75. Regarding the second sentence of Argentina's reply to question 39, what precisely is the "procedure" (for supporting documentation) followed by the investigating authority? How was an interested party to know what supporting documentation it was required to provide? Where exactly has the "procedure" been specified? Where exactly is the request for supporting documentation set forth? Please provide copies of the relevant sources.

Reply

Regarding the procedure followed by the investigating authority to obtain supporting documentation, attached to the questionnaire are instructions explaining how it should be completed and stating that it should be accompanied by supporting documentation. At the same time, the instructions state that where it is not possible to provide supporting documentation, the source of the information should be indicated. By supporting documentation, the authority means documentation that backs the statements or arguments of the interested parties. For example, if the implementing authority is expected to make an adjustment for freight, it would be helpful for the interested party to attach the contract with the shipping company or any other documentation at its disposal which records the value or percentage that should be discounted for freight.

These instructions can be found in the first part of the questionnaire to be completed by the exporter.

A blank copy of the questionnaire for exporters is provided as Annex ARG-LXIII.

Claim 20

76. Regarding question 43, please indicate precisely what normal value data Catarinense was asked to provide. Please specify the document(s) in which the request was made. Furthermore, for what period of time was Catarinense asked to provide the relevant normal value data?

Reply

The information that the company Catarinense was asked to supply was the information requested in Note DCD No. 273-001065/99, provided by Brazil in Exhibit BRA-13, in which it can be seen that the period for which the information was requested was 1998 - January 1999. We recall in this connection that independently of the documentation requested, in the last note sent by the implementing authority - Note DCD No. 273-001321/99 provided in Exhibit BRA-27 - the companies were reminded that they were to comply with the requirements of the National Law on Administrative Procedures, particularly as regards certification of legal status, a basic prerequisite for a party to be considered in an investigation.

77. With regard to Catarinense's normal value data, Argentina asserts that those data were submitted in an aggregate form. However, it is apparently stated in Section VII.3.2 of the Final Dumping Determination that Catarinense

Report of the Panel

had submitted information on sales made in the domestic market corresponding to 1998 and January 1999 disaggregated by transaction. Please comment.

Reply

As stated, in Section VII.3.2 of the Final Report on the Determination of the Margin of Dumping there is a reference to Annex VIII: "Sales in the domestic market for 1998 and January 1999, disaggregated by transaction" at folio 3023. That is, with respect to normal value for the requested period, Catarinense submitted a list of domestic market sales transactions without providing any supporting documentation and without any magnetic media. Finally, we repeat that Catarinense at no time provided any certification of legal status although this had been requested in Note DCD No. 273-001321/99.

Section VIII.1.3.3.5 of the Report on the Final Determination on the Margin of Dumping, at folios 3053/3054, states that the values reproduced at folio 3054 were obtained from the information from the exporting company in aggregate form in Annexes V and VI of the questionnaire for exporters and that it covered a longer period than that requested by the implementing authority. Thus, the processing of the information in Annexes V and VI yields the detailed values in the table appearing at folio 3054. As indicated in the footnotes to Annexes V and VI, in the case of 1999 the information was accumulated until September. We attach as Annex ARG-LXIV a copy of Annexes V and VI, as submitted by Catarinense.

78. Please comment on the first two sentences of para. 53 of Brazil's Second Oral Statement.

Reply

With respect to the first two sentences of paragraph 53, there is no contradiction whatsoever as Brazil tries to suggest, since Argentina said that the export price information was indeed provided, but since for the reasons already given the determination of normal value could not be made, the notified export prices could not be considered. In this connection, Argentina had official information on export prices for both companies which is the information that was used in the final determination.

Claim 21

79. It would seem from para. 185 of Argentina's First Written Submission that parties were informed of the 'essential facts' through the Report on Action Taken of 4 January 2002. Could Argentina confirm that this is the only instrument on the record of the investigation through which the investigating authority informed interested parties of the 'essential facts'?

Reply

Yes, the Report on Action Taken is the document by which the investigating authority informed the interested parties of the essential facts. In this connection, Argentina reaffirms what it stated in paragraph 185 of its first written submission.

80. The Panel notes Argentina's reply to question 47(a). As a follow-up question, the Panel would appreciate it if Argentina could reply the following questions:

(1) In the investigation at stake, which were the 'essential facts' informed by the investigating authority to interested parties?

(2) Where, if at all, the information referred to in paras. 340-350 of Brazil's First Written Submission and para. 87 of Brazil's Second Written Submission can be found?

In replying to these questions, Argentina is requested to point out with precision the paragraph or page number where the information is contained on the record of the investigation, if any, and to provide a copy of the relevant documents.

Reply

The essential facts are those which appear throughout the Report on Action Taken of January 2000 (folio 2757).

However, to be more precise with respect to the normal value and the export price, we refer by way of example to Section VIII.1 and VIII.1.3.3 of the said report, which explains the methodology used by Sadia for the calculation of normal value. The same is done for Avipal SA in Section VIII.1.3.3.2, which contains detailed information and a description of the methodology applied to calculate normal value for that company. Corresponding information is also provided for Nicolini (folios 2819 and 2820) and for Seara (folio 2821).

Consequently, what Brazil stated in paragraphs 340-350 of its first written submission does not correspond to reality. Indeed, the interested parties were given ample opportunity to express their views with respect to the essential facts that the authority considered for the calculation of normal value and the export price.

Concerning the copy of the essential facts report, see Exhibit BRA-28.

Claim 23

81. At para. 73 of ASS, Argentina suggests that the exporter had ample opportunity to inform the DCD of any adjustments that needed to be made when it submitted the invoices requested by the DCD. Why should Sadia have requested an adjustment for freight costs when submitting its invoices if it had already requested that adjustment in its questionnaire response?

Reply

Argentina reaffirms what it said in paragraphs 210 and 211 of its first written submission. Indeed, Sadia replied to the questionnaire item concerning internal freight, but never provided any supporting documentation for that item. Nor do the invoices submitted provide any indication of the percentage and/or amount of the adjustment to be made.

In other words, although in Annex X Sadia provided a US$/Ton value to be discounted for freight, and also did so in Annex VIII - Sales in the domestic market - these values were presented in annualized form without any supporting documentation that would have enabled the authority to verify whether they corresponded to the reality and hence carry out the said adjustment.

In this connection, a "*nota fiscal*" (tax receipt) from SADIA has been provided showing clearly that the box corresponding to cost of freight does not contain any figure at all. And the box corresponding to "*frete por conta*" contains the indication "1", which corresponds to "*emitente*".

The kind of supporting documentation to which we refer in this case would be, for example, a contract between Sadia and a shipping company or any other documentation from the company which clearly indicates the amount to be discounted for freight. We insist that the "*notas fiscales*", which did not reveal the indicative amount of the requested adjustment, were the only documentation on hand.

Attached hereto as Annex ARG-LXV is a photocopy of the invoice and a photocopy of Annexes VIII and X of the Questionnaire for Exporters.

82. Argentina has asserted that it did not grant Sadia's request for a freight cost adjustment because Sadia failed to support its request with documentary evidence. Please indicate precisely (page number, paragraph number, line number) where the investigating authority explained the reason for rejecting Sadia's request in its final determination, or in any other document prepared by the investigating authority at the time of its determination. If the Panel does not already have a copy of the relevant document, please provide a copy thereof.

Reply

The relevant explanation can be found in Section VIII.1.3.3.1 of the Report on Action Taken. In that report, the DCD identified the information that it would use for the determination of normal value, which did not include any adjustment for freight.

Claim 22

83. Please comment on para. 59 of Brazil's Second Oral Statement.

Reply

To begin with, it should be noted with respect to Brazil's question as to why the authority did not proceed in the same manner with Catarinense and Frangosul, that Catarinense never provided certification of legal status, i.e. it did not comply with an essential requirement that must be met by any interested party wishing to participate in the investigation in accordance with the National Law on Administrative Procedures (Law No. 19.49) which, pursuant to Article 76 of Decree No. 2121/94, applies on a residual basis in investigation proceedings.

This law was duly notified to the WTO Anti-Dumping Committee, which is why the last note sent to Catarinense, which appears in Exhibit BRA-27, states that it should comply with the requirements of the National Law on Administrative Procedures. Instead, not only did Catarinense persist in not making any submission, but as mentioned, it failed to provide certification of legal status.

In the case of Frangosul, in spite of the successive extensions granted and the numerous requests for information from the implementing authority (see the summary table for the company in question, which was transmitted to the Panel together with Argentina's replies to the questions posed following the first meeting), no information was available in connection with domestic market sales transactions, needed by the authority to determine the individual margin of dumping.

We recall in this connection that, as can be seen in the summary table for Frangosul, by Note DCD No. 272-001181/99 of 12 October 1999 and Note DCD No.

273-001412/99 of 18 November of 1999, the implementing authority asked Frangosul for the last time to provide lists of domestic market sales. In the second of these two notes, it granted a maximum of five days to do so. The purpose of this time-limit was to ensure that the implementing authority would have sufficient time to analyse and process the requested information.

However, Frangosul, once the time-limit for the submission for the information had elapsed, provided, in magnetic form only (diskette), the list of *notas fiscales*. Indeed, Frangosul failed to provide a hard copy of the list as required under the National Law on Administrative Procedures. This Law applies on a residual basis to anti-dumping proceedings pursuant to Article 76 of Decree No. 2121/94.

For the sake of clarity, we cite below Articles 7 and 15 of Decree No. 1759/72 which regulates the mentioned Law.

"Article 7 - The identification under which a record of proceedings is initiated shall be retained throughout successive proceeding regardless of the bodies participating in them. All of the units are under obligation to provide information from a file on the basis of its initial identification.

The title page shall indicate the body with primary responsibility for the proceedings and the time-limit for its settlement."

"Article 15 - Documents shall be typed or legibly handwritten in ink, in the national language" …The top of the page shall contain a summary of the pleadings. They shall be signed by the interested parties, or their legal representatives or attorneys. Each document, with the sole exception of the document initiating the proceedings, shall be headed by the identification of the file to which it corresponds, and where appropriate, shall contain a precise indication of the representation exercised …".

Administrative proceedings in Argentina are written.

Once again, Argentina would like to draw the Panel's attention to the numerous requests by the implementing authority to the exporting companies concerning documentation to be submitted, and is ready to provide the Panel with any documents that it may consider relevant in this respect.

Claim 24

84. In respect of claim 24, please indicate precisely (page number, paragraph number, line number) where the investigating authority gave the reasons for not making the various adjustments to the JOX domestic price data, either in the investigating authority's final determination, or in any other document prepared by the investigating authority at the time of its determination. If the Panel does not already have a copy of the relevant document, please provide a copy thereof.

Reply

At folio 3040 of the Report on the Final Determination, Section VIII.1.3, there is an explanation of the circumstances of the request for information by the implementing authority to the President of the JOX publication.

85. Did the investigating authority ask JOX to provide a Spanish translation of its letter of 3 August 1999 through which JOX had given information in

Portuguese? If so, please provide a copy of the document containing that request.

Reply

The translation was not requested because it was assumed that the parties to the anti-dumping proceedings, to which the National Law on Administrative Procedures applies on a residual basis, would know what was required under that Law.

86.   Please comment on para. 68 of Brazil's second oral statement.

Reply

We agree with Brazil in theory that to conduct a fair comparison, all of the appropriate adjustments need to be made both to the normal value and the export price.

However, in the case at issue, with respect to the JOX publication, the information that would have made it possible to carry out some of the adjustments that Brazil mentions did not comply with the requirements of the National Law on Administrative Procedures (Law No. 19549) in that under Article 28 of Decree No. 1759/72 regulating the said Law, documentation in a foreign language must be translated into Spanish by a registered translator.

Claim 32

87.   Please indicate precisely (page number, paragraph number, line number) where the investigating authority explained why it looked at 1999 data for only certain injury factors and not others, either in the investigating authority's final determination, or in any other document prepared by the investigating authority at the time of its determination. If the Panel does not already have a copy of the relevant document, please provide a copy thereof.

Reply

Lines 1 to 6 in the second paragraph of Section V (State of the Domestic Industry) of Record No. 576 of 23 December 1999, which appears in CNCE File No. 43/1997 (folio 7313), clearly state that:

> "The 'period under analysis' corresponds to the period from January 1996 to December 1998. For certain variables, such as domestic production, prices, imports, national exports and apparent consumption, data is included for the first half of 1999. Data for 1995 is provided for reference purposes. Variations for the first half of 1999 are against the same period for the previous year." (Emphasis added)

Nevertheless, Argentina reiterates what it stated in its two previous submissions, and for a better understanding of the overall context, we repeat our reply that:

> "First of all, there is no obligation to analyse any indicator outside the period established by the authorities as the investigation period.
>
> In accordance with international practice in certain countries, Argentina considered a number of variables accessible to the public in order to double check the trends observed during the investigation period. If we were to insist

on the constant updating of all indicators during the investigation, as Brazil seems to suggest in this case, the investigation would be endless. We repeat that this is not the objective of the AD Agreement, nor is it the practice of those countries which, like Argentina, examine certain relevant indicators of reference data."

It should be noted that the determination of threat of injury was based on the period from January 1996 to December 1998, and the other data, as stated in previous replies and in the Record in question, was used for reference purposes.

Claim 38

88. Please explain precisely how Table 16 of Act No. 576 (para. 292 of Argentina's first written submission) constitutes an evaluation of "factors affecting domestic prices" within the meaning of Article 3.4 of the AD Agreement. Please provide a more detailed explanation than that set forth in paragraph 74 of Argentina's second oral statement.

Reply

Table No. 16, which belongs to Technical Report GEGE/1TDF No. 03/99 and is an integral part of Record No. 576, provides the average sales revenue for one kilogram of eviscerated poultry, fresh or chilled, and the relative prices of the comparable product, with regard to the price of industrial goods taken as a whole and of bovine meat - represented respectively by the Wholesale Industrial Price Index for Manufactured Goods and the simple average of the consumer price indices for fresh bovine meat, front and hind cuts.

The comparison made with respect to the Wholesale Industrial Price Index for Manufactured Goods was based on the need to assess whether the price of the product in question was following the same trend as the other manufactured goods.

With regard to the second index, Argentina has traditionally been a consumer of red meat, so that it was considered appropriate to use this index to analyse the impact of variations in that product on poultry meat as from a certain degree of substitution between bovine meat and poultry meat.

As can be seen from the table, the two relative prices analysed followed the same trend as average sales revenue for the product in question, although in the case of the price in relation to the simple average for bovine meat the annual variations reflected a stronger decrease in 1998 as a result of the increase in the price of bovine meat recorded that year. Indeed, as indicated in the Market Chapter of Technical Report GEGE/ITDF No. 03/99, Section VI.5 (Recent evolution of the market), folio 7371, paragraph 3: "During 1998 there was a further increase in the demand for poultry as a result of the substitution effect following the sharp increases in the price of bovine meat, which reached its peak in the middle of 1998. No decline in the consumption of poultry was recorded following the subsequent fall in the price of bovine meat. This because the market perception is that the price of poultry is so low that it is even pushing the price of bovine meat downwards".

Consequently Article 3.4 was clearly taken into consideration where it provides that "[t]he examination of the impact of the dumped imports on the domestic industry concerned shall include an evaluation of all relevant economic factors and indices having a bearing on the state of the industry, including ... factors affecting domestic prices ...".

89. **Regarding Argentina's reply to question 59 concerning paragraph 80 of Brazil's first oral statement, please provide exact citations (e.g., page number, paragraph number, line number) for the various extracts from Act No. 576.**

Reply

Concerning the citations referred to in paragraph 80:

- The citation "An econometric exercise was conducted which showed that for the period from January 1995 to June 1999, the price of the product on the domestic market depended on the volume of imports for the previous month, the price of the imported product and the price of bovine meat. The inclusion of the price of maize in the mentioned model did not produce satisfactory results, indicating that the considerable variability of the price of whole eviscerated poultry does not coincide with the price of maize. Nevertheless, both variables showed similar patterns ... " can be found in Section VIII (Conditions of Competition between the Like Product and the Imported Product), § 1, folio 7328, last paragraph, and folio 7329, first paragraph.

- The citation according to which "[t]he economic recession did not particularly affect the consumption of whole eviscerated poultry, which continued to increase (in 1998 it increased by 14 per cent)" can be found in Section VIII (Conditions of Competition between the Like Product and the Imported Product), § 1, folio 7329, second paragraph.

- Finally, the citation "...with regard to the price of industrial goods taken as a whole and of bovine meat - represented respectively by the Wholesale Industrial Price Index for Manufactured Goods and the simple average of the consumer price indices for fresh bovine meat, front and hind cuts - followed the same trend as the sales revenue described above, although in the case of bovine meat, the annual variations reflected a stronger decrease in 1998 as a result of the increase in the price of bovine meat recorded that year" can be found in Section V (State of the Domestic Industry), at folio 7318, last paragraph.

Questions to Brazil

Claim 22

90. **It is stated in para. 319 of Brazil's First Written Submission that 'Frangosul and Catarinense submitted the requested information on normal value and export price, which was disregarded by the DCD without explanation.' Would Brazil agree that, if the data submitted by Frangosul and Catarinense had been disregarded in accordance with relevant provisions of the ADA, the investigating authority would not have been required to calculate an individual dumping margin for Frangosul and Catarinense? Please explain.**

91. **It is stated in para. 324 of Brazil's First Written Submission that 'the DCD provided no explanation, either in the final determination or in any other document on the record of the investigation, as to why, in this case, it was not possible to determine an individual margin for Frangosul and Catarinense.' Would Brazil agree that, if the investigating authority had disregarded the data**

submitted by Frangosul and Catarinense in accordance with relevant provisions of the ADA, it would not have been required to explain in the final determination or in any other document on the record of the investigation why an individual dumping of margin for those exporters had not been calculated?

Claim 23

92. Please comment on para. 210 of Argentina's first written submission.

Claim 24

93. Please comment on paras 77 - 79 of ASS.

Claim 27

94. Does Brazil consider that the investigating authority would have violated Article 2.4.2 if the exporters had agreed that the investigating authority could calculate normal value on the basis of those domestic transactions for which invoices had been requested?

Questions to both parties

Claim 21

95. What are 'essential facts under consideration which form the basis for the decisions whether to apply definitive measures' within the meaning of Article 6.9 ADA? In particular, would 'essential facts' cover only facts or also reasoning supporting a certain conclusion?

Reply

> They are the facts upon which the implementing authority bases its conclusions.

96. At para. 8.229 of its report, the Panel in Guatemala - Cement II found that:

> 'An interested party will not know whether a particular fact is "important" or not unless the investigating authority has explicitly identified it as one of the "essential facts" which form the basis of the authority's decision whether to impose definitive measures.'

Would you agree with the above finding? Please explain.

Reply

> Argentina agrees with the position of the Panel in *Guatemala - Cement II* - indeed, all that is reported in the Report on Action Taken makes up the facts which will form the basis of the authority's decision, a circumstance of which the implementing authority informs the interested parties.

Claim 22

97. What do parties understand by the words "for each known exporter or producer concerned of the product under investigation" contained in the first sentence of Article 6.10? In the view of the parties, would the cited portion of the first sentence of Article 6.10 require the calculation of an individual margin of

dumping for each exporter known to the investigating authority? Would that also be the case when a known exporter does not provide relevant information requested by the investigating authority? Please explain.

Reply

A condition for the determination of an individual margin of dumping for each exporter is that the exporter should be known, and should supply the documentation needed to reach such a determination.

98. In the view of the parties, would the findings in paras. 6.86 to 6.101 (both included) of the panel Argentina - Ceramic tiles be applicable to the facts in this dispute? In particular, would the following finding of the Panel be relevant to the current dispute: 'The basis of the normal value determination has no bearing on the ability to calculate an individual dumping margin for the producer whose normal value is in question'? Would the lack of information on normal value, export price or cost of production, automatically allow the non-calculation of an individual dumping of margin in accordance with Article 6.10? Please explain, identifying and providing relevant factual support to the Panel.

Reply

It does not apply to the present case, since in the arguments of the *Ceramic Tiles* case, the investigating authority, in calculating the margin of dumping, took account of circumstances relating to "cases where the number of exporters, producers, importers or types of products involved is so large as to make such a determination impracticable ...". In other words, the considerations on which the Panel relied were related to the fact that the Argentine authority had decided to determine the margin of dumping on the basis of "a reasonable number of interested parties ... using samples which are statistically valid on the basis of information available to the authorities at the time of the selection, ...". Thus, the findings are not applicable to this case.

ANNEX B-7

REPLIES OF ARGENTINA TO QUESTIONS OF BRAZIL - SECOND MEETING

(26 November 2002)

Questions from Brazil to Argentina

Brazil understands that right after the investigation was initiated the DCD sent questionnaires to the Brazilian exporters Sadia, Avipal, Frangosul, Seara and Nicolini, which required export price and normal value data for the years 1996, 1997, 1998 and the months in 1999 where data was available. On 15 September 1999, the DCD sent notifications of the investigation and the questionnaires to the Brazilian exporters CCLP, Catarinense, Chapecó, Minuano, Perdigão, Comaves and Pena Branca, requiring dumping data for the period 1998 through January 1999. With that in mind, please provide:

1. When did the investigating authority decide that the dumping period of data collection for Sadia, Avipal and Frangosul would be from January 1998 through January 1999, and not the years 1996, 1997 and 1998?

2. When did the investigating notify Sadia, Avipal and Frangosul that the dumping period of data collection would be from January 1998 through January 1999, and not the years 1996, 1997 and 1998?

Reply

1 and 2. The Brazilian exporters were informed of the period of data collection at the preliminary determination stage of the investigation.

As can be seen in the annexes to the Report on the Preliminary Determination, the implementing authority had already decided that the investigation period would be January 1998 to January 1999.

All of the exporting companies could clearly see what investigation period was being examined by the authority. In the case of AVIPAL, SADIA and FRANGOSUL, the requests for documentation by the DCD provided indications of what the investigation period to be examined would be.

Likewise, we refer to the Summary Table attached as a supplement to Argentina's replies to the questionnaire provided by the Panel following the First Meeting of the Panel with the Parties.

3. What basis did the investigating authority use to select January 1998 through January 1999 as the period of data collection for dumping purposes, as opposed to the period 1996 through 1998, indicated in the dumping questionnaires sent to Sadia, Avipal and Frangosul?

Reply

The authority based its determination of the period of investigation on the principle that the information to be submitted should correspond to a period as close as possible to the initiation of the investigation.

ANNEX B-8

COMMENTS OF ARGENTINA ON THE REPONSES OF BRAZIL TO THE PANEL'S QUESTIONS - SECOND MEETING
(28 November 2002)

Questions to Brazil

Claim 22

90. It is stated in para. 319 of Brazil's First Written Submission that 'Frangosul and Catarinense submitted the requested information on normal value and export price, which was disregarded by the DCD without explanation.' Would Brazil agree that, if the data submitted by Frangosul and Catarinense had been disregarded in accordance with relevant provisions of the ADA, the investigating authority would not have been required to calculate an individual dumping margin for Frangosul and Catarinense? Please explain.

Regarding Brazil's response to question 90, Argentina wishes to point out once again that Brazil is mistaken in claiming that FRANGOSUL and CATARINENSE submitted all the information and in therefore believing that the implementing authority was required to make an individual determination of the margin of dumping. In this connection, reference is made to Argentina's response to question 83 regarding Claim 22.

Argentina wishes to emphasize that the reply given by Brazil does not answer the question posed by the Panel. Nevertheless, Brazil attempts to justify the fact that the implementing authority should have determined the individual margin of dumping and seeks to draw an analogy with the implementing authority's handling of the information submitted by SADIA and AVIPAL.

In Argentina's view, such a comparison is not appropriate because the information supplied by SADIA and AVIPAL satisfied the requirements for it to be considered in the final determination. It should be noted that, in their submissions, neither SADIA nor AVIPAL objected to the methodology used for calculating the margin of dumping, particularly as regards the export price. Argentina therefore does not see why at this stage Brazil insists on stating its failure to understand and disagreement with the handling of the export price in the case of SADIA and AVIPAL.

In other words, when the parties had the opportunity to express their views on the methodology used by Argentina for determining the export price, SADIA and AVIPAL made no comment in that regard.

Lastly, we note that Brazil does not reply to the Panel's question; following the above reasoning, Brazil should therefore explain - as requested by the Panel in question 90 - the methodology which it believes should be used in determining the individual margin of dumping when information is disregarded for not having been submitted in accordance with the requirements of the Agreement on Implementation of Article VI of the General Agreement on Tariffs and Trade 1994, its Regulatory Decree No. 2121/94, the National Law on Administrative Procedures and its

Regulatory Decree No. 1759/72, all of which were notified to the WTO Anti-Dumping Committee.

91. **It is stated in para. 324 of Brazil's First Written Submission that 'the DCD provided no explanation, either in the final determination or in any other document on the record of the investigation, as to why, in this case, it was not possible to determine an individual margin for Frangosul and Catarinense.' Would Brazil agree that, if the investigating authority had disregarded the data submitted by Frangosul and Catarinense in accordance with relevant provisions of the ADA, it would not have been required to explain in the final determination or in any other document on the record of the investigation why an individual dumping of margin for those exporters had not been calculated?**

It would not appear to make sense for the implementing authority to report that it did not intend to make an individual determination of the margin of dumping if it had already been explained that normal value and export price information would not be taken into account because of the lacunae in the documentation submitted. Hence it was obvious that there would be no determination of the individual margin of dumping, meaning that Brazil's arguments in that respect are unnecessary.

Claim 23

92. **Please comment on para. 210 of Argentina's first written submission.**

Argentina refers the Panel to its response to question 81 regarding Claim 23.

Claim 24

93. **Please comment on paras 77 - 79 of ASS.**

The Panel is referred to Argentina's response to question 86 regarding Claim 24.

Claim 27

94. **Does Brazil consider that the investigating authority would have violated Article 2.4.2 if the exporters had agreed that the investigating authority could calculate normal value on the basis of those domestic transactions for which invoices had been requested?**

Brazil errs in maintaining that the determination of normal value could have been distorted as a result of the use of a statistically valid sample of invoices from the exporting firms that substantiated domestic sales transactions in order to establish normal value.

Secondly, Brazil's position on the subject is, again, surprising, because this argument was not put forward by the Brazilian Government either during the course of the investigation or in its final submission. Nor did the exporters claim that the methodology for calculating normal value, on the basis of the data supplied by the exporting firms, was - as the Brazilian Government now submits - questionable or inconsistent with Article 2.4 of the Agreement on Implementation of Article VI of the General Agreement on Tariffs and Trade 1994.

Claim 21

95. **What are 'essential facts under consideration which form the basis for the decisions whether to apply definitive measures' within the meaning of**

Article 6.9 ADA? In particular, would 'essential facts' cover only facts or also reasoning supporting a certain conclusion?

Argentina reiterates the response given to this question at the time.

96.   At para. 9.229 of its report, the panel in *Guatemala - Cement II* found that:

> 'An interested party will not know whether a particular fact is "important" or not unless the investigating authority has explicitly identified it as one of the "essential facts" which form the basis of the authority's decision whether to impose definitive measures.'

Would you agree with the above finding? Please explain.

As regards Brazil's claims regarding the information submitted by FRANGOSUL and CATARINENSE in the investigation, the line of reasoning is once again wrong. In this connection, it should be mentioned that the Report on Action Taken specifies the lacunae in the information furnished by FRANGOSUL and CATARINENSE. Furthermore, the parties' right of defence was not impaired at any time, since FRANGOSUL offered comments on the content of that report in its final submission.

Lastly, the paragraph from *Guatemala - Cement II* cited by Brazil is superfluous, because Argentina made the relevant report on essential facts available to all interested parties.

Claim 22

97.   What do parties understand by the words "for each known exporter or producer concerned of the product under investigation" contained in the first sentence of Article 6.10? In the view of the parties, would the cited portion of the first sentence of Article 6.10 require the calculation of an individual margin of dumping for each exporter known to the investigating authority? Would that also be the case when a known exporter does not provide relevant information requested by the investigating authority? Please explain.

It would be important for Brazil to explain how it calculates individual margins of dumping when the information submitted - as in the case of FRANGOSUL and CATARINENSE - is not consistent with the requirements of the Anti-Dumping Agreement, or in a specific case such as that of CATARINENSE, whose submission presented the added problem of the firm never having provided certification of legal status in the proceedings, as required by the National Law on Administrative Procedures, which applies on a supplementary basis to anti-dumping investigation procedures and was duly notified to the WTO.

98.   In the view of the parties, would the findings in paras. 6.86 to 6.101 (both included) of the panel *Argentina - Ceramic tiles* be applicable to the facts in this dispute? In particular, would the following finding of the panel be relevant to the current dispute: 'The basis of the normal value determination has no bearing on the ability to calculate an individual dumping margin for the producer whose normal value is in question.'? Would the lack of information on normal value, export price or cost of production, automatically allow the non-calculation of an individual dumping of margin in accordance with Article 6.10? Please explain, identifying and providing relevant factual support to the Panel.

Brazil is now mentioning issues that were not raised in the course of the investigation. Moreover, it continuously insists on stating its point of view regarding the information submitted by FRANGOSUL and CATARINENSE. This is confusing the Panel with considerations that are not appropriate insofar as they do not correspond to the Panel's questions. Furthermore, Argentina has provided ample and repeated evidence as regards the nature of and the lacunae in the information supplied by these two exporting firms, during the investigation and throughout the course of these proceedings.

Once again, Argentina reiterates the need for Brazil to explain how the individual margin of dumping would be determined when the information is not in conformity with the Anti-Dumping Agreement.

Brazil's response does not apply to the paragraph cited since the analysis conducted by that particular panel refers to the sample and the data in that sample as submitted by the exporters.

Lastly, it is surprising that, in view of the numerous explanations offered by Argentina in all of its responses, Brazil still fails to understand the situation at issue, the more so since it did not report such circumstances in the course of the investigation.

ANNEX B-9

COMMENTS OF ARGENTINA ON THE SECOND ORAL STATEMENT OF BRAZIL

(26 November 2002)

I. INTRODUCTION

1. Argentina thanks the Panel for the opportunity to offer its comments on the oral statement of Brazil at the second meeting of the Panel with the parties.

2. Argentina will also comment briefly on Brazil's oral statement at the second meeting with the Panel.

II. PRELIMINARY ARGUMENTS

3. Argentina first of all wishes to provide some clarification regarding Brazil's arguments in the section entitled "Ruling by the MERCOSUL Ad Hoc Arbitral Tribunal".

4. Argentina will also provide clarifications regarding the issues raised by Brazil in connection with the current dispute before the WTO, which, as both parties have already acknowledged, is "similar"[1] to that brought in the framework of MERCOSUR.

5. Brazil itself recognizes that the object of its complaint is the alleged inconsistency of the Argentine measure with the WTO Anti-Dumping Agreement.[2] However, what Brazil fails to mention is that, in its prior submission to the MERCOSUR Ad Hoc Tribunal, it included in the MERCOSUR regulatory framework a reference to the WTO Anti-Dumping Agreement.[3]

6. As Argentina has already noted[4], the arbitral award rendered by the Ad Hoc Tribunal constituted to hear and settle the dispute brought before MERCOSUR states that the WTO Anti-Dumping Agreement stands as a reference *"(...) by virtue of Article 19 of the Protocol of Brasilia as an applicable principle of international law (...), in this case to shed light on the meaning and purpose of anti-dumping proceedings"*.[5]

---

[1] Oral statement of Brazil at the second meeting with the Panel, 26 November 2002, para. 4.
[2] *Ibid.*, para. 6.
[3] *Laudo sobre pollos* (Award on poultry) - Award of the MERCOSUR Ad Hoc Arbitral Tribunal constituted to rule on the dispute between the Federative Republic of Brazil and the Argentine Republic regarding the imposition of anti-dumping measures on exports of whole poultry from Brazil (Res. 574/2000 of the Ministry of the Economy of the Argentine Republic)". Date: 21 May 2001. Paragraph 30.
[4] Rebuttal submission of Argentina, 17 October 2002, para. 3.
[5] *Laudo sobre pollos* (Award on poultry), end of para. 159.

7. Argentina rejects Brazil's claim[6] that "[w]e have shown that the disputes are not the same" and reiterates[7] that the dispute refers to the same measure and that the legal grounds claimed by Brazil before each forum are the same.

8. Argentina notes that a reading of the arbitral award - in its entirety - clarifies the scope of the paragraphs of the award cited by Brazil.[8] In Argentina's opinion, these should be read in the context of the full text of the award, and in particular section II-F-3-c) entitled "*Conclusiones sobre el modo como ha sido llevado el procedimiento antidumping*" (Conclusions regarding the conduct of the anti-dumping procedure).

9. Argentina also rejects Brazil's claim[9] regarding the principle of estoppel. It affirms that Brazil's conduct, in successively bringing the same complaint before different forums - first before MERCOSUR, and then, in view of the unfavourable outcome, before the WTO - claiming violations of the same provisions of the WTO Anti-Dumping Agreement in both forums, runs counter to the principle of good faith requiring full observance of treaties and is a case for estoppel.

10. Argentina rejects Brazil's claims[10] and affirms that the proceedings conducted in the context of MERCOSUR and the arbitral award are relevant, because the rules forming part of the MERCOSUR regulatory framework - which includes the Protocol of Brasilia and the award rendered by the Ad Hoc Tribunal - are pertinent rules applicable to the case, within the meaning of Article 3.2 of the DSU and Article 31.3(c) of the Vienna Convention on the Law of Treaties.

---

[6] Oral statement of Brazil at the second meeting with the Panel, 26 November 2002, paras. 7 and 12.
[7] Oral intervention by Argentina at the first meeting with the Panel, 25 September 2002, para. 8.
[8] Oral statement of Brazil at the second meeting with the Panel, 26 November 2002, para. 8.
[9] *Ibid.*, para. 12.
[10] Oral Statement of Brazil at the second meeting with the Panel, 26 November 2002, paras. 14, 15 and 16.

ANNEX C

Third Parties

Contents		Page
Annex C-1	Third Party Submission of Canada	C-2254
Annex C-2	Third Party Submission of the European Communities	C-2258
Annex C-3	Third Party Submission of Guatemala	C-2271
Annex C-4	Third Party Submission of Paraguay	C-2276
Annex C-5	Third Party Submission of the United States	C-2278
Annex C-6	Third Party Oral Statement of Paraguay	C-2284
Annex C-7	Third Party Oral Statement of Chile	C-2286
Annex C-8	Third Party Oral Statement of the United States	C-2287
Annex C-9	Third Party Oral Statement of Canada	C-2289
Annex C-10	Third Party Oral Statement of the European Communities	C-2290
Annex C-11	Replies of the European Communities to Questions of the Panel	C-2293
Annex C-12	Replies of the United States to Questions of the Panel	C-2295

ANNEX C-1

THIRD PARTY SUBMISSION OF CANADA

(5 September 2002)

I. INTRODUCTION

1. In letter dated April 24, 2002 to H.E. Carlos Pérez del Castillo, Chairman of the Dispute Settlement Body, Canada expressed its wish to participate as a third party in *Argentina - Definitive Anti-Dumping Duties on Poultry from Brazil* (WT/DS241). Canada makes this submission in accordance with Article 10.2 of the *Understanding on Rules and Procedures Governing the Settlement of Disputes* (DSU). At this point, Canada restricts its comments to the interpretation of Article 9.3 of the *Agreement on the Implementation of Article VI of the General Agreement on Tariffs and Trade 1994* (Anti-dumping Agreement). However, Canada may make additional submissions on this and other legal issues at the Substantive Meeting of the Panel with the Third Parties.

II. LEGAL ARGUMENT

A. Brazil's Arguments

2. In its claims 28 and 29, as set out and developed in its First Written Submission, Brazil argues that the imposition by Argentina of a "variable anti-dumping duty" violates Articles 9.2 and 9.3 of the Anti-dumping Agreement.

3. According to Brazil, the variable duty at issue is an anti-dumping duty that is equal to the "absolute different between the f.o.b. price invoiced in any one shipment and a designated 'minimum export price' also fixed in f.o.b. terms ...". Because the amount of the duty is variable, the result can be the imposition of duties on each shipment that "can exceed the margin of dumping established in the final determination". In its First Written Submission, Brazil does not adequately set out a legal analysis of the relevant provisions of the Anti-dumping Agreement. It only asserts that Argentina's anti-dumping duties are not collected in "an appropriate amount" as required by Article 9.2 and are, in addition, in violation of Article 9.3 because they exceed the margin of dumping "established in the final determination".

B. Canada's Submission

1. The Scope of this Submission

4. Canada is interested in ensuring that the Panel arrives at the correct legal interpretation of Articles 9.2 and 9.3. This is because if the Panel accepts Brazil's assertions, the consequence would be a serious dilution of the rights of WTO Members under the Anti-dumping Agreement.

5. Canada does not express any views on the application of the provisions at issue on the specific facts of this case.

2. An appropriate amount: Article 9.2 of the Anti-Dumping Agreement

6. Brazil purports to argue that with respect to the amount of an anti-dumping duty, there are *two* obligations on WTO Members: Article 9.2, which requires the collection of "an appropriate amount", and Article 9.3, which restricts the "amount" of an anti-dumping duty to the "margin of dumping as established under Article 2".

7. Brazil does not explain what would constitute an "appropriate" amount for the purposes of Article 9.2. The context of Article 9 as a whole is cogent evidence, however, that the appropriateness of an amount under the second paragraph of that Article is to be determined in accordance with the criteria set out in the third. Simply put, it is inconceivable that an "amount" arrived at following the detailed instructions of Article 9.3 (in conjunction with Article 2) would be considered not "appropriate" for the purposes of Article 9.2. Accordingly, as a starting point, unless Brazil can demonstrate otherwise, the Panel should consider that an amount permitted under Article 9.3 is "appropriate" under Article 9.2.

3. Margin of dumping: Article 9.3 of the Anti-Dumping Agreement

8. Article 9.3 provides that the "amount of an anti-dumping duty" must not exceed the "margin of dumping as established under Article 2." Relying on Article 2.4.2 of the Anti-dumping Agreement, Brazil argues that, "the dumping margin as established under Article 2 of the Anti-dumping Agreement is that established *during the investigation phase.*" [emphasis added] Accordingly, Brazil seems to argue, even if Brazilian exporters export poultry at prices that result in dumping that is *more egregious* than during the investigation phase, Argentina may impose anti-dumping duties only if they do not exceed the original margin of dumping.

9. Article 9.3 has no such requirement. Indeed, the very fact situation set out by Brazil in its submission underlines the illogic of Brazil's proposed interpretation.

10. In determining the "margin of dumping" for the purposes of Article 9.3, the Panel should examine Article 2 in its entirety. Article 2 provides that under normal market conditions, the margin of dumping is simply the difference between the export price and the "comparable price ... in the exporting country" as set out in Article 2.1. The prices must be *comparable* in the sense of Article 2.4; the comparison must be made at the same level of trade and *around the same time*. Nothing in Article 2 limits the margin of dumping to a static amount found during the period of investigation. Indeed, any such reading appears to directly contradict the fair comparison requirement in Article 2.4.

11. Brazil quotes Article 2.4.2 in support of its position that the "margin of dumping" is fixed in time. However, Article 2.4.2 deals with the situation where a weighted average dumping margin needs to be established *during the period of investigation*. Nowhere does it fix the "margin of dumping" to that found in the period of investigation. Article 2.4.2 does not appear immediately relevant to this case.

12. Finally, Brazil's interpretation is fundamentally at odds with the object and purpose of Article VI of the GATT 1994 and the Anti-dumping Agreement.

13. Article VI:1 provides that:

> The contracting parties recognize that dumping, by which products of one country are introduced into the commerce of another country at less than the normal value of the products, *is to be condemned* if it causes or threatens material injury .... [emphasis added]

14. The object and purpose of the Anti-dumping Agreement, as can be seen in Article VI:1 and also in the terms of the Anti-dumping Agreement, is to provide a mechanism to address unfair trade situations where products are sold at prices below their "normal value" in the export market. This can be achieved through the imposition of anti-dumping duties equal to the difference between the two prices (the margin of dumping), or through price undertakings. If it were to prevail, Brazil's interpretation would result in the perverse outcome that an exporter will be able to undermine anti-dumping duties legitimately imposed by an importing country, through dumping at even *larger* margins than those found during the investigation period. Nothing in the Anti-dumping Agreement prevents a Member from imposing anti-dumping duties equivalent to the actual margin of dumping to prevent precisely such an outcome.

15. The "margin of dumping" under Article 9.3 is the price difference set out in Article 2, and in this case, Article 2.1. Such a margin by definition varies in accordance with the pricing strategy of an exporter found to have engaged in dumping. An export price that equals or exceeds the normal value does not attract an anti-dumping duty. At the same time, an export price below the normal value will attract an amount equal to the difference between the normal value and export price of those goods (that is, the actual margin of dumping). While Members may choose, for their own reasons, to apply a rate of duty equal to the margin of dumping found in the original investigation, nothing in Article 9.3 compels them to do so.

III. CONCLUSION

16. Brazil's interpretation of Articles 9.2 and 9.3 of the Anti-dumping Agreement is flawed and should be rejected because:

- the "appropriate amount" in Article 9.2 is the same as the amount found under Article 9.3 and Article 9.2 does not impose an additional calculation obligation on Members;
- read in context, the "margin of dumping" in Article 9.3 is not limited to the margin found during the period of investigation; and
- Brazil's interpretation seriously vitiates the right of Members to ensure that anti-dumping measures address the actual margin of dumping.

17. Making a determination of dumping in accordance with Article 2 is one of the requisite elements for the imposition of anti-dumping measures. The margin of dumping found in the course of the original investigation does not, however, cap the amount of anti-dumping duties that may be imposed when future imports take place. When such future imports are dumped at a margin higher than that determined to exist at the time of the final determination, the importing Member may impose anti-dumping measures equal to that margin.

18. Canada stresses that it does not have any views on the application of the provisions of the Anti-dumping Agreement to the specific facts of this case. Canada may make additional remarks on this and other aspects of this dispute at the Substantive Meeting of the Panel with the Third Parties.

Report of the Panel

ANNEX C-2

THIRD PARTY SUBMISSION OF THE EUROPEAN COMMUNITIES
(9 September 2002)

I. INTRODUCTION

1. The European Communities (the "EC") intervene in this dispute because of their systemic interest in the correct interpretation of the *Agreement on Implementation of Article VI of the General Agreement on Tariffs and Trade 1994* (the "*Anti-Dumping Agreement*").

2. Many of the claims submitted by Brazil raise factual issues on which the EC is not in a position to comment. Accordingly, in this submission the EC will limit itself to provide its views with respect to a number of issues of legal interpretation to which it attaches particular importance. More specifically, the EC will argue in this submission that:

- in so far as the issue arises in connection with Claim 21, the Panel should confirm the interpretation of Article 6.9 made by the panel in *Guatemala - Cement II* to the effect that the disclosure obligation imposed by that provision cannot be satisfied simply by allowing access to the file;

- Article 2.4 does not address the issue raised by Brazil under Claim 24;

- contrary to Brazil's Claims 28 and 29, the imposition of variable duties equal to the difference between the normal value established during the investigation and the export prices of the shipments made after the imposition of the duties is not inconsistent with Articles 9.2 and 9.3;

- the term "dumped imports", as used in Article 3, may be interpreted as referring to all imports from the country concerned, contrary to Brazil's Claims 32, 33, 34, 35 and 36; and

- contrary to Brazil's Claim 41, the term "major proportion" used in Article 4.1 does not mean at least 50 per cent of the domestic production, but rather an important proportion thereof, which may be less than 50 per cent.

3. Before addressing the above issues, the EC will comment on the preliminary objection raised by Argentina on the basis of the existence of a ruling issued by an Ad Hoc Arbitral Tribunal established under the MERCOSUR Agreement in connection with the same measure.

II. PRELIMINARY OBJECTION

A. *Relevance of the Ruling by the MERCOSUR Ad Hoc Arbitral Tribunal with Respect to the same Measure*

4. The anti-dumping measure in dispute in this case has already been the subject of another dispute before an Ad Hoc Arbitral Tribunal ("Tribunal Arbitral Ad Hoc") established at the request of Brazil under Article 7 of the *Protocol of Brasilia*[1] to the *Treaty of Asunción* establishing the MERCOSUR[2], which issued a ruling ("laudo arbitral") rejecting Brazil's complaint on 21 May 2001.[3]

5. Citing the existence of the above mentioned arbitration ruling, Argentina has requested the Panel to dismiss Brazil's complaint. The grounds for that request are, nevertheless, somewhat unclear. In essence, Argentina appears to be arguing the following:

- the dispute has already been "debated and resolved".[4] This suggests that Argentina takes the view that the arbitration ruling has the effect of *res iudicata* between the parties. Nevertheless, Argentina does not invoke expressly that notion;

- the arbitration ruling is part of the relevant "normative framework"[5] and must be "taken into account"[6] by the Panel in accordance with the last part of the second sentence of Article 3.2 of the *DSU* (which provides that the dispute settlement mechanism serves to "clarify the existing provisions of those agreements in accordance with customary rules of interpretation of public international law")[7];

- by bringing this dispute, Brazil has abused its rights under the *WTO Agreement*[8];

- given Brazil's earlier decision to bring the same dispute before a MERCOSUR Ad Hoc Arbitral Tribunal, as well as Brazil's previous practice of resorting exclusively to the MERCOSUR dispute settlement mechanism, Brazil is *estopped* from bringing this case before a WTO Panel.[9]

---

[1] Protocol of Brasilia on the Settlement of Disputes of 17 December 1991 (the "Protocol of Brasilia").
[2] Tratado para la Constitución de un Mercado Común between the Republic of Argentina, the Federative Republic of Brazil, the Republic of Paraguay and the Oriental Republic of Uruguay of 26 March 1991 (the "MERCOSUR Treaty").
[3] Laudo del Tribunal Ad Hoc del MERCOSUR constituido para decidir sobre Controversia entre la República Federativa de Brasil y la República Argentina sobre "Applicación de Medidas Antidumping contra la exportación de pollos enteros provenientes de Brasil (Res. 574/2000) del Ministerio de Economía de la Republica Argentina" de 31 de Mayo de 2001.
[4] Argentina's Submission, paras. 23 and 17.
[5] Argentina's Submission, para. 22. See also para. 18.
[6] *Ibid.*
[7] *Ibid.*, para. 18.
[8] *Ibid.*, paras. 17 and 23
[9] *Ibid.*, paras. 22 and 24.

(a) Res iudicata

6. The applicability of the principle of *res iudicata* to the disputes arising under the *WTO Agreement* has been examined by the panel in *India - Autos*[10], which nevertheless did not consider it necessary to rule on that issue. Likewise, this Panel need not reach this issue because it is plain that, in any event, the requirements for the existence of *res iudicata* are not met. As noted by the panel in *India - Autos*,

> for *res iudicata* to have any possible role in WTO dispute settlement, there should, at the very least, be in essence identity between the matter previously ruled on and that submitted to the subsequent panel. This requires identity between both the measures and the claims pertaining to them.[11]

7. The measure before this Panel is the same as the measure in dispute before the MERCOSUR Ad Hoc Arbitral Tribunal. But the claims are different because they involve a different legal basis. The claims raised by Brazil before this Panel are based on the *Anti-Dumping Agreement*. On the other hand, the claims ruled upon by the MERCOSUR Ad Hoc Arbitral Tribunal were based on MERCOSUR law.

8. Indeed, the jurisdiction of the dispute settlement mechanism established by the *Protocol of Brasilia* is limited to disputes concerning the application and interpretation of MERCOSUR law. Article 1 of the *Protocol of Brasilia* states in this regard that

> Las controversias que surjan entre los Estados Partes sobre la interpretación, aplicación o incumplimiento de las disposiciones contenidas en el Tratado de Asunción, de los acuerdos celebrados en el marco del mismo, así como de las Decisiones del Consejo del mercado Común y de las Resoluciones del Grupo del Mercado Común, serán sometidas a los procedimientos de solución establecidos en el presente protocolo.

9. Brazil argued before the Ad Hoc Arbitral Tribunal that since all the Party States of Mercosur were parties to the *WTO Agreement*, the *Anti-Dumping Agreement* was part of the relevant MERCOSUR law.[12] This view, however, was rejected by the Ad Hoc Arbitral Tribunal, which declined to rule on the consistency of the measure in dispute with the *Anti-Dumping Agreement*.[13]

(b) Article 3.2 of the DSU

10. The relevance of Article 3.2 of the *DSU* to Argentina's request is difficult to understand. The language of Article 3.2 relied upon by Argentina is concerned exclusively with the interpretation of the *WTO Agreement*, and not with the sources of WTO law. Yet, Argentina's position appears to be, not that the ruling of the Ad Hoc Arbitral Tribunal is a relevant element for the interpretation of the *Anti-Dumping Agreement* to be made by this Panel, but rather that the existence of such ruling would preclude this Panel from making such interpretation.

---

[10] Panel Report, India - Measures Affecting the Automotive Sector, WT/DS146/R, WT/DS175/R ("India - Autos").
[11] *Ibid.*, para.7.66
[12] Arbitration ruling, para. 30.
[13] *Ibid.*, paras. 127-130.

11. In any event, it is difficult to see how the interpretation of the provisions of MERCOSUR law made by the Ad Hoc Arbitral Tribunal could become relevant, in accordance with the rules laid down in Articles 31 and 32 of the *Vienna Convention*, for the interpretation of the provisions of the *Anti-Dumping Agreement* at issue in this dispute.

(c) *Abuse of rights and estoppel*

12. Although Argentina has made these two arguments separately, they raise essentially the same issues. Therefore, the EC will consider them together.

13. As recalled by Argentina, Article 3.10 of the *DSU* provides that

> if a dispute arises, all Members will engage in these procedures in good faith in an effort to resolve the dispute…

14. In *United States - FSC*, the Appellate Body relied upon Article 3.10 in order to conclude that the United States was precluded from raising at the appellate stage a defence which it had failed to invoke in a timely manner during the panel proceedings.[14] This case shows that Article 3.10 of the *DSU* is more than a mere exhortation. Members are under a positive duty to exercise their procedural rights under the *DSU* in good faith and may forfeit those rights if they fail to do so.

15. The EC does not consider it necessary to take a position on the issue of whether a Member would abuse its right to a panel under the *DSU* and, hence, act inconsistently with Article 3.10 if it were to request the establishment of a panel in violation of the principle of *estoppel*.[15] Indeed, this Panel need not reach this issue because, in any event, Brazil's conduct is not contrary to that principle.

16. As noted by the panel in *EC - Bananas I*, *estoppel* can only "result from the express, or in exceptional cases implied consent of the complaining parties".[16] The same panel noted that, in particular,

> The decision of a contracting party not to invoke a right vis-à-vis another contracting party at a particular point in time can, therefore, by itself, not reasonably be assumed to be a decision to release that other contracting party from its obligations under the General Agreement.[17]

17. The facts alleged by Argentina are not sufficient to conclude that Brazil has "consented", whether explicitly or implicitly, not to bring this dispute before the WTO. The *Protocol of Brasilia* contains no provision which limits in any manner the right of the parties to request a panel under the *WTO Agreement* with respect to a

---

[14] Appellate Body Report, United States - Tax Treatment for "Foreign Sales Corporation", WT/DS108/AB/R, DSR 2000:III, 1619, para. 166.

[15] The panel in *India - Autos* (at footnote 364) suggested that a Member may be estopped from requesting the establishment of a panel with respect to a matter which has been the subject of a mutually agreed solution.

[16] Panel Report, EEC - Member States' Import Regimes for Bananas, DS32/R ("EC - Bananas I") (unadopted), para 361. See also Panel Report, Guatemala - Definitive Anti-Dumping measures on Grey Portland Cement from Mexico, WT/DS156/R, DSR 2000:XI, footnote 791, ("it is clear that not any silence can be considered to constitute consent").

[17] Panel Report, EC - Bananas I, para.362.

Report of the Panel

measure that has already been the subject of a dispute under that Protocol.[18] Thus, the mere fact that Brazil requested first the establishment of an Ad Hoc Arbitral Tribunal under the *Protocol of Brasilia* does not amount to a renunciation by Brazil to bring a dispute settlement action under the *WTO Agreement*.

18. Similarly, the mere fact that Brazil did not consider it necessary to take dispute settlement action under the *WTO Agreement* following the arbitration rulings issued in a number of other cases cited by Argentina cannot be construed as an implicit renunciation by Brazil to its right under the *WTO Agreement* to take such action in this case.

III. CLAIMS

A. Claim 21: Article 6.9

19. Brazil alleges that the report issued by the DCD prior to the Final Determination (the so-called "*Relevamiento de lo Actuado con Anterioridad al Cierre de la Etapa probatoria*") did not provide sufficient information with respect to certain facts that Brazil considers to be essential facts which formed the basis for the decision whether to apply definitive measures.[19] Brazil claims that, by failing to provide such information to the exporters, Argentina violated Article 6.9.

20. The EC does not wish to express any views with respect to the largely factual issues of whether Argentina provided the information in question and of whether the omitted information, if any, constituted "essential facts" within the meaning of Article 6.9.

21. The EC would like, nevertheless, to restate its well known position with respect to the scope of the disclosure obligation imposed by Article 6.9. Brazil has relied[20] on the panel report in *Argentina - Ceramic Tiles*.[21] The EC considers that the interpretation of Article 6.9 made in that report is incorrect in so far as the panel found that the disclosure requirements imposed by that provision could be met

---

[18] Unlike the more recent *Protocol of Olivos on Dispute Settlement*, which provides in its Article 1.2 that

Las controversias comprendidas en el ámbito de aplicación del presente Protocolo que puedan también ser sometidas al sistema de solucián de controversias de la Organización Mundial de Comercio o de otros esquemas preferenciales de comercio de que sean parte individualmente los Estados Partes del Mercosur, podrán someterse a uno u otro foro a elección de la parte demandante. Sin perjuicio de ello, las partes en la controversia podrán, de común acuerdo, convenir el foro.

Una vez iniciado un procedimiento de solución de controversias de acuerdo al párrafo anterior, ninguna de las partes podrá recurrir a los mecanismos establecidos en los otros foros respecto del mismo objeto ...

The Protocol of Olivos was signed on 18 February 2002 and has not entered into force yet. The question might be raised whether the request for the establishment of the panel made by Brazil on 25 February 2002, i.e. after the signature of the Protocol of Olivos, was consistent with Brazil's obligation under Article 18 of the Vienna Convention not to defeat the object and purpose of a signed treaty prior to its entry into force. However, Article 50 of the Protocol of Olivos appears to suggest that it does not apply to disputes already decided in accordance with the Protocol of Brasilia.

[19] Brazil's Submission, para. 342.

[20] *Ibid.*, paras. 346-347.

[21] Panel Report, Argentina - Definitive Measures on Imports of Ceramic Floor Tiles from Italy, WT/DS189/R ("Argentina - Ceramic Tiles") DSR 2001:XII, 6241.

through the inclusion in the record of documents - such as verification reports, a preliminary determination, or correspondence exchanged between the investigating authorities and individual exporters - which actually disclose to the interested parties the essential facts which, being under consideration, are anticipated by the authorities as being those which will form the basis for the decision whether to apply a definitive measure.[22]

22. The EC agrees with the panel in *Argentina - Ceramic Tiles* that Article 6.9 "does not prescribe the precise manner in which the authority is to comply with its disclosure obligation".[23] Thus, for example, the authorities may provide disclosure by sending a disclosure document to the exporters, or by holding a disclosure hearing, or by placing a disclosure document in the file.

23. The EC considers, nevertheless, that Article 6.9 requires that, regardless of the form of the disclosure, the authorities take active steps in order to identify and point to the exporters the relevant "essential facts". Accordingly, merely giving access to the file is not sufficient to satisfy the requirements of Article 6.9, unless the file contains a disclosure document specifically prepared by the authorities which clearly identifies the "essential facts".

24. For the above reasons, the EC considers that a more correct interpretation of Article 6.9 is to be found in the panel report on *Guatemala - Cement - II*.[24] In particular, the EC agrees with the following views expressed by that panel and would urge this Panel to endorse them :

> We now turn to Guatemala's argument that the Ministry disclosed the "essential facts" by making copies of the file available to interested parties. We note that an investigating authority's file is likely to contain vast amounts of information, some of which may not be relied on by the investigating authority in making its decision whether to apply definitive measures. For example, the file may contain information submitted by an interested party that was subsequently shown to be inaccurate upon verification. Although that information will remain in the file, it would not form the basis of the investigating authority's decision whether to apply definitive measures. The difficulty for an interested party with access to the file, however, is that it will not know whether particular information in the file forms the basis of the authority's final determination. One purpose of Article 6.9 is to resolve this difficulty for interested parties. This has been acknowledged by Guatemala, which has itself asserted that "[t]he object and purpose of Article 6.9 is to allow exporters a fair opportunity to comment on the important issues in an investigation after the record is closed to new facts". An interested party will not know whether a particular fact is "important" or not unless the investigating authority has explicitly identified it as one of the "essential facts" which form the basis of the authority's decision whether to impose definitive measures.

---

[22] *Ibid.*, para. 6.125.
[23] *Ibid.*
[24] Panel Report, Guatemala - Definitive Anti-Dumping Measures on Grey Portland Cement from Mexico, WT/DS156R/, DSR 2000:XI, 5295, paras. 8.229-8.230.

Furthermore, if the disclosure of "essential facts" under Article 6.9 could be undertaken simply by providing access to all information in the file, there would be little, if any, practical difference between Article 6.9 and Article 6.4. Guatemala is effectively arguing that it complied with Article 6.9 by complying with Article 6.4, *i.e.*, by providing "timely opportunities for interested parties to see all information that is relevant to the presentation of their cases ... and that is used by the authorities ...". We do not accept an interpretation of Article 6.9 that would effectively reduce its substantive requirements to those of Article 6.4. In our view, an investigating authority must do more than simply provide "timely opportunities for interested parties to see all information that is relevant to the presentation of their cases ... and that is used by the authorities ..." in order to "inform all interested parties of the essential facts under consideration which form the basis for the decision whether to apply definitive measures". In light of these considerations, we do not consider that the Ministry could comply with the requirement to "inform all interested parties of the essential facts under consideration which form the basis for the decision whether to apply definitive measures" simply by offering to provide interested parties with copies of all information in the file.

25. The EC notes that in its First Submission Argentina appears to argue that it disclosed the "essential facts" by issuing to the exporters the above mentioned *"Relevamiento de lo Actuado con Anterioridad al Cierre de la Etapa probatoria"*.[25] Thus, unlike in *Argentina - Ceramic Tiles*, Argentina does not seem to take the position that merely giving access to the file can be sufficient to comply with Article 6.9. If confirmed, the Panel would not need to address the issue discussed in the above paragraphs. The above comments, therefore, are submitted in the event that, in subsequent submissions, Argentina were to take the view that, in examining Brazil's claim, the Panel should take into account not only the *"Relevamiento de lo Actuado con Anterioridad al Cierre de la Etapa probatoria"* but also any other facts "disclosed" in other documents contained in the file.

B.   Claim 26:   Article 2.4

26. Brazil alleges that the DCD did not establish the data collection period for the dumping investigation until nine months after the investigation was initiated.[26] Brazil argues that, by doing so, Argentina acted inconsistently with Article 2.4, which provides that the authorities "shall indicate to the parties in question what information is necessary to ensure a fair comparison and shall not impose an unreasonable burden of proof".

27. The EC is of the view that Article 2.4 does not address the issue raised by Brazil. As recently recalled by the panel report in *Egypt - Steel Rebar*[27], Article 2.4 is concerned exclusively with the comparison between the normal value and the export

---

[25] Argentina's Submission, para. 185.
[26] Brazil's Submission, para. 407.
[27] Panel Report, Egypt - Definitive Anti-Dumping Measures on Steel Rebar from Turkey, WT/DS211/ para. 7.335 (not adopted yet).

price. It does not to apply to the determination of the normal value and the export price.

28. The EC would suggest that the relevant provisions to examine the issue raised by Brazil are Article 6.1, which states that

> All interested parties in an anti-dumping investigation shall be given notice of the information which the authorities require ...

and the first paragraph of Annex II, which provides that

> As soon as possible after the initiation of the investigation, the investigating authorities should specify in detail the information required from any interested party, and the manner in which that information should be structured by the interested party in its response.

C. Claims 28 and 29: Articles 9.2 and 9.3

29. The Argentinean authorities have imposed anti-dumping duties in the form a specific duty equal to the difference between the FOB price invoiced in any one shipment and a designated "minimum export price", also fixed in FOB terms.

30. Brazil claims that the duties imposed by Argentina are inconsistent with Articles 9.2 and 9.3 of the *Anti-Dumping Agreement* because they may lead to the collection of duties in excess of the dumping margin (expressed as a percentage of the export price) established for the investigation period.

31. The EC considers that Brazil's claim under Article 9.3 (and, consequently, also its claim under Article 9.2, which appears to be entirely dependent upon a violation of Article 9.3) is based on a misinterpretation of that provision. Article 9.3 provides that "the amount of the anti-dumping duty shall not exceed the margin of dumping established under Article 2". It does not provide that such margin must be the margin established for the investigation period. Nor is this required by Article 2.

32. Brazil suggests that the "dumping margin" referred to in Article 9.3 is the margin established for the investigation period because Article 2.4.2 applies in order to determine "the existence of margins of dumping during the investigation phase". This is an obvious *non-sequitur*. From the fact that Article 2.4.2 applies to the investigation phase, it does not follow that the application of all the other provisions of Article 2 is also restricted to the investigation phase. Nor does Article 2.4.2 imply that dumping margins can be calculated only for the investigation period.

33. Brazil's interpretation is contradicted by the immediate context of Article 9.3. Article 9.3.1 envisages the possibility to collect duties on a retrospective basis, which, by definition, presupposes the possibility to calculate the dumping margins on the basis of data for individual shipments or for time-periods outside the investigation period. Similarly, Article 9.3.2 provides that, where duties are assessed prospectively, the authorities shall refund the duties "paid in excess of the dumping margin". That "dumping margin" is not the margin established for the investigation period, but rather the margin established for individual shipments or time-periods after the imposition of the duties.

34. Furthermore, Brazil's claim would seem to imply that the application of variable anti-dumping duties, or indeed the application of any kind of specific duties, is contrary *per se* to Articles 9.2. The EC strongly disagrees with that proposition.

The *Anti-Dumping Agreement* does not require to express the margin of dumping as a percentage of the export price (except for the purpose of establishing whether it is *de minimis*[28]). Nor does it prescribe any particular type of duties.

35. The collection of variable duties equal to the difference between the normal value established for the investigation period and the export prices of the shipments made after the imposition of the duties is expressly contemplated in Article 9.4 of the *Anti-dumping Agreement*, which provides in pertinent part that

> When the authorities have limited their examination in accordance with the second sentence of paragraph 10 of Article 6, any anti-dumping duty applied to imports from exporters or producers not included in the examination shall not exceed:
>
> [...]
>
> (ii) where the liability for payment of anti-dumping duties is calculated on the basis of a prospective normal value, the difference between the weighted average normal value of the selected exporters or producers and the export prices of producers or exporters not individually examined.

36. Article 9.4 (ii) lays down rules to calculate the "all-others" rate where the duties applied to the exporters included in the sample are calculated on the basis of prospective normal values. It presupposes, therefore, that the use of such prospective normal values is not inconsistent *per se* with the *Anti-Dumping Agreement*, including with Articles 9.2 and 9.3.

37. The precise method followed by the Argentinean authorities in order to calculate the so-called "minimum export prices" is unclear to the EC. In particular, it is unclear whether, and if so how, those "minimum export prices" relate to the normal values established during the investigation. The EC would observe, nevertheless, that the "minimum export prices" set out in the table included at pages 112 and 113 of Brazil's Submission appear to be lower than the corresponding normal values shown in the table at page 111. In the EC's view, if it were confirmed that the "minimum export prices" applied by Argentina are equal to, or lower than the relevant normal values established during the investigation, the collection of a variable duty equal to the difference between those "minimum export price" and the export prices of the shipments made after the imposition of the duties would not be inconsistent with Articles 9.2 and 9.3 of the *Anti-Dumping Agreement*.

D. Claims 34, 35, 36 and 37: Articles 3.1, 3.2, 3.4 and 3.5

38. The DCD found that imports from two exporters (Nicolini and Seara) were not dumped.[29] Brazil argues that the CNCE did not exclude those imports from the "dumped imports" analysed in the injury determination.[30] Brazil claims that, by failing to do so, Argentina violated Articles 3.1, 3.2, 3.4 and 3.5 of the *Anti-Dumping Agreement*.

---

[28] Cf. Article 5.8 of the *Anti-Dumping Agreement*.
[29] Brazil's Submission, para. 445.
[30] *Ibid.*, paras. 450-451.

39.   Argentina appears to argue that, in fact, it did exclude imports from Nicolini and Seara from the injury determination.[31] The comments below are submitted in the event that the Panel were to find that, contrary to Argentina's contention, imports from those exporters were included in the injury analysis.

40.   For the reasons explained below, the EC considers that Argentina was entitled to treat all imports from Brazil as "dumped imports" for the purposes of the injury determination and, therefore, did not act inconsistently with the provisions invoked by Brazil.

41.   The *Anti-Dumping Agreement* is concerned with dumping between countries. This is reflected in the definition of dumping contained in Article VI:1 of the *GATT* and in Article 2.1 of the *Anti-Dumping Agreement*, as well as in the following basic features of the anti-dumping investigations:

- investigations are opened with respect to countries and not with respect to individual exporters. This is evident from Article 12.1, which provides that the notice of initiation shall contain "the name of the exporting country or countries";

- once the investigation is open, all exports of the product from the named country must be examined in order to determine dumping and injury, subject to the possibility to resort to sampling in accordance with Article 6.10;

- although Article 6.10 provides that, as a rule, an individual dumping margin must be established for each exporter (*inter alia* to ensure that the measures are effective), there is normally always a general duty (the "residual" or "all others" duty) applicable to all unnamed exporters on a country-by-country basis. This practice is comforted by Article 9.2 which provides that, where duties are imposed, if it is impracticable to name all the suppliers from one country, the authorities may name the supplying country.

42.   The wording of Article 3.3 confirms that the notion of "dumped imports", as used in Article 3, refers to all the imports of the product under consideration from each country concerned. It provides that

> Where imports of a product from more than one country are simultaneously subject to anti-dumping investigations, the investigating authorities may cumulatively assess the effects of such imports only if they determine that (a) the margin of dumping established in relation to the imports from each country is more than de minimis as defined in paragraph 8 of Article 5 and the volume of imports from each country is not negligible and (b) a cumulative assessment of the effects of the imports is appropriate in light of the conditions of competition between the imported products and the conditions of competition between the imported products and the like product.

43.   There are no corresponding rules to address the cumulation of imports from several exporters, although this would be just as necessary if the term "dumped

---

[31] Argentina's Submission, paras. 266-273.

imports" were taken to require separate consideration of the imports from different exporters.

44. Additional support is provided by Article 5.7 of the *Anti-Dumping Agreement*, which provides that dumping and injury must be examined simultaneously during the course of the investigation. Since injury has to be investigated before it is established which exporters are dumping, it is clear that the term "dumped imports" used in connection with the injury provisions of Article 3 must be referring to all imports of the product under investigation (although the finding of injury is, of course, conditional upon dumping being found).[32]

E. Claim 41: Article 4.1

45. Brazil alleges that the assessment of the impact of the dumped imports upon the domestic industry was based on the data supplied by ten domestic producers that responded to the CNCE's questionnaires, out of the thirteen producers that had supported the application.[33] According to Brazil, those ten producers accounted for 46 per cent of the total domestic production in 1998.[34]

46. Brazil claims that 46 per cent of the total domestic production does not constitute a "major proportion" of the total domestic production within the meaning of Article 4.1 of the *Anti-Dumping Agreement*. According to Brazil, "a major proportion" means at least 50 per cent of the total production.[35]

47. As explained below, the EC disagrees with Brazil's interpretation of the terms "a major proportion". In the EC's view, "a major proportion" does not mean the majority of the domestic production, but rather an important part thereof, which may be less than 50 per cent. In any event, assuming that "a major proportion" meant at least 50 per cent of the domestic production, this would not imply that the determination of injury must be based necessarily on data pertaining to domestic producers representing that proportion.

(a) The meaning of "a major proportion"

48. Brazil asserts that the ordinary meaning of the term "major proportion" is "the majority".[36] That is indeed one of the ordinary meanings of "major", but not the only one. The *New Shorter Oxford Dictionary* gives another meaning of "major":

---

[32] In addition, the EC would like to point out that its interpretation is also warranted in view of the fact that a joint injury analysis is possible or even warranted when anti-dumping and anti-subsidy proceedings concerning the same country run in parallel. The salmon Panel has recognized that the injury analysis can be carried out jointly for both such proceedings (see paras 572 and 573 of the Panel Report on *United States - Imposition of Anti-Dumping Duties on Imports of Fresh Atlantic Salmon from Norway*, ADP/87, adopted on 27 April 1994). Indeed, since the starting point for such analysis is the volume and the prices of the imports concerned (and not the level of dumping or subsidization), it does not seem appropriate to distinguish at company level. If the EC's interpretation were not accepted, two different injury examinations would have to be carried out if a company is found to be dumping but not to be subsidized or *vice versa*. This makes injury examinations often unworkable and that cannot have been the intention of the drafters of the *Anti-Dumping Agreement*.
[33] Brazil's Submission, para. 509.
[34] *Ibid.*, para. 510.
[35] *Ibid.*, paras 512-519.
[36] Brazil's Submission, para. 514.

"unusually important, serious or significant".[37] Similarly, *Le Petit Robert* defines the word "majeur" as "très grand, très important".[38]

49.   The EC submits that in the context of Article 4.1 the phrase "a major proportion" does not mean "the majority", but rather an important part. Article 4.1 alludes to "*a* major proportion", rather than "*the* major proportion". The use of the indefinite article "a" indicates that there may be more than one "major proportion" and, therefore, that it is not necessary that "a major proportion" represents "the majority" of domestic production. Confirmation of this is provided by the Spanish version of the *Anti-Dumping Agreement*, where the term "major" has been rendered as "importante".

50.   The EC's interpretation is supported by Article 5.4, which provides that an investigation shall not be initiated unless the authorities determine that the application has been made "by or on behalf of the domestic industry". Article 5.4 goes on to state that

> The application shall be considered to have been made "by or on behalf of the domestic industry" if it is supported by those domestic producers whose collective output constitutes more than 50 per cent of the total production of the like product produced by that portion of the domestic industry expressing either support for or opposition to the application. However, no investigation shall be initiated when domestic producers expressly supporting the application account for less than 25 per cent of the total production of the like product produced by the domestic industry.

51.   Thus, in accordance with Article 5.4, an application may be considered to have been made "on behalf of the domestic industry" even if the producers which support it represent less than 50 per cent of the domestic production. The term "domestic industry" has the same meaning throughout the *Anti-Dumping Agreement*.[39] If a number of producers which accounts for less than 50 per cent of the domestic production may, in certain circumstances, be considered to constitute "a major proportion" of the domestic production for the purposes of Article 5.4, then the same should be true also for the purposes of the other provisions of the *Anti-Dumping Agreement*.

52.   Moreover, it would be illogical to allow the opening of an investigation on the basis of an application filed by producers which represent less than 50 per cent of the domestic production only to conclude subsequently that the injury suffered by those producers does not, by reason of the percentage of the domestic production accounted by those producers, amount to injury to the "domestic industry".

>   *(b)   Must the injury determination be based on data for producers representing a "major proportion" of domestic production ?*

53.   Brazil assumes that if the term "a major proportion" means at least 50 per cent of the domestic production, then the fact of basing the injury analysis on data for

---

[37] The New Shorter Oxford Dictionary, Clarendon Press Oxford, 1993.
[38] Le Petit Robert, 1976.
[39] Cf. The introductory clause of Article 4.1 ("For the purposes of this agreement…").

producers which represent less than that percentage amounts necessarily to a violation of Article 4.1.

54. As explained above, the EC disagrees with the premise of Brazil's claim, i.e. that "major proportion" means at least 50 per cent. In any event, the EC takes issue also with the consequence attached by Brazil to that premise. The EC submits that, even if "a major proportion" meant at least 50 per cent of the domestic production, there are circumstances in which the authorities could base an injury finding on data pertaining to producers accounting for less than that percentage.

55. In the first place, if a domestic producer which is part of the domestic industry fails to cooperate in the investigation, as indeed happened in the case under consideration, the authorities may, in accordance with the provisions of Article 6.8 and Annex II, resort to "facts available" in order to establish whether such producer has been injured. For that purpose, the relevant "facts available" may include the data collected from other producers which have co-operated in the investigation.

56. Second, when assessing the state of the domestic industry, the authorities may resort to sampling techniques. In other words, the investigating authorities may consider that data for some domestic producers are representative of the state of the whole of the domestic industry. The possibility to use sampling techniques is expressly envisaged in Article 6.10 with respect to the dumping determination. There is no reason why similar sampling techniques should not be allowed also for the purposes of the injury determination, subject to the general requirement of Article 3.1 that the determination of injury must be based on "positive evidence" and involve an "objective examination" of the relevant facts.

ANNEX C-3

THIRD PARTY SUBMISSION OF GUATEMALA

(9 September 2002)

INTRODUCTION

1. Guatemala presents this third-party submission because of its systemic interest in the correct interpretation of the Agreement on Implementation of Article VI of the General Agreement on Tariffs and Trade 1994 (hereinafter "the Anti-Dumping Agreement").

2. The Government of Guatemala understands that most of the procedural errors arising in the course of anti-dumping investigations are due to the very complexity of the procedure, with which Members that are only sporadically involved in its application are not usually familiar. However, Guatemala holds the view that, in implementing such measures, the Members must fully guarantee observance of the rules of the WTO Agreements governing such mechanisms.

3. Many of the issues in this dispute refer to factual points on which Guatemala is not in a position to comment. Guatemala will therefore limit itself to addressing a matter of legal interpretation stemming from its interest. In any case, it reserves the right to amplify the views put forward in this submission.

ARTICLE 4.1 OF THE ANTI-DUMPING AGREEMENT

4. The Spanish version of Article 4.1 establishes that:

   "A los efectos del presente Acuerdo, la expresión "rama de producción nacional" se entenderá en el sentido de abarcar el conjunto de los productores nacionales de los productos similares, o aquellos de entre ellos cuya producción conjunta constituya una proporción importante de la producción nacional total de dichos productos."

5. The English version of Article 4.1 establishes that:

   "For the purposes of this Agreement, the term "domestic industry" shall be interpreted as referring to the domestic producers as a whole of the like products or to those of them whose collective output of the products constitutes a major proportion of the total domestic production of those products."

ARGUMENTS OF BRAZIL

6. In its first written submission, Brazil notes that Article 4.1 defines the term "domestic industry" as the domestic producers as a whole of the like products or

Report of the Panel

those of them whose collective output of the products constitutes a major proportion of the total domestic production of those products.[1]

7. Brazil also notes that the issue before the Panel is whether 46 per cent of the total domestic production of poultry in Argentina constitutes a major proportion of the total domestic production of that product.[2]

8. Brazil then suggests that, in order to examine the issue, the Panel must interpret the meaning of the term "major proportion" in Article 4.1 of the Agreement.[3]

9. In paragraph 514 of its first written submission, Brazil notes that:

"According to ordinary meaning interpretation, the term "major part"[4] is defined as "the majority"[5]. "Majority" is understood to mean "the greater number or part"[6]. From these definitions, the phrase "major proportion" can be understood as the greater part in relation to the whole. If the whole in question is 100 per cent of the total domestic production of the like product, 46 per cent cannot be considered as the greater part in relation to the whole."

10. In the light of the foregoing, Brazil notes that Article 4.1 provides that the domestic industry can be represented by 100 per cent of the domestic producers of the like products or by those of them whose production, jointly considered, constitutes more than half of the domestic production. If the collective output of those whose domestic production, jointly considered, is less than 50 per cent of the total domestic production, the domestic producers do not comply with the definition of Article 4.1 of the Agreement.

11. Consequently, Brazil argues that the CNCE's determination that 46 per cent of the collective output of those whose production, jointly considered, of the like product constitutes a major proportion of the collective output of the domestic producers is inconsistent with Article 4.1 of the Agreement.[7]

ARGUMENTS OF ARGENTINA

12. In paragraphs 302 to 304 of its first written submission, Argentina notes that:

"302. The definition of 'domestic industry' was consistent with the WTO rules because Argentina considers that 46 per cent of total production is "a major proportion". Brazil's contention that "a major proportion" can only represent at least 50 per cent of the domestic industry is a subjective opinion and is not based on Article 4 of the Anti-Dumping Agreement.

303. According to Record No. 576, the firms concerned represented 46.2 per cent of the domestic industry in 1998, so the CNCE

---

[1] Paragraph 511 of Brazil's first written submission.
[2] Paragraph 512 of Brazil's first written submission.
[3] Paragraph 513 of Brazil's first written submission.
[4] The terms "proportion" and "part" are viewed and used as synonyms. Concise Oxford Dictionary - Ninth Edition, Oxford University Press, 1995, pages 995 and 1098.
[5] Concise Oxford Dictionary - Ninth Edition, Oxford University Press, 1995, page 822.
[6] Ibid.
[7] Paragraph 519 of Brazil's first written submission.

considered that it had complied with the requirement in Article 4.1 of the Anti-Dumping Agreement.

304. For the Argentine Republic, as for other WTO Members (in accordance with previous, consistent decisions in this respect), 46 per cent represents a major proportion because it is not by accident that the Anti-Dumping Agreement did not establish a fixed percentage in order to show what is meant by 'major proportion'."

GUATEMALA'S SUBMISSION

13. Guatemala concurs with paragraph 517 of Brazil's first written submission, stating that the establishment of the domestic industry is important, particularly with respect to the injury analysis. Because the injury examination takes into account the impact of the dumped imports on the domestic industry, if the domestic industry is not properly constituted, the impact examination in the injury analysis may be flawed.

14. Guatemala also holds the view that the requirement to make a determination of injury to the domestic industry read in the light of the definition of the domestic industry of Article 4.1 implies that the injury must be analysed with regard to the domestic producers as a whole or to those of them whose collective output constitutes a major proportion of the total domestic production of those products.

15. The injury test being one of the prerequisites for the adoption of anti-dumping measures, the taking of such measures must logically encompass the producers that are, or deem themselves to be, injured by dumping practices, hence the importance of Article 4.1 in defining what is meant by "domestic industry".

16. There is a difference between the Spanish and the English version of paragraph 1 of Article 4. Indeed, the words "proporción importante" in the Spanish version are translated as "major proportion" in the English version.

17. According to Brazil's interpretation, the term "major proportion" is defined as "the majority", which is understood to mean "the greater number or part".

18. According to that interpretation, the phrase is understood to mean the greater part in relation to a "whole". Brazil suggests that the "whole" in question is 100 per cent of the total domestic production of the like products.

19. In other words, Brazil understands Article 4.1 to provide that the domestic industry can be represented by 100 per cent of the domestic producers of the like products or by those of them whose production, jointly considered, constitutes more than half of the domestic production. Thus, if the collective output of those whose domestic production, jointly considered, is less than 50 per cent of the total domestic production, the domestic producers do not comply with the definition of Article 4.1 of the Anti-Dumping Agreement.

20. Guatemala understands the term "major" to mean "muy importante, serio, a fondo"[8] (very important, serious, thorough). Likewise, it understands the term "importante" to mean "la cualidad de lo importante, de lo que es muy conveniente o interesante, o de mucha entidad o consecuencia"[9] (the quality of that which is

---

[8] Oxford Spanish Dictionary, Oxford University Press, 2001, page 1293.
[9] Diccionario de la Lengua Española. Real Academia Española, XXII Edición, 2001, page 1255.

important, very appropriate or interesting, or of considerable importance or consequence)."

21. In view of the above, Guatemala acknowledges that the term "major" used in the English version could involve a more exacting criterion than that implied by the term "importante" used in the Spanish version. However, it is of the opinion that the term "importante" in the Spanish version of Article 4.1 could on no account be defined as representing more than half of a "whole", as Brazil suggests.

22. Guatemala considers that this difference should not be interpreted as Brazil has suggested, because this would have significant practical implications.

23. Attempts to find a solution should in any event be based on the recognition that the Article in question does not expressly establish any percentage indicative of a "proporción importante" or a "major proportion."

24. For the Argentine Republic, as for other WTO Members (in accordance with previous, consistent decisions in this respect), 46 per cent represents a major proportion ("proporción importante"). In this respect, Guatemala considers that the practice of the Members does not, in and of itself, guarantee the consistency of a measure with a WTO Agreement.

25. Guatemala understands that the aforementioned provision leaves the authority some room for discretion in determining, with regard to the facts and in the light of the circumstances specific to each industry, what is meant by the expression "domestic industry". We thus consider that this expression encompasses a great deal more than the definition of a percentage.

26. Moreover, the Report of the Group of Experts that examined anti-dumping and countervailing duties states the following:

"The Group then discussed the term "industry" in relation to the concept of injury and agreed that, even though individual cases would obviously give rise to particular problems, as a general guiding principle judgements of material injury should be related to total national output of the like commodity concerned or a significant part thereof."[10] (Emphasis added).

27. It seems to us that Article 4.1 allows the investigating authority to determine, depending on the complexity of the case, what is meant by the phrase "*those of them whose collective output of the products constitutes a major proportion of the total domestic production of those products*." The investigating authority's discretionary power is not unlimited, however, since it would not be able to invoke this phrase alone.

28. Likewise, our understanding is that this provision is not intended to give the investigating authority unlimited discretion in the determination of the domestic industry and that such a determination must necessarily be examined in relation to the notion of injury, without prejudice to the other assumptions to be gathered and verified prior to the final determination of injury.

---

[10] L/978, adopted on 13 May 1959, 8S/145, para. 18.

29. Guatemala thus urges the Panel to refrain from implying, in any context whatsoever, that the reference to "a major proportion" in Article 4.1 requires reaching the percentage of 50 per cent.

30. In any event, and pursuant to the examination rule in Article 17.6 of the Anti-Dumping Agreement, the Panel can assess the grounds for the Argentine authority's decision according to the decision's degree of consistency with that which an unbiased and impartial authority would have made in this case.

ANNEX C-4

THIRD PARTY SUBMISSION OF PARAGUAY
(9 September 2002)

Background

1. At its meeting on 17 April 2002, the DSB established a panel in accordance with Article 6 of the DSU to examine the matter referred to the DSB by Brazil (WT/DS241/3).

2. At that meeting, the parties to the dispute also agreed that the Panel should have standard terms of reference. The terms of reference are, therefore, the following:

> "To examine, in the light of the relevant provisions of the covered agreements cited by Brazil in document WT/DS241/3, the matter referred by Brazil to the DSB in that document, and to make such findings as will assist the DSB in making the recommendations or in giving the rulings provided for in those agreements."

3. At that meeting, Paraguay reserved the right under Article 10 of the DSU to participate as a third party in the procedure.

4. In this submission, Paraguay wishes to convey its preliminary views on the case, without prejudice to any other oral or written submission it may make at the substantive meeting of the Panel with the third parties.

Rules and principles of public international law relevant to and applicable in this case

5. Paraguay considers that, in accordance with the general principles of public international law, this case is "res judicata" because it has already been brought under the dispute settlement procedure established within the framework of MERCOSUR, and under the Brasilia Protocol in particular.

6. In this regard, Article 21[1] of the Brasilia Protocol clearly establishes the unappealable and binding nature of awards rendered by the Ad Hoc Arbitral Tribunal, which are deemed to be "res judicata" - a principle that should prevail in addressing this case.

7. As noted in paragraph 20 of Argentina's written submission, the fact that the States party to MERCOSUR resorted to the Protocol of Brasilia mechanism demonstrates their full acceptance of that mechanism as a part of the MERCOSUR legal framework and as a dispute settlement procedure *in totum*, which is why it

---

[1] Article 21
1. The decisions of the Arbitral Tribunal cannot be appealed, and are binding on the State Parties to the controversies from the moment the respective notification is received and will be deemed by them to have the effect of res judicata.
2. The decisions should be complied with within a time-limit of fifteen (15) days, unless the Arbitral Tribunal fixes a different time-limit.

should be considered that the Award rendered by the MERCOSUR Ad Hoc Arbitral Tribunal[2] gives res judicata effect to this case.

8. In Paraguay's view, it is also relevant to mention the signing of the Olivos Protocol for the settlement of disputes within MERCOSUR among the four States party to MERCOSUR. Although not yet in force, the Protocol provides in Article 1.2 that: " ... *Disputes within the scope of this Protocol that can also be addressed under the dispute settlement system of the World Trade Organization or those of other preferential trade arrangements entered into by the States Parties to MERCOSUR on an individual basis may be brought before any one of those forums, at the complainant's discretion. Without prejudice to the foregoing, the parties to the dispute may jointly agree on the forum.*

Once a dispute settlement procedure has been initiated pursuant to the preceding paragraph, none of the parties may resort to the mechanisms established in the other forums in respect of the same subject-matter."[3]

This instrument, negotiated and signed by the States Parties to MERCOSUR, allows them to choose the forum in which they wish disputes to be settled, with the restriction constituted by the exclusion clause, which stipulates that once a procedure has been initiated in one forum, this precludes resorting to any of the other forums provided for in the Protocol.

9. Paraguay also wishes to draw the Panel's attention to a rule of public international law in force, namely Article 18 of the Vienna Convention on the Law of Treaties of 1969, which reads as follows:

A State is **obliged to refrain**[4] from acts which would defeat the object and purpose of a treaty when:

(a) it has signed the treaty or has exchanged instruments constituting the treaty subject to ratification, acceptance or approval, until it shall have made its intention clear not to become a party to the treaty; or

(b) ... ".

10. In view of the foregoing, Paraguay considers this case as having been subject to a prior dispute settlement procedure, as recognized by both parties and resolved by a ruling that is binding on and mandatory for those parties. Hence this case should not be addressed by this Panel, for if it were, this would constitute a violation of the principles and rules of public international law and failure to abide by decisions handed down by MERCOSUR institutions, in this instance the award of an Ad Hoc Arbitral Tribunal constituted under the Brasilia Protocol.

---

[2] Award of the MERCOSUR Ad Hoc Arbitral Tribunal constituted to rule on the dispute between the Federative Republic of Brazil and the Argentine Republic regarding the imposition of anti-dumping measures on exports of whole poultry from Brazil (Res. 574/2000) of the Ministry of the Economy of the Argentine Republic. Date: 21 May 2001.
[3] Emphasis added.
[4] *Ibid.*

Report of the Panel

ANNEX C-5

THIRD PARTY SUBMISSION OF THE UNITED STATES
(9 September 2002)

TABLE OF CONTENTS

		Page
I.	INTRODUCTION	C-2278
II.	ARTICLE 5.7 OF THE AD AGREEMENT DOES NOT REQUIRE MEMBERS DECIDING WHETHER TO INITIATE AN ANTI-DUMPING INVESTIGATION TO EVALUATE DUMPING AND INJURY DATA FROM "SIMULTANEOUS" TIME PERIODS	C-2279
III.	THE TERM "A MAJOR PROPORTION" IN THE DEFINITION OF THE DOMESTIC INDUSTRY IN ARTICLE 4.1 OF THE AGREEMENT DOES NOT MEAN "THE MAJORITY"	C-2280
IV.	A MEMBER'S DECISION TO EVALUATE CERTAIN FACTORS UNDER ARTICLE 3.4 USING A TIME PERIOD DIFFERENT THAN THAT USED FOR OTHER FACTORS WOULD NOT *PER SE* BREACH ARTICLE 3.1	C-2281
V.	AN INVESTIGATING AUTHORITY'S FAILURE TO DISCUSS A PARTICULAR ARTICLE 3.4 FACTOR DOES NOT NECESSARILY BREACH ARTICLE 12.2.2	C-2282
VI.	THE PANEL SHOULD DECLINE TO PROVIDE VIEWS ON THE PROPER INTERPRETATION OF ARTICLE 18.2 OF THE DSU	C-2282
VII.	CONCLUSION	C-2283

I. INTRODUCTION

1. The United States welcomes the opportunity to present its views in this proceeding on *Argentina - Definitive Anti-Dumping Duties on Poultry from Brazil* (DS241). The United States is limiting its comments to certain issues relating to the proper legal interpretation of various articles of the *Agreement on Implementation of Article VI of the General Agreement on Tariffs and Trade 1994* (the "AD Agreement").[1]

---

[1] The United States has not had an opportunity to review fully Argentina's written submission in this dispute and is therefore limiting itself to addressing Brazil's written submission at this time. The United States will address Argentina's written submission, as appropriate, at the first Panel meeting.

II. ARTICLE 5.7 OF THE AD AGREEMENT DOES NOT REQUIRE MEMBERS DECIDING WHETHER TO INITIATE AN ANTI-DUMPING INVESTIGATION TO EVALUATE DUMPING AND INJURY DATA FROM "SIMULTANEOUS" TIME PERIODS

2. Brazil claims that Argentina breached Article 5.7 of the AD Agreement because its investigating authorities evaluated dumping and injury data that covered non-identical time periods when it determined whether to initiate the challenged investigation.[2] Brazil's argument is based on a misinterpretation of the term "simultaneously" as that term is used in Article 5.7.

3. Article 5.7 states that in deciding whether to initiate an investigation, the "evidence of both dumping and injury shall be considered simultaneously. . . ." Brazil appears to believe that this language obligates a Member to ensure that its investigating authorities consider dumping and injury information from simultaneous (*i.e.*, identical) time periods. Viewed in context, however, the term "simultaneously" is linked to the term "considered," not the term "evidence." Thus, the obligation in Article 5.7 is to *consider* the evidence of dumping and injury simultaneously (for example, in concurrent investigations), not to consider *evidence* of dumping and injury collected from simultaneous (or identical) time periods.

4. As the Committee on Anti-Dumping Practices has recognized, the AD Agreement "does not establish any period of investigation" or establish guidelines for determining an appropriate period of investigation "for the examination of either dumping or injury."[3] The Committee has adopted a non-binding recommendation, however, which calls for a twelve-month period of investigation for analyses of dumping, and a three-year period of investigation for analyses of injury.[4] On its face, the Committee's recommendation indicates the lack of any basis for requiring Members to examine dumping and injury information from "simultaneous" time periods. The lack of congruity in the recommended time periods reflects the inherent differences in the nature of the analyses that administering authorities conduct for determining the existence of dumping, on the one hand, and injury, on the other.

5. For example, a Member's determination of dumping normally need not consider trends over time. An injury determination, by contrast, will normally require an investigating authority to gather information covering more than one year in order to evaluate volume and price changes. An importing Member's consideration of whether there is sufficient evidence relating to injury, such as whether there have been significant absolute or relative increases in the volume of dumped imports, must be made in the context of an appropriate time frame, which will almost always extend longer than the period of investigation for making a dumping calculation.[5]

---

[2] *See, e.g.,* Brazil's first written submission at para. 168.

[3] Committee on Anti-Dumping Practices, *Recommendation Concerning the Periods of Data Collection for Anti-Dumping Investigations*, G/ADP/6, adopted by the Committee on 5 May 2000.

[4] *Ibid.*

[5] Indeed, the effects of import volume increases or price undercutting often take longer than a year to reach the level where they would be significant, and the impact of those effects on the domestic industry's condition may take even longer to become apparent. Furthermore, the fact that execution of sales in some industries can take as long as a year, and that in some industries sales are made pursuant to annual contracts, further demonstrates the appropriateness of examining a multi-year period in injury investigations.

Report of the Panel

6. The US views on this issue are not meant to suggest, however, that an investigating authority is free to examine dumping and injury information from entirely unrelated time periods. Article 3.5 of the AD Agreement clearly requires a Member to demonstrate a causal relationship between the dumped imports and injury to the domestic industry.[6] It is entirely possible that the particular time periods that a Member chooses to examine in a particular investigation could call into question whether the Member has demonstrated such a causal link. Article 5.7 of the AD Agreement, however, does not bear on this matter.

III. THE TERM "A MAJOR PROPORTION" IN THE DEFINITION OF THE DOMESTIC INDUSTRY IN ARTICLE 4.1 OF THE AGREEMENT DOES NOT MEAN "THE MAJORITY"

7. Article 4.1 of the AD Agreement defines the term "domestic industry" as:

> the domestic producers as a *whole* of the like products *or* . . . those of them whose collective output of the products constitutes *a major proportion* of the total domestic production of those products . . . .

(emphasis added). Brazil claims that the term "major proportion" is synonymous with "majority," and that Argentina breached Article 4.1 because its investigating authority examined data for 46 per cent of the domestic industry, which is less than a majority.[7] The United States respectfully submits that Brazil's argument is based upon a misinterpretation of Article 4.1.

8. As an initial matter, Article 4.1 is just a definition. As a definition, it does not impose an independent obligation on WTO Members.[8] For this reason alone, there is no basis for Brazil's claim that Argentina's injury analysis breached Article 4.1.

9. Even if this were not the case, however, Brazil's claim would find no support in the text of Article 4.1. First, the AD Agreement does not define the term "major," and the ordinary meaning of the term is "[d]esignating the greater *or relatively greater* of . . . two things" - the opposite of "minor."[9] It can also mean "unusually important, serious, or significant."[10] None of these meanings necessarily connotes "the majority."

10. Second, Brazil's argument that "major proportion" actually means "majority" directly conflicts with the fact that the drafters were quite explicit, elsewhere in the Agreement, when they intended to impose a majority requirement for a particular obligation. Specifically, Article 5.4 of the Agreement provides that an application is made "by or on behalf of the domestic industry" if it is supported by those domestic producers whose collective output constitutes "more than 50 per cent" of the total production of the specified portion of the industry. Unlike Article 4.1, Article 5.4

---

[6] Similarly, Article 5.2 of the AD Agreement requires an application for an investigation to include evidence of dumping, injury, and causal link.
[7] Brazil's first written submission, paras. 511-519.
[8] See Appellate Body Report on *United States - Tax Treatment for "Foreign Sales Corporations", Recourse to Article 21.5 of the DSU by the European Communities*, WT/DS108/AB/RW, adopted 29 January 2002, DSR 2002:I, 55, para. 85 (stating that the definition of the term "subsidy" in Article 1.1 of the *Agreement on Subsidies and Countervailing Measures* "does not impose any obligation on Members with respect to the subsidies it defines.").
[9] *The New Shorter Oxford English Dictionary*, vol. 1 at 1670 (1993) (emphasis added).
[10] Ibid.

clearly imposes a majority requirement. Article 4.1 establishes a different standard: "a major proportion."

11. Viewing the term in context also provides support for the conclusion that "major proportion" was not meant to establish a "majority" requirement. The term appears in Article 4.1 as an alternative to the industry "as a whole." The definition reflects the reality in many anti-dumping investigations that it will not be possible to obtain the requested information from all domestic producers of the like product, and confirms that an injury determination would not be rendered inadequate simply because an investigating authority was unable to obtain information from all such producers. The AD Agreement does not establish a numerical benchmark for what constitutes a "major" proportion of a domestic industry. It will vary from case to case.

IV. A MEMBER'S DECISION TO EVALUATE CERTAIN FACTORS UNDER ARTICLE 3.4 USING A TIME PERIOD DIFFERENT THAN THAT USED FOR OTHER FACTORS WOULD NOT *PER SE* BREACH ARTICLE 3.1

12. Brazil claims that Argentina committed a *per se* breach of Article 3.1 by evaluating certain Article 3.4 factors over the period January 1996 through June 1999, and other factors over the period January 1996 through December 1998.[11] The United States takes no position on the question whether Argentina's decision to base its analysis on two different time periods breached its obligations in the particular case at issue. The United States disagrees, however, with Brazil's contention that an analysis of differing time periods *cannot* be objective, and thus *per se* breaches Article 3.1.

13. The panel report in *United States - Hot Rolled Steel* is instructive in this regard.[12] In that investigation, the United States gathered information on all factors over the entire three year period of investigation, and it evaluated the various factors, at various instances, over the three year period.[13] With regard to certain factors pertaining to impact, however, the United States compared data for 1998 with data for 1997, without explicitly discussing the data for 1996.[14] The Panel concluded that the United States' failure to explicitly address the data for 1996 did not "undermine the adequacy of the [United States'] evaluation of the relevant economic factors, in light of its analysis and explanations, so as to render its examination of the impact of dumped imports on the domestic industry inconsistent with the AD Agreement."[15] The Panel's finding is consistent with the US view that the use of differing time periods to evaluate injury does not *per se* mean the investigating authority failed to carry out an objective examination.

---

[11] *See* Brazil's first written submission, paras. 425-430.
[12] Panel Report on *United States - Anti-Dumping Measures on Certain Hot-Rolled Steel Products from Japan,* WT/DS184/R, adopted 23 August 2001 ("*United States - Hot Rolled Steel*"), DSR 2001:X, 4769.
[13] *Ibid.*, at para. 7.227.
[14] *Ibid.*, at para. 7.228.
[15] *Ibid.*, at para. 7.234.

V. AN INVESTIGATING AUTHORITY'S FAILURE TO DISCUSS A PARTICULAR ARTICLE 3.4 FACTOR DOES NOT NECESSARILY BREACH ARTICLE 12.2.2

14. Brazil asserts (claims 38-40) that Argentina failed to evaluate or refer to several of the factors set out in Article 3.4, and that Argentina's failure to do so breached Articles 3.1, 3.4, and 12.2.2 of the Agreement.[16] The United States agrees with Brazil that the AD Agreement requires an investigating authority to evaluate each of the Article 3.4 factors, and we take no position on the issue whether Argentina did, in fact, evaluate each of the factors in the challenged investigation.

15. The United States does not agree, however, that a failure to refer to a particular factor in the published determination necessarily breaches Article 12.2.2. Article 12.2 requires only that the authorities set forth "in sufficient detail the findings and conclusions reached on all issues of fact and law *considered material by the investigating authorities.*"[17] While all enumerated factors must be evaluated, not all are necessarily material in any particular case.

16. Given the requirement to evaluate all of the Article 3.4 factors, however, it should be discernible from the published determination that the authorities have done so. This obligation may be achieved when a determination, through its demonstration of why the authorities relied on the specific factors they found to be material in the case, thereby discloses why other factors on which they did not make specific findings were accorded little weight or were deemed not relevant at all. "[A]s long as the lack of relevance or materiality of the factors not central to the decision is at least implicitly apparent from the final determination, the Agreement's requirements are satisfied." [18]

VI. THE PANEL SHOULD DECLINE TO PROVIDE VIEWS ON THE PROPER INTERPRETATION OF ARTICLE 18.2 OF THE DSU

17. In a letter dated 8 August 2002, Brazil submitted a letter to the Panel stating its intention to release to the public a non-confidential version of its first written submission. On 15 August 2002, Argentina submitted a letter expressing its view that Brazil's proposed action would be inconsistent with Article 18.2 of the DSU. On 21 and 23 August 2002, Brazil and Canada, respectively, submitted letters opposing Argentina's views. Finally, on 27 August 2002, Argentina submitted a second letter supporting the "spirit of transparency" and requesting the Panel's views on the proper interpretation of Article 18.2.

18. The United States agrees with Brazil and Canada that nothing in Article 18.2 of the DSU would prevent a Member from releasing its own WTO submissions to the public. We have long done so as a matter of course, and we would welcome a decision by Argentina to do the same. Argentina does not need permission to make its own submissions available to the public. The United States is concerned, however, that Argentina's request for the Panel's views on this matter is, in essence, a request for an advisory opinion since there is no measure before the Panel. Furthermore,

---

[16] Brazil's first written submission, paras. 475-507.
[17] *See* Article 12.2 (emphasis added).
[18] Panel Report on *European Communities - Anti-Dumping Duties on Imports of Cotton-Type Bed Linen from India*, WT/DS141/R, adopted 12 March 2001, para. 6.163.

Article 18.2 is not within the Panel's terms of reference. The United States notes that to the extent that Argentina is asking the Panel to interpret Article 18.2, that would be incompatible with the exclusive authority of the Ministerial Conference and General Council under Article IX:2 of the *Marrakesh Agreement Establishing the World Trade Organization* to interpret the WTO agreement. We respectfully request the Panel to decline Argentina's request for views on the proper interpretation of Article 18.2.

VII. CONCLUSION

19.   The United States thanks the Panel for providing an opportunity to comment on the issues at stake in this proceeding, and hopes that its comments will prove to be useful.

ANNEX C-6

THIRD PARTY ORAL STATEMENT OF PARAGUAY
(26 September 2002)

Mr Chairman,

As one of the four States party to MERCOSUR, Paraguay wishes to convey its views on this case and defend the integration institutions created under the Treaty of Asunción of 1991, as mentioned in our third party submission a few weeks ago.

Paraguay considers that, in accordance with the general principles of public international law, this case is "res judicata" because it has already been brought under the dispute settlement procedure established within the framework of MERCOSUR, and under the Brasilia Protocol in particular.

In this regard, Article 21 of the Brasilia Protocol clearly establishes the unappealable and binding nature of awards rendered by the Ad Hoc Arbitral Tribunal, which are deemed to be "res judicata" - a principle which my delegation considers should prevail in addressing this case.

As noted in paragraph 20 of Argentina's written submission, the fact that the States party to MERCOSUR resorted to the Protocol of Brasilia mechanism demonstrates their full acceptance of that mechanism as a part of the MERCOSUR legal framework and as a dispute settlement procedure *in totum*, which is why it should be considered that the Award rendered by the MERCOSUR Ad Hoc Arbitral Tribunal gives res judicata effect to this case.

In Paraguay's view, it is also relevant to mention the signing of the Olivos Protocol for the settlement of disputes within MERCOSUR among the four States party to MERCOSUR. Although not yet in force, the Protocol provides in Article 1.2 that: "**… Disputes within the scope of this Protocol that can also be addressed under the dispute settlement system of the World Trade Organization or those of other preferential trade arrangements entered into by the States Parties to MERCOSUR on an individual basis may be brought before any one of those forums, at the complainant's discretion. Without prejudice to the foregoing, the parties to the dispute may jointly agree on the forum.**

> Once a dispute settlement procedure has been initiated pursuant to the preceding paragraph, none of the parties may resort to the mechanisms established in the other forums in respect of the same subject-matter, …"

This instrument, negotiated and signed by the States Parties to MERCOSUR, allows them to choose the forum in which they wish disputes to be settled, with the restriction constituted by the exclusion clause, which stipulates that once a procedure has been initiated in one forum, this precludes resorting to any of the other forums provided for in the Protocol.

Paraguay also wishes to draw the Panel's attention to a rule of public international law in force, on which my delegation bases the arguments set forth in this statement, namely Article 18 of the Vienna Convention on the Law of Treaties of 1969, which reads as follows:

"A State is obliged to refrain from acts which would defeat the object and purpose of a treaty when:

(a) it has signed the treaty or has exchanged instruments constituting the treaty subject to ratification, acceptance or approval, until it shall have made its intention clear not to become a party to the treaty; ..."

In view of the foregoing, Paraguay considers this case as having been subject to a prior dispute settlement procedure, as recognized by both parties and resolved by a ruling that is binding on and mandatory for those parties. Hence this case should not be addressed by this Panel, for if it were, this would constitute a violation of the principles and rules of public international law and failure to abide by decisions handed down by MERCOSUR institutions, in this instance the Award of an Ad Hoc Arbitral Tribunal constituted under the Brasilia Protocol.

Lastly, Paraguay trusts that this Panel will rule on the arguments put forward both by my delegation and by that of the Republic of Argentina, for my country's government accords vital importance to the institutions created under the international agreements and treaties to which it is party, and in this case in particular, to the MERCOSUR institutions. Compliance with and recognition of these institutions strengthens, and assures predictability and security for, the Members in general and the multilateral trading system in particular.

Thank you.

ANNEX C-7

THIRD PARTY ORAL STATEMENT OF CHILE
(26 September 2002)

Thank you, Mr Chairman.

1. Chile thanks the Panel for the opportunity to present its views in this dispute. We are making use of the right provided for in Article 10 of the Dispute Settlement Understanding, on account of our systemic interest in the correct application of Article VI of the GATT 1994 and the Anti-Dumping Agreement in order to avoid abusive use of anti-dumping measures as protectionist barriers to trade.

2. We do not wish at this stage to take any view on Brazil's numerous complaints, most of which concern procedural aspects that would require us to undertake a more careful study of the investigation conducted by the Argentine authorities.

3. Instead, Chile would like to refer to one of the preliminary arguments put forward by Argentina in its first written submission, which is that an international tribunal has ruled on this same case, which would disqualify this Panel from hearing Brazil's complaint.

4. Without knowing the details of the arbitral procedure followed by the parties in dispute under the MERCOSUR dispute settlement rules, Chile understands, on the one hand, that the Arbitral Tribunal ruled against Brazil because no anti-dumping disciplines exist in the MERCOSUR framework and, on the other, that there is no precedent of Brazil having renounced its rights before the WTO, and specifically that to invoke the WTO dispute settlement mechanism, as might have been the case if the Olivos Protocol, which contains a forum exclusion clause (*cláusula sobre opción excluyente de foro*), had been in force.

5. On that understanding, and in the absence of legal identity, Brazil legitimately brought its subsequent complaint before the forum in which anti-dumping disciplines impose obligations on Argentina and Brazil, and the rest of the WTO Members.

6. What has been invoked in this dispute is the violation or failure to abide by the rules of the WTO, which is a distinct regulatory system that imposes its own rights and obligations on its Members, and these are different from the rights and obligations imposed by a bilateral agreement.

7. Consequently, Chile considers that Argentina's preliminary claim is unfounded since Brazil has invoked, before the WTO and this Panel in particular, the violation of obligations undertaken by Argentina within the framework of the WTO Agreements - and the Anti-Dumping Agreement and the GATT 1994 in particular - and not of obligations entered into in the MERCOSUR framework. Accordingly, this Panel is the forum with jurisdiction to hear the complaint lodged by Brazil in its request for the establishment of a panel and in its first written submission.

ANNEX C-8

THIRD PARTY ORAL STATEMENT OF THE UNITED STATES
(26 September 2002)

Mr Chairman, members of the Panel,

1. It is my honour to appear before you to present the views of the United States as a third party in this proceeding. As the Panel will recall, the United States has already filed a third-party submission in this dispute. Today, my comments will be limited to Argentina's preliminary request that the Panel not address any of Brazil's claims. We would be happy to receive any questions the Panel may have on either our written submission or our statement today.

Preliminary Objection

2. Mr. Chairman, in Argentina's first written submission, Argentina argues that the Panel should refuse to make findings on the claims that Brazil has raised in this dispute. In the view of the United States, there is no basis in the DSU for the Panel to grant Argentina's request.

3. Argentina argues that the Panel should refuse to make findings on Brazil's claims because Brazil previously challenged the Argentine measure under MERCOSUR dispute settlement rules. In Argentina's view, the Panel must take account of those rules and consider the consequences of Brazil's decision to use them. Alternatively, Argentina argues that the Panel should apply the principle of estoppel because Brazil has, in the past, accepted the scope of those rules. Mr. Chairman, neither argument provides a basis for the Panel to refuse to make findings on Brazil's claims.

4. Turning first to Argentina's initial point, the United States respectfully submits that the MERCOSUR dispute settlement rules are not within the Panel's terms of reference. Article 7.1 of the DSU makes quite clear that a Panel's role in a dispute is to make findings in light of the relevant provisions of the "covered agreements" at issue. The *Protocol of Brasilia* is not a covered agreement, and Argentina has not claimed that Brazil's actions with respect to the *Protocol* breach any provision of a covered agreement. Rather, Argentina's claim appears to be that Brazil's actions could be considered to be inconsistent with the terms of the *Protocol*. A claim of a breach of the *Protocol* is not within this Panel's terms of reference, and there are no grounds for the Panel to consider this matter. Argentina may, however, be able to pursue that claim under the MERCOSUR dispute settlement system.

5. Turning to Argentina's second point, its request for a finding of estoppel against Brazil, the United States first notes that this alternative claim again appears to relate to Brazil's obligations under MERCOSUR rather than to any provision of the DSU or the other covered agreements. As a result, the matter is not within the Panel's terms of reference and the Panel has no basis for making the requested finding. The United States also disagrees with Argentina that the Panel may apply what Argentina calls the principle of estoppel. The fact that Argentina cites to no textual basis for its request reflects the fact that Members have not consented to provide for the

application of any such principle of estoppel in WTO dispute settlement. The term estoppel appears nowhere in the text nor does Argentina cite to any provision which in substance provides Argentina the type of defense it asserts.

6.   The United States also notes that the lack of any textual basis is reflected in the fact that no panel to date has applied a principle of estoppel. Moreover, there is no basis for attempting to import into WTO dispute settlement proceedings legal concepts with no grounding in the DSU. The lack of any textual basis is further emphasized by the lack of consistent description of the concept when panels have had occasion to discuss estoppel in the past. In *Bananas I*, for example, the panel stated that estoppel can only "result from the express, or in exceptional cases implied, consent of the complaining parties."[1] In *Asbestos* and *Guatemala Cement*, by contrast, the panels stated that estoppel is relevant when a party "reasonably relies" on the assurances of another party, and then suffers negative consequences resulting from a change in the other party's position.[2] These inconsistencies illustrate the dangers of seeking to identify purportedly agreed-upon legal concepts beyond the only source all Members *have* agreed to - the text of the DSU itself.

7.   Finally, Argentina's citation of Article 3.2 of the DSU in support of its position is misplaced. By its plain terms, Article 3.2 is limited to the rules of *interpretation* used to clarify the existing provisions of the *WTO Agreement*. Argentina's request that the Panel refuse to consider Brazil's claims does not present an issue of the proper interpretation of a provision of the *WTO Agreement*.

8.   For the foregoing reasons, the United States respectfully urges the Panel to reject Argentina's request that it not consider Brazil's claims.

Conclusion

9.   This concludes my presentation. Thank you again for this opportunity to express our views.

---

[1] See Third Party Submission of the European Communities, citing Report of the Panel on *EEC - Member States' Import Regimes for Bananas*, DS32/R, unadopted, para. 361.

[2] See Report of the Panel on *European Communities - Measures Affecting Asbestos and Asbestos-Containing Products*, WT/DS135/R, adopted April 5, 2001, DSR 2001:VIII, 3305, para. 8.60 (citations omitted); Panel Report on *Guatemala - Definitive Anti-Dumping Measures on Grey Portland Cement from Mexico*, WT/DS156/R, adopted 17 November 2000, , DSR 2000:XI, 5295, para. 8.23-24. One could also argue that these panels are describing the concept of "detrimental reliance."

ANNEX C-9

THIRD PARTY ORAL STATEMENT OF CANADA
(26 September 2002)

Thank you Mr. Chairman.

In starting, I would like to express Canada's appreciation and thank the Members of the Panel for having accepted to take on the responsibility of aiding the Parties in resolving this dispute.

Canada made a written Third Party submission in this matter on 5 September 2002. In that submission, Canada limited its arguments to the interpretation of Articles 9.2 and 9.3 of the Antidumping Agreement.

Also, 23 August, Canada submitted a letter to the Chairman, outlining Canada's position with respect to the procedural issue that arose between the Parties pertaining to the public release of a Party's own written submissions.

As you may recall, in its written Third Party submission Canada indicated that it may wish to raise further substantive points at a later time. However, Canada has decided to limit its Third Party submissions in this matter to what is contained in its two previous written communications to the Panel.

Nonetheless, although Canada does not wish to raise any further substantive points at this time, I would be pleased to receive from the Panel or the Parties any questions regarding Canada's positions.

Thank you Mr. Chairman.

ANNEX C-10

THIRD PARTY ORAL STATEMENT OF THE EUROPEAN COMMUNITIES
(26 September 2002)

I. INTRODUCTION

1. The European Communities (the "EC") thanks the Panel for this opportunity to submits its views orally in this dispute.

2. In its written submission, the EC has limited its comments to certain issues of legal interpretation. Specifically, the EC has argued that:

- the Panel should dismiss Argentina's preliminary objection based on the existence of an arbitration award issued by a MERCOSUR Ad Hoc Arbitration Tribunal with respect to the same anti-dumping measure;

- in so far as the issue arises in connection with **Claim 21**, the Panel should confirm the interpretation of Article 6.9 made by the panel in *Guatemala - Cement II* to the effect that the disclosure obligation imposed by that provision cannot be satisfied simply by allowing access to the file;

- Article 2.4 does not address the issue raised by Brazil under **Claim 24**;

- contrary to Brazil's **Claims 28 and 29**, the imposition of a variable duty equal to the difference between the normal value established during the investigation and the export prices of the shipments made after the imposition of the duties is not inconsistent with Articles 9.2 and 9.3;

- the term "dumped imports", as used in Article 3, may be interpreted as referring to all imports from the country concerned, contrary to Brazil's **Claims 32, 33, 34, 35 and 36**; and

- contrary to Brazil's **Claim 41**, the term "major proportion" used in Article 4.1 does not mean at least 50 per cent of the domestic production, but rather an important proportion thereof, which may be less than 50 per cent.

3. In our statement of this morning we will not repeat the comments already made in our written submission. Instead, we will comment briefly on some of the arguments submitted by the other third parties to this dispute.

II. ARGUMENT

A. Article 18.2 DSU

4. The EC agrees with Canada[1] and with the United States[2] that Article 18.2 of the *DSU* does not prevent Brazil from making its written submissions available to the public.

5. The EC would recall, nevertheless, that the right of a Member to disclose its own submissions to the public is subject to the third sentence of Article 18.2, which provides that "Members shall treat as confidential information submitted by another Member to the panel ... which that Member has designated as confidential". Therefore, to the extent that a Member's submission incorporates or refers to confidential information provided to the panel by another party to the dispute, such information should be omitted from the version disclosed to the public or replaced by a non-confidential summary requested from the party concerned in accordance with the fourth sentence of Article 18.2. We understand, however, that this issue does not arise here, as Argentina's complaint concerned Brazil's first submission to the panel.

6. Also, to the extent that Brazil's submission contained information received by the Brazilian Government on a confidential basis from the Argentinean investigating authorities during the underlying investigation, the Brazilian Government would be bound to comply with any applicable provisions of Argentinean law which protect such confidentiality. However, again, we understand that this issue does not arise in this dispute. In any event, it would be beyond the Panel's jurisdiction to enforce the provisions of Argentinean law on confidentiality.

7. Finally, the EC also agrees with the United States[3] that the Panel should reject Argentina's request that the Panel gives its "opinion" on the correct interpretation of Article 18.2 of the *DSU*.[4] As noted by the United States[5], it would be beyond the Panel's terms of reference to give such an advisory opinion.

B. RES iudicata and Article 18 of the Vienna Convention

8. Paraguay has argued that, since under the *Protocol of Brasilia* the award issued by an Ad Hoc Arbitration Tribunal is binding upon the parties to the arbitration, it has the effect of *res iudicata* between them, with the consequence that Brazil would be barred from bringing this dispute.[6]

9. As explained in our written submission, the EC disagrees with that view. The existence of *res iudicata* requires identity between the claims. While the measure at issue in this dispute is the same as the measure before the Ad Hoc Arbitration Tribunal in the case cited by Argentina and Paraguay, the claims are different because they involve different legal bases. The claims before this Panel are based on the *WTO Agreement*. In contrast, the claims ruled upon by the Ad Hoc Arbitration Tribunal were based on MERCOSUR law.

10. Furthermore, the EC would recall that Article 23.1 of the *DSU* provides that:

---

[1] Canada's Letter to the Panel of 23 August 2002.
[2] US Submission, para. 18.
[3] *Ibid.*
[4] Argentina's Letter to the Panel of 27 August 2002.
[5] US Submission, para. 18.
[6] Paraguay's Submission, para. 7.

When Members seek the redress of a violation of obligations or other nullification or impairment of benefits under the covered agreements or an impediment to the attainment of any objective of the covered agreements, they shall have recourse to, and abide by, the rules and procedures of this Understanding.

11. This suggests that the Members of the WTO are not free to refer the adjudication of a dispute concerning their rights and obligations under the *WTO Agreement* to a body outside the WTO. Thus, although Article 25 of the *DSU* allows Members to resort to arbitration as an alternative means of dispute settlement, it envisages that such arbitration will take place "within" the WTO.

12. Paraguay further suggests that, by bringing this dispute, Brazil would have acted in violation of Article 18 of the *Vienna Convention on the Law of the Treaties*, because the *Protocol of Olivos* (which in its Article 1.2 requires the complainant to make a choice between bringing the dispute before a WTO panel or a MERCOSUR Arbitration Tribunal) had already been signed before Brazil brought this dispute, even if it has not entered into force yet.[7] However, as noted in our written submission, it seems that even if the *Protocol of Olivos* had already entered into force, it would not apply to the facts at issue. Article 50 of that protocol provides that:

> Las controversias en trámite iniciadas de acuerdo con el régimen del Protocolo de Brasilia se regirán exclusivamente por el mismo hasta su total conclusión.

13. It seems that, by the same logic, and indeed *a fortiori*, the *Protocol of Olivos* cannot be applied to disputes which have already been adjudicated under the *Protocol of Brasilia* as of the date of entry into force of the *Protocol of Olivos*. If the *Protocol of Olivos*, including its Article 1.2, was not meant to apply to the current dispute, it is clear that, by bringing it before this Panel, Brazil cannot defeat the object and purpose of that protocol. The EC considers that, in view of that, this Panel need not reach the issue of whether, by bringing a dispute in violation of Article 18 of the *Vienna Convention*, a Member would act inconsistently with Article 3.10 of the *DSU*.

C. Article 5.7 of the Anti-Dumping Agreement

14. The EC agrees with the United States that the mere fact that the reference period used for the purposes of the injury determination does not coincide with that used for the dumping determination does not amount *per se* to a violation of Article 5.7 of the *Anti-Dumping Agreement*.[8] That provision is concerned exclusively with the *timing* of the examination of dumping and injury and not with the scope of such examination.

Thank you for your attention.

---

[7] *Ibid.*, para. 9.
[8] US Submission, paras. 2-6.

ANNEX C-11

REPLIES OF THE EUROPEAN COMMUNITIES TO QUESTIONS OF THE PANEL

(3 October 2002)

Question 1

Please comment on the distinction apparently made between the terms "written submissions" and "statements of [a member's] own positions" in the first two sentences of Article 18.2 of the DSU.

Reply

The *DSU* does not limit in any manner the form, content or length of the "statements" referred to in the second sentence of Article 18.2. Accordingly, a Member is free to make a "statement" of its positions by disclosing its written submissions to the Panel.

Question 2

Please explain how your investigating authorities treat imports for the purpose of investigating injury. In particular, does your investigating authority presume from the outset that all imports are dumped? Is so, what is the basis for such presumption, and is the presumption rebuttable under any circumstances? For example, is that presumption rebutted if the investigating authority finds that imports from a given exporter are not dumped?

If your investigating authority does not presume from the outset that all imports are dumped, how does your investigating authority distinguish between dumped and non-dumped imports during its injury investigation?

If your investigating authority determines that imports from a given exporter are not dumped, are imports from that exporter excluded for the purpose of the Article 3 injury determination.

Reply

In accordance with Article 5.7 of the *Anti-Dumping Agreement*, the EC authorities examine simultaneously the existence of both dumping and injury. The examination of injury must, of necessity, be based on the assumption that all the imports under investigation are dumped. If the authorities did not make that assumption, it would be impossible to examine the existence of injury simultaneously with the examination of dumping. Instead, the authorities would have to wait until the examination of dumping has been completed and a final determination has been reached with respect to the existence of dumping before starting the injury examination.

If, as a result of the dumping examination, the EC authorities reach a negative determination of dumping for a country, the investigation will be terminated with respect to that country and the imports from that country "decumulated" from the imports of the other countries under investigation for the purposes of the injury determination.

As explained in paragraphs 41 to 44 of the EC's first submission, the EC considers that the determination of dumping is made with respect to countries and, therefore, that the authorities are entitled to treat all imports from a given country as "dumped" for the purposes of Article 3, even if one or more exporters from that country are found not to be dumping.

The exclusion from the injury examination of the imports from the exporters that have been found not to be dumping would often require a substantial re-examination of the injury, contrary to the requirement imposed by Article 5.7. This is an additional reason for considering that, as submitted by the EC, the terms "dumped imports" in Article 3 must be interpreted as including all the imports from a country.

Question 3

Is it possible to exclude non-dumped imports for the purposes of an injury determination while still complying with the Article 5.7 obligation to consider the evidence of dumping and injury "simultaneously". Please explain. Does the word "simultaneously" in Article 5.7 mean that the determination of dumping and injury must be made at exactly the same point in time? Please explain.

Reply

See above the answer to Question 2.

ANNEX C-12

REPLIES OF THE UNITED STATES TO QUESTIONS OF THE PANEL
(17 October 2002)

Q1. Please comment on the distinction apparently made between the terms "written submissions" and "statements of [a Member's] own positions" in the first two sentences of Article 18.2 of the DSU.

1. The second sentence of Article 18.2 of the *Understanding on Rules and Procedures Governing the Settlement of Disputes* ("DSU") recognizes that Members are entitled to release "statements" of their own positions to the public. The provision places no limitations on the form or manner in which a Member may choose to do so, including by making its "submissions" available to the public in their entirety. Public disclosure of submissions contributes to better public understanding of - and support for - the WTO dispute settlement system.

2. The ordinary meaning of the term "statement" supports the US interpretation. The *New Shorter Oxford English Dictionary* defines the term in pertinent part as "A formal written or oral account, setting down facts, an argument, a demand, etc.; *esp.* an account of events made to the police or in a court of law.[1] This is, in essence, what a Member does when it prepares a submission in a WTO dispute: It creates a formal written account setting down arguments in support of its position. That these "statements" also constitute "submissions" when Members provide them to panels does not mean they are no longer "statements" which may be disclosed to the public.

3. Finally, it is worth noting that panels routinely attach parties' written submissions (or detailed summaries of the same) to the final versions of their written reports before releasing the reports to the public. If Argentina's interpretation of Article 18.2 were correct, panels have been breaching Article 18.2 of the DSU whenever they have done so.

Q2. Please explain how your investigating authorities treat imports for the purpose of investigating injury. In particular, does your investigating authority presume from the outset that all imports are dumped? If so, what is the basis for such presumption, and is that presumption rebuttable under any circumstances? For example, is that presumption rebutted if the investigating authority finds that imports from a given exporter are not dumped?

If your investigating authority does not presume from the outset that all imports are dumped, how does your investigating authority distinguish between dumped and non-dumped imports during its injury investigation?

If your investigating authority determines that imports from a given exporter are not dumped, are imports from that exporter excluded for the purpose of the Article 3 injury determination?

4. The investigating authority of the United States makes no presumption regarding whether imports are dumped (or subsidized) at the outset of the investigation. In the preliminary injury determination, the US investigating authority makes a determination regarding the imports *alleged* to be dumped without

---

[1] The New Shorter Oxford English Dictionary 3037 (1993).

presuming that the imports are dumped in fact. In the final injury determination, the US investigating authority excludes from the volume of dumped imports merchandise that is determined to have a zero or *de minimis* rate of dumping.

Q3: Is it possible to exclude non-dumped imports for the purpose of an injury investigation while still complying with the Article 5.7 obligation to consider the evidence of dumping and injury "simultaneously". Please explain. Does the word "simultaneously" in Article 5.7 mean that the determinations of dumping and injury must be made at exactly the same point in time? Please explain.

5. Article 5.7 of the Antidumping Agreement provides that:

> The evidence of both dumping and injury shall be considered simultaneously (*a*) in the decision whether or not to initiate an investigation, and (*b*) thereafter, during the course of the investigation, starting on a date not later than the earliest date on which in accordance with the provisions of this Agreement provisional measures may be applied.

6. Addressing the Panel's second question first, the use of the term "simultaneously" in Article 5.7 does not mean that a Member must make its determinations of dumping and injury at the same time. The obligation in Article 5.7 is to simultaneously "consider" the evidence of dumping and injury, not to make simultaneous "determinations" of dumping and injury. The term "determination" is not even present in Article 5.7. Moreover, the obligation to simultaneously consider both dumping and injury is limited to the decision whether to initiate an investigation and then arises again only after the date on which provisional measures may be applied.

7. With respect to the Panel's first question, it is possible to exclude non-dumped imports for the purpose of an injury determination while still complying with the Article 5.7 obligation to consider the evidence of dumping and injury "simultaneously." Inherent to the exclusion of non-dumped imports for purposes of an injury determination is that the final determination of dumping be made before the final determination of injury. However, the fact that *determinations* are made at different times does not prevent the simultaneous *consideration* of evidence of dumping and injury "during the course of the investigation." If a Member's investigating authorities simultaneously consider the evidence of dumping and injury "during the course of the investigation," the authorities satisfy the requirement of Article 5.7. As noted in response to question 2, there is no additional obligation to make the determinations of dumping and injury simultaneously.

Cumulative Index of Published Disputes

Argentina – Definitive Anti-Dumping Measures on Imports of Ceramic Floor Tiles from Italy
 Complaint by the European Communities (WT/DS189)
  Report of the Panel ....DSR 2001:XII, 6241

Argentina – Definitive Safeguard Measure on Imports of Preserved Peaches
 Complaint by Chile (WT/DS238)
  Report of the Panel .... DSR 2003:III, 1037

Argentina - Measures Affecting Imports of Footwear, Textiles, Apparel and Other Items
 Complaint by the United States (WT/DS56)
  Report of the Appellate Body .... DSR 1998:III, 1003
  Report of the Panel .... DSR 1998:III, 1033

Argentina - Measures Affecting the Export of Bovine Hides and the Import of Finished Leather
 Complaint by the European Communities (WT/DS155)
  Report of the Panel .... DSR 2001:V, 1779
  Award of the Arbitrator under Article 21.3(c) of the DSU ......DSR 2001:XII, 6013

Argentina - Safeguard Measures on Imports of Footwear
 Complaint by the European Communities (WT/DS121)
  Report of the Appellate Body ....DSR 2000:I, 515
  Report of the Panel .... DSR 2000:II, 575

Australia - Measures Affecting Importation of Salmon
 Complaint by Canada (WT/DS18)
  Report of the Appellate Body .... DSR 1998:VIII, 3327
  Report of the Panel .... DSR 1998:VIII, 3407
  Award of the Arbitrator under Article 21.3(c) of the DSU ....DSR 1999:I, 267
  Report of the Panel - Recourse to Article 21.5 of the DSU....... DSR 2000:IV, 2031

Australia - Subsidies Provided to Producers and Exporters of Automotive Leather
 Complaint by the United States (WT/DS126)
  Report of the Panel .... DSR 1999:III, 951
  Report of the Panel - Recourse to Article 21.5 of the DSU....... DSR 2000:III, 1189

Brazil - Measures Affecting Desiccated Coconut
 Complaint by the Philippines (WT/DS22)
  Report of the Appellate Body ....DSR 1997:I, 167
  Report of the Panel ....DSR 1997:I, 189

Brazil - Export Financing Programme for Aircraft
Complaint by Canada (WT/DS46)
   Report of the Appellate Body .... DSR 1999:III, 1161
   Report of the Panel .... DSR 1999:III, 1221
   Report of the Appellate Body - Recourse to Article 21.5
   of the DSU .... DSR 2000:VIII, 4067
   Report of the Panel - Recourse to Article 21.5 of the DSU....... DSR 2000:IX, 4093
   Report of the Panel - Second Recourse to
   Article 21.5 of the DSU .... DSR 2001:XI, 5481
   Decision by the Arbitrators - Recourse to Arbitration by Brazil under
   Article 22.6 of the DSU and Article 4.11 of the SCM Agreement...DSR 2002:I, 19

Canada - Certain Measures Affecting the Automotive Industry
Complaint by the European Communities (WT/DS142);
complaint by Japan (WT/DS139)
   Report of the Appellate Body .... DSR 2000:VI, 2985
   Report of the Panel .... DSR 2000:VII, 3043
   Award of the Arbitrator under Article 21.3(c) of the DSU .... DSR 2000:X, 5079

Canada - Certain Measures Concerning Periodicals
Complaint by the United States (WT/DS31)
   Report of the Appellate Body .... DSR 1997:I, 449
   Report of the Panel .... DSR 1997:I, 481

Canada - Export Credits and Loan Guarantees for Regional Aircraft
Complaint by Brazil (WT/DS222)
   Report of the Panel .... DSR 2002:III, 849
   Decision by the Arbitrator under Article 22.6 of the DSU
   and Article 4.11 of the SCM Agreement   DSR 2003:III, 1187

Canada - Measures Affecting the Importation of Milk and the Exportation of Dairy Products
Complaint by New Zealand (WT/DS113); complaint by the United States (WT/DS103)
   Report of the Appellate Body .... DSR 1999:V, 2057
   Report of the Panel .... DSR 1999:VI, 2097
   Report of the Appellate Body - Recourse to Article 21.5
   of the DSU .... DSR 2001:XIII, 6829
   Report of the Panel - Recourse to Article 21.5 of the DSU.... DSR 2001:XIII, 6865
   Report of the Appellate Body - Second Recourse to
   Article 21.5 of the DSU .... DSR 2003:I, 213
   Report of the Panel - Second Recourse to Article 21.5
   of the DSU .... DSR 2003:I, 255

Canada - Measures Affecting the Export of Civilian Aircraft
Complaint by Brazil (WT/DS70)
   Report of the Appellate Body .... DSR 1999:III, 1377
   Report of the Panel .... DSR 1999:IV, 1443

Report of the Appellate Body - Recourse to Article 21.5
of the DSU .... DSR 2000:IX, 4299
Report of the Panel - Recourse to Article 21.5 of the DSU .... DSR 2000:IX, 4315

Canada - Patent Protection of Pharmaceutical Products
Complaint by the European Communities (WT/DS114)
Report of the Panel .... DSR 2000:V, 2289
Award of the Arbitrator under Article 21.3(c) of the DSU .... DSR 2002:I, 3

Canada - Term of Patent Protection
Complaint by the United States (WT/DS170)
Report of the Appellate Body .... DSR 2000:X, 5093
Report of the Panel .... DSR 2000:XI, 5121
Award of the Arbitrator under Article 21.3(c) of the DSU ...... DSR 2000:IX, 4537

Chile – Price Band System and Safeguard Measures Relating to Certain Agricultural Products
Complaint by Argentina (WT/DS207)
Report of the Appellate Body .... DSR 2002:VIII, 3045
Report of the Panel .... DSR 2002:VIII, 30127
Award of the Arbitrator under Article 21.3(c) of the DSU .... DSR 2003:III, 1237

Chile - Taxes on Alcoholic Beverages
Complaint by the European Communities (WT/DS87), (WT/DS110)
Report of the Appellate Body .... DSR 2000:I, 281
Report of the Panel .... DSR 2000:I, 303
Award of the Arbitrator under Article 21.3(c) of the DSU .... DSR 2000:V, 2583

Egypt – Definitive Anti-Dumping Measures on Steel Rebar from Turkey
Complaint by Turkey (WT/DS211)
Report of the Panel .... DSR 2002:VII, 2667

European Communities - Anti-Dumping Duties on Imports of Cotton-Type Bed Linen from India
Complaint by India (WT/DS141)
Report of the Appellate Body .... DSR 2001:V, 2049
Report of the Appellate Body (Recourse to Article 21.5 of
the DSU by India) .... DSR 2003:III, 965
Report of the Panel .... DSR 2001:VI, 2077
Report of the Panel - Recourse to Article 21.5 of the DSU .... DSR 2003:IV, 1269

European Communities - Customs Classification of Certain Computer Equipment
Complaint by the United States (WT/DS62); complaint by the United States – Ireland (WT/DS68); complaint by the United States – United Kingdom (WT/DS67)
Report of the Appellate Body .... DSR 1998:V, 1851
Report of the Panel .... DSR 1998:V, 1891

European Communities - Measures Affecting Asbestos and Asbestos-Containing Products
Complaint by Canada (WT/DS135)

Report of the Appellate Body ....DSR 2001:VII, 3243
Report of the Panel .... DSR 2001:VIII, 3305

European Communities - Measures Affecting the Importation of Certain Poultry Products
Complaint by Brazil (WT/DS69)
Report of the Appellate Body .... DSR 1998:V, 2031
Report of the Panel .... DSR 1998:V, 2089

European Communities - Measures Concerning Meat and Meat Products (Hormones)
Complaint by Canada (WT/DS48); complaint by the United States (WT/DS26)
Report of the Appellate Body ....DSR 1998:I, 135
Report of the Panel (Canada)... DSR 1998:II, 235
Report of the Panel (United States)..DSR 1998:III, 699
Award of the Arbitrator under Article 21.3(c) of the DSU .... DSR 1998:V, 1833
Decision by the Arbitrators under Article 22.6 of the DSU
(Canada) .... DSR 1999:III, 1135
Decision by the Arbitrators under Article 22.6 of the DSU
(United States) .... DSR 1999:III, 1105

European Communities - Regime for the Importation, Sale and Distribution of Bananas
Complaint by Ecuador; Guatemala; Honduras; Mexico; and the
United States (WT/DS27)
Report of the Appellate Body .... DSR 1997:II, 589
Report of the Panel (Ecuador)... DSR 1997:III, 3
Report of the Panel (Guatemala, Honduras) .... DSR 1997:II, 695
Report of the Panel (Mexico).. DSR 1997:II, 803
Report of the Panel (United States).. DSR 1997:II, 943
Award of the Arbitrator under Article 21.3(c) of the DSU ....DSR 1998:I, 3
Decision by the Arbitrators under Article 22.6
of the DSU (US) .... DSR 1999:II, 725
Report of the Panel - Recourse to Article 21.5 of the DSU
(European Communities) .... DSR 1999:II, 783
Report of the Panel - Recourse to Article 21.5 of the DSU
(Ecuador) .... DSR 1999:II, 803
Decision by the Arbitrators under Article 22.6
of the DSU (Ecuador) .... DSR 2000:V, 2237

European Communities – Trade Description of Sardines
Complaint by Peru (WT/DS231/R)
Report of the Appellate Body .... DSR 2002:VIII, 3359
Report of the Panel .... DSR 2002:VIII, 3451

European Communities – Trade Description of Scallops
Complaint by Canada (WT/DS7); complaint by Chile (WT/DS14); complaint by Peru (WT/DS12)
Report of the Panel (Canada)...DSR 1996:I, 89

Report of the Panel (Chile, Peru) .... DSR 1996:I, 93

Guatemala – Anti-Dumping Investigation Regarding Portland Cement From Mexico

Complaint by Mexico (WT/DS60)

Report of the Appellate Body .... DSR 1998:IX, 3767

Report of the Panel .... DSR 1998:IX, 3797

Guatemala - Definitive Anti-Dumping Measures on Grey Portland Cement from Mexico

Complaint by Mexico (WT/DS156)

Report of the Panel .... DSR 2000:XI, 5295

India – Measures Affecting the Automotive Sector

Complaint by European Communities (WT/DS146,) complaint by the United States (WT/DS175)

Report of the Appellate Body .... DSR 2002:V, 1821

Report of the Panel .... DSR 2002:V, 1827

India - Patent Protection for Pharmaceutical and Agricultural Chemical Products

Complaint by European Communities (WT/DS79); complaint by the United States (WT/DS50)

Report of the Appellate Body (United States) .... DSR 1998:I, 9

Report of the Panel (European Communities) .... DSR 1998:VI, 2661

Report of the Panel (United States) .... DSR 1998:I, 41

India - Quantitative Restrictions on Imports of Agricultural, Textile and Industrial Products

Complaint by the United States (WT/DS90)

Report of the Appellate Body .... DSR 1999:IV, 1763

Report of the Panel .... DSR 1999:V, 1799

Indonesia - Certain Measures Affecting the Automobile Industry

Complaint by European Communities (WT/DS54); complaint by Japan (WT/DS55, WT/DS64); complaint by the United States (WT/DS59)

Report of the Panel .... DSR 1998:VI, 2201

Award of the Arbitrator under Article 21.3(c) of the DSU ...... DSR 1998:IX, 4029

Japan - Measures Affecting Agricultural Products

Complaint by the United States (WT/DS76)

Report of the Appellate Body .... DSR 1999:I, 277

Report of the Panel .... DSR 1999:I, 315

Japan - Measures Affecting Consumer Photographic Film and Paper

Complaint by the United States (WT/DS44)

Report of the Panel .... DSR 1998:IV, 1179

Japan – Taxes on Alcoholic Beverages

Complaint by Canada (WT/DS10); complaint by the European Communities (WT/DS8); complaint by the United States (WT/DS11)

Report of the Appellate Body .... DSR 1996:I, 97

Report of the Panel ....DSR 1996:I, 125
Award of the Arbitrator under Article 21.3(c) of the DSU ....DSR 1997:I, 3

Korea - Definitive Safeguard Measure on Imports of Certain Dairy Products
Complaint by the European Communities (WT/DS98)
Report of the Appellate Body ....DSR 2000:I, 3
Report of the Panel ....DSR 2000:I, 49

Korea – Measures Affecting Imports of Fresh, Chilled and Frozen Beef
Complaint by Australia (WT/DS169); complaint by the United States (WT/DS161)
Report of the Appellate Body ....DSR 2001:I, 5
Report of the Panel ....DSR 2001:I, 59

Korea - Measures Affecting Government Procurement
Complaint by the United States (WT/DS163)
Report of the Panel .... DSR 2000:VIII, 3541

Korea - Taxes on Alcoholic Beverages
Complaint by the European Communities (WT/DS75); complaint by the United States (WT/DS84)
Report of the Appellate Body ....DSR 1999:I, 3
Report of the Panel ....DSR 1999:I, 44
Award of the Arbitrator under Article 21.3(c) of the DSU .... DSR 1999:II, 937

Mexico - Anti-Dumping Investigation of High Fructose Corn Syrup (HFCS) from the United States
Complaint by the United States (WT/DS132)
Report of the Panel .... DSR 2000:III, 1345
Report of the Appellate Body - Recourse to Article 21.5 of the DSU .... DSR 2001:XIII, 6675
Report of the Panel - Recourse to Article 21.5 of the DSU.... DSR 2001:XIII, 6717

Thailand – Anti-Dumping Duties on Angles, Shapes and Sections of Iron or Non-Alloy Steel and H-Beams from Poland
Complaint by Poland (WT/DS122)
Report of the Appellate Body ....DSR 2001:VII, 2701
Report of the Panel ....DSR 2001:VII, 2741

Turkey - Restrictions on Imports of Textile and Clothing Products
Complaint by India (WT/DS34)
Report of the Appellate Body ....DSR 1999:VI, 2345
Report of the Panel ....DSR 1999:VI, 2363

United States - Anti-Dumping Act of 1916
Complaint by the European Communities (WT/DS136); complaint by Japan (WT/DS162)
Report of the Appellate Body .... DSR 2000:X, 4793
Report of the Panel (European Communities) .... DSR 2000:X, 4593
Report of the Panel (Japan)... DSR 2000:X, 4831
Award of the Arbitrator under Article 21.3(c) of the DSU .... DSR 2001:V, 2017

Cumulative Index

United States-Anti-Dumping and Countervailing Measures on Steel Plate from India
Complaint by India (WT/DS206)
Report of the Panel .... DSR 2002:VI, 2073

United States - Anti-Dumping Duty on Dynamic Random Access Memory Semiconductors (DRAMS) of One Megabit or Above from Korea
Complaint by Korea (WT/DS99)
Report of the Panel .... DSR 1999:II, 521

United States – Anti-Dumping Measures on Certain Hot-Rolled Steel Products from Japan
Complaint by Japan (WT/DS184)
Report of the Appellate Body .... DSR 2001:X, 4697
Report of the Panel .... DSR 2001:X, 4769
Award of the Arbitrator under Article 21.3(c) of the DSU .... DSR 2002:IV, 1389

United States – Anti-Dumping Measures on Stainless Steel Plate in Coils and Stainless Steel Sheet and Strip from Korea
Complaint by Korea (WT/DS179)
Report of the Panel .... DSR 2001:IV, 1295

United States – Continued Dumping and Subsidy Offset Act of 2000
Complaint by Australia, Brazil, Canada, Chile, the European Communities, India, Indonesia, Japan, Korea, Mexico and Thailand (WT/DS217)
Report of the Appellate Body .... DSR 2003:I, 375
Report of the Panel .... DSR 2003:II, 489
Award of the Arbitrator under Article 21.3(c) of the DSU .... DSR 2003:III, 1163

United States – Countervailing Duties on Certain Corrosion-Resistant Carbon Steel Flat Products from Germany
Complaint by European Communities (WT/DS213)
Report of the Appellate Body .... DSR 2002:IX, 3781
Report of the Panel .... DSR 2002:IX, 3835

United States – Countervailing Measures Concerning Certain Products from the European Communities
Complaint by European Communities (WT/DS212)
Report of the Appellate Body .... DSR 2003:I, 5
Report of the Panel .... DSR 2003:I, 73

United States – Definitive Safeguard Measures on Imports of Circular Welded Carbon Quality Line Pipe from Korea
Complaint by Korea (WT/DS202)
Report of the Appellate Body .... DSR 2002:IV, 1403
Report of the Panel .... DSR 2002:IV, 1473
Award of the Arbitrator under Article 21.3(c) of the DSU .... DSR 2002:V, 2061

United States – Definitive Safeguard Measures on Imports of Wheat Gluten from the European Communities
Complaint by the European Communities (WT/DS166)
    Report of the Appellate Body .... DSR 2001:II, 717
    Report of the Panel .... DSR 2001:III, 779

United States – Import Measures on Certain Products from the European Communities
Complaint by the European Communities (WT/DS165)
    Report of the Appellate Body .... DSR 2001:I, 373
    Report of the Panel .... DSR 2001:II, 413

United States - Imposition of Countervailing Duties on Certain Hot-Rolled Lead and Bismuth Carbon Steel Products Originating in the United Kingdom
Complaint by the European Communities (WT/DS138)
    Report of the Appellate Body .... DSR 2000:V, 2595
    Report of the Panel .... DSR 2000:VI, 2623

United States - Import Prohibition of Certain Shrimp and Shrimp Products
Complaint by India (WT/DS58); complaint by Malaysia (WT/DS58); complaint by Pakistan (WT/DS58); complaint by Thailand (WT/DS58)
    Report of the Appellate Body ....DSR 1998:VII, 2755
    Report of the Panel ....DSR 1998:VII, 2821
    Report of the Appellate Body - Recourse to Article 21.5
    of the DSU (Malaysia) .... DSR 2001:XIII, 6481
    Report of the Panel - Recourse to Article 21.5
    of the DSU (Malaysia)... DSR 2001:XIII, 6529

United States - Measure Affecting Imports of Woven Wool Shirts and Blouses from India
Complaint by India (WT/DS33)
    Report of the Appellate Body .... DSR 1997:I, 323
    Report of the Panel ....DSR 1997:I, 343

United States - Measures Treating Export Restraints as Subsidies
Complaint by Canada (WT/DS194)
    Report of the Panel ....DSR 2001:XI, 5767

United States – Preliminary Determinations with Respect to Certain Softwood Lumber from Canada
Complaint by Canada (WT/DS236)
    Report of the Panel ....DSR 2002:IX, 3597

United States - Restrictions on Imports of Cotton and Man-made Fibre Underwear
Complaint by Costa Rica (WT/DS24)
    Report of the Appellate Body ....DSR 1997:I, 11
    Report of the Panel ....DSR 1997:I, 31

Cumulative Index

United States – Safeguard Measures on Imports of Fresh, Chilled or Frozen Lamb Meat from New Zealand and Australia
Complaint by Australia (WT/DS178); complaint by new Zealand (WT/DS177)
Report of the Appellate Body .... DSR 2001:IX, 4051
Report of the Panel .... DSR 2001:IX, 4107

United States - Section 110(5) of the US Copyright Act
Complaint by the European Communities (WT/DS160)
Report of the Panel .... DSR 2000:VIII, 3769
Award of the Arbitrator under Article 21.3(c) of the DSU .... DSR 2001:II, 657
Award of the Arbitrator under Article 25 of the DSU................. DSR 2001:II, 667

United States - Sections 301-310 of the Trade Act of 1974
Complaint by the European Communities (WT/DS152)
Report of the Panel .... DSR 2000:II, 815

United States – Section 211 Omnibus Appropriations Act of 1998
Complaint by the European Communities (WT/DS176)
Report of the Appellate Body .... DSR 2002:II, 589
Report of the Panel .... DSR 2002:II, 683

United States- Section 129(c)(1) of the Uruguay Round Agreements Act
Complaint by Canada (WT/DS221)
Report of the Panel .... DSR 2002:VII, 2581

United States – Standards for Reformulated and Conventional Gasoline
Complaint by Brazil (WT/DS4); complaint by Venezuela (WT/DS2)
Report of the Appellate Body .... DSR 1996:I, 3
Report of the Panel .... DSR 1996:I, 29

United States - Tax Treatment for "Foreign Sales Corporations"
Complaint by the European Communities (WT/DS108)
Report of the Appellate Body .... DSR 2000:III, 1619
Report of the Panel .... DSR 2000:IV, 1675
Report of the Appellate Body - Recourse to Article 21.5
of the DSU .... DSR 2002:I, 55
Report of the Panel - Recourse to Article 21.5
of the DSU .... DSR 2002:I, 119
Decision by the Arbitrator under Article 22.6 of the DSU
and Article 4.11 of the SCM Agreement .... DSR 2002:VI, 2517

United States – Transitional Safeguard Measure on Combed Cotton Yarn from Pakistan
Complaint by Pakistan (WT/DS192)
Report of the Appellate Body .... DSR 2001:XII, 6027
Report of the Panel .... DSR 2001:XII, 6067